THE HARPERCOLLINS
DICTIONARY OF
AMERICAN GOVERNMENT AND POLITICS
Concise Edition

THE HARPERCOLLINS DICTIONARY OF AMERICAN GOVERNMENT AND POLITICS

Concise Edition

Jay M. Shafritz

HarperPerennial
A Division of HarperCollins*Publishers*

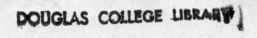
HarperCollins books may be purchased for educational, business, or sales promotional
use. For information, please write: Special Markets Department, HarperCollins Publishers,
Inc., 10 East 53rd St., New York, NY 10022.

FIRST HARPERPERENNIAL EDITION

Library of Congress Cataloging-in-Publication Data

Shafritz, Jay M.
    The HarperCollins dictionary of American government and politics / Jay M. Shafritz. —
Concise ed.; 1st ed.
    p. cm.
    ISBN 0-06-461021-7
    1. United States—Politics and government—Dictionaries.
    I. Title.
JK9.S43 1993
320.973—dc20   92-26224

95 96 97 ◆/RRD 10 9 8 7 6 5 4 3

CONTENTS

PREFACE

This dictionary is a tool for those who seek information on American national, state, or local government and politics. You will find here all commonly used terms and concepts of American government, such as the presidency, Congress, and the courts. Also included are the vocabularies of other key aspects of American governance, such as foreign policy, public administration, political economy, and taxation.

Beyond listing generally accepted and established terms, I have specifically included political terms found in newspapers and mass-market journals that have not yet found their way into text, reference, and scholarly books. Generally excluded were those terms whose meaning in the context of American governance did not differ from definitions to be found in any college-level dictionary of the English language. When a word has multiple meanings, I often thought it useful to provide a brief standard English meaning first. I excluded those terms that once were, but no longer are, part of the language of American politics. With minor exceptions, for entries considered historically important, a term had to be relevant to modern American governance in order to merit a place in this dictionary.

This book is based upon *The Dorsey Dictionary of American Government and Politics*. About half of the material here originally appeared there. Suggestions for enhancements, new entries, and additional citations will always be welcome.

Jay M. Shafritz
Graduate School of Public and International Affairs
University of Pittsburgh
Pittsburgh, Pennsylvania 15260

HOW TO USE THIS BOOK

This dictionary includes several features designed to make it easy for the reader to use.

Alphabetization

The dictionary is arranged in continuous alphabetical order. This organization is especially useful for comparing entries that sound similar. It also allows for quick comparison of terms with the same root. For example, the entry for *bill* is followed by more than a dozen variants of bill, such as "bill, companion"; "bill, deficiency"; "bill, omnibus"; and so on. The entry for *democracy* is followed by "democracy, direct"; "democracy, economic"; "democracy, Jacksonian"; and so on. This format is followed as often as possible so that if the root of a term is known, all of its variants can readily be found. All terms that begin as numbers, such as the constitutional amendments, are alphabetized as if the number were spelled out; thus, the Second Amendment is under *S*, the Third under *T*, and so on.

Cross-References

No event or term of American government and politics is an island unto itself. No dictionary would be optimally useful if it did not suggest the related terms, laws, court cases, or personalities significant to a fuller understanding of the initial term. The many hundreds of cross-references provide threads the reader can use to follow the connections between and evolution of political concepts. Cross-references were indicated by SMALL CAPITALS within an entry only when it was felt that reading the cross-reference would significantly enhance the understanding of the original entry.

Court Cases

Among the entries are more than a hundred Supreme Court decisions. Often they will be integrated with a related entry. Such judicial decisions are originally many pages long, so be cautious! A brief summary of a case, no matter how succinct, may not be sufficient information upon which to base formal action. These summaries were written to identify the case and its significance to American governance, not to make less work for lawyers.

HOW TO USE THIS BOOK

Federal Laws

Choosing from among thousands of federal legislative acts those most significant to contemporary government proved very difficult. Rather than attempt to compile an encyclopedia of federal law, I selected over 100 of those laws that have had a major and continuing impact on American governance, such as the National Labor Relations Act of 1935, the Civil Rights Act of 1964, or the Tax Reform Act of 1986.

Government Agencies

Close to 100 entries on federal government agencies, from the Agency for International Development, to the National Railroad Passenger Corporation (Amtrak), to the Tennessee Valley Authority, as well as all cabinet departments, have been included.

Slang

More than 150 slang terms (such as "big mo" and "teflon president") and informal processes (such as "logrolling" and "spin control") are described. Each entry includes the historical background, if one could be determined. Only those expressions that have developed a specialized meaning and usage in the practice of American politics were included.

The Appendixes

Since the Constitution of the United States is the core document of American government, a copy is provided in Appendix B. The Declaration of Independence (the other core document) is reprinted in Appendix A.

The HarperCollins
Dictionary of
AMERICAN GOVERNMENT AND POLITICS
Concise Edition

A

ABA *See* AMERICAN BAR ASSOCIATION.

ability to pay   1. The principle of taxation that holds that the tax burden should be distributed according to wealth. It is based on the assumption that, as a person's income increases, that person (whether an individual or a CORPORATION) can and should contribute a larger percentage of income to support government activities. The first major analysis comes from Adam Smith's *The Wealth of Nations* (1776): "The subjects of every state ought to contribute towards the support of the government, as nearly as possible, in proportion to their respective abilities; that is, in proportion to the revenue which they respectively enjoy under the protection of the state." The progressive income tax is based on the ability-to-pay principle. **2.** A concept from labor relations and collective bargaining that refers to an employer's ability to tolerate the costs of requested wage and benefit increases.

Abington School District v Schempp   *See* SCHOOL DISTRICT OF ABINGTON TOWNSHIP V SCHEMPP.

Ableman v Booth (1859) The Supreme Court case that held that a prisoner in federal custody could not be released by a writ of habeas corpus issued by a state court. This case helped establish the independence of the state and federal courts from each other by asserting that no judicial process can have any authority outside its own jurisdiction.

abortion   The artificial termination of a pregnancy. This is the single most emotional issue in American politics today because opponents associate it with murder while proponents associate it with women's rights. In 1973 the Supreme Court in ROE V WADE made the option of abortion a constitutional right during the first trimester of pregnancy and a limited right during the second trimester. Ever since, as the Court has grown more conservative, this right to abortion has been increasingly curtailed. Finally in *Webster v Reproductive Health Services* (1989), the Court stopped just short of reversing *Roe v Wade* when it held that states could regulate or abolish a woman's right to have an abortion. Justice Harry Blackmun, who wrote the Court's opinion in *Roe v Wade,* wrote a stinging dissent in the *Webster* case. He said the Court "casts into darkness the hopes and visions of every woman in this country who had come to believe that the Constitution guaranteed her the right to exercise some control over her unique ability to bear children."

The *Webster* decision suddenly made abortion *the* issue of state politics. Now many candidates for a governorship or state legislature must take a stand. This is vexing for politicians of both parties because abortion is not clearly an issue of the left or right. Nevertheless, during the 1992 presidential campaign abortion was a central issue. The Republican Party candidate, President George Bush (running for reelection) was opposed to abortion while the Democratic Party candidate, Governor Bill Clinton of Arkansas, believed abortion was a choice that each woman had to make for herself. Immediately after his inauguration in 1993 Clinton reversed federal restrictions on abortion counseling and on abortion services at military hospitals.

See also BOYCOTT; PRO-CHOICE; PRO-LIFE.

Abrams v United States (1919) The Supreme Court case that upheld the federal government's authority, under the Sedition Act of 1918, to restrict the circulation of pamphlets, during World War I, calling for munitions workers to strike. In doing this, the Court invoked the "bad tendency" rule, which holds that free speech and other First Amendment rights can be curtailed if their exercise might lead to such evils as sedition, riots, or rebellion. In a famous dissenting opinion, Justice Oliver Wendell Holmes, Jr. argued for the "free trade of ideas." He said "that the best test of truth is the power of the thought to get itself accepted in the competition of the market." It was in a previous decision, *Schenck v United States* (1919), that Holmes, speaking for a unanimous Court, enunciated his famous CLEAR AND PRESENT DANGER doctrine. *Compare to* GITLOW V NEW YORK.

abrogation 1. The repeal of a law. **2.** The termination of an agreement by the mutual consent of the parties involved. **3.** The unilateral termination of a formal agreement. The founders of the United States abrogated their formal ties to England when they stated in the Declaration of Independence "that these United Colonies are, and of right ought to be free and independent states; that they are absolved from all allegiance to the British Crown, and that all political connection between them and the State of Great Britain, is and ought to be totally dissolved."

abstention 1. The policy of the federal courts of withholding jurisdiction, even though it may lawfully be claimed, until a state court has rendered judgment of those aspects of state law that bear on the case. *Compare to* COMITY. **2.** Refraining to vote when one is entitled to do so. This is often a diplomatic expedient, especially in the United Nations. While Article 27 of the UN Charter holds that Security Council decisions "shall be made by an affirmative vote of nine members including the concurring votes of the permanent members," the Charter does not deal directly with abstention by those five permanent members who must concur. However, over time an abstention has been interpreted to be neither a veto nor a bar to the passage of a proposal.

abstraction 1. Something that exists only as an intellectual construct. Political scientists often use abstractions such as systems theory, the BALANCE OF POWER, or DETERRENT EFFECT to explain the behavior of political actors. **2.** Taking something, usually illegally, as in the phrase "abstraction of funds."

abuse 1. The use of an existing authority for purposes that extend beyond or even contradict the intentions of the grantors of that authority. It was

President James Madison who warned in a December 2, 1829 speech in the Virginia constitutional convention at Richmond: "The essence of Government is power; and power, lodged as it must be in human hands, will ever be liable to abuse." **2.** The furnishing of excessive services to beneficiaries of government programs, violating program regulations, or performing improper practices, none of which involves prosecutable fraud. Fraud, a more serious offense, involves obtaining something of value by unlawful means through willful misrepresentation.

abuse of right The COMMON LAW concept, also used in international law, that one party should not exercise a right if in so doing it violates the rights of other parties.

abuser fees 1. Additional taxes on tobacco products or alcoholic beverages justified on the basis that abusers of these products, in consequence of their abuse, use a disproportionate share of the nation's health care resources. **2.** Additional charges added to fines of ticketed drivers; the logic is that they should be charged for the services they make necessary.

access 1. The ability to gain the attention and to influence the decisions of key political agents. Political party leaders, the heads of major interest groups, and those who make large campaign contributions are typically said to have access. **2.** LOBBYING; getting information to key decision makers at critical times. This concept was extensively developed by political scientist DAVID B. TRUMAN.

acclamation Overwhelming approval by voice vote. At a political convention, when it becomes obvious that a particular candidate will win a nomination, it is often suggested that the nomination be approved by acclamation to create the appearance of party unity and to generate a sense of total enthusiasm.

accommodation A foreign policy approach that lessens tensions by allowing other actors in the international system room to maneuver into face-saving positions; in essence, not backing an opponent into a diplomatic or political corner. *Compare to* APPEASEMENT.

accord 1. An informal diplomatic understanding. **2.** An international agreement that is for all practical purposes a TREATY except that it is not practical to call it one, such as the CAMP DAVID ACCORDS. **3.** An agreement reached by two previously conflicting parties (such as labor and management). **4.** An agreement by one side to pay, and another side to accept, less than full payment for a debt or obligation.

accountability 1. The extent to which one must answer to higher authority—legal or organizational—for one's actions in society at large or within one's particular organization. Elected public officials are theoretically accountable to the political sovereignty of the voters. In this sense, appointed officials—from file clerks to cabinet secretaries—are less accountable than elected officials. The former are accountable mainly to their organizational supervisors, while the latter must answer to the people of their jurisdiction. The President, especially one in a second term, is in a uniquely unaccountable position. Nevertheless, James MacGregor Burns reminds us that: "One constraint on the President may be his realization that obscure historians, burrowing into the records, will, in their own way, hold him accountable for word and deed, and the relation between word and deed" (*Wall Street Journal*, April 12, 1971). **2.** An obligation for keeping accurate records of property, documents, or funds. *See also* ADMINISTRATIVE ACCOUNTABILITY.

accreditation 1. The process by which a person is invested with credit as a diplomatic representative. The formal vehicle for this is a letter of credence signed by a head of state and personally presented by an AMBASSADOR to the head of the receiving state. Lower ranks may present their letters merely to a foreign minister. **2.** A letter of credence itself.

Acheson, Dean Gooderham (1893–1971) The U.S. Secretary of State (1949–1953), under President Harry S Truman, who was the prime architect of the policy of CONTAINMENT of Soviet expansion and a major influence on the development of NATO and the MARSHALL PLAN. Acheson was Secretary of State when the Chinese Communists forced Chiang Kai-shek and his Nationalists off the mainland to Taiwan in 1949. In spite of the fact that Acheson maintained that "nothing that this country did or could have done within the reasonable limits of its capabilities would have changed the results," he and the Truman administration were blamed for having "lost" China to the Communists. This seemed like the bankruptcy of the containment policy that was actually working quite well in Western Europe. Acheson was further criticized when, in a January 1950 speech to the National Press Club, he excluded Korea from the American "defense perimeter." Six months later, when North Korea invaded the South, his critics blamed him for precipitating the invasion. Nevertheless, Acheson remains one of the few men who actually shaped the post-World War II world order.

Acheson's Rule That a government memorandum is written not to inform the reader but to protect the writer. Dean Acheson wrote in his memoirs, *Present at the Creation* (1969): "I have never yet read a memorandum of conversation in which the writer came off second best."

acid rain Rainfall contaminated by industrial pollution. Such rain, because of its acidity, adversely affects inland aquatic life and forests. Since the pollutants causing acid rain come from one place and the rain itself falls on another, this has become an important interregional and international environmental issue. Acid rain is an especially contentious problem between the United States and Canada.

ACIR *See* ADVISORY COMMISSION ON INTERGOVERNMENTAL RELATIONS.

ACLU *See* AMERICAN CIVIL LIBERTIES UNION.

acquittal The judgment of a court, based on the verdict of either a jury or a judge, that a defendant is not guilty of the offense that was charged. *See* DOUBLE JEOPARDY.

act 1. A written piece of legislation formally passed by a legislature, such as the U.S. Congress. An act is a BILL from its introduction until its passage by a legislature. An act becomes a LAW, a formal statute, when it is signed by (or passed over the veto of) a chief executive, such as the U.S. President. **2.** A bill that has been passed by only one house of a legislature.

ACTION The federal agency, created by the Domestic Volunteer Service Act of 1973, that coordinates and administers all domestic volunteer activities sponsored by the federal government. ACTION is the administrative home of Volunteers in Service to America (VISTA), the Foster Grandparent Program, the Retired Senior Volunteer Program (RSVP), and related programs. (While ACTION is correctly written with all capital letters, it is not an acronym—just a matter of federal government style.) *Compare to* PEACE CORPS.

actionable Something that provides adequate reason for a grievance or lawsuit.

activist 1. One who is seriously and passionately involved in politics by running for office, mobilizing support for issues, participating in campaigns, and so on. **2.** One who is so impatient with the normal or existing processes of political change that he or she resorts to more active methods, such as street demonstrations or sit-ins. Activists of both types subscribe to the philosophy of OLIVER WENDELL HOLMES, Jr. (1841–1935), which he stated in a May 30, 1884 speech: "Life is action and passion. I think it is required of a man that he should share the action and passion of his time at peril of being judged not to have lived" (*Speeches*, 1934).

act of Congress A statute; a law passed by the U.S. Congress and signed (or passed over the veto of) the President. All of the acts passed by the Congress are published, in chronological order according to term and session of Congress, in the *United States* STATUTES-AT-LARGE. The statutes are organized by subject in the *United States* CODE.

act of state Governmental actions for which individual citizens cannot be held accountable; activities that only the state has the legal right to perform: for example, declaring war, passing laws, punishing criminals.

act of state doctrine The judicial policy that a court in one nation should not rule on the legality of the internal acts of a foreign country.

action–reaction 1. An explanation of the behavior of political actors during international crises, which implies that each actor responds to the behavior of others with preplanned moves; thus, the sequence of actions taken are not necessarily reflective of long-term goals or genuine motivations. The classic example is the beginning of World War I. The initial response to the assassination of Archduke Ferdinand of Austria in 1914 set off a chain reaction: mobilization by Russia sparked mobilization by Germany, which in turn led to mobilization by others. In each case, one participant was reacting in a more or less automatic way to another, rather than making a deliberately thought-out move. **2.** In an arms race context, the action-reaction pattern occurs when the deployment of a new weapons system by one side leads to the development of an equivalent or superior system by the opposition.

actual malice What a public figure must prove to exist if he or she is to successfully sue someone for LIBEL or SLANDER. *See* NEW YORK TIMES MAGAZINE V SULLIVAN.

Adams, Herbert Baxter (1850–1901) The American historian who helped revolutionize higher education with his introduction of the seminar method and his "germ theory of politics," which sought to trace American political institutions back to their roots in ancient Anglo-Saxon villages. Adams stressed the historical-comparative approach, which called for scholars to use original sources.

Adams, John (1735–1826) The first Vice President (1789–1797) and the second President (1797–1801) of the United States. Adams, the lawyer who defended the British soldiers responsible for the Boston Massacre, represented Massachusetts in the Continental Congress. He was a major influence in the appointment of George Washington as the commander of the revolutionary forces, because he felt it was essential for national unity that the war, at first fought mainly in New England, actively involve all the colonies—especially Washington's native Virginia. Although Thomas Jefferson drafted the Declaration of Independence, many of its principles were formulated by Adams; and it was Adams who led the fight for its adoption by the Continental Congress.

Adams failed to win reelection to a second presidential term largely because of the controversy over the ALIEN AND SEDITION LAWS. His replacement by Thomas Jefferson is often hailed as the "real" American Revolution, because it was the first major instance of a party in power (the Federalists) peacefully yielding government control to its political opposition (the Democratic-Republicans). Adams' defeat also marks the beginning of a viable two-party system in the United States. John Adams is the only President of the United States whose son (John Quincy Adams) became President.

Adams, John Quincy (1767–1848) The President of the United States (1825–1829) who is considered the United States' foremost diplomatic strategist and negotiator in the pre-Civil War era. He helped negotiate the 1814 Treaty of Ghent which ended the War of 1812 between the United States and Great Britain. As United States Secretary of State under President James Monroe, Adams drafted much of the MONROE DOCTRINE. He negotiated the Adams-Onis Treaty of 1817, by which the United States acquired Florida from Spain, and the settlement of the United States-Canadian boundary through the Convention of 1818. Nevertheless, he accomplished little as President and thereafter served the rest of his life in the House of Representatives (1831–1848).

ad hoc committee A committee created by the SPEAKER of the House of Representatives for a specific task or purpose, whose existence ceases with the attainment of its goal, and whose members are drawn from the several House committees having jurisdictional claims over the issue or question involved.

ad interim A Latin term meaning "in the meantime." A public official is ad interim when serving the unexpired term of a predecessor (who has died, resigned, or been removed) until a permanent official can be appointed or elected.

adjournment The putting off of business to another time or place; the decision of a court, legislature, or other group to stop meeting either temporarily or permanently.

adjournment sine die The adjournment of a legislature that does not fix a day for reconvening. (Sine die is a Latin term meaning "without a day.") It is used to indicate the final adjournment of a session of the Congress or of a state legislature.

adjournment to a day certain Legislative adjournment under a motion or resolution fixing the date for a next meeting. Neither house of the U.S. Congress can adjourn for more than three days without the concurrence of the other. *Compare to* RECESS.

adjudication **1.** The resolution of a dispute by means of judicial or quasi-judicial proceedings in which the parties are able to present evidence and reasoned arguments. **2.** The formal pronouncing and recording of the decision of a court or quasi-judicial entity.

administration **1.** The management and direction of the affairs of governments and institutions. **2.** A collective term for all policy making officials of a government. **3.** The execution and implementation of public policy. But this is never value-free. Governor Adlai E. Stevenson, while campaigning for the presidency in Los Angeles on September 11, 1952 explains: "In the tragic days of Mussolini, the trains in Italy ran on time as never before and I am told in their way, their horrible way, that the Nazi concentration-camp system in Germany was a model of horrible efficiency. The really basic thing in government is policy. Bad administration, to be sure, can destroy good policy, but good administration can never save bad policy." **4.** The time in office of a chief executive such as a President, governor, or mayor. Thus, "the Reagan Administration" refers to those years (1981–1989) when Ronald Reagan was President of the United States. **5.** The supervision of the estate of a dead person to pay taxes and assign assets to heirs. *Compare to* PUBLIC ADMINISTRATION.

administrative accountability The concept that officials are to be held answerable for general notions of democracy and morality as well as for specific legal mandates. The two basic approaches to administrative accountability were first delineated by Carl J. Friedrich (1901–1984) and Herman Finer (1898–1969). Friedrich argued that administrative responsibility can be assured only internally, through professionalism or professional standards or codes, because the increasing complexities of modern policies require extensive policy expertise and specialized abilities on the part of bureaucrats. Finer, on the other hand, argued that administrative accountability could be maintained only externally, through legislative or popular controls, because internal power or control would ultimately lead to corruption. *See also* ACCOUNTABILITY.

administrative adjudication The settlement of disputes by QUASI-JUDICIAL means.

administrative advocacy The presentation of alternative policies to an administrative agency. This practice recognizes that public administration is a highly political process involving significant differences of judgment. The most feasible course of action often emerges from the competition produced when each interested group pleads the cause it represents, whether that cause be more funds to carry out agency policies, the survival of a particular program, or the desire for a more efficient system of administrative decision making. *Compare to* LOBBYING.

administrative agency **1.** A government organization set up to implement a law. **2.** Any civilian government body (board, bureau, department, or individual), other than a court or legislature, that deals with the rights of private parties by adjudication, rule making, investigation, prosecuting, and so on. **3.** In the context of labor relations, any impartial private or government organization that oversees or facilitates the labor relations process.

administrative assistant **1.** A vague title for an executive's aide who can be little more than a secretary or as powerful as an assistant boss. **2.** A legislator's chief assistant; the person who manages the legislative office and is the legislator's chief source of advice on political and legislative issues. *Compare to* LEGISLATIVE ASSISTANT.

Administrative Conference of the United States A permanent independent agency established by the Administrative Conference Act of 1964 that seeks to develop improvements in the legal procedures by which federal agencies administer regulatory, benefit, and other government programs.

administrative due process Term encompassing a number of points in ADMINISTRATIVE LAW that require that the administrative procedures of government agencies and regulatory commissions, as they affect private parties, be based upon written guidelines that safeguard individual rights and protect against the arbitrary or inequitable exercise of government authority. *Compare to* DUE PROCESS.

administrative law *See* LAW, ADMINISTRATIVE.

administrative law judge A government official who conducts hearings in the place of or on behalf of a more formal body, such as the National Labor Relations Board, the Merit Systems Protection Board, or the Social Security Administration. He or she may also be known as a *hearing examiner* or *hearing officer*.

administrative legislation The rules made by regulatory agencies or commissions.

administrative order A directive carrying the force of law issued by an administrative agency after ADJUDICATION.

Administrative Procedure Act of 1946 (APA) The basic law governing the way federal government agencies operate, intended to safeguard agency clients and the general public. The APA specifies the conditions under which administrative agencies: (1) publicize information about their operations; (2) make rules; (3) engage in adjudication; and (4) are subject to judicial review. Major amendments to the APA include the FREEDOM OF INFORMATION ACT OF 1966, the PRIVACY ACT OF 1974, and the Sunshine Act of 1976. *See also* SUNSHINE LAWS.

administrative remedy A means of enforcing a right by appealing to an administrative agency, either for help or for a decision. People are often required to "exhaust all administrative remedies" by submitting their problems to the proper agency before taking their cases to court.

administrator 1. A manager. **2.** The head of a government agency. **3.** Someone appointed by a court to handle a deceased person's estate. **4.** Anyone with a FIDUCIARY responsibility.

admonition of rights *See* MIRANDA RIGHTS.

advance man/advance woman A person who travels to a location preceding a political candidate to arrange for campaign appearances, hotels, rental cars, publicity, and so on. To "advance" is to arrange for a campaign's logistics.

adversary proceeding Any formal hearing, trial, or legal contest in which both sides are appropriately represented and challenge each other's view of fact or law before an impartial decision-maker or jury.

adversary system The Anglo-American system of law, in which a judge or jury acts as an impartial decision maker between opposite sides, each of which has an opportunity to prove its assertion of guilt or innocence. The adversary system contrasts with the inquisitional system, in which accused parties must exonerate themselves before a judge (or judges), who function as both judge and public prosecutor. Under the adversary system it is generally the lawyers for each side that argue the case. According to trial lawyer F. Lee Bailey: "I get paid for seeing that my clients have every break the law allows. I have knowingly defended a number of guilty men. But the guilty never escape unscathed. My fees are sufficient punishment for anyone" (*Los Angeles Times*, January 9, 1972).

adverse action 1. An act against someone else's interests. **2.** A personnel action unfavorable to an employee, such as discharge, suspension, or demotion. **3.** A use of land that harms local property values, such as the construction of a gas station or a prison on land zoned for and occupied by single-family homes.

advice and consent The right of the U.S. Senate, granted in Article II, Section 2 of the Constitution, to review treaties and major presidential appointments. For these to take effect they must be approved by two thirds of the senators present or a simple majority, respectively. While much is made of the Senate's right to confirm designated presidential appointees, it is only on the rarest occasion that a nominee is rejected. (More often, a controversial nomination is withdrawn.) Historically, rejections have been based far more on questions of qualifications and scandals in the nominee's past than on disapproval of the nominee's political, judicial, or managerial philosophy. This attitude on the part of the Senate has had the effect of giving the President a relatively free hand in appointments.

Advisory Commission on Intergovernmental Relations (ACIR) The federal commission created by the U.S. Congress in 1959 to monitor the operation of the federal system and to recommend improvements. The ACIR is a permanent national bipartisan body composed of 26 members, who serve two-year terms and are representative of the federal, state, and local governments and the public.

AFDC *See* AID TO FAMILIES WITH DEPENDENT CHILDREN.

affidavit A written statement made under oath before a person permitted by law to administer such an oath (e.g., a NOTARY PUBLIC). Such statements are frequently used in legal proceedings, labor arbitrations, and other formal hearings.

affirmative action A term that first gained currency in the 1960s, when it meant the removal of "artificial barriers" to the employment of women and minority group members. Toward the end of that decade, however, the term was altered to mean compensatory opportunities for hitherto disadvantaged groups. In a formal, legal sense, affirmative action now refers to specific efforts to recruit, hire, and promote disadvantaged groups for the purpose of eliminating the present effects of past discrimination.

affirmative action groups Also known as *protected groups*, segments of the population that have been identified by federal, state, or local laws to be specifically protected from employment discrimination. Such groups include women, identified minorities, the elderly, and the handicapped. *See also* RACE CATEGORIES.

AFL-CIO *See* AMERICAN FEDERATION OF LABOR-CONGRESS OF INDUSTRIAL ORGANIZATIONS.

Afroyim v Rusk (1967) The Supreme Court case that held unconstitutional a portion of the Nationality Act of 1940, under which U.S. citizens would forfeit their citizenship by voting in a foreign election. This reversed *Perez v Brownell,* 356 U.S. 44 (1958), which held that certain acts in a foreign country could cause automatic forfeiture of U.S. citizenship. In *Afroyim,* the Court held that a citizen has a constitutional right to remain a citizen unless that right is specifically relinquished.

AFSCME *See* AMERICAN FEDERATION OF STATE, COUNTY AND MUNICIPAL EMPLOYEES.

agency 1. Any department, office, commission, authority, administration, board, government-owned corporation, or other independent establishment of any branch of government in the United States. **2.** A formal relation whereby one person is authorized to act for another. **3.** In intelligence usage, an organization or individual engaged in collecting and/or processing information. **4.** A slang term for the CIA.

Agency for International Development (AID) A unit of the U.S. International Development Cooperation Agency that is authorized by the Foreign Assistance Act of 1961 to carry out assistance programs designed to help the people of certain less-developed countries nurture their human and economic resources, increase their productive capacities, and improve their quality of life. AID was a part of the U.S. Department of State until 1979.

agency shop A union security provision, found in some collective bargaining agreements, that requires that nonunion employees of the bargaining unit must pay for the union's representational services as a condition of continuing employment. The agency shop was designed as a compromise between the union's desire to eliminate free riders by means of compulsory membership (the union shop) and management's wish that union membership be voluntary. Its constitutionality was upheld by the Supreme Court in *Abood v Detroit Board of Education,* (1977). Later, in *Chicago Teachers Union v Hudson* (1986), the Court held against making nonmembers of the union pay for union activities other than representation.

agenda setting 1. The process of deciding what issues will be considered at a formal meeting. **2.** The process by which ideas or issues bubble up through the various political processes to wind up on the agenda of a political institution, such as a legislature or court. Extensive use of the mass media can take a relatively unknown or unsupported issue and, through publicity, expand the numbers who care about the issue so an institution, whether it be a city hall or the U.S. Congress, is forced to take some action. **3.** The process by which the mass media decides what is news, and therefore decides what issues will be brought to the public for attention.

agent 1. A person authorized to act on behalf of another, such as a bargaining agent or a business agent. **2.** In intelligence usage, a person who is recruited, trained, controlled, and employed to obtain and report information. **3.** An intelligence agent employed in a covert operation; a spy. **4.** A saboteur.

agent of influence 1. A person of one presumed loyalty who is actually under the control of a competitor, not to spy or to engage in illegal activities, but to affect public opinion. **2.** Japanese agents who buy influence in Washington (and in universities and think tanks) to keep American trade and economic policies favorable to Japan. The usage comes from Pat Choate's 1990 book *Agents of Influence.*

Agnew, Spiro T. (1918–   ) President Richard M. Nixon's Vice President from 1969 to 1973. Agnew resigned amid charges that he had accepted bribes during his previous tenure as Governor of Maryland. He pleaded NOLO CONTENDERE to related income tax violations and was found guilty.

Agriculture, U.S. Department of (USDA) The federal department, created in 1862, that works to improve and maintain farm income, to develop and expand markets abroad for agricultural products, to enhance the environment, and to maintain U.S. production capacity by helping landowners protect their soil, water, forests, and other natural resources. The department, through inspection and grading services, also assures that certain standards are met in food products.

AID *See* AGENCY FOR INTERNATIONAL DEVELOPMENT.

Aid to Families with Dependent Children (AFDC) The largest federal WELFARE program after FOOD STAMPS. As part of the Social Security Act of 1935, the Aid to Dependent Children program was expanded by 1962 amendments to the Social Security Act and renamed. AFDC provides federal funds, administered by the states, for children living with a parent or a relative who meets state standards of need. The program has been controversial because of charges that it promotes illegitimacy and encourages fathers to abandon their families so their children can become eligible for AFDC. In 1988 about 3.7 million families were receiving AFDC. The Family Support Act of 1988 revised AFDC requirements to emphasize WORKFARE and child support from absent fathers.

AIDS (Acquired Immune Deficiency Syndrome) A disease, unknown until 1981, that has killed approximately 100,000 persons in the United States alone. An estimated two and a half million Americans are infected with the Human Immunodeficiency Virus (HIV), and many will develop AIDS (which is usually fatal) in the future. AIDS has considerable political significance because governments have been forced to respond to the disease by funding massive research, treatment, and prevention programs. For example, because the AIDS virus is often transmitted through sexual relations, many school districts have vastly expanded their sex education programs. Some, such as New York City, even distribute free condoms to students in an effort to curtail the spread of the disease.

Air Force One Not one aircraft, but any of the aircraft in the presidential fleet that the President is currently using.

Albany Congress A 1754 meeting of delegates from seven of the American colonies. It was there that Benjamin Franklin proposed the Albany Plan of Union, which would have united the colonies in a federation. While the colonies, fearing the loss of powers inherent in a federation, rejected the plan, the meeting helped lead to the later calling of the Continental Congresses.

Albertson v Subversive Activities Control Board (1965) The Supreme Court case that held that the compulsory registration of members of American communist groups was self-incrimination, in violation of the Fifth Amendment. This decision invalidated a major portion of the Internal Security (McCarran) Act of 1950. The Subversive Activities Control Board, which was created by the act to monitor communist groups, individuals, and activities, was abolished in 1973. *Compare to* APTHEKER V SECRETARY OF STATE.

alderman/alderwoman 1. Title for members of some local legislatures, from the Anglo-Saxon *ealdorman*, meaning an "elder person." **2.** A member of the upper house of a bicameral city council.

alien A legal visitor or resident in a nation of which he or she is not a citizen; a citizen of one nation living in another. A RESIDENT ALIEN is allowed permanent residence by a nation of which he or she is not a citizen. Since no nation can demand that its nationals be allowed to visit or reside in another, the laws governing aliens are domestic matters for each nation.

alien and sedition laws A series of 1798 laws approved by President John Adams and passed by the last FEDERALIST-controlled Congress. These laws made it a crime to criticize the federal government, made it more difficult to become a naturalized American citizen, and gave the President the power to deport undesirable aliens. They were enacted to quiet the pro-French activities of the Jeffersonian Republicans and were repealed after Thomas Jefferson and his party took control of both the Congress and the presidency in 1801. President Harry S Truman would later write that these "extreme and arbitrary security measures strike at the very heart of our free society and that we must be eternally vigilant against those who would undermine freedom in the name of security" (*The Words of Harry S Truman*, 1984).

Alien Registration Act of 1940 The federal law, also known as the *Smith Act*, that requires the annual registration of aliens and prohibits advocating the violent overthrow of the U.S. government.

alien, resident One who is not a citizen of the country in which he or she lives. Resident aliens in the United States have as a matter of right the full protection of the laws but do not have all of the privileges of citizenship, such as the right to vote, the opportunity to hold many government jobs, the right to many welfare benefits, and so on.

alienation 1. Marxist term for the inevitable dissociation felt by industrial workers because of their lack of control over their work. (They would thus be ripe for revolution.) The word has largely lost its Marxist meaning and now refers to any feelings of estrangement from one's work, family, government, society, and the like. In the context of politics and voting behavior, alienation refers to a voluntary dropping out of the political process, to nonvoting, or to feelings of contempt or indifference toward government. *Compare to* ANOMIE. **2.** The legal transfer of real property.

all deliberate speed *See* DELIBERATE SPEED.

allegiance 1. The LOYALTY and devotion that a citizen owes his or her country; the positive obligation that a citizen has to safeguard the country's interests. **2.** The bond, whether emotional, coercive, or legal, that binds a subject to the nation's sovereign.

allegiance, pledge of The affirmation of devotion recited when the American flag is presented on ceremonial occasions. It reads: "I pledge allegiance to the flag of the United States of America and to the republic for which it stands, one nation under God, indivisible, with liberty and justice for all." The original version (which did not include the words "under God") was written by Francis Bellamy in 1892 and published in the September 8 issue of *Youth's Companion,* a weekly magazine. In 1942 the Congress made the pledge officially part of the U.S. Code. In 1954 the Congress added "under God." The Supreme Court has held in *West Virginia State Board of Education v Barnette* (1943) that children cannot be compelled to salute the flag while reciting the pledge of allegiance. Because 1988 Democratic presidential candidate Michael Dukakis, as Governor of Massachusetts, vetoed a state bill that would have been in violation of this ruling, the question of which candidate was more patriotic became a campaign issue. Republican presidential nominee George Bush said he would have found a way to sign the bill; Dukakis countered by asserting that it was his patriotic duty as Governor to respect Supreme Court precedents.

alliance A formal agreement between two or more nations for mutual assistance in case of war. The FOUNDING FATHERS warned against alliances. George Washington in his Farewell Address of September 17, 1796, proclaimed that, "It is our true policy to steer clear of permanent alliance with any portion of the foreign world." Thomas Jefferson in his Inaugural Address of March 4, 1801, put forth the policy of "peace, commerce, and honest friendship with all nations—entangling alliances with none." Nevertheless, the modern world has forced the United States into many an entangling alliance. The main reason for peacetime alliances, such as NATO, is to deter war. By that criterion, the Western alliance, as NATO is often called, has been a resounding success because of the fact that there has been no European war since its founding in 1949.

ambassador A diplomat of the highest rank who is sent as the personal representative of one head of state to another. Not all ambassadors are equal. The most powerful is an ambassador extraordinary and plenipotentiary, who has the broadest mandate of authority. Then follows an ambassador extraordinary, who has lesser powers, an ambassador plenipotentiary, who has authority of a specific nature, and an ambassador ordinary, who is the chief of a diplomatic mission without specifications as to authority. Sir Henry Wotton (1568–1639), Queen Elizabeth I's ambassador to Venice, was the first of many wits to note that "an ambassador is an honest man sent to lie abroad for the commonwealth." Camillo Benso (1810–1861), an Italian statesman, took a different approach toward lying. "I have discovered the art of deceiving diplomats. I speak the truth, and they never believe me." The modern ambassador dates from the fifteenth century when the Italian city-states began establishing permanent representatives in each other's capitals. By the next century all the monarchies of Europe were exchanging resident ambassadors. The 1815 Congress of Vienna codified diplomatic ranks with ambassadors (along with papal nuncios and legates) at the top. *See also* COUNTRY TEAM; DIPLOMATIC PRIVILEGES AND IMMUNITIES.

amendment **1.** A change in a prior law by the enactment of a new law. **2.** An addition to a bill during its time of consideration in a legislature. **3.** A provision of a constitution adopted after its original ratification. The United States Constitution has had only 26 amendments in over 200 years (each of which has its own entry in this book). A large part of the reason for this is that many Americans have Senator Barry Goldwater's attitude: "Our constitutional government is the finest thing ever devised by man. Why screw around with it?" (*Wall Street Journal*, August 3, 1981). The first 10 amendments to the United States Constitution are called the BILL OF RIGHTS.

America First An isolationist motto first used by President Woodrow Wilson in a speech on April 20, 1915; later used by those who did not want the United States government to help Great Britain before the United States formally entered World War II.

American Bar Association (ABA) Since 1878 this has been *the* professional association for lawyers. Located in Chicago with over 300,000 members nationwide, it is always a major voice in the public debate over changing any aspect of the civil or criminal justice system. Its Committee on Federal Judiciary evaluates federal judicial nominations and rates the nominees according to their qualifications. These ratings may become a significant factor in the Senate confirmation or nonconfirmation of the nominees. But this is very rare. Consequently, the ABA evaluations are in reality little more than a formality.

American Civil Liberties Union (ACLU) The quarter-million-strong New York-based public interest group dedicated to the promotion and protection of the civil liberties that all Americans have under the U.S. Constitution. Its main activity is the testing of civil rights issues in the courts. Thus, it has played a vital role in cases on school prayer, loyalty oaths, illegal search and seizure, and the right of free speech for members of the American Nazi party and other unpopular groups. The ACLU evolved from the American Civil Liberties Bureau started by attorneys Norman Thomas (1884–1968) and Roger Baldwin (1884–1981) in 1917 to defend World War I conscientious objectors. It expanded to become the ACLU in 1920 to fight the egregious violations of civil rights and due process by U.S. Attorney General A. Mitchell Palmer (1872–1936) during the postwar RED SCARE. By taking more cases to the Supreme Court than any other private organization, the ACLU has been in the forefront of civil rights and free speech constitutional issues.

American Commonwealth *See* JAMES BRYCE.

American Federation of Government Employees (AFGE) The largest union of federal government employees. Founded in 1932, it has grown to 700,000 members in 1,380 locals around the world; headquartered in Washington, D.C.

American Federation of Labor-Congress of Industrial Organizations (AFL-CIO) A voluntary federation of over a hundred national and international labor UNIONS operating in the United States and representing in total over 13 million workers. The AFL-CIO is not itself a union; it does no bargaining. It is perhaps best thought of as a union of unions. The affiliated unions created the AFL-CIO to represent them in the creation and execution of broad national and international policies and to coordinate a wide range of joint activities. The American Federation of Labor (organized in 1881 as a federation of craft unions, the Federation of Organized Trade and Labor Unions), changed its name in 1886 after merging with those craft unions that had become disenchanted with the Knights of Labor. In 1955, the AFL merged with the Congress of Industrial Organizations to become the AFL-CIO. Each member union of the AFL-CIO remains autonomous, conducting its own affairs in the manner determined by its own members. Each has its own headquarters, officers, and staff. Each decides its own economic policies, carries on its own contract negotiations, sets its own dues, and provides its own membership services. Each is free to withdraw at any time. But through such voluntary participation, the AFL-CIO, based in Washington, plays a role in establishing overall policies for the U.S. labor movement, which in turn advances the interests of every union.

American Federation of State, County and Municipal Employees (AFSCME) The largest union of state and local government employees. Founded in 1936 and headquartered in Washington D.C., it has grown to 1,100,000 members in 3,000 locals in 46 states. It represents virtually every category of public employee from computer programmers to firefighters to garbage collectors to police officers to teachers to sewage workers, among others. It is the second largest union in the AFL-CIO; only the Teamsters are bigger.

American Legion A private organization of veterans of the U.S. armed forces. Created in 1919 in the wake of World War I, it has long been an effective lobby for veterans' concerns.

American Political Science Association (APSA) Since 1903, the leading academic organization for American political scientists. APSA, located in Washington, D.C., publishes the *American Political Science Review*, *PS* (a quarterly which contains political analysis, articles, and news of interest to professionals in political science), directories of political scientists and college programs in political science, and a wealth of other materials relating to the teaching and practice of political science. Its annual conventions provide an opportunity for political scientists to meet and present their research findings.

American Revolution The war fought by the British colonies in America for freedom from British rule. The fighting is usually dated from the 1775 clashes at Lexington and Concord in Massachusetts to the British surrender at the 1781 Battle of Yorktown, Virginia. The 1776 DECLARATION OF INDE-

PENDENCE was a justification for war which was formally ended by the Treaty of Paris of 1783. However, President John Adams maintained in a February 13, 1818 letter to Hezekiah Niles: "The Revolution was effected before the war commenced. The Revolution was in the minds and hearts of the people; a change in their religious sentiments of their duties and obligations . . . This radical change in the principles, opinions, sentiments, and affections of the people, was the real American Revolution."

American Spectator, The   A conservative monthly of political analysis known for its wit and bite.

American system   1. The essential principles of American government. Alexander Hamilton wrote in *Federalist* No.11: "Let the thirteen states, bound together in a strict and indissoluble union, concur in erecting one great American system." Thomas Jefferson wrote in a letter of October 24, 1820, to Joseph Correa de Serra that "nothing is so important as that America shall separate herself from the systems of Europe and establish one of her own." **2.** The American economic policy in the nineteenth century, which emphasized protective tariffs and public works. Henry Clay (1777–1852), as Speaker of the House of Representatives and later a leader in the Senate, was the most famous advocate of an "American system" of protective domestic industries combined with internal improvements to what we now call infrastructure. **3.** Inventor Eli Whitney's (1765–1825) system of manufacturing, the first to make major use of interchangeable parts.

Americanism   1. Something, such as a word or practice, that is uniquely American. **2.** A vague term for the practice and advocacy of virtuous patriotism. **3.** The belief that American ideals, values, and practices are better than those of any other country. President Theodore Roosevelt in a January 10, 1917 letter to S. Stanwood Menken wrote: "Americanism means the virtues of courage, honor, justice, truth, sincerity, and hardihood—the virtues that made America. The things that will destroy America are prosperity-at-any-price, peace-at-any-price, safety-first instead of duty-first, the love of soft living and the get-rich-quick theory of life."

amicus curiae   A Latin term meaning "friend of the court"; any person or organization allowed to participate in a lawsuit who would not otherwise have a right to do so. Participation is usually limited to filing a brief on behalf of one side or the other.

amnesty   The act of "forgetfulness" by a government for crimes, usually political, committed by a group of people. After the U.S. Civil War, President Andrew Johnson granted amnesty to all Confederates. When the Congress tried to limit its effects, the Supreme Court ruled in *Ex parte Garland* (1867) that this was an invalid interference with the President's power to pardon, given in Article II, Section 2, of the U.S. Constitution. In 1977, President Jimmy Carter granted an amnesty to all Vietnam War draft evaders (but not to military deserters). A PARDON, in contrast, is usually granted to individuals. For example, in 1974 President Gerald R. Ford granted a pardon to former President Richard M. Nixon for any crimes he may have committed while in office.

Amtrak *See* NATIONAL RAILROAD PASSENGER CORPORATION.

anarchism The belief that government and its administrative institutions are intrinsically evil and should be abolished (typically by violence) so they can be replaced by arrangements not "corrupted" by exploitative and oppressive governments. The word comes from the ancient Greek *anarkhia*, meaning "nonrule."

anarchy A social context in which legitimate political authority does not exist; the absence of formal legal order. The international system of sovereign states is often referred to as anarchic because there is no over-reaching power above them; because, while there are international organizations, alliances, and understandings, sovereign states do not recognize any greater authority than their own. This is why political scientist Hedley Bull entitled his analysis of international relationships *The Anarchical Society* (1977).

Annapolis Convention A 1786 meeting at Annapolis, Maryland, called by the states to discuss interstate commerce. Its significance lies in its only recommendation: that a larger convention—which turned out to be the Constitutional Convention of 1787—be held in Philadelphia the following year.

annexation 1. The formal extension of sovereignty over new territory. For example, the United States annexed the Republic of Texas in 1845. **2.** The acquisition of adjacent settlements by a city. After annexation, these settlements are part of the city. Though, in the past, most cities grew by annexation, it is difficult for most cities to annex now because the suburbs are typically incorporated entities not usually subject to involuntary annexation. Nevertheless, annexation is still a major issue in municipal politics in the western United States, where cities often have the state-legislated right to annex adjacent unincorporated areas. These unincorporated areas are often rightfully fearful that annexation will adversely affect their municipal services and tax rates, while the central city is often anxious to annex lands so as to expand its tax and service bases. Sometimes, however, this strategy backfires when an annexed area fails to attract significant business and industry and becomes a tax and service drain.

annuit coeptis A Latin term meaning "he [God] has favored our undertakings." This motto is on the Great Seal of the United States and on the back of the one-dollar bill.

anomie A social condition in which previously established norms of behavior have been dissipated or rejected; consequently, there is no effective social control of individual behavior. The concept was named and explicated by the French sociologist Emile Durkheim (1858–1917). *Compare to* ALIENATION.

antifederalists Those opposed to the adoption of the new U.S. Constitution in the late 1780s. They were against a strong central government and preferred the retention of powers by the state governments. Their concerns helped bring into life the BILL OF RIGHTS.

Anti-Ku Klux Klan Act *See* CIVIL RIGHTS ACT OF 1871.

Anti-Trust Act of 1914 *See* CLAYTON ACT OF 1914.

antitrust laws Those federal and state statutes that limit the ability of businesses and unions to exercise monopoly control and to cause the restraint of trade. They are thought necessary because, as Adam Smith observed in *The Wealth of Nations* (1776): "People of the same trade seldom meet together, even for merriment and diversion, but the conversation ends in a conspiracy against the public, or in some contrivance to raise prices." The Sherman Anti-Trust Act of 1890 was the first significant American break with the economic philosophy of LAISSEZ-FAIRE. It asserted that law could create and control conditions in the marketplace and that it was sometimes in the public interest for government to exercise substantial indirect control over economic conditions. The American policy of antitrust enforcement contrasts sharply with those of most other nations, which encourage and tolerate cartels as the normal order of things. Thus, commercial competitors of the United States have industries that are able, with their government's sanction and assistance, to compete as one against the fractioned industries of the United States.

apolitical **1.** Outside of politics; not concerned with political dominance; apathetic toward voting or politics. **2.** nonpartisan; not affiliated with a political party. *Compare to* POLITICAL APATHY.

appeal **1.** Any request to a higher authority that a lower authority's decision be reviewed. **2.** A formal request to a higher court that it review the actions of a lower court. *Compare to* CERTIORARI. **3.** A challenge to a ruling made by a presiding officer of a legislature. If the challenge is supported by a majority vote of the legislators, the initial ruling is overridden.

appeasement **1.** The practice of giving in to the demands of those making explicit or implicit threats. The term is most associated with the 1938 incident in which England and France permitted Germany to occupy the Sudetenland in Czechoslovakia. Thereupon, British Prime Minister Neville Chamberlain (1869–1940) said there would be "peace in our time," and German Chancellor Adolf Hitler (1889–1945) declared that he had no further territorial ambitions in Europe. Because the policy of appeasement only encouraged Hitler's aggression, which led to World War II, the word has taken on a decidedly negative connotation. **2.** A description of a foreign policy in which aggressive acts by a potential enemy are allowed to pass unpunished. But as George Orwell (*New Leader*, March 29, 1947) warned: "In international politics . . . you must either be ready to practice appeasement indefinitely, or at some point you must be ready to fight." Appeasement has been seen as an intrinsic evil by American politicians ever since President Franklin D. Roosevelt warned in a message to Congress (January 6, 1941) that, "We must always be wary of those who . . . preach the 'ism' of appeasement."

appellant One who appeals a case to a higher authority.

appellate Any court that considers appeals concerning a lower court's actions.

appellate jurisdiction The power of a court, board, or commission to review cases previously decided by a lower authority.

appellee The defendant in an appeal (usually the victor in a lower-court case).

applause line Statements that are deliberately inserted into a political speech to encourage "spontaneous" applause. Often lead clappers are planted in the audience to start clapping at the desired times.

apportionment 1. A determination of how many legislators should be sent to a legislative body from a given jurisdiction. The U.S. Constitution provides that each state is entitled to two senators and at least one representative. Beyond the minimum, representatives are apportioned among the states according to population. This apportionment is adjusted after every 10-year census. Under the Apportionment Act of 1929, the Congress fixed the size of the House of Representatives at 435 seats, and after each census the Congress assigns the appropriate number of seats to each state. The states themselves carry on from there: the actual redistributing process is a matter of state law, with one major exception. In 1967 Congress prohibited at-large elections in all states entitled to more than one seat in the House. *See also* BAKER V CARR; REYNOLDS V SIMS. *Compare to* REDISTRICTING. **2.** An executive budget function that takes place after passage of an appropriations bill in which a jurisdiction's budget office creates a plan for expenditures to reconcile agency or department programs with available resources. **3.** A requirement, written into the Pendleton Act of 1883, that all federal government merit system jobs in headquarter offices of agencies in metropolitan Washington, D.C., were to be distributed among the residents of the states on the basis of population. This requirement was repealed by Congress in 1977. Today, voting residence is not a valid factor for ranking applicants for federal employment.

appropriation 1. Funds set aside by a legislature to pay for something authorized by law. **2.** An act of the U.S. Congress that permits federal agencies to incur obligations and to make payments out of the Treasury for specified purposes. An appropriation usually follows the enactment of authorizing legislation and is the most common form of budget authority, but in some cases the authorizing legislation also provides the budget authority. Appropriations are categorized in a variety of ways, such as by their period of availability (one-year, multiple-year, no-year), the time of congressional action (current, permanent), and the manner of determining the amount of the appropriation (definite, indefinite).

appropriation, advance An appropriation provided for use beyond the fiscal year for which the appropriation act is passed.

appropriation limitation A statutory restriction (or limitation amendment) in appropriation acts that establishes the maximum or minimum amount that may be obligated or expended for specified purposes.

appropriation, supplemental An appropriation enacted as an addition to a regular annual appropriation act. It provides additional budget authority beyond original estimates for programs or activities (including new programs authorized after the date of the original appropriation act) for which the need for funds is too urgent to be postponed until the next regular appropriation.

APSA *See* AMERICAN POLITICAL SCIENCE ASSOCIATION.

Aptheker v Secretary of State (1964) The Supreme Court case that held that the passport restrictions placed on American communists by the Internal Security (MCCARRAN) Act of 1950 were unconstitutional because the Fifth Amendment guarantees the right to travel. *Compare to* ALBERTSON V SUBVERSIVE ACTIVITIES CONTROL BOARD.

arbiter/arbitrator One chosen to settle a disagreement. In a formal sense, an arbiter is one who already has the power to decide, such as a judge, while an arbitrator is one chosen to decide by the parties to the dispute; but the words tend to be used interchangeably.

arbitration 1. The means of settling a dispute by having an impartial third party (the arbitrator) hold a formal hearing and render a decision that may or may not be binding on both sides. The arbitrator may be a single individual or a board of three, five, or more (usually an uneven number). When boards are used, they may include, in addition to impartial members, representatives from both of the disputants. In the context of labor relations, arbitrators are selected jointly by labor and management, recommended by the Federal Mediation and Conciliation Service, by a state or local agency offering similar referrals, or by the private American Arbitration Association. **2.** In the context of international law, arbitration is a process sometimes used to peacefully resolve a dispute between two (or more) states. Basically, the parties agree to submit their case to a third party for resolution and at the same time agree to be bound by the decision. The formal agreement to use arbitration is called the compromis or compromis d'arbitrage. The decision or verdict in the case is called the award.

arbitration acts Laws that encourage (and sometimes require) the submission of certain types of problems (often labor disputes) to an arbitrator.

arbitration, compulsory A negotiating process whereby the parties are required by law to arbitrate their dispute. Some state statutes concerning collective bargaining impasses in the public sector mandate that parties who have exhausted all other means of achieving a settlement must submit their dispute to an arbitrator. The intent of such requirements for compulsory arbitration is to induce the parties to reach agreement by presenting them with an alternative that is certain, even though it may be unpleasant in some respects to everyone involved.

ARISTOCRACY

aristocracy **1.** Rule by a relatively small, elite group. ARISTOTLE believed aristocracy to be rule by the most virtuous of a society. By medieval times the concept had degenerated to mean rule by the upper classes—those, it was thought, who were chosen by God to lead. Thomas Jefferson got back to the Aristotelian notion when he spoke of rule by a "natural aristocracy," whose talent entitled them to govern. Article I, Section 9 of the U.S. Constitution sought to inhibit traditional aristocracies when it proclaimed that "No Title of Nobility shall be granted by the United States." **2.** Any group with great (usually hereditary) wealth and influence. ALEXIS DE TOCQUEVILLE's 1835 observation on aristocracy from *Democracy in America* remains equally true today: "The surface of American society is covered with a layer of democratic paint, but from time to time one can see the old aristocratic colors breaking through."

Aristotle (384–322 B.C.) The Greek philosopher who originated much of the study of logic, science, and politics. For several years, Aristotle, who was a student of Plato, served as the tutor of the boy who would become Alexander the Great. In 323 B.C., after Alexander the Great had died, Aristotle's former association with the Macedonians caused Athenians to indict him for "impiety." Remembering what had happened to Socrates some years earlier, Aristotle, who had no stomach for hemlock, fled from Athens, maintaining that he would not give the city a second chance to sin against philosophy.

In *Politics,* Aristotle presented the first comprehensive analysis of the nature of a state, of a polity, and of a political community. To Aristotle, the state was a natural product because "man is by nature a political animal." The state was even more important than family because, while a family exists for comfort, the state can be a vehicle for glory and the good life.

Aristotle was the ancient world's foremost authority on a CONSTITUTION, for which he had a dual definition: first, a constitution was the formally established and written rules of governance; second, a constitution also consisted of the informal processes of politics—in effect, the POLITICAL CULTURE of the community. Perhaps Aristotle's most famous analytical construct is his classification of the three basic forms of government and their perversions. He found that every political community had to be governed by either the one, the few, or the many. This corresponds to his three governing types: kingship, aristocracy, and polity (majority rule). Unfortunately, each of these has its perversions, the conditions to which it degenerated when the rulers ceased ruling in the interests of the whole community. Kingship often degenerates into tyranny; aristocracy (rule by a talented and virtuous elite) into an oligarchy (rule by a small group in its own interest); and a polity or constitutional system (where a large middle class rules for the common interest) into democracy (mob rule in the interests of the lower classes). Overall, Aristotle favored a mixed constitution (in the sense of political culture)—one in which all citizens "rule and are ruled by turn," where no class monopolizes power and a large middle class provides stability.

arms control 1. Any international agreement governing the numbers, types, and performance characteristics of weapon systems or armed forces. **2.** A general reference to any measures taken to reduce international military instability. Arms control can be divided into two types: control over existing weapons systems; and pre-emptive arms control, which tries to prevent the deployment of a new or potential weapon. Arms controls may be self-imposed or unilateral; but more often they are the result of bilateral or multilateral agreements or treaties. **3.** Any measures taken by potential adversaries to reduce the likelihood or scope of a future war.

arms race 1. The competition between opposing states or alliances to increase military and/or naval capabilities to gain parity with or superiority over the opposition. The justification for being armed or maintaining parity with a rival is age-old and thoroughly tied up with concepts of defense, deterrence, national honor, prestige, and the elusive glory of war. **2.** A process by which potential enemies adjust their arms procurement policies to each other's military development, with the intention of gaining a specific level of comparative military strength. Critics contend that arms races inevitably lead to war, but others see arms races as stabilizing factors in the balance of power.

arraignment 1. A hearing before a court having jurisdiction in a criminal case in which the identity of the defendant is established, the defendant is informed of his or her rights, and the defendant is required to enter a plea. **2.** Any appearance in court prior to trial in criminal proceedings.

arrest The taking of a person into physical custody by authority of law for the purpose of charging that person with a criminal offense.

arrest, citizen's The taking of a person into physical custody by a witness to a crime other than a law enforcement officer for the purpose of delivering that person into the custody of law enforcement authorities.

arrest warrant A document issued by a judicial officer directing a law enforcement officer to arrest an identified person who has been accused of a specific crime. For an arrest warrant to be issued, there must be either a sworn complaint or evidence of probable cause that the person being arrested committed a crime. When arrest warrants do not identify a person by name, they are often called John Doe warrants or no-name warrants.

arsenal of democracy President Franklin D. Roosevelt's phrase, first used in a December 29, 1940 speech, to describe the U.S. role in supplying arms to the nations opposed to the Axis powers in World War II. When the United States came into the war a year later, the phrase became even more significant and literal.

Arthur, Chester A. (1829–1886) The Republican Vice President who succeeded to the presidency (1881–1885) after President James A. Garfield was murdered by an assassin. Arthur is known for signing into law the Civil

Service Reform (Pendleton) Act of 1883. This surprised his political supporters because he was previously an unabashed supporter of the SPOILS SYSTEM; but Arthur felt honor bound to sign a law that Garfield, had he lived, would have wanted. After all, Garfield was murdered by a disappointed office seeker.

articles 1. The various parts of a document or law. For example, the U.S. Constitution is divided into seven Articles. **2.** A system of rules, such as the ARTICLES OF WAR. **3.** A contract, as in articles of partnership.

Articles of Confederation The original framework for the government of the United States; it went into effect in 1781 and was superseded by the U.S. Constitution in 1789. The Articles said that the states were entering into a "firm league of friendship" and a "perpetual union for the common defense, the security of their liberties, and their mutual and general welfare." The Articles provided for a weak central government, which could not compel states to respect treaties, could not regulate interstate and foreign commerce, could neither collect taxes directly from the people nor compel the states to pay for the costs of the national government, and could not create a sense of national unity and national purpose. It nonetheless provided the experience of state cooperation out of which the consciousness of the need for a stronger union could emerge.

articles of war The laws under which the U.S. military force governed itself from 1775 until 1950, when these laws were superseded by the Uniform Code of Military Justice.

art of the possible A definition of politics that implies the necessity for compromise and accommodation and suggests the limits of the application of science in the practice of politics. It is the nineteenth-century chancellor of Germany, Otto von Bismarck, who is usually credited with first observing that "politics is not an exact science" and that "politics is the art of the possible."

Ashwander rules A definition of the Supreme Court's jurisdiction put forth by Justice Louis D. Brandeis in a concurring opinion in the case of *Ashwander v TVA* (1936). Brandeis asserted that the Court would not decide constitutional questions unless they were absolutely essential, would avoid a constitutional question if the case could be decided on other grounds, and would not make a constitutional ruling broader than required by a case at hand. The case also upheld the construction of dams and the selling of electric power by the federal government.

assembly 1. Any large meeting. **2.** The right to meet for political or other purposes, guaranteed by the First Amendment to the U.S. Constitution. Freedom of assembly is as fundamental as the freedoms of speech and press, all three freedoms being inseparable parts of freedom of expression. While the assembly clause adds little to the protection of the rights to assemble, picket, or parade that would not already be protected by the speech clause, it does reaffirm the breadth of those rights. **3.** Any legislature. **4.** The lower, more numerous, house of a legislature.

assessment 1. The valuation of property for the purposes of TAXATION. **2.** The contributions to political parties determined according to a schedule of rates and made in order to retain a civil service patronage appointment. **3.** An extra payment required by law, such as an assessment for additional taxes. **4.** The financial damages charged to the loser of a lawsuit. **5.** Amounts paid by labor union members in addition to their regular dues when a union needs funds urgently to support a strike or some other union-endorsed cause. The amount of these assessments is usually limited by a union's constitution or bylaws. **6.** Financial contributions made by a government (such as the United States) to the regular budget of an international organization (such as the United Nations) to which it belongs.

assessment ratio A property tax computation; the ratio between the market value and assessed value. Assessment ratios vary tremendously, because some jurisdictions value property at or close to actual market value and others use formulas calling for assessed values to be various fractions of market value.

assessor 1. In ancient Rome, a legal expert who advised the governor of a province on the technical details of the law. **2.** An official of a jurisdiction who determines the value of property for the purpose of taxation. **3.** An expert who sits with a court to provide technical advice but has no right to decide issues. **4.** An insurance investigator who determines the amount of a loss and whether the loss is genuine.

assigned counsel A lawyer, not regularly employed by government, assigned by a court to represent a person in a criminal case who cannot afford to pay for counsel. An assigned counsel may or may not be paid by a government agency.

asylum 1. Originally, a protected place for those fleeing authority and whose forced removal would be sacrilege. In ancient Greece, temples were inviolate, and those inside had the protection of the gods and could not be removed by force. Under Christianity, churches became places of asylum. **2.** A charitable refuge for the afflicted or others unable to care for themselves. **3.** Protection for those fleeing political persecution. The United States has often granted political asylum for those fleeing foreign tyrannies—especially those who would be unjustly persecuted if forced to return. In recent years the question of asylum has been caught up in a controversy over whether "economic" refugees are as worthy of asylum as "political" refugees. Normal immigration to the United States is in effect a grant of asylum.

asylum, diplomatic The right to offer asylum within the grounds of a diplomatic mission. Diplomatic asylum, which is not recognized as a legal right by all nations, is generally a function of local custom, humanitarian practice, and diplomatic expediency.

at large An election in which one or more candidates for a legislature are chosen by all of the voters of a jurisdiction. This is in contrast to an election by legislative district, in which voters are limited to selecting one candidate to represent their district. Minority candidates have more difficulty gaining office in at-large elections than in district elections.

Atomic Energy Commission *See* NUCLEAR REGULATORY COMMISSION.

attaché A French word meaning "one assigned to." This person is usually a technical, military, economic, or cultural specialist assigned to a diplomatic mission abroad.

attack PAC *See* TARGETING.

attorney 1. A lawyer; a person trained in the law, admitted to practice before the bar of a given jurisdiction, and authorized to advise, represent, and act for others in legal proceedings. Lawyers, as a profession, have been vilified since antiquity. When a character in William Shakespeare's *Henry VI, Part 2* (1589) says, "Let's kill all the lawyers," audiences still offer a knowing laugh.

But in spite of popular feeling, lawyers remain, as Jane Bryant Quinn suggests, "operators of toll bridges across which anyone in search of justice must pass" (*Newsweek*, October 9, 1978). **2.** Any person who formally represents another. *Compare to* ASSIGNED COUNSEL; PROSECUTOR; PUBLIC DEFENDER.

attorney general 1. The appointed head of the U.S. Department of Justice; the chief legal advisor to the President and the federal government. **2.** The chief legal officer of a state, usually elected. While the U.S. attorney general in effect supervises the work of all of the nation's federal prosecuting attorneys and the federal prison system, a state attorney general typically has no authority over local district attorneys or state prisons.

attorney general's list A list of purportedly subversive organizations initially compiled during the Harry S Truman administration by the attorney general of the United States as part of the loyalty program created to weed communists out of government positions. It was abolished by executive order in 1974.

attorney, power of A document that gives one person the formal authority to act for another in a legal matter.

audit 1. The official examination of a financial report submitted by an individual or organization to determine whether it accurately represents expenditures, deductions, or other allowances determined by laws and regulations. **2.** The final phase of the government budgetary process, which reviews the operations of an agency, especially its financial transactions, to determine whether the agency has spent its money in accordance with the law, in the most efficient manner, and with desired results.

auditing, expanded scope Evaluating the results and effectiveness of a government activity in addition to delving into the traditional financial compliance concerns of auditing.

authoritarianism Rule by an individual whose claim to sole power is supported by subordinates who sustain control of the system by carrying out the ruler's orders and by a public that is unwilling or unable to rebel against that control. The ruler's personality may be a significant element in maintaining the necessary balance of loyalty and fear. Authoritarianism differs from TOTALITARIANISM only in that the latter has a specific ideology that rationalizes it, although it may require a leader who embodies that ideology to sustain public support. An authoritarian state may be further distinguished from a totalitarian one by the fact that under some circumstances an authoritarian state could allow limited freedom of expression and political opposition so long as the regime does not feel threatened. *See also* DICTATOR.

authoritative source A journalism term applied to a public official whose particular position implies special closeness to information, even though neither the official nor the position is identified. The information thus gets to the public even though the source may be "off the record."

authority **1.** The right to do something. **2.** The feature of a leader or an institution that compels others to grant it obedience, usually because of some ascribed legitimacy. **3.** A government corporation, such as the Tennessee Valley Authority or the Port Authority of New York and New Jersey. **4.** The POWER inherent in a specific position or function that allows an incumbent to perform assigned duties and assume delegated responsibilities. *See also* BUREAUCRACY.

authority, backdoor Legislation enacted outside the normal APPROPRIATION process that permits the obligation of funds. The most common forms of backdoor authority are borrowing authority (authority to spend debt receipts) and contract authority. Entitlement programs may sometimes take the form of backdoor authority, since the enactment of the basic benefit legislation may, in effect, mandate the subsequent enactment of the appropriations to pay the statutory benefits.

authorization Basic substantive legislation enacted by a legislature that sets up or continues the legal operation of a government program or agency, either indefinitely or for a specific period of time, or sanctions a particular type of obligation or expenditure within a program. Such *authorization legislation* is normally a prerequisite for subsequent appropriations or other kinds of budget authority to be contained in appropriation acts. It may limit the amount of budget authority to be provided subsequently or may authorize the appropriation of "such sums as may be necessary"; in a few instances, budget authority may be provided in the authorization.

authorization election Poll conducted by the NATIONAL LABOR RELATIONS BOARD (or other administrative agency) to determine if a particular group of employees will be represented by a particular union or not. The term is used interchangeably with "certification election" (because, if the union wins, it is certified as the representative of the workers by the administrative agency) and "representative election" (because a winning union becomes just that, the representative of the workers).

authorizing committee A STANDING COMMITTEE of the U.S. House of Representatives or Senate with legislative jurisdiction over the subject matter of those laws, or parts of laws, that set up or continue the legal operations of designated federal programs or agencies. An authorizing committee also has jurisdiction in those instances where "backdoor authority" is provided in the substantive legislation.

automatic stabilizer A government mechanism or standing policy with a COUNTERCYCLICAL effect, continually moderating changes in incomes and outputs in the economy without specific changes in government policy. Unemployment insurance and the progressive income tax are among the most important of the automatic, or built-in, stabilizers in the United States. They are established to modify the severity of economic downturns.

autonomy 1. Political independence. A self-governing independent state is said to have autonomy. **2.** Less than full political independence; a situation in which a region within a larger sovereign state has some degree of authority in the conduct of its internal affairs. **3.** Local control over nonpolitical affairs; for example, a region could be granted cultural or religious autonomy.

B

backbencher **1.** Any legislator of low seniority or rank who also has no formal leadership position. **2.** A member of the British House of Commons who literally sits in the back benches (there are no assigned seats) and is expected to be completely supportive of his party's leadership.

back channel Any informal method for government-to-government communications in place of normal or routine methods.

background, deep Information given to the press that can be neither quoted directly nor attributed to any source, however official the source may be. *Compare to* OFF THE RECORD.

backgrounder A meeting with the press by a government official in which the information revealed can be used but attributed only to an unnamed source. (In Britain, such information is said to be on *lobby terms*.)

backlash **1.** A negative reaction by whites to the civil rights efforts of blacks and other protected classes when the whites feel threatened. Busing (to achieve school integration) and compensatory hiring practices are two situations that often create a backlash. **2.** Any counterreaction by any group—sexual, ethnic, national, and so on—to preference shown toward another group.

backslider Originally, a religious believer who slipped back into sin (and hence slid back toward hell); today, anyone who reneges on a doctrinal commitment of any kind.

bad tendency rule *See* ABRAMS V UNITED STATES.

bagman **1.** The intermediary in a political payoff; he or she carries the money in a bag from the one offering the bribe to the one accepting it. **2.** Someone who transports illegal campaign contributions, usually in cash, from one place to another. **3.** The military officer who constantly attends the President, carrying the secret codes through which the President could launch an immediate retaliatory nuclear strike. *Compare to* BLACK BAG JOB.

bail **1.** To arrange the release of an accused person from custody in return for a promise that the defendant will appear at a place and time specified and submit to the jurisdiction of the court, guaranteed by a pledge of money or property that is forfeited to the court if the defendant does not appear. The amount of bail is determined by a judge and should be appropriate to the crime. **2.** The money or property involved in such a pledge. The Eighth Amendment prohibits excessive bail—that is, any amount greater than is necessary to assure subsequent appearance in court. This amendment does not specifically provide that all citizens have a right to bail, but only that bail will not be excessive. In a few instances, as when a capital offense, such as murder, is charged, bail may be denied altogether. *Also see* JUMP BAIL.

bail bond A document guaranteeing the appearance of a defendant in court as required and recording the pledge of money or property to be forfeited to the court if the defendant does not appear.

bail bondsperson A person, usually licensed, whose business it is to arrange releases on bail for persons charged with crimes by pledging to pay a sum of money if the defendant fails to appear in court as ordered. In effect, the defendant pays to borrow bail money from the bondsperson. Actually, what is usually being borrowed is not money but the bondsperson's credit with the court. The bail amount must be paid only if the defendant does not show up for trial.

bail revocation The decision of a court to withdraw the status of release on bail previously given to a defendant. Bail status may be revoked if the defendant fails to appear in court when required, is arrested for another crime, or violates a condition of bail release.

bailiff 1. The court officer whose duties are to keep order in the courtroom and to maintain physical custody of the jury. A bailiff's duties might include seating witnesses, announcing the judge's entrance, or resolving disturbances in the courtroom. In some jurisdictions a bailiff may be called a court officer. Federal court bailiffs are U.S. marshalls. **2.** A sheriff's aide or deputy. **3.** Any low-level court official.

bailiwick 1. A bailiff's office or jurisdiction. **2.** The dimensions of a public official's jurisdiction whether expressed as a set of responsibilities or a physical district. The expression "stay in your own bailiwick" means narrowly to stay within your legal jurisdiction; broadly, to mind your own business.

bailout A government-sponsored rescue (by providing loans or LOAN GUARANTEES) of a failing private-sector enterprise. The best-known government bailout of recent years was the federal government's rescue of the Chrysler Corporation in order to prevent its bankruptcy. *See* CHRYSLER CORPORATION LOAN GUARANTEE ACT OF 1979.

Baker v Carr (1962) The Supreme Court case that held that under the equal protection clause of the Fourteenth Amendment the federal courts have jurisdiction in cases involving state legislative apportionment. Apportionment thus became justiciable (*see* JUSTICIABILITY). *Baker* reversed *Colegrove v Green,* (1946), opened the federal courts to the problem of malapportionment, and established the basis for the one person, one vote decision in REYNOLDS V SIMS and WESBERRY V SANDERS. *See also* POLITICAL QUESTION.

balance 1. A state of equilibrium. **2.** A condition in which the armed forces and equipment of one nation do not have an advantage or a disadvantage in relation to the military posture of another nation. **3.** The internal military adjustments that a nation may make to cope with remaining threats to its security after an arms control agreement is implemented.

balance law Any law which requires (or sets as a goal) an equal number of men and women to be appointed to government boards and commissions.

In 1990 only Iowa and North Dakota had such laws on the books. The rationale for balance laws is that ultimate policies will be different (and presumedly better) if women are more fully represented among policy makers; and such appointed posts are frequently stepping stones to other political jobs. Those who oppose balance laws hold that any such quotas are inherently offensive and discriminatory.

balance of payments 1. A tabulation of a nation's debt and credit transactions with foreign countries and international institutions. A favorable balance, more money coming in from other countries than going out, is an economic advantage. An unfavorable balance over a significant time is one indication of problems within a nation's economy. **2.** A tabulation of what a state as a whole pays in taxes to the federal government compared to what it as a whole gets back from the federal government. In 1989, 27 states received more money from the federal government than they paid in federal taxes.

balance of power 1. The international relations policy on the part of rival states whose goal is to prevent any one nation or alliance of nations from gaining a preponderance of power in relation to the rival nation or alliance; thus, an approximate military balance is maintained. **2.** A principle of international relations that asserts that when any nation seeks to increase its military potential, neighboring or rival nations will take similar actions to maintain the military equilibrium. This is why HENRY KISSINGER asserts in *The White House Years* (1979) that: "The management of a balance of power is a permanent undertaking, not an exertion that has a foreseeable end." **3.** A purely descriptive way to describe the actual distribution of power in the world, without implying that an equally "balanced" distribution exists. **4.** The system of relations in nineteenth-century Europe in which a relatively stable international system was maintained because whenever a state or coalition appeared to be reaching a position in which they could dominate a weaker state or coalition, most of the other states gave their support to the weaker power. Balance-of-power strategy assumes that nations have no ideological preference—that they will just as happily oppose or support any member of the international system. Secondly, it assumes that each nation thinks it is in its self-interest to maintain the existence of each other member state as well as its own. One can see remnants of traditional balance-of-power politics, for instance, in the U.S. courtship of the People's Republic of China during the Nixon Administration when U.S. attitudes shifted from seeing it as an unacceptable partner to trying to use its potential as a third superpower to alter the balance between the U.S. and U.S.S.R.

balance of terror British Prime Minister Winston Churchill's (1874–1965) phrase for the nuclear stalemate between the United States and the Soviet Union. Because the terror is in balance, neither country, in theory, would risk nuclear war because neither could win. While the classic balance of power actually involved occasional recourse to war in order to restore an equilibrium, in which no nation dominated the international system, the balance of terror freezes that system by making war impossible because of the probability of utter destruction. "Balance" has a different meaning here; with nuclear weapons two sides do not need to be equally powerful, as long as the weaker can still guarantee to devastate the stronger; so long as it retains a second strike capability.

balance of trade The amount by which the value of merchandise exports exceeds (creating a trade surplus) or falls short of (creating a trade deficit) the value of merchandise imports. The balance of trade is the visible element of a nation's balance of payments.

balanced budget A budget in which receipts are equal to or greater than outlays. Senator Phil Gramm, speaking of the federal budget, said: "Balancing the budget is like going to heaven: Everybody wants to balance the budget, but nobody wants to do what you have to do to balance the budget" (*U.S. News & World Report*, July 13, 1987). The advantages of a balanced budget, of not spending more than you take in, are obvious. But there are also advantages to "unbalanced" budgets, those that require public borrowing. The "extra" spending can stimulate the economy during economic downturns (*See* KEYNES, JOHN MAYNARD) and provide needed public works and public support for the less fortunate. But these considerations must be weighed against the danger that large deficits over a significant period can devalue the currency, kindle inflation, and have such a CROWDING OUT effect on capital markets that an economic depression (or recession) occurs. Note that it is only the federal government that has the option of long-term deficit spending. The states all have constitutional or statutory provisions mandating balanced budgets. *Compare to* FISCAL POLICY; MONETARY POLICY.

balanced budget amendment Any of a variety of proposals to force an end to DEFICIT spending by the federal government by passing a constitutional amendment mandating a balanced budget. Many critics think that this is an exercise in futility because the Congress could easily create any number of mechanisms to meet the letter, but violate the spirit, of any such amendment. In 1986, the Senate was only one vote short of approving a balanced budget amendment, which read, in part, "Outlays of the United States for any fiscal year shall not exceed receipts to the United States for that year, unless three fifths of the whole number of both houses of Congress shall provide for a specific excess of outlays over receipts."

balanced ticket A slate of candidates whose characteristics mesh for maximum appeal to the voters in terms of geographic origin, race, religion, and so on.

ballot 1. The means by which votes are officially recorded. The word has its origin in the balls (white meaning yes and black meaning no) that the ancient Greeks anonymously put in a container to register their votes. **2.** The sheet of paper on which a voter indicates preferences. **3.** The array of choices presented to a voter by a voting machine.

ballot, absentee A device that allows qualified voters who anticipate being unable to appear at the polls in person on election day (because of military service, illness, and so on) to vote in advance by mail. Such ballots are then opened and integrated with the rest of the vote on election day. Absentee voting was first used during the Civil War to allow Union troops to vote.

ballot, advisory A nonbinding referendum usually in the form of a question to which a voter answers yes or no. When an advisory ballot is used in a presidential primary, it is often known as a preferential primary.

ballot, Australian A ballot printed by a government (as opposed to being printed by a political party) and distributed and collected by that government's officials at a polling place. In this way, a voter's vote is secret and not known to those who collect and tabulate the votes; thus, such information cannot be used to punish or reward. The ballot lists the names of all candidates lawfully nominated and provides room for write-in candidates. First used in Australia in 1858, it was introduced in the United States in 1888. It has generally been modified by the Massachusetts or Indiana ballot format.

ballot box stuffing **1.** Putting illegal ballots into a ballot box to affect an election. Voting machines were designed in part to eliminate this practice. **2.** Any rigging of an election.

ballot, Indiana A party-column ballot, which lists all candidates under their party designation; this makes it easy to vote for all of the candidates of one party by pulling a single lever on a voting machine. *Compare to* BALLOT, MASSACHUSETTS.

ballot, long Any ballot containing a large number of offices for which candidates must be selected by the voter; also known as a bedsheet ballot. The longer the ballot, the more difficult it is for voters to make discriminating decisions and the easier it is for others to influence results with prepared lists of names. Jacksonian democracy favored a greater number of elected offices to insure greater participation in government, while progressive reform and the rise of professionalism in many fields of public service favored shorter ballots and more appointments of specialists in fields like public health and educational administration. The debate over the selection of judges by ballot or appointment is still active in many parts of the country. *Compare to* BALLOT, SHORT.

ballot, Massachusetts An office-block ballot, which lists all candidates under the office for which they are running. This ballot passively encourages ticket splitting. *Compare to* BALLOT, INDIANA.

ballot, nonpartisan A ballot not designating the political party of the candidates. The progressive movement encouraged it in order to lessen the influence of political party commitment.

ballot, preferential An advisory ballot used in an election whose results are not binding. As used in a presidential preference primary, this ballot tells the delegates to the national nominating convention the preferences of the voters at the time of the election. See also PRIMARY, PREFERENCE.

ballot propositions Policy questions that must be decided by the voters during a primary or general election. There are two basic kinds of ballot propositions: a REFERENDUM in which a legislature submits a new law or constitutional amendment to the voters; or an INITIATIVE which is placed on the ballot by a PETITION of a prescribed percentage of the voters.

ballot, short Any ballot containing relatively few offices for which candidates must be selected by the voter. The shorter the ballot, the more likely it is that the voters will be able to make a discriminating decision. The short ballot was advocated by the progressive reform movement so that the voters would be able to know who the rascals were when it was time to throw them out. In general, the short ballot, which presumes that competent technicians and professionals will be appointed by those who are elected, was an effort to hold elected public officials more accountable to their public. *Compare to* BALLOT, LONG.

ballyhoo **1.** Noisy, sensational advertising, a carnival barker's speech, general blarney, and the like. **2.** The artificial enthusiasm created by political campaigns. Ballyhoo is short for Ballyhooly, a village in Cork County, Ireland, long famous for raucous behavior.

bandwagon effect **1.** The gaining of additional support by a candidate or proposal because it seems to be winning. In the days before television, a real bandwagon was popular in political campaigns. As the musician-laden wagons were pulled through the streets, supporters of the candidate (or the music) would literally climb on or march along with the bandwagon as a gesture of enthusiasm and support. **2.** Any demonstration of the herd instinct in politics.

banner district The electoral jurisdiction that gave a candidate the most, or greatest percentage of, votes. In the last century, such districts would literally receive a banner, which signified their enthusiastic support.

bar, the **1.** The legal profession; a jurisdiction's community of lawyers. **2.** The once real but now imaginary partition across a court: lawyers stood at this bar to argue their cases. Thus, to be "called to the bar" meant that you were thought to be enough of a lawyer to plead a case in court. *Compare to* AMERICAN BAR ASSOCIATION.

bar examination A written test set by state bar associations that new lawyers must pass to be certified by the state to practice law. They differ from state to state. Strange as it may seem, most law school graduates are unable to pass a bar examination without a special cram course on the minutiae of the law. However, once a lawyer passes the exam in one state, it is possible to have the exam in some other states waived. Thus, a lawyer can become a member of the bar in one state after proving he or she knows the law in a differing state. The federal government, one of the nation's largest employers of new lawyers, is forbidden by law to give civil service examinations for legal positions. The Congress, mostly a group of lawyers, does not want the federal government to create what could lead to, in effect, a national bar exam. Consequently, federal government lawyers are not chosen on the basis of objective merit, but on subjective considerations alone.

Barber, James David *See* PRESIDENTIAL CHARACTER.

bargaining chip **1.** Anything one might be willing to trade in a negotiation; a deliberately produced point of negotiation designed to provide an advantage. **2.** Any military force, weapons system, or other resource, present or projected, that a nation is willing to downgrade or discard in return for a concession by a military rival. The phrase was first used in this context during the SALT talks (1969–1979) between the United States and the Soviet Union. The bargaining chip strategy has been attacked on two fronts: first, because it is too expensive to develop weapons systems just to trade them away at the negotiating table; and, second, because it is inflammatory to the arms race to develop weapons systems merely as a hedge in negotiations.

bargaining strength The relative power each party holds during negotiation. One government has great bargaining strength vis-à-vis another if both sides know that it has the military power to impose its will regardless of the outcome of negotiations; management has great bargaining strength over labor if it has so much excess inventory that a short strike would be desirable. The final settlement often reflects the bargaining power of each side.

barnburners Political opponents who fail to measure the ultimate or long-range cost of the tactics they are committed to using, despite the fact that these tactics may prove more costly than the benefits they may actually achieve. The term is derived from the story of a farmer who was so determined to get rid of the rats in his barn that he burned them out—by burning down his barn.

barnstorm To make an election campaign trip with many brief stops, after the fashion of traveling players who would perform from barn to barn.

Barron v Baltimore *See* INCORPORATION.

baseline **1.** A specific value used for purposes of comparison; beginning data. **2.** Budget estimates at current levels of expenditure, sometimes adjusted for inflation.

bashing Extreme public criticism (often unwarranted and irrational) of a person, policy, or nation. Bashing can be international or domestic in focus. For example, while the United States thoroughly bashed Japan during World War II in the traditional sense of striking it with a crushing blow, the new style of "Japan-bashing" has Americans berating Japan verbally for its illegal selling of sensitive submarine technology to the Russians (in the Toshiba case), for what Americans perceive to be its unfair trade practices, and for its "hiding" behind the U.S. defense umbrella in the Pacific without paying its "fair share." Domestically, bashing has often followed the word bureaucrat. During the 1980s the constant complaints and jokes about the competence of government employees—led by President Ronald Reagan—helped to create a general acceptance of bureaucrat-bashing.

Battle Act of 1951 The Mutual Defense Assistance Control Act of 1951, which calls for the automatic embargo of military and strategic materials to states that the U.S. government declares to be a threat. This law also forbids foreign aid both to designated "threat" states and their military suppliers.

Bay of Pigs 1. The landing site in 1961 of the American-sponsored invasion of Cuba by expatriate Cubans trained by the CIA to overthrow the government of Fidel Castro. It was a total failure and a major embarrassment to the John F. Kennedy administration. Theodore C. Sorensen's *Kennedy* (1965) quotes the President assessing his judgment on the Bay of Pigs: "All my life I've known better than to depend on the experts. How could I have been so stupid, to let them go ahead?" **2.** Any fiasco or major flop. Just as Napoleon had his Waterloo, Kennedy had his Bay of Pigs. But there's a major difference. Napoleon nearly won; it was an honest try. Kennedy's failure was an embarrassment because it was such an incompetent effort. The invasion was based on grossly inaccurate intelligence, was poorly planned and led, and lacked adequate air cover. So, if you have a Bay of Pigs, you haven't merely lost—you've disgraced yourself as well.

Beard, Charles A. *See* CONSTITUTION, ECONOMIC INTERPRETATION OF.

beggar-thy-neighbor policy A course of action through which a country tries to reduce unemployment and increase domestic output by raising tariffs and instituting nontariff measures that impede imports. Countries that pursued such policies in the early 1930s found that other countries retaliated by raising barriers against the first country's exports, which tended to worsen the economic difficulties that precipitated the initial protectionist action. *Compare to* PROTECTIONISM.

behavioralism 1. A philosophical disposition toward the study of the actions of people in political situations, as opposed to studying the institutional structures of politics. Thus, for example, a behavioralist would maintain that one should not study the structure of the Congress, because what is really important is the behavior of its members. **2.** The scientific study of politics that emphasizes the use of the scientific method for empirical investigations and the use of quantitative techniques.

behavioralism, post The critical response to behavioralism that complained that, as political science adopted the orientation of behavioralism, it became less relevant to the study of politics. Because of the overemphasis on being empirical and quantitative, too much attention was being devoted to easily studied trivial issues at the expense of important topics. Post-behavioralism as a movement within political science does not advocate the end of the scientific study of politics; it mainly suggests that there is more than one way of advancing knowledge and that methodologies should be appropriate to the issue under study.

behavioral sciences A general term for all of the academic disciplines that study human and animal behavior by means of experimental research. The phrase was first put into wide use in the early 1950s by the Ford Foundation to describe its funding for interdisciplinary research in the social sciences, and by faculty at the University of Chicago seeking federal funding for research, and concerned that in an era of MCCARTHYISM their social science research might be confused with socialism.

bellwether 1. A leading political indicator. A bellwether is literally a ram, the leader of the flock, with a bell hung about its neck. So in politics a bellwether can be a district that historically votes for the winning side, an endorsement from a political figure who has always backed winners, and so on. **2.** A decoy candidate whose nomination is designed to split a vote or conceal the intentions of another candidate.

beltway bandits Consulting firms in the Washington, D.C., area located about the interstate beltway, Route 495, that surrounds the capital.

beltway issue A political affair of little concern to the general public; mainly of concern to the national political community in Washington, D.C.

bench 1. The courts in general. **2.** All judges.

bench trial A nonjury trial; one where a judge decides the issue.

benefit district A method for financing construction of public works in which those who directly benefit are charged for the construction costs. For example, sidewalks are often financed through increases in property taxes of residents through whose property the sidewalk passes; that is, those owners are members of a sidewalk benefit district that levies a tax, which is dissolved when the construction costs have been recovered.

benefit theory The belief that those who gain from a government action should pay for it. Thus, gasoline taxes paid by drivers help pay for highway repair and construction, fees for fishing licenses help pay for restocking lakes, and so on.

benign neglect A policy of allowing a situation to improve, or at least not to get worse, by leaving it alone for a while. The phrase was first used by the Earl of Durham in an 1839 report to the British Parliament, in which he observed that "Through many years of benign neglect by Britain, Canada had become a nation much more prosperous than England itself." *See also* DANIEL PATRICK MOYNIHAN.

Bentham, Jeremy (1748–1832) A utilitarian philosopher who held that self-interest was the prime motivator and that a government should strive to do the greatest good for the greatest numbers. Bentham held that governments were created because of man's desire for happiness, not by divine intervention. Because of his beliefs, writings, and actions, Bentham is considered the major social reformer of nineteenth-century England. He is also credited with coining the word "international," and wrote extensively on the futility and irrationality of war; he called for rational international laws and institutions for the arbitration of disputes. His most important work was *Principles of Morals and Legislation* (1780). *See also* UTILITARIANISM.

BENTLEY, ARTHUR F.

Bentley, Arthur F. (1870–1957) The political scientist who was one of the pioneering voices in the behavioral analysis of politics and the intellectual creator of modern INTEREST GROUP THEORY. In *The Process of Government* (1908), Bentley argued that political analysis has had to shift its focus from forms of government to actions of individuals in the context of groups, because groups are the critical action mechanisms that enable numbers of individuals to achieve their political, economic, and social desires. Bentley's work was effectively "lost" until it was rediscovered and publicized by political scientist DAVID B. TRUMAN.

Bentsen, Lloyd (1921–   ) The United States Senator from Texas (1970–1993) who was the Democratic vice presidential nominee in 1988. The high point of his campaign for the vice presidency occurred during a televised debate with the Republican nominee for Vice President, Senator Dan Quayle. Just after Senator Quayle compared his qualifications for office to that of 1960 presidential candidate John F. Kennedy, Bentsen countered: "Senator, I served with Jack Kennedy. Jack Kennedy was a friend of mine. Senator, you're no Jack Kennedy." Bentsen's reproachful tone made it among the best and most memorable SOUND BITES in a campaign of sound bites. In 1993 Bentsen became President William J. Clinton's Secretary of the Treasury.

best and the brightest A description of the intellectual and managerial talent each new national administration claims it will bring to Washington to solve the nation's problems. The phrase is now used almost cynically since David Halberstam's book, *The Best and the Brightest* (1972), showed how all that talent still managed to lead the nation into the morass of Vietnam. The story is often repeated of Speaker of the House Sam Rayburn being told by Vice President Lyndon B. Johnson of the great brilliance and tremendous intellects of the new leaders of the Kennedy Administration in the early 1960s. Rayburn responded: "That may be true, but I'd feel a helluva lot better if just one or two of them had ever run for sheriff."

Betts v Brady See GIDEON V WAINWRIGHT.

beyond a reasonable doubt The criterion of proof in a criminal case. It does not amount to absolute certainty but leaves an unbiased person with the belief that the defendant has committed the alleged crime; that is, a standard of proof in which the evidence offered precludes every sensible hypothesis except the one it supports—that of the defendant's guilt. In civil cases, judgment is supposed to rest on the weight of the evidence. This less-strict standard of proof is called "preponderance of the evidence." The legal rationale for the "beyond a reasonable doubt" standard goes back at least as far as 1783 when Sir William Blackstone in his *Commentaries on the Laws of England* wrote: "For the law holds, that it is better that ten guilty persons escape, than that one innocent suffer." Yet this was an old maxim long before. Benjamin Franklin wrote in a March 14, 1785 letter to Benjamin Vaughn: "That it is better 100 guilty persons should escape than that one innocent person should suffer, is a maxim that has been long and generally approved."

bicameral legislature A representative lawmaking body that consists of two separate chambers or houses. A unicameral legislature has only one. Nebraska is the only state with a unicameral legislature. Historically, bicameral legislatures arose as a means of representing both the elite and the common members of a society. Thus, an upper house (like the House of Lords in England) would represent the nobility, while a lower house (like the House of Commons in England) would represent the other interests, including the common people. This distinction has faded somewhat in the United States, where representatives to both houses are popularly elected. But in the beginning—and until the Seventeenth Amendment in 1913 mandated the popular election of U.S. senators—the U.S. Senate represented not the people of their state, but the individual states themselves. This anecdote is often offered as an explanation and justification for a bicameral legislative system: Thomas Jefferson was in France during the Constitutional Convention. Upon returning, he met with George Washington for breakfast. The story goes that Jefferson asked Washington why the Convention, which Washington had chaired, had agreed to a second chamber, the Senate. "Why do you pour your coffee into your saucer?" Washington is supposed to have asked Jefferson. "To cool it," Jefferson replied. "Even so," concluded Washington, "we pour legislation into the senatorial saucer to cool it." Benjamin Franklin wrote a more formal defense of bicameralism in 1789: "A plural Legislature is as necessary to good Government as a single Executive. It is not enough that your Legislature should be numerous; it should also be divided. Numbers alone are not a sufficient Barrier against the Impulses of Passion, the Combinations of Interest, the Intrigues of Faction, the Haste of Folly, or the Spirit of Encroachment. One Division should watch over and control the other, supply its Wants, correct its Blunders, and cross its Designs, should they be criminal or erroneous" (reprinted in *The Writings of Benjamin Franklin*, A. H. Smith, ed., Vol. 10, 1907).

big A term connoting threat or malevolence when used in conjunction with political terms: big government, big business, big labor. Louis Brandeis (1856–1941), as a progressive reform advocate before he became a Supreme Court justice, often used the "curse of bigness" to describe the malevolence of industrial giantism. This helped justify the antitrust policies called for by the progressives. And President Gerald R. Ford told a joint session of Congress, August 12, 1974: "A government big enough to give you everything you want is a government big enough to take from you everything you have." President Ford was quoting one of Senator BARRY GOLDWATER's favorite sayings from the 1964 presidential campaign.

big lie **1.** An untruth so great or so audacious that it is bound to have an effect on public opinion. Both Adolf Hitler (1889–1945) in Germany and

Senator Joseph R. McCarthy (1908–1957) in the United States were skill-ful users of this dishonorable but long-practiced political tactic. Hitler wrote in *Mein Kampf* (1927) that "the great masses of the people will more easily fall victim to a great lie than to a small one." But he was only mimicking NICCOLO MACHIAVELLI, who wrote in *The Prince* (1532) that "it is necessary that the prince should know how to color his nature well, and how to be a great hypocrite and dissembler. For men are so simple, and yield so much to immediate necessity, that the deceiver will never lack dupes." **2.** PLATO's concept of the royal lie, the noble lie, the golden lie from book 3 of *Republic*, in which he asserts that the guardians of a soci-ety may put forth untruths necessary to maintain social order. Plato wrote: "The rulers of the State are the only ones who should have the privilege of lying, either at home or abroad; they may be allowed to lie for the good of the state." Plato's noble lie was simply a poetic or allegorical way of telling ordinary people difficult truths. It is absolutely incompati-ble with the big lie of fascist propaganda. **3.** Criticisms from a political opponent. There is much truth in journalist Hunter S. Thompson's obser-vation from *Fear and Loathing on the Campaign Trail* (1973) that: "Skilled professional liars are as much in demand in politics as they are in the advertising business."

big mo Significant momentum in an election campaign often gained by a key primary victory or a good performance in a televised debate. Ever since George Bush used the phrase in 1980, all presidential candidates have been seeking big mo on the campaign trail.

big stick President Theodore Roosevelt's foreign policy, derived from the adage, "Speak softly and carry a big stick." The best example of his big stick policy was the dismemberment of the Isthmus of Panama from Colombia to create a government that would be more cooperative in the American effort to build a canal. When Roosevelt met with his cabinet to report what had happened, he asked Attorney General Philander C. Knox (1853–1921) to construct a defense. The attorney general is reported to have remarked, "Oh, Mr. President, do not let so great an achievement suffer from any taint of legality." Later, when Roosevelt sought to defend his heavily criti-cized actions to the cabinet, he made a lengthy statement and then asked, "Have I defended myself?" Secretary of War Elihu Root (1845–1937) replied, "You certainly have. You have shown that you were accused of seduction, and you have conclusively proved that you were guilty of rape." (For more on this incident, see David McCullough, *The Path Between the Seas: The Creation of the Panama Canal: 1870–1914*, 1977.)

The big stick still refers to an American foreign policy with a threat of force behind it. Even today it is part of the everyday rhetoric of American politics. President Gerald Ford in a campaign speech of October 16, 1976: "Teddy Roosevelt . . . once said 'Speak softly and carry a big stick.' Jimmy Carter wants to speak loudly and carry a fly swatter." Former Secretary of

State Alexander M. Haig, Jr., was quoted in *USA Today* (December 2, 1986) as saying, "We've tended to forget Teddy Roosevelt's advice. Speak softly and carry a big stick. We've tended to speak too threateningly while we carried a feather."

big tent The heterogeneous major American political party because it contains within itself a figurative "big tent"; a very wide spectrum of political opinion. *Compare to* UMBRELLA PARTY.

big three The World War II leaders of the major allied powers—Winston Churchill, Joseph Stalin, and Franklin D. Roosevelt; or the states they represented: Great Britain, the Soviet Union, and the United States.

bilateral "Two party" or "two-country," as in a bilateral trade agreement between the United States and one other country.

bilateralism **1.** Joint economic policies between nations; specifically, the agreement to extend to each other privileges (usually relating to trade) that are not available to others. *Compare to* MOST-FAVORED NATION. **2.** Joint security policies between nations; specifically, treaties of alliance in the event of war. **3.** Joint diplomatic postures or actions by nations, whether or not in the form of a formal alliance. This is in contrast to unilateralism, in which each state goes its own way without necessarily regarding the interests of the others.

bill **1.** A legislative proposal formally introduced for consideration; unfinished legislation. After a bill is passed and signed into law, it becomes an ACT. **2.** A law passed by a legislature when it is functioning in a judicial capacity; for example, a bill of impeachment. **3.** A negotiable instrument; for example, a dollar bill. **4.** A statement of details in a legal proceeding; for example, a bill of indictment. **5.** A petition or statement to an appellate court; for example, a bill of exceptions. **6** An important listing; for example, the Bill of Rights.

bill, administration A legislative proposal that has the formal backing of the President or one of his cabinet agencies.

bill, appropriation A bill granting the monies approved by an authorization bill, but not necessarily the total amount. Congressional appropriation bills must originate in the House, and these normally are not acted on until a corresponding authorization measure is enacted. General appropriations bills are supposed to be enacted by the seventh day after Labor Day, before the start of the fiscal year to which they apply. *Compare to* APPROPRIATION.

bill, authorization A bill that creates a program, specifies its general aims and how they are to be achieved, and (unless open-ended) puts a ceiling on monies that can be used to finance it. *Compare to* AUTHORIZATION.

bill, by request A bill introduced by a legislator at the request of an executive branch agency or private organization. Such an introduction does not necessarily imply an endorsement by the introducing legislator.

bill, Christmas tree Any bill to which many amendments, typically conferring benefits to certain groups, have been added.

bill, clean A bill that has been revised by a legislative committee and then reintroduced as a new, or clean, bill.

bill, committee A bill introduced under the name of the chair of a committee on behalf of the entire committee which has prepared it. In the Congress, all appropriations bills are committee bills.

bill, companion A bill introduced in one house of a bicameral legislature identical to a bill submitted in the other house.

bill, deficiency A bill carrying an appropriation to supplement an appropriation that has proved insufficient. An appropriation is normally made on the basis of estimates for a year, but conditions may arise that exhaust the appropriation before the end of the fiscal year.

bill drafting The writing of legislative proposals. Most legislatures have the assistance of legislative counsel to aid with technical aspects of taking proposals and forging them into appropriate legal documents.

bill, engrossed The final copy of a bill as passed by one house of the Congress, with the text as amended by floor action and certified to by the clerk of the House or the secretary of the Senate.

bill, enrolled The final copy of a bill that has been passed in identical form by both houses of the Congress. It is certified by an officer of the house of origin and then sent on for signatures of the House speaker, the Senate president, and the President of the United States. An enrolled bill is printed on parchment.

bill, fetcher A bill introduced by a state or local legislator solely to encourage a bribe, from an adversely affected party, to withdraw the bill. Mike Royko's *Boss: Richard J. Daley of Chicago* (1971) discusses Mayor Daley's early years as a state legislator in Illinois: "If a day passed without profit, some legislators would dream up a 'fetcher' bill. A 'fetcher' bill would, say, require that all railroad tracks in the state be relaid six inches farther apart. It would 'fetch' a visit from a lobbyist, bearing a gift." Journalist Brad Kessler in *The New York Times Magazine* (June 3, 1990) explained how the process worked in Alabama: "Some ally of his [the governor's] would get a friendly legislator to draft a bill that would hurt a given economic interest—say dog tracks, or coal miners, or electric utilities—and then offer to have the bill killed in exchange for a fee."

bill, free-standing A bill that does not amend existing legislation; one that initiates a new government program.

bill, housekeeping A bill dealing with minor legislative technicalities with no real bearing upon policy.

bill, juice A bill that will cause lobbyists on both sides of the issue to squeeze out a lot of "juice," meaning money, to influence it.

bill, marking up a The process of revising a bill in committee by reexamining and editing every section, phrase, word, and so on. An extensively marked-up bill is often reintroduced as a new—or clean—bill.

bill, no The opposite of a true bill; what a grand jury issues when it finds that there is not sufficient evidence to hold a suspect for a criminal trial. *Compare to* BILL, TRUE.

bill of attainder A legislative act declaring an individual guilty of a crime without a trial and sentencing him or her to death. (A punishment less than the death penalty was called a bill of pains and penalties.) A bill of attainder has come to mean any legislatively instrumented punishment without a trial. This is forbidden by Article I, Sections 9 and 10, of the Constitution.

Bill of Rights 1. The first 10 amendments to the U.S. Constitution, concerning basic individual liberties. Only a few individual rights were specified in the Constitution ratified in 1788. Shortly after its adoption, however, 10 amendments—called the Bill of Rights—were added. There was great sentiment that, as expressed by Thomas Jefferson in a December 20, 1787 letter to James Madison: "A bill of rights is what the people are entitled to against every government on earth, general or particular; and what no just government should refuse, or rest on inference." The Bill of Rights originally restricted only the actions of the federal government; it did not prevent state and local governments from taking action that might threaten an individual's civil liberties. States had their own constitutions, some of which contained their own bills of rights guaranteeing the same or similar rights. These rights, however, were not guaranteed by all the states; and where they did exist, they were subject to varying interpretations by state courts. In short, citizens were protected only to the extent that the states themselves recognized their rights. In 1868, the Fourteenth Amendment was added to the Constitution. In part, it provides that no state shall "deprive any person of life, liberty, or property without due process of law." It was not until 1925, in the case of *Gitlow v New York*, that the Supreme Court interpreted due process of law to mean, in effect, "without abridgement of certain of the rights guaranteed by the Bill of Rights." Since that decision, the Supreme Court has ruled that a denial by a state of certain of the rights contained in the Bill of Rights actually represents a denial of due process of law. While the Court has not ruled that all rights in the Bill of Rights are contained in the notion of due process, neither has it limited that notion to the rights enumerated in the Bill of Rights. It simply has found that there are concepts in the Bill of Rights so basic to a democratic society that they must be recognized as part of due process of law and made applicable to the states as well as to the federal government. *Compare to* INCORPORATION. **2.** The British Bill of Rights of 1689; one of the major documents which make up the unwritten constitution of the United Kingdom. It deals with many of the same items (such as the right to petition, to bear arms, to speak freely) as the U.S. Bill of Rights, which it influenced.

bill, omnibus A bill containing various disparate elements, although they may deal with a common theme.

bill, one-house Proposed legislation that is never intended to go beyond a single house of a legislature. Such bills are introduced so politicians or lobbyists can tell their constituents or clients that an effort was made on their behalf.

bill, private A bill that deals with individual matters (claims against the government, immigration and naturalization cases, land titles, and the like) and that becomes a private law if passed. A private bill essentially provides an exception to a law for an individual rather than trying to change the entire law. Most private bills in the past dealt with immigration matters. Nowadays relatively few private bills are passed in large measure because federal agencies now work informally to resolve problems that years ago might have led to a private bill. In addition, the 1946 Legislative Reorganization Act created the Federal Tort Claims Court to relieve Congress of the burden created by the increasing number of such cases.

bill, public A bill that deals with general questions and that becomes a public law if passed.

bill, readings of The traditional parliamentary requirement that bills be read three times before they can be passed. Today in the Congress, a bill is considered to have had its first reading when it is introduced and printed in the *Congressional Record*. In the House, the second reading comes when floor consideration begins and may include an actual reading of the bill or portions of it; in the Senate, the second reading is supposed to take place on the legislative day after the bill is introduced but before it is referred to committee. The third reading in both houses takes place when action has been completed on amendments.

bill, referral The sending of a bill to the committee whose jurisdiction it is in. In the U.S. Congress, although bills are formally referred by the Speaker of the House and by the presiding officer in the Senate, the PARLIAMENTARIANS of the House and Senate usually do the referrals on their behalf.

bill, sleeper A bill whose import is not known or fully appreciated when passed, but which becomes surprisingly significant once passed into law. Sleeper bills are often created by last-minute amendments inserted almost secretly into a bill.

bill, true An indictment made and endorsed by a grand jury when it finds that there is sufficient evidence to bring a person to trial.

bipartisanship **1.** Cooperation by two political parties on political issues. Bipartisanship occurs when the leaders of interested parties wish to assure that a given topic will not become the subject of partisan disputes. **2.** Consultation and cooperation between the President and the leaders of both parties in the Congress on major foreign policy issues. The high point of this occurred after World War II when the Republicans under the leadership of Senator Arthur H. Vandenberg (1884–1951) supported the Harry S Truman administration's efforts to rebuild Europe and contain Soviet expansionism. This bipartisan attitude—that politics ends "at the water's edge"—continued until the American foreign policy consensus broke down over the Vietnam War during the Lyndon B. Johnson administration.

According to Representative Lee H. Hamilton: "As long as I've been in the Congress, the President, every President, calls for bipartisanship in foreign policy. But bipartisanship requires Congress' informed consent. It cannot merely be a call to support the President's policy" (*Los Angeles Times*, May 15, 1987).

Bircher *See* JOHN BIRCH SOCIETY.

black 1. Bad; for example, black Friday was the day the stock market crashed in 1929, a BLACKLIST is one no one wants to be on, and BLACK MONEY is illegal income. **2.** Dark. Because people of African ancestry had dark colored skin, they were called blacks. Because this term was related to slavery, it fell out of fashion in favor of "colored" or "Negro." But starting in the 1960s as part of the CIVIL RIGHTS MOVEMENT, a companion black pride movement asserted that "black is beautiful." Very quickly black became the preferred term of reference. The black pride movement had removed the negative connotations from the word. However, starting in the late 1980s, some black leaders began objecting to the word black and asserting that African-American is the correct term of reference. **3.** In intelligence handling, a term used in certain phrases (e.g., living black, black border crossing) to indicate reliance on illegal concealment rather than on cover. **4.** Secret; for example the black economy is the hidden (from tax collectors) UNDERGROUND ECONOMY.

black bag job 1. An FBI term for illegal searches to gather intelligence. **2.** The bribing of someone to obtain information. **3.** A CIA nonmilitary covert operation. *Compare to* BAGMAN.

black caucus A caucus of black legislators formed to discuss and advance issues of concern to the black community. There is a black caucus in the U.S. Congress (since 1969) and in some state legislatures.

black codes 1. Laws passed in some southern states after the Civil War that had the effect of forcing many freed blacks into a state of peonage. *Compare to* JIM CROW; *see also* PRIVILEGES AND IMMUNITIES CLAUSE. **2.** Unwritten laws set by black society that certain blacks feel bound to obey as opposed to the laws of society at large. According to Michael McGee, a Milwaukee alderman and leader of a black militia in that city: "My moral code is that I don't feel there are any laws that the United States has made that I'm bound to respect because I consider myself to be at a state of war. I consider the white structure to be the enemy. I live by a set of codes that are accepted and condoned by my community. I call them black laws. There are white laws, and there are black laws. The black code is set by black society. . . . " (*The Washington Post National Weekly*, July 30–August 5, 1990).

blacklist 1. Originally, lists prepared by merchants containing the names of men who had gone bankrupt. Later, employers' "don't hire" lists of men who had joined unions. The National Labor Relations (Wagner) Act of 1935 made such blacklisting illegal. **2.** The denial of employment to members of the entertainment industry for alleged un-American activities. This was a component of the MCCARTHYISM of the 1950s. One of the factors that killed the entertainment-industry blacklist was John Henry Faulk's successful 1962 libel suit against AWARE, an organization which sought out and publicized the names of people in the industry who were supposedly sympathetic to communism. Among the "proofs" that justified Faulk's blacklisting was the fact that he attended a 1946 meeting also attended by a known communist. The meeting was a tribute to the United Nations co-sponsored by the American Bar Association. The communist who attended "with" Faulk was the Soviet Representative to the United Nations.

black militancy Confrontational politics organized by certain groups within the black community. Black militancy can take many forms: (1) traditional disruptive demonstrations to achieve political goals, (2) direct action efforts such as boycotts, or (3) the creation of urban militia to threaten widespread violence if black political demands are not met. In 1990, Milwaukee Alderman Michael McGee got much publicity and criticism when he organized such a militia and threatened the city with violence if RACIAL PARITY was not achieved in five years.

black money Illegal campaign contributions, usually in cash. This is far more common in state and local elections than at the federal level.

black ops Black operations; the most secret, and often illegal, covert operations of an intelligence agency.

Black Panthers A radical Left political party, founded in Oakland, California in 1966, that espoused black control of the black community in America. Its rhetoric of violence got its relatively few members an astounding amount of publicity as well as attention from the police.

black power 1. A political slogan of militant black leaders first heard in the mid-1960s. It implied black control and self-determination of all the political and social institutions that affected the black community. The first usage is generally credited to Stokely Carmichael (1941–), an important figure in the student protest movement. **2.** A general phrase for black political influence.

bleeding heart conservative 1. A Republican who makes an effort to alleviate poverty and inadequate housing through conservative programs that empower people to help themselves as opposed to traditional government handouts. **2.** A Republican who wants to restart the "war on poverty"—this time with Republican generals and Republican tactics.

bleeding hearts A conservative's term of invective for liberals whose hearts bleed so easily at stories of misfortune that they have an overwhelming desire to raise taxes to cure social problems.

bloc 1. An amorphous term for any group or coalition of groups organized to promote an interest; for example, farm bloc, civil rights bloc. **2.** A temporary coalition of legislators that transcends party lines and is designed to further or to obstruct a legislative initiative.

bloc voting *See* VOTING, BLOC.

blockade A military action in which one country attempts to prevent another from importing either some or all goods by use of force. Traditionally, a blockade involves the exercise of sea power, where one navy patrols the coastline of another, stopping shipping from entering and preventing the enemy's merchant and naval ships from leaving harbor. Because a blockade has historically been considered an act of war, softer words are often used. For example, during the 1962 CUBAN MISSILE CRISIS the United States used a "quarantine" to prevent some Russian missiles from getting to Cuba by sea; and in 1990 during the PERSIAN GULF WAR the United States "interdicted" ships going to Iraq. In each instance the softer word was used to indicate the United States did not seek further military action—at that time.

BLS *See* BUREAU OF LABOR STATISTICS.

Blue Eagle *See* NATIONAL INDUSTRIAL RECOVERY ACT OF 1933.

blue flu An informal strike by police officers who call in sick en masse, the blue referring to their uniforms.

blue laws State and local legislation banning commercial and related activities on particular days, usually Sunday, for religious reasons; or a law against anything a community considers immoral. According to David Walker's *Oxford Companion to Law* (1980), the name "may have been derived from an account purporting to list the Sabbath regulations of New Haven, Connecticut, printed on blue paper and published in 1781."

blue ribbon jury A jury specially chosen for some particular expertise.

blue ribbon panel A committee of eminent or distinguished citizens. For example, a presidential commission is often referred to a a blue ribbon panel. Of course, many of these panelists may be distinguished only for their political connections.

blue sky laws Government regulations designed to prevent fraud in the sale of land and securities by calling for full disclosure, clear title, and so on.

blue slip A letter or form sent to an individual senator requesting the approval of a presidential nomination. If the senator does not sign off on the blue slip, especially if he or she is of the President's party and the nominee is from the senator's state, the nomination is likely to be withdrawn.

blue smoke and mirrors **1.** A metaphorical description of how political campaigns manipulate images and perceptions to influence voters one way or another. The phrase is usually credited to journalist Jimmy Breslin in *How the Good Guys Finally Won: Notes from an Impeachment Summer* (1975): "All political power is primarily an illusion. . . . Mirrors and blue smoke, beautiful blue smoke rolling over the surface of highly polished mirrors, first a thin veil of blue smoke, then a thick cloud that suddenly dissolves into wisps of blue smoke, the mirrors catching it all, bouncing it back and forth." **2.** Political deception in general. For example, Charles A. Bowsher, the Comptroller General of the United States told the Federal Advi-

sory Council on Social Security: "The use of growing Social Security surpluses to mask the deficit in Federal operations amounts to blue smoke and
mirrors" (*The New York Times*, July 28, 1990).

board **1.** A group charged with directing a government function such as a
county government or school district. **2.** An administrative body within a
larger organization appointed to act as a fact-finding or as an advisory body.
For example, a selection board may make recommendations on merit system promotions. Boards, also known as *commissions*, are used when it is
desirable to have bipartisan leadership or when their functions are of a
quasi-judicial nature.

boat people **1.** A term used to describe the more than one million refugees
who have fled Indochina since communist regimes rose to power there in
1975, and who have increasingly resorted to the use of small boats as a means
of escape. The refugees are from Vietnam, Laos, and Kampuchea (Cambodia) and include a large proportion of ethnic Chinese families. **2.** Refugees
from Haiti or Cuba seeking to illegally enter the United States by boat.

Bob Jones University v United States *See* FREE EXERCISE CLAUSE.

body politic **1.** A government. **2.** Any collectivity organized for political purposes. **3.** The citizens of a jurisdiction. John Adams defined the body politic
in the 1776 Constitution of Massachusetts as "a social compact, by which
the whole people covenants with each citizen, and each citizen with the
whole people, that all shall be governed by certain laws for the common
good." But JEAN-JACQUE ROUSSEAU warned in *The Social Contract* (1762):
"The body politic, as well as the human body, begins to die as soon as it is
born, and carries in itself the cause of its destruction." *Compare to* POLITY.

Boland Amendment Any of a series of amendments beginning in 1982 that
were attached to various defense-related appropriations acts to prohibit
U.S. funding of the CONTRAS in Nicaragua beyond what was specifically
authorized by Congress. The amendments, sponsored by Edward Boland,
the Chairman of the House Intelligence Committee, were intended to prevent executive branch covert support of Contra operations. Much of the
controversy over the IRAN-CONTRA AFFAIR was over the question of whether
or not the Boland Amendment was violated when the Reagan administration used the profits or "residuals" (as they called these profits) from arms
sales to Iran to fund Contra activities.

boiler room *See* TELEPHONE BANK.

boll weevils **1.** A long-used term for southern Democrats in the U.S. House
of Representatives who support conservative policies. **2.** Southern
Democrats in the U.S. House of Representatives who supported President
Ronald Reagan's economic programs. Boll weevils are insects that feed on
cotton. *Compare to* GYPSY MOTHS.

bond A certificate of indebtedness issued by a borrower (usually a company
or government) to a lender that constitutes a legal obligation to repay the
principal of the loan plus accrued interest.

bond anticipation notes (BANs) A form of short-term borrowing commonly used to accelerate progress on approved capital construction projects. Once the revenues for a project have been realized from the sale of long-term bonds, the BANs are repaid. BANs also may be used to allow a jurisdiction to wait until the bond market becomes more favorable for the sale of long-term securities.

bond bank An arrangement whereby small units of government within a state are able to pool their long-term debt to create a larger bond issue at more advantageous rates.

bonds, callable Bonds that can be repaid totally or in part prior to the maturity date. For this reason, callable bonds ordinarily carry higher interest rates. Noncallable bonds, on the other hand, may not be repurchased until the date of maturation.

bonds, general obligation Bonds that are backed by the jurisdiction's FULL FAITH AND CREDIT with repayment, usually from general revenues.

bonds, industrial development State or local government bonds issued to finance the building of a factory or installation that will be used by a private company. While such bonds are popular as a means of attracting new industry to a community, they are essentially fronts for private borrowing. The Congress, sensing the loss of tax revenue from these fronts, has in recent years put a variety of constraints on their use.

bonds, junk A bond issued by a company or government with a poor credit rating; thus, it pays higher than normal interest to compensate for the additional risk.

bonds, moral obligation State or local government bonds that are backed only by the jurisdiction's promise to repay; they are specifically not backed by a jurisdiction's FULL FAITH AND CREDIT. Moral obligation bonds often carry a higher interest rate than other municipal bonds, because full faith and credit bonds will always be paid first.

bonds, mortgage revenue State or local government bonds used to create low-interest mortgages for low-income home buyers.

bonds, municipal The debt instruments of subnational governments; the main means of local public borrowing and debt financing. Their name causes confusion because they appear to refer only to bonds issued by a local government. Yet bonds issued by states, territories, or possessions of the United States, or by any municipality, political subdivision (including cities, counties, school districts, and special districts for fire prevention, water, sewer, irrigation, and other purposes), or public agency or instrumentality (such as an authority or commission) are subsumed under the "rubric municipal bonds." While the interest on municipal bonds is exempt from federal taxes, state and local exemptions may vary. *Tax-exempt municipal bonds* allow jurisdictions to borrow money at lower than commercial market interest rates. The buyers of the bonds find them an attractive investment because their high marginal tax rates make a tax-free investment more advantageous than a taxable one paying even higher interest. *See also* MCCULLOCH V MARYLAND.

bonds, revenue Municipal bonds whose repayment and dividends are guaranteed by revenues derived from the facility constructed from the proceeds of the sale of the bonds (e.g., stadium bonds, toll road bonds). As revenue bonds are not pledged against the tax base of the issuing jurisdiction, they are usually not regulated by the same debt limitations imposed by most states on the sale of general obligation bonds. Additionally, revenue bond questions usually do not have to be submitted to the voters for approval as they do not commit the FULL FAITH AND CREDIT of the jurisdiction.

bonds, serial Bonds that are sold in such a way that a certain number of them are retired each year.

bonds, sovereign junk High yield bonds issued by third-world countries that are already heavily in debt.

bonds, special tax Bonds backed by a specific tax such as one on gasoline or sales; revenues from these sources are pledged to the bond obligation.

bonds, term Bonds that all mature on the same date.

boom 1. The relatively sudden, short-lived, and spontaneous efforts of supporters to advance a candidate. **2.** Artificially induced (via advertising and propaganda) temporary enthusiasm for a candidate. **3.** A strong upturn in the economy.

boomlet 1. A boom that failed. **2.** A boom never intended to succeed, undertaken for strategic purposes (such as a campaign for a favorite son at a nominating convention).

boondoggle 1. A wasteful or unproductive government program. **2.** Make-work projects undertaken to stimulate the economy. The term has long been used to describe trifling but very time-consuming work, such as saddle ornaments made by cowboys out of odd pieces of leather. In the 1930s it was applied to New Deal make-work programs. President Franklin D. Roosevelt in a Newark, New Jersey speech on January 18, 1936, said: "If we can 'boondoggle' ourselves out of this depression, that word is going to be enshrined in the hearts of the American people for years to come." Since then it has been synonymous with wasteful government activities.

boro An Americanized spelling of borough.

borough 1. A local government unit smaller than a city. New York City, for example, is divided into five boroughs: Manhattan, Brooklyn, Bronx, Queens, and Richmond (Staten Island). **2.** In Alaska, a borough is similar to a county. *See also* TOWN.

bossism An informal system of local government in which public power is concentrated in the hands of a central figure, called a political boss, who may not have a formal government position. The power is concentrated through the use of a POLITICAL MACHINE, whereby a hierarchy is created and maintained through the use of PATRONAGE and government largesse to assure compliance with the wishes of the boss. It was a dominant system in

American city government after the Civil War and was the main target of the American urban reform effort. Few authentic bosses exist today.

Boston Massacre The incident on March 5, 1770, in Boston, when British soldiers fired into a taunting crowd, killing five. The soldiers were tried for murder and acquitted. (John Adams, later President of the United States, was their defense attorney.) The incident was widely and effectively used by revolutionary agitators to generate anti-British feelings.

Boston Tea Party Perhaps the most famous act of civil disobedience in American history. On December 16, 1773, colonists dressed as Indians dumped over 300 chests of tea belonging to the British East India Company into Boston harbor as a protest against British taxation on tea. This was the beginning of the violence that led to the American Revolutionary War and ended with British recognition of the creation of the United States of America.

boycott 1. Ostracize. During the mid-nineteenth century, Charles C. Boycott, a retired English army captain, managed the Irish estate of an absentee owner. His methods were so severe and oppressive that the local citizens as a group refused to deal with him in any manner. When Captain Boycott was forced back to England, the first boycott, or nonviolent intimidation through ostracism, was a success. **2.** In the context of labor relations, a refusal to deal with or buy the products of a business, as a means of asserting pressure in a labor dispute. **3.** A tactic in diplomacy wherein one nation or group of nations pointedly ignores the diplomatic efforts of another. **4.** A foreign policy of not buying the products of, or doing business with, a hostile country—or with a nonhostile country, as a means of influencing its domestic or foreign policies. **5.** A national policy of refusing to do business with companies who also do business with a specified country. This is a kind of economic warfare. For example, the Arab states of the Middle East have long had a policy of boycotting companies who also do business with Israel. The Export Agreement Act of 1977 prohibits American companies from "refusing, or requiring any other person to refuse, to do business with or in the boycotted country . . . pursuant to an agreement with, a requirement of, or a request from or on behalf of the boycotting country." **6.** A mass consumer tactic to force companies to change a particular policy. For example, a two-year boycott on canned tuna fish was successful in forcing the major producers to announce that they would only buy "dolphin-safe" tuna in the future (tuna that was caught without inadvertently killing dolphins). **7.** A political tactic to change or influence a government policy. For example, when the Idaho legislature in 1990 passed a bill severely restricting abortion, pro-choice groups threatened to boycott Idaho potatoes if the governor signed the bill. The governor then found "other" reasons to veto it.

boys on the bus The media people that follow a political candidate. The phrase comes from the title of journalist Timothy Crouse's 1972 book about reporters attending the 1972 presidential candidates.

brag sheet A brief (one- to two-page) biography of a candidate produced as part of a larger campaign media kit.

brains trust **1.** Expert advisors to a candidate or office holder. **2.** The Columbia University professors who first advised President Franklin D. Roosevelt during the 1932 presidential campaign. The original usage was plural (brains) but it is now common to see it singular (brain). **3.** A sarcastic reference to any group of experts or advisors. *Compare to* CABINET, KITCHEN.

brainwashing The altering of a person's social and political views by severe physical and psychological conditioning. The phrase came into English to describe the way the North Koreans "re-educated" some American prisoners during the Korean War of 1950–1953. The term is now applied to the techniques used by religious cults to indoctrinate new converts. Brainwashing is countered by "de-programming." There has been one instance in which brainwashing destroyed a serious presidential candidacy. George Romney, Governor of Michigan, speaking in Detroit, Michigan, on September 4, 1967, said: "I just had the greatest brainwashing that anyone can get when you go over to Vietnam, not only by the generals, but also by the diplomatic corps over there, and they do a very thorough job." This statement destroyed Romney's chances for the Republican presidential nomination in 1968. According to General William C. Westmoreland, *A Soldier Reports* (1976): "I cannot . . . understand the about-face on the war of Michigan's Governor George Romney, except that as a man prominently mentioned as a presidential candidate he listened to too many antiwar dissidents and deemed it politically expedient to say he had been 'brainwashed' while visiting Vietnam." According to David Halberstam's *The Best and the Brightest* (1972), Romney would be "jumped on by all sorts of people, like Robert Kennedy, who had been brainwashed themselves and never known it or admitted it."

branches of government The three main divisions of American government at all levels: executive, legislative, and judicial.

Brandeis brief *See* BRIEF, BRANDEIS.

brethren The old-fashioned plural of brother. Historically, the Supreme Court has referred to its members as the brethren. This usage is all the more outdated now that the Court is no longer all male.

bribery **1.** The giving or offering of anything of value with intent to unlawfully influence an official in the discharge of his or her duties. **2.** A public official's receiving of or asking for anything of value with the intent to be unlawfully influenced. As a crime, bribery is usually restricted to the giving or offering of bribes; the solicitation or accepting of bribes is often called corruption. Viewed systemically, bribery is an important element in the American political system. It supplements the salaries of various public officials. Many policemen and building inspectors, for example, would be unable to maintain their standard of living if it were not for such informal salary increments. Additionally, such income supplement programs forestall the need for politically unpopular, precipitous tax hikes that would bring the legal wages of such officers up to reasonable levels. Systematic bribery allows business owners, dependent upon the discretionary powers of public officials for their livelihoods, to stabilize the relationships essential for the smooth functioning of their businesses. After all, many regulations that govern safety or conditions of business operation may not be universally applicable, reasonably enforceable, or economically feasible. Bribery's occasional exposure by the press serves to foster the political alienation of the electorate, which in turn encourages cynicism and reduces support for the democratic processes of government. While it is possible to quibble over the particulars of any given instance or noninstance of bribery, its pervasiveness in too many American communities is generally not contested, except by the most naive or the most corrupt. **3.** An important and time-honored tool of foreign policy. Of course, the United States would never bribe a foreign government to gain its support on some international issue. It achieves the same effect by granting or withholding military or economic aid. *Compare to* CORRUPTION, POLITICAL; POLITICAL CULTURE.

brief A written statement prepared by each side in a formal lawsuit or hearing, summarizing the facts of the situation and making arguments about how the law should be applied. Copies of briefs submitted to the Supreme Court in most of its important cases can be found in the more than 100 volumes of *Landmark Briefs and Arguments of the Supreme Court of the United States* (Philip B. Kurland and Gerhard Caspar, eds., 1975 onward).

brief, Brandeis A legal brief that takes into account not only the law but the technical data from social or scientific research that have economic and sociological implications for the law as well as society. This kind of legal argument was pioneered by Louis D. Brandeis (1856–1941), who later served on the Supreme Court (1916–1939). It was a Brandeis brief that helped win the *Brown v Board of Education* case when, with testimony from psychologists about the effects of segregation on black children, the lawyers for Brown proved that separate educational facilities were inherently unequal.

briefing book A candidate's notebook containing statements of policy positions and other useful data; this is studied in preparation for news conferences or debates.

brinkmanship 1. Taking very large risks in negotiations to force the other side to back down; this tactic is always reckless and sometimes a bluff. According to Thomas C. Schelling's *The Strategy of Conflict* (1963), brinkmanship is the "deliberate creation of a recognizable risk of war, a risk that one does not completely control. It is the tactic of deliberately letting the situation get somewhat out of hand, just because its being out of hand may be intolerable to the other party and force his accommodation." **2.** A critical description of the foreign policies of President Dwight D. Eisenhower's secretary of state, John Foster Dulles, who advocated going to the brink of war as a negotiating tactic. In a famous *Life* magazine interview (January 16, 1956), he asserted that "the ability to get to the verge without getting into the war is the necessary art. If you cannot master it, you inevitably get into war. If you try to run away from it, if you are scared to go to the brink, you are lost." *Time* reported on January 23, 1956, that Democratic presidential candidate ADLAI STEVENSON responded to this by saying, "I am shocked that the Secretary of State is willing to play Russian roulette with the life of our nation." **3.** A tactic in trade negotiations. Major and seemingly disproportionate disruptions in international commerce are threatened unless one side gives way. **4.** A tactic—generally a threat to default on loans—that some third-world countries, notably Brazil, have used to get more favorable terms for the repayment of debt to Western Banks.

brokered convention *See* NATIONAL CONVENTION.

Brownlow Committee A committee appointed by President Franklin D. Roosevelt in 1936 for the purpose of diagnosing the staffing needs of the President and making appropriate recommendations for the reorganization of the executive branch; formally known as the President's Committee on Administrative Management. The committee of three was chaired by Louis Brownlow (1879–1963), a major figure in the development of city management as a profession. Overall, the committee recommended a major reorganization of the executive branch. The President agreed, and appropriate legislation was submitted to the Congress in 1938. But the Congress, in the wake of the President's efforts to "pack" the Supreme Court and fearful of too much power in the presidency, killed the bill. The President resubmitted a considerably modified reorganization bill the following year, and the Congress passed the Reorganization Act of 1939, authorizing the President, subject to congressional veto, to redistribute and restructure executive branch agencies. President Roosevelt subsequently created the EXECUTIVE OFFICE OF THE PRESIDENT (EOP). The EOP began with six top-level assistants in 1939 but has expanded to over a hundred.

Brown v Board of Education of Topeka, Kansas (1954) The landmark Supreme Court decision holding that the separation of children by race and according to law in public schools "generates a feeling of inferiority as to their [the minority group's] status in the community that may affect their hearts and minds in a way unlikely ever to be undone." Consequently, it held that "separate educational facilities are inherently unequal" and therefore violate the equal protection clause of the Fourteenth Amendment. According to Chief Justice Earl Warren, "We come then to the question presented: does segregation of children in public schools solely on the basis of race, even though the physical facilities and other 'tangible' factors may be equal, deprive the children of the minority group of equal educational opportunities? We believe that it does." This decision, one of the most significant in the century, helped create the environment that would lead to the modern CIVIL RIGHTS MOVEMENT. *See also* SEPARATE BUT EQUAL.

Bryce, James (1838–1922) The British historian and ambassador to the United States (1907–1913) who wrote a classic analysis of the American political system, *The American Commonwealth* (1888; final revised ed., 1922), which held that the American political experience was a continuation and enlargement of British traditions. Bryce was a keen observer of American political culture. He noted that civil service reform received the support of both parties, "a lip service expressed by both with equal warmth and by the average professional politician of both with equal insincerity." The most famous part of his landmark book is his chapter "Why Great Men Are Not Chosen Presidents." About most American Presidents (the founders, Lincoln, and Grant excluded), Bryce concluded that "the only thing remarkable about them is that being so commonplace they should have climbed so high." He found that: "Great men are not chosen President, firstly, because great men are rare in politics; secondly, because the method of choice does not bring them to the top; thirdly, because they are not, in quiet times, absolutely needed."

Bubba vote The conservative rural vote in parts of the South—especially Texas.

Buchanan, James (1791–1868) The President of the United States from 1857 to 1861. Buchanan is generally considered one of the least effective leaders ever to serve in the White House, mainly because he did practically nothing to prevent the Civil War which started a month after he left office. When in 1845 former President Andrew Jackson learned that President James K. Polk had appointed Buchanan Secretary of State, he was incensed and let Polk know it. Polk responded by saying that "you [Jackson] appointed him minister to Russia in your first term [as President]." "Yes, I did, [Jackson replied]. It was as far as I could send him out of my sight and where he could do the least harm! I would have sent him to the North Pole if we had kept a minister there" (quoted in Augustus C. Buell, *History of Andrew Jackson*, 1904).

buck 1. Responsibility. President Harry S Truman was famous for the sign on his desk that read "The Buck Stops Here." Buck, a term from poker, refers to the marker put in front of the player who next had to deal. To avoid a problem or a responsibility is to pass the buck. Bureaucrats in many jurisdictions refer to the form memos that they use to direct paper from one to another as buck slips. **2.** The lowest in a series of grades: for example, a buck private. **3.** To work hard at something, as in "he's bucking for promotion."

Buckley v Valeo (1976) The Supreme Court case upholding the constitutionality of the Federal Election Campaign Act except for provisions that limited campaign spending and limited what an individual candidate could spend on his or her own campaign. The Court held that: "Being free to engage in unlimited political expression subject to a ceiling on ex-penditures is like being free to drive an automobile as far and as often as one desires on a single tank of gasoline." The court explained that the "First Amendment denies government the power to determine that spending to promote one's political views is . . . excessive. In the free society ordained by our Constitution, it is not the government but the people . . . who must retain control over the quantity and range of debate . . . in a political campaign." Thus, wealthy individuals may spend unlimited amounts on their own campaigns and PACs can spend unlimited amounts so long as their spending is independent of the formal campaign structure of the candidate they support.

budget A financial plan serving as a pattern for and control over future operations—hence, any estimate of future costs or any systematic plan for the utilization of the workforce, material, or other resources.

Budget and Accounting Act of 1921 The law which (1) mandated that the President prepare and submit to the Congress a budget for the federal government, and (2) created the Bureau of the Budget (later called the Office of Management and Budget) and the General Accounting Office.

budget, balanced *See* BALANCED BUDGET.

Budget, Bureau of the The central budget agency of the United States from 1921 to 1970. *See* OFFICE OF MANAGEMENT AND BUDGET.

budget, current services A budget that projects estimated budget authority and outlays for the upcoming fiscal year at the same program level (and without policy changes) as the fiscal year in progress. To the extent mandated by existing law, estimates take into account the budget impact of anticipated changes in economic conditions (such as unemployment or inflation), pay increases, and benefit changes. The Congressional Budget and Impoundment Control Act of 1974 requires that the President submit a current services budget to the Congress by November 10 of each year.

budget cycle The timed steps of the budget process, which includes preparation, approval, execution, and audit.

budget, executive 1. The budget document for an executive branch of government that a jurisdiction's chief executive submits to a legislature for review, modification, and enactment. **2.** The process by which agency requests for appropriations are prepared and submitted to a budget bureau under the chief executive for review, alteration, and consolidation into a single budget document that can be compared to expected revenues and executive priorities before submission to the legislature.

budget, line-item The classification of budgetary accounts according to narrow, detailed objects of expenditure (such as motor vehicles, clerical workers, or reams of paper) used within each particular agency of government, generally without reference to the ultimate purpose or objective served by the expenditure.

budget, operating A short-term plan for managing the resources necessary to carry out a program. Short term can mean anything from a few weeks to a few years. Usually an operating budget is developed for each fiscal year, with changes made as necessary.

budget, president's The executive budget for a particular fiscal year transmitted to the Congress by the President in accordance with the Budget and Accounting Act of 1921, as amended. Some elements of the budget (such as the estimates for the legislative branch and the judiciary) are required to be included without review by the Office of Management and Budget or approval by the President.

budget surplus The amount by which a government's budget receipts exceed its budget outlays for any given period.

budget, unified The present form of the budget of the federal government, in which receipts and outlays from federal funds and trust funds (such as social security) are consolidated. When these two fund groups are consolidated to display budget totals, transactions from one fund group to the other fund group (interfund transactions) are deducted to avoid double counting. The fiscal activities of off-budget federal agencies (such as the Federal Financing Bank) are not included in the unified budget.

budget year The fiscal year for which the budget is being considered; the fiscal year following the current year.

budgeting The single most important decision-making process in U.S. public institutions today. The budget itself is also a jurisdiction's most important reference document. In their increasingly voluminous formats, budgets simultaneously record policy decision outcomes, cite policy priorities as well as program objectives, and delineate a government's total service effort.

A public budget has four basic dimensions. First, it is a political instrument that allocates scarce public resources among the social and economic needs of the jurisdiction. Second, a budget is a managerial or administrative instrument: it specifies the ways and means of providing public programs and services; it establishes the costs of programs and the criteria by which these programs are evaluated for efficiency and effectiveness; it ensures that the programs will be reviewed or evaluated at least once during each year (or cycle). Third, a budget is an economic instrument that can direct a jurisdiction's economic growth and development. Certainly at the national level—and to a lesser extent at the state and regional levels—government budgets are primary instruments for redistributing income, stimulating economic growth, promoting full employment, combating inflation, and maintaining economic stability. Fourth, a budget is an accounting instrument that holds government officials responsible for the expenditure of the funds with which they have been entrusted. Budgets also hold governments accountable in the aggregate. The very concept of a budget implies that there is a ceiling, or a spending limitation, which literally (but theoretically) requires governments to live within their means.

The classic comment on federal budgeting is usually credited to Senator Everett M. Dirksen (1896–1969): "A billion here, a billion there, and pretty soon you're talking about real money."

budgeting, capital A budget process that deals with planning for large expenditures for long-term investment items, such as bridges and buildings, which yield returns for years after they are completed. Capital budgets typically cover five- to 10-year periods and are updated yearly. Items included in capital budgets may be financed through borrowing (including tax-exempt municipal bonds), savings, grants, revenue sharing, special assessments, and so on. A capital budget provides for separating the financing of capital, or investment, expenditures from current, or operating, expenditures. The federal government has never had a capital budget in the sense of financing capital programs separately from current expenditures.

budgeting, incremental A method of budget review that focuses on the amount of increase or decrease in the budgets of existing programs. Incremental budgeting, which is often called traditional budgeting, is a counter school of thought to more rational, systems-oriented approaches, such as zero-based budgeting. But this old approach nicely takes into account the inherently political nature of the budget process and so will continue to be favored by legislative appropriations committees, if not by budget theorists. As Aaron Wildavsky wrote in *The Politics of the Budgetary Process* (1964): "The largest determining factor of the size and content of this year's budget is last year's budget."

budgeting, planning programming *See* PLANNING PROGRAMMING BUDGETING SYSTEM.

budgeting, zero-based A budgeting process that is, first and foremost, a rejection of the incremental decision-making model of budgeting. It demands a rejustification of the entire budget submission (from ground zero, hence its name), whereas incremental budgeting essentially respects the outcomes of previous budgetary decisions (collectively referred to as the budget base) and focuses examination on the margin of change from year to year. In 1976, presidential candidate Jimmy Carter made the installation of zero-based budgeting (ZBB) a campaign promise, and in 1977, as President, he ordered its adoption by the federal government. In large part, ZBB failed because the conditions that had prevailed for most of the previous budgeting system reforms had changed. In an era of acute resource scarcity, ZBB had little utility because there was little real chance that funding could be provided for any program growth. Critics assaulted ZBB as a fraud; some called it a nonsystem of budgeting. ZBB's fate in the federal government was tied to the Carter presidency. After the inauguration of a new President in 1981, it was quietly rescinded. Still, numerous state and local governments use ZBB techniques or some adaptation of it. Now that the hype has subsided, it remains an important part of public budgeting.

bull moose party The informal name for the Progressive Party in 1912 when former President Theodore Roosevelt was its presidential candidate. It was one of Roosevelt's pet phrases to compare his level of physical fitness to that of a bull moose. Even after he was wounded in an assassination attempt while giving a campaign speech in Milwaukee on October 14, 1912, he told the crowd: "I have been shot; but it takes more than that to kill a Bull Moose."

bully pulpit **1.** President Theodore Roosevelt's definition of the American presidency, because the office provided its occupant an unparalleled opportunity to preach to and to inspire the national congregation. Bully is an informal interjection of approval that has fallen into disuse, except among those who do impersonations of Teddy Roosevelt. **2.** By analogy, any highly visible public office whose incumbent uses it as a platform to influence public opinion.

buncombe Insincere public utterings of politicians; speechmaking undertaken to please constituents; political nonsense (also appearing as *bunkum* or *bunk*). The word has its origin in a statement by Felix Walker (1753–1828), the U.S. Representative from Buncombe County, North Carolina, who in 1820 rose in the House "to make a speech for Buncombe." It was so obviously insincere and irrelevant, his home county's name was transformed into a term for inconsequential political speech. This is the basis of automaker Henry Ford's (1863–1947) famous 1919 assertion that "history is bunk."

burden of proof The requirement that a party to an issue show that the weight of evidence is on his or her side to have the issue decided in his or her favor.

bureau A government department, agency, or a subdivision of same. It was former Secretary of State James F. Byrnes (1879–1972) who wrote that "The nearest approach to immortality on earth is a government bureau" (*Speaking Frankly*, 1947).

bureaucracy **1.** The totality of government offices or bureaus (a French term meaning "office") that constitute the permanent government of a state; that is, those people and functions that continue irrespective of changes in political leadership. Modern Western-style bureaucracies originated in Europe when the governing affairs of centralized autocratic regimes became so complicated that it became necessary to delegate the king's authority to his representatives. American bureaucracy has never fully recovered from its nondemocratic European origins, and some politicians rejoice in attacking the "unresponsive" bureaucracy. At the same time, "good government" groups often contend that, once in office, politicians make the bureaucracy all too responsive to special interests instead of leaving them alone to impartially administer the programs for which they were originally established. **2.** All of the public officials of a government. **3.** A general invective to refer to any inefficient organization encumbered by

RED TAPE. **4.** A specific set of structural arrangements. **5.** "The giant power wielded by pigmies," according to *Bureaucracy* by French author Honore de Balzac (1901).

The dominant structural definition of bureaucracy, indeed the point of departure for all further analyses on the subject, is that of the German sociologist MAX WEBER, who used an "ideal type" approach to extrapolate from the real world the central core of features that would characterize the most fully developed bureaucratic form of organization. This ideal type is neither a description of reality nor a statement of normative preference; it is merely an identification of the major variables or features that characterize bureaucracy. The fact that such features might not be fully present in a given organization does not necessarily imply that the organization is not bureaucratic. It may be an immature rather than a fully developed bureaucracy. At some point, however, it may be necessary to conclude that the characteristics of bureaucracy are so lacking in an organization that it could neither reasonably be termed bureaucratic nor be expected to produce patterns of bureaucratic behavior.

Weber's ideal type of bureaucracy possesses the following characteristics: (1) The bureaucrats must be personally free and subject to authority only with respect to the impersonal duties of their offices. (2) The bureaucrats are arranged in a clearly defined hierarchy of offices. (3) The functions of each office are clearly specified. (4) The bureaucrats accept and maintain their appointments freely—without duress. (5) Appointments to office are made on the basis of technical qualifications, which ideally are substantiated by examinations administered by the appointing authority, a university, or both. (6) The bureaucrats receive money salaries and pension rights, which reflect the varying levels of the hierarchy. While the bureaucrats are free to leave the organization, they can be removed from their offices only under previously stated, specific circumstances. (7) The office must be the bureaucrat's sole or at least major occupation. (8) A career system is essential; while promotion may be the result of either seniority or merit, it must be premised on the judgment of hierarchical superiors. (9) The bureaucrats do not have property rights to their office nor any personal claim to the resources that go with it. (10) The bureaucrat's conduct must be subject to systematic control and strict discipline.

While Weber's structural identification of bureaucratic organization, first published in 1922, is perhaps the most comprehensive statement on the subject in the literature of the social sciences, it is not always considered satisfactory as an intellectual construct. For example, Anthony Downs, in *Inside Bureaucracy* (1967), argued that at least two elements should be added to Weber's definition. First, the organization must be large. According to Downs, "any organization in which the highest ranking members know less than half of the other members can be considered large." Second, most of the organization's output cannot be "directly or indirectly evaluated in any markets external to the organization by means of voluntary quid pro quo transactions." *See also* FOURTH BRANCH OF GOVERNMENT; RED TAPE; REPRESENTATIVE BUREAUCRACY.

bureaucracy, contract All those employees of private firms whose jobs involve performing government services on a contract basis. *Compare to* CONTRACTING OUT.

bureaucratic freelancing The activities of agency heads who call for policy initiatives seemingly without the approval of their elected political superiors. When the secretary of this calls for a new program on that, he or she may be freelancing. Alternatively, he or she may merely be floating a TRIAL BALLOON for the President.

bureaucrats, street-level Those public officials who are literally closest to the people by being in almost constant contact with the public; for example, police officers, welfare case workers, teachers.

Bureau of Labor Statistics (BLS) The agency responsible for the economic and statistical research activities of the U.S. Department of Labor.

Burger, Warren Earl (1907–) The Chief Justice of the United States from 1969 to 1986. He was appointed by President Richard M. Nixon in the expectation that he would lead a conservative court that would reverse many of the liberal rulings of the Warren court. But the conservative revolution was slow in coming and would not become generally evident until after Burger's retirement. While Burger's philosophy of judicial restraint is evident by his voting record, he never developed a reputation as a great legal draftsman. However, he was an outspoken advocate for administrative reform of the federal court system.

burgess 1. An elected member in the lower house of the legislature in colonial Virginia or Maryland. Burgess simply means a citizen of an English borough. **2.** A modern-day member of the governing board of some boroughs.

Burke, Edmund (1729–1797) The British political philosopher and member of Parliament who is often referred to as the father of modern conservative thought. Burke, in his 1770 pamphlet "Thoughts on the Cause of the Present Discontents," provided the first modern definition of a political party as a group united on public principle that could act as a link between the executive branch (the king) and the legislative branch (Parliament), providing consistency and strength while in power and principled criticism when out of power. But Burke is best known for his 1774 "Speech to the Electors of Bristol," in which he asserted that the role of an elected member of a legislature should be that of a representative or trustee (free to exercise his own best judgment) rather than that of a delegate (bound by prior instructions from a constituency). *Compare to* POLITICO.

Bush, George Herbert Walker (1924–) The President of the United States from 1989 to 1993. After serving eight years as Vice President under

President Ronald Reagan, Bush became the first serving Vice President to be elected President since Martin van Buren in 1836. After extensive combat as a Navy pilot in World War II, he earned a bachelor's degree in economics from Yale in 1948, then moved to Texas and prospered in the oil business. He served two terms representing Texas in the House of Representatives (1967–1971), then was appointed Ambassador to the United Nations (1971–1973) by President Richard M. Nixon. After a stint as Chairman of the Republican National Committee (1973–1974), he was appointed Chief of the U.S. Liaison Office (effectively ambassador) in China (1974–1975). He returned to be Director of the CIA (1976–1977) for President Gerald Ford.

Bush was Ronald Reagan's main competition for the Republican presidential nomination in 1980. After accepting Reagan's offer of the Vice Presidency, Bush proved so supportive and loyal to his President that a conservative columnist such as George Will was comparing him to a "lap dog" (*The Washington Post*, January 30, 1986). Nevertheless, in the 1988 Republican primaries he quickly knocked out all rivals, and after overcoming a WIMP image waged an aggressive, successful campaign against Democratic challenger, Michael Dukakis, the Governor of Massachusetts.

As President, Bush continued to wind down the Cold War with the Soviet Union, used military force in 1989 to overthrown and arrest the Panamanian dictator Manuel Noriega, and after the Iraqi invasion of Kuwait in 1990, committed massive American forces to the defense of Saudi Arabia and the other Persian Gulf states. By general agreement, Bush's finest hour was his orchestration of the diplomatic and military alliance against Iraq. For the first time since the KOREAN WAR, the UNITED NATIONS (again under United States leadership) sanctioned a combat force in the field. The ensuing short and highly successful PERSIAN GULF WAR that followed in early 1991 liberated Kuwait, and sent Bush's popularity ratings to new highs.

Domestically, Bush was plagued by the financial problems left over by the SAVINGS AND LOAN and HUD scandals of the Ronald Reagan Administration, by continuing large deficits, and by a lengthy recession. Bush was defeated for reelection in 1992 by Governor William J. Clinton of Arkansas. *See* BIG MO; DEEP DOO-DOO; HORTON, WILLIE; VOODOO ECONOMICS.

business cycle, political The manipulation of an economy for political purposes by means of government expenditures and monetary policy. A political business cycle would ideally seek to maintain the greatest prosperity just before elections and to suffer through the seemingly inevitable periods of economic decline just after elections. While many politicians have tried to manipulate economic activity for political advantage (increased government spending just before an election is an obvious example), there is no hard evidence that their success is more related to calculated policies than to luck.

business cycles The recurrent phases of expansion and contraction in overall business activity. Although no two business cycles are alike, they are all thought to follow a pattern of prosperity, recession (or depression), and recovery.

busing The transporting of children to schools at a greater distance from their homes than those they would otherwise attend to achieve racial desegregation. Busing has often been mandated by the federal courts as a remedy for past practices of discrimination. Parents who want their children to attend neighborhood schools have strongly objected to it and it has, in consequence, been a major factor in WHITE FLIGHT from central cities. Busing is often used as an example of government by the judiciary, because even though it has been one of the most controversial domestic policies in the history of the United States, it has never been specifically sanctioned by the Congress. *Compare to* SWANN V CHARLOTTE-MECKLENBURG BOARD OF EDUCATION.

button, the The figurative ignition device that would start a full-scale nuclear war. Thus, "pushing the button" has become a metaphor for ending the world.

buy American acts Various state and national laws that require government agencies to give a preference to American-made goods when making purchases. Similar "buy national" practices are also being used by all the major trading partners of the United States.

by-election A type of special election. *See* ELECTION, SPECIAL.

bylaws 1. The regulations adopted by a corporation's stockholders for its internal governance. **2.** The rules and regulations adopted by an organization, such as a social club or professional association. **3.** The laws enacted by subordinate legislative bodies, such as municipalities.

C

cabinet The heads of the executive departments of a jurisdiction who report to and advise its chief executive; for example, the President's cabinet, the governor's cabinet, the mayor's cabinet.

cabinet council A subgroup of the federal cabinet departments used to coordinate and develop policy in an area of common concern; it is chaired by the President or a cabinet member of his or her designation.

cabinet government 1. The British system, whereby the cabinet as a whole, rather than only the prime minister who heads it, is considered the executive, and the cabinet is collectively responsible to the Parliament for its performance. In addition, while in the United States the cabinet secretaries are only of the executive branch, in Britain the cabinet ministers are typically drawn from among the majority party's members in Parliament. **2.** A concept informally applied to an American President's assertion that he and his cabinet are going to work together as a team. Such team spirit rarely lasts beyond an administration's HONEYMOON PERIOD.

cabinet, inner Usually refers to the federal departments of State, Defense, Treasury, and Justice—because they (and their secretaries) tend to be more prominent and influential in every administration than the rest of the cabinet (the outer cabinet). While all cabinet secretaries are equal in rank and salary, the missions of those in the inner cabinet give them an advantage in prestige, access, and visibility.

Cabinet, Kitchen The informal advisors of a chief executive. First used derisively for some of President Andrew Jackson's advisors, "kitchen" implying they were not respectable enough to meet in the more formal rooms of the White House. Over the years the term has lost its derisive quality. *Compare to* BRAINS TRUST.

cabinet, president's An institution whose existence rests upon custom rather than constitutional provision, even though its chief members, the secretaries of the federal executive departments, must be approved by the Senate. It came into being as a single body, because President George Washington found it useful to meet with the chiefs of the several executive departments. While all subsequent Presidents have considered it necessary to meet with the cabinet, their attitudes toward the institution and its members have varied greatly. Some Presidents have convened their cabinet only for the most formal and routine matters, while others have relied upon it for advice and support. The President's cabinet differs from the cabinet in the British parliamentary system in that, in the United States, the executive power is constitutionally vested in the President alone, so the cabinet members are responsible to him or her.

At the present time, cabinet membership consists of the secretaries of 14 executive departments, the newest member being the Secretary of Veterans Affairs. A substantial part of the executive branch is not represented in the cabinet. From the earliest days, Presidents have accorded to others the privilege of attending and participating in cabinet meetings. In recent years, the U.S. ambassador to the United Nations and the director of the Office of Management and Budget, among others, have been accorded cabinet rank. According to Edward Weisband and Thomas M. Frank's *Resignation in Protest* (1975): "Cabinet meetings in the United States, despite occasional efforts to make them into significant decision-making occasions, have, at least in this century, been characterized as vapid non-events in which there has been a deliberate non-exchange of information as part of a process of mutual nonconsultation."

cadre **1.** The most dedicated members of a political party. **2.** The founding members of a political organization who thereupon expand the organization by enlisting new members. **3.** A detachment from an existing organization capable of being the training nucleus about which a new large organizational unit can be built. In a military context, cadres of commissioned as well as noncommissioned officers have always been critical for rapidly expanding an army.

calendar An agenda or list of pending business awaiting action by a legislature. The House of Representatives uses five legislative calendars: CONSENT CALENDAR, HOUSE CALENDAR, PRIVATE CALENDAR, UNION CALENDAR, and DISCHARGE CALENDAR (see below). In the Senate, all legislative matters reported from committee are listed in order on a single calendar, but they may be called up irregularly by the majority leader, either by motion or by obtaining the unanimous consent of the Senate. The Senate also uses one nonlegislative calendar, known as the executive calendar, for presidential nominations and treaties.

calendar, call of *See* CALL OF THE CALENDAR.

calendar, consent The calendar on which members of the House of Representatives may place any noncontroversial bill appearing on the union or house calendars. Bills on the consent calendar are normally called on the first and third Mondays of each month. On the first occasion that a bill is called in this manner, consideration may be blocked by the objection of any member. The second time, if there are three objections, the bill is stricken from the consent calendar. If fewer than three members object, the bill is given immediate consideration. A bill on the consent calendar may be postponed in another way. A member may ask that the measure be passed over "without prejudice." In that case, no objection is recorded against the bill, and its status on the consent calendar remains unchanged. A bill stricken from the consent calendar remains on the union or house calendars.

calendar, discharge The House of Representatives calendar to which motions to discharge committees are referred when the necessary 218 signatures have been obtained. *See* DISCHARGE A COMMITTEE.

calendar, executive A nonlegislative calendar in the Senate, on which presidential documents, such as treaties and nominations, are listed.

calendar, House The listing of public bills, other than appropriations or revenue measures, awaiting action by the House of Representatives.

calendar, private The calendar on which House of Representative bills dealing with individual matters—such as claims against the government, immigration, and land titles—are put. Two members may block consideration of a private bill in the chamber. If blocked, it is then recommitted to committee. An omnibus claims bill is several private bills considered as one. As with any bill, no part of an omnibus claims bill may be deleted without a vote. When a private bill goes to the floor in this form, it can be defeated only by a majority of those present. The private calendar can be called on the first and third Tuesdays of each month.

calendar, union The calendar in the House of Representatives on which bills that directly or indirectly appropriate money or raise revenue are placed according to the date they are reported from committee.

calendar Wednesday Certain Wednesdays when the House of Representatives is in session. On these Wednesdays, committees may be called (in the order in which they appear in House Rule 10) for the purpose of bringing up any of their bills from the House or the union calendars, except privileged bills. General debate is limited to two hours. Bills called up from the union calendar are considered in the Committee of the Whole. Calendar Wednesday is not observed during the last two weeks of a session and may be dispensed with at other times by a two-thirds vote. On the whole, it is a cumbersome and largely ineffective device for calling up a bill for floor consideration.

Calhoun, John C. (1782–1850) The leading political voice of the South in the first half of the nineteenth century and the only Vice President (1825–1832) to resign over policy differences with a President (Andrew Jackson). Calhoun is most associated with the concept of nullification, which held that a state could nullify an act of the Congress within its own borders. This was later referred to as interposition, because a state might interpose its sovereignty to void a law of the United States. The whole nullification-interposition controversy was settled by the Civil War, and these concepts are now only of historical significance. In the 1950s some southern politicians tried to revive the interposition doctrine as a way of avoiding federal court desegregation mandates. But the federal courts have rejected interposition as a violation of the supremacy clause of Article VI of the U.S. Constitution.

In his *Disquisition on Government* (1848), Calhoun, the leading states' rights and proslavery advocate of his era, ironically argued for the protection of minorities in a democratic society. He suggested that binding political decisions be made only by a "concurrent majority" representing all major elements of society. Decisions made only by a simple majority, Calhoun asserted, could not be binding on groups whose interests they violated. In effect, Calhoun was pleading for consensus government.

call of the calendar The means by which those Senate bills not brought up for debate by a motion or a unanimous consent agreement are brought before the Senate for action when the calendar listing them in order is "called." Bills considered in this fashion are usually noncontroversial, and debate is limited to five minutes for each Senator on a bill or on amendments to it.

Camelot King Arthur's legendary city, which became a retrospective symbol of the John F. Kennedy administration's style after Jacqueline Kennedy, the President's widow, told journalist Theodore H. White in an interview for *Life* magazine how much the late President loved the music from the Broadway musical *Camelot* ("For President Kennedy, An Epilogue," *Life*, December 6, 1963). Because of some negative reassessment of Kennedy's presidency, the term is sometimes used sarcastically.

campaign Continuous operations leading toward a known goal, a clearly defined single objective. The traditional military campaign began when the combatant force left its home base to engage the enemy and ended when it returned home—victorious or defeated. Much of the language of political contests has its origins in military campaigning. *See* POLITICAL CAMPAIGN.

campaign biography 1. A largely uncritical, indeed often adoring, life of a presidential candidate written so that it is available during the campaign season. When these books are autobiographies, they are almost always ghost-written. The writing of campaign biographies is a tradition that goes back far in American history. In the 1850s novelist Nathaniel Hawthorne wrote what he referred to as "the necessary book" for Franklin Pierce, a friend from college days. The prose is appropriately purple. Hawthorne wrote that Pierce's possible election as President "comes, not like accident, but as a consummation which might have been anticipated, from its innate fitness, and as the final step of a career which, all along, has tended thitherward." For his efforts Hawthorne was rewarded with an appointment as the American consul in Liverpool. Modern biographers dream of similar presidential patronage rewards. **2.** A damning indictment of a candidate in the form of a life story published in time to encourage his or her defeat.

campaign buttons A general category for political advertising on any number of novelty items, such as hats, key rings, pens, and especially buttons—usually round plastic pins with the candidate's picture or slogan. These are among the oldest forms of political advertising. And they're free—except of course for the cost of the button.

campaign card A single piece of cardboard with the candidate's picture, slogan, and ad on one side, and something useful (such as a calendar, football schedule, etc.) on the other side so that people will keep it around.

campaign, front-loaded *See* FRONT LOADED.

campaign literature All the printed materials distributed by a political campaign to convince voters of the merits of the candidate; they range from fliers to be stuck in doors or on mailboxes to the most professionally prepared brochures. Campaign literature has recently taken on new importance as part of DIRECT MAIL solicitations for campaign funds.

campaign manager The individual who functions as the executive officer of a political campaign. Theoretically, the candidate is responsible for all of the major decisions of a campaign. But a manager can free him or her from campaign details and administration so that maximum FACE TIME is given to potential voters.

campaign message The major theme of a political campaign. It could be the qualities of the candidate ("experience counts"), the candidate's policy positions ("no new taxes"), or any other factor that will appeal to voters.

campaign promise What candidates say they will do "if elected." There has often been a tenuous relation between the promise and the performance. Most citizens are astute enough not to believe many promises. This has been true since ancient times. Quintus Tullius Cicero (102–43 B.C.) in his "Handbook of Electioneering" advised those seeking public office in ancient Rome: "Human nature being what it is, all men prefer a false promise to a flat refusal. At the worst the man to whom you have lied may be angry. That risk, if you make a promise, is uncertain and deferred, and it affects only a few. But if you refuse you are sure to offend many, and that at once,"(quoted in H.J. Haskell, *The New Deal in Old Rome*, 1939). The best known campaign promise of the 1988 presidential election was George Bush's assertion: "Read my lips: no new taxes." Yet a *New York Times* poll (May 27, 1990) reported that 63 percent of the population did not believe him or thought it only meant that he would raise taxes "later rather than sooner." Less than a month later, in June 1990, President Bush announced that he would be raising taxes after all. At his first news conference following this announcement on June 29, 1990, he said that he expected to hear "some campaign words played back to me." In his defense he cited other Presidents who had to break campaign promises, such as President Abraham Lincoln, who did so in freeing the slaves. According to journalist David Wise: "Campaign promises are made to be broken. The voter wants to hear pie-in-the-sky, and the politician knows that he or she has to make promises to get elected. So it's a kind of mutual con game, although neither side will ever admit that" (*The New York Times*, July 2, 1990). Financier Bernard Baruch (1870–1965) is usually credited with the advice to "vote for the man who promises least; he'll be the least disappointing." For an assessment of presidential campaign promises after the candidate has won, see Jeff Fishel, *Presidents and Promises: From Campaign Pledge to Presidential Performance* (1984).

campaign spending limitations Federal or state laws which put limits on what candidates can spend seeking a given political office. For example, the FEDERAL ELECTION CAMPAIGN ACT provides about $50 million to each major party's presidential candidate. If they agree to accept the money, they are prohibited from raising additional funds. The states are experimenting with similar laws. For example, in Minnesota the state will pay up to 25 percent of the campaign costs of U.S. House and Senate candidates, provided they spend no more than a prescribed limit.

campaign strategy The plan of a political campaign; how it spends its money and uses other resources, how it creates an overall tone or theme, and ultimately how it expects to win. Author Hedrick Smith in *The Power Game* (1988) suggests that: "[The] modern campaign is mass marketing at its most superficial. It puts a premium on the suggestive slogan, the glib answer, the symbolic backdrop. Television is its medium. Candidates must have razzle-dazzle. Boring is the fatal label. Programs and concepts that cannot be collapsed into a slogan or a 30-second sound bite go largely unheard and unremembered."

Camp David The U.S. President's private resort in the Catoctin Mountains in Maryland. Called Shangri-La by President Franklin D. Roosevelt (after James Hilton's mystical place of enchantment in his 1933 novel, *Lost Horizons*), its name was changed to Camp David by Dwight D. Eisenhower in honor of his grandson. Camp David is no Spartan camp; it has a swimming pool, a bowling alley, tennis courts, and a movie theater, among other luxuries.

Camp David Accords The agreements negotiated and signed by Egyptian President Anwar Sadat and Israeli Prime Minister Menachem Begin in September 1978 at Camp David. These agreements led to the formal Egyptian-Israeli peace treaty in March 1979. President Jimmy Carter sequestered the two heads of state at Camp David while he and his staff mediated an agreement.

Camp David, Spirit of The temporary thaw in the cold war brought about by the 1959 summit meeting at Camp David between President Dwight D. Eisenhower and Soviet Premier Nikita S. Khrushchev.

candidate 1. One who seeks elective office. The word came from the Latin *candida* (white) for the white togas worn by *candidati* (candidates for elective office in the ancient Roman republic). Because a formal candidate for U.S. public office may have to abide by a variety of campaign spending and other limitations, many probable candidates do not announce their formal candidacy until a strategic moment, even though it is perfectly obvious to everybody that he or she is running for office. **2.** An applicant for a civil service position.

candidate, captive A political party's nominee who is perceived to be a captive of specific interest groups—to be working more in their interests than in the interests of the electorate. During the 1984 presidential campaign the Republicans were quite successful at labeling Walter Mondale as the "captive" of special interests because of his formal endorsements by the AFL-CIO and other organizations.

candidate committee A POLITICAL COMMITTEE authorized in writing by a candidate to receive campaign contributions and to make expenditures on his or her behalf.

candidate escrow funding A campaign fund-raising technique whereby potential supporters are sent a check for a small amount (such as $25); they are then told (in small print) that endorsement and cashing of the check creates a contract which allows the campaign committee to deduct a small amount (such as $12.50) from the supporter's checking account each month. The original check is considered a "refund" of the first two months' contribution and the gimmick to get the potential supporter to sign on.

candidate services The stock in trade of firms that sell professional services to political campaigns. Typical services available to candidates include polling, advertising, fund raising, speech writing, and so on.

candidate, write-in A candidate who is not on a printed ballot; whose supporters must write his or her name on the ballot. Write-in campaigns are usually futile.

canvass **1.** An election. **2.** A political campaign. **3.** To count votes. **4.** To assess public opinion.

canvassing The process of contacting voters, either by a candidate or by a political worker, to solicit their vote on election day. There are two basic kinds of canvassing: door-to-door and telephone.

canvassing board The state or local government agency that receives the vote counts from the various election precincts, tabulates the count, and certifies the winners.

capital **1.** The city in which a central government is located. New York City became the first capital of the United States (1789); Philadelphia became the capital in 1790; since 1800, the capital has been Washington, D.C. *Compare to* CAPITOL. **2.** Wealth; one of the three traditional factors of production, the others being land and labor.

capital offense **1.** A crime punishable by death. **2.** A crime punishable by death or life imprisonment.

capital punishment The death penalty. The word capital is derived from the Latin word for head, *caput;* thus, "head punishment" once meant you had to give up your head—that it would be cut off. Today, most countries applying capital punishment, except those that still use the sword or guillotine, allow those who are condemned to retain their heads after all life is taken from it. While capital punishment is much discussed in the United States, it has been rarely practiced in recent years. For example, while 2,124 prisoners were legally condemned to death and awaiting execution in the various states in 1988, there were only 11 executions—all for murder. Yet polls have consistently shown great public support for capital punishment. For example, the *Gallup Report* of January/February 1986 showed that 77 percent of all Americans favored the death penalty. While many states have capital punishment on the books, only a few states (Texas,

Florida, Louisiana, Georgia, Virginia, and Alabama) conduct the vast majority of actual executions. The following states and the District of Columbia do not have capital punishment on the books: Alaska, Hawaii, Iowa, Kansas, Maine, Massachusetts, Michigan, Minnesota, New York, North Dakota, Rhode Island, West Virginia, and Wisconsin. A common attitude on capital punishment was expressed by Frank L. Rizzo when he was Mayor of Philadelphia: "I don't know if it will stop this type of activity [murder] by taking the life of the individual who commits this vicious crime, but I'm certain of one thing: he won't be around to commit another one" (*Newsweek*, January 24, 1972). *Compare to* CRUEL AND UNUSUAL PUNISHMENT.

capitalism **1.** The private ownership of most means of production and trade, combined with a generally unrestricted marketplace of goods and services. **2.** An economic system where there is a combination of private property, a generally unrestricted marketplace of goods and services, and a general assumption that the bulk of the workforce will be engaged in employment by private (nongovernmental) employees engaged in producing goods to sell at a profit. It was the Scottish economist Adam Smith (1723–1790) who provided the first systematic analysis of the economic phenomena of laissez-fare capitalism. In *The Wealth of Nations* (1776), Smith describes an "invisible hand" that automatically promotes the general welfare as long as individuals are allowed to pursue their self-interest. To believers in capitalism, this form of economic organization provides the greatest chance of maximizing economic performance and defending political liberty while securing something approaching equality of opportunity. However, classic unrestrained laissez-faire capitalism is today only a theory because all of the capitalistic societies of the West have mixed economies that temper capitalism with government regulation and social welfare measures. *Compare to* MARXISM.

Capitol **1.** The domed building in which the Congress of the United States meets. The dome of the Capitol was built during the Civil War. When people complained that it was "an extravagance during wartime," President Abraham Lincoln responded: "If people see the Capitol going on, it is a sign we intend the Union shall go on" (quoted in Carl Sandburg, *Abraham Lincoln* II, 1939). **2.** Any building in which a state legislature meets; also called a statehouse. *Compare to* CAPITAL.

Capitol Hill **1.** The site, originally known as Jenkins Hill, on which the U.S. Capitol is situated. **2.** A reference to the U.S. Congress as a whole in such phrases as "What does Capitol Hill think?"

card-carrying A zealous supporter of an organization that issues membership cards. The term gained political currency during the RED SCARE when it meant "enthusiastic" when used in front of "communist." During this time the worst thing you could be called, if you were a mainstream American, was a "card-carrying member of the Communist Party."

CARPETBAGGERS

During the 1988 presidential race the Democratic nominee, Michael Dukakis, inadvertently shot himself in the political foot when he proudly asserted: "I am a card-carrying member of the A.C.L.U. [AMERICAN CIVIL LIBERTIES UNION]." Card-carrying carries too many bad subliminal messages to Americans. They don't mind people carrying cards; but they still seem to mind "card-carriers."

carpetbaggers **1.** Northerners who went into the defeated South after the Civil War to seek their fortunes by taking advantage of the corrupt and unstable conditions of the times. **2.** A candidate who seeks elective office in a jurisdiction of which he or she is not considered a native. When Robert Kennedy moved to New York specifically to run for U.S. senator and when Jay Rockefeller moved to West Virginia to run for secretary of state (and later governor and senator), they were carpetbaggers. But they both won, anyway, proving that the term has lost some of its negative connotations—or that enough campaign money can wash the stain away. President George Bush had one of the best defenses for carpetbagging. He recalled that when he first ran for Congress in the 1960s in Texas he was attacked for having been born in New England. He responded: "I said, 'Wait a minute, I couldn't help that. I wanted to be near my mother at the time'"(*The Washington Post*, February 16, 1988).

Carter Doctrine The policy announced by President Jimmy Carter in his State of the Union address to Congress on January 23, 1980: "An attempt by any outside forces to gain control of the Persian Gulf region will be regarded as an assault on the vital interests of the United States of America, and such an assault will be repelled by any means necessary, including military force." The press labeled the statement the Carter Doctrine, and characterized it as a reversal of the Nixon Doctrine. President Ronald Reagan's 1987 military buildup and President George Bush's PERSIAN GULF WAR of 1990–1991 certainly supported the substance if not the title of the Carter Doctrine.

Carter, Jimmy (1924–   ) The President of the United States from 1977 to 1981. He was hard working, bright, earnest, and honest; but he seemed to bring such political and decisional ineptness to the office that he became the first elected President to be defeated for reelection since Herbert Hoover in 1932. (Gerald Ford, who was defeated by Carter in 1976, was not running for reelection, since he was never elected President in the first place but was appointed under provisions of the Twenty-Fifth Amendment.) Carter, born James Earl Carter in Plains, Georgia, graduated from the U.S. Naval Academy in 1946. After a brief career as a nuclear engineer in the U.S. Navy, he returned to Georgia to become a peanut farmer, entered local politics, and won election as governor (1971–1974). Carter was the first President to be elected from the Deep South since the Civil War (discounting Woodrow Wilson, who was born in Virginia but elected from New Jersey, and Lyndon Johnson of Texas, who became President only when John F. Kennedy was assassinated). Carter's basic tactic was to run against Washington, to use the fact that he was an outsider and not in any way associated with WATERGATE. But with both inflation and interest rates around twenty percent, and the year-long insult of the IRANIAN HOSTAGE CRISIS, Republican candidate Ronald Reagan was able to devastate Carter's hope for reelection with a simple, but oft-repeated, question: "Are you better off today than you were four years ago?" While Carter was disdained by many as President, he has since become widely admired for the manner in which he conducts his "ex-presidency." Instead of retiring or generating personal wealth, he has continued with an active life of good works by, for example, building homes for the homeless and mediating conflicts in the Third World.

Carter, Rosalynn (1927–   ) The wife of President Jimmy Carter who, as First Lady, was a strong advocate of the Equal Rights Amendment, the most politically influential presidential wife since ELEANOR ROOSEVELT, and the first First Lady to regularly attend cabinet meetings. In 1990 President and Mrs. Carter met with Nicaraguan President Daniel Ortega a few hours after Ortega's electoral defeat. According to *Newsweek* (March 26, 1990), President Carter offered this soothing advice: "I won one and lost one. It feels terrible to lose, but you'll get over it. I did." Thereupon Mrs. Carter snapped: "I didn't."

case **1.** A legal dispute, whether criminal or civil, that goes to court. **2.** A judge's opinion deciding a case. **3.** The evidence and arguments presented by each side in a legal dispute. **4.** Any systematic presentation of arguments in favor of or in opposition to any position or circumstances.

case law All recorded judicial and administrative agency decisions.

casework **1.** The services performed by legislators and their staffs at the request of and on behalf of constituents. For example, a U.S. senator may be asked to discover why a social security check has been delayed or why a veteran's claim for benefits has been denied. Casework is an important means by which legislators maintain oversight of the bureaucracy and solidify their political base with constituents. *Compare to* HOME STYLE. **2.** Generally any method of providing services that proceeds on the basis of a case-by-case treatment of individuals or groups, as in social work or medicine.

caseworker An employee of a government welfare agency with responsibility for determining and administering individual entitlement benefits.

cattle show Joint appearances by candidates early in the presidential primary season; candidates are willing to be treated like "cattle" to gain additional media exposure or concomitant name recognition.

caucus **1.** A private meeting of political party members in order to seek agreement on a common course of action, to select delegates for a state or national nominating convention, and so on. The caucus was an early method of selecting presidential candidates before its replacement by party conventions. Today's caucus method for choosing delegates to the national party conventions (and for nominating state and local candidates) rests on a series of party meetings that begin at the precinct level and extend to the state convention. The first-round caucuses are especially important, for they often establish the share of delegates awarded to each candidate. Those in favor of the caucus system for selecting delegates hold that caucuses are good tests of a candidate's ability to run a campaign, that face-to-face debate within a party is a good in itself, and that citizens should be willing to take the time to attend caucuses. Those who oppose the caucus system argue that caucuses tend to be dominated by those with a strong ideological bias, that attendance does not represent the party as a whole, and that candidates who have no real chance of winning are nominated. *Compare to* IOWA CAUCUS; PRIMARY, PRESIDENTIAL. **2.** An organization of members of the House of Representatives or Senate. The organizations may be officially recognized, as are the House majority and minority caucuses, or they may be unofficial groups of members having shared legislative interests. It is the congressional caucuses that vote for the LEADERSHIP. Congressman Morris K. Udall tells the story in his *Too Funny to be President* (1988) of how he received "firm assurances" from many colleagues in the House that they would support him for MAJORITY LEADER. After he lost big in his party's caucus, he told reporters: "I have learned the difference between a cactus and a caucus. On a cactus, the pricks are on the outside." *Compare to* BLACK CAUCUS.

caucus, special Another name for LEGISLATIVE SERVICE ORGANIZATION.

cause The reason given for removing someone from an office or job (short for "just cause"). The cause cited may or may not be the real reason for the removal.

CBO *See* CONGRESSIONAL BUDGET OFFICE.

CEA *See* COUNCIL OF ECONOMIC ADVISERS.

cease-and-desist order A ruling, frequently issued in unfair labor practice and regulatory cases, that requires the charged party to stop conduct held to be illegal and to take specific action to remedy the unfair or illegal practice. *Compare to* CONSENT ORDER.

censure 1. A formal expression of disapproval. **2** A note by a legislature reprimanding one of its members. It is a disciplinary action short of expulsion and more serious than a formal reprimand. Article I, Section 5 of the Constitution provides that "Each house may . . . punish its own members for disorderly behavior, and with the concurrence of two-thirds, expel a member." In the Congress expulsion has been rare. In recent decades formal censure has only involved about a dozen members-typically on charges of financial or sexual misconduct. Recently, the Senate has taken to using the word "denouncement" instead of censure, but in effect it means the same thing.

census In ancient Rome, the registration of citizens and their property to determine who owed what taxes and who was entitled to vote. The modern census seeks a vast array of statistical information and is not directly concerned with taxation or suffrage. Article I, Section 2, of the U.S. Constitution requires that a census be conducted every 10 years so that seats in the House of Representatives shall be appropriately apportioned among the states.

Census, Bureau of the The general-purpose statistical agency of the federal government located within the Department of Commerce, created as a permanent office in 1902. It collects, tabulates, and publishes a wide variety of statistical data about the people and the economy of the nation. These data are utilized by the Congress, by the executive branch, and by the public generally in the development and evaluation of economic and social programs.

census undercount The contention that people are missed by the census count because they move, are fearful of filling out government forms, are illiterate, or for other reasons. Because the count is critical for congressional districting and for the funding level of many intergovernmental grant programs, jurisdictions are apt to make an issue of what they consider to be an undercount.

center **1.** The middle of something. **2.** The broad core of a political constituency whose support or suppression is essential to a regime if it is to maintain itself in power. **3.** Elites or ruling classes within a polity. **4.** As used by DEPENDENCY theorists, the center or core refers to the industrialized states of Europe, North America, and Japan.

central bank In most countries, the central monetary authority. Functions may include issuing a country's currency, carrying out a nation's monetary policy, and managing the country's foreign exchange reserves and the external value of its currency. In the United States, the Federal Reserve System functions as the nation's central bank, although it is not formally a bank and is subject to only limited influences by the executive and legislative branches.

central clearance The Office of Management and Budget's (OMB) coordination and assessment of recommendations and positions taken by the various federal departments and agencies on legislative matters as they relate to a President's program. The first form of central clearance is substantive bill clearance. This concerns bills dealing with policy as opposed to money. Drafts of these bills from departments and agencies must clear the OMB before going to the Congress. Congressional committees also solicit views from interested agencies on substantive legislative bills emanating from sources other than the executive branch. However, executive agency responses are expected to be cleared by the OMB.

The second form of central clearance is financial bill clearance. Since the Budget and Accounting Act of 1921, federal agencies have not had the authority to decide for themselves what appropriations to ask of the Congress. Instead, their proposed spending measure must clear the OMB.

The third form of central clearance is enrolled bill clearance. When enrolled bill enactments come from the Congress to the President for signature or veto, the OMB solicits agency opinion on the merits of the congressionally approved legislation, evaluates these opinions, and prepares its own report to the President recommending either approval or veto and the reasons.

Central Intelligence Agency (CIA) The federal agency created by the NATIONAL SECURITY ACT in 1947 to coordinate the various intelligence activities of the United States. The director of Central Intelligence is a member of the President's cabinet and is the principal spokesperson for the American intelligence community. Both the director and the deputy director of the CIA are appointed by the President by and with the advice and consent of the Senate.

The CIA has no police, subpoena, or law enforcement powers, and has no internal security functions. George Bush, speaking as the Director of the CIA once said: "I think the American people support the concept of a strong Central Intelligence Agency, and if they don't, they'd better . . . " (*The New York Times*, May 9, 1976). *See also* COVERT OPERATIONS; FINDING.

certification of eligibles The procedure whereby those who have passed competitive civil service examinations have their names ranked in order of score and placed on a list of those eligible for appointment. When a government agency has a vacancy, it requests its personnel arm to provide a list of eligibles for the class to which the vacant position has been allocated. The personnel arm then certifies to the appointing authority the names of the highest ranking eligibles. Usually, only a few of the qualified eligibles are certified. An agency requirement that three eligibles be certified to the appointing authority is called the RULE OF THREE.

certiorari An order or writ from a higher court demanding that a lower court send up the record of a case for review. Except for a few instances of original jurisdiction, most cases that reach the Supreme Court do so because the Court itself has issued such a writ, or has granted certiorari. If certiorari is denied by the Court, it means that the justices are content to let the lower court's decision stand. Frequently, a U.S. court of appeals case citation will include "cert. denied," meaning that certiorari has been denied by the Supreme Court, which has reviewed the case to the extent that it has made a judgment not to review the case further. It takes the votes of four justices to grant certiorari. However, at least five votes are normally needed for a majority opinion on the substance of a case.

CETA *See* COMPREHENSIVE EMPLOYMENT AND TRAINING ACT OF 1973.

CFR *See* CODE OF FEDERAL REGULATIONS.

Chadha case *See* VETO, LEGISLATIVE.

change of venue The movement of a case from the jurisdiction of one court to that of another court that has the same subject-matter jurisdiction but is in a different geographic location. The most frequent reason for a change of venue is a judicial determination that an impartial jury cannot be found in the original jurisdiction, usually because of widely publicized, prejudicial pretrial statements.

channel The route of official communication between headquarters and field offices of military or bureaucratic units. "To go through channels" is to follow the regularly established means for getting things done.

Chappaquiddick The incident that effectively ended Senator EDWARD M. KENNEDY's presidential prospects. On the night of July 19, 1969 Kennedy drove off a bridge on Chappaquiddick Island, Massachusetts, into the water. The young staff aide with him in the car, Mary Jo Kopechne, drowned while Kennedy was able to swim to safety. His lack of candor on this incident continues to fuel countless speculations, books, and articles.

character issue 1. A polite way of referring to the concerns people have with a political figure's excessive drinking or nontraditional sexual activity. But as former Senator Barry Goldwater said of Washington, D.C.: "If . . . everybody in this town connected with politics had to leave town because of [chasing women] and drinking, you'd have no government"(*Newsweek*, March 13, 1989). **2.** A persistent criticism of welfare payments to the poor—that they are bad for their character.

charisma Leadership based on the compelling personality of the leader rather than upon formal position. The word is derived from the Greek word meaning "divine grace." The concept was first developed by MAX WEBER, who distinguished charismatic authority from both the traditional authority of a monarch and the legal authority given to someone by law. Charismatic leadership, if it is to survive, must eventually be institutionalized or routinized. Thus, the founder of a movement or organization may be a charismatic spellbinder, but his or her successors are often, of necessity, comparatively dull bureaucrats. American political leaders didn't have charisma until Daniel Bell applied the term to labor leader John L. Lewis (1880–1969) in a 1949 article in *Fortune*.

charter 1. Originally a document issued by a monarch granting special privileges to groups or individuals, as in the MAGNA CHARTA of 1215 or the Charter of Liberties, which preceded it. Some of the original American colonies were created by such charters granted to trading companies or to other groups to establish governments in the New World. The charters themselves ultimately came to symbolize independent powers of self-government. **2.** A document that spells out the purposes and powers of a municipal corporation. To operate, a municipal corporation must have a charter like any other corporation. The municipality can perform only those functions and exercise only those powers that are in the charter. If the particular state permits home rule, a city can develop and implement its own charter. Otherwise, it is limited to statutory charters spelled out by the state legislature. **3.** The constitution of an international body, such as the United

Nations. **4.** The government document that allows a group of people to create a corporation.

cheap shot A political attack aimed at an opponent who is unable to properly defend himself. The term comes from football, where it refers to a move against a player unable to defend himself because he has just been tackled by another player or is in distress for some other reason. The classic cheap shot in politics is to accuse an opponent of something so vile and untrue that it is embarrassing even to deny it.

Checkers speech A speech given by a politician to exculpate himself from allegations of wrongdoing. The original Checkers speech was given by Republican vice presidential candidate RICHARD M. NIXON on September 23, 1952, in response to charges that he had a secret political SLUSH FUND. In a live televised speech, he thoroughly explained the legitimate uses of the so-called secret fund and appealed to the public to support his staying on the ticket with Dwight D. Eisenhower. The speech was a great success. It generated overwhelming support for Nixon to stay on the ticket, and he went on to become Vice President under Eisenhower for eight years. But what made the speech so memorable and poignant was Nixon's reference to his dog named Checkers: "We did get something—a gift. . . . It was a little cocker spaniel dog in a crate . . . sent all the way from Texas. Black and white spotted. And our little girl, Tricia, the six-year-old, named it Checkers. And you know, the kids love that dog, and I just want to say this right now, that regardless of what they say about it, we're going to keep it."

checks and balances The notion that constitutional devices can prevent any power within a nation from becoming absolute by being balanced against, or checked by, another source of power within that same nation. First put forth by the French philosopher Charles de Montesquieu (1689–1755) in his *The Spirit of the Laws* (1734), this notion was further developed by Thomas Jefferson (1743–1826) in his *Notes on the State of Virginia* (1784), in which he asserted that "the powers of government should be so divided and balanced among several bodies of magistracy, as that none could transcend their legal limits, without being effectively checked and restrained by the others." James Madison wrote: "In all political societies, different interests and parties arise out of the nature of things, and the great art of politicians lies in making them checks and balances to each other" (*National Gazette*, January 23, 1792). The U.S. Constitution is often described as a system of checks and balances. For example, it allows the President to check the Congress by vetoing a bill, and the Congress to check the President by overriding a veto or refusing to ratify treaties or confirm nominees to federal office; the Supreme Court can check either by declaring law passed by Congress or actions taken by the President to be unconstitutional. President Franklin D. Roosevelt during his "fireside chat" radio address of March 9, 1937, described the American system of government as "a three horse team provided by the Constitution to the American people so that their field might be plowed. . . . Those who have intimated that the President of the United States is trying to drive the team, overlook the simple fact that the President of the United States, as Chief Executive, is himself one of the horses." As Justice Antonin Scalia told the Senate Judiciary Committee on August 5, 1986 during his confirmation hearings: "What makes it [the U.S. Constitution] work, what assures that those words are just not hollow promises, is the structure of government that the original Constitution established, the checks and balances among the three branches of government so no one of them is able to run roughshod over the liberties of the people." *Compare to* FEDERALIST NO. 51; SEPARATION OF POWERS.

chicken in every pot General economic prosperity; a political and economic situation in which the whole nation is well fed. The phrase is usually traced back to the French king, Henry IV (1553–1610), who was supposed to have said: "I wish that there would not be a peasant so poor in all my realm who would not have a chicken in his pot every Sunday." In the United States, the phrase is often credited to President HERBERT HOOVER, who often denied he ever said it.

chief executive *See* EXECUTIVE, CHIEF.

chief justice The presiding member of a court with more than one judge. A chief justice has no more power than other judges on the same court in deciding cases. However, a chief justice can often influence the legal reasoning behind a decision if he or she has the authority, as does the chief justice of the United States, to decide which justice will write a majority opinion. The office also provides considerable mediating authority with other justices, great prestige, and a platform for leadership in the legal community.

Chief Justice of the United States The presiding member of the Supreme Court, who is appointed effectively for life ("during good behavior," according to Article III, Section 1, of the Constitution) by a President with the consent of the Senate. This consent must be obtained even if a President's nominee is already an associate justice on the Supreme Court.

chief of state The ceremonial head of a government, such as a king, queen, or President. This is in contrast to the chief executive of a government, such as a prime minister, chancellor, or President. The American presidency combines in one office, one person, the roles of chief of state and chief executive. According to Howard K. Smith (*Time*, January 18, 1971): "The 'chief of state' is like the flag—you have to be deferential. The 'head of government' is nothing but a politician—and you can be rough and relentless with him. We [the United States] combine the two in one person . . . and suffer all the psychological stresses usual when you adopt two contradictory attitudes. [In England] you bow and scrape to the monarch—but you raise hell with the Prime Minister." Journalist Jimmy Breslin in *How the Good Guys Finally Won* (1975) put it differently: "The Office of President is such a bastardized thing, half royalty and half democracy, that nobody knows whether to genuflect or spit." *Compare to* COMMANDER IN CHIEF.

chilling **1.** Any policies or practices that inhibit others from exercising legal rights or professional responsibilities. In *Dombrowski v Pfister* (1965) the Supreme Court first used the phrase "chilling effect" to describe the inhibition of First Amendment rights. Then in *United States v Jackson* (1968), the Court asserted: "If the provisions had no other purpose or effect than to chill the assertion of Constitutional rights by penalizing those who choose to exercise them, then it would be patently unconstitutional." **2.** Employment practices, government regulations, court decisions, or legislation (or the threat of these) that inhibit the free exercise of individual employment rights. A chilling effect tends to keep minorities and women from seeking employment and advancement in an organization even in the absence of formal bars. Other chilling effects may be positive or negative, depending upon the "chillee's" perspective. For example, even discussion of proposed regulations could chill employers or unions into compliance. **3.** Political activities that consciously or unconsciously inhibit judges from dealing with some cases fairly and impartially. **4.** The effect of legislative redistricting that so weakens one party that it is discouraged from even trying to win the district in the next election.

choice, not an echo A meaningful (usually ideological) difference in what political candidates or parties stand for. In asserting that a candidate or policy is a choice, not an echo, supporters seek to refute charges of "me-tooism." BARRY GOLDWATER, asserting that "I will offer a choice, not an echo," first used this phrase in 1963 when he announced he would be a candidate for President in 1964. Phyllis Schlafly then gave the phrase wide currency when she used it as the title of her 1964 campaign polemic attacking both Republican and Democratic party leaderships and national administrations. According to columnist George Will: "Conservatives had . . . the 'conservatives in the woodwork' theory . . . : One reason millions of Americans do not vote is that they are forced to choose between two liberals; give them a choice, not an echo, and conservatives will pour out of the woodwork, into voting booths" (*The New Season*, 1988).

chop **1.** Bureaucratic or political clearance or approval on something; the right to participate in a policy's development. **2.** To sign off on a policy or document to indicate such approval.

Chrysler Corporation Loan Guarantee Act of 1979 The law that authorized the federal government to guarantee up to $1.5 billion in loans to the Chrysler Corporation to prevent the bankruptcy of the company, which would have had a widespread negative impact on the economy. Within four years, Chrysler became profitable again and repaid all of its federally guaranteed loans—seven years ahead of schedule. This kind of policy was long ago summed up by Will Rogers (1879–1935), who said that "The business of government is to keep the government out of business—that is, unless business needs government aid." *Compare to* BAILOUT.

CIA *See* CENTRAL INTELLIGENCE AGENCY.

Cincinnatus, Lucius Quinctius (519–439? B.C.) A Roman general who has become the symbol of republican virtue and personal integrity. In 458 B.C., when Rome was threatened with military defeat, Cincinnatus, a farmer, was appointed dictator by the Senate to deal with the emergency. Legend has it that he literally abandoned his plow in mid-field to take command. Within 16 days he defeated the enemy, resigned from the dictatorship, and returned to his plow. Ever since, politicians have been insincerely asserting how much they yearn to give up power and return to the farm, as Cincinnatus did. This is a very strong theme in American political history. Until recent decades, it was thought politically indecent to publicly lust after power. Politicians were expected to sit contentedly on the farm until they were called. George Washington is one of the few genuine Cincinnatus figures in world history. Author Garry Wills writes in *Cincinnatus: George Washington and the Enlightenment* (1984): "[On December 23, 1783 at the end of the Revolutionary War General George Washington] spoke what he took to be his last words on the public stage; 'Having now finished the work assigned me, I retire from the great theater of Action . . . I here offer my commission, and take my leave of all the employments of public life.' At that moment the ancient legend of Cincinnatus—the Roman called from his plow to rescue Rome, and returning to this plow when danger had passed—was resurrected as a fact of modern political life." The example of Cincinnatus is still with us today. It is even unconsciously evoked for a modern public that never heard of the ancient Roman general. For example, Ronald Reagan is quoted in E.G. Brown's, *Reagan*: "One thing our founding fathers could not foresee . . . was a nation governed by professional politicians who had a vested interest in getting reelected. They probably envisioned a fellow serving a couple of hitches and then looking early forward to getting back to the farm."

Circuit court of appeals *See* COURT OF APPEALS.

circuit rider A government official who travels from jurisdiction to jurisdiction providing any of a variety of technical services. The term is derived from the fact that, in the days before modern transportation, judges, preachers, and others with occupational specialties would travel a circuit, from their home base to clients in various locations and back home again.

citizen 1. A person who owes allegiance to, and in turn receives protection from, a nation. 2. A person born or naturalized in the United States. All U.S. citizens are also citizens of the state in which they permanently reside; corporations, which are artificial persons, are citizens of the state in which they were legally created. A citizen may take an active or passive role in the government process. The right to vote gives the citizen the opportunity to help select those who will determine public policy. Beyond simply voting, the citizen can assist in electoral campaigns, lobby his or her representatives, or join with others to form interest groups—all to advance personal interests or to further his or her conception of the public interest. **3.** A person with special privileges. Roman citizens in their ancient empire had special legal rights. That is why President John F. Kennedy, in his speech in Berlin on June 26, 1963, said: "Two thousand years ago the proudest boast was 'civis Romanus sum' [I am a Roman citizen]." **4.** A person who is a normal resident of a country in which sovereignty is supposed to belong to the people. This is in contrast to a monarchy wherein a normal resident is a subject owing allegiance to a king or queen.

citizen, natural born According to Article II, Section 1 of the Constitution, the only kind of citizen who may be President. The Supreme Court has never had to interpret the constitutional provision that "no person except a natural born citizen" can be President. So there is no ruling on whether a naturalized citizen or someone born of American parents living abroad is eligible.

citizen participation A means of empowering individuals or groups with bargaining power to represent their own interests and to plan and implement their own programs with a view toward social, economic, and political power and control. Some government programs have enabling legislation specifically requiring that citizens affected by the program be involved in its administrative decisions. Presumably, the greater the level of citizen participation in a program, the more responsive the program will be to the needs of the community and the more responsive the community will be to the needs of the program. *See also* INTEREST GROUP THEORY; LOBBY.

citizens' councils Groups of whites who created private schools, private swimming pools, and so on to avoid racial integration in the 1950s and 1960s.

citizenship The dynamic relation between a citizen and his or her nation. The concept of citizenship involves rules of what a citizen might do (such as vote), must do (pay taxes), and can refuse to do (pledge allegiance). Increasingly, the concept involves benefits or entitlements that a citizen has a right to demand from government. In some jurisdictions, citizenship is a requirement for public employment. *See also* AFROYIM V RUSK; FOURTEENTH AMENDMENT.

citizenship, dual **1.** Having citizenship in two jurisdictions at the same time. For example, all citizens of the United States are citizens of both the United States and the state in which they reside. **2.** Having citizenship in two separate nations at the same time. This is not uncommon. For example, the children of American citizens born abroad are usually considered citizens of the countries in which they were born as well as of the United States.

citizens' ticket A slate of candidates running in opposition to the undesired offerings of the established parties.

city A MUNICIPAL CORPORATION chartered by its state. A central city is the core of a metropolitan area, whereas an independent city is outside of, or separate from, a metropolitan area. A political subdivision must meet various state requirements before it can qualify for a city CHARTER; for example, it must usually have a population above a state-established minimum level. There has long been a bias in American government and American political thought against cities. For example, Thomas Jefferson expressed a common opinion when he wrote in a December 20, 1787 letter to James Madison: "I think our governments will remain virtuous for many centuries; as long as they are chiefly agricultural; and this will be as long as there shall be vacant lands in any part of America. When they get piled upon one another in large cities, as in Europe, they will become corrupt as in Europe." But the real harm to cities was not in thinking ill of them, but in state and federal policies of denying them their fair share of representatives in the Congress and in state legislatures. This bias existed until the Supreme Court, beginning in 1962 with BAKER V CARR, issued a series of decisions that finally ended malapportionment in favor of rural areas. The cities were finally politically equal.

city beautiful movement The late nineteenth century and early twentieth century city-planning influence, which emphasized neoclassical architecture, parks, open spaces, monuments, boulevards, and other structures that would create a more benign urban environment.

city charter *See* CHARTER.

city clerk A title for a municipal administrator. The duties and responsibilities of a city clerk vary tremendously, from recording minutes at council meetings to having many of the duties of a city manager.

city council The legislative branch, typically unicameral, of a municipal government. The duties of city council members vary greatly; but in almost all cases the most significant functions include passing ordinances (local laws) and controlling expenditures.

city-county consolidation The merger of several governments within a county to form one new government unit. Consolidation offers considerable cost savings by reducing overlap. Many consolidated cities and counties have the same name; for example, the City and County of Los Angeles, the City and County of Philadelphia.

city manager The chief executive of the council-manager (originally commission-manager) system of local government. In contrast to the heads of other types of government, the city manager is an appointed chief executive serving at the pleasure of the council. The concept was created by Richard Childs, an urban reformer, who wanted to replace political bosses with municipal experts. To do this effectively, he created the concept of an administrative chief executive armed with critical administrative powers, such as appointment and removal of administrative officials, but denied any political powers, such as the veto. The dichotomy between administration and politics upon which the system was premised was implemented by putting all of the policymaking and political functions into the city council, essentially abolishing any separation of powers in the traditional sense at the local level. The decision-making ability of the council was assured by creating a small council, typically from five to nine members, elected through at-large, nonpartisan elections; and by permitting the council to hire and fire the city manager, their expert in the implementation of community policies.

Present council-manager systems, found in about half of all U.S. cities, often deviate from this traditional model. Many have large councils, partisan elections, and separately elected mayors, and some if not all of the council members are elected from wards or districts. In fact, some recent federal court decisions have required ward elections in some cities. The council-manager system has been criticized by some political scientists as being unresponsive to some elements of the community and supported by public administration experts for its effective management in the public interest. In some larger cities, a variant of the system has evolved, utilizing a chief administrative officer often appointed by the mayor.

city upon a hill An ideal political community thoroughly fit for others to observe as an example. It comes from a discourse written by John Winthrop, Governor of the Massachusetts Bay Colony, in 1630, which was itself a Biblical reference (Mathew 5:14). Robert C. Winthrop in *Life and Letters of John Winthrop* reprints the text, in part, as follows: "For we must consider that we shall be as a city upon a hill. The eyes of all people are upon us." This is a famous quote in Massachusetts history and both Presidents Kennedy and Reagan favored using it in speeches.

civic Belonging to citizens as a whole.

civic action **1.** The use of military forces for projects useful to a local population. This has the dual effect of providing needed services in areas, such as education, transportation, health, sanitation, and so on; and improving the standing of the military forces with the population. **2.** The use of organized volunteers to provide certain community services.

civic center **1.** An amorphous term for the location of a city's major public buildings and cultural institutions. **2.** A specific grouping of municipal and other public buildings.

civic culture *See* POLITICAL CULTURE.

civic duty The responsibility to vote. Angus Campbell, Philip E. Converse, Warren E. Miller, and Donald E. Stokes's landmark study *The American Voter* (1960) found that "wide currency in American society is given to the idea that the individual has a civic responsibility to vote." This "sense of citizen duty," a major factor in individual turnout decisions, tends to increase with educational levels.

civic organization A formal association of local citizens that works to further its concept of the public interest. Such groups may be purely local, such as a parent-teacher association, or a chapter of a national organization, such as the Rotarians or the LEAGUE OF WOMEN VOTERS.

civics **1.** That part of political science which deals with the rights and responsibilities of citizenship. **2.** The study of American government. According to Bruce Chapman, speaking as Director of the Bureau of the Census: "The baby-boom generation's voting participation is lower than its predecessors' was at the same age ... I personally attribute a large part of the change to the elimination or diminution of school instruction in what used to be called 'civics'", *U.S. News & World Report*, May 31, 1982).

civic virtue A demonstrable pride in a city by its citizens, evidenced by their willingness to take responsibility for its public affairs, its physical development, its cultural activities, and so on.

Civil Aeronautics Board (CAB) The federal agency that promoted and regulated the civil air transport industry within the United States and between the United States and foreign countries. Created in 1938, it was abolished on January 1, 1985. *See* DEREGULATION.

civil affairs **1.** Military government; the administrative process by which an occupying power exercises executive, legislative, and judicial authority over occupied territory. **2.** A general term for all those matters concerning the relation between military forces and the surrounding civil authorities.

civil defense **1.** The mobilization, organization, and direction of the civilian population, designed to minimize, by passive measures, the effects of enemy action against all aspects of civilian life. **2.** The emergency repairs to, or the restoration of, vital utilities and facilities destroyed or damaged by enemy action.

civil disobedience Henry David Thoreau's (1817–1862) notion, described in his essay *On the Duty of Civil Disobedience* (1849), that one should not support a government by paying taxes if it sanctions policies with which one disagrees (in his case, slavery). Thoreau's civil disobedience implied a willingness to publicly stand up and accept the consequences of one's disobedience, such as going to jail. Now the phrase is used to refer to acts of lawbreaking designed to bring public attention to laws of questionable morality and legitimacy. The most famous practitioners of civil disobedience in this century were Mohandas K. Gandhi (1869–1948) in India and MARTIN LUTHER KING, JR., (1929–1968) in the United States. Those who practice civil disobedience often cite a HIGHER LAW as their reason. Consider the justification of Martin Luther King, Jr., from his *Why We Can't Wait* (1964): "I submit that an individual who breaks a law that conscience tells him is unjust, and who willingly accepts the penalty of imprisonment in order to arouse the conscience of the community over its injustice, is in reality expressing the highest respect for the law." *Compare to* CONFRONTATIONAL POLITICS.

Civil Liberties Act of 1988 The law that authorized the payment of $20,000 to all living Japanese-Americans who were interned by the U.S. government during World War II. The Act authorized a total of $1.25 billion in reparation payments. Of the 120,000 Japanese-Americans who were interned, about 70,000 were still alive when the Act was passed. *See also* EMERGENCY POWERS.

Civil Liberties Union *See* AMERICAN CIVIL LIBERTIES UNION.

civil liberty 1. A freedom to which an individual has a right, such as personal security, the right to own property, and the right to have children. **2.** Freedom from government interference that violates the law.

civil religion 1. A belief in the "American way of life" and an acceptance of and reverence for its icons (such as the flag), symbols (such as the Constitution), rituals (such as the pledge of allegiance), and secular saints (such as George Washington and Abraham Lincoln). Civil religion, which exists in parallel harmony with traditional religious beliefs, provides a society with a common set of unifying ideals that give the overarching political culture cohesiveness and form. While the concept was first used by JEAN-JACQUES ROUSSEAU in *The Social Contract* (1762), it was revived by American sociologists in the late 1960s. **2.** A state-sponsored secular religion designed to replace the "corrupting" aspects of traditional religious practices, such as those implemented after the French Revolution of 1789 and the Russian Revolution of 1917.

civil rights 1. The protections and privileges given to all U.S. citizens by the Constitution and the Bill of Rights; for example, freedom of assembly and freedom of religion. **2.** Those positive acts of government that seek to make constitutional guarantees a reality for all citizens; for example, the CIVIL RIGHTS ACT OF 1964. **3.** Whatever rights a citizen possesses, even if those rights are slight.

Civil Rights Act of 1866 The first civil rights law after the Civil War and the adoption of the Thirteenth Amendment, which outlawed slavery. It granted citizenship to all people (former slaves) born in the United States and granted these new citizens the same rights "as is enjoyed by white citizens."

Civil Rights Act of 1870 The reenactment of the Civil Rights Act of 1866 (with minor changes in wording), following the ratification of the Fourteenth Amendment, to allay any doubts about the act's constitutionality.

Civil Rights Act of 1871 A law enacted to enforce the Fourteenth Amendment's equal protection concerns against secret, conspiratorial, and terrorist organizations, such as the Ku Klux Klan, which were thwarting black voter registration, voting, jury service, and office holding after the Civil War. The act also provided civil remedies for the denial of constitutional rights and provided for damages or injunctive relief against any person who "under color of law" deprives another of any right, privilege, or immunity secured by federal law or the Constitution. Thus, it has become the basis for lawsuits by anyone who feels their constitutional rights have been violated by any government official at any level. This act is often called Section 1983, after its numerical designation in Title 42 of the U.S. Code.

Civil Rights Act of 1875 The civil rights law that first provided for equality in public accommodations. The Supreme Court held the act to be unconstitutional in *Civil Rights Cases* (1883), and no subsequent civil rights legislation was passed until 1957. Yet the essence of the 1875 act was incorporated into the Civil Rights Act of 1964, which was later held constitutional by HEART OF ATLANTA MOTEL V UNITED STATES.

Civil Rights Act of 1957 The first federal civil rights legislation enacted since the post-Civil War Reconstruction period; significant primarily as an indication of renewed federal legislative concern with the protection of civil rights. As finally enacted (following lengthy and turbulent debate), the act accomplished essentially three things: it established the U.S. Commission on Civil Rights to investigate civil rights violations and make recommendations; it created the Civil Rights Division in the Department of Justice; and it enacted limited provisions to enforce the Fifteenth Amendment's guarantee of the right to vote. The most enduring feature of the act may well be the creation of the U.S. Commission on Civil Rights. As originally enacted, the commission was only temporary and due to terminate within two years of its establishment. However, subsequent legislation in 1959, 1961, 1963, 1964, 1967, 1972, and 1978 extended the life of the commission. As the result of the controversy stirred by President Ronald Reagan's firing of three sitting commissioners, and his appointment of new members strongly opposed to racial quotas or entitlement programs, the Congress acted in 1983 to reconstitute the panel and extend its life once again. As signed by the President on November 30, 1983, P.L. 98–183 replaced the original six-member presidentially appointed commission with an eight-member panel appointed half by the President and half by the Congress. The commissioners are removable only for cause under this new legislation.

Civil Rights Act of 1960 This century's second installment of federal civil rights legislation. The act of 1960 emerged from a sharply divided Congress to reinforce certain provisions of the 1957 law, but it also included limited criminal provisions related to racially motivated bombings and burnings and to obstruction of federal court orders; a clause to enlarge the powers of the Civil Rights Commission; and a section providing for the desegregated education of children of U.S. military personnel. The most important new provision made a remedy available to those improperly denied the right to vote: a voter-referee procedure enforced by the federal courts.

Civil Rights Act of 1964 By far the most significant civil rights legislation in American history, with the possible exception of the VOTING RIGHTS ACT OF 1965. Forged during the CIVIL RIGHTS MOVEMENT of the early 1960s, the act consists of 11 titles, of which the most consequential are titles II, VI, and VII. Title II bars discrimination in all places of public accommodation, whose operations affect commerce (including hotels and other places of lodging of more than five rooms, restaurants and other eating places, gasoline stations, theaters, motion picture houses, stadiums, and other places of exhibition or entertainment. In Title VI, the Congress made broad use of its spending power to prohibit racial discrimination in any program or activity receiving federal financial assistance. More important, Title VI goes on to provide that compliance with the nondiscrimination requirement is to be effected by the termination or refusal to grant federal funds to any recipient who has been found guilty of racial discrimination. TITLE VII makes it an unfair employment practice for any employer or labor organization engaged in commerce to refuse to hire, to fire, or to otherwise discriminate against any person because of race, religion, sex, or national origin. Title VII is enforced by the Equal Employment Opportunity Commission, which was also created by the act. *Compare to* AFFIRMATIVE ACTION; EQUAL EMPLOYMENT OPPORTUNITY.

Civil Rights Act of 1968 A law that prohibited discrimination in housing rentals and sales, defined the rights of American Indians, and prescribed penalties for interfering—through violence, intimidation, or other means—with any person's enjoyment of federally protected rights.

Civil Rights Act of 1991 The law which overturned a series of Supreme Court decisions (most notably the 1989 WARDS COVE V ANTONIO ruling) that made it more difficult for employees to sue employers for job discrimination.

Civil Rights Cases *See* CIVIL RIGHTS ACT OF 1875.

civil rights clause That portion of the Fourteenth Amendment which reads: "No State shall make or enforce any law which shall . . . deny to any person within its jurisdiction the equal protection of the laws."

Civil Rights Commission *See* COMMISSION ON CIVIL RIGHTS.

civil rights movement The continuing effort of minorities and women to gain the enforcement of the rights guaranteed by the Constitution to all citizens. The modern civil rights movement is often dated from 1955, when Rosa Parks, a black seamstress, refused to sit in the back of a bus (where blacks were required by local law to sit) and was arrested. MARTIN LUTHER KING, JR., then led the Montgomery, Alabama, bus boycott, the first of a long series of nonviolent demonstrations that eventually led to the passage of the civil rights acts of 1957, 1960, and 1964. The civil rights movement, while still a major force in American politics, has lost much of the energy, support, and organization that it had in the 1960s.

Civil Rights Restoration Act of 1988 The law which reversed the Supreme Court decision in *Grove City College v Bell* (1984), which held that laws prohibiting discrimination in school programs financed in part by federal aid apply only to the specific program and not to the entire school. The new act bans federal funds to an entire institution if even one of its programs or units is guilty of illegal discrimination.

civil servant A government employee; a member of a civil service.

civil service A collective term for all nonmilitary employees of a government. Paramilitary organizations, such as police and firefighters, are always included in civil service counts in the United States. This practice may be confusing to citizens of countries where there is less distinction between the police and the military. Civil service employment is not the same as merit system employment, because all patronage positions (those not covered by merit systems) are included in civil service totals. *Compare to* MERIT SYSTEM.

civil service commission A government agency charged with the responsibility of promulgating the rules and regulations of the civilian personnel management system. Depending upon its legal mandate, a civil service commission may hear employee appeals and take an active or a passive role in the personnel management process. *See* UNITED STATES CIVIL SERVICE COMMISSION.

civil service reform 1. Efforts to improve the status, integrity, and productivity of the civil service at all levels of government by supplanting the SPOILS SYSTEM with the MERIT SYSTEM. 2. Efforts to improve the management and efficiency of the public service. 3. The historical events, the movement, leading up to the enactment of the PENDELTON ACT OF 1883.

Civil Service Reform Act of 1883 *See* PENDLETON ACT.

Civil Service Reform Act of 1978 The law that mandated that the U.S. Civil Service Commission would be divided into two agencies—an OFFICE OF PERSONNEL MANAGEMENT (OPM) to serve as the personnel arm of the chief executive, and an independent MERIT SYSTEMS PROTECTION BOARD (MSPB) to provide recourse for aggrieved employees. In addition, the act created the FEDERAL LABOR RELATIONS AUTHORITY (FLRA) to oversee federal labor-management policies. On March 2, 1978, President Jimmy Carter, with the enthusiastic support of his Civil Service Commission leadership, submitted his civil service reform proposals to the Congress. On that same day, before the National Press Club, he further called his proposals to the attention of the Congress by charging that the present federal personnel system had become a "bureaucratic maze which neglects merit, tolerates poor performance, and permits abuse of legitimate employee rights, and mires every personnel action in red tape, delay and confusion." The reform bill faced considerable opposition from federal employee unions (which thought the bill was too management-oriented) and from veterans' groups (which were aghast at the bill's curtailment of veterans' preferences). The unions lost. The veterans won. The bill passed almost intact thanks in great measure to the efforts of Alan K. "Scotty" Campbell (1923–   ), the last chairman of the U.S. Civil Service Commission, who was both the architect of the reform act and its most fervent advocate before Congress. Campbell served as the first director of the new Office of Personnel Management during 1979 and 1980. *See also* SENIOR EXECUTIVE SERVICE.

civil war 1. An armed conflict between military units of the same nation or political entity. Most of organized warfare since World War II has been civil war. Examples include: the Korean conflict, the Vietnam War,

Nicaragua in the 1980s, Northern Ireland. **2.** The American Civil War between the North and the South fought from 1861 to 1865, initially over the issue of secession; later over the issue of slavery as well. **3.** A very polite war.

Civil War Amendments The Thirteenth, Fourteenth, and Fifteenth Amendments to the U.S. Constitution providing, respectively, for the abolition of slavery, equal protection and due process of the law, and the right of all citizens to vote. These amendments were adopted immediately after the Civil War.

civilian control The subordination of a nation's military to its civil authorities. The U.S. Constitution (Article II, Section 2) by making the President "commander in chief of the army and the navy" mandates civilian control in the United States. Even though some generals have become President, they were elected as civilians. Of course, as Richard J. Walton's *Cold War and Counterrevolution* warns: "Civilian control versus military control is a distinction without a difference if the civilians think the same way the military does." President John F. Kennedy in a West Point Commencement Address (June 7, 1962) called for continued civilian control: "I wish all of you the greatest success. While I say that, I am not unmindful of the fact that two graduates of this Academy [Grant and Eisenhower] have reached the White House and neither was a member of my party. Until I'm more certain that this trend will be broken, I wish that all of you may be generals and not commanders in chief."

class **1.** A grouping of people or things. **2.** A stratum in a hierarchical social structure. **3.** A social rank. The United States has often been referred to as a classless society because there are no formal, legal class distinctions— even though there are many informal, subtle ones. The most famous pronouncement on class in the United States was made by Supreme Court Justice John Marshall Harlan in a dissenting opinion in *Plessy v Ferguson* (1896): "There is in this country no superior, dominant, ruling class of citizens. There is no caste here. Our Constitution is color-blind, and neither knows nor tolerates classes among citizens. In respect of civil rights, all citizens are equal before the law."

class action A search for a judicial remedy that one or more persons may undertake on behalf of themselves and all others in similar situations. Class action suits are common against manufacturers who have sold defective products that have later harmed significant numbers of people who were unaware that there was any danger.

classified information **1.** Secrets, usually military. **2.** Any matter in any form that requires protection in the interests of national security.

classify **1.** To group bureaucratic positions according to their duties and responsibilities and to assign a class title. **2.** To make secret; to determine that official information requires, in the interests of national security, a certain level of protection against unauthorized disclosure.

class struggle The conflict between competing economic groups in a capitalist society; the continuous competition between social classes over resources and power. Karl Marx (1818–1883) and Friedrich Engels (1820–1895) wrote in their 1848 *Communist Manifesto*: "The history of all hitherto existing society is the history of class struggles." Marxists believe that the tension between the exploiting bourgeoisie and the exploited working-class masses (the proletariat) eventually leads to revolution. This has not happened in American society, in large measure because the economic system has made many working-class people middle class in both income and outlook. *See also* MARXISM

class warfare **1.** Armed conflict between social classes; classically, the peasants against the aristocracy. **2.** Conflict over tax policies. In the 1980s it began to be commonly suggested that those who wanted to raise taxes on the wealthy were seeking to instigate class warfare—the poor against the rich. The logic of the suggestion was that such "warfare" could be avoided by avoiding any talk about the prevailing tax policies that favored the rich.

Clayton Act of 1914 The federal law that extended the SHERMAN ANTITRUST ACT's prohibition against monopolies and price discrimination. It also sought to exempt labor unions from antitrust laws and to limit the jurisdiction of courts in issuing injunctions against labor organizations. Subsequent judicial construction limited its effectiveness in this area, and new laws were necessary to achieve the original intent.

Clean Air Act The federal statute (passed in 1963 and amended in 1965, 1967, 1970, 1977, and 1990) intended to protect the public's health and welfare from the effects of air pollution. The act established national air quality standards. It specified automobile emission standards, among other things, to achieve these goals.

clean hands A legal phrase meaning freedom from guilt or dishonesty. A legal maxim holds: "He who comes to equity must come with clean hands." Thomas Jefferson wrote in a March 29, 1807 letter to Count Diodati: "I have the consolation . . . of having added nothing to my private fortune during my public service, and of retiring with hands as clean as they are empty."

clear **1.** To approve or authorize or to obtain approval or authorization. For example, a bill may clear one house of a legislature meaning that it has been approved by that house. *Compare to* CENTRAL CLEARANCE. **2.** To be no longer suspected of committing a crime. **3.** To pass a security clearance. **4.** The final approval of a check by the bank upon which it was drawn. **5.** Free of taxes; a house may be clear for sale after its back taxes have been paid.

clear and present danger The Supreme Court's test on whether the exercise of the First Amendment's right of free speech should be restricted or punished. This was first articulated by Associate Justice Oliver Wendell Holmes in *Schenck v United States* (1919), when he wrote that "the most stringent protection of free speech would not protect a man in falsely shouting 'fire' in a theatre and causing a panic." Holmes created the test that has been often used in free-speech cases: "The question in every case is whether the words used are used in such circumstances and are of such a nature as to create a clear and present danger that they will bring about the substantive evils that Congress has a right to prevent."

cleared by arrest The condition of a criminal case after the suspect has been arrested but before any trial or other legal determination of guilt.

clerk of the House The chief administrative officer of the U.S. House of Representatives responsible for taking votes, certifying the passage of bills, and processing legislation. The clerk prepares the House budget and serves as the contracting officer of the House. *Compare to* SECRETARY OF THE SENATE.

Cleveland, Grover (1837–1908) The only President of the United States to serve two nonconsecutive terms: from 1885 to 1889, and from 1893 to 1897. Cleveland was the Democratic Mayor of Buffalo, New York in 1882. As a reform candidate he was elected governor of his state later that year and in 1884 became the first Democratic President since the Civil War. When he ran for reelection in 1888, he won the popular vote but lost in the ELECTORAL COLLEGE to Benjamin Harrison. The panic of 1893, one of the worst depressions in American history, created the conditions for his second successful run for the presidency that same year. According to Dean Acheson's *A Democratic Look at His Party* (1955): "Grover Cleveland was a man of honor, courage, and integrity. He followed the right as he saw it. But he saw it through a conservative and conventional cast of mind."

clientele Individuals or groups who benefit from the services provided by an agency.

clientele agency A loose term for any government organization whose prime mission is to promote, serve, or represent the interest of a particular group.

clientitis A common malady of administrators and diplomats; the symptoms are a greater concern for the people that are served by the agency or live in the country in which a diplomatic mission is located than for the interests of the political figures or nation that appointed them in the first place. Clientitis is an occupational hazard for cabinet members who sometimes forget that they are in office to serve their chief executive first and their clients second.

Clinton, Hillary Rodham (1947–   ) The wife of President Bill Clinton. Since marrying her Yale Law School classmate in 1975, she has been his closest and most intimate political advisor. A nationally recognized attorney in her own right, she campaigned almost as a co-candidate at the beginning of her husband's bid for his party's nomination. But this "vote for one, get one free" attitude so turned off voters that she quickly retreated into the more traditional role of the adoring wife. However, as soon as the Clintons moved into the White House, it was announced that Mrs. Clinton, while she would have no title but that of First Lady, would have major domestic policy responsibilities.

Clinton, William Jefferson "Bill" (1946–) The President of the United States since 1993. After earning a bachelor's degree in international relations from Georgetown University in 1968, he attended Oxford University as a Rhodes Scholar (1968–1970) and Yale Law School (graduating in 1973). He then returned to his native state of Arkansas to teach at the University of Arkansas School of Law and campaign for public office. After serving as his state's Attorney General (1977–1979), he then became the youngest governor in the United States. As the Governor of Arkansas (1979–1981; 1983–1993) he gained a reputation as an innovator in domestic policy. After winning the nomination of the Democratic Party, he conducted a campaign that stressed the comparatively poor performance of the American economy under incumbent President GEORGE BUSH. After decisively defeating Bush in the electoral college but only winning a plurality of the popular vote (third party candidate ROSS PEROT took almost twenty percent of the vote), Clinton asserted that the domestic economy would be his first priority. In his inaugural address of January 20, 1993 he called on his fellow citizens to have the "courage to reinvent America." But on assuming office he was faced with continuing international crises in Somalia, the Middle East, and the former Yugoslavia.

cloak and dagger A melodramatic phrase for the covert operations of intelligence agents.

cloakroom A private legislative antechamber, originally used for hanging cloaks, where members may informally meet and negotiate with each other. Some cloakrooms are quite elaborate, with telephones, dining facilities, and so on. The U.S. Senate has separate Republican and Democratic cloakrooms. Senator Bill Bradley told *Cosmopolitan* (August 1985): "I was here a couple of months when I was in the Democratic cloakroom in the Senate. It was 1 or 2 A.M. I looked around and there was a senator pacing back and forth, another quietly reading, another telling a joke; and my reaction was, you know, this isn't a lot different from the Knicks locker room." (Bradley used to play professional basketball for the New York Knicks.)

cloture The process by which a filibuster can be ended in the U.S. Senate, other than by unanimous consent. A motion for cloture can apply to any measure before the Senate, including a proposal to change the chamber's rules. It requires 16 senators' signatures for introduction and the votes of three fifths of the entire Senate membership (sixty, if there are no vacancies), except that to end a filibuster against a proposal to amend the standing rules of the Senate, a two-thirds vote of senators present and voting is required. Cloture is put to a roll-call vote one hour after the Senate meets on the second day following introduction of the motion. If voted, cloture limits debate on the matter for a total of 30 hours more.

clout To hit someone with one's fist. It has grown to be a slang term for influence or power and it implies an ability to get things done through informal, nonlegal, personal (as opposed to official) channels, whether the thing is the passage of a bill, a patronage job for a constituent, or the getting of some important person on the phone.

coalition 1. A temporary joining of political actors to advance legislation or to elect candidates. It is often the case that the actors in a coalition are poles apart on many issues but are able to put their continuing differences aside in the interest of joining to advance (or defeat) the issue at hand. Legislative coalitions tend to form around specific issues as the legislators sort themselves out, for or against a bill or policy. The leaders of a coalition may or may not occupy formal leadership positions in the legislature or their party. The best-known coalition in recent congresses has been the conservative coalition, an informal alliance of southern Democrats and Republicans. **2.** An agreement between political parties in a PARLIAMENTARY SYSTEM to form a government. **3.** A group of Supreme Court justices who tend to take the same philosophical approach to judicial decision making. **4.** A group of international actors that temporarily combine to further a common interest, such as the waging of war against a common enemy or the passing of a proposal in an international conference.

coalition defense The basic long-term security strategy of the United States. It means that the United States recognizes its inability to defend all areas of the world which affect its vital interests without assistance. NATO is the linchpin, though not the whole, of the U.S. coalition defense strategy.

coattails The ability of the head of an electoral ticket to help attract voters to other members of the ticket. A winning presidential candidate is said to have coattails if the election also sweeps into office a significant number of new House and Senate members from his party. Abraham Lincoln as a congressman in 1848 originally popularized this metaphor when he referred to the military coattails of generals-turned-president Andrew Jackson and Zachary Taylor. In recent national elections, the coattail effect has been weak. Congressional incumbents tend to be reelected irrespective of the popularity of the presidential ticket. *See also* INCUMBENCY EFFECT.

code A comprehensive collection of statutory laws. For example, the U.S. Code is the official compilation of federal laws. A code differs from a collection of statutes in that codes are organized by topics for easy reference rather than in the chronological order in which the various laws were passed.

code of conduct 1. A compendium of ethical norms promulgated by an organization to guide the behavior of its members. Many government agencies have formal codes of conduct for their employees. **2.** The rules governing how soldiers should conduct themselves if captured by the enemy. These vary from nation to nation but usually imply a duty to try to escape, a refusal to make disloyal statements, and a refusal to give information beyond personal identification. **3.** An international instrument that specifies acceptable international behavior by nation-states or multinational corporations.

code of ethics A statement of professional standards of conduct to which the practitioners of a profession say they subscribe. Codes of ethics are usually not legally binding, so they should not be taken too seriously as constraints on behavior. They sometimes become significant factors in political campaigns when questionable behavior by one side or the other is attacked or defended as being within or without a professional code. Professional groups also hide behind codes as a way of protecting (or criticizing) a member subject to public attack. President Ronald Reagan took the attitude "that people shouldn't require a code of ethics if they're going to be in government. They should be determined, themselves, that their conduct is going to be beyond reproach" (*U.S. News & World Report*, January 19, 1981). Nevertheless, the problem remains that some people need help in determining just what constitutes ethical behavior.

Code of Federal Regulations (CFR) The annual accumulation of executive agency regulations published in the daily *Federal Register*, combined with regulations issued previously that are still in effect. Divided into 50 titles, each representing a broad subject area, individual volumes of the CFR are revised at least once each calendar year and issued on a staggered quarterly basis. An alphabetical listing, by agency, of subtitle and chapter assignments is provided in the back of each volume under the heading "Finding Aids" and is accurate for the revision date of that volume.

code word 1. A word or phrase whose use in a political context alters its meaning. Code words are often used when it is not politic or respectable to address an issue directly. For example, in the early days of the civil rights movement, many southern politicians emphasized that they were in favor of states' rights, a code word for opposition to full civil rights for blacks. In early 1986, when world oil prices started to fall dramatically, politicians from oil-producing states started talking about the need for stable oil prices. In this context, stable became a code word for higher prices. As President Dwight D. Eisenhower said in his State of the Union Address of January 7, 1960: "We live . . . in a sea of semantic disorder in which old labels no longer faithfully describe. Police states are called 'people's democracies.' Armed conquest of free people is called 'liberation.'" **2.** A word which has been assigned a classified meaning to safeguard intentions and information regarding a secret plan or operation. **3.** A word or phrase in another language which means one thing literally, but has a different meaning to most of its native speakers. For example, the Japanese phrase "zensho shimasu" literally means "I will do my best," which sounds like an accommodating answer during diplomatic negotiations. But to many Japanese the phrase really means "no way"—quite a different answer. Code words should be distinguished from buzz words, which merely refer to the technical vocabularies of various occupational specialties.

coexistence **1.** An international situation wherein nations with differing social systems and conflicting ideologies refrain from war. Coexistence is less than peace, but preferable to war. It is often used to refer to strained relations between the Soviet Union and the West. **2.** Any contentious relation in which genuine rivals (political, organizational, and so on) purposely refrain from a direct confrontation, which might otherwise be logically expected of them.

COG *See* COUNCIL OF GOVERNMENT.

Cohens v Virginia (1821) The Supreme Court case that held that state court decisions involving federal questions could be appealed to a federal court. *Compare to* NATIONAL SUPREMACY.

cohort **1.** One tenth of a Roman legion. **2.** In the social sciences, a group identified as having common characteristics for the purposes of study, usually over time. Cohorts can be identified by age of the year they first had a common experience, such as graduating college, entering the military, or winning election to the Congress.

COLA *See* COST-OF-LIVING ADJUSTMENT.

cold war **1.** War by other than military means (a "hot war") that emphasizes ideological conflict, BRINKMANSHIP, and consistently high international tension. This idea is not new. THOMAS HOBBES wrote in *Leviathan* (1651) that: "War consists not in battle only, or the act of fighting; but in a tract of time, wherein the will to contend by battle is sufficiently known: and therefore the notion of time, is to be considered in the nature of war; as it is in the nature of weather. For as the nature of foul weather, lyeth not in a shower or two of rain; but in an inclination thereto of many days together; so the nature of war, consists not in actual fighting; but in the known disposition thereto, during all the time there is no assurance to the contrary. All other time is peace." **2.** The hostile but nonlethal relations between the United States and the Soviet Union in the post-World War II period. The phrase was first used by Herbert Bayard Swope (1882–1958) in speeches he wrote for financier and presidential advisor Bernard Baruch (1870–1965). After Baruch told the Senate War Investigating Committee on October 24, 1948, "Let us not be deceived—today we are in the midst of a cold war," the press picked up the phrase, and it became part of everyday speech. By the late 1980s the cold war had thawed to the point of almost disappearing. The Soviet Union made the pivotal decision. As Georgi Arbatov, the leading Soviet American expert, put it: "We are going to do something terrible to you—we are going to deprive you of an enemy" (*Time*, May 23, 1988). While once Presidents talked of winning the cold war, President George Bush told a news conference on January 27, 1989: "I want to try to avoid words like cold war if I can because . . . that doesn't properly give credit to the advances that have taken place in this relationship. So I wouldn't use that term." In an editorial, the *New York Times* (April 2, 1989) declared: "The cold war of poisonous Soviet-American feelings, of domestic political hysteria, of events enlarged and distorted by East-West confrontation, of almost perpetual diplomatic deadlock is over."

collective good Anything of value (such as clean air, safe streets, or tax loopholes) that cannot be denied to a group member. The size of the group can vary from all of society to any subset of it. Mancur Olson's in *The Logic of Collective Action* (1965) found that small groups are better at obtaining collective goods. The larger the potential group, the less likely it is that most will contribute to obtain the "good." Just as in military strategy, concentration is the key. Thus, a particular industry is better able to obtain tax loopholes for itself than the general public is able to obtain overall tax equity.

comity **1.** The constitutional provision that "the citizens of each state shall be entitled to all privileges and immunities of citizens in the several states." **2.** A courtesy by which one nation, court, house of a legislature, and so on, defers the exercise of some authority to some other nation, court, house.

commander in chief **1.** The military or naval officer in charge of all allied forces in a theater of operations. **2.** The authority granted under Article III, Section 2, of the U.S. Constitution that "the president shall be commander in chief of the army and the navy of the United States and of the militia of the several states when called into the actual service of the United States." The last President to exercise his authority as commander in chief to command troops in the field was James Madison during the War of 1812. At Bladensburg, Maryland, the Americans under their President met the British and were soundly defeated. The British then marched on Washington, D.C., to burn the White House and all other public buildings. No subsequent President, while in office, has sought to lead men in battle. **3.** The officer in charge of a branch of a service, or of all services in a given area. For example, CINCPAC is the Commander in Chief, Pacific, commanding all U.S. military and naval units in the Pacific Region. *See also* CIVILIAN CONTROL.

commerce clause The power (Article I, Section 8, of the U.S. Constitution) that allows the Congress to control trade with foreign countries and among the states. If anything "affects interstate commerce" (such as labor unions and product safety), it is fair game for federal government regulation. *See* GIBBONS V OGDEN.

Commerce, U.S. Department of The cabinet-level federal agency created in 1913, when the Congress split the Department of Commerce and Labor (founded in 1903) into two departments. The Department of Commerce encourages, serves, and promotes the nation's economic development and technological advancement.

commercial speech Communications for business purposes; for example, advertising. Under the U.S. Constitution, commercial speech is given the same protection as political speech. However, commercial speech to propose a business transaction, such as advertising, may be subjected to regulations designed to insure that it is truthful and legitimate. *Compare to* FREE SPEECH CLAUSE.

commission **1.** A group charged with directing a government function, whether on an ad hoc or a permanent basis. Commissions tend to be used (1) when it is desirable to have bipartisan leadership, (2) when their functions are of a quasi-judicial nature, or (3) when it is deemed important to have wide representation of ethnic groups, regions of the country, differing skills, and so on. **2.** In the international context, a United Nations group, numbering from 28 to 36 members, that meets once a year or every two years, and is charged with a particular subject area, such as human rights. **3.** A written authorization assigning rank or authority to either a civilian or military officer. **4.** To put into use, as when the navy commissions a ship. **5.** A payment based on a percentage of sales or profit.

commission form of government The structure of urban governance that replaced the city council, as a reform measure, in the early 1900s. It put all the executive, legislative, and administrative powers into a single group, a board of commissioners. Collectively, the board acts as the local legislature, while each member individually serves as an administrator of a department or set of departments. The obvious coordination problems of such a system led to its decline. It was first used in 1900 in Galveston, Texas, following a devastating hurricane; many of these commissioners were appointed by the governor. The commission form of local government has suffered a steady decline in popularity in recent decades.

Commission on Civil Rights The federal agency whose role is to encourage constructive steps toward equal opportunity for all. The commission, created by the CIVIL RIGHTS ACT OF 1957, investigates complaints, holds public hearings, and collects and studies information on denials of equal protection of the laws because of race, color, religion, sex, or national origin. The commission can make findings of fact in cases involving, for example, voting rights, administration of justice, and equality of opportunity in education, employment, and housing; but it has no enforcement authority. Its findings and recommendations are submitted to both the President and the Congress. Many of the commission's recommendations have been enacted by statute, executive order, or regulation. In addition, the commission evaluates federal laws and the effectiveness of the government's equal opportunity programs. It also serves as a national clearinghouse for civil rights information.

Commission on Intergovernmental Relations *See* KESTNBAUM COMMISSION.

Commission on the Organization of the Executive Branch *See* HOOVER COMMISSION OF 1947–1949; HOOVER COMMISSION OF 1953–1955.

commission, presidential A committee sanctioned by the President of the United States to investigate a matter of public concern and to issue recommendations for improvement. Ever since the Civil War, Americans have found it a useful means of dealing with important national issues. There is great public satisfaction to be had in the bringing together of a group of responsible, respected, supposedly objective but knowledgeable citizens to examine and report upon a national problem or major disaster. Such commissions have proven to be handy devices for modern Presidents. When faced with an intractable problem, such as crime, pornography, or urban riots, they can, at slight expense, appoint commissions as a gesture to indicate their awareness of constituent distress. Whether that gesture has meaning or sincerity beyond itself is inconsequential for its immediate effect. By the time a commission makes its report, six months to a year later, attention will have been diverted to other issues, and the recommendations can be safely pigeonholed or curtailed.

commissioner 1. A member of the governing board of a government regulatory agency, such as the Federal Trade Commission. **2.** One member of a multi-headed executive in some local governments, especially counties. **3.** The manager of a municipal agency, such as a commissioner of police.

committee 1. A part of a larger group appointed to perform a specialized service on a one-time or continuous basis. **2.** A subdivision of a legislative house that prepares legislation for action by that house or that makes investigations as directed by the house. Most standing (full) committees are divided into subcommittees, which study legislation, hold hearings, and report their recommendations to the full committee. Only the full committee can report legislation for action by the entire legislature. In 1990 there were 270 committees and subcommittees in both houses of Congress.

committee, ad hoc *See* AD HOC COMMITTEE.

committee bill *See* BILL, COMMITTEE.

committee, conference A meeting between the representatives of the two houses of a legislature to reconcile the differences over the provisions of a bill. The most usual case is when a bill passes one house with amendments unacceptable to the other. In such a case, the house that disagrees generally asks for a conference. In the U.S. Congress, the Speaker of the House of Representatives and the Vice President of the Senate appoint the managers, as the conferees are called. Generally, they are selected from the committee having charge of the bill, and they usually represent majority and minority positions on the bill. After attempting to resolve the points in disagreement, the conference committee issues a report to each house. If the report accepted by both houses, the bill is then passed and sent to the President. If rejected by either house, the matter in disagreement comes up for disposition anew, as if there had been no conference. Unless all differences between the houses are finally adjusted, the bill fails. The conference committee process can sometimes have a dramatic effect on a bill. As President Ronald Reagan once said: "You know, if an orange and an apple went into conference consultations, it might come out a pear" (*The New York Times*, December 18, 1982).

committee, credentials *See* CREDENTIALS COMMITTEE.

committee, joint A U.S. congressional committee whose members are chosen from both the House of Representatives and the Senate, generally with the chair rotating between the most senior majority party senator and representative. These committees can be created by statute or by joint or concurrent resolution. However, all existing joint committees have been established by statute, the oldest being the Joint Committee on the Library, which dates from 1800.

committeeman/committeewoman 1. The front-line workers of a political party who are assigned several city blocks or a neighborhood to recruit and service members of the party. Their single most important function is to get out the vote on election day by making sure that sympathetic voters have previously registered, by driving people to the polls, by arranging for babysitters while parents vote, and so on. **2.** A worker, usually elected by co-workers, to represent the union membership in the handling of grievances and the recruitment of new union members, among other duties.

Committee of the Whole The working title of what is known formally as the Committee of the Whole House [of Representatives] on the State of the Union. Unlike other committees, it is composed of all members of the body—now 435. It debates measures that have passed through the regular committees and that are placed on the calendar, usually made "in order" by a "rule" from the Rules Committee. Because in the Committee of the Whole a quorum is only 100 members, business is expedited. When the full House resolves itself into the Committee of the Whole, it supplants the Speaker with a chair. The measure is debated or amended, with votes on amendments as needed. When the committee completes its action on the measure, it dissolves itself by "rising." The Speaker returns, and the full House hears the chair of the Committee of the Whole report that group's recommendations. The full House then acts upon the recommendations. At this time, members may demand a roll-call vote on any amendment adopted in the Committee of the Whole.

committee on committees *See* COMMITTEE, STANDING.

Committee on the Present Danger A nonprofit citizens' group founded in 1976 that views the principal threat to U.S. security to be "the Soviet drive for dominance based upon an unparalleled military buildup." The committee urged a stronger U.S. military position and more defense spending to counter the Soviet buildup. Some members of the committee later became prominent in the Reagan Administration: National Security Advisor Richard Allen, CIA director William Casey, United Nations Ambassador Jeane Kirkpatrick, Ambassador Paul Nitze, and defense policy expert Richard Pipes, for example.

committee, recommit to A simple motion, made on the floor of the Congress after deliberation on a bill, to return it to the committee that reported it. If approved, recommittal usually is considered a death blow to the bill. A motion to recommit may include instructions to the committee to report the bill again with specific amendments or by a certain date. Or the instructions may be to make a particular study, with no definite deadline for final action.

committee, select A committee established by the House of Representatives or the Senate, usually for a limited period and generally for a strictly temporary, usually investigative, purpose. When that function has been carried out, the select committee automatically expires. This is also known as a special committee.

committees of correspondence Citizen committees created in the American colonies after 1772 to exchange information and arouse resistance to English rule.

committee, standing A regular committee of a legislature that deals with bills within a specified subject area. In the U.S. Congress, each of the two principal parties has a committee on committees, which recommends committee assignments subject to caucus or conference approval. At the beginning of each Congress, members can express assignment preferences to their respective committee on committees. This committee then prepares and approves an assignment slate of members for each committee and submits it to the caucus or conference for approval. Normally, the recommendations are approved without challenge, but procedures exist by which other members can be nominated for vacant committee posts. The House, generally by strict party vote, adopts the slates presented by the two parties. The proportion of Republicans to Democrats is fixed by the majority party of the House. A similar method is used in the Senate. The influence of the standing committees of the Congress cannot be overstated. As Woodrow Wilson declared almost a hundred years ago: "I know not how better to describe our form of government in a single phrase than by calling it a government by the Chairmen of the Standing Committees of Congress."

committee staff Aides employed by legislative committees as opposed to the personal staff of the legislators.

committee system The means by which legislatures organize themselves; all proposed policies and laws are reviewed by various committees before formal consideration by the entire body. The committee system allows legislators to develop expertise and influence in particular areas.

common carrier Any organization (such as a trucking company, railroad, or airline) whose transportation services for moving things or people are available to the general public. Consequently, they are subject to extensive government regulation.

common law *See* LAW, COMMON.

common man The ordinary citizen; someone who is typical—just like everybody else. Politicians often talk about what policies are good for the common man. Vice President Henry A. Wallace said in a May 8, 1942 speech that: "The century on which we are entering can be and must be the century of the common man." Politicians also find it advantageous to put themselves forth as common people. This annoyed President Herbert Hoover, no common man himself, who commented: "It is a curious fact that when we get sick, we want an uncommon doctor. If we have a construction job, we want an uncommon engineer. When we get into a war, we dreadfully want an uncommon admiral and an uncommon general. Only when we get into politics are we content with the common man" (*The New York Times*, October 21, 1964). *Compare to* FORGOTTEN MAN.

commonwealth The notion of THOMAS HOBBES (1588–1679) and other seventeenth-century philosophers that the members of a social order have a "common weal," or good, which is in their collective interest to preserve and protect. Common weal evolved into commonwealth, which came to mean the state. Thus, the republic established in Britain under Oliver Cromwell from 1649 to 1660 was called the Commonwealth. Four American states (Pennsylvania, Virginia, Massachusetts, and Kentucky) are formally commonwealths rather than states.

communique 1. A formal announcement by a government. 2. Joint statements made by parties during or after diplomatic sessions. They are especially popular during U.S.-Soviet summit meetings when the world's press hungers for news of any kind. Seldom is it reported that these statements are usually drafted and negotiated in advance by staff members so that they can be blessed and dispensed at the appropriate time.

communism *See* MARXISM.

community 1. A group of people living in an identifiable area. This can range from the world community, which occupies the planet called Earth, to the community of San Antonio, Texas, or the Jewish community of Miami, Florida. 2. A group having common interests, such as the medical community, the Catholic community, and so on. 3. A housing development. 4. Descriptive of shared goods, such as a community swimming pool in a city, or community property in a marriage. 5. A euphemism for the vote. Thus, if a candidate asks his or her campaign manager, "How is the Hispanic community today?" the question does not inquire about their general health or economic welfare; it merely asks, "How many of them plan to vote for me today?" 6. A recognized ESTABLISHMENT of influential individuals or organizations; for example, the intelligence community.

community action programs Local organizations mandated by the Economic Opportunity Act of 1964, which provided that special programs to alleviate poverty could be funded by the federal government but operated by community agencies exempt from political review or control at the state or local level. While these programs were effectively abandoned by the Richard M. Nixon administration, many still exist with other than federal funding.

community control An extreme form of citizen participation in which democratically selected representatives of a neighborhood-sized government jurisdiction are given administrative and financial control over such local programs as education, land use, and police protection.

community development **1.** An approach to the administration of social and economic development programs in which government officials are dispatched to the field to act as catalysts at the local level, encouraging local residents to form groups, to define their own needs, and to develop self-help projects. The government then provides technical and material assistance and helps the community establish institutions (such as farm cooperatives) to carry on the development programs after the officials have left. **2.** Local government efforts to plan for and finance the physical development of the jurisdiction. In this context, community development block grants have been available from the U.S. Department of Housing and Urban Development for a variety of activities, such as land acquisition, new parks and playgrounds, historic preservation, and street and drainage improvements.

community power Usually, the study or description of the political order, both formal and informal, of a local segment of U.S. governance. In the 1960s, such studies used behavioral methodologies and were considered the cutting edge of political science.

community service A punishment mandated by a court for people convicted of crimes that do not warrant a prison sentence. These are almost always nonviolent offenders who at their own expense must work a predetermined number of weeks or months in nursing homes, drug rehabilitation programs, and so on. Community service often becomes controversial when high profile figures receive what some consider to be very lenient sentences.

competitiveness The ability of the United States to compete economically with the other developed nations in the western world—especially Japan. In the late 1980s, the term became an abbreviated way of referring to the concern for a comprehensive national INDUSTRIAL POLICY, to the persistent problem of lagging productivity of American workers, and to an increasingly unfavorable BALANCE OF TRADE. Competitiveness goes beyond the concerns of international trade to a concern for, indeed a reevaluation of, the entire American business structure. This is because the nations with which the United States mainly competes, ironically its closest military allies in most cases, play the competitiveness game by radically different rules using business-government partnership in ways that are for all practical purposes unknown in the United States. *See also* CORPORATISM.

compliance **1.** Acting in accordance with the law. Voluntary compliance is the basis of a civil society. No government has the resources to force all of its citizens to comply with all of the criminal and civil laws. Consequently, all governments are more dependent upon compliance than they would ever like to admit. The best single example of massive voluntary compliance is the U.S. federal income tax system, which is essentially administered by self-assessment and voluntary payment. **2.** A technical term used by funding agencies as a criterion to judge whether a grantee is acting (i.e., spending their grant funds) in accordance with the grantor's policies or preset guidelines.

Comprehensive Employment and Training Act of 1973 (CETA) The law that, as amended, established a program of financial assistance to state and local governments to provide job training and employment opportunities for economically disadvantaged, unemployed, and underemployed people. The CETA provided funds for state and local jurisdictions to hire unemployed and underemployed people in public service jobs. The CETA reauthorization legislation expired in September 1982. It was replaced by the Job Training Partnership Act of 1982, which provides for job-training programs to be planned and implemented under the joint control of local elected officials and private industry councils in service delivery areas designated by the governor of each state.

compromise Resolving differences through mutual concessions; this is often considered to be the very essence of politics. Legislatures are often referred to as institutions of compromise. Representative Gerald R. Ford, during his vice presidential confirmation hearings in the House of Representatives, said on November 15, 1973: "I believe in friendly compromise. I said over in the Senate hearings that truth is the glue that holds government together. Compromise is the oil that makes governments go."

comptroller *See* CONTROLLER.

comptroller general of the United States *See* GENERAL ACCOUNTING OFFICE.

comptroller of the currency The officer of the U.S. Department of the Treasury responsible for monitoring the operations of all national banks. *Compare to* CONTROLLER.

compulsory process *See* WITNESS.

concession speech The traditional speech by the losing candidate in an election, wherein the winner is congratulated, the supporters thanked, and every effort is made to exit with grace. Some concession speeches are memorable. For example, Adlai E. Stevenson, conceding his defeat in the 1952 presidential election, said: "Someone asked me, as I came in, down on the street, how I felt and I was reminded of a story that a fellow townsman of ours used to tell—Abraham Lincoln. They asked him how he felt once after an unsuccessful election. He said he felt like a little boy who had stubbed his toe in the dark. He said that he was too old to cry, but it hurt too much to laugh." Some concession speeches are witty. For example, when Senator Bob Dole lost his race for Vice President (on the ticket with Gerald Ford) in 1976, he said: "Contrary to reports that I took the loss badly, I want to say that I went home last night and slept like a baby— every two hours I woke up and cried." And some are just bitter, as when Richard M. Nixon told reporters after his 1962 defeat for the governorship of California: "You won't have Richard Nixon to kick around any more because, gentlemen, this is my last press conference" (*The Washington Post*, November 8, 1962).

conciliation 1. The process of bringing together two sides to agree on a voluntary compromise. **2.** An international dispute-settling process whereby a disagreement is submitted to a standing or ad hoc independent commission which examines the facts of the case and makes a recommendation for settlement. However, this recommendation is merely advisory and the parties, unlike a similar process in ARBITRATION, are under no formal obligation to accept it.

concurrent jurisdiction A legal situation in which two or more court systems (such as state and federal) or two or more agencies (such as the local police and the FBI) both have the power to deal with a problem or case.

concurrent majority *See* JOHN C. CALHOUN.

concurrent power A power held jointly by both federal and state governments. Taxation is a major example.

concurrent resolution *See* RESOLUTION, CONCURRENT.

concurrent resolution on the budget *See* RESOLUTION ON THE BUDGET, CONCURRENT.

condemn 1. To pronounce a negative judgment of an individual, an action, or an event. **2.** To pronounce a negative judgment in a criminal case. **3.** To impose the death penalty. **4.** To exercise public domain by taking over private property with payment to the owner, who may or may not have been willing to sell. **5.** To declare that a property is unfit for use or occupancy. This usually means that it must be vacated, renovated, or torn down.

Confederate States of America The short-lived confederation formed by the 11 states that sought to secede from the Union. That they could not do so was decided by the Civil War of 1861 to 1865. Those states, in order of secession, were South Carolina, Mississippi, Florida, Alabama, Georgia, Louisiana, Texas, Virginia, Arkansas, North Carolina, and Tennessee.

confederation 1. A league of sovereign states that delegates powers on selected issues to a central government. In a confederation, the central government is deliberately limited and thus may be inherently weak because it has few independent powers. The United States was a confederation from 1781 to 1789. **2.** A military alliance. **3.** A private sector alliance of interests that form to exert pressure on a government or advance the welfare of its members. The Confederation of British Industry is an example. *Compare to* ARTICLES OF CONFEDERATION.

conferee A legislator who has been appointed to a conference committee, usually a senior member on the committee that originated the bill being considered.

confirmation 1. The confirming of a previously existing treaty by a new regime. **2.** The required consent of a legislature to high-level appointments of the executive branch. *See also* ADVISE AND CONSENT.

conflict of interest 1. The classic conflict facing a member of a national legislature when the narrow interests of constituents conflict with the broader interests of the nation as a whole. *See also* BURKE, EDMUND. **2.** Any situation in which the personal interest of an officeholder may influence or appear to influence that officeholder's decision on a matter of public interest. The classic statement on conflict of interest was made by Charles E. Wilson during his January 15, 1953, confirmation hearing for the position of Secretary of Defense in the Eisenhower Administration. Wilson, who had just resigned as president of General Motors, was asked if he could make a decision in the interests of the United States if that decision was adverse to the interests of General Motors, a corporation in which he still held considerable stock. Wilson replied: "For years I thought what was good for our country was good for General Motors, and vice versa. The difference did not exist." This is often misquoted as: "What's good for General Motors is good for the country." Today many high-level officials avoid such questions of conflicting interests by putting their investments in blind trusts. Officeholders are wise to avoid both actual conflict and appearance of conflict. A common means of avoiding conflict is for the officeholder to abstain from voting or acting on an issue in which a personal benefit may exist. Thus, a judge or an administrator may withdraw from a case or the making of a decision in a situation where his or her ownership of stock or other interest might be perceived as being benefited. The ETHICS IN GOVERNMENT ACT OF 1978 seeks to avoid conflict of interest by high-level federal employees even after they cease government employment by putting postemployment restrictions on their relations with the agencies for which they once worked. The most common means of avoiding conflict—that is, by abstaining—is not practical for many elected officeholders. A major election campaign for the Congress, for example, involves so many diverse contributors and supporters that a legislator would be severely restricted in voting if the automatic criteria for abstaining was the fact that a campaign contributor would be affected.

conflict of laws 1. Having the laws of more than one jurisdiction apply to a case. The judge must then choose which jurisdiction's laws are most applicable. This is a particularly thorny problem when a state law precedes federal legislation; the conflict comes after the federal legislation takes effect. **2.** Having the laws of more than one nation apply to a case involving private parties (as opposed to the nations themselves); the problem then becomes one of international law.

confrontation clause The Sixth Amendment provision that an accused person "be confronted with the witnesses against him." This implies a right of cross-examination. The Supreme Court applied this right to state courts in *Pointer v Texas* (1965), through the due process clause of the Fourteenth Amendment.

confrontation politics Political action premised on the notion that change can best be achieved by dramatic acts, such as sit-ins, demonstrations, and obstructionism. The end purpose is to alert the larger political community to the problem in order to generate a consensus for change. *Compare to* AGENDA SETTING.

congress **1.** The legislative branch of the U.S. government created and defined by Article I of the Constitution. The U.S. Congress is composed of the House of Representatives and the Senate. *See also* CONGRESS, UNITED STATES. **2.** The two-year-long cycle of federal legislative meetings beginning on January 3 of each odd-numbered year. **3.** Any large representative assembly.

Congress, Continental The delegates from the 13 original colonies who first met in 1774 in Philadelphia. The second Continental Congress instigated the American Revolution by adopting the DECLARATION OF INDEPEN-DENCE in 1776 and continued to function until the adoption of the ARTI-CLES OF CONFEDERATION in 1781.

Congress, do-nothing President Harry S Truman's insult to the "notorious 'do-nothing' Republican 80th Congress," first used in a September 18, 1948 campaign speech. Since then the phrase has been used by anyone impatient with the Congress' slow way with legislation.

Congress, gridlock Republican President George Bush's phrase from the 1992 presidential campaign for the Democratically controlled U.S. Congress that would not pass legislation exactly the way he wanted it. This gridlock was presumably broken when William J. Clinton became President in 1993 and both the White House and the Congress came under control of the same party.

Congress, member of A person elected to either the U.S. Senate or the U.S. House of Representatives. A member of the Senate is usually referred to as senator and a member of the House of Representatives as congress-man or congresswoman. The qualifications for members of the Congress are established by the Constitution (Article I, Sections 2 and 3). A member of the House of Representatives must be at least 25 years of age, must have been a U.S. citizen for at least seven years, and must reside in the state from which he or she is elected to the Congress. When vacancies occur, special elections are held to fill them; members of the House of Represen-tatives are never appointed—vacancies are filled only by election. (*Compare to* DELEGATE.) A member of the Senate must be at least 30 years of age, must have been a U.S. citizen for at least nine years, and must be a res-ident of the state he or she represents in the Congress. Until the Seven-teenth Amendment was ratified in 1913, senators were elected by their state legislatures. The amendment required that they be popularly elected. When a vacancy occurs in the Senate for any reason, the Seventeenth Amendment directs the governor of the State to call an election to fill it and authorizes the state legislature to make provision for an immediate appoint-ment (if lawful) pending such election. The senator appointed serves only until either the next general election or a special election. The senator chosen in a special election serves only the remainder of the original term.

The traditional advice given to new members who are often in awe of their politically famous colleagues, recounted by President Harry S Truman in his *Memoirs* (Vol. I, 1955), is: "Don't start out with an inferiority complex. For the first six months you'll wonder how you got here, and after that you'll wonder how the rest of us got here."

Many political scientists hold that there are really two Congresses (the first being the national policymaking body and the second being "a collectivity of independently chosen political entrepreneurs"). An analysis of this concept can be found in Roger H. Davidson and Walter J. Oleszek's, *Congress and Its Members* (2d ed., 1985).

To find basic data on, and the voting records of, all members of the Congress, seek out the latest editions of the *Almanac of American Politics*, published by the *National Journal*; or *Politics in America: Members of Congress in Washington and at Home*, published by Congressional Quarterly.

Congress, permanent **1.** A critical description of the U.S. Congress because the overwhelming majority of members use the advantages of incumbency to ensure reelection. **2.** A merely descriptive phrase for the U.S. Congress because it now meets virtually year round. *Compare to* INCUMBENCY EFFECT.

Congress, session of Each Congress is composed of two sessions. A new session of the Congress begins each January 3 at noon and continues until adjourned sine die later that year. Congress is also said to be in session during the hours of the day when it is formally meeting. Woodrow Wilson wrote in *Congressional Government* (1885) that: "Congress in session is Congress on public exhibition, whilst Congress in its committee-rooms is Congress at work."

Congress, United States The legislative branch of the U.S. government. The Congress of the United States was created by Article I, Section 1, of the Constitution, which provides that "all legislative powers herein granted shall be vested in a Congress of the United States, which shall consist of a Senate and House of Representatives."

The Senate is composed of 100 members, two from each state, who are elected to serve for a term of six years. Senators were originally chosen by the state legislatures. This procedure was changed by the Seventeenth Amendment to the Constitution, adopted in 1913, which made the election of senators a function of the people. There are three "classes" of senators, and a new class is elected (or re-elected) every two years. James Madison wrote of the Senate in *Federalist* No. 62 that "such an institution may be sometimes necessary as a defense to the people against their own temporary errors and delusions."

The House of Representatives now comprises 435 representatives. The number representing each state is determined by population, but every state is entitled to at least one representative. Members are elected by the people for two-year terms, all terms running for the same period. James Madison wrote of the importance of the House in *Federalist* No. 52:

> As it is essential to liberty that the government in general should have a common interest with the people, so it is particularly essential that the [House of Representatives] should have an immediate dependence on, and an intimate sympathy with, the people. Frequent elections are unquestionably the only policy by which this dependence and sympathy can be effectually secured.

A resident commissioner from Puerto Rico (elected for a four-year term) and delegates (elected for a two-year term) from American Samoa, the District of Columbia, Guam, and the Virgin Islands complete the composition of the Congress. The resident commissioner and delegates may take part in committee and floor discussions and vote in committees but cannot vote on the floor.

Congress has always been subject to vigorous criticism. But as Representative Barber B. Conable, Jr., reminds us, it is "functioning the way the Founding Fathers intended—not very well. They understood that if you move too quickly, our democracy will be less responsible to the majority" (*Time*, October 22, 1984).

congressional budget The U.S. budget as set forth by the Congress in a CONCURRENT RESOLUTION on the budget. These resolutions include: (1) the appropriate level of total budget outlays and of total new budget authority; (2) an estimate of budget outlays and new budget authority for each major functional category; (3) the amount, if any, of the surplus or deficit in the budget; (4) the recommended level of federal revenues; and (5) the appropriate level of the public debt.

Congressional Budget and Impoundment Control Act of 1974 A major restructuring of the congressional budgeting process. The act's Declaration of Purposes states that it is essential: to assure effective congressional control over the budgetary process; to provide for yearly congressional determination of the appropriate level of federal revenues and expenditures; to provide a system of impoundment control; to establish national budget priorities; and to provide for the furnishing of information by the executive branch in a manner that will assist the Congress in discharging its duties.

The significant features of the act are: (1) the creation of the House and Senate budget committees; (2) the creation of the Congressional Budget Office to support the Congress just as the OFFICE OF MANAGEMENT AND BUDGET serves the President; (3) the adoption of a new appropriations process for the Congress; (4) the adoption of a new budget calendar for the Congress; (5) the establishment of a new fiscal year (October 1 through

September 30) to more rationally deal with the timing of the budget cycles; (6) the creation of a current services budget; and (7) the creation of two new forms of IMPOUNDMENTS—recisions and deferrals—both of which must be submitted to the Congress.

Congressional Budget Office (CBO)   A support agency of the U.S. Congress created in 1974 by the Congressional Budget and Impoundment Act to provide the Congress with basic budget data and with analyses of alternative fiscal, budgetary, and programmatic policy issues, independent of the executive branch and of the OFFICE OF MANAGEMENT AND BUDGET.

congressional district   A division of a state, based on population, that elects one member to the U.S. House of Representatives. There are 435 congressional districts in the United States. Some have only one member of the House; therefore, the entire state is the congressional district.

congressional government   1. A government dominated by the legislature. This was the condition of American government during most of the nineteenth century (the Civil War being the major period of exception). **2.** A government in which the legislature is separate from the executive and independent of it. This is in contrast to a cabinet form of government, in which an executive is chosen by, and responsible to, a legislature. Woodrow Wilson, while a college professor, published the classic account of congressional government, *Congressional Government: A Study in American Politics* (1885; reprinted 1981), in which he observed that authority "is perplexingly subdivided and distributed, and responsibility has to be hunted down in out-of-the-way corners." Some things haven't changed much in the hundred years since!

congressional groups   *See* LEGISLATIVE SERVICE ORGANIZATIONS.

congressional immunity   *See* IMMUNITY, CONGRESSIONAL.

congressional oversight   *See* OVERSIGHT, CONGRESSIONAL.

Congressional Record   The publication containing the proceedings of the Congress and issued daily when the Congress is in session. On March 4, 1873, the *Record* began to be officially reported, printed, and published directly by the federal government; prior to that time, the proceedings had been recorded by private reporters. (The *Record* superseded the privately published *Congressional Globe*, which started in 1830.) The *Record* is a verbatim transcript; but that's the least of it. It is mostly whatever members choose to put into it—long speeches they never made, testimonials to constituents, articles from newspapers back home, and so on. According to Robert Sherrill's *Why They Call It Politics* (1990): "An extreme example of *Congressional Record* 'ghosting' was a day when it ran to 112 pages. Yet the Senate had met for only eight seconds, the House not at all. The *Record* was done by remote control—by adding, by revising, by expanding from the comfort of the members' offices—and often was done not by the members themselves but by their staffs."

congressional veto   *See* VETO, LEGISLATIVE.

congressman/congresswoman A member of the U.S. House of Representatives. This title is preferred over representative.

Connecticut compromise The proposal put forth by the Connecticut delegation to the Constitutional Convention of 1787 that melded elements of the VIRGINIA PLAN and the NEW JERSEY PLAN into the present arrangement of the U.S. Congress: one house in which each state has an equal vote (the Senate) and one house in which representation is based on population (the House).

consensus Agreement; a convergence of public opinion; a time of temporary truce between normally hostile political parties and factions. A political consensus is not necessarily total agreement and harmony, but it does represent agreement enough that action can be taken knowing that there is far more than majority support behind it. The concept of consensus was first analyzed by Marcus Tullius Cicero (106–43 B.C.), the Roman politician and philosopher who wrote that a consensus was a prerequisite for the creation and endurance of a republican form of government. Since the 1950s, some historians and political scientists have argued from various perspectives that the American polity did not need either an IDEOLOGY or ideological confrontation because the nation, fortunately, possessed a common set of values and beliefs (a consensus) that obviated the need for such conflict. Others, such as journalist Henry Fairlie in *The Life of Politics* (1968), have argued that: "Consensus has, or should have, little place in politics. American Presidents (some more than others) feel it necessary to pretend that consensus is both desirable and possible, because they have no organized party on which they can rely to sustain them in the day-to-day political conflict."

consent of the governed The notion that the institutions of government must be based on the will of the people. The Declaration of Independence asserts that "governments are instituted among men, deriving their just powers from the consent of the governed, that whenever any form of government becomes destructive of these ends, it is the right of the people to alter or abolish it." While this theme can be traced back to PLATO, it was JOHN LOCKE's development of the idea that most influenced the Founding Fathers. As journalist Walter Lippmann observed in *A Preface to Politics* (1914): the consent of the governed "is more than a safeguard against ignorant tyrants: it is an insurance against benevolent despots as well."

consent order A regulatory agency procedure to induce voluntary compliance with its policies. A consent order usually takes the form of a formal agreement whereby an industry or company agrees to stop a practice in exchange for the agency's cessation of legal action against it. *Compare to* CEASE-AND-DESIST ORDER.

conservation The protection, preservation, replenishment, and prudent use of natural resources, which indicates the planned use of public lands, forests, wildlife, water, and minerals. Theodore Roosevelt was the first

President to be really serious about conservation. He wrote in *The Outlook* (August 27, 1910): "Here in the United States we turn our rivers and streams into sewers and dumping-grounds, we pollute the air, we destroy forests, and exterminate fishes, birds, and mammals—not to speak of vulgarizing charming landscapes with hideous advertisements. But at long last it looks as if our people . . . are doing all they can for the Conservation movement." Not quite all! This was the same era when the Speaker of the House (from 1903–1911), Joseph G. Cannon, had a policy of "not one cent for scenery."

Federal conservation programs and policies have a long history: the greatest efforts at conservation in the continental United States were made during the administrations of Theodore Roosevelt (1901–1909) and Franklin D. Roosevelt (1933–1945). The Department of the Interior, established in 1849, is the custodian of the national government's natural resources. Conservation policy over the years has tended to be a fight for the soul—or control—of that department. Since the 1970s, conservation groups, such as the Sierra Club and the National Audubon Society, have joined with other groups interested in environmental policy to take a more active role in lobbying for conservation issues. The basic policy issue in conservation has always been whether preservation or controlled use would win out over industrial exploitation or vice versa.

conservatism Adherence to a political disposition that tends to prefer the status quo and accepts change only in moderation. Both major parties have historically had a substantial number of conservatives, but since the 1960s many of the conservatives in the Democratic party (especially from the South) have been shifting to the Republicans. Conservatives are most often found among those who have, or have the potential to have, wealth and property. They naturally resist change, because they have something to lose. As John Kenneth Galbraith wrote in *American Capitalism* (1956): "It is a simple matter of arithmetic that change *may* be costly to the man who has something: it cannot be so to the man who has nothing." If modern conservatism can be said to have a founding father, that person would be EDMUND BURKE (1729–1797), the British politician who asserted that a political community should conserve the best policies of the past by carefully, slowly, blending them into the ever-evolving future. Conservatism's founding document is often held to be Burke's *Reflections on the Revolution in France* (1790), in which he said that "it is with infinite caution that any man ought to venture upon pulling down an edifice which has answered in any tolerable degree for ages the common purposes of society." The seminal book for post World War II conservatism is generally considered to be Russell Kirk's *The Conservative Mind* (1953). *Compare to* REACTIONARY; RIGHT.

conservatism, cultural Support for traditional western Judeo-Christian values not just as a matter of comfort and faith, but out of a firm belief that the secular, the economic, and the political success of the western world is rooted in these values. Cultural conservatives feel that if these values are destroyed, then the material and political success they spawned cannot last.

conservatism, new 1. Historian (and poet) Peter Viereck's conception of a "non-Republican, non-commercialist, non-conformist" conservatism that would synthesize the "ethical New Deal social reforms with the more pessimistic, anti-mass insights of America's Burkean founders" (see his 1949 *Conservatism Revisited*). Unfortunately, in an author's note to the 1962 edition, Viereck found that "the new conservatism has at least halfway degenerated into a facade for either plutocratic profiteering or fascist-style thought-control nationalism." **2.** The resurgence of the Republican party under the leadership of Ronald Reagan in the 1970s and 1980s. This built upon the foundation established by BARRY GOLDWATER in his 1964 presidential bid. According to Representative Jack Kemp, the new conservatism "trusts people and markets. It is more optimistic about the future. And it is activist. It isn't content with the status quo. The new conservatives . . . want to make change" (*The Christian Science Monitor*, March 18, 1986). **3.** NEOCONSERVATISM. *Compare to* RIGHT, NEW.

conservative One who believes in conservatism. But conservatives are seldom pure. The new right is a major variant and many conservatives are closet LIBERALS. For example, Republican Representative Trent Lott of Mississippi said: "Americans think of themselves as conservatives; they want government reduced. But in their hearts they're liberals; they want money for sewers and libraries and all the goodies coming in. It's a fact" (*The New York Times*, November 18, 1982). Another Republican Representative, Clay Shaw of Florida, confessed: "Every conservative becomes a liberal when he talks about his own district" (*The New York Times*, January 18, 1981). Even the nation's leading conservative officeholder, President George Bush, once admitted that he was "a conservative but . . . not a nut about it" (*The Washington Post*, November 3, 1984). The reality is that most Americans, the mainstream of society, have both conservative and liberal inclinations depending upon a given issue and how they perceive their economic circumstances. Purity is to be found only among the LUNATIC FRINGE. *See also* RIGHT; RIGHT, NEW.

conservative coalition *See* COALITION.

conservatives in the woodwork theory *See* CHOICE, NOT AN ECHO.

conservative, neo *See* NEOCONSERVATISM.

conservative, paleo A traditional conservative as opposed to a member of the new right. *Compare to* RIGHT, NEW.

consolidated government *See* METROPOLITAN GOVERNMENT.

constable A law enforcement officer in a town or township. The word comes from the Latin *comes*, meaning a companion, and *stabulum*, meaning stable. So the first constables were stable attendants. Over the centuries, they worked themselves up to be guards; thus, the modern meaning.

constituent **1.** One who lives in a legislator's district. **2.** One of a group that an elected representative or elected political executive represents.

constituent power **1.** The right of the people as the ultimate sovereign to amend a constitution as exercised by their representatives in a legislature. **2.** The authority of a constitutional convention.

constituency **1.** A legislator's geographical district. **2.** The voters to whom an elected official is responsible. The constituency for a U.S. congressman is a district; for a U.S. senator, a state; and for the President, the entire nation. **3.** The campaign contributors to whom an elected official feels responsible. All too often officials are torn between the demands of two, sometimes competing, constituencies: the people who elected him or her and the people who contributed the money that made the electoral victory possible. *See also* HOME STYLE.

constitution **1.** The basic political and legal structures prescribing the rules by which a government operates. THOMAS PAINE in *The Rights of Man* (1792) noted that: "A constitution is a thing antecedent to a government, and a government is only the creature of a constitution. The constitution of a country is not the act of its government, but of the people constituting a government." There are three kinds of constitutions: (1) written, which are based upon a specific document supplemented by judicial interpretations and traditional practices; (2) unwritten, where there is no specific document but many laws, judicial decisions, and accepted practices that in their totality establish the principles of governance; and (3) autocratic, where all power is in the hands of a dictator or elite, which defines governance as it wills—even though the state may have a legal document called a constitution calling for democratic governance. James Madison wrote in *Federalist* No. 57 that "the aim of every political constitution is, or ought to be, first to obtain for rulers men who possess most wisdom to discern, and most virtue to pursue, the common good of the society; and in the next place, to take the most effectual precautions for keeping them virtuous whilst they continue to hold their public trust." **2.** The Constitution of the United States (see Appendix B). It is the oldest written constitution continuously in force and a constant example to the rest of the world of the benefits and effectiveness of such a well-crafted document. Its famous beginning, "We the people," asserts that the source of its authority is the people as opposed to the states. It then assigns powers to the various branches of government and in doing so structures the government. It limits the powers that any branch may have and allows each branch to CHECK AND BALANCE the others. Most significantly, it denies certain powers to the national government, reserving them for the states and the people. But aside from its force as law the U.S. Constitution is more than just a piece of fading parchment in the National Archives—it is the national icon, the premier symbol of American freedom and governance; above all, it represents the collective political will of the American people over two centuries to maintain their republican form of government.

Nevertheless, because of the nature of JUDICIAL REVIEW, the Constitution is ultimately, as Chief Justice Charles Evans Hughes asserted in a May 3, 1907 speech, "what the judges [of the Supreme Court] say it is." It is as Thomas Jefferson wrote in a September 6, 1819 letter to Spencer Roane: "a mere thing of wax in the hands of the judiciary, which they may twist and shape into any form they please." **3.** A constitution of an American state. They tend to parallel the national constitution in that they declare what powers the state does and does not have, provide for three branches of government, and have a bill or declaration of rights. **4.** The political culture of a community or nation. *Compare to* ARISTOTLE. **5.** The formal rules prescribing the governance practices of a club, an association, a union, a political party, and so on, even though the rules may be called charters, by-laws, articles of association, and the like.

constitutional   Consistent with and reflective of the U.S. Constitution, which lies at the very heart of the American political system and establishes the framework and rules of the game within which that system operates. It defines the roles and powers of the legislative, judicial, and executive branches, delineates the extent of federal political power, and places limitations on the authority of the states. Moreover, American politics have grown up around the Constitution and have been, thereby, "constitutionalized." Many domestic political issues are eventually treated in constitutional terms; for example, civil rights, crime, pornography, abortion, women's rights, and impeachment, to name but some of the more obvious cases. Only the realm of foreign affairs has substantially escaped this tendency. In addressing matters of government and politics, Americans are likely to pose as the first question, "Is it constitutional?" Only afterward are the desirabilities of policies and government arrangements considered on their own merits. In the 1819 case of MCCULLOCH V MARYLAND, the Supreme Court explained how to tell if something is constitutional: "Let the end be legitimate, let it be within the scope of the Constitution, and all means which are appropriate, which are plainly adapted to that end, which are not prohibited, but consist with the letter and spirit of the Constitution, are constitutional."

But what is constitutional is often a matter of political debate and considerable conflict. In October 1986, U.S. Attorney General Edwin Meese renewed the debate on what is constitutional when he proclaimed in a speech at Tulane University that the rulings of the Supreme Court were not "the supreme law of the land." The Constitution was. Therefore, Meese argued, citizens might be obligated to obey only the "original intent" and not the intent as the Court interprets it. After all, Court rulings are not definitive; it has reversed itself several hundred times. But if the Court is not the national referee of what is or is not constitutional, who or what will be? In spite of Meese's attack on the Court, it remains solidly ensconced as the referee in the constant battle over what is constitutional. *See also* BILL OF RIGHTS.

constitutional amendment 1. An addition to a constitution. **2.** A proposed change to the U.S. Constitution or to a state constitution. *See also* AMENDMENT.

constitutional convention A group chosen either by popular vote or legislative appointment to create or revise a constitution. After a new or revised constitution has been produced by the constitutional convention, it must be ratified either by the people or their legislature. The various states have had more than 200 constitutional conventions in the last two centuries; the United States has had only one, the Constitutional Convention of 1787, even though the U.S. Constitution in Article V provides for the calling of a convention at the request of two thirds of the states.

A constitutional convention is one way of amending the constitution. In recent years, political conservatives have been urging a convention to enact a BALANCED BUDGET AMENDMENT, and by 1985 over half the states had passed bills requesting such a convention. However, no convention could be limited to one amendment: if one were held, it might open up a Pandora's box of new troubles, or it might be the means of fine-tuning one of the greatest political instruments in world history—if the delegates collectively have the same political acumen as the founders.

Constitutional Convention of 1787 The meeting in Philadelphia, May 25 to September 18, at which 55 delegates from the various states designed the U.S. Constitution. The convention was called to revise the ARTICLES OF CONFEDERATION. Instead, the convention, presided over by George Washington, discarded the articles and designed an entirely new framework for American governance. *See also* CONNECTICUT COMPROMISE; FEDERALIST PAPERS; JAMES MADISON; NEW JERSEY PLAN; VIRGINIA PLAN.

constitutional court Any court specifically authorized by a constitution; for example, the Supreme Court, which is authorized by Article III of the Constitution. This is in contrast to a legislative court, which is created by statute without specific constitutional authorization, such as the U.S. Court of Military Appeals.

constitutional government A form of limited government in which a constitution, whether written, as is the case in the United States, or unwritten, as is the case in Britain, establishes who has the right to what powers; and in which any officer who violates constitutional provisions ceases to hold power legitimately and thus is removable from office by constitutional provisions for IMPEACHMENT or the people's right of REVOLUTION.

constitutional initiative *See* INITIATIVE, CONSTITUTIONAL.

constitutionalism The evolution of constitutional thinking through the ages. While theorizing on constitutions goes back to ARISTOTLE, modern theory stems from the seventeenth-century social contract theorists. The hallmark of modern thinking on constitutions is the notion of a limited government whose ultimate authority is the consent of the governed.

constitutionalist 1. One who believes that the U.S. Constitution, more than anything else, has guided the development of American politics and culture; that the existence of the document and its revered place in the American consciousness largely differentiates the United States from other nations. What better example is there of the constitutionalist view of American society than the discussions of public policy innovations that start or end with the question: "Is it constitutional?" **2.** A lawyer or political scientist who is an authority on the Constitution.

constitutional law See LAW, CONSTITUTIONAL.

constitutional officers Those positions in a government specifically established by its constitution (such as President or governor) as opposed to positions created by subsequent legislation or executive order.

constitutional right A prerogative guaranteed to the people by a constitution. For example, the Fourth Amendment of the U.S. Constitution guarantees "the right of the people to be secure in their persons, houses, papers, and effects, against unreasonable searches and seizures," and the Eighth Amendment guarantees that "excessive bail shall not be required."

constitution, economic interpretation of A reference to the contention of historian Charles A. Beard (1874–1948), in *An Economic Interpretation of the Constitution of the United States* (1913), that the founders wrote the U.S. Constitution in large measure to protect their economic interests and that it is "an economic document drawn with superb skill by men whose property interests were immediately at stake." While best known for explaining how the founders developed a political system to protect their economic interests, Beard was one of the most influential of all American historians in part because of the sheer number of his books (more than 50), often written with his wife, Mary (1876–1958), and which in their totality sold many millions. In addition to being both a major scholar and popular historian, Beard was also an important figure in the early evolution of PUBLIC ADMINISTRATION.

Constitution, living The governing document of the United States whose meaning changes and evolves over time in response to new circumstances. This evolution takes place mainly in the minds of the justices of the Supreme Court, not to mention other officials, whose actions and decisions constantly forge the written Constitution into directions never imagined by the framers. Yet this is in accord with their intent. In 1789 Thomas Jefferson wrote to James Madison that "no society can make a perpetual constitution, or even a perpetual law. The earth belongs always to the living generation." Ultimately, the Constitution is whatever each succeeding Supreme Court says it is.

constructive engagement A diplomatic phrase for maintaining political and economic ties with regimes with which a nation has many disagreements in the hope that the ties will gradually lead to changes in the regime's objectionable policies and practices. It has often been used to describe the relations of the United States with South Africa.

consumer movement The continuous efforts of citizen pressure and government action for such things as the wholesomeness and safety of consumer products, consumer representation on government boards, truth in labeling, and hospital cost containment. While the movement has its roots in the progressive movement, its modern impetus is usually traced to the 1960s auto safety efforts of RALPH NADER.

consumer price index (CPI) The Bureau of Labor Statistics' cost-of-living index, the monthly statistical measure of the average change in prices over time in a fixed-market basket of goods and services. The CPI is one of the nation's most important measures of INFLATION/DEFLATION. Many employment and labor union contracts relate wage increases directly to changes in the CPI.

Consumer Product Safety Commission (CPSC) The federal commission created by the Consumer Product Safety Act of 1972 to protect the public against unreasonable risks of injury from consumer products; to assist consumers to evaluate the comparative safety of consumer products; to develop uniform safety standards for consumer products and minimize conflicting state and local regulations; and to promote research and investigation into the causes and prevention of product-related deaths, illnesses, and injuries.

containment The underlying basis of U.S. foreign and military policy during the COLD WAR, which sought to restrict the expansion of communist influence. It was first espoused by George F. Kennan in a June 1947 *Foreign Affairs* article, "The Sources of Soviet Conduct," in which he asserted that "Soviet pressure against the free institutions of the Western World is something that can be contained by the adroit and vigilant application of counterforce." (The official author of this article was X because Kennan wrote it while serving as a Foreign Service officer; but it was never a secret who the actual author was.)

contempt of Congress The criminal act of refusing to testify or produce documents when formally requested by a Congressional committee to do so. Contempt of Congress is a misdemeanor punishable by a fine of at least $100 and one to 12 months' imprisonment. In the 1950s a variety of witnesses called by the HOUSE UN-AMERICAN ACTIVITIES COMMITTEE were held in contempt and eventually imprisoned.

contempt of court The intentional obstruction of a court in the administration of justice; or an action calculated to lessen a court's authority or dignity; or the failure to obey a court's lawful orders. Flight to avoid prosecution or to avoid prison following conviction is usually prosecuted as contempt of court.

continuing appropriations The means by which the U.S. Congress allows federal agencies to continue operations when their annual budget appropriations has been delayed because of the usual political crisis over the budget. When a fiscal year begins and the Congress has not yet enacted all the regular appropriation bills for that year, it passes a joint resolution continuing appropriations at rates generally based on the previous year's appropriations for government agencies not yet funded.

continuing resolution Legislation that provides budpecific ongoing activities when the regular fiscal-year appropriation for such activities has not been enacted by the beginning of the fiscal year. The continuing resolution usually specifies a maximum rate at which the agency may incur an obligation based on the rate of the prior year, the President's budget request, or an appropriation bill passed by either or both houses of the Congress.

contract clause That portion of Article I, Section 10 of the U.S. Constitution which asserts that no state shall pass any "law impairing the obligation of contracts."

contract theory *See* SOCIAL CONTRACT.

contracting out Having work performed outside an organization's own workforce. Contracting out is often an area of union-management disagreement, especially in the public sector. While many unions recognize management's right to occasionally subcontract a job requiring specialized skills and equipment not possessed by the organization or its employees, they oppose the letting of work that could be done by the organization's own workforce. In particular, unions are concerned if work normally performed by its members is contracted out to firms providing inferior wages or working conditions or if such action may result in reduced earnings or layoffs of regular employees. Contracting out is one of the major means of privatizing and thus reducing the size of the public sector.

contras The U.S.-backed "democratic resistance movement" in Nicaragua. The contras opposed the communist Sandinista government. They were called contras during the 1980s by their government because they were *contra* (against) the Sandinistas' revolution. President Ronald Reagan preferred to call them "freedom fighters" and had consistent problems getting funding for their guerilla operations from the Congress. The essence of the problem was succinctly put by Senator John P. East: "The average American doesn't know the difference between a Contra and a caterpillar or between a Sandinista and a sardine" (*The New York Times*, October 12, 1984). The Contras disbanded in 1990 after a democratically elected government replaced the Sandinista regime. *See also* IRAN-CONTRA AFFAIR.

controllability The ability of the U.S. Congress or the President under existing law to control spending during a given fiscal year. Uncontrollable spending—spending that cannot be increased or decreased without changes in existing substantive law—is usually the result of open-ended programs and fixed costs, such as social security and veterans' benefits (sometimes called entitlements), but also includes payments due under obligations incurred during prior years.

controller The financial officer of a company or a government agency, sometimes known as a *comptroller*. For example, the comptroller general of the United States heads the GENERAL ACCOUNTING OFFICE, which audits government agencies. Normally, a controller has the technical skills of an accountant. The basic functions of the office are to supervise accounting and to make sure that funds are spent for acceptable purposes. The AUDIT function comes afterward; it is a review to see that funds were expended correctly.

convention 1. A political meeting of the members of one party (*see* NATIONAL CONVENTION). Author Norman Mailer in *Some Honorable Men* (1976) defined a political convention as "a fiesta, a carnival, a pig-rooting, horse-snorting, band-playing, voice-screaming medieval get-together of greed, practical lust, compromised idealism, career-advancement, meeting, feud, vendetta, conciliation of rabble-rousers, fist fights (as it used to be), embraces, drunks (again as it used to be) and collective rivers of animal sweat." **2.** A CONSTITUTIONAL CONVENTION. **3.** An international agreement on matters less significant than those regulated by treaty. The best-known conventions are probably the Geneva conventions of 1864, 1906, and 1949, which concern the treatment of prisoners of war.

convergence The notion that socialist and capitalist societies will inexorably grow more and more alike in response to similar bureaucratic and technological development. The imperatives of planning, and the response of bureaucrats and planners charged with achieving particular goals, are seen as transcending overt ideological differences between the two societies. But the thesis generally ignores the crucial difference between bureaucracies which are, and those which are not, subject to electoral power. In one sense, however, the model could be regarded as correct. The end of the Cold War has shown that there has been convergence on the importance of capitalism and free market economies.

cooking the books 1. Creating financial records that do not reflect the truth. **2.** Preparing the federal budget. President Ronald Reagan's former director of the Office of Management and Budget, David Stockman, said of the federal budget: "We have increasingly resorted to squaring the circle with accounting gimmicks, evasions, half-truths and downright dishonesty in our budget numbers, debate and advocacy. Indeed, if the SEC had jurisdiction over the Executive and Legislative branches, many of us would be in jail" (*Time*, July 22, 1985).

Cooley v Board of Wardens (1851) The Supreme Court case that established the Cooley Doctrine—that the states had the right to regulate foreign and interstate commerce if the Congress hadn't dealt with the area of concern. However, once the Congress took action, state legislation could not validly contradict federal law.

Coolidge, Calvin (1872–1933) The Vice President who became President (1923–1929) upon the death of President Warren G. Harding. Coolidge was a traditional conservative who believed that "the business of America is business." Known as Silent Cal, Coolidge would often sit through entire dinner parties without saying a word. Legend has it that a woman dinner companion told him she made a large bet with her friends that she could get him to say more than three words. Coolidge responded, "You lose." Actress Ethel Barrymore (1879–1959) said that during a visit to the White House Coolidge told her: "I think the American public wants a solemn ass as a President. And I think I'll go along with them" (*Time*, May 16, 1955).

cooling-off period **1.** Any legal provision that postpones a labor strike or lockout for a specific time to give the parties an additional opportunity to mediate their differences. While the device has great popular appeal, it has proven to be of doubtful value because more time will not necessarily resolve a labor dispute. The first federal requirements for a cooling-off period were set forth in the War Labor Disputes Act of 1943. This was superseded by the national emergency provisions of the Labor-Management Relations (Taft-Hartley) Act of 1947, which called for an 80-day cooling-off period in the event of a national emergency. **2.** A legally mandated period of time before a person seeking to buy a rifle or pistol can gain possession of it; the period both (1) allows police to do a background check on the purchaser and (2) allows the purchaser to "cool off" if he or she is buying the weapon in anger.

cooptation The inclusion of new potentially dissident group members into an organization's policymaking process to prevent such elements from being a threat to the organization or its mission. The classic analysis of cooptation is found in *TVA and the Grass Roots* by Philip Selznick (1949).

coordination with In consultation with. The expression means that government agencies "coordinated with" one another shall participate actively; their concurrence shall be sought; and that if concurrence is not obtained, the disputed matter shall be referred to the next higher authority.

copyright An author's exclusive right to control the duplication of books, articles, movies, and so on. Article I, Section 8, of the U.S. Constitution provides that the Congress shall "promote the progress of science and useful arts, by securing for limited times to authors and inventors the exclusive right to their respective writings and discoveries." According to the Copyright Act of 1976, the legal life of a copyright is the author's life plus 50 years and a flat 75 years for one held by a company. The symbol for copyright is $ad. Copyrights are registered in the copyright office of the Library of Congress.

coroner The county official responsible for determining the causes of deaths occurring under violent, unusual, or suspicious circumstances. Ideally, a coroner (whose title comes from the fact that such officers originally represented the crown) should be both a medical examiner (who performs autopsies) and a trained criminal investigator. Unfortunately, many jurisdictions have no particular qualifications for the office, and it is often a political plum. Coroners usually have the power to hold a formal hearing into suspicious deaths, or inquest. If evidence of wrongdoing is discovered, the case is then turned over to an appropriate prosecutor or grand jury.

corporation An organization formed under state or federal law which exists, for legal purposes, as a separate being or an artificial person. It may be public (set up by the government) or private (set up by individuals), and it may be set up to carry on a business or to perform almost any function. It may be owned by the government, by a few persons, or by the general public through purchases of stock. A "publicly owned corporation" is not owned by government but by members of the public who buy its shares on an open market.

corporation counsel An attorney for a municipal corporation (a city).

corporatism 1. The designation for a form of social organization in which corporations, nongovernment bodies with great authority over the lives and professional activities of their members, play an intermediary role between public and state. The practice goes back to medieval times when trade guilds or corporations controlled the activities of craftsmen and traders; at the height of their power the guilds represented a third force in society along with the Church and the nobility. **2.** A theoretical concept developed by the French sociologist Emile Durkheim (1858–1917) which found political expression in the fascist institutions of the 1930s and 1940s. Fascist corporatism suggested that people engaged in a particular trade—employers as well as workers—had more in common with one another than with people of the same class or status in other trades. Thus, in Spain and Italy legislative assemblies and councils of state were organized around trade corporations rather than around geographic constituencies. Corporatist theory appealed to the fascists because it by-passed both class-conflict issues and democratic elections. **3.** The modern meaning of corporatism refers to the increasing tendency for states to work closely with major business corporations and trade unions to enhance international competitiveness. This is sometimes called neocorporatism.

correcting the record The method by which members of the U.S. Congress may change recorded votes. Rules prohibit members from changing their votes after the result has been announced, but frequently, hours, days, or months after a vote has been taken, a member might announce that he or she was incorrectly recorded. In the Senate, a request to change one's vote almost always receives unanimous consent. In the House of Representatives, members are prohibited from changing their votes if the votes were tallied by the electronic voting system. If they were taken by a roll call, a vote may be changed if consent is granted. "Errors" in the text of the *Congressional Record* may be corrected by unanimous consent.

corrupt and contented MUCKRAKER Lincoln Steffens' (1866–1936) famous description, from his *The Shame of the Cities* (1904), of BOSSISM in Philadelphia at the turn of the century.

corruption, political The unauthorized use of public office for private gain. The most common forms of corruption are bribery, extortion, and the misuse of inside information. While there are isolated pockets of rectitude, just as there are instances of abject venality, many communities come to tolerate the systematic corruption of their officials through one of three patterns:

1) *Nonenforcement policies for officials high in an organization.* For obvious reasons, police departments tend to be the bell wethers of systematic corruption, the only surprise being the shock of political leaders when confronted with the evidence. The most publicized police exposés of recent years were the 1972 Knapp Commission hearings in New York City, yet the hearings turned up nothing that had not been well-documented about big city police operations since the Wickersham Commission in the early 1930s. While it is more comforting to dwell upon just justices and honest police, thoughtful citizens do not have to be cynics to support Senator Daniel P. Moynihan's contention that "Corruption by organized crime is a normal condition of American local government and politics" (*Reporter*, July 6, 1961).

2) *Community indifference.* This sort of toleration of corruption amounts to consent, and a community unwilling to devote the necessary resources to weed out corrupting influences deserves the conditions it tacitly supports.

3) *Encouragement by "leading citizens."* A society cannot reasonably maintain moral standards for its public officials that grossly differ from those of the leaders of the community. If a plumbing inspector arrives two hours later than his appointment, this could cost the contractor thousands of dollars in unnecessary payroll, since the brickmasons, carpenters, and plasterers, for example, cannot begin their work until the plumbing has been inspected. It is simply good business sense for the contractor to tip the plumbing inspector $20 to show up on time, rather than risk having a variety of skilled workers idle for several expensive hours. But, once started, this tipping of government officials frequently has no end: building plans must be expedited through city architectural reviewers; police must allow construction equipment to be illegally parked on side streets. It is estimated that about 5 percent of the cost of construction in New York City goes for bribes of public officials. *Compare to* BRIBERY; HONEST GRAFT/DISHONEST GRAFT.

cosponsor To jointly submit a bill for legislative consideration. In the U.S. Congress there is no limit to the number of cosponsors a bill may have; a very popular bill may even have more cosponsors than is needed for eventual passage. The first senator or representative listed on a bill is the sponsor; all that follow are cosponsors.

cost-of-living adjustment (COLA) An increase in compensation in response to increasing inflation. Some labor union contracts and some entitlement programs (such as social security) provide for automatic COLAs if inflation reaches predetermined levels.

cost-of-living index *See* CONSUMER PRICE INDEX.

cost overrun A situation in the procurement of big-ticket, usually defense, items such as tanks and fighter planes when the cost to the government is greater than originally planned. Cost overruns, usually due to a change in contract specifications requested by the government or to the need to respond to the latest technology, are the butt of countless jokes because the overruns have sometimes been enormous and sometimes occasioned by corruption.

council-manager plan A form of municipal government in which an elected city council appoints a professional CITY MANAGER to administer the city government. A county-manager system offers the same essential structure at the county level.

Council of Economic Advisers (CEA) The U.S. President's primary source of economic advice. It assists the President in preparing various economic reports, including the annual *Economic Report of the President*. Established in the Executive Office of the President by the Employment Act of 1946, the CEA consists of three economists (one of whom is designated chair) appointed by the President, with the advice and consent of the Senate, who formulate proposals to "maintain employment, production and purchasing power." While council members are now usually professional economists, the Congress initially objected to them and preferred practical businessmen.

council of government (COG) A multijurisdictional cooperative arrangement to permit a regional approach to planning, development, transportation, environment, and other problems that affect a region as a whole. The COGs are substate regional planning agencies established by states and are responsible for areawide review of projects applying for federal funds and for development of regional plans and other areawide special-purpose arrangements. They are composed of designated policymaking representatives from each participating government within the region. Some COGs have assumed a more enterprising role in the 1980s by acting as contractors for and service providers to their local governments.

Council of State Governments (CSG) The joint agency of all state governments—created, supported, and directed by them. The purpose of the CSG, which is located in Lexington, Kentucky, is to strengthen all branches of state government and preserve the state government role in the federal system through catalyzing the expression of states' views on major issues; to conduct research on state programs and problems, assisting in federal-state liaison and state-regional-local cooperation; to offer training, reference, and consultation services to state agencies, officials, and legislators; and to serve as a broad instrument for bringing together all elements of state government. Originally created as the American Legislators Association in 1925, it took its present name in 1933. *See* PUBLIC INTEREST GROUPS.

Council on Environmental Quality The federal advisory council that develops and recommends to the President national policies to further environmental quality; continually analyzes changes or trends in the national environment; administers the environmental impact statement process; provides an ongoing assessment of the nation's energy research and development from an environmental and conservation standpoint; and assists the President in the preparation of the annual environmental quality report to the Congress. It was established by the National Environmental Policy Act of 1969 within the Executive Office of the President.

Council on Foreign Relations A private nonpartisan membership organization which, since 1921, has functioned as a U.S. foreign policy establishment. One cannot simply join the Council; one must be nominated and then elected to membership. In its 1990 *Annual Report* it is stated that "election to the Council is based on an estimate of a candidate's special intellectual pursuits, experience, and involvement in American foreign policy; active interest in the council and its programs; and standing in his or her own professional community." Thus, the organization limits its membership to the 2,670 (in 1990) movers and shakers of American foreign policy. While headquartered in New York, it holds meetings throughout the United States. Its major journal is *Foreign Affairs*.

council ward A legislative district from which a person is elected to a city council.

councilor A member of a council. This is in contrast to a counselor—one who gives advice, such as a lawyer.

countercyclical Descriptive of government actions aimed at smoothing out swings in economic activity. Countercyclical actions may take the form of monetary and fiscal policy (such as countercyclical revenue sharing or jobs programs). Automatic (built-in) stabilizers have a countercyclical effect without necessitating changes in government policy.

countertrade An international trade transaction whereby the exporting country agrees to purchase products or services from the importing country so that the latter can offset some or all of the foreign exchange costs of the imports. In countertrade, the exporting party is usually a First World country and the purchaser either a Communist state or a developing nation. In the 1980s countertrade accounted for 25 percent of world trade. *Compare to* MANAGED TRADE.

countervailing theory The notion that when one group gets too powerful in a pluralist society another group or coalition springs up to counter or oppose its power.

country desk The unit within the U.S. Department of State that has the daily responsibility of monitoring and analyzing the activities of a given foreign country. The person in charge of a country desk is the "desk officer."

country team In a foreign country, the coordinating and supervisory body headed by the chief of the U.S. diplomatic mission, usually an ambassador, and composed of the senior member of each represented U.S. department or agency.

county The basic unit for administrative decentralization of state government. Although it is typically governed by an elected board or commission, there is a movement at present toward government by a county administrator or executive (sometimes elected). In Louisiana, the comparable unit is called a parish; in Alaska, it is a borough. In 1987, the United States had 3,042 county governments. Each state determines for itself how many counties it will have; two states, Connecticut and Rhode Island, have no counties at all. The elected officials of county government hold a bewildering array of titles. According to Dade County, Florida, Commissioner Harvey Ruvin, county officials "are supervisors in California, judges in Texas, jurors in Louisiana, freeholders in New Jersey, county legislators in New York, commissioners in Dade. If I tell somebody from New York I'm a commissioner, they think I'm the dog catcher. No wonder the public and the media focus on governors and mayors" (*Governing*, May 1989).

county agent A field officer of the U.S. Department of Agriculture and one of over 3,000 county government officials who is responsible for disseminating information about new agricultural techniques developed by research funded by the U.S. Department of Agriculture and state land-grant universities. The county agent is the grassroots officer of the Cooperative Extension Service, a partnership of all three levels of government authorized by the Smith-Lever Act of 1914.

county board The generic term for the governing board of a county.

county chairman/county chairwoman The head of a political party organization at the county level who supervises the activities of the party precinct leaders and who helps select (along with other chairs in the state) the state party officials.

county clerk The secretary to a county board. An elected office in more than half the states, a county clerk's job ranges from maintaining county records to a bewildering variety of other duties as well.

county commissioner An elected member of the governing body of a county government, often called a county board or board of supervisors. In some southern states, the elected county commissioners are formally called judges, even though their judicial duties are minimal.

county committee A political party's governing apparatus at the county level; typically composed of people elected at the precinct level.

county coroner *See* CORONER.

county court Local trial courts variously called district, superior, or circuit courts. They handle criminal cases other than misdemeanors. In some states there are separate county courts for criminal and civil cases.

county-manager system *See* COUNCIL-MANAGER PLAN.

county seat The capital of a county, where the courts and administrative offices are located. In much of the United States, the county seat was so located in the geographical center of the county that it would not be more than one day's ride on horseback from the farthest part of the county.

county single-executive plan A county government structure which calls for the election of one individual to administer all county programs and services. This county equivalent to a strong mayoral form of municipal government is particularly popular in urban areas.

court **1.** An agency of the judicial branch of government authorized or established by statute or constitution that consists of one or more judicial officers and that has the authority to decide upon controversies in law and disputed matters of fact brought before it. There are two basic types of courts: those having original jurisdiction to make decisions regarding matters of fact and law (trial courts), and those having appellate jurisdiction to review issues of law in connection with decisions made in specific cases previously adjudicated by other courts and administrative agencies (appeals courts). Article III of the U.S. Constitution outlines the structure and power of the federal court system and establishes a federal judiciary, which helps maintain and define the rights of American citizens. Article III, Section 2, also contains a guarantee that the trial of all federal crimes, except cases of impeachment, shall be by jury. The Supreme Court has interpreted this guarantee as containing exceptions for "trials of petty offenses," cases rightfully tried before court-martial or other military tribunal, and some cases in which the defendant has voluntarily relinquished his or her right to a jury. This section also requires that a federal criminal trial be held in a federal court sitting in the state where the crime was committed. Thus, citizens are protected against being tried without their consent in a place distant from where their alleged violation of federal laws occurred. State constitutions establish parallel court systems at the state level. **2.** A judge. When it is said that "the court decided . . . " the reference is to the judge of the court.

court, appellate A court whose primary function is to review the judgments of other courts and of administrative agencies.

court, district *See* DISTRICT COURT.

court, divided An appeals court, such as the Supreme Court, whose judges have reached a decision by a narrow majority, say five to four. "Divided" applies only to the case at hand, not to the court in general. Any opinion by a divided court is subject to continued legal debate; but it is just as legally binding as if the court had been unanimous. An equally divided court results in the affirmation of the lower court's decision.

court, juvenile A local court that specializes in cases dealing with delinquent or neglected children. The Supreme Court has held in *In re Gault* (1967) that children accused of crimes have the same procedural protections (right to counsel, right to confront witnesses, etc.) as adults. In serious cases, such as murder, a juvenile court may waive jurisdiction and allow a teenager to be tried as an adult.

court, kangaroo A phony court in which principles of justice are mocked and perverted.

court-martial **1.** A military court that tries members of the armed forces for violations of military law. **2.** To force someone to be tried by a military court. The Supreme Court held in *Ex parte Milligan* (1866), that in the United States it is illegal to try civilians by military court when regular courts are available. *See* WRIT OF HABEAS CORPUS.

court of appeals **1.** A court that hears appeals from a trial court. In most states, it is the midlevel court between the trial courts and the state supreme court. However, in some states, the supreme court is the midlevel court, and the appeals court is the highest (in effect, the supreme) state court. **2.** One of 12 U.S. courts of appeals, the appellate courts below the U.S. Supreme Court, which hear appeals from cases tried in federal district courts. In most cases, a decision by a court of appeals is final, since only a small fraction of its decisions are ever reviewed by the Supreme Court. Before 1948, these courts were called circuit courts of appeals. They were created in 1891 to relieve the Supreme Court of considering all appeals in cases originally decided by the federal trial courts. The United States is divided into 12 judicial circuits, each of which has a court of appeals. At present, each court of appeals has from four to 23 permanent judgeships, depending upon the amount of judicial work in that circuit. The judge senior in commission who has not reached his or her seventieth birthday is the chief judge. One of the justices of the Supreme Court serves as circuit justice for each circuit. Divisions of three judges usually hear cases, but all the judges of the circuit may sit EN BANC.

court of first instance **1.** A COURT OF ORIGINAL JURISDICTION. **2.** A trial as opposed to an appellate court.

court of general jurisdiction A trial court having original jurisdiction over all subject areas not specifically assigned to a court of limited jurisdiction. These are often called superior or district courts.

court of last resort **1.** An appellate court having final jurisdiction over appeals in a given state. **2.** The Supreme Court of the United States. **3.** The last authority from whom one can hope for a reversal of judgment or opinion. Thus, public opinion or history may be perceived as a court of last resort.

court of limited jurisdiction A trial court having original jurisdiction over only that subject area specifically assigned to it by law; for examples: traffic court, small claims court, and probate court.

court of original jurisdiction A trial court where cases are initially heard.

court packing **1.** President Franklin D. Roosevelt's unsuccessful 1937 attempt to enlarge the Supreme Court by appointing additional justices who would be more sympathetic to NEW DEAL legislation. Roosevelt sought congressional approval to appoint one new Supreme Court justice for each sitting justice over the age of 70 years. This would have allowed him to immediately put six new justices on the Court for a total of 15. The Congress would not approve, but the issue soon became moot because the court suddenly started approving New Deal legislation, a change often referred to as "the switch in time that saved nine." **2.** Any administration's efforts to fill judicial vacancies with appointees philosophically sympathetic to the administration, rather than with the best qualified candidates, regardless of party affiliation. President Ronald Reagan has been accused of court packing, because his administration was said to impose an ideological LITMUS TEST for potential judicial appointments.

court, small claims A court that handles civil cases with a value under a specified limit (usually $500 to $1,000). Such courts are designed to allow the "little person" to take even a large corporation to court. Sessions are often at night, and plaintiffs do not need to be represented by a lawyer— although corporations usually are.

court, special Specialized federal courts created by the U.S. Congress to deal with special classes of cases: (1) the U.S. Tax Court handles disputes between citizens and the Internal Revenue Service; (2) the U.S. Court of Military Appeals is the final appellate tribunal to review court-martial convictions in all the military services; (3) the U.S. Court of International Trade has jurisdiction over any civil action against the United States arising from federal laws governing import transactions; (4) the U.S. Claims Court has original jurisdiction to render judgment on a claim against the United States, an act of the Congress, and expressed or implied contracts with the United States; (5) a bankruptcy court system, which operates under the supervision of the U.S. district courts. All decisions of these courts are appealable to a court of appeals or directly to the Supreme Court.

court, supreme **1.** The highest U.S. court. *See* SUPREME COURT, UNITED STATES. **2.** The highest state court. **3.** A midlevel state court of appeals in states such as New York, where the highest state court is a court of appeals.

court, trial A court whose primary function is to initially hear and decide cases. All U.S. district courts are trial courts.

courthouse gang A derisive phrase for the dominant political figures in rural county politics; the political machine of county government.

covenant **1.** The religious belief that God has promised salvation to humanity. **2.** The biblical tradition of a promise sanctioned by an oath with an appeal to the deity to punish any violation of it. **3.** A legally binding instrument, such as a restriction in a deed. While covenants as legal tools are neutral devices, they were once widely used to prevent land and houses from being sold to blacks and Jews. Such restrictive covenants are now illegal through a variety of federal and state civil rights and equal housing laws. **4.** An international treaty, such as the Covenant of the League of Nations, the first part of the Treaty of Versailles of 1919, which formally ended World War I. **5.** A political compact.

COVERT OPERATIONS

covert operations Military, police, or intelligence activities that are planned and executed to conceal the identity of, or permit plausible denial by, the sponsor. They differ from clandestine operations in that emphasis is placed on concealment for the sponsor, rather than on concealment of the operation itself. Since World War II covert operations have become an inherent part of American foreign policy.

cozy triangles The mutually supportive relations among government agencies, interest groups, and the legislative committee or subcommittee with jurisdiction over their areas of common concern; also known as *iron triangles*. Such coalitions constantly exchange information, services, and money (in the form of campaign contributions from the interest groups to the members of the legislative committee and budget approval from the committee to the agency). As a whole, they tend to dominate policymaking in their areas of concern. The triangles are considered to be as strong as iron, because the supportive relations are so strong that others elected or appointed to control administrative policy as representatives of the public's interest are effectively prohibited from interfering on behalf of the public. *Compare to* ISSUE NETWORKS.

cradle to the grave Slang phrase that refers to the total security offered citizens in the fully realized welfare state; sometimes used as "womb to tomb." "Cradle to the grave" may have first been used in Edward Bellamy's novel *Looking Backward* (1888), in which he stated: "The nation guarantees the nurture, education, and comfortable maintenance of every citizen from cradle to the grave." Historically, the term was applied to the postwar program President Franklin D. Roosevelt announced in 1943, intended as a promise of an expanded postwar NEW DEAL. President Harry S Truman attempted to pick up the pieces of it in his FAIR DEAL program.

credentials committee The committee of a political party that rules on any challenges to the right of convention delegates to vote. The work of the credentials committee is relatively routine unless rival groups assert the right to represent their district or state. In *Cousins v Wigoda* (1975) the Supreme Court held that national political parties have the right to determine credential disputes between rival delegations. The national party's position was further strengthened in *Democratic Party v LaFollette* (1981) when the Court held states could not force a national party to recognize a delegation selected in violation of the party's rules.

credibility gap The difference between official description of events and the public's understanding of those events from other sources, chiefly the news media and political critics. A credibility gap engenders public mistrust and disbelief of elected officials. Credibility was an especially acute problem for the Lyndon B. Johnson and Richard M. Nixon administrations, the first for lies about the Vietnam War, the second for lies over Watergate. Public trust tended to increase during the Ronald Reagan administration, at least until the IRAN-CONTRA AFFAIR.

crisis 1. An unstable situation ripe for decisive change. As the then-Senator John F. Kennedy said in a speech on April 12, 1959: "When written in Chinese, the word 'crisis' is composed of two characters—one represents danger and the other represents opportunity." **2.** A foreign policy problem involving a threat to the security of the state and dealt with by the highest level of a government forced to make crucial decisions within a short time frame.

cross-examination The questioning of witnesses by opposition counsel during a trial or formal hearing. The right of cross-examination is implied by the Sixth Amendment to the Constitution which holds, in part, that: "In all criminal prosecutions, the accused shall enjoy the right . . . to be confronted with the witnesses against him."

cross-filing Formally becoming a candidate for elective office in the primary elections of more than one party, as permitted in some states, particularly for judicial offices.

crowding out The displacement of private investment expenditures by increases in public expenditures financed by the sale of government securities. It is often suggested that, as the federal deficit increases, the money borrowed from the public to pay for it is therefore unavailable for private investment. Such crowding out could thus lead to a recession.

cruel and unusual punishment Criminal penalties not considered appropriate by a society; inhumane punishment involving torture; any punishment that could result in death when the death penalty had not been ordered. This is the criminal penalty prohibited by the Eighth Amendment, which not only bars government from imposing punishment that is barbarous but, as the Supreme Court has announced, forbids punishment that society's "evolving standards of decency" would mark as excessive. It also bars punishment disproportionate to the offense committed, based on the facts of the particular case.

In *Gregg v Georgia* (1976), the Court ruled that the death penalty as a punishment for murder does not necessarily constitute cruel and unusual punishment. But the Court held in *Woodson v North Carolina* (1976) that the death penalty may not be made mandatory. The jury or the judge must be given discretion, structured by legislative determination of the factors looking toward imposition of death, to consider the individual defendant, the particular crime, mitigating circumstances, and the treatment of similarly situated defendants. The Court has closely reviewed the substantive and procedural rules and practices associated with the determination of whether to put a convicted murderer to death. The most recent trend appears to be the enlargement of the discretion of the jury, which many find to be inconsistent with the 1972 decision of *Furman v Georgia*, which temporarily struck down the death penalty because of the arbitrary, capricious, and racist manner in which it was usually applied by juries and judges. Race was considered again in *McCleskey v Kemp* (1979) when the

Court ruled that statistics showing race-related disparities in death sentences are not sufficient grounds to constitutionally challenge capital punishment.

Death as a penalty for any crime other than the actual commission of murder is of doubtful status. For example, it was held to be disproportionate, and thus not permitted, for the crime of rape of an adult woman in *Coker v Georgia* (1977). Finally, punishment for narcotics addiction has been held to be cruel and unusual in *Robinson v California* (1962), on the grounds that addiction is an illness and therefore cannot be properly categorized as a crime. However, the Court held in *Tison v Arizona* (1987) that it is constitutional to execute accomplices to murder.

Cuban missile crisis The 1962 confrontation between the United States and the Soviet Union over the Soviet placement of nuclear missiles in Cuba. President John F. Kennedy demanded the removal of the missiles, imposed a naval blockade on Cuba, and waited for the Soviet response. In the end, the Soviets removed their missiles in exchange for a U.S. promise not to invade Cuba and an understanding that the United States would also remove its nuclear missiles in Turkey. Secretary of State Dean Rusk offered his now famous summary of the crisis: "We were eyeball-to-eyeball and the other fellow just blinked" (*Saturday Evening Post*, December 8, 1962). The Russian perspective is quite different. Nikita Khrushchev, who led the Soviet Union at the time, wrote in his memoirs, *Khrushchev Remembers* (1971) that: "[In] bringing the world to the brink of atomic war, we won a Socialist Cuba. . . . We achieved, I would say, a spectacular success without having to fire a single shot!"

cult of personality A concentration of political power and authority in one individual, rather than in the office. The phrase came from the 1956 meeting of the Russian Communist party, where Joseph Stalin (1879–1953), the Soviet dictator from 1924 until his death, was denounced for his excesses in office.

cult of the robe The notion that the lawyers who become judges, once they put on their judicial robes, are suddenly somehow wiser, purer, and better than the ordinary mortals in other parts of government. Supreme Court justices in particular have been accused from time to time of believing too much in the "cult of the robe."

custom duties Taxes on imports or exports. *See also* DUTY.

customs The authorities designated to collect duties levied by a country on imports and exports. The term also applies to the procedures involved in such collection.

Customs Service, U.S. The agency of the Department of the Treasury that collects revenue from imports and enforces customs and related laws. The service was established in 1973; its forerunner was the Bureau of Customs, created in 1789 and placed in the Treasury Department in 1927.

customs union A group of nations that has eliminated trade barriers among themselves and imposed a common tariff on all goods imported from all other countries. The European Common Market is a customs union, as are the United States in themselves.

cutting Working against one particular candidate of one's party while supporting the rest of the ticket. This is sometimes done by local party workers who are obligated to the entire ticket but feel they have strong reason for "opposing" an unfavored candidate.

cycles of American history The concept popularized by historian Arthur Schlesinger, Jr., in his 1986 book of the same title, that American politics operate in 30-year cycles which alternate between conservative and liberal periods of politics.

czar 1. Title of the absolute monarch of Russia; also anglicized as tzar. **2.** A nickname for any high-ranking administrator who is given great authority over something; for example, an energy czar, a housing czar.

D

damage control 1. In naval usage, measures necessary aboard a ship after it has sustained damage from enemy action or accident to keep it afloat and maintain its ability to fight. **2.** Applied to politics, efforts to contain the effects of a mistake or scandal so that the political actors involved will once again find themselves in a stable situation with an ability to continue fighting the political wars. Henry Kissinger offered this theory of damage control when the IRAN-CONTRA AFFAIR broke: "One iron rule in situations like this is, whatever must happen ultimately should happen immediately. Anybody who eventually has to go should be fired now. Any fact that needs to be disclosed should be put out now, or as quickly as possible, because otherwise . . . the bleeding will not end" (*Time*, December 8, 1986).

dark horse 1. A relatively unknown candidate nominated for political office. **2.** A long-shot candidate who is not given much chance to win a party's nomination for office. **3.** A compromise candidate, being the first choice of few but the final choice of the majority. The phrase came from and is still used in racing, where it refers to a horse about whom little is known but who has a reasonable chance to win. Under the democratizing reforms of the major parties in recent years, it has become increasingly unlikely that a dark horse can be nominated for President.

Dartmouth College v Woodward (1819) The Supreme Court case that upheld the legal sanctity of contracts under the Constitution. The State of New Hampshire wanted to unilaterally change Dartmouth College's 1769 charter, but the Court held that the charter was a contract and could be changed only by the mutual consent of the parties. Daniel Webster (1782–1852), who argued the case for the college before the Court, summarized his case with the words: "It is, sir . . . a small college, and yet there are those that love it." *Compare to* FLETCHER V PECK.

de minimus Short form of *de minimus non curat lex,* Latin for "the law does not bother with trifles." This means that a court will not waste its time on a matter it considers ridiculously trivial.

dealignment A decline in political party loyalty and a rise in political independence. In a period of party dealignment, group ties to parties are weakened, and the electorate becomes more volatile in its behavior. *Compare to* REALIGNMENT.

death penalty *See* CAPITAL PUNISHMENT; CRUEL AND UNUSUAL PUNISHMENT.

debate 1. A formal contest during which opposing speakers take either the affirmative or the negative side of a proposition. **2.** The discussion of a public issue in a legislature. **3.** A political media event. Generations ago candidates met on the campaign trail to actually debate the questions of the day.

But today most campaign debates are little more than joint news conferences. *Compare to* PRESIDENTIAL DEBATES.

debriefing 1. Interrogating someone (a spy, a soldier, a diplomat, etc.) after he or she has returned from a mission. **2.** Formally instructing someone about his or her responsibilities in dealing with government secrets as he or she leaves a position dealing with classified information.

debt, general obligation A long-term full-faith-and-credit obligation other than one payable initially from nontax revenue. It includes a debt payable in the first instance from earmarked taxes, such as motor fuel sales taxes or property taxes.

debt limit The official ceiling established by Congress on the total amount of money the federal government can borrow. Because the debt limit must be raised every few years to accommodate the growing national debt, many members of Congress use the needed legislation as an opportunity to make speeches about the evils of the budget deficit and to attach unrelated RIDERS. Without the new legislation raising the debt limit, the federal government can literally come to a standstill because no funds can be legally spent for anything. Consequently, a President is under great pressure to sign such legislation even if it has unappealing riders.

debt, nonguaranteed Long-term debt payable solely from pledged specific sources; for example, from earnings of revenue-producing activities (such as university and college dormitories, toll highways and bridges, electric power projects, and public building authorities) or from specific nonproperty taxes. It includes only debt that does not constitute an obligation against any other resources if the pledged sources are insufficient.

debt service The regular payment of principal, interest, and other costs (such as insurance) to pay off a financial obligation.

declaration 1. A document stating a course of action and usually the reasons for it to which the signatories (either individuals or nations) bind themselves. Perhaps the most famous of all political declarations is the American Declaration of Independence of 1776. **2.** A declaration of war (or neutrality) expresses to the world a nation's intentions on these matters. **3.** A statement of intention by a political leader. The leader can be either in power, speaking for the government, or out of power, speaking for an opposition party. **4.** A customs form on which, upon entering a country, one must list items for which duty should be paid.

Declaration of Independence The document that heralded the birth of the United States of America (see Appendix A for text). In 1776, during the Second Continental Congress, Richard Henry Lee (1732–1794) of Virginia made the motion that "these United Colonies are, and of right ought to be, free and independent states." In response, a committee of five was appointed to write a Declaration of Independence. But one member of the committee, Thomas Jefferson, drafted almost all of it. The Declaration starts off with a philosophical discussion of the nature of law and the rights of men. Then the influence of JOHN LOCKE and other social contract theorists is seen, as Jefferson provides the philosophical justification for breaking with a tyrannical king. This is followed by a long list of the king's abuses and a statement of how the colonists constantly petitioned for redress with no effect. The attack on the king was thought necessary to justify breaking with the long-held notion that it was a citizen's responsibility to be loyal to the monarch. Then the "Representatives of the United States of America" declare their independence and "mutually pledge to each other our lives, our fortunes and our sacred honor." Jefferson would later write in a May 8, 1825 letter to Henry Lee that: "This was the object of the Declaration of Independence. Not to find out new principles, or new arguments, never before thought of, not merely to say things which had never been said before; but to place before mankind the common sense of the subject, in terms so plain and firm as to command their assent, and to justify ourselves in the independent stand we are compelled to take." The Declaration, which was approved by the convention in July 1776, was the first significant political—as opposed to philosophical—statement that the people of a nation had a right to choose their own government. It was the beginning of the independence of the United States and has been a significant influence on revolutionary movements ever since.

Legend has it that when the Declaration of Independence was formally signed, John Hancock signed first and used large letters so that King George III could read it without putting on glasses. This is true enough. He is then supposed to have warned: "We must be unanimous; there must be no pulling different ways; we must all hang together." Then Benjamin Franklin is supposed to have replied: "Yes, we must, indeed, all hang together, or most assuredly we shall all hang separately." However, according to Ronald W. Clark's *Benjamin Franklin* (1983), "No contemporary record substantiates the story, which first surfaced in 1840."

declaration of war The legal obligation (under international law) on the part of a nation to formally notify another sovereign nation that a "state of war" exists between them if the first nation intends to commence hostilities. The last time the United States declared war was during World War II, when President Franklin D. Roosevelt called December 7, 1941 "a date which will live in infamy" in the wake of the Japanese attack on Pearl Harbor, Hawaii, and asked "that the Congress declare that since the unprovoked and dastardly attack on Sunday, December 7th, 1941, a state of war has existed between the United States and the Japanese empire." The United States was then at war with both Japan and Germany, because Germany, as an ally of Japan, promptly declared war on the United States.

Formal declarations of war seem to be rapidly becoming quaint relics of diplomatic history. The phrase "undeclared war" was used by American policymakers in the 1930s to define the illegality of the Japanese action against China. President Harry S Truman's actions in Korea (*see* KOREAN WAR) told the world that, when a war was not a war, it was a "police action." President Dwight D. Eisenhower's request for a congressional resolution empowering action in defense of Formosa set the stage for President Lyndon B. Johnson's GULF OF TONKIN RESOLUTION—that is, the prior approval by the Congress for a war action. There has been a real transformation of the concept of war power, which has led to the WAR POWERS Resolution through a series of transforming stages. Consequently, today the American President as commander in chief can commit American forces without congressional approval until after the fact.

declaratory judgment **1.** A court ruling on the rights of parties in a particular case, without a judicial order that any particular action be taken in consequence. Thus, the legal issues of a dispute can be examined and ruled in an effort to forestall more complicated lawsuits. A declaratory judgment differs from an advisory opinion in that there exists a real controversy, even though no actual injuries have yet to occur. The Declaratory Judgments Act of 1934 empowers the federal courts to issue such judgments. **2.** A judicial decision in a case or controversy in which no party has yet suffered specific harm or injury through the enforcement of a law or administration regulation. However, such harm or injury is considered sufficiently likely to make a court decision on the issue reasonable before any harm or injury occurs. *Compare to* OPINION, ADVISORY.

de facto **1.** A Latin phrase meaning "in fact"; actual. For example, *de facto* segregation has occurred without the formal assistance of government; it evolved from social and economic conditions. In contrast, *de jure* ("by law") segregation in schools was once a legal requirement in many states. While segregation practices are no longer sanctioned by government (are no longer *de jure*), they often remain *de facto*. **2.** Diplomatic recognition that implies acceptance but falls short of formal, legal (*de jure*) recognition.

deep doo-doo President George Bush's wholesome way of avoiding a traditional vulgarity to refer to someone who has stepped into a serious political problem. According to *Newsweek* (May 23, 1988), he first used this phrase in front of reporters in 1985.

deep pockets **1.** Legal slang which refers to a person or organization with enough money to be worthy of being sued. **2.** By analogy, a reference to candidates for public office who have so much money in campaign contributions that others are discouraged from running against them.

deep throat A secret leaker; someone within an organization who gives secrets to an outsider. The original "Deep Throat" was the title of a pornographic film popular at the time of the 1972 WATERGATE scandal. When *The Washington Post* reporters needed a code name for their most secret "deep background" source on the illegal activities of President Richard M. Nixon and his associates, their managing editor humorously chose "deep throat." The identity of this source has never been formally revealed.

defamation of character The injuring of the good name or reputation of another. When this is done in writing, it is LIBEL. When done orally, it is SLANDER.

defendant Someone formally accused of a crime. A person becomes a defendant when a formal accusation is entered into the record of a court and remains so until the charge is dropped, the case is dismissed, or the court pronounces judgment (either acquittal or conviction).

defense 1. The armed forces of a state. **2.** All of the means, both overt and covert, by which a state defends and extends its military, economic, and social influence. **3.** NATIONAL SECURITY. **4.** A credible threat to other states that forestalls aggressive action. Such a credible threat takes varied forms. It could be the massive strategic and conventional forces maintained by the U.S. It could be strong allies. Or it could be a social and military reserve system which insures that the entire population, not just the regular military, would vigorously resist attack, as in Israel and Switzerland. **5.** An offense, in keeping with the military maxim that the best defense is a good offense. **6.** War, due to the fact that a nation's department of defense is in reality a department for war even though only defensive wars are contemplated.

Defense Intelligence Agency (DIA) A less well-known counterpart to the CENTRAL INTELLIGENCE AGENCY (CIA), which is a major actor in the U.S. intelligence community. The DIA is essentially an analysis and research organization whose major source of intelligence comes from the service attachés in U.S. embassies. It employs a large staff of mainly civilian analysts, who report on all aspects of foreign countries (including U.S. allies) which might affect their military posture.

Defense, U.S. Department of (DOD) The federal agency, created by the NATIONAL SECURITY ACT amendments of 1949, responsible for providing the military forces needed to deter war and protect U.S. security. The major elements of these forces are the army, navy, marine corps, and air force, consisting of over a million men and women on active duty. The creation of a single Department of Defense to replace the separate departments of the War and Navy was a major effort to consolidate and integrate the military services and to obviate interservice rivalry. Critics of the Defense Department argue that interservice consolidation has not been achieved in any meaningful way because the department tends to function as a holding company for the individual services. One illustration of this is the fact that the individual service secretaries (army, navy, air force) are still retained.

deficit The amount by which an entity's expenditures exceed its revenues. With the federal government this is not a straightforward exercise in arithmetic because all sorts of budgetary gimmicks are used to make the deficit look smaller than it really is. For example, a ROSY SCENARIO typically overestimates tax revenues so the deficit will appear smaller.

deficit financing A situation in which a government's excess of outlays over receipts for a given period is financed primarily by borrowing from the public. Deficit financing, and especially the general acceptance of it by economic theorists, is largely a twentieth-century phenomenon. Depending on the economist you listen to, a large deficit is either considered to be a major drag on the economy or a significant stimulus. The national debt is the sum total of all federal deficits and interest currently owed to holders of federal government securities, such as Treasury bills and savings bonds. *Compare to* CROWDING OUT; KEYNES, JOHN MAYNARD.

defining moment **1.** An incident in a political campaign that establishes for the public the nature of the campaign or the candidate. Defining moments may be spontaneous, but more often are planned. An example of a planned moment during the 1988 presidential campaign is Vice President George Bush's visit to a flag factory where he draped himself with the flag as a photo opportunity for reporters. **2.** The pivotal event of a new era. The German invasion of Poland in 1930 was certainly a defining moment because it started World War II. Whether the Iraqi invasion of Kuwait in 1990 is a defining moment because it led to the creation of a NEW WORLD ORDER, as Secretary of State James Baker has suggested, remains to be seen.

de jure A Latin phrase meaning "by right; by law." *See also* DE FACTO.

delegate **1.** An accredited representative to a national nominating convention. **2.** A member of the lower house of the legislature in Maryland, Virginia, and West Virginia. **3.** A representative to the U.S. House of Representatives from the District of Columbia (since 1971), Guam (since 1973), the Virgin Islands (since 1973), and American Samoa (since 1981). Delegates can participate in House debates but are not permitted to vote on the floor. They can serve on committees, and they possess the powers and privileges of committee members. Puerto Rico has had similar representation in the House since 1946, but its representative is called a resident commissioner. **4.** A legislator who assumes the role of a conduit for constituency opinions as opposed to a Burkean TRUSTEE. *See* BURKE, EDMUND; FIDUCIARY.

delegate, super A new category of national convention delegate created by the Democrats in 1984 to make sure that elected public officials as well as party officials are able to attend the convention as delegates. Super delegates are chosen by congressional caucuses and state conventions and are intended to give the party leadership a greater voice at the convention.

delegated powers The ENUMERATED POWERS and the IMPLIED POWERS that the Constitution of the United States grants to the national government. These are often contrasted with the RESERVED POWERS granted to the state governments.

delegation **1.** A group sent to represent a larger group. For example, a state level political party would send a delegation to its party's national convention. **2.** The official party sent to an international conference. **3.** The specific powers granted to an agency or individual. For example, a diplomat's authority in a given situation is his or her "delegation."

delegation of power The empowering of one to act for another. The delegation of power from one part of government to another and from one official to another is fundamental to American government. Article I, Section 8, of the U.S. Constitution enumerates the powers of the Congress and then grants to the Congress the power "to make all laws which shall be necessary and proper for carrying into execution the foregoing powers, and all other powers vested by this Constitution in the government of the United States, or in any department or officer thereof." But how explicit must such laws be? If the Congress were to attempt to legislate in such a fashion to give complete direction to administrative officials, it would result in an unworkable government. Every contingency would have to be anticipated in advance; the legislature would have to be expert in all phases of all policy areas. Moreover, changes in the nature of implementing statutes would have to be accomplished by new laws; the congressional work load would be crushing. Consequently, the Congress typically avoids writing highly detailed legislation, preferring to state broad policy objectives and allowing administrators to choose the means of attaining them.

While administrative discretion is clearly necessary, it can raise important constitutional questions. If the delegation is so broad as to allow administrators to exercise legislative power without congressional guidance or standards, then the requirements of the separation of powers may be breached. This issue is of great importance, because the Congress does tend to delegate important questions of public policy to administrative officials, rather than come to grips with the questions itself. Excellent examples of this can be found in the areas of equal opportunity for minorities, women, and the handicapped. Certainly, the administratively chosen means of affirmative action have been more controversial and politicized than the legislatively enacted end of equal opportunity.

deliberate speed The pace of new policy implementation; for example, of school integration. The Supreme Court held in *Brown v Board of Education of Topeka, Kansas* that school integration should proceed "with all deliberate speed." This is a good example of the Court's use of a vague word to avoid dealing head on with a difficult policy problem. While this phrase is most associated with the *Brown* decision, it has a long history. For example, Justice OLIVER WENDELL HOLMES, JR., in *Virginia v West Virginia* (1911), said: "A question like the present should be disposed of without undue delay. But a State cannot be expected to move with the celerity of a private business man; it is enough if it proceeds, in the language of the English Chancery, with all deliberate speed."

demagogue 1. A political leader accused of seeking or gaining power through the use of arguments designed to appeal to a mass public's sentiments, even though critics may consider those arguments exaggerated or spurious. The term is loaded and is never considered a compliment except as an indirect way of referring to a politician's rhetorical powers. Derived from the Greek *demagogos,* meaning a leader of the people, the term is one of the most time-honored epithets thrown at successful opposition politicians. **2.** The archetypal ruthless but charismatic politician who longs for power for its own sake and is loose with the truth, the law, and the public's purse. Well-known American demagogues include Huey R. Long (1893–1935) of Louisiana and Joseph McCarthy (1903–1957) of Wisconsin (see MCCARTHYISM). Of course, one person's demagogue may be another's honorable advocate of good government. Dead demagogues often make good subjects for writers. Robert Penn Warren (1905–) won the Pulitzer Prize for fiction for his 1946 novelization of Huey Long's life, *All the King's Men.* And when it was made into a movie, it won an Academy Award for best picture of 1949. More than 20 years later, T. Harry Williams (1909–) won the Pulitzer Prize in biography for his definitive account of Long's life, *Huey Long* (1969). **3.** According to author James Fenimore Cooper in *The American Democrat* (1838), a "demagogue is . . . a detractor of others, a professor of humility and disinterestedness, a great stickler for equality as respects all above him, a man who acts in corners, and avoids open and manly expositions of his course, calls blackguards gentlemen, and gentlemen folks, appeals to passions and prejudices rather than to reason, and is in all respects, a man of intrigue and deception, of sly cunning and management."

democracy   The Greek concept of rule by the ordinary populace, the plebian public, whose well-being was necessary for the stability of the state but whose judgment could not necessarily be trusted in the management of the state. The growth of democracy as an ideal thus depended upon the slow evolution of classes of educated and experienced citizens, whose capacity to govern themselves and others depended on the transformation of ways of understanding and interpreting the will of the people—although not necessarily giving the people the power to exercise that will for themselves.

The development of concepts of popular or universal democracy in the nineteenth century, known in various parts of the world as POPULISM, rested on a much stronger faith in individual intuition and universal rights, regardless of education or social status, and led in turn to new revolutionary conceptions of democracy that called for the placing of all power in the people. The problem of constructing a state that could exercise that power resulted in debates over the definition of the state that ranged from anarchy, or total absence of the state, through socialism and various forms of state control of industrial production and public welfare, to totalitarianism, or total control of all the people by an all-powerful state acting on their behalf. Thus, the term democracy is often used by totalitarian regimes and their people's democracies. One person's democratic regime is another's totalitarian despotism; democracy, like beauty, is in the eye of the beholder.

DEMOCRACY, BOURGEOIS

By becoming a term that could be used to describe so broad a range of institutional possibilities, democracy has thus tended to lose its meaning in political debate—but not its vitality. It continues to serve as an ideal over which political debate can take place. As novelist and essayist George Orwell wrote in "Politics and the English Language" (*Selected Essays*, 1957): "In the case of a word like democracy not only is there no agreed definition but the attempt to make one is resisted from all sides . . . . The defenders of any kind of regime claim that it is a democracy, and fear that they might have to stop using the word if it were tied down to any one meaning."

The founders of the United States were rightly suspicious of the pure democracy available to the free male citizens of ancient Athens. As Aristotle had warned, time and again throughout history pure democracies had degenerated into dictatorial tyrannies. John Adams wrote in an April 15, 1814 letter to John Taylor: "Remember, democracy never lasts long. It soon wastes, exhausts, and murders itself. There never was a democracy yet that did not commit suicide." This well-justified fear of the mob led the founders to create a REPUBLIC, a form of government one step removed from democracy, that presumably protects the people from their own passions. The frustration of coming to grips with the concept and the reality of democracy is illustrated by Winston Churchill's remark in the House of ElCommons on November 11, 1947, that "no one pretends that democracy is perfect or allwise. Indeed, it has been said that democracy is the worst form of government except all those other forms that have been tried from time to time."

democracy, bourgeois A Marxist phrase of contempt for modern western-style democratic government because it only really represents the middle and upper classes at the expense of the poor proletariat.

democracy, constitutional Any system of democratic governance that places formal limits, by means of a constitution, on what government can do. The United States, while a REPUBLIC in structure, is a constitutional democracy in concept. Thomas Jefferson wrote in 1798: "In questions of power, then, let no more be heard of confidence in man, but bind him down from mischief by the chains of the Constitution." *Compare to* CONSTITUTIONALISM.

democracy, direct Any governing system in which decisions are made directly by the people, as opposed to being made by elected representatives. Examples of direct democracy include the political meetings of male citizens in the ancient Greek city-states and the New England town meeting. More modern forms of direct democracy include such processes as the initiative, the referendum, and the recall, which allow citizens to directly enact laws or to remove officials by voting.

democracy, economic An equality of economic rights, which parallels the equality of political rights possessed by all citizens. In an economic democracy, citizens would have a right to a job, decent housing, and so on.

Democracy in America *See* TOCQUEVILLE, ALEXIS DE.

democracy, Jacksonian The move toward equalitarianism in American politics and social life, dating from Andrew Jackson's election as President in 1828. It signaled the disappearance of the aristocratic tradition in politics by rejecting Thomas Jefferson's notion of a natural aristocracy and upheld in its place the notion that the desires of the common people should rule in all things.

democracy, Jeffersonian Thomas Jefferson's ideals of a limited government for an agrarian society: freedom of religion, speech, and the press; a natural aristocracy, who ought to rule; laissez-faire economic policies; and strong state governments allied with a relatively weak constitutional government at the national level.

democracy, participatory The direct involvement of individuals and groups in the decision-making processes of government. This is often manifested by citizen participation in the planning and implementation activities of the various government agencies by interest groups and individuals. Many laws have built-in features of participatory democracy, such as hearings (where the public may testify) preliminary to changes, such as in rules, regulations, and tax rates. The new LEFT picked up on this theme when, in the 1960s, it called for citizen control of local public services. The main problem with participatory democracy is that self-appointed spokespersons for the people often have a disproportionate impact on public policy; the situation may all too quickly turn oligarchic, rather than democratic.

democracy, people's A communist regime. This is in no way comparable to democracy as practiced in the western world.

democracy, pluralistic A governing system in which real power is held by various groups and institutions that, from time to time, combine to advance the interests, the causes, and the people they represent. American government is often analyzed as a pluralistic democracy. *Compare to* PLURALISM.

democracy, procedural The elective process whereby citizens reaffirm their commitment to popular government and confer legitimacy on elected political leaders.

democracy, representative A form of governance in which the citizens rule through representatives, who are periodically elected in order to keep them accountable. The United States, as a REPUBLIC, is a representative democracy.

democrat A person who espouses belief in the core principles of democracy—that all power in government is ultimately derived from the will of the people. *Compare to* REPUBLICAN.

Democrat A member of the Democratic party.

Democrat party A mildly offensive REPUBLICAN term for the Democratic party, a way of reminding the Democrats that they may not be the only democratic party.

Democrat, tory A pro-business conservative Democrat. A tory is a conservative in modern Britain. Historically, the tories were the strongest supporters of the British monarchy.

Democrat, yellow dog A really loyal Democrat. How loyal? So loyal he'd vote for a yellow dog if it ran as a Democrat.

Democratic-Farmer-Labor Party (DFL) The name of the Democratic Party in Minnesota. This came about in 1944 when the Democrats merged with a local third party, the Farmer-Labor Party. The key person in the successful merger was HUBERT H. HUMPHREY, who was elected Mayor of Minneapolis on the DFL ticket in 1945.

democratic government Any form of government which is effectively able to translate citizen preferences into actual government policies.

Democratic Leadership Council (DLC) Washington-based organization formed in 1985 by Democratic senators, representatives, governors; it seeks to establish an intellectual and philosophical basis for a new national leadership by appealing to the political mainstream.

Democratic Party One of the two main parties in American politics. The Democratic party traces its origins to the Democratic-Republican party of Thomas Jefferson. In 1828, under Andrew Jackson, the party took its current name. The ideals of the party have from the beginning tended toward greater egalitarianism and the abolition of special privilege, but it had difficulty living up to its ideals so long as the party favored slavery. Once that issue was decided by the Civil War, the party in the South took a "whites only" orientation. The first major change in this attitude came about when, under the leadership of HUBERT H. HUMPHREY and President Harry S Truman, the party accepted a civil rights plank in the platform approved at the 1948 national convention. This was the first major split in the traditionally SOLID SOUTH, which defected and formed its own third party that year, the DIXIECRATS. But the Democratic party was able to win the White House without them. The party's appeal to blacks was solidified when the Democrats under President Lyndon B. Johnson sponsored the Civil Rights Act of 1964 and the Voting Rights Act of 1965. Now, most black Americans are solidly and influentially in the Democratic camp. Since the New Deal coalition of Franklin D. Roosevelt, the Democrats have been the leading party (*see* PARTY IDENTIFICATION) in terms of sheer numbers; but since the election of Ronald Reagan in 1980, their lead has grown much smaller. The Democratic party in recent decades has had a reputation for being liberal, for appealing to low-income groups, for expanding civil rights protection, and for believing that government is a legitimate vehicle for solving social problems.

democratic socialism Socialism achieved by democratic means (through honest elections), as opposed to socialism imposed by force. *Compare to* SOCIAL DEMOCRACY.

Democratic Study Group *See* LEGISLATIVE SERVICE ORGANIZATIONS.

democratization The gradual installation of collective choice and majority rule in social institutions (schools, churches, factories), not just in the government institutions.

deniability The prearranged insulation of a political executive from a decision that he or she actually made, but is later able to plausibly deny because there is no paper or other trail that would lead to him or her. Arrangements for deniability are important parts of covert actions and diplomacy. As John M. Poindexter, the former national security adviser to President Ronald Reagan, testified in the Iran-Contra hearings on July 15, 1987: "I made a very deliberate decision not to ask the President so that I could insulate him from the decision [to use funds from arms sales to Iran to pay for CONTRA operations] and provide some future deniability for the President if it ever leaked out."

denouncement *See* CENSURE.

department **1.** A CABINET-level agency of the U.S. government. **2.** One of the three branches of government: executive, legislative, or judicial. **3.** A general term for any administrative subdivision. **4.** Usually the largest and most important administrative agencies at all levels of government. **5.** A ministry in a country using a PARLIAMENTARY SYSTEM of government.

department head The chief executive officer of a government department; sometimes called a secretary, as in secretary of State.

depression *See* RECESSION, GREAT DEPRESSION.

deregulation The lifting of restrictions on business, industry, and other professional activities for which government rules were established and bureaucracies created to administer. The modern movement toward deregulation, which really began during the Carter Administration under the leadership of the Civil Aeronautics Board, was supported by both parties, but for different reasons. Republicans tended to support it because they were inclined to be philosophically hostile toward government interference with business in the first place. Democrats tended to support it because they felt that greater market competition would bring down prices for the consumer. *See also* REGULATION.

détente **1.** A French word meaning "the easing of strained relations." In diplomatic usage, this refers to the lessening of military and diplomatic tensions between two countries. **2.** The term used to describe Soviet-American relations in the 1970s, which included political summit conferences, economic agreements leading to increased trade, and strategic arms limitations (SALT) agreements. It is generally conceded that this era of détente ended with the Soviet invasion of Afghanistan in December 1979, American retaliatory sanctions against the Soviet Union in 1980 (notably the grain embargo and the boycott of the Moscow Olympic Games), the shelving by the Senate of the SALT II treaty, and the election of Ronald Reagan as President in November 1980. *Compare to* COLD WAR; CONTAINMENT.

deterrence The prevention of an action by fear of the consequences. Deterrence is a state of mind brought about by the existence of a credible threat of unacceptable counteraction; it is the foundation of American defense policy. The basic argument is that, as long as a potential enemy believes that the United States is capable of responding to an attack with a devastating counterattack, there will be no war. Therefore, a massive defense establishment is essential to maintain the peace. In some ways deterrence has always been the role of all military forces except those specifically intended for wars of conquest. In its broadest use, deterrence means any strategy, force position, or policy which is intended to persuade a potential enemy not to attack.

deterrent effect Discouraging people from doing something through policies or laws designed to prevent the unwanted behavior. Deterrence, which seems to have worked well as a matter of defense policy, has had a poorer record of success in the domestic arena: some people will violate the law no matter how severe the penalties. A classic example of a sentence designed to have a deterrent effect concerned Alferd E. Packer, who had murdered and eaten five companions during an 1873 Colorado blizzard. Packer's cannibalism was tainted with politics, so the judge at Packer's trial, M. B. Gerry, said: "Stand up, you man-eating son-of-a-bitch, and receive your sentence! There were seven Democrats in Hinsdale County, but you, you voracious, man-eating son-of-a-bitch, you ate five of them. I sentence you to be hanged by the neck until you're dead, dead, dead, as a warning against reducing the Democratic population of the state." *American Heritage* (October 1977) reports that while the judge's outburst was probably apocryphal, Packer was hanged.

devaluation 1. The lowering of the value of a nation's currency in relation to gold, or to the currency of other countries, when this value is set by government intervention in the exchange market. Devaluation normally refers to fixed exchange rates. In a system of flexible rates, if the value of the currency falls, it is referred to as depreciation; if the value of the currency rises, it is referred to as appreciation. **2.** A diplomatic stratagem whereby something once considered of great value in negotiations is deliberately, as a matter of policy, considered of less value than it was before. For example, after the Iran-Contra scandal broke, the Reagan administration "devalued" the American hostages held in Lebanon.

DHHS *See* HEALTH AND HUMAN SERVICES, DEPARTMENT OF.

dicta 1. A synonym for obiter dictum, a digression of a court. **2.** In the context of arbitration, an opinion or recommendation an arbitrator expresses in making an award that is not essential to the resolution of the dispute.

dictator The ancient Roman republic's term for the leader to whom was given extraordinary powers in times of crisis. Under the republic, the office was inherently temporary, but Julius Caesar and the Caesars who followed him gave the term its modern definition as a government in which one person or party controls all political action. In this century, the classic dictators, Adolf Hitler (1889–1945) of Germany and Benito Mussolini (1883–1945) of Italy, came to power as the leaders of mass movements. Others, such as Joseph Stalin (1879–1953) of the Soviet Union, rose to power by taking over a party that was already in control of a government. One should also differentiate between the dictators mentioned above, whose power was based on their personalities and control of force, and many modern dictators, such as the recent leaders of China and the Soviet Union, who tend to be just the "first among equals" within a ruling elite.

The United States has never had a dictator, although some political bosses have sometimes approached such powers at the local level and some Presidents, most notably Franklin D. Roosevelt, have been accused of seeking to become a dictator. The only President who had to face the real possibility of a dictatorship was Abraham Lincoln. During the Civil War, General Joseph Hooker (1814–1878) publicly stated that the country needed a dictator. Lincoln responded by writing to him on January 26, 1863, that "I have heard, in such a way as to believe it, of your recently saying that both the army and the government needed a dictator. Of course, it was not for this, but in spite of it, that I have given you the command. Only those generals who gain successes can set up dictators. What I now ask of you is a military success, and I will risk the dictatorship." Because Hooker wasn't a very successful general, the question never came up again.

dilatory motion A legislative motion, usually made upon a technical point, for the purpose of killing time and preventing action on a bill. Legislative rules usually outlaw dilatory motions, but enforcement is largely within the discretion of the presiding officer.

Dillon's rule The criteria developed by state courts to determine the nature and extent of powers granted to municipal corporations. It is a very strict and limiting rule, stating that municipal corporations have only those powers (1) expressly granted in the city charter, (2) necessarily or fairly implied by or incidental to formally expressed powers, and (3) essential to the declared purposes of the corporation. "Any fair, reasonable, substantial doubt" about a power is to result in denying that power to the corporation. The rule was formulated by Iowa judge John F. Dillon (1831–1941) in his *Commentaries on the Law of Municipal Corporations* (5th ed., 1911). In some states, the rule has been relaxed, especially in dealing with home rule cities. The essence of Dillon's rule was upheld by the Supreme Court in *City of Trenton v State of New Jersey* (1913).

diminishing marginal utility of income The principle that the value of an additional dollar of income to a rich person is less than its worth to a poor person. This concept underlies progressive taxation—proportionally larger tax payments by those with higher incomes. *Compare to* ABILITY TO PAY.

diplomacy 1. A state's foreign policy. While this is the most popular usage of the term, a policy in itself is not diplomacy. Foreign policies, made by governments or heads of state, represent the ends or goals of a nation's diplomacy. The word comes from the Greek *diploma*, which means a document that has been folded twice. This was a reference to the format of state papers and letters historically carried by diplomats. **2.** The formal relations that independent nations maintain with each other; in effect, all of the normal and idiosyncratic intentional communications between nations short of war. Indeed, it is often said that diplomacy has failed when war begins. On the other hand, many nations throughout history have taken Karl von Clausewitz's attitude that war is only the continuation of diplomacy "by other means." **3.** The art of maintaining and conducting international relations and negotiations. **4.** According to Ambrose Bierce's *The Devil's Dictionary* (1911), "The patriotic art of lying for one's country."

diplomacy, dollar **1.** The expansion of American business overseas. **2.** A pejorative term for those diplomatic and military efforts that seek to help American business penetrate into foreign markets. **3.** The foreign policy of the William Howard Taft administration (1909–1913), which actively sought to expand American trade in Latin America. **4.** Diplomatic efforts to stabilize the American dollar in international currency markets.

diplomatic privileges and immunities The special rights accorded to formally accredited diplomatic officials, particularly immunity from the civil and criminal laws of the nation to which they are assigned. This immunity also applies to the physical grounds of an embassy, which is technically considered the soil of the foreign government. Abuses of diplomatic immunity often receive widespread publicity. They range from the unpaid parking tickets of United Nations diplomats in New York City to the use of diplomatic offices as centers for terrorism against the host country. The most outrageous abuse of diplomatic immunity by a host government in recent times was the IRANIAN HOSTAGE CRISIS.

diplomatic recognition The establishment of formal diplomatic relations with a regime. The granting or withholding of such recognition is a powerful tool of foreign policy. The whole history of the United States might have been different if the United Kingdom had recognized the Confederacy during the American Civil War. The new state of Israel achieved immediate international legitimacy because of United States recognition. Whether or not to recognize communist China was a major issue of American politics from the late 1940s to the Nixon Administration's rapprochement in the 1970s. British Prime Minister Winston Churchill, in a November 17, 1949, speech in the House of Commons on the recognition of Communist China, said: "Recognizing a person is not necessarily an act of approval. ... One has to recognize lots of things and people in this world of sin and woe that one does not like. The reason for having diplomatic relations is not to confer a compliment, but to secure a convenience."

diplomatic service That branch of a nation's civil service which provides the personnel who staff its foreign missions. In the United States, the employees who represent their nation overseas are often members of the Department of State's FOREIGN SERVICE and are known as foreign service officers.

direct legislation The use of techniques of direct democracy, such as the INITIATIVE, the REFERENDUM, or the RECALL.

direct mail 1. A method of selling a product directly to a customer, using the mail as the vehicle for both advertising and solicitation. **2.** An increasingly popular way to solicit political campaign contributions and volunteers. It is often thought that large donors are the prime financial supporters of candidates for major offices. Not so. The reality is that the small donor is the backbone of most modern campaign finances—and the best, most economical, most efficient, and most cost effective way to reach them is through direct mail. But direct mail may also ask for campaign volunteers and ask that letters be written to members of Congress opposing or supporting a given issue. Or it could simply ask that the recipient vote for a particular candidate and send money to pay for more direct mail.

dirty tricks 1. The covert operations of an intelligence agency. Former Secretary of State Dean Rusk once said: "Dirty tricks form about 5 percent of the CIA's work—and we must have full control over dirty tricks" (*New York Times*, January 22, 1971). **2.** Dishonorable acts during a political campaign by the opposition or by pranksters. Examples include starting false rumors, creating scandals with forged evidence, and disrupting campaign schedules. Milder dirty tricks may be classified as jokes or political humor. For example, during the 1968 presidential contest the slogan widely used by Richard Nixon's supporters during the national convention was "Nixon's the One!" In response a prankster hired an obviously pregnant woman to picket the hotel where Nixon had his convention headquarters carrying a "Nixon's the One!" sign.

disarmament The recurring efforts of the major powers to put limits on their war-making capabilities. General and complete disarmament has never made much progress, although the United Nations does have it as an official policy goal. Clearly it runs into tremendous definitional problems, as well as being simply utopian in its impracticality. The classic statement on disarmament comes from *The Bible*: "They shall beat their swords into plowshares, and their spears into pruning-hooks; nation shall not lift up sword against nation, neither shall they learn war any more" (Isaiah, 11,4). But Niccolo Machiavelli in *The Prince* (1513) warned: "Among other evils which being unarmed brings you, it causes you to be despised." Winston Churchill in speech in the House of Commons, July 13, 1934 felt that: "It is the greatest possible mistake to mix up disarmament with peace. When you have peace you will have disarmament." *Compare to* ARMS CONTROL.

discharge a committee To relieve a legislative committee from jurisdiction over a measure that is before it. In the U.S. House of Representatives, if a committee does not report a bill within 30 days after the bill is referred to it, any member may file a discharge motion to bring the bill to the floor for consideration. This motion, treated as a petition, needs the signatures of 218 members (a majority of the House). If a resolution to consider a bill is held up in the Rules Committee for more than seven legislative days, any member may enter a motion to discharge the committee. The motion is handled like any other discharge motion in the House. Occasionally, to expedite noncontroversial legislative business, a committee is discharged upon unanimous consent of the House, and a petition is not required. Discharge motions are rarely successful.

discharge resolution In the U.S. Senate, a special motion that any senator may introduce to relieve a committee from consideration of a bill that is before it. The resolution can be called up on motion for approval or disapproval, in the same manner as other matters of Senate business.

discomfort index *See* MISERY INDEX.

discount rate The interest rate paid by a commercial bank when it borrows from a Federal Reserve Bank. The discount rate is one of the tools of monetary policy used by the Federal Reserve System. The Federal Reserve customarily raises or lowers the discount rate to signal a shift toward restraining or toward easing its money and credit policy.

discrimination 1. Bigotry in practice; intolerance towards those who have different beliefs or different religions. **2.** In employment, the failure to treat equals equally. Whether deliberate or unintentional, any action that has the effect of limiting employment and advancement opportunities because of an individual's sex, race, color, age, national origin, religion, physical handicap, or other irrelevant criteria, is discrimination. Because of the equal employment opportunity and civil rights legislation of recent years, people aggrieved by unlawful discrimination now have a variety of administrative and judicial remedies open to them. **3.** Inequity of trade treatment accorded one or more exporting nations by an importing nation. This may take the form of preferential tariff rates for imports from particular countries, or trade restrictions that apply to the exports of certain countries but not to similar goods from other countries. *Compare to* MOST-FAVORED-NATION.

disinformation 1. A term used in intelligence work to refer to the purposeful lies that a government overtly or covertly releases to the international mass media in order to mislead or embarrass adversary nations. For example, it was a Soviet disinformation campaign that spread the rumor that the deadly AIDS virus was created in a U.S. military laboratory and is now being spread around the world by U.S. servicemen. The Americans use disinformation too. After the 1986 U.S. air raid on Libya the Reagan administration purposely planted news stories that the Libyan leader Colonel Muammar al-Qaddafi had top aides that were plotting a coup and that the U.S. was planning another raid, all in an effort to destabilize the Libyan government. **2.** The secret transmitting of false information to rival intelligence agencies. **3.** The lies that a government tells its own people in order to hide actions that would be considered unacceptable and possibly "checked" by another branch of government if known. As NICCOLO MACHI-AVELLI advises in *The Prince* (1513): "men are so simple and so ready to obey present necessities, that one who deceives will always find those who allow themselves to be deceived." *Compare to* PROPAGANDA.

dissent **1.** Political disagreement. President Dwight D. Eisenhower in a May 31, 1954 speech said: "Here in America we are descended in blood and in spirit from revolutionaries and rebels—men and women who dared to dissent from accepted doctrine. As their heirs, may we never confuse honest dissent with disloyal subversion." Earlier, on a March 7, 1954 TV news program, *See It Now*, journalist Edward R. Murrow attacked Senator Joseph McCarthy by saying: "We must not confuse dissent with disloyalty." **2.** A minority opinion of a court. *See* OPINION, MINORITY. **3.** The title of a liberal journal.

distinguished **1.** Eminent or famous. **2.** What all U.S. Senators are; at least that is how they address each other—as the "distinguished Senator from" this or that state. Senator Edward W. Brooke once said: "If we [in the Senate] stop calling each other 'distinguished,' we might save 10 working days [a year]" (*Los Angeles Times*, January 1, 1971).

district A subdivision of an area (such as a country, state, or county) for judicial, political, or administrative purposes. Districting is the process of drawing a district's boundary lines for purposes of APPORTIONMENT.

district attorney The county official, usually elected, who initiates prosecutions against criminals. Variously called county attorney or county prosecutor as well. Federal government prosecutions in federal courts, in contrast, are undertaken by U.S. Attorneys. Prosecuting attorneyships, whether county or federal, offer great visibility to ambitious lawyers. Many a national political career started in the district attorney's office.

district, competitive An electoral district in which a challenger to the incumbent has a chance to win; a seat that is not safe.

district court Also known as federal district court or U.S. district court, the court of original jurisdiction for most federal cases. This is the only federal court that holds trials in which juries and witnesses are used. Each state has at least one district court. Altogether, there are 89 district courts in the 50 states, plus one in the District of Columbia. In addition, the Commonwealth of Puerto Rico has a U.S. district court with jurisdiction corresponding to that of district courts in the various states. At present, each district court has from one to 27 federal district judgeships, depending upon the amount of judicial work within its territory. In districts with more than one judge, the judge senior in commission who has not reached his or her seventieth birthday acts as chief judge. There are altogether 485 permanent district judgeships in the 50 states and 15 in the District of Columbia. There are seven district judgeships in Puerto Rico. *Compare to* COURT OF APPEALS.

district cracking Drawing legislative district lines so as to minimize a party's strength by splitting its most likely supporters among several districts. *Compare to* DISTRICT PACKING.

district, majority-minority A legislative district in which the majority of the voters are members of a minority group; such districts are in consequence highly likely to elect a minority group member to represent them. *See also* GERRYMANDERING, AFFIRMATIVE.

district, multimember Any electoral district that elects more than one candidate to a legislature at the same time. This is often the case with AT-LARGE seats on a city council. The Supreme Court has held in *White v Register* (1973) that it is unconstitutional for a multimember district to deprive a racial minority within the district of meaningful access to political representation. But multimember districts, according to *Whitcomb v Chavis* (1971), are not automatically unconstitutional simply because minorities would do better politically under a single-member district system.

district, open A legislative district in which the incumbent legislator is not running for reelection. This means that none of the candidates will have the advantage of the INCUMBENCY EFFECT.

district packing Drawing legislative district lines so as to include as many of one party's voters as possible. This makes the seat safe for an incumbent. *Compare to* DISTRICT CRACKING.

district, single-member Any electoral district that elects only one candidate (chosen by a plurality) to a legislature, such as a city council, state assembly, or the U.S. House of Representatives.

diversity of citizenship The situation that exists when the parties in a lawsuit come from different states. Article III, Section 2, of the U.S. Constitution gives jurisdiction in such cases to the federal courts. But the Congress has since given exclusive jurisdiction for these cases to state courts if no federal question is involved and any amount in question is less than $10,000. Above that, there is CONCURRENT JURISDICTION.

Dixiecrats Southern Democrats who opposed their party's presidential nomination of Harry S Truman in 1948 because of his civil rights policies. They subsequently ran their own candidate for President (J. Strom Thurmond, now a Republican senator from South Carolina) and lost; but they carried five Southern states.

doctrine **1.** A legal principle or rule, such as the FAIRNESS DOCTRINE. **2.** A foreign policy, such as the MONROE DOCTRINE or TRUMAN DOCTRINE. **3.** The principles by which military forces guide their actions in support of objectives. *See also* CARTER DOCTRINE; EISENHOWER DOCTRINE; NIXON DOCTRINE; REAGAN DOCTRINE.

DOD *See* DEFENSE, U.S. DEPARTMENT OF.

DOE *See* EDUCATION, U.S. DEPARTMENT OF; ENERGY, U.S. DEPARTMENT OF.

do gooders A derisive term for social and political reformers. Do gooders are often joined by goo-goos, advocates of good government.

DOI *See* INTERIOR, U.S. DEPARTMENT OF THE.

DOL *See* LABOR, U.S. DEPARTMENT OF.

domicile A person's permanent legal residence. While a person can legally have many residences, he or she can have only one domicile. Some government jurisdictions require their employees to be domiciled within the bounds of that jurisdiction. *Compare to* VOTING RESIDENCE.

domino theory The notion that if a critically situated country falls to communism, its neighbors will soon follow. This was a major element in the rationale for American involvement in the Vietnam War. Biographer Doris Kearns quotes President Johnson in *Lyndon Johnson and the American Dream* (1976): "I knew that if the aggression succeeded in South Vietnam, then the aggressors would simply keep on going until all of Southeast Asia fell into their hands, slowly or quickly." President Richard M. Nixon would later say: "Now I know there are those that say, 'Well, the domino theory is obsolete.' They haven't talked to the dominoes" (*The New York Times*, July 3, 1970). The domino metaphor was first popularized by President Dwight D. Eisenhower in a press conference on April 7, 1954, with reference to the strategic importance of Indochina. He said: "You have a row of dominoes set up. You knock over the first one, and what will happen to the last one is a certainty that it will go over very quickly." The domino theory has not proved very useful as a predictor of communist expansion, because it is sometimes true and sometimes not. Most recently, the Reagan Administration analyzed the dangers presented by the left-wing government in Nicaragua in the same way: if Nicaragua stayed communist, they believed the rest of Central America would follow, and eventually Mexico as well, leaving the United States with an enemy at its southern border. Nevertheless, the domino theory remains a general justification for taking action in a given instance, because failure to do so would produce effects on neighboring nations.

donkey The symbol of the Democratic party, first used by caricaturist Thomas Nast (1840–1902) in 1874 in a series of cartoons that expounded upon Republican politician Ignatius Donnelly's (1831–1901) critical comment that "the Democratic party is like a mule—without pride of ancestry nor hope of posterity." *Compare to* ELEPHANT.

double jeopardy The Fifth Amendment requirement that no person "be subject for the same offense to be twice put in jeopardy of life or limb." This clause prevents retrials in either state or federal court of those already tried once—and thus placed in "jeopardy" once. Jeopardy attaches not only after a prior conviction or acquittal but also in jury trials once the jury is sworn in and, in trials without juries, once the introduction of evidence has begun. Thereafter, if for some reason the trial is terminated, a second trial is barred, except in limited circumstances. Such circumstances include those cases in which mistrials are declared at the request or with the consent of the defendant or in cases of manifest necessity, such as when the jury deadlocks or when illness or death prevents continuation of a trial. A second trial is also permissible when an appellate court sets aside a guilty verdict and orders a new trial.

The double jeopardy clause offers no protection when conduct violates both federal and state law; the Supreme Court has held in *Bartkus v Illinois* (1958) that an offender may be prosecuted in the courts of both jurisdictions. Neither does the clause prevent the multiple prosecutions of a suspect for conduct that constitutes more than one offense, though factual issues decided by one jury may prevent relitigation of those factual issues in a subsequent trial. Furthermore, if a defendant obtains a reversal of a conviction and is retried, the clause does not prevent an increase of penalty in the event that the defendant is reconvicted, although due process requires the sentencing judge to demonstrate that the penalty was not increased to penalize the defendant for exercising the right to appeal. The Supreme Court held in *Benton v Maryland* (1969) that the Fifth Amendment prohibition on double jeopardy applies to the states through the Fourteenth Amendment.

double riding The giving of campaign contributions to both major candidates in an election; thus, the giver is assured of ACCESS no matter which side wins.

draft 1. The conscription of citizens into the armed services. The unpopularity of the Vietnam War made the draft politically untenable. Congress mandated that it end in 1973. However, draft registration is still required by law. The problem with conscription was summed up by Chesterfield Smith, then president of the American Bar Association: "A citizen of a free country should not be forced to fight in a war that neither he nor his elected representatives chose to initiate or declare" (*The Washington Post*, August 13, 1974). Muhammad Ali, heavyweight boxing champion, explained why he was refusing to be drafted thusly: "I ain't got no quarrel with them Viet Cong" (*New York Times*, January 11, 1967). The draft was also grossly unfair. According to Arthur T. Hadley's *The Straw Giant* (1986): "So pervasive was this practice of college deferment [during Vietnam] that the chief of Selective Service, General Lewis B. Hershey, bitterly remarked: 'In the Civil War it required $300 to escape service. In this war it requires sufficient funds to attend college.'" **2.** The nomination of a political candidate who has claimed disinterest by refusing to announce his or her candidacy or to go through the normal procedures that involve announced candidacy. It is a device that can be used to suggest vast popular support and an unwillingness to incur political indebtedness to obtain support. Only in the rarest of cases is someone drafted who was not encouraging the process from behind the scenes. One such rare person was William Tecumseh Sherman (1820–1891), the Civil War general who, upon being asked to be the Republican presidential nominee in 1884, said: "I will not accept if nominated and I will not serve if elected." The Shermanesque refusal is now the classic manner in which to genuinely refuse a draft.

Dred Scott v Sandford (1857) The second case in which the Supreme Court declared an act of the Congress (the Missouri Compromise) to be unconstitutional (the first was MARBURY V MADISON in 1803). Dred Scott (1795–1858) was a slave who was taken to a free state in the North. The question before the Court was whether residence in a free state was sufficient basis for declaring Scott a free man. The Supreme Court in a 7 to 2 ruling said no. The Chief Justice, Roger Brook Taney, wrote in the Court's opinion: "The right of property in a slave is distinctly and expressly affirmed in the Constitution. . . . No word can be found in the Constitution which gives Congress a greater power over slave property, or which entitles property of that kind to less protection than property of any other description." While it helped to further entrench the Court's right to judicial review, the Court's holdings—that blacks could not become citizens and that the United States could not prohibit slavery in unsettled territories—did much to make the Civil War inevitable, especially because the decision made a legislative solution to the slavery issue virtually impossible. The Dred Scott decision was overturned by the Thirteenth and Fourteenth Amendments.

duck test An empirical aid to the clarity of political discourse: "If it looks like a duck, quacks like a duck, and walks like a duck, then it must be a duck." This was a fashionable way of divining communists in the 1950s and taxes in the 1980s.

due process The constitutional requirement that "no person shall be deprived of life, liberty, or property without due process of law." While the specific requirements of due process vary with Supreme Court decisions, the essence of the idea is that people must be given adequate notice and a fair opportunity to present their side in a legal dispute, and that no law or government procedure should be arbitrary or unfair.

due process of law A right guaranteed by the Fifth, Sixth, and Fourteenth Amendments and generally understood to mean that legal proceedings will follow rules and forms established for the protection of private rights. The Fourteenth Amendment's provision that "no person shall be deprived of life, liberty, or property without due process of law" is considered to be a powerful restraint on government interference in the rights or property interests of citizens. However, the concept raises considerable questions regarding both the procedures themselves and the kinds of rights and interests protected by them. For the most part, these two elements are related, in that the more fundamental the right or interest, the greater the procedural protections. The degree of protection ranges from a jury trial and appellate processes to a hearing, perhaps including a right to counsel, confrontation, and cross-examination of adverse witnesses before an impartial examiner. Of course, there are instances in which citizens are adversely affected by administrative decisions but have no right or opportunity to be heard. In recent years, the most interesting developments in this area of constitutional law have been (1) the extension of the procedural safeguards afforded citizens at the hearing stage and (2) the extension of the right to have a hearing in situations previously not deemed sufficiently important to warrant such protections. Consider the procedural protections afforded public employees in dismissals; it has now been found that where constitutionally protected rights and interests are at stake, there may be a right to an open hearing, including counsel, confrontation, and cross-examination.

due process, procedural The legal process and machinery that ensures due process. Daniel Webster (1782–1852) gave the classic description of due process as that "which hears before it condemns, which proceeds upon inquiry, and renders judgment only after trial." Procedural due process thus requires the legal system to follow the rules.

due process, substantive The formal legal requirement that due process requirements be observed by government or its agents. Thomas M. Cooley's *Constitutional Limitations* (Boston: Little, Brown, 1868) is considered the doctrinal foundation of substantive due process in the United States. According to historian Bernard Schwartz in *The Law in America: A History* (1974), "Cooley identified due process with the doctrine of vested rights drawn from natural law, which had been developed to protect property rights. This meant that due process itself was the great substantive safeguard of property." It was "Cooley's analysis which prepared the way for the virtual takeover of American public law by the Due Process Clause of the Fourteenth Amendment." Thus, the threads of Cooley's analysis can be found whenever an American court strikes down an executive or legislative act for being arbitrary or unreasonable and thus lacking in substantive due process.

Dukakis, Michael (1933–   ) The Governor of Massachusetts (1975–1979; 1983–1991) who was the Democratic nominee for the presidency in 1988. He came out of the nominating convention with a significant lead in the polls over his Republican challenger, Vice President George Bush, but managed his campaign so ineptly that he allowed Bush, previously considered a waffling-on-the-issues WIMP, to win by a landslide.

dumping 1. Getting rid of a political candidate or supporter who has proven useless, unpopular, or embarrassing. **2.** Selling a product in export markets below that product's selling price in domestic markets. Rules created by countries to protect themselves from this practice are called antidumping laws. Additional tariffs that may be imposed on imports that have been dumped are called antidumping duties.

duty 1. A tax imposed on imported products. A duty is distinguished from a tariff solely by the fact that the duty is the actual tax imposed or collected, while the tariff, technically speaking, is the schedule of duties. However, in practice the words are often used interchangeably. **2.** A legal obligation to do something because of an office one holds, a profession one practices, and so on. But as George Bernard Shaw warns in *Caesar and Cleopatra,* Act III (1899): "When a stupid man is doing something he is ashamed of, he always declares that it is his duty." **3.** A moral obligation that, if left unfulfilled, would cause only a bruised conscience. **4.** The obligation of a person in military service to die for his or her country if circumstances warrant. According to Richard A. Gabriel and Paul L. Savage's, *Crisis in Command* (1978): "Military life . . . is unique in that it clearly levels upon the officer . . . responsibilities which transcend his career or material self-interest. . . . at some point an officer may be called upon to do his duty and 'be faithful unto death.'"

Duverger's law French political scientist Maurice Duverger's (1917–   ) assertion, from his *Political Parties: Their Organization and Activity in the Modern State* (1951, 1963), that "the simple-majority single-ballot system favours the two-party system. Of all the hypotheses that have been defined in this book, this approaches the most nearly perhaps to a true sociological law. An almost complete correlation is observable between the simple-majority single-ballot system and the two-party system: dualist countries use the simple-majority vote, and simple-majority vote countries are dualist. The exceptions are very rare and can generally be explained as the result of special conditions." Thus, according to Duverger's law, the strong American TWO-PARTY SYSTEM is very much a product of the simple-majority winner-take-all voting system, the norm in American elections. Any newly installed system of proportional representation in American politics would necessarily weaken the two-party system.

DWEMs Dead, White, European Males; a belittling reference to the great political thinkers and literary figures of western civilization.

dyed in the wool The most partisan of the partisans; one who cannot be converted; one who goes all out for his or her party. The phrase comes from the fact that wool dyed while still raw retains its color better than wool dyed after processing.

dynasty **1.** The passing of political power through a succession of rulers directly related by blood. **2.** An American political family, such as the Adamses, the Roosevelts, or the Kennedys, whose various members seek and gain political office over a long period of time.

E

e pluribus unum A Latin phrase meaning "one out of many": the motto on the Great Seal of the United States. The original use was from a poem, "Moretum," by the ancient Roman poet, Virgil (70–19 B.C.); his "e pluribus unus" was a salad composed of many ingredients.

early money The best kind of contribution a political campaign can have. It allows for rational planning, for buying the best media slots, and for early visibility so that the candidate can break out of the pack. Because early money is so critical, its contributors often have far more access and influence than those who later contribute as part of a BANDWAGON EFFECT.

Economic Advisers, Council of *See* COUNCIL OF ECONOMIC ADVISERS.

economic growth The increase in a nation's productive capacity, leading to an increase in the production of goods and services. Economic growth usually is measured by the annual rate of increase in real (constant dollars) GROSS NATIONAL PRODUCT.

economic indicators Measurements of various economic and business movements and activities in a community, such as employment, unemployment, hours worked, income, savings, volume of building permits, and volume of sales, whose fluctuations affect and may be used to determine overall economic trends. The various economic time series can be segregated into leaders, laggers, and coinciders in relation to movements in aggregate economic activity. *Compare to* LEADING INDICATORS.

economic nationalism 1. A desire to make a nation completely self-sufficient in terms of trade, so that it requires neither imports nor exports for its economic well-being; also known as autarchy or national self-sufficiency. **2.** Economic policies based on a nation's self-interest as opposed to those more concerned with the economic health of a larger sphere, such as a region, a political grouping (e.g., the third world, etc.), or the world economy in general. Economic nationalism often comes into effect through trade restrictions and other protectionist policies.

Economic Opportunity Act of 1964 The keystone of the Lyndon B. Johnson administration's WAR ON POVERTY. The act created the Job Corps, the office of Economic Opportunity, community action programs, and other work incentive programs. *See also* GREAT SOCIETY.

economic policy The processes by which a nation manages its trade, business, and finances. Economic policy generally consists of three dimensions—fiscal policy, monetary policy, and those other facets of public policy with economic implications (such as energy policy, farm policy, and labor union policy). The interaction of these policy dimensions is crucial, since none operate in a vacuum. While monetary policy basically exercises control over the quantity and cost (interest rates) of money and credit in the economy, fiscal policy deals with the sizes of budgets, deficits, and taxes. Other policy areas, such as housing policy (also dependent upon interest rates) and programs dependent upon deficit spending, involve aspects of both monetary and fiscal policy, and vice versa. However, their interrelationship does not exist with regard to implementation. Monetary policy, while receiving major inputs from the President and other executive agencies, is the responsibility of the Federal Reserve Board, an independent agency. Fiscal policy, while receiving similar inputs from the Federal Reserve Board, is primarily the responsibility of the President and the Congress. The degree of equality and subsequent share of responsibility varies within a stable range. While a President may wish to spend this or that amount, only the Congress has the constitutional ability to levy taxes (although tax laws, like any others, must be signed or vetoed by the President). Also limiting a President's discretion over economic policy is the fact that so much of it is controlled by prior funding decisions (e.g., welfare, entitlement, and pension programs), which are not easily changed. *See also* FISCAL POLICY; MONETARY POLICY; POLITICAL ECONOMY.

economic royalists Big business interests hostile to the concerns of ordinary people. President Franklin D. Roosevelt used this as a term of invective against the wealthy who opposed his NEW DEAL policies. In his acceptance speech at the Democratic National Convention in Philadelphia, June 27, 1936, he said: "The economic royalists complain that we seek to overthrow the institutions of America. What they really complain of is that we seek to take away their power. Our allegiance to American institutions requires the overthrow of this kind of power. . . . The royalists of the economic order have conceded that political freedom was the business of government, but they have maintained that economic slavery was nobody's business."

economic warfare **1.** An aggressive use of economic means to achieve national objectives. There are many levels of intensity to economic warfare. They range from freezing a foe's assets and confiscating its property during a formally declared war to using clandestine methods to destabilize an opponent's economy during a cold war. **2.** The normal peaceful competition between nations for markets and trade advantages.

economics, voodoo *See* VOODOO ECONOMICS.

economy, underground *See* UNDERGROUND ECONOMY.

Education, U.S. Department of (DOE) The cabinet-level department that establishes policy for, administers, and coordinates most federal assistance to education; created on October 17, 1979 by the Department of Education Organization Act, when the Department of Health, Education, and Welfare was divided in two. The Ronald Reagan administration pledged to eliminate DOE but bowed to political pressures and retained it as a platform for conservative stands on education policy.

EEO *See* EQUAL EMPLOYMENT OPPORTUNITY.

EEOC *See* EQUAL EMPLOYMENT OPPORTUNITY COMMISSION.

egghead An intellectual; a politician with a highbrow image; someone who reads serious books on a regular basis—when he or she doesn't have to for school. The term was first used in American politics to derisively refer to Adlai Stevenson (1900–1965) when he was the Democratic presidential nominee in 1952. It fit Stevenson because he was all that the word implied, and worse—he had a balding, egg-shaped head. Stevenson responded in good humor by paraphrasing Karl Marx: "Eggheads of the world unite; you have nothing to lose but your yolks."

Eighteenth Amendment The 1919 amendment to the U.S. Constitution that enacted prohibition—a legal ban on alcoholic beverages.

Eighth Amendment The amendment to the U.S. Constitution that prohibits excessive BAIL, excessive fines, and CRUEL AND UNUSUAL PUNISHMENTS. *See also* booth v maryland

Eisenhower Doctrine The 1957 statement of U.S. policy in the Middle East, which asserted that the United States would use force "to safeguard the independence of any country or group of countries in the Middle East requesting aid against aggression" from a communist country. This differs from other presidential doctrines in that it was adopted as a joint resolution of the Congress.

Eisenhower, Dwight David "Ike" (1890–1969) The President of the United States (1953–1961) who, as commander of U.S. forces in Europe, orchestrated the defeat of Germany in World War II. The returning war hero could have had the nomination of either major party. While he won the Republican nomination narrowly, he won the 1952 election overwhelmingly. In the midst of the frustrating "limited war" of Korea (*see* KOREAN WAR), Americans flocked to support a winning general who pledged: "I will go to Korea." Eisenhower wrote in his memoirs that the end to the war was achieved only after he threatened to use atomic weapons. "The lack of progress ... demanded, in my opinion, definite measures on our part to put an end to these intolerable conditions. One possibility was to let the Communist authorities understand that, in the absence of satisfactory progress, we intended to move decisively without inhibition in our use of weapons .... we dropped the word, discreetly, of our intention ....

Soon the prospects for armistice negotiations seemed to improve" (*The White House Years*, Vol. I, 1963). With the war over within six months (through a negotiated armistice), the rest of the Eisenhower years were noted for COLD WAR diplomacy and the lack of domestic initiatives. Yet this belies the fact that the Eisenhower administration was basically one of peace abroad and prosperity at home. In recent years, Eisenhower's reputation as a President has risen sharply, as the decade of the 1950s is compared to the years that followed. Analyses, like Fred Greenstein's *The Hid-*

den-Hand Presidency: Eisenhower as Leader (1982), have looked anew at Eisenhower's "hidden hand" style of leadership, which combined deft behind-the-scenes maneuvering with a public posture of a leader above the political fray. One innovation of the Eisenhower years that is still with us was a new candor about the President's health. After a heart attack in his first term, the President's bodily functions (or nonfunctions) became news. Now, any President's physical maladies are as legitimate a news story as a major foreign policy decision.

elastic clause *See* NECESSARY AND PROPER CLAUSE.

election 1. A process of selecting one person or more for an office, public or private, from a wider field of candidates. Thus, the public of a jurisdiction elects its highest officials, a corporation's stockholders elect their board of directors, and the members of a club or honorary society elect new members. In essence, an election is an aggregation of individual preferences and occurs whenever selection is not the will of a single decision maker. **2.** The government-administered process by which people, whether opposed or unopposed, seek a political party's nomination for, or election to, public office. In most of today's world, elections are the only legitimate way by which governments can claim the right to power. Consequently, even totalitarian regimes and military dictatorships use elections (though fraught with fraud and hardly free) to justify their remaining in power. Thus, there are two basic kinds of elections: (1) *free,* where parties of competing philosophies compete for power in a fair contest; and (2) *sham,* where rulers hold cynically staged elections in order to justify their rule.

Gerald M. Pomper's *Elections in America* (2d ed., Dodd, Mead, 1980) classifies U.S. presidential elections into the following four categories. (1) *Maintaining:* party loyalties remain stable and the majority party wins. (2) *Deviating:* the majority party loses. (3) *Converting:* the majority party wins, but there are basic changes in the distribution of party membership. (4) *Realigning:* the majority party may lose because of changing party loyalties. *See also* REALIGNMENT.

election, authorization *See* AUTHORIZATION ELECTION.

election board *See* CANVASSING BOARD.

election, certification *See* AUTHORIZATION ELECTION.

election, contested An election in which more than one person claims to have won. In such cases, a recount is often undertaken, and if there is still ambiguity as to the winner, the dispute may be settled in court or by a legislature.

election, contesting An election in which there is more than one candidate on the ballot from which to choose.

election, converting *See* ELECTION.

election, critical An election that heralds a new political alignment, that produces a new political majority, or that indicates a long-term shift in electoral behavior.

election day The first Tuesday after the first Monday in November in an election year. The U.S. Constitution provides in Article II, Section 1, that the Congress may determine the time of choosing the electors and the day on which they shall give their votes, "which day shall be the same throughout the United States." In 1792, the Congress by law designated the first Wednesday in December as the date for presidential electors to meet and cast their vote for President and Vice President. This same act required the states to "appoint" their electors within 34 days of the date set for the electors to vote. Following this act, until 1845, there was no national election day, and each state fixed its own date, usually in November, for the selection of presidential electors. The decision to create a single national day for the selection of presidential electors grew out of the need to prevent election abuses resulting from electors being selected on separate days in neighboring states. Thus, in 1845, the Congress established by law that in each state the electors were to be selected on the "Tuesday next after the first Monday in the month of November of the year in which they are to be appointed." In 1872, the Congress adopted legislation requiring states to hold their elections for members and delegates to the U.S. House of Representatives on this same day. After the adoption of the Seventeenth Amendment, providing for the direct popular election of U.S. senators, the Congress enacted legislation in 1914 to require that U.S. senators also be elected on the same Tuesday in November.

Tuesday was selected to protect the rights of persons opposed for religious reasons to holding elections on Sunday or to traveling to the polls on that day. Therefore, it was desirable to have at least one day intervening between Sunday and election day. The first Tuesday of the month was eliminated, because it might fall on the first day of the month and cause inconvenience to business. But Tuesday has proved inconvenient for many, in that it is a working day, not a holiday. Many advocate Sunday elections for that reason.

election, deviating An election in which a new party wins, not because there has been a realignment in political party preferences but because the winning party just happened to have an attractive candidate or some other factor in its favor (such as a scandal in the other party). In a deviating election, existing party loyalties are temporarily displaced by short-term forces.

election, general An election held to choose among candidates nominated in a primary (or by convention or caucus) for federal, state, and local office.

election, indirect An electoral process whereby voters first vote for delegates or "electors" who in turn will decide the actual election at issue. The U.S. presidential election, because of the ELECTORAL COLLEGE, is an example of an indirect election.

election judges Local officials who supervise balloting at the precinct level. Duties and titles vary. They are also known as election inspectors and election commissioners. But these are the officials who basically determine the eligibility of voters, monitor the voting, and officially count the votes.

election, maintaining An election that reaffirms the existing patterns of political party support. In other words, the party dominant in the electorate wins.

election, midterm The U.S. congressional election that occurs in the middle of a President's four-year term. It is usually the case that the party of the President in power loses seats in the House of Representatives and Senate. This has so often been the case that the President's party now declares it a victory when they lose only a few seats. While the pattern of midterm elections is clear, one can only speculate on the reasons for it. Some analysts contend that many voters who turn out to vote only in presidential contests tend to vote also for congressional nominees from the President's party. These voters are absent at midterm elections. Other analysts suggest that voters exercise rational judgment on individual candidates and turn out of office those whom they perceive as not having delivered on their promises; thus, a decline in the party in the White House. Still others contend that a midterm congressional election is a de facto referendum on a President's performance for the previous two years.

election, nonpartisan A local election in which a candidate runs for office without formally indicating political party affiliation. Judges and members of school boards, for example, are often elected in nonpartisan elections. The rationale for nonpartisan local elections has often been attributed to New York Mayor Fiorello LaGuardia (1882–1947): "There is no Democratic or Republican way of cleaning the streets."

election, off year An election held in any year other than a presidential election year.

election, representation *See* AUTHORIZATION ELECTION.

election, runoff A second election held in some states if no one candidate for an office receives a majority (or a specified percentage) of votes. Voters then choose in a runoff election between the two candidates who received the most votes in the first election.

election, special An election specially scheduled to fill an office that has become vacant before the term of its expiration.

election, uncontested An election in which a candidate has no opposition.

electioneering **1.** Campaigning actively on behalf of a candidate; the total efforts made to win an election. Many polling places have signs reminding political workers that electioneering is prohibited within a specified distance from the polls. **2.** The specific efforts that interest groups make to help a political candidate, such as formal endorsements, providing campaign workers, and making campaign contributions.

elector **1.** A qualified voter. **2.** One of the 538 members of the electoral college.

electoral college The 538 electors who, on the first Monday after the second Wednesday in December of a presidential election year, officially elect the President and Vice President of the United States. Each state chooses in the November general election—in a manner determined by its legislature—a number of electors equal to the total of its senators and representatives in the Congress. The District of Columbia, under the Twenty-Third Amendment, chooses a number of electors equal to the number chosen by the least populous states. All 51 jurisdictions provide that presidential electors be elected by popular vote.

The electoral college never meets as one body, but state electors usually meet in their state's capital and the District of Columbia. Once the electors have voted and the results have been certified by the chief executive of each state, the results are sent to Washington, D.C., to be counted before a joint session of the newly elected Congress, meeting the first week in January. If no candidate for President or Vice President has received a majority, the House, voting by states, elects the President; and the Senate, voting as individuals, elects the Vice President.

It was originally thought that electors would exercise their own judgment in selecting the President and Vice President; nobody expected that political parties would arise and create the situation whereby electors were no longer independent voters but the representatives of a party. (In six of the last nine elections, however, one elector has cast an electoral vote for someone other than the person he or she was pledged to.)

Supporters of the electoral college argue that it should be kept—because it works. Even though it has failed in three instances to elect a President (1800, 1824, and 1876), the Congress was able to resolve the disputes peaceably. Critics of the electoral college have charged it with being undemocratic, because it permits candidates to win the presidency without having most of the popular votes, and dangerous, because whenever the election is thrown into the House of Representatives the choice must be made from among the three top candidates. Critics believe it is a threat to the legitimacy of the American political system, and they periodically demand its abolition and a system of direct election put in its place.

electoral vote The votes cast for President and Vice President by presidential electors in what is known popularly as the electoral college. The total electoral vote is 538, with 270 needed to win the election. The candidate who wins the most popular votes in a state wins all of that state's electoral votes. In 1984, Ronald Reagan won 525 electoral votes to Walter Mondale's 13; in 1988 George Bush won 426 electoral votes to Michael Dukakis' 111.

elephant The symbol of the Republican Party, first used by caricaturist Thomas Nast (1840–1902) in a *Harper's Weekly* cartoon on November 7, 1874. Nast labeled the elephant "The Republican Vote" because it was the biggest vote in the politcal jungle. *Compare to* DONKEY.

Eleventh Amendment The 1798 amendment to the U.S. Constitution that prohibits the federal courts from hearing cases brought against a state by citizens of other states or of foreign countries. This reversed the Supreme

Court's decision in *Chisholm v Georgia* (1793), which held that citizens of one state could sue the citizens of other states in federal court.

elite party *See* MASS PARTY.

elite theory *See* C. WRIGHT MILLS; PLURALISM.

Emancipation Proclamation President Abraham Lincoln's formal declaration that all slaves residing in the states still in rebellion against the United States on January 1, 1863, would be free once those states came under the military control of the Union army. It did not abolish slavery (that was done by the Thirteenth Amendment in 1865); but it did ensure that slavery would be abolished once the war concluded with a Northern victory. Lincoln showed his cabinet the draft of the proclamation about half a year earlier, on July 22, 1862, but felt that he had to keep it secret until the military situation improved for the North. While the battle of Antietam of September 17, 1862, was essentially a draw, Lincoln considered it enough of a victory to announce the proclamation.

embargo A government prohibition of the import or export of commodities or of the vessels of specific nations. An embargo is a mildly hostile act, more related to foreign policy than to trade policy. For example, shortly after the communists came to power in Cuba, the United States embargoed sugar from Cuba in an effort to disrupt the Cuban economy. And after the Soviet Union invaded Afghanistan, the United States embargoed grain shipments to the Soviets in an effort to make them aware of American displeasure with their aggressive actions. This infuriated many farmers. According to Senator Edward Zorinsky of Nebraska, "With the embargo, this country pointed a gun at the Soviet Union and shot the U.S. farmer in the foot" (*U.S. News & World Report*, February 16, 1981). The Cuban sugar embargo is still in effect, but the Soviet grain embargo was lifted by the Reagan Administration.

embargoed Information given to the news media that may not be released to the public until a pre-set time; thus, the information may be "embargoed" until 5:00 P.M. or until, for example, the Secretary of Defense starts his congressional testimony. Typically, major reports or budgets are embargoed so that the media may have time to analyze the material and to allow all media sources time to obtain the items. Often someone violates the embargo; then everyone is free to use the material—and the violator may have trouble getting similar materials next time.

embassy 1. The highest class of diplomatic mission, headed by an AMBASSADOR. In this context, the embassy refers to all of the diplomatic staff as well as to all of their support personnel. **2.** The physical building or buildings (also called the mission) used to house the office (the chancery) and personal quarters of the embassy staff, including the ambassador. **3.** The job (also called the mission) of an ambassador. Thus, an ambassador's embassy or mission (the job) might be to negotiate a treaty, which might be signed in the mission (a building), which is also known as the embassy.

EMERGENCY POWERS

emergency powers **1.** Those special powers granted to a government or executive agency which allow normal legislative procedures and/or judicial remedies to be suspended. In western democracies, such emergency powers are usually strictly controlled by the legislature and permitted only for a limited period. In nondemocratic countries, emergency powers are frequently referred to as states of siege, and all civil liberties are suspended. **2.** The enlarged authority that the President of the United States is deeded to have, either by statute, from the U.S. Constitution (Article II, Sections 2 & 3), or because of the nature of the emergency, to deal with the problem at hand. An exercise of emergency powers may or may not be later upheld by the Supreme Court. In the case of *Korematsu v United States* (1944), the Court affirmed President Franklin D. Roosevelt's World War II decision to forcibly relocate American citizens of Japanese origin. (However, the CIVIL LIBERTIES ACT OF 1988 apologized to these citizens for their mistreatment and provided that they should each, if still living at the time of the act, be paid $20,000 in reparations.) Yet in the case of YOUNGSTOWN SHEET AND TUBE V SAWYER, the Court denied President Harry S Truman's assertion that he had inherent emergency powers to seize civilian steel mills to maintain wartime production. The President can pretty much do what he wants under the rubric of emergency powers until he is checked by one of the other branches of government. The fact that such checks exist goes a long way in keeping a President's emergency powers "in the closet" until there is substantial agreement that they are needed. *Compare to* NATIONAL EMERGENCY ACT OF 1976.

Emily's List A political action committee that raises campaign funds for female candidates for the U.S. Congress and state legislatures. "Emily" is an acronym for "Early Money Is Like Yeast"—it helps things rise. Not only does Emily's List donate money early in a campaign when it is most needed, but it also allows its chosen candidates to use its national network of campaign contributors. Emily's List has been an important factor in increasing the number of women in major elected offices.

eminent domain **1.** A government's right to take private property for the public's use. The Fifth Amendment requires that, whenever a government takes an individual's property, the property acquired must be taken for public use, and the full value thereof paid to the owner. Thus, a government cannot take property from one person simply to give it to another. However, the Supreme Court has held that it is permissible to take private property for such purposes as urban renewal, even though ultimately the property taken will be returned to private ownership, since the taking is really for the benefit of the community as a whole. Property does not have to be physically taken from the owner to acquire Fifth Amendment protection. If government action leads to a lower value of private property, that may also constitute a "taking" and therefore require payment of compensation. Thus, the Supreme Court has held that the disturbance of chickens' egg-laying on a man's poultry farm, caused by the noise of low-level flights by military aircraft from a nearby airbase, lessened the value of the farm and that, accordingly, the landowner was entitled to receive compensation equal to his loss. **2.** In the context of international law this can mean EXPRO-PRIATION.

Employment Act of 1946 The federal statute that created the Council of Economic Advisers in the Executive Office of the President and asserted that it was the federal government's responsibility to maintain economic stability and promote full employment.

empowerment 1. Giving a person or organization the formal authority to do something. **2.** In the context of antipoverty programs, for example, giving the poor more power over their lives by allowing public housing tenants, for example, to manage or buy their homes. Secretary of Housing and Urban Development Jack Kemp defined empowerment as: "Giving people the opportunity to gain greater control over their own destiny through access to assets of private property, jobs and education" (*The New York Times Magazine*, July 15, 1990). The concept of empowerment has had a strange political history. It first surfaced during the GREAT SOCIETY programs of the 1960s among black power advocates. By the 1990s it had become the backbone of conservative efforts to help the poor. **3.** In the context of education, the right of citizens to choose what schools their children would attend. This is usually part of a VOUCHER SYSTEM.

en banc A French term meaning "on the bench"; a case heard and decided by all of the judges of a court as opposed to judges acting individually. The Supreme Court always sits en banc.

enabling act Legislation permitting cities or districts to engage in particular programs. Enabling acts prescribe some of the administrative details of implementation. As cities are the creatures of their state, their ability to participate in particular types of programs, especially those of the national government, depends upon state enabling acts.

enacting clause The first part of a statute that begins "Be it enacted . . . ." This phrase gives a bill legal force once it becomes law.

endorsement Formal approval of a candidate by, among others, a political party, by a newspaper editorial, by a PAC, or by celebrities from the political and entertainment world. Some endorsements carry greater weight than others. Too many can backfire and have the candidate branded the tool of special interests.

enemies list 1. Generally, any list of political enemies. In this sense all administrations maintain informal lists of those in the political community that are persona non grata, not to be invited to social functions, etc. **2.** Specifically, a list maintained by the Nixon Administration of its critics so that they could be targeted for harassment, income tax audits, etc. The list included many of the biggest names of the day in journalism (e.g., Jack Anderson, James Reston, Richard H. Rovere, and Gary Wills) and was first revealed by John Dean in testimony to the Senate Watergate Committee on June 26, 1973. Journalist Morton Kondracke wrote (*The New Republic*, April 30, 1990): "In 1973 I made it onto his White House enemies list, and it was one of the high points of my youth. . . . for a journalist to be singled out by Nixon—this was very heaven. Maybe I wasn't Woodward or Bernstein or I.F. Stone or Seymour Hersh, but I was part of that noble band saving humanity from evil—and, what's more, Satan noticed!"

Energy, U.S. Department of (DOE) The cabinet-level department created by the Department of Energy Organization Act of 1977 that provides the framework for a national energy plan through the coordination and administration of the energy functions of the federal government. The DOE absorbed some of the functions of the now disbanded Atomic Energy Commission (most AEC functions were assigned to the NUCLEAR REGULATORY COMMISSION).

enterprise zone Originally, an area of high unemployment and poverty that is granted business tax reductions by a state to lure industry and concomitant prosperity. By the end of the 1980s, over 37 states had enterprise zones of one kind or another; however, the trend has been to use them less as a means to help poor neighborhoods and more as part of overall regional economic development programs geared equally to retaining old businesses and attracting new ones. Also known as *urban enterprise zone*.

entitlement authority Legislation that requires the payment of benefits to any person or government meeting the requirements established by such law (such as social security benefits and veterans' pensions). Section 401 of the Congressional Budget and Impoundment Control Act of 1974 places certain restrictions on the enactment of new entitlement authority. *See also* AUTHORITY, BACKDOOR.

entitlement program Any government program that pays benefits to individuals, organizations, or other governments that meet eligibility requirements set by law. Social security is the largest federal entitlement program for individuals. Others include farm price supports, Medicare, Medicaid, unemployment insurance, and food stamps. Entitlement programs have great budgetary significance, in that they lock in such a great percentage of the total federal budget each year that changes in the budget can only be made at the margin.

entrapment Inducing a person to commit a crime that the person would not have committed without such inducement. When done by government agents, usually police, for the purposes of prosecuting a person, it is generally unlawful. In most cases, a criminal charge based on entrapment will fail.

enumerated powers Those rights and responsibilities of the U.S. government specifically provided for and listed in the Constitution. *Compare to* IMPLIED POWER; RESERVED POWER.

environmental movement A spontaneous grassroots mobilization of citizens that grew out of the earlier CONSERVATION movement and that is concerned with the quality of the natural and human environment. Earth Days in 1970 and 1990, which launched nationwide parades, teach-ins, and demonstrations, were high points in the environmental movement. The movement receives its organizational expression through interest groups that engage in lobbying, court litigation, and public information activities. Major organizations of the environmental movement include the Environmental Defense Fund, Friends of the Earth, National Audubon Society, National Parks and Conservation Association, National Wildlife Federation, Natural Resources Defense Council, Sierra Club, and Wilderness Society.

environmental policy Processes by which a nation manages and protects its natural resources. The National Environmental Policy Act of 1969 declared that the federal government had responsibility for the protection of the environment. The act, which created the President's Council on Environmental Quality, provides for the preparation of an environmental impact statement (a document assessing the impact of a new program upon the environment) for all major federal actions significantly affecting the quality of the human environment. *Compare to* CONSERVATION.

Environmental Protection Agency, U.S. (EPA) The federal agency created by Reorganization Plan no. 3 of 1970 to permit coordinated and effective government action on behalf of the environment. The EPA endeavors to abate and control pollution systematically, by proper integration of research, monitoring, standard setting, and enforcement activities. As a complement to its other activities, the EPA coordinates and supports research and antipollution activities by state and local governments, private and public groups, individuals, and educational institutions.

Equal Access Act of 1984 The law that requires public secondary schools to allow the religious and political clubs of students to use school facilities just as any other extra curricular activity. This was upheld by the Supreme Court in *Board of Education v Mergens* (1990).

equal employment opportunity (EEO) A set of employment procedures and practices that effectively prevents any individual from being adversely excluded from employment opportunities on the basis of race, color, sex, religion, age, national origin, or other factors that cannot lawfully be used in employing people. While the ideal of EEO is an employment system devoid of both intentional and unintentional discrimination, achieving this ideal may be a political impossibility because of the problem of definition. One man's equal opportunity may be another man's institutional racism or a woman's institutional sexism. Because of this problem of definition, only the courts have been able to say if, when, and where EEO exists.

Equal Employment Opportunity Act of 1972 An amendment to TITLE VII of the 1964 Civil Rights Act strengthening the authority of the Equal Employment Opportunity Commission and extending antidiscrimination provisions to state and local governments and labor organizations with 15 or more employees, and to public and private employment agencies.

EQUAL EMPLOYMENT OPPORTUNITY COMMISSION

Equal Employment Opportunity Commission (EEOC) A five-member commission created by Title VII of the Civil Rights Act of 1964. The EEOC members (one designated chair) are appointed for five-year terms by the President, subject to the advice and consent of the Senate. The EEOC's mission is to end discrimination based on race, color, religion, sex, or national origin in hiring, promotion, firing, wages, testing, training, apprenticeship, and all other conditions of employment, and to promote voluntary action programs by employers, unions, and community organizations to make equal employment opportunity an actuality.

equality The American ideal as stated in the 1776 Declaration of Independence that "all men are created equal, that they are endowed by their Creator with certain unalienable rights"; the principle of egalitarianism that each citizen, regardless of economic resources or personal traits, deserves and has a right to be given equal treatment by the political system. Even though the United States has not lived up to this ideal, has not provided equality to all its men and women throughout its history, its history is nevertheless one of constantly moving in that direction. Political theorists such as JEAN-JACQUES ROUSSEAU have often warned: "It is precisely because the force of circumstances tends always to destroy equality that the force of legislation must always tend to maintain it" (*The Social Contract*, 1762). However, such economists as Arthur Okun have asserted with equal vigor that "any insistence on carving the pie into equal slices would shrink the size of the pie" (*Equality and Efficiency*, 1975).

equalization The adjustment of assessments and taxes on real estate to make sure that properties are properly valued and are fairly taxed according to value.

Equal Pay Act of 1963 An amendment to the Fair Labor Standards Act of 1938 prohibiting pay discrimination because of sex and providing that men and women working in the same establishment under similar conditions must receive the same pay if their jobs require equal or similar skill, effort, and responsibility.

equal protection of laws The constitutional requirement that a government will not treat people unequally, nor set up illegal categories to justify treating people unequally, nor give unfair or unequal treatment to a person based on that person's race or religion. The Fourteenth Amendment prohibits states from denying their residents the equal protection of the law. The due process clause of the Fifth Amendment has also been held, in *Bolling v Sharpe* (1954), to include a requirement of equal protection.

While equal protection has been the law since the ratification of the Fourteenth Amendment in 1868, it was largely a dormant concept until awakened by the Warren Court in the 1950s. It can truly be said that landmark decisions, such as BROWN V BOARD OF EDUCATION OF TOPEKA, KANSAS and BAKER V CARR, used the equal protection clause of the Fourteenth Amendment to revolutionize American society. The United States is an increasingly more equal nation because of it. Without it, the peaceful changes that have come about in race relations might not have been possible. *Compare to* REVERSE DISCRIMINATION.

Equal Rights Amendment (ERA) A proposed amendment to the U.S. Constitution passed by the Congress in 1972 that never became law because too few states ratified it. The proposed Twenty-Seventh Amendment read in part: "Equality of rights under the law shall not be denied or abridged by the United States or any state on account of sex." At first, the ERA seemed headed for quick passage. It was approved in both houses of the Congress with overwhelming majorities; both major party platforms endorsed it. By the end of 1972, over 22 states had ratified it. But when it became apparent that ERA would eventually become law, a conservative opposition organized. It argued that the ERA would not only subject women to a potential military draft, but also to combat duty; and that women would lose the legal advantages they hold under many state domestic relations laws and labor codes. As ERA became more controversial, fewer states moved to ratify it. In 1980 the Republican party platform became officially neutral on it. As the issue became more and more controversial, the states that had not acted on it held hearings and encountered delay after delay. On March 27, 1982, the final deadline, three states were still needed for ratification, and the ERA was dead.

Equal Rights Amendment, State An amendment to a state constitution paralleling the proposed federal Equal Rights Amendment.

equal-time rule The Federal Communication Commission's rule that broadcasters do not have to sell air time to any candidates but those for federal offices; however, if they do sell to any, they must make equal time available to opposing candidates on equal terms. News programs and debates sponsored by good government groups are exempt from this rule. *See also* FAIRNESS DOCTRINE.

equity 1. A principle of justice. **2.** A legal system that deals with the spirit of the law when no statute or precedent is directly applicable. **3.** What a borrower may own on a mortgaged property; the amount of the debt that has been paid.

equity jurisdiction The authority of a court to administer justice when no specific laws exist to cover the case at hand.

equity law *See* CODE LAW.

ERA *See* EQUAL RIGHTS AMENDMENT.

escalation An increase in scope or violence of a military conflict, deliberate or unpremeditated. Using the analogy of a ladder, strategists think of potential conflict arrayed as a series of steps from minimum to maximum violence. The word became particularly associated with American policy during the Vietnam War because of the constant debate over whether that war should be expanded. For example, President Lyndon B. Johnson was quoted in *Time* (March 4, 1966): "Our numbers have increased in Vietnam because the aggression of others has increased in Vietnam. There is not, and there will not be, a mindless escalation." He may not have thought that his subsequent escalation of the war was mindless, but many others certainly did.

Escobedo v Illinois (1964) The Supreme Court case that held that a criminal defendant must be allowed to consult an attorney if he or she requests to do so. Denying this is a violation of the "assistance to counsel" provision of the Sixth Amendment.

establishment 1. Those who hold the real power in society; a basically conservative and secretive ruling class. The term first surfaced in England during the 1950s, but it soon crossed the Atlantic and by the 1960s there was much talk of an "Eastern Establishment" and a "Protestant Establishment." Now the word has become so trite and overused that "establishments" are to be found all over; or not found because secretiveness is part of their essence. **2.** The collective holders of power in a segment of society: political, military, social, academic, religious, or literary. It is always the establishment that revolutionaries—whether political, intellectual, organizational, or others—wish to overthrow, so they can become the new establishment.

establishment clause The first part of the First Amendment that asserts that "Congress shall make no law respecting an establishment of religion." The clause is the basis for the separation of church and state in the United States. Yet the Supreme Court has held in *Everson v Board of Education* (1947) that it is not a violation of the establishment clause for the government to pay for the cost of busing children to religious schools; nor is the tax-exempt status of religious property—at issue in *Walz v Tax Commission of the City of New York* (1970)—a violation. Increasingly, the Court is taking an attitude of "benevolent neutrality" toward religion. Government activity that has the purpose or primary effect of advancing or inhibiting religion or that results in excessive government entanglement with religion is proscribed. Moreover, the establishment clause guards against measures that would foster political divisiveness on religious grounds in the general community. One continuing problem with the establishment clause is that, traditionally, many welfare and educational services in local communities have been provided by privately funded religious groups. This has posed a problem as far back as the New Deal in the 1930s. A significant part of the public-private controversy in the United States rests on the problem raised by the religious interests in such services and what happens when the federal government begins funding them. *Compare to* FREE EXERCISE CLAUSE.

Ethics in Government Act of 1978 The federal statute that seeks to deal with possible conflicts of interest by former federal executive branch employees by imposing postemployment prohibitions on their activities. The restrictions in the law are concerned with former government employees' representation or attempts to influence federal agencies, not with their employment by others. What is prohibited depends on how involved a former employee was with a matter while with the government and whether he or she was one of a specified group of senior employees.

ethnic politics **1.** The workings and activities of FACTIONS when those factions are ethnic groups. **2.** The politics within a minority ethnic community of a larger polity. **3.** Specific political appeals to ethnic group members. Politicians may be said to be practicing ethnic politics when they tell their Irish constituents of their support for a united Ireland, their Jewish constituents of their support for a strong state of Israel, and their Hispanic constituents of strong support for bilingual education. Ethnic politics does not have to be so substantive; sometimes it is nothing more than a "photo opportunity" of the politician eating ethnic food or attending an ethnic cultural festival or wedding. **4.** Any appeal to racism. It is racism for candidates to imply that people should vote for them because of their ethnic background. **5.** The resurging pride in ethnicity that came about since the civil rights movement of the 1960s. This has radically affected how minorities view themselves and their roles in the polity. **6.** Laying claim to a significant ethnic constituency largely because of one's ethnic origins.

Ethnic politics isn't what it used to be. Originally, the term applied only to European ethnics. The term is now more likely to refer to the new ethnics, both those that have long been here and those that are more recent arrivals, for example, Hispanics and Vietnamese. Technically, every American is a member of an ethnic group except for white Anglo-Saxon Protestants. And now that they are in the minority, many of them have begun to claim that they are an ethnic group, too.

ex officio A Latin phrase meaning "by virtue of the office." Many people hold positions on boards, commissions, councils, and so on because of another office they occupy. For example, the mayor of a city may be an *ex officio* member of the board of trustees of a university in that city.

ex parte A Latin phrase meaning "with only one side present." It usually refers to a hearing or trial in which only one side is present because the other side failed to show up, was not given notice, and so on.

Ex parte McCardle See MCCARDLE, EX PARTE.

Ex parte Milligan See WRIT OF HABEAS CORPUS.

ex post facto law A law that makes something retroactively illegal—makes unlawful an act that was not a crime when it was committed. The U.S. Constitution prohibits *ex post facto* laws by the federal government (Article I, Section 9) and by the states (Article I, Section 10). These prohibitions have been interpreted to prevent the imposition of a greater penalty for a crime than that in effect when the crime was committed. However, laws that retroactively determine how a person is to be tried for a crime may be changed, as long as no important rights are lost. Laws are not considered ex post facto if they make the punishment less severe than it was when the crime was committed.

exclusionary rule The constitutional ruling that evidence obtained through an illegal search or seizure may not be used in a criminal trial. The exclusionary rule, which is premised upon the Fourth Amendment prohibition against unreasonable searches and seizures, was established for the federal courts in the Supreme Court case of *Weeks v United States* (1914). It was extended to state courts in *Mapp v Ohio*. In recent years, the exclusionary rule has been increasingly refined and limited by the Supreme Court. In *United States v Calandra* (1974), the Court held that the rule does not extend to grand jury proceedings where witnesses might be required to answer questions about illegally obtained evidence. *United States v Havens* (1980) allowed the use of illegally obtained evidence to contradict a defendant's testimony; and in *United States v Salvucci* (1980) the Court restricted a defendant's "automatic standing" to challenge searches and seizures. The trend continues.

exclusive power Powers that constitutionally belong to only one level of government. For example, the federal government has exclusive power over currency, postal service, and foreign policy. This is in contrast to a CONCURRENT (or shared) POWER, such as taxation.

executive 1. Any of the highest managers in an organization. **2.** That branch of government concerned with the implementation of the policies and laws created by a legislature.

executive action 1. The implementation of a public policy; the last stage of the policymaking process. This is what happens after a law is passed and the executive branch is charged with putting it into effect. **2.** An intelligence community term for assassination.

executive agreement A term that applies to a wide variety of international agreements and understandings that are reached by the governments concerned in the course of administering their relations. The executive agreement device permits a U.S. President to enter into open or secret arrangements with a foreign government without the advice and consent of the Senate. There are two broad categories of executive agreements: presidential agreements and congressional-executive agreements. Presidential agreements are those made solely on the basis of the constitutional authority of the President; congressional-executive agreements cover all international agreements entered into under the combined authority of the President and the Congress. The executive agreement is used for significant political agreements, such as an aid-for-naval-bases agreement with Spain, as well as routine, nonpolitical agreements, such as reciprocal postal arrangements with England. The former are usually made under the President's sole power to faithfully execute the laws or under his diplomatic or commander-in-chief powers. The latter are usually made under authority of the Congress and the President. The vast majority of executive agreements are entered into in pursuit of specific congressional authority.

The Supreme Court in *United States v Belmont* (1937) unanimously held an executive agreement to be a valid international compact, state policy notwithstanding. The Court said in part: "In respect of all international negotiations and compacts, and in respect of our foreign relations generally, state lines disappear." The Court has ruled, however, that the President is not free to enter into executive agreements that violate constitutional provisions.

By the Case Act of 1972, Congress required that the U.S. Secretary of State transmit to the Congress all executive agreements to which the United States is a party no later than 60 days after such agreement has entered into force. The President need report secret agreements only to the foreign relations committees of the two houses. The act did not give the Congress the authority to disapprove an executive agreement. Because there is often a thin line between what constitutes an executive agreement a President can make on his own and a treaty that must be ratified by the Senate, there is often considerable concern that a President might be using executive agreements to avoid the Senate's constitutional role in the foreign relations process. Executive agreements have been published since 1950 in a series entitled *United States Treaties and Other International Agreements*.

executive branch In a government with SEPARATION OF POWERS, that part which is responsible for applying or administering the law. Thus, a President, governor, or mayor and their respective supporting bureaucracies are the executive branches of their respective jurisdictions. But not all of the federal bureaucracy is part of the executive branch. Some agencies such as the General Accounting Office are directly responsible to Congress. Others, such as the Federal Trade Commission (and other regulatory agencies), have been held by the Supreme Court not to be part of the executive branch. *See* HUMPHREY'S EXECUTOR V UNITED STATES.

executive budget *See* BUDGET, EXECUTIVE.

executive calendar *See* CALENDAR, EXECUTIVE.

executive, chief 1. The highest elected office in a jurisdiction, whether it be the mayor of a city, the governor of a state, or the President of the United States. **2.** The highest level manager of an organization no matter what the formal title might be. **3.** The President of the United States. All chief executives, because they occupy a highly visible office, have significant public relations responsibilities. As President Calvin Coolidge wrote in his *Autobiography* (1929): "It has become the custom in our country to expect all Chief Executives, from the President down, to conduct activities analogous to an entertainment bureau. No occasion is too trivial for its promoters to invite them to attend and deliver an address."

executive department Any cabinet-level agency in the federal government.

executive document A written agreement, usually a treaty, sent to the Senate by the President of the United States for consideration or approval. These are identified for each session of Congress as, for example, Executive

A, 97th Congress, 1st Session; Executive B, and so on. They are referred to committee in the same manner as other measures. Unlike legislative bills, however, treaties do not die at the end of a Congress but remain live proposals until acted on by the Senate or withdrawn by the President.

Executive Office of the President (EOP) The umbrella office consisting of the top presidential staff agencies that provide the President help and advice in carrying out his major responsibilities. The EOP was created by President Franklin D. Roosevelt under the authority of the Reorganization Act of 1939. Since then, Presidents have used executive orders, reorganization plans, and legislative initiatives to reorganize, expand, or contract the EOP. *See also* BROWNLOW COMMITTEE; PRESIDENCY, AMERICAN; PRESIDENTIAL POWER.

executive officer A military term, now commonly if informally used in government offices, for the person who is just under the boss and runs the day-to-day operations of the agency.

executive order **1.** Any rule or regulation issued by a chief administrative authority that, because of precedent and existing legislative authorization, has the effect of law. **2.** The principal mode of administrative action on the part of the President of the United States. The power of a President to issue executive orders emanates from the constitutional provision requiring the President to "take care that the laws be faithfully executed," the commander-in-chief clause, and express powers vested in the office by congressional statutes.

executive oversight The total process by which executives attempt to control their organization and to hold individual managers responsible for the implementation of their programs.

executive, plural **1.** The de facto arrangement of most state governments because most GOVERNORS share executive authority with other independently elected officers, such as secretary of state, treasurer, attorney general, or auditor. **2.** Any formal arrangement whereby more than one individual or office shares executive power; county commissioners, for example.

executive privilege The presidential claim that the executive branch may withhold information from the Congress or its committees and the courts to preserve confidential communications within the executive branch or to secure the national interest. Although the Constitution does not explicitly grant the executive a privilege to withhold information from the Congress, Presidents have from the beginning of the Republic claimed it. President George Washington withheld from the House of Representatives papers and documents connected with the Jay Treaty because, he argued, the House had no constitutional role in the treaty-making process. The presidential claim of executive privilege was not seriously challenged until President Richard M. Nixon sought to use executive privilege to sustain immunity from the judicial process. In 1974, the Supreme Court restricted the privilege when it held that, in a criminal case before a court, a concrete need for evidence takes precedence over a generalized assertion of executive privilege unrelated to defense or diplomacy. The Court did acknowledge a constitutional protection for the "president's need for complete candor and objectivity from advisors" and for "military, diplomatic, or sensitive national security secrets." *See also* UNITED STATES V NIXON.

executive session **1.** A secret meeting. **2.** A confidential meeting of any governing body. **3.** A meeting of a U.S. Senate or a House of Representatives committee (or, occasionally, of the entire membership) that only the group's members are privileged to attend. Frequently, witnesses appear before committees meeting in executive session and other members of the Congress may be invited, but the public and press are not allowed to attend. As a result of SUNSHINE RULES, most committee meetings in the Congress are now open to the public. **4.** A meeting of the U.S. Senate when it is dealing with executive functions, such as the confirmation of presidential nominations and the ratification of treaties. In this context, an executive session is distinguished from a legislative session.

executive summary A brief description (usually a few pages) of a much larger report (usually a few hundred pages).

exempt A short form of "tax-exempt," referring to nonprofit organizations not usually subject to taxation.

expectations game The manipulation of voter and media predictions about an election in order to influence perceptions about the results. The classic case concerns the New Hampshire presidential primary of 1968. Most opinion polls thought that Senator Eugene McCarthy's challenge to President Johnson would lose big. So when he far surpassed expectations with 42 percent of the vote, the media and public perception was that he had won—when, in fact, he lost. Ever since campaign managers have sought to manipulate expectations for strategic gains.

expenditures The actual spending of money, as distinguished from its APPROPRIATION. Expenditures are made by the disbursing officers of a government; appropriations are made by a legislature. The two are rarely identical: in any fiscal year, expenditures may represent money appropriated one, two, or more years previously.

Export-Import Bank (Eximbank) An autonomous agency of the U.S. government created by the Export-Import Bank Act of 1945 to facilitate international trade. Under various programs, the Eximbank provides export credits and direct loans to foreign buyers and sells insurance and export guarantees to U.S. manufacturers.

expressed powers Those powers specifically stated, or expressed in a constitution. *See also* NECESSARY AND PROPER CLAUSE.

expropriation The confiscation of private property by a government, which may or may not pay a portion of its value in return. *Compare to* NATIONALIZATION.

EXTENSION OF REMARKS

extension of remarks That portion of the CONGRESSIONAL RECORD that contains speeches and other material not immediately germane to the current debate but that a member of the Congress wants printed as part of the *Record*.

externalities *See* SPILLOVER EFFECTS.

extradition The surrender by one nation or state to another of a person accused or convicted of an offense in the second nation or state.

extraordinary majority Any vote that is required to be more than a simple majority: more than half plus one. The ratification of constitutional amendments, for example, requires extraordinary majorities.

extraterritoriality A nation's exercise of its authority and laws outside of its physical limits, such as on its ship at sea, over its own soldiers in foreign countries, and in the residences of its diplomats stationed abroad.

extremism **1.** The doctrine of the far left or far right of the political spectrum. **2.** A belief in going to extremes in political matters. The most famous use of this word in American politics occurred when Senator Barry Goldwater said in accepting the nomination for President at the Republican national convention in San Francisco on July 16, 1964: "Extremism in the defense of liberty is no vice. Moderation in the pursuit of justice is no virtue." The use of this word helped to create such high negative perceptions of Goldwater that he was trounced in the general election by President Lyndon Johnson.

F

face time **1.** The time that a bureaucrat spends making an impression on someone that can help his or her career, such as an immediate boss or an influential member of Congress. **2.** The time that a campaign worker gets alone with the candidate. **3.** The time a candidate or any public figure gets on national television.

faction **1.** In English political history, any group whose motives for supporting a given action were inherently suspect because of the assumption of selfish interest, as opposed to the welfare of the community as a whole. **2.** The term used by James Madison in *Federalist* No. 10 to describe "a number of citizens, whether amounting to a majority or minority of the whole, who are united and actuated by some common impulse of passion or of interest, adverse to the rights of other citizens, or to the permanent and aggregate interests of the community." **3.** Any subgroup within a larger organization; for example, the moderate faction of the Republican party, the conservative faction of the Democratic party.

factoid A false statement, statistic, or fact that is accepted as true because of its dissemination by the mass media. Many an unsubstantiated allegation increasingly gains factoid status as it bounces from one media outlet to another.

Fair Deal President Harry S Truman's domestic programs. He first used the phrase in an address to the Congress in 1949. The Fair Deal was in essence an effort on the part of the Truman administration to sustain and extend the NEW DEAL.

fair employment practice commission A generic title for any state or local government agency responsible for administering or enforcing laws prohibiting employment discrimination because of race, color, sex, religion, national origin, or other factors.

fair employment practice laws All government requirements designed to prohibit discrimination in the various aspects of employment.

fair housing laws State, local, and federal statutes prohibiting discrimination in the sale, rental, or financing of housing.

Fair Labor Standards Act of 1938 (FLSA) The federal statute, also called Wages and Hours Act, that, as amended, established standards for minimum wages, overtime pay, equal pay, recordkeeping, and child labor.

fairness doctrine The now abandoned policy of the Federal Communications Commission that radio and television stations must present all sides on important public issues. This meant that all candidates for political office had to have an equal opportunity to present their views. The fairness doctrine was upheld by the Supreme Court in *Red Lion Broadcasting v FCC*

(1969). But in 1986 a federal court of appeals ruled that the doctrine was not law and thus could be repealed without congressional approval. In response, Congress passed a bill in 1987 which would have made the fairness doctrine permanent. President Ronald Reagan vetoed the bill citing the first amendment's requirement for freedom of the press and observing that: "In any other medium besides broadcasting, such federal policing of the editorial judgment of journalists would be unthinkable." When the veto was not overridden, the FCC promptly negated the fairness doctrine which it had first enunciated in 1949. *Compare to* EQUAL TIME RULE.

fairness question **1.** An abbreviated way of referring to concerns over the fairness of the domestic budget cuts made by the Reagan and Bush administrations. This concern, which has been expressed mainly by Democrats, basically asked the question of whether it was fair to cut funds from welfare programs to pay for a peacetime defense buildup. And, additionally, whether the cutbacks in social programs combined with benefits for middle and upperclass citizens resulted in an equitable distribution of benefits. **2.** The concern over the equity of tax rates. Beginning in 1990, the Democrats increasingly asserted that high income earners don't pay their fare share of taxes according to the ABILITY TO PAY principle.

fait accompli **1.** Something that has been accomplished, is in place, and is unchangeable without extraordinary effort. **2.** A one-sided act that creates a new political and diplomatic situation.

fallback position **1.** A military term for a defensive position taken up after an initial position has been overrun. **2.** By analogy in political bargaining, a position taken up after one has to retreat from an earlier stand.

family policy A vague term for the totality of current or future legislation (or corporate policies) aimed at reconciling the role of women as both mothers and members of the workforce. Family policies seek to help working mothers better cope with their family responsibilities through paid maternity leave, subsidized or free day-care programs for children, and so on. A main difference in attitudes toward family policy is that liberals, as opposed to conservatives, seek policies that call for additional government spending; while conservatives, as opposed to liberals, seek policies that emphasize traditional religious values and the enforcement of their standards of morality (e.g., in regard to abortion and pornography) for the entire society.

Family Support Act of 1988 *See* WELFARE.

family values A vague phrase used by conservative Republicans to refer to policies that are anti-abortion, favorable toward prayer in schools, and so on.

farewell address A political leader's last major speech while in high office and made in anticipation of retirement from public life. Just as deathbed confessions are given special credence, farewell addresses have a similar poignancy. Many Presidents of the United States have made farewell addresses: George Washington used his to urge the nation "to steer clear of permanent alliance with any portion of the foreign world"; Dwight D. Eisenhower used his to warn the nation about the MILITARY-INDUSTRIAL COMPLEX.

fascism 1. A political philosophy that advocates governance by a dictator, assisted by a hierarchically organized, strongly ideological party, in maintaining a totalitarian and regimented society through violence, intimidation, and the arbitrary use of power. **2.** A mass-based REACTIONARY political movement in an industrialized nation that, through the means of a charismatic leader, espouses nationalism in the extreme. The main difference between totalitarian fascism and totalitarian communism is that fascism professes sympathy toward many aspects of private capitalism and would resolve the conflict between capital and labor by using the government to enforce their relations to one another in the interest of full employment and high productivity. Charismatic leadership is believed to appeal to the irrational and would cement the loyalty of the mass public to the nation through its emotional commitment to an individual. Italy's Benito Mussolini (1883–1945) created the prototype of the modern fascist state in the 1920s. According to Mussolini, in *The Doctrine of Fascism* (1932), "The key stone of the Fascist doctrine is the conception of the State, of its essence, of its functions, its aims. For Fascism the State is absolute, individuals and groups relative." In the early 1930s, Huey P. Long (1893–1935), the political boss of Louisiana, predicted that "if fascism came to America, it would be on a program of Americanism." Sinclair Lewis (1885–1951), the first American to win the Nobel Prize for literature, showed exactly how this could happen in his 1935 novel *It Can't Happen Here*. The word "fascism" is derived from the official symbol of power and justice of ancient Roman magistrates: a bundle of sticks (fascis) with an ax protruding. This symbol can be seen on the wall of the U.S. House of Representatives and on the stairs of the Lincoln Memorial. Mussolini used this ancient symbol of justice to represent his modern style of tyranny.

fat cats Major contributors to political causes. When Governor of California, President Ronald Reagan spoke at a Republican fund-raiser: "We've heard a great deal about Republican fat-cats—how the Republicans are the party of big contributions. I've never been able to understand why a Republican contributor is a fat-cat and a Democratic contributor of the same amount of money is a public-spirited philanthropist" (*Los Angeles Times*, August 5, 1974).

favorite son/favorite daughter A presidential aspirant at a national nominating convention who seeks to keep the votes of his or her state's delegation together behind his or her candidacy to maintain a strong political bargaining position. Such candidates seldom have any real support beyond their own states. They are of lessening significance since the adoption of party democratizing rules in the 1970s.

FBI *See* FEDERAL BUREAU OF INVESTIGATION.

FCC *See* FEDERAL COMMUNICATIONS COMMISSION.

FDIC *See* FEDERAL DEPOSIT INSURANCE CORPORATION.

Fed *See* FEDERAL RESERVE SYSTEM.

federal assistance programs The totality of federal financial aid programs available to state and local governments, including counties, cities, and metropolitan and regional governments; schools, colleges, and universities; health institutions; nonprofit and for-profit organizations; and individuals and families. Current federal assistance programs are listed in the annual *Catalogue of Federal Domestic Assistance*.

Federal Bureau of Investigation (FBI) The principal investigative arm of the U.S. Department of Justice, established in 1908 as the Bureau of Investigation. It is charged with gathering and reporting facts, locating witnesses, and compiling evidence in matters in which the federal government is, or may be, a party in interest. Cooperative services of the FBI for other duly authorized law enforcement agencies include fingerprint identification, laboratory services, police training, and the National Crime Information Center. J. Edgar Hoover (1895–1972), as director of the FBI from 1924 to his death, created the modern identity and functions of the FBI; the FBI achieved its greatest prestige and public support under Hoover, and the FBI agent became a national symbol of incorruptible law enforcement. But toward the end of his reign, Hoover's reputation and that of the FBI were hurt when a variety of scandals came to light about illegal wiretapping, burglaries, and violations of the civil rights of citizens. Since then, the FBI has been kept on a tighter rein by the Justice Department. *Compare to* G-MEN.

Federal Communications Commission (FCC) The independent federal agency created by the Communications Act of 1934 that regulates interstate and foreign communications by radio, television, wire, and cable. It is responsible for the orderly development and operation of broadcast services and the provision of nationwide and worldwide communications services at reasonable rates. The FCC also has the responsibility for establishing and monitoring moral standards in broadcasting. *See also* FAIRNESS DOCTRINE.

Federal Court of Appeals *See* COURT OF APPEALS.

Federal Deposit Insurance Corporation (FDIC) The federal agency established in 1933 to promote and preserve public confidence in banks and to protect the money supply through provision of insurance coverage for bank deposits.

federal district court *See* DISTRICT COURT.

Federal Election Campaign Act of 1972 (FECA) The basic law that, as amended in 1974, 1976, and 1979, regulates the federal election process, including primaries, general elections, special elections, caucuses, and conventions. The FECA and its amendments establish strict reporting requirements for all candidates for federal office, their campaign committees, and others spending money to influence federal elections. Contributions are limited but expenditures, in general, are not. Furthermore, full—though optional—public financing is provided for major-party presidential candidates in the general election and major-party national nominating conventions, and matching public funding is provided in presidential primary elections. Minor-party presidential candidates may receive partial public funding in the general election. Expenditures by candidates accepting federal funds are limited, as are the personal funds such a candidate may spend on his or her own campaign. *See* BUCKLEY V VALEO.

Federal Election Commission The principal enforcement agency for the Federal Election Campaign Act established by the Federal Election Campaign Act of 1971. This six-member commission has the power to prescribe regulations to implement and clarify campaign laws and to issue advisory opinions to guide compliance with the federal election laws. Naturally beset by intense political pressures, it is often in the middle of a storm of controversy.

Federal Election Commission v National Conservative Political Action Committee (1985) The Supreme Court case that invalidated a portion of the Federal Election Campaign Act which limited a political action committee's (PAC) independent expenditure on behalf of presidential candidates. The Court reasoned that to do otherwise would infringe on free speech because PACs allow ordinary people to "amplify their voices." *Compare to* BUCKLEY V VALEO.

Federal Emergency Management Agency (FEMA) The agency, established by Reorganization Plan no. 3 of 1978, that plans for and coordinates emergency preparedness and response for all levels of government and for all kinds of emergencies—natural, industrial, and nuclear. This is the organization that decides what the various governments should be doing after such a catastrophe.

federalese *See* GOBBLEDYGOOK.

federal funds rate The interest rate at which depository institutions, such as banks, lend each other reserve funds on an overnight or temporary basis.

Federal Home Loan Bank Board The federal agency, created by the Federal Home Loan Bank Act of 1932, to supervise and regulate savings and loan associations. The board operated the Federal Savings and Loan Insurance Corporation (FSLIC). In the wake of the SAVINGS AND LOAN SCANDAL the FSLIC became insolvent and its functions were assumed by the FEDERAL DEPOSIT INSURANCE CORPORATION.

Federal Labor Relations Authority (FLRA) The agency created by the Civil Service Reform Act of 1978 to oversee the creation of bargaining units, to supervise elections, and to otherwise deal with labor-management issues in federal agencies. The FLRA is headed by a three-member panel—a chair and two members—who are appointed on a bipartisan basis to staggered five-year terms. The FLRA replaced the Federal Labor Relations Council (FLRC). A general counsel, also appointed to a five-year term, investigates alleged unfair labor practices and prosecutes them before the FLRA. Also within the FLRA, and acting as a separate body, the Federal Service Impasses Panel (FSIP) acts to resolve negotiation impasses.

Federal Maritime Commission (FMC) The independent agency, created by Reorganization Plan no. 7 of 1961, that regulates the waterborne foreign and domestic offshore commerce of the United States, assures that U.S. international trade is open to all nations on fair and equitable terms, and guards against unauthorized monopoly in the waterborne commerce of the United States.

Federal Mediation and Conciliation Service (FMCS) The labor-management mediation agency created by the Labor-Management Relations (Taft-Hartley) Act of 1947 as an independent agency of the federal government. The FMCS helps prevent disruptions in the flow of interstate commerce caused by labor-management disputes by providing mediators to assist disputing parties in the resolution of their differences. The FMCS can intervene on its own motion or by invitation of either side in a dispute. Mediators have no law enforcement authority and rely wholly on persuasive techniques. The FMCS also helps provide qualified third-party neutrals as factfinders or arbitrators.

federal office The positions of Vice President or President of the United States, or of senator or representative in, or delegate or resident commissioner to, the United States Congress.

Federal Open Market Committee The seven members of the Federal Reserve Board plus five of the 12 Federal Reserve Bank presidents. The committee meets every four to six weeks to set Federal Reserve guidelines regarding purchases and sales of government securities in the open market as a means of influencing the volume of credit and money. It also sets Federal Reserve policy relating to foreign exchange markets. *See also* FEDERAL RESERVE SYSTEM.

federal question An aspect of a legal case that involves rights or privileges guaranteed by the U.S. Constitution or federal laws. A legal matter must involve a federal question if it is to be heard in a federal court.

Federal Reserve notes Paper money; obligations of the Federal Reserve backed by the FULL FAITH AND CREDIT of the U.S. government. Nearly all of the nation's circulating paper currency consists of Federal Reserve notes printed by the Treasury Department and issued to the Federal Reserve banks, which place them in circulation through depository institutions. Federal Reserve notes contrast with paper money backed by gold or silver payable on demand. While some silver certificate dollar (or higher) notes are still in circulation, the Congress revoked the right to redeem them for silver in 1968.

Federal Reserve System Colloquially known as the Fed, this is in effect the central bank of the United States, created by the Federal Reserve Act of 1913 and charged with administering and making policy for the nation's credit and monetary affairs. Run by a seven-member board of governors appointed by the President (who also appoints their chairperson), the system includes 12 Federal Reserve banks, 24 branches, all national banks, and many state banking institutions. Three major monetary tools are available to the Federal Reserve System to control the economy's supply of money and credit: (1) open-market operations, which, through the purchase or sale of government bonds, increase or decrease the availability of dollars to member banks; (2) discount-rate adjustments, which increase or decrease the interest rate charged to member banks for the money they borrow; (3) reserve requirements, which, through changes in levels of reserve, increase or decrease the number of dollars a bank may make available for loan. Two less significant tools, moral suasion and selective controls over stock purchase margin requirements, are also used to help manage the economy. *See also* FISCAL POLICY; MONETARY POLICY.

Federal Savings and Loan Insurance Corporation *See* FEDERAL HOME LOAN BANK BOARD.

Federal Service The totality of the civilian MERIT SYSTEM employees of the federal government.

Federal Service Impasses Panel (FSIP) *See* FEDERAL LABOR RELATIONS AUTHORITY.

Federal Trade Commission (FTC) The independent regulatory agency, created by the Federal Trade Commission Act of 1914, whose objective is to prevent the free enterprise system from being stifled, substantially lessened, fettered by monopoly or restraints on trade, or corrupted by unfair or deceptive trade practices. The commission deals with trade practices on a continuing and corrective basis. It has no authority to punish; its function is to prevent, through cease-and-desist orders and other means, those practices condemned by the law of federal trade regulation. *See* HUMPHREY'S EXECUTOR V UNITED STATES.

federalism A system of governance in which a national, overarching government shares power with subnational or state governments. History indicates clearly that the principal factor in the formation of federal systems of government has been a common external threat. Tribes, cities, colonies, or states have joined together in voluntary unions to defend themselves. However, not all systems so formed have been federal. A federal system has the following features: (1) a written constitution that divides government powers between the central government and the constituent governments, giving substantial powers and sovereignty to each; (2) levels of government, through their own instrumentalities, exercising power directly over citizens (unlike a confederation, in which only subnational units act directly on citizens while the central government acts only on the subnational governments); and (3) a constitutional distribution of powers that cannot be changed unilaterally by any level of government or by the ordinary process of legislation.

FEDERALISM, COOPERATIVE

federalism, cooperative **1.** The notion that the national, state, and local governments are interacting agents, jointly working to solve common problems, rather than conflicting, sometimes hostile competitors, pursuing similar or, more likely, conflicting ends. While some cooperation has always been evident in spite of the conflict, competition, and complexity of intergovernmental relations, cooperation was most prominent between the 1930s and the 1950s. The emergency funding arrangements of the depression years (known collectively as the New Deal) and the cooperation among federal, state, and local authorities during World War II to administer civilian defense, rationing, and other wartime programs are noteworthy examples of cooperative federalism in the United States. **2.** The fiscal arrangements whereby the federal government offers states and localities grants to encourage them to pursue national goals.

federalism, creative The Lyndon B. Johnson administration's term for its approach to intergovernmental relations, which was characterized by joint planning and decision making among all levels of government (as well as the private sector) in the management of intergovernmental programs. Many new programs of this period had an urban-metropolitan focus, and much attention was given to antipoverty issues. Creative federalism sought to foster the development of a singular GREAT SOCIETY by integrating the poor into mainstream America. Its expansive efforts were marked by the rapid development of categorical grant programs to state and local governments and direct federal grants to cities, frequently bypassing state governments entirely.

federalism, dual The nineteenth-century concept, now no longer operational, that the functions and responsibilities of the federal and state governments were theoretically distinguished and functionally separate from each other. Some analysts suggest that this kind of federalism, which went out when the New Deal of 1933 came in, is the system to which the Ronald Reagan administration sought (at least rhetorically) to return. The basic idea of dual federalism was expressed succinctly in *The American Commonwealth* (Vol. 1, 2nd ed., 1891) by JAMES BRYCE, a British scholar who visited the United States in the 1880s to observe its political system:

The characteristic feature and special interest of the American Union is that it shows us two governments covering the same ground yet distinct and separate in their action. It is like a great factory wherein two sets of machinery are at work, their revolving wheels apparently intermixed, their bands crossing one another, yet each doing its own work without touching or hampering the other.

federalism, fiscal The fiscal relations between and among units of government in a federal system. The theory of fiscal federalism, or multiunit government finance, is one part of the branch of applied economics known as public finance.

federalism, horizontal State-to-state interactions and relations. Interstate relations take many forms, including compacts and commissions established for specific purposes: river basin management, transportation, extradition of criminals, conservation of forests and wildlife, and administration of parks and recreation. Horizontal relations between local governments also are numerous. Cities frequently contract for services from various neighboring local governments (and even from private providers). The Lakewood plan, established in southern California in 1954, has been the most comprehensive example of interlocal contracting for services to date. Under this plan, the City of Lakewood contracted for a rather comprehensive package of services from Los Angeles County, where Lakewood is located. *See also* SERVICE CONTRACT.

federalism, marble-cake The concept that the cooperative relations among the varying levels of government result in an intermingling of activities; in contrast to the more traditional view of layer-cake federalism, which holds that the three levels of government are totally or almost totally separate. Marble-cake federalism is usually associated with political scientist Morton Grodzins (1917–1964), who in *The American System* (Daniel J. Elazar, ed., 1966) pointed out the case of rural county health officials called sanitarians: sanitarians are appointed by the state government under merit standards established by the federal government, and while their base salaries come from state and federal funds, the county provides them with offices and office amenities and pays a portion of their expenses.

federalism, new **1.** The reconceptualization of federalism as INTERGOVERNMENTAL RELATIONS. **2.** The actual relations between the levels of government as they shared in the performance of expanding government functions in the early 1970s. The term has its origins in the liberal Republican effort to find an alternative to the centralized state perceived as having been set up by the New Deal, but an alternative that nonetheless recognized the need for effective national government. During the Richard M. Nixon administration, new federalism referred to the style of decentralized management at the federal level, symbolized by such programs as Federal Assistance Review, General Revenue Sharing, and the decentralization of federal regional management to 10 coterminous regions, each with a common regional center. New federalism as developed by the Ronald Reagan administration disregarded the Nixon approach of decentralized federal regional management and turned to development of direct relations between the federal government and the state governments. The intent was to return power and responsibility to the states and to dramatically reduce the role of the federal government in domestic programs, reminiscent of the dual federalism that prevailed in the United States in the last century. Reagan's new federalism had two phases: phase one consisted of the President's economic recovery program, which included reductions in the federal budget, the use of new block grant programs to give states greater flexibility in using federal monies, the reduction of the volume of new federal regulations, and tax reductions to stimulate the economy; phase two was the return from the federal to state governments of some authority to tax, thereby increasing the revenue capacity of state governments. These goals have had mixed success. The main problem is that federal funding has been cut at the same time that the states have been mandated to undertake hundreds of new functions relating to health, the environment, factory safety, and education. *See also* FEDERALISM, DUAL.

federalism, picket fence The concept that implies that bureaucratic specialists at the various levels of government (along with clientele groups) exercise considerable power over the nature of intergovernmental programs. Bureaucratic or program specialists at national, state, and local government levels for such fields as public housing, vocational education, health and hospitals, and higher education represent the pickets in the picket fence. They communicate with each other in daily work, belong to the same professional organizations, and have similar professional training. They are likely to be in conflict with general-purpose government officials (mayors, governors, the President), who attempt to coordinate the vertical power structures. The general-purpose officials are the cross pieces of the fence. The metaphor is credited to Terry Sanford, former governor of North Carolina, in his book *Storm Over the States* (1967).

federalism, vertical State-national government interactions. Such interactions are not limited to the executive branches of the national and state governments; close coordination also exists between the federal and state court systems. Crisscrossing vertical relations also have become more common. For example, the executive branch of the national government embarked upon several programs for assistance to state courts and state legislatures in the 1970s.

Federalist Papers The commentary on the U.S. Constitution and the theories behind it, published in 1787–1788, and considered by many political scientists to be the most important work of political theory written in the United States—the one product of the American mind counted among the classics of political philosophy. The papers were originally newspaper articles written by ALEXANDER HAMILTON, JAMES MADISON, and John Jay (under the name Publius) to encourage New York to ratify the new Constitution. The papers reflect the genius of the balance achieved in the American system between the views of Madison, an exponent of limited government, and Hamilton, an admirer of an energetic national government. It has been suggested that the papers reflected the thinking of the minority of Americans, who wanted a more nationalist government than most of the postrevolutionary generation wanted. They succeeded in getting it, in part, through JOHN MARSHALL's influence on the Supreme Court. Indeed, the Court has frequently cited the *Federalist Papers* as evidence of the ORIGINAL INTENT of the framers of the Constitution. *Compare to* ANTIFEDERALISTS.

Federalist No. 10 The Federalist paper in which James Madison discusses the problem of FACTIONS and the danger they pose to a political system. Madison feared that the interests of parties and pressure groups could destabilize a government; but he believed that an overarching representative government, with a functional as well as territorial separation of powers, could prevent this. Madison's brief essay, a defense of a pluralistic society, is the best known of the *Federalist Papers*. In the federal union he advocated, Madison envisioned "a republican remedy for the diseases most incident to republican government." The essay is one of the first attempts by an American to explain the political nature of humans. Madison found the causes of political differences and the creation of factions to be "sown in the nature of man." The essay is the classic explanation of why it is not easy to achieve change in the American political system. The constitutional structure is purposely designed to protect minorities from the possible tyranny of 50 percent plus one. The essay was more or less rediscovered by historian Charles A. Beard and other political analysts early in this century, when they sought to build an historical justification for modern interest group theory. Beard wrote in his *An Economic Interpretation of the Constitution* (*see* CONSTITUTION, ECONOMIC INTERPRETATION OF) that "The most philosophical examination of the foundations of political science is made by Madison in the tenth number."

Federalist No. 35 The Federalist paper in which James Madison discusses the nature and advantages of a legislature representing all classes of society, something he considered "altogether visionary." Madison concluded that, as long as the votes of the people are free, "the representative body . . . will be composed of landholders, merchants, and men of the learned professions," who out of their own self-interest would look after the interests of those not directly represented.

Federalist No. 51 The Federalist paper in which James Madison explains how the federal constitution provides for a SEPARATION OF POWERS whereby "those who administer each department [have] the necessary constitutional means and personal motives to resist encroachments of the others." This is achieved by "contriving the interior structure of the government as that its several constituent parts may, by their mutual relations, be the means of keeping each other in their proper places." *Compare to* CHECKS AND BALANCES.

Federalist No. 78 *See* JUDICIAL REVIEW; LEAST DANGEROUS BRANCH.

federalists 1. Those who supported the U.S. Constitution before its ratification. *Compare to* ANTIFEDERALISTS. **2.** After ratification of the Constitution, the term was applied to members of the Federalist political party of George Washington, John Adams, and Alexander Hamilton. The party disappeared from national politics in 1816.

federalists, anti *See* ANTIFEDERALISTS.

federated government *See* METROPOLITAN GOVERNMENT.

feeding frenzy Overwhelming attention by the press. When a major story breaks that has a single focus on one individual, the mass media's interest can be so intense that it has been compared to a hungry animal's attack on food. When, for example, in 1988 Senator Dan Quayle was unexpectedly made the Republican vice presidential nominee, the media is said to have descended on him in a "feeding frenzy."

felony A serious crime. In most jurisdictions, felonies are one of two major classes of crimes, the other being misdemeanors. With felonies, the upper limit of potential penalties depends upon the particular crime and ranges from a few years in prison to death. One year in prison is almost always the minimum scheduled penalty for a felony conviction. *Compare to* MISDEMEANOR.

FEMA *See* FEDERAL EMERGENCY MANAGEMENT AGENCY.

Ferraro, Geraldine (1935–   ) The New York congresswoman (1979–1985) who was the first female nominee for the vice presidency on the 1984 Democratic party ballot with Walter Mondale. While the Democrats lost by a landslide that year, Ferraro wrote in her memoir, *Ferraro: My Story* (1985), that: "The fallout from my candidacy gave new strength and a sense of purpose to women no matter what situations they were in. I got letters from secretaries who had finally summoned the courage to ask their bosses for raises, from women who for years had meant to go back to school and now were enrolling. . . . It was like a giant light bulb going on. A lot of the general public and a lot of women as well had not been aware that they were missing out on something. . . . A new political consciousness was born that no longer asked 'why' a woman candidate, but 'why not?'"

fiduciary 1. A person who manages money or property for others. Anyone who has discretionary authority or responsibility for the administration of a pension plan is a fiduciary. **2.** A concept in the theory of representation. A "fiduciary" is a representative who votes as the voters he or she represents would vote if they were present to vote for themselves; that is, the representative acts as a fiduciary for constituents. *Compare to* DELEGATE; TRUSTEE.

Fifteenth Amendment The 1870 amendment to the U.S. Constitution that guarantees to all citizens the right to vote regardless of "race, color, or previous condition of servitude." This is the legal source of federal voting rights legislation. *See also* VOTING RIGHTS ACT OF 1965.

Fifth Amendment The amendment to the U.S. Constitution that provides for the grand jury, prohibits DOUBLE JEOPARDY and the compelling of self-incrimination, requires that citizens will not "be deprived of life, liberty, or property, without due process of law," and mandates that private property shall be taken only for public use (EMINENT DOMAIN) with "just compensation." While the guarantees of the Fifth Amendment originally applied only to the federal government, they have been extended to the states through the due process clause of the Fourteenth Amendment. A person who "takes the Fifth Amendment" before a congressional committee or court is exercising his or her privilege against compulsory self-incrimination. *See also* JURY, GRAND.

fifth column Traitors within a country who wait to join the forces of invading enemy soldiers. The term dates from the Spanish Civil War when General Emilio Mola advanced on Madrid in 1936 with four columns of troops and boasted that a fifth column awaited him within the city. During World War II, the term came to be used in America for anyone secretly sympathetic with the Germans. Peter Wyden's *The Passionate War* (1983) notes: "Mola made the phrase famous but did not coin it. . . . It was first applied to Russian sympathizers within the besieged fortress of Ismail in 1790."

fighting words Insults that are not covered by the First Amendment's protection of free speech. When a man caused a fight by calling a city official "a damned fascist," he was arrested and convicted for his choice of words. The Supreme Court in *Chaplinsky v New Hampshire* (1942) upheld the conviction and said: "There are certain well-defined and narrowly limited classes of speech, the prevention and punishment of which have never been thought to raise any Constitutional problem. These include the lewd and obscene, the profane, the libelous, and the insulting or 'fighting' words—those which by their very utterance inflict injury or tend to incite an immediate breach of the peace. It has been well observed that such utterances are no essential part of any exposition of ideas, and are of such slight social value as a step to truth that any benefit that may be derived from them is clearly outweighed by the social interest in order and morality."

filibuster A time-delaying tactic used by a legislative minority in an effort to prevent a vote on a bill. The most common method is unlimited debate, but other forms of parliamentary maneuvering may be used. The stricter rules in the U.S. House of Representatives make filibusters most difficult, but they may be attempted through various delaying tactics. True filibusters are not possible in the House, because no member is permitted to speak for longer than one hour without unanimous consent. Moreover, a majority can call for the "previous question" and bring a bill to an immediate vote. In the Senate a member can filibuster without speaking continuously; he or she may yield to a colleague for a question or call for a quorum without losing the floor. In the event a recess is called, he or she is entitled to regain the floor when the Senate reassembles. A filibuster is a kind of guerrilla warfare on the part of a minority to prevent a majority from exercising its will. In this sense, it is antidemocratic, especially notorious for being used by U.S. senators from the South to delay or defeat civil rights bills. But it is in reality no more antidemocratic than any other parliamentary delaying tactic. The word originally meant a kind of pirate who waged irregular warfare for private gain. In 1917, the Senate adopted the first CLOTURE rule. As amended in 1975, it provides that the Senate may end debate—that is, end a filibuster—on a pending bill by a three-fifths vote of the entire Senate membership. In the modern Senate, filibusters—and cloture—are more common than ever.

filing 1. The formal process by which a candidate seeks a position on a jurisdiction's ballot. Filing requirements vary widely; some states require only a nominal fee, others require a petition signed by a small percentage of voters. Filing requirements are usually designed to discourage frivolous candidates. *Compare to* CROSSFILING. **2.** The initiation of a court case by formally submitting, or filing, the appropriate documents.

Fillmore, Millard (1800–1874) President of the United States from 1850 to 1853. Elected as Vice President on a ticket with Zachary Taylor, he became President upon Taylor's death. Virtually unknown today, Fillmore is famous for two things, only one of which is true. He opened trade with Japan; and he is said to be the first President to put a bathtub in the White House. This is totally false and derives from a 1917 hoax by H.L. Mencken who, on a slow day, simply made up a story about the history of the bathtub. Published in the New York *Evening Mail* on December 28, 1917, this "joke" about Fillmore and the bathtub found its way into history books.

financial disclosure Requirements under various federal laws that top federal officials and candidates for federal office disclose the sources of their personal income as well as sources of campaign contributions.

Financial Institutions Reform, Recovery, and Enforcement Act of 1989 The federal law passed in response to the SAVINGS AND LOAN SCANDAL which transferred the responsibilities of the former Federal Savings and Loan Insurance Corporation (FSLIC) to the FDIC. As a result, the FDIC now insures deposits in banks (using the "Bank Insurance Fund") as well as savings associations (using the "Savings Association Insurance Fund"). The new law also required the FDIC to eliminate differences that existed in deposit insurance coverage at banks and savings associations.

finding 1. A decision (by a judge or jury) on a question of fact or law. **2.** A formal, written, signed, presidential determination that a covert operation of the CIA is legal, important to national security, and (according to law) will be reported to the appropriate congressional committee in a timely fashion. Title XXII of the Intelligence Oversight Act of 1980 mandates "a report to the Congress concerning any finding or determination under any section of this chapter. That finding shall be reduced to writing and signed by the President."

fire in the belly The overwhelming desire to gain political office; the motivation to do all that has to be done to get elected.

fireside chat 1. President Franklin D. Roosevelt's radio talks to the nation. Part of the effectiveness of FDR's fireside chats was in their novelty; for the first time, the President could visit every home (via the radio) and in a very real sense "chat" with each citizen. **2.** Any informal address by a political leader to constituents via radio or television.

First Amendment The amendment to the U.S. Constitution that asserts that the "Congress shall make no law respecting an establishment of religion, or prohibiting the free exercise thereof; or abridging the freedom of speech, or of the press; or the right of the people peaceably to assemble, and to petition the government for a redress of grievances." This, the first part of—and the backbone of—the BILL OF RIGHTS, originally applied only to the federal government but has been extended to the states through the due process and equal protection clauses of the Fourteenth Amendment. It was Justice Hugo Black who wrote in *New York Times v Sullivan* (1964): "An unconditional right to say what one pleases about public affairs is what I consider to be the minimum guarantee of the First Amendment." *See also* ASSEMBLY; ESTABLISHMENT CLAUSE; FREE EXERCISE CLAUSE; FREE PRESS CLAUSE; FREE SPEECH CLAUSE; GRISWOLD V CONNECTICUT; INCORPORATION.

first branch 1. The U.S. Congress, established by Article I of the Constitution. **2.** A legislature in any government with separation of powers. The legislature is first because it is the branch most representative of and closest to the people.

First Lady 1. The wife of the President of the United States. **2.** The wife of a state governor.

first use *See* NO FIRST USE.

fiscal Having to do with taxation, public revenues, or public debt.

fiscal federalism *See* FEDERALISM, FISCAL.

fiscal policy The manipulation of government finances by raising or lowering taxes or levels of spending to promote economic stability and growth. Stability and growth must be combined, since stability without growth is stagnation. The use of fiscal policy for economic objectives is a decidedly recent phenomenon. For the greater part of the 200-year history of the United States, fiscal policy was not a factor. The national budgetary policy was premised upon expenditures equaling revenues (a balanced budget). In fact, with the exception of war years, budgeting before the 1900s was primarily an exercise in deciding how to get rid of excess revenues, generated primarily by tariffs. This is not to say that modern fiscal policies would not have saved the nation considerable distress from assorted recessions and depressions. Nineteenth-century economic thought held that the economy followed a natural order. The first major tampering with the natural order of things came in 1913, with the advent of the federal income tax and the establishment of the FEDERAL RESERVE SYSTEM. In 1921, the Budget and Accounting Act provided for a unified federal executive budget. The Great Depression of the 1930s, along with the initiation of social security and unemployment compensation programs, provided the first recognitions of the need for a national economic policy. However, legitimization of the goal of a national economic policy came with the passage of the Full Employment Act of 1946. The act not only created a Council of Economic Advisers for the President, but it prescribed objectives for economic prosperity and charged the President with insuring their achievement.

Basically, fiscal policy offers two courses of action, discretionary and built in. The first involves changing policy decisions. Discretionary fiscal policy has two major facets—the level of receipts and the level of expenditures. The major fiscal policy actions of recent years are replete with tax cuts and temporary reductions. Given the time lags involved in legislating tax changes, it is easy to see why Presidents have preferred to wage fiscal policy battles in terms of government spending. The second dimension involves built-in fiscal stabilizers—that is, preset or automatic policy. These are the transfer payments, the progressive tax rates, and the changing federal budget deficits and surpluses that move automatically to counter economic downturns or to control excessive periods of demand and business activity. For example, as people are laid off from work in a recessionary period, payments for unemployment compensation mount automatically. This increases the federal budget deficit, which in turn stimulates the economy and moves to offset the economic downswing. If the economy heats up, both regular and overtime wages increase, fueling demand for goods and services and creating inflation. As personal income increases, however, more and more people move into higher tax brackets; the tax structure thus functions as an automatic stabilizer by absorbing more personal income and thus restraining demand for goods and services. *See also* BUDGETING; ECONOMIC POLICY; MONETARY POLICY; POLITICAL ECONOMY.

fiscal year Yearly accounting period without regard to a calendar year. The fiscal year for the federal government through fiscal year 1976 began on July 1 and ended on June 30. Since fiscal year 1977, fiscal years for the federal government begin on October 1 and end on September 30. The fiscal year is designated by the calendar year in which it ends (e.g., fiscal year 1990 was the fiscal year ending September 30, 1990).

flag A cloth, with distinguishing color or design, which has a special meaning or serves as a signal. The American flag, the stars and stripes, is a major icon in the CIVIL RELIGION of the United States. Despite the fact that it is a revered symbol, the Supreme Court in *Texas v. Johnson* (1989) held that the public desecration of the flag is a protected form of free speech under the U.S. Constitution. Justice William J. Brennan, in the majority opinion, said: "We can imagine no more appropriate response to burning a flag than waving one's own, no better way to counter a flag-burner's message than by saluting the flag that burns, no surer means of preserving the dignity even of the flag that burned than by—as one witness here did—according its remains a respectful burial. We do not consecrate the flag by punishing its desecration, for in doing so we dilute the freedom that this cherished emblem represents." In response to this ruling Congress passed the Flag Protection Act of 1989 which made it a crime to desecrate the flag. The Court then held in *United States v Eichman* that the Act was an unconstitutional violation of free speech. This created an immediate national debate over the desirability of a constitutional amendment to prohibit flag burning.

With unintentional humor, President George Bush on June 12, 1990 warned that [flag burning] "endangers the fabric of our country."

flag of convenience The registration of a merchant ship in a foreign country, rather than in the country where it is owned or does business, to avoid high fees, high safety requirements, and so on; the ship then must legally fly the flag (the flag of convenience) of the country in which it is registered. This is different from reflagging, which is a diplomatic undertaking designed to qualify previously ineligible merchant ships for naval protection from friendly powers—whose flag they then fly.

flag, show the **1.** A state's efforts to make its presence known by sending troops or ships flying its flag to participate in an action. **2.** High profile involvement in something by a country, a government agency, or a private company.

Fletcher v Peck (1810) The first case in which the Supreme Court declared a state law to be unconstitutional. It held that a state's legislatively conferred charter (in effect, a contract) could not be unilaterally rescinded by a subsequent session of the legislature. *Compare to* DARTMOUTH COLLEGE V WOODWARD.

floater **1.** Anyone who sells their vote. **2.** Anyone who illegally votes in different places during the same election; usually for pay. *Compare to* VOTE, FLOATING.

floor **1.** The main part of a legislative chamber; that portion of a legislative chamber reserved for members; the place where legislators vote. **2.** The exclusive right to speak; a legislator who "has the floor" may usually continue to speak until willing to "yield the floor."

floor fight Disputes at a national nominating convention, often concerning the party platform or delegate credentials, that cannot be resolved in committee and must be taken to the floor of the full convention for resolution.

floor manager A legislator, usually representing sponsors of a bill, who attempts to steer the bill through debate and revision to a final vote in the chamber. Floor managers in the U.S. Congress are frequently chairs or ranking members of the committee that reported the bill. Increasingly, subcommittee chairs are being selected to manage legislation on the floor. Floor managers are responsible for apportioning the time granted to supporters of the bill for debating it. The minority leader or the ranking minority member of the committee often apportions time for the opposition.

FLRA *See* FEDERAL LABOR RELATIONS AUTHORITY.

FLSA *See* FAIR LABOR STANDARDS ACT OF 1938.

FMC *See* FEDERAL MARITIME COMMISSION.

FMCS *See* FEDERAL MEDIATION AND CONCILIATION SERVICE.

focus groups A relatively small number (6–20) of people with a common characteristic brought to a neutral setting to participate in a discussion on products or politics led by a trained researcher. Focus groups are a major tool of marketing research. They allow analysts to delve deeply into the motivations for buying a product or voting for a politician. Increasingly, reporters will assemble focus groups to help analyze elections or policies.

Food and Drug Administration The federal agency within the Department of Health and Human Services that is responsible for insuring the safety of food, drugs, cosmetics, and medical devices sold to the public. While the present name dates from 1931, other agencies had performed similar functions since the enactment of the Food and Drug Act of 1906.

food stamps A welfare program designed to improve the nutrition of the poor. Administered by the Department of Agriculture and state and local welfare organizations, the program provides coupons (stamps) that can be exchanged for food at many grocery stores. This is the nation's single largest welfare program; in 1990 some 20 million people were food stamp recipients. It is a good example of an ENTITLEMENT PROGRAM. The idea of food stamps originated in the late New Deal as a way of providing food to the poor from surpluses held by the government.

footprints One's impact on events. A political figure who is said to have "no footprints" is one who, though active in public life, has never made a memorable contribution. This negative usage is frequently used to describe an incumbent who hasn't much of a record.

Ford, Gerald R. (1913–) The President of the United States (1974–1977) after Richard M. Nixon was forced to resign because of the Watergate scandals. Ford was appointed Vice President by Nixon in 1973, with the consent of the Congress, to replace Spiro Agnew, who had resigned in disgrace. Ford was narrowly defeated for election in his own right when he ran against Jimmy Carter in 1976. He is the only person to have served as President without election to that office by the people. Ford, who had served in the U.S. House of Representatives since 1948, was the popular leader of the House Republicans when Nixon appointed him to the vice presidency. This meant that his confirmation would go smoothly and quickly and that Ford might prove useful to Nixon in the then-surfacing call for Nixon's impeachment over Watergate. When Ford succeeded to the presidency he said in his inaugural address of August 9, 1974: "If you have not chosen me by secret ballot, neither have I gained office by any secret promises." This was immediately called into question, as he pardoned Nixon a few weeks later. But no serious commentator has suggested that there was a direct deal concerning a pardon. Nevertheless, many analysts feel that Ford might have won election to the presidency in his own right if he had not pardoned Nixon for "all crimes he may have committed while in office." For his memoirs, see Gerald Ford, *A Time to Heal: The Autobiography of Gerald R. Ford* (1979).

Foreign Agents Registration Act of 1938 The federal law that requires all lobbyists, public relations consultants, political consultants, and so on, working for foreign governments, to register with the U.S. attorney general. Exempted from the registration requirement are foreign diplomats, attorneys, and those engaged in international trade and humanitarian, religious, academic, and cultural activities.

foreign aid All official grants and concessional loans (i.e., loans made on softer than commercial terms), in currency or in kind, broadly aimed at transferring resources from developed to less-developed countries for the purposes of economic development or income distribution. Foreign aid may be bilateral (from one country to another) or multilateral (distributed through international financial institutions, such as the World Bank or the International Monetary Fund). Foreign aid, also referred to as economic assistance, may be given as project aid (where the donor provides money for a specific project, such as a dam or a school) or as program aid (where the donor does not know what projects the money will be spent on). Economic assistance consists of both hard loans (those at commercial bank interest rates) and soft loans (concessional, or at low interest rates). Aid may be tied to multilateral aid agencies (i.e., the loans may be partially financed by the recipient country), or to bilateral arrangements (i.e., the money must be spent on procurement in the donor country or must be transported by the donor country's shipping).

Countries give foreign aid for various reasons: to give humanitarian assistance after wars or natural disasters; to militarily strengthen allies against external or internal threats; to promote the economic development of the recipient country; or to simply meet the basic human needs of the poor citizens of the recipient country. The first significant instance of foreign aid was that given by the United States to its allies during and right after World War I. But this was ad hoc. Not until the Harry S Truman administration did foreign aid become institutionalized and a continuous part of American foreign policy. It was and remains motivated both by humanitarian concerns and a desire to allow grantees to achieve the kind of economic and social growth that would allow their governments to withstand the efforts of communists to take them over. *See also* MARSHALL PLAN.

foreign policy The totality of a state's relations with and policies toward other states. A nation's foreign policy, even though it may be largely the prerogative of an executive branch, is always grounded in its domestic policy. There seems to be bipartisan support for this notion. For example, two-time Democratic presidential nominee (1952 and 1956) Adlai E. Stevenson wrote in *What I Think* (1956): "We cannot be any stronger in our foreign policy—for all the bombs and guns we may heap up in our arsenals—than we are in the spirit which rules inside the country. Foreign policy, like a river, cannot rise above its source." Secretary of State (under Republican Presidents Nixon and Ford) Henry Kissinger has said essentially the same thing: "No foreign policy—no matter how ingenious—has any chance of success if it is born in the minds of a few and carried in the hearts of none" (*Washington Post*, August 4, 1973). The other major tenet of foreign policy on which there is general agreement is political theorist Hans J. Morgenthau's assertion from *Politics Among Nations* (5th ed.,

1978) that: "The objectives of foreign policy must be defined in terms of national interest."

foreign service **1.** A corps of professional diplomats. The Rogers Act of 1924 combined U.S. diplomatic and consular services into the present U.S. Foreign Service, the diplomatic corps, known as Foreign Service Officers (FSOs), responsible for administering U.S. foreign policies. While most American ambassadors gain their positions through a long career in the Foreign Service, historically a significant number of them are patronage appointees whose only outward qualification for the job is a demonstrated ability to make large campaign contributions to the party in power. While many distinguished outsiders have been appointed to ambassadorships, the de facto sale of these offices is a continuous, if quiet, bipartisan national scandal. **2.** Military or civilian service in foreign locations.

Forest Service, U.S. The agency within the U.S. Department of Agriculture, created in 1905, that has the responsibility for national leadership in forestry. While inexorably associated with the CONSERVATION movement, it has also at times been at odds with conservationists over the commercial use of national forests.

forgotten man President Franklin D. Roosevelt's term for the ordinary citizen who had not been served well by the previous Republican administrations and for the millions left in desperate destitution by the Great Depression. The "forgotten man" was first mentioned by Yale University economics professor William Graham Sumner (1840–1910) in 1883, but Roosevelt made it one of the most potent political symbols of the twentieth century. While Sumner's forgotten man was the "quiet virtuous, domestic citizen, who pays his debts and his taxes and is never heard of out of his little circle," Roosevelt's was "at the bottom of the economic pyramid."

forward funding The practice of obligating funds in one fiscal year for programs that are to operate in a subsequent year.

Founding Fathers **1.** An imprecise phrase for all of those individuals who played a major role in declaring U.S. independence, fighting the Revolutionary War, and writing and adopting the U.S. Constitution. **2.** Those who framed and signed the U.S. Constitution. While these men are now generally revered in American history, the presiding officer of the Constitutional Convention, George Washington, was not so impressed. He wrote in a November 10, 1787 letter to Bushrod Washington: "I do not think we are more inspired, have more wisdom, or possess more virtue, than those who will come after us." Historians such as Merrill Jensen remind us that: "When it comes to logrolling, dirty politics, hanky-panky, bribery—you name it—our Founding Fathers often behaved in a way that would make many twentieth-century politicians look like saints" (*The New York Times*, March 16, 1978).

Fourteenth Amendment The post-Civil War amendment to the U.S. Constitution that defines citizenship and mandates due process as well as equal protection of the laws for all citizens. Through the due process and equal protection clause of the Fourteenth Amendment, the Supreme Court has gradually applied most of the protections of the Bill of Rights to the states. The Fourteenth Amendment, which has produced more litigation and court interpretation than any other part of the Constitution, was enacted originally to protect the freed slaves from abrogations of their rights by the southern states.

When the Congress met in 1866, it faced several unprecedented circumstances: the Confederacy had recently surrendered, President Abraham Lincoln had been assassinated, and Andrew Johnson had taken over the presidency and had moved to begin the reconstruction of the South. These conditions contributed, either directly or indirectly, to the eventual framing of the Fourteenth Amendment. The Congress was dominated by a strong coalition of pro-civil rights and anti-Confederate congressmen. This coalition, the Radical Republicans, disagreed with almost every point of President Johnson's reconstruction program. They felt that Johnson's plan did not provide for adequate protection against state infringements of the former slaves' civil rights. In addition, they protested that the Johnson plan was not severe enough in reprimanding former Confederates. Finally, the Radicals feared that the President's plan would allow the southern states to regain their congressional seats too quickly, enabling the former Confederates to block the Radicals' own plan for reconstruction. Ultimately, the Radicals turned to amending the Constitution as a means of implementing their reconstruction program, without fear of veto by the President or opposition by former Confederate states.

Fourth Amendment The amendment to the U.S. Constitution that protects individuals and their properties from unreasonable searches and seizures by generally prohibiting state acts that invade one's reasonable expectation of privacy. This provision applies both to arrests of persons and to searches of their person or properties for evidence. *See also* EXCLUSIONARY RULE; MAPP V OHIO.

fourth branch of government 1. The bureaucracy. While technically under the control of the executive branch, it sometimes seems to function as if it had a will, power, and legal authority all its own. **2.** The independent regulatory agencies. **3.** The press; the mass media in general. *Compare to* FOURTH ESTATE.

fourth estate The press; the media in general; the journalistic profession. The term is usually credited to EDMUND BURKE (1729–1797), who observed that in the reporters' gallery in the British Parliament "there sat a Fourth Estate more important by far than them all." The word estate is used here to mean class—the other three estates being the nobility, the commoners, and the clergy.

framers, the The men who wrote the U.S. Constitution in 1787.

franchise 1. A privilege of some sort. **2.** The right to vote.

frank The facsimile signature of a member of the U.S. Congress used on envelopes in lieu of stamps on official outgoing mail. The franking privilege is a major political advantage for congressional incumbents. While designed to allow members of the Congress to freely communicate with their constituents, it has grown to be a significant element in most members' reelection campaigns. While it is illegal to use the frank for other than official business, or to solicit political support or campaign contributions, it is perfectly legal for members to communicate with their constituents on a massive basis. Common Cause once estimated that, during an election year, about 40 million pieces of franked mail is sent out each month by the House of Representatives alone.

fraud *See* ABUSE.

freedom **1.** The liberty to do or not do something; for example, to speak or to practice religion. **2.** The condition of not being in the power of others. **3.** The capacity to perform legal acts; for example, to vote or to buy property. In this sense, children in the United States under 18 years of age are generally not free; they are still subject to the power of others. Freedom is one of the most important of America's intellectual icons. It implies the political independence of the nation and of each of its individual citizens. Yet there are those who would argue that political freedom is only one side of the issue, the other being economic freedom. What good are political rights, they contend, if one must go to sleep hungry in a public park? **4.** The right to think freely. Justice Oliver Wendell Holmes, Jr., in *United States v Schwimmer* (1929) wrote: "If there is any principle of the Constitution that more imperatively calls for attachment than any other it is the principle of free thought—not free thought for those who agree with us but freedom for the thought that we hate."

freedom of choice A phrase usually used in the context of ABORTION to mean a woman's right to make personal decisions on abortion without government interference; usually shortened to PRO CHOICE.

Freedom of Information Act of 1966 The law that provides for public availability of information held by federal agencies, unless the information falls within one of the specific categories exempt from public disclosure. Exempt records are those whose disclosure would impair rights of privacy or national security. Virtually all agencies of the executive branch of the federal government have issued regulations to implement the Freedom of Information Act. These regulations inform the public where certain types of information may be readily obtained, how other information may be obtained on request, and what internal agency appeals are available if the request for information is refused. To locate specific agency regulations pertaining to freedom of information, consult the *Code of Federal Regulations* index under Information Availability. *See also* PRIVACY ACT OF 1974.

freedom of religion *See* ESTABLISHMENT CLAUSE.

free exercise clause That portion of the First Amendment to the U.S.

Constitution that prevents the Congress from "prohibiting the free exercise of" religion. However, the Supreme Court held in *Reynolds v United States* (1879) that this freedom does not extend to "religious acts which are crimes or contrary to generally accepted public morals" (in this case the polygamous practices of some Mormons). In another case, *Bob Jones University v United States* (1983), the Court denied tax-exempt status to a private school because it practiced racial discrimination that was grounded in religious doctrine. In interpreting the free exercise clause, the Court has held that if the purpose or effect of a statute is to impede the observance of religion, or to discriminate invidiously among religions, then the free exercise of religion is abridged. Indeed, only a compelling government interest, such as nondiscrimination in higher education, can legitimize a statute restrictive of the free exercise of religion. In this regard, it is clear that no statute can validly impinge upon religious thought—that is, religious belief devoid of conduct. Moreover, by applying the compelling interest test, the Court has assured that forms of conduct based on religious belief are to receive increasing protection. Thus, when a Seventh-Day Adventist was fired for refusing to work on Saturdays (her sabbath), the Supreme Court in *Thomas v Review Board of the Indiana Employment Security Division* (1981) ruled that she was fully entitled to unemployment benefits.

free press clause   That portion of the First Amendment to the U.S. Constitution that protects the liberty and independence of the media from being abridged by government. Thomas Jefferson wrote on the subject to Edward Carrington on January 16, 1787, "Were it left to me to decide whether we should have a government without newspapers, or newspapers without a government, I should not hesitate a moment to prefer the latter." The Supreme Court has also interpreted the amendment to prohibit PRIOR RESTRAINT, that is, prepublication censorship. In the leading case on prior restraint, *Near v Minnesota* (1931), the Court declared unconstitutional a State of Minnesota gag law, which allowed judges to bar publication of newspapers considered "malicious, scandalous or defamatory." This ruling was reinforced by *New York Times v United States* (1971), when the Court dissolved an injunction against the *New York Times* that had halted publication of the Pentagon Papers.

The concept of a free press is often confused with the notion of free access. While government in the United States cannot prevent the press from printing (or broadcasting) the information it has, it can and often does deny the press access to information. The best recent example of this occurred when the Ronald Reagan administration, as a matter of policy, refused to allow reporters to accompany American forces in the invasion of Grenada. Nor does freedom of the press insulate the press, as corporations, from those economic regulations applied to all business—such as taxation, equal employment opportunity, labor management, and antitrust laws. Because television and radio station owners are licensees of scarce frequencies, they have been held subject to additional government regulation in a number of areas. *Compare to* FAIRNESS DOCTRINE.

free ride **1.** The seeking of office by an incumbent officeholder who campaigns for a higher office without giving up his or her present one. For example, an incumbent governor who runs for President in a year when he or she is not up for reelection as governor is getting a free ride. **2.** According to some, the U.S. policy of providing a defense umbrella for its allies in Western Europe and Asia. They then have more resources to devote to developing their economics. Meanwhile, the United States has vast deficits, caused in part by providing for their defense.

free rider One who does not belong to an organized group, such as a union or a political party, but who nevertheless benefits from its activities. For example, a worker in a given organization who does not belong to a union, when most of the other workers do, may receive all of the wage increases and fringe benefits bargained for by the union without paying dues to the union. *See also* AGENCY SHOP.

free speech clause That portion of the First Amendment to the United States Constitution that prevents the Congress from passing any law that would inhibit the open discussion of issues. While the English common law concept of freedom of speech meant freedom from PRIOR RESTRAINT only, the present American theory of freedom of speech generally establishes both freedom from prior restraint and freedom from subsequent punishment for the exercise of these rights. Some Supreme Court justices have, in fact, suggested that freedom of speech is absolute; but a majority of the Court always has maintained that it must be balanced against other legitimate interests. In short, the Court has attempted to preserve the greatest degree of expression consistent with the protection of overriding and compelling government interests. President Woodrow Wilson said in a May 10, 1919 speech at the institute of France in Paris: "I have always been among those who believed that the greatest freedom of speech was the greatest safety, because if a man is a fool, the best thing to do is to encourage him to advertise the fact by speaking. It cannot be so easily discovered if you allow him to remain silent and look wise, but if you let him speak, the secret is out and the world knows that he is a fool. So it is by the exposure of folly that it is defeated . . . . " *Compare to* FIGHTING WORDS; CLEAR AND PRESENT DANGER; COMMERCIAL SPEECH.

free trade A theoretical concept that refers to international trade unhampered by government restrictions or tariffs. Since World War II, American policy has been in favor of free trade—with a variety of politically expedient limitations. In 1924, English historian Lord Macaulay (1800–1859) wrote that "free trade, one of the greatest blessings which a government can confer on a people, is in almost every country unpopular." This is still true today. *Compare to* PROTECTIONISM.

free trade area A cooperative arrangement among a group of nations that agree to remove barriers to trade with each other, while each maintains its own differing schedule of tariffs applying to all other nations. The best example is the European Free Trade Association. *Compare to* CUSTOMS UNION.

free trade protectionist A member of the U.S. Congress who believes in free trade "in principle" but seeks protectionist legislation on a "temporary" basis for industries in his or her district that are adversely affected by foreign imports.

friend of the court *See* AMICUS CURIAE.

friends and neighbors effect V.O. KEY's description from his *Southern Politics in State and Nation* (1949) of a local voting pattern in which candidates for statewide offices gain large majorities in their home counties, heavy support in nearby counties, and slight support in the rest of the state. To Key, this points out the "absence of stable, well-organized, statewide factions of like-minded citizens formed to advocate measures of common concern."

frontage assessment A tax to pay for neighborhood improvements (such as sidewalks or sewage lines) charged in proportion to the frontage (number of feet bordering the road) of each property.

front loaded 1. Presidential primaries that are scheduled disproportionately early in the primary season, presumably increasing the influence of these early states in the selection process and making it more difficult for new candidates to emerge later in the season. **2.** A labor agreement that provides for a greater wage increase in its first year of effect than in subsequent years.

front runner The candidate who seems to be leading in a major race for a political party's nomination. Because early front runners have so often stumbled and fallen out of the political race, no candidate wants to be called a front runner; they prefer the UNDERDOG label. Indeed, candidates nowadays spend considerable time accusing each other of being the front runner. It's what all candidates want to be but don't want to be called.

frostbelt *See* RUSTBELT; SUNBELT-SNOWBELT TENSION.

FTC *See* FEDERAL TRADE COMMISSION.

full faith and credit 1. The clause in Article IV, Section 1, of the U.S. Constitution that requires states to legally recognize (i.e., to give full faith and credit to) the official acts of other states. This ensures that property rights, wills, deeds, and so on will be honored for all citizens in all states. However, the clause is limited to civil judicial proceedings. **2.** The descriptive term for those debt obligations, such as certain bonds, that have first claim upon the resources of the state.

furlough issue *See* HORTON, WILLIE.

fusion 1. The temporary joining of two or more political parties to support a common candidate or ticket. **2.** The process underlying thermonuclear weapons.

G

gag rule **1.** Any formal instruction from a competent authority, usually a judge, to refrain from discussing or advocating something, or both; also known as a *gag order*. The Supreme Court held in *Nebraska Press Association v Stuart* (1976) that a judge could not gag the press about what could be reported prior to a trial. Perhaps the most famous gag rules are President Theodore Roosevelt's executive orders in 1902 and 1904 that forbade federal employees, on pain of dismissal, to seek pay increases or to attempt to influence legislation before the Congress, either as individuals or as members of organizations, except through the heads of their departments. Roosevelt's gag orders were repealed by the Lloyd-LaFollette Act of 1912, which also granted federal employees the right to organize unions. **2.** A judge's order that a disruptive defendant literally be gagged. This was upheld in the case of *Illinois v Allen* (1970). **3.** A judge's order to witnesses and lawyers that they not discuss a case with people who are not directly involved with it. **4.** A legislative rule that limits debate on a bill. *Compare to* CLOTURE; RULE. **5.** The policy of the Reagan and Bush Administrations which forbade employees of federally-supported family planning organizations from discussing the option of abortion with their female clients. This was reversed by the Clinton administration in 1993.

Gallup, George Horace (1901–1984) The best known of American pollsters, whose Gallup poll has become synonymous with the measurement of public opinion. He was a pioneer of scientific polling techniques that use a small sample of respondents from a large population. Gallup first came to national attention when his poll correctly predicted the results of the 1936 presidential election—quite in contrast to the badly flawed *Literary Digest* prediction of that year. Because the Gallup poll (compiled by the American Institute of Public Opinion, located in Princeton, New Jersey), which covers all aspects of public opinion, not just politics, has been published continuously since the mid-1930s, it contains a wealth of baseline data about American social attitudes. (For example, in 1939 a survey asked about topless bathing suits—for men; over one third of all Americans found them objectionable.) Many serious studies of changing American social and political attitudes during the last half-century necessarily start with historical data from the Gallup poll. *Compare to* SAMPLE.

game plan A phrase borrowed from football for an overall strategy designed to achieve a goal. According to columnist Alan Otten in the *Wall Street Journal* (December 23, 1970): "Officials in both foreign and economic policy areas have too eagerly embraced the 'game plan' image of the sports world. They now constantly project their 'economic game plan' or 'Vietnam game plan' even though the phrase carries overtones of fun and frivolity that don't quite suit the serious business of ending the war in Southeast Asia or restoring economic vigor at home."

game theory A mathematical approach to problems of conflict and collaboration between rational actors. The essence of game theory is that, given assumptions about preferences, possession of information, and psychological tendency to risk, it is possible to figure out how people will react to the possible actions of others. Game theory is often illustrated by the "Prisoners' Dilemma" paradigm. It supposes that two men have been arrested on a suspicion of having committing a crime together and are being held in separate cells. There is not enough evidence to prosecute unless one confesses and implicates the other. Both of them know this, but cannot talk to each other. The dilemma is that the best outcome, not being convicted, is only available if they trust each other. So if X decides to trust Y, but Y fears X may not be trustworthy, Y may confess to get a lesser sentence; X then gets a worse one. The best solution to this dilemma is for both to cooperate, to minimize the worst that can happen, rather than trying for the outcome that is maximum. This is called the "Minimax" strategy; it is considered by game theorists to be the most probable outcome.

GAO *See* GENERAL ACCOUNTING OFFICE.

Garfield, James A. (1831–1881) Twentieth President of the United States, elected in 1880 and assassinated on July 2, 1881, by Charles Guiteau, an insane self-styled attorney who had worked for Garfield's election and was angry about not receiving a patronage appointment. Garfield's death from his wounds on September 19, 1881 gave new life to the CIVIL SERVICE REFORM movement, culminating in the passage of the Pendleton or Civil Service Act of 1883. Garfield, after only a few months in office, was succeeded by his Vice President, Chester A. Arthur.

gatekeeper **1.** A critical decision maker in a political system. Such a person or institution decides who shall and who shall not get political rewards and can effectively veto a person's advance in a political or social system. For example, a local political leader may be the gatekeeper for nominations for city council membership; a legislative committee chair may be a gatekeeper for certain kinds of bills. **2.** A mass media decision maker who decides what stories will be printed or broadcast; in effect, what will become news. **3.** A staff member of an executive or legislator who screens problems and issues to decide which ones will be reviewed by the boss. *Compare to* AGENDA SETTING.

gay rights movement The efforts to achieve full civil rights for homosexuals, to repeal laws that hold that homosexual acts are illegal, and to create a more positive image of homosexuals. A landmark in the gay rights movement was the 1975 decision of the American Psychiatric Association to remove homosexuality from its list of mental disorders. Some jurisdictions, such as San Francisco and New York City, have enacted laws making it illegal to discriminate against someone because of sexual orientation. The increasing demands for acceptance of homosexual lifestyles is a direct result of the CIVIL RIGHTS MOVEMENT, which made it possible for all minorities to insist upon their full rights as citizens.

gender balance 1. A situation that will exist only when women hold half of all positions of political power. **2.** A reference to laws in some states (such as Iowa, North Dakota, and Delaware) that require a governor's appointments to state boards and commission to be evenly divided between the sexes.

gender gap The difference in political opinions between men and women. During the 1984 presidential election, the gender gap was a big issue—which turned out in the end to be a nonissue because it didn't make any real difference in the end. Men and women voted pretty much alike, but there was a slight gap in preferences. For example, in the 1984 election, eight percent more men voted for Ronald Reagan than women. In the 1988 election, men supported George Bush by seven percentage points more than women did. Nevertheless, there are significant differences: women are more likely to be registered voters and more likely to be Democrats.

General Accounting Office (GAO) A support agency created by the Budget and Accounting Act of 1921 to audit federal government expenditures and to assist the Congress with its legislative oversight responsibilities. The GAO is directed by the comptroller general of the United States, who is appointed by the President with the advice and consent of the Senate for a term of fifteen years. While the GAO originally confined itself to auditing financial records to see that funds were properly spent, since the 1960s it has redefined its mission to include overall program evaluation.

General Assembly 1. The largest unit of the United Nations, in which all member nations are represented and each has a single vote. While the General Assembly, which meets annually each fall, is a continuing international conference that has many U.N. housekeeping responsibilities and generates a goodly number of resolutions, it has no real power to affect the behavior of sovereign states. It functions mainly as a forum for international propaganda and debate. *Compare to* SECURITY COUNCIL. **2.** A legislature in some state governments.

general manager The administrative official, also known as *city administrator* or *chief administrative officer*, appointed in a MAYOR-COUNCIL SYSTEM of government. He or she is typically appointed by the mayor and shares powers with that office. *Compare to* CITY MANAGER.

general revenue All the taxes or fees paid to a government whose use is unrestricted. Excluded from general revenue are funds that can only be used for specified purposes, such as earmarked taxes or categorical grants.

general revenue sharing *See* REVENUE SHARING.

general schedule The basic pay system for federal white-collar employees. It is the largest of the civilian pay systems, covering approximately half of the almost three million civilian employees.

General Services Administration (GSA) The federal agency, created by the Federal Property and Administrative Services Act of 1949, which establishes policy and provides for the management of the federal government's property and records, including construction and operation of buildings, procurement and distribution of supplies, utilization and disposal of property, transportation, traffic and communications management, stockpiling of strategic materials, and the management of a government-wide automatic data-processing resources program.

general welfare clause That part of Article I, Section 8, of the U.S. Constitution that authorizes the Congress to "provide for the common Defense and general Welfare of the United States." It has long been argued whether this is an unlimited grant of power to spend or whether its power is limited to spending on those activities specifically mentioned in other parts of the Constitution. A liberal interpretation has prevailed, and the spending power of the Congress has never been successfully challenged in the courts.

general will JEAN JACQUES ROUSSEAU's idea from *The Social Contract* (1761) that there is a collective will or consensus among the people, which is the ultimate locus of all political power. Only majority rule can define the general will. However, there are instances when politicians pointedly ignore the general will, such as when the Congress grants itself a pay increase. When then Speaker of the House Thomas P. "Tip" O'Neill was asked why the Congress authorized a pay raise for itself without a formal vote, he said "There are instances where it is in the best interests of the nation not to vote the will of the people."

gentrification The gradual replacement of the poor of a neighborhood by people with middle and upper incomes; the upgrading of inner-city neighborhoods when well-to-do families refurbish vacant or abandoned properties to move into them. Gentrification can have many social and political implications. The most intractable problem is that, once gentrification starts, poorer residents are forced out because they cannot pay increased rents or property taxes.

germane Pertaining to the subject matter of the measure at hand. All U.S. House of Representatives amendments must be germane to the bill. The Senate requires that amendments be germane only when they are proposed to general appropriation bills, bills being considered under cloture, or, often, when proceeding under an agreement to limit debate.

gerrymander To reshape an electoral district to enhance the political fortunes of the party in power (or incumbents), as opposed to creating a district with geographic compactness. The term first arose in 1811, when Massachusetts Governor Elbridge Gerry (1744–1814) reluctantly signed a redistricting bill that created a district shaped like a salamander. Gerrymandering is often called an abuse of political power by the party out of power. Actually, it is simply the use of political power by the party in control of the redistricting process. The only thing abused is geography. But in 1986, the

Supreme Court ruled in *Davis v Bandemer* that partisan gerrymandering is unconstitutional "when the electoral system is arranged in a manner that will consistently degrade a voter's or a group of voters' influence on the political process as a whole." According to Representative Vic Fazio, gerrymandering is "like obscenity. Some people see it and some people don't. It is often something that is a purely partisan attack on what is a purely partisan process, and no party is guilty or without guilt" (*The New York Times*, May 9, 1990). *Compare to* REDISTRICTING.

gerrymandering, affirmative Redistricting to consolidate minority votes so that a minority group member will most likely win the next election. This was encouraged by the VOTING RIGHTS ACT and upheld by the Supreme Court in *United Jewish Organizations of Williamsburgh v Carey* (1977).

get out the vote Campaigns, both partisan and nonpartisan, which are designed to increase turnout on election day.

ghetto **1.** Those areas of European or Middle Eastern cities where Jews were once legally forced to live. **2.** An area of a city inhabited almost exclusively by members of an ethnic, racial, religious, or social group. It often carries connotations of low income. The black urban ghettos of the nation have long been centers of social unrest and sometimes of disorder. After a series of urban riots during the mid-1960s, President Lyndon B. Johnson appointed an Advisory Commission on Civil Disorders (the Kerner Commission) to investigate the problem. It reported that "what white Americans have never fully understood—but what the Negro can never forget—is that white society is deeply implicated in the ghetto. White institutions created it, white institutions maintain it, and white society condones it." MARTIN LUTHER KING, JR. concurred. He wrote in *The Trumpet of Conscience* (1967) that "the slums are the handiwork of a vicious system of the white society; Negroes live in them, but they do not make them, any more than a prisoner makes a prison."

Gibbons v Ogden (1924) The Supreme Court case in which Chief Justice JOHN MARSHALL first put forth a broad interpretation of the COMMERCE CLAUSE by defining interstate commerce to include all navigable waters—even those within a state.

Gideon v Wainwright (1963) The Supreme Court case that held that the due process clause of the Fourteenth Amendment required that persons brought to trial in state courts on felony charges are entitled to have a court-appointed lawyer if they cannot afford to pay for one of their own. Previously, state courts were required to provide legal counsel to indigent defendants only in cases where the death penalty was at issue (*Powell v Alabama* [1932]) or when the defendant was young or mentally incompetent (*Betts v Brady* [1942]). *Gideon v Wainwright* extended the right to legal assistance to all felony defendants in all state criminal trials. Justice Hugo Black wrote that "reason and reflection require us to recognize that, in our adversary system of criminal justice, any person hauled into court, who is too poor to hire a lawyer, cannot be assured a fair trial unless counsel is provided for him. This seems to be an obvious truth."

Gitlow v New York (1925) The Supreme Court case that held that the freedom of speech and press as guaranteed by the First Amendment "are among the fundamental personal rights and 'liberties' protected by the due process clause of the Fourteenth Amendment from impairment by the states." This case is a landmark because it was the first time that the Court said that a portion of the Bill of Rights was applicable to the states by means of the Fourteenth Amendment.

give 'em hell What all candidates strive to do to the opposition on the campaign trail. The phrase is particularly associated with President Harry S Truman. As he tells the story in his memoirs: "It was in 1948, and we were holding an enthusiastic meeting [in Seattle] when some man with a great big voice cried from the galleries, 'Give 'em hell, Harry!' I told him at that time, and I have been repeating it ever since, that I have never deliberately given anybody hell. I just tell the truth on the opposition—and they think it's hell" (*Mr. Citizen*, 1960).

G-men 1. FBI agents. Legend has it that the term originated in 1933 when public enemy George "Machine Gun" Kelly (1895–1954), upon being surrounded by FBI agents in a Memphis, Tennessee, boarding house, screamed, "It's the government men—don't shoot, G-men, don't shoot!" Well, don't believe it. First, the FBI didn't capture Kelly; local Memphis police did. Second, the term was long in use as slang to describe government workers and agents. Nevertheless, in the public's mind, G-men became synonymous with the FBI, especially after the 1935 James Cagney movie, *G-Men*. **2.** Secret Service agents. Interestingly, the U.S. Secret Service is today located on G Street in Washington, D.C. Because the Secret Service is part of the Treasury Department, their agents have also been known at T-men. *See also* SECRET SERVICE, UNITED STATES. **3.** Relatively low-level civil servants who are members of the FBI's special support group. These G's, as they are known, relieve the higher-paid FBI agents of the drudgery of routine surveillance work.

GNP *See* GROSS NATIONAL PRODUCT.

go negative A policy decision by a political campaign to use NEGATIVE ADVERTISING.

goals Within the context of equal employment opportunity, realistic objectives that an organization endeavors to achieve through AFFIRMATIVE ACTION. Quotas, in contrast, restrict employment or development opportunities to members of particular groups by establishing required numbers of proportionate representation, which managers are obligated to attain without regard to equal employment opportunity.

gobbledygook Slang terms—along with *officialese, federalese,* and *baffle-gab*—for the obtuse language so frequently used by bureaucrats. Gobbledygook was coined by World War II administrator Maury Maverick

(1896–1954). Maverick, a former Representative from Texas (1934–1938), was so angered by the convoluted language he found in so many government documents that he invented the special word for it. He told *The New York Times* (May 21, 1944): "People ask me where I got gobbledygook. I do not know. It must have come in a vision. Perhaps I was thinking of the old bearded turkey gobbler back in Texas who was always gobbledy-gobbling and strutting with ludicrous pomposity. At the end of this gobble there was a sort of gook." Officialese and federalese are obvious derivatives of the long standing "legalese." This construction, which means language only a lawyer can understand, is applied to language only an official or a member of the federal government can understand. The construction has since been extended to Pentagonese. Bafflegab surfaced in the 1950s to mean almost unintelligible jargon.

Goldwater, Barry M. (1909–   ) The U.S. Senator from Arizona (1952–1964 and 1969–1986) who was the Republican presidential nominee in 1964 and later the "grand old man" of American conservatism. Widely perceived as a "right wing nut" during his presidential bid, he later became widely respected for personal integrity and a penchant for speaking unpopular truths. His *The Conscience of a Conservative* (1960) helped create the modern conservative movement that eventually led to the election of President Ronald Reagan in 1980.

Goldwater-Nichols Military Reform Act of 1986 The Pentagon Reorganization Act which gave the chairman of the JOINT CHIEFS OF STAFF greater power and responsibility in order to reduce the problems of interservice rivalry.

Goldwater Republican A conservative as opposed to a moderate Republican.

good faith Honest; honesty in fact. In the context of equal employment opportunity, good faith is the absence of discriminating intent. Good-faith bargaining is a requirement of the National Labor Relations Act, which makes it illegal for an employer to refuse to bargain in good faith about wages, hours, and other conditions of employment with the representative selected by a majority of the employees in a unit appropriate for collective bargaining.

good life, the The end or goal of political community. This notion goes back to ARISTOTLE, who wrote in his *Politics* (fourth century B.C.): "When several villages are united in a single complete community, large enough to be nearly or quite self-sufficing, the state comes into existence, originating in the bare needs of life, and continuing in existence for the sake of a good life."

good neighbor policy A phrase first used by President Herbert Hoover but best known for describing President Franklin D. Roosevelt's policies toward Central and South America. Roosevelt said, in his inaugural address of March 4, 1933: "I would dedicate this nation to the policy of the good neighbor—the neighbor who resolutely respects himself and, because he does so, respects the rights of others—the neighbor who respects his obligations and respects the sanctity of his agreements in and with a world of neighbors."

Goodnow, Frank J. (1859–1939) A leader of the progressive reform movement and one of the founders and first president (in 1903) of the American Political Science Association. Goodnow is now best known as one of the principal exponents, along with Woodrow Wilson, of public administration's politics-administration dichotomy. Goodnow's most enduring work is *Politics and Administration* (1900).

good offices The disinterested use of one's official position, one's office, to help others settle their differences; an offer to mediate a dispute.

good samaritan law Any statute that gives malpractice protection to medical specialists when they use their skills to help people in an emergency—when they might not be covered by the regular malpractice insurance.

GOP Grand Old Party; the REPUBLICAN PARTY.

Gore, Albert Jr. (1948–   ) The Vice President of the United States since 1993. The son of Albert Gore, Sr. (the U.S. Senator from Tennessee from 1952 to 1970), Harvard educated Gore the younger, after military service in Vietnam and a brief career in journalism, was elected to the House of Representatives from 1976 to 1984. Tennessee then sent him to the U.S. Senate in 1984. After actively seeking the Democratic Party nomination for President in 1988, he declined to run in 1992—until the 1992 Democratic Party presidential nominee, Governor William J. Clinton of Arkansas, selected him as his vice presidential running mate.

governance **1.** The process of government; the exercise of government power; government action. **2.** PUBLIC ADMINISTRATION. **3.** A system or method of government, for example, democracy or fascism. **4.** The state of being under the control of a higher legal or political authority. Thus, citizens are under the governance of their national government, agencies are under the governance of their jurisdictions, and police officers are under the governance of their department. **5.** The collective actions of a board of directors, board of trustees, or a board of governors in providing policy guidance to the organization that the board was established to manage.

governing class **1.** A vague term for those citizens both in and out of office who take an active and effective interest in public affairs. **2.** A pejorative term for the rich special interests who manipulate republican institutions for their own ends. According to President Theodore Roosevelt, speaking at Harvard University on February 23, 1907: "In a republic like ours the governing class is composed of the strong men who take the trouble to do the work of government; and if you are too timid or too fastidious or too careless to do your part in this work, then you forfeit your right to be considered one of the governing and you become one of the governed instead—one of the driven cattle of the political arena."

government **1.** The formal institutions and processes through which binding decisions are made for a society. A government can be as small as a tribal council or as vast and complex as the U.S. government. It can be democratic and responsive to its people or it can consist of a despot and a surrounding clique. It is still a government so long as it rules a defined land area and group of people. Essayist Henry David Thoreau (1817–1862) wrote in *Civil Disobedience* (1849) that "that government is best which governs least." This statement is often attributed to Thomas Jefferson; but while it certainly reflects his philosophic sentiments, it has never been found in any of Jefferson's writings. British historian Thomas Carlyle observed: "In the long-run every Government is the exact symbol of its People, with their wisdom and unwisdom; we have to say, Like People like Government" (*Past and Present*, 1843). This is what French diplomat Joseph de Maistre (1753–1821) meant when he wrote in a letter of August 15, 1811: "Every country has the government it deserves" (*Lettres et Opuscules Inedits*, 5th ed., 1869). Unfortunately, as Jeane J. Kirkpatrick, former Ambassador to the United Nations, warns: "The truth is that most of the governments of the world are, by our standards, bad governments. Corrupt, inefficient. Sometimes we are going to have to support and associate with governments that do not meet our standards" (*The Christian Science Monitor*, March 30, 1982). **2.** The apparatus of a state, consisting of executive, legislative, and judicial branches. **3.** A political entity that has taxing authority and jurisdiction over a defined geographic area for some specified purpose, such as fire protection or schools. **4.** The individuals who temporarily control the institutions of a state or subnational jurisdiction. **5.** The United States government, especially as in "the government." **6.** The RULE OF LAW. British courtier James Harrington (1611–1677) was the first to describe government as "the empire of laws and not of men" in his *The Commonwealth of Oceana* (1656). **7.** A necessary evil. THOMAS PAINE wrote in *Common Sense* (1776): "Society in every state is a blessing, but government, even in its best stage, is but a necessary evil; in its worst state an intolerable one." However, President Andrew Jackson, in a veto message to Congress July 10, 1832, said: "There are no necessary evils in government. Its evils exist only in its abuses." *Compare to* BODY POLITIC. **8.** The problem. According to President Ronald Reagan, speaking of inflation and unemployment in his first inaugural address, January 20, 1981: "In this present crisis, government is not the solution to our problem. Government is the problem." This is the man who also said during his 1965 campaign for governor of California: "Government is like a big baby—an alimentary canal with a big appetite at one end and no sense of responsibility at the other" (*The Reagan Wit*, Bill Adler, ed., 1981). **9.** The people. According to President Theodore Roosevelt in a speech at Asheville, North Carolina on December 5, 1905: "The government is us; we are the government, you and I." **10.** "A contrivance of human wisdom to provide for human wants," EDMUND BURKE,

Reflections on the Revolution in France (1790). **11.** According to ADAM SMITH 's, *The Wealth of Nations* (1776): "Government, so far as it is instituted for the security of property, is, in reality instituted for the defense of the rich against the poor, or of those who have some property against those who have none at all."

government corporation A government-owned corporation or an agency of government that administers a self-supporting enterprise. Such a structure is used (1) when an agency's business is essentially commercial, (2) when an agency can generate its own revenue, and (3) when the agency's mission requires greater flexibility than government agencies normally have. Examples of federal government corporations include the Saint Lawrence Seaway Development Corporation, the Federal Deposit Insurance Corporation, the National Railroad Passenger Corporation (AMTRAK), and the Tennessee Valley Authority. At the state and municipal levels, corporations (often bearing different names, such as authorities) operate such enterprises as turnpikes, airports, and harbors.

government, divided A government in which different political parties control the legislative and executive branches.

government, popular **1.** A government supported by public opinion; one that is liked by its citizens. **2.** An elected democratic government as opposed to one that imposes its rule on the people. It was Walter Lippmann who warned in *The Public Philosophy* (1955): "Popular government has not yet been proved to guarantee, always and everywhere, good government."

government of laws, not of men *See* RULE OF LAW.

government, positive An administration that believes in actively influencing the economy and social fabric of its jurisdiction to achieve benefits for the general welfare. The development of the modern welfare state during the NEW DEAL was the triumph of positive government in the United States. Because the WELFARE STATE has continued through subsequent liberal as well as conservative administrations, positive government is now the norm in the United States.

government, seat of **1.** A capitol building. **2.** Washington, D.C. This was late FBI director J. Edgar Hoover's favorite phrase for the District of Columbia. Critics contend that he thought his personal power was so great that this "seat," this font of power, was literally the chair behind his own desk.

government relations **1.** Corporate contacts with government. **2.** A euphemism for LOBBYING of government by corporations.

government, unitary A system of governance in which all authority is derived from a central authority, such as a parliament, an absolute monarch, or a dictator. The United States is not a unitary government. *Compare to* CONFEDERATION; FEDERALISM; LIMITED GOVERNMENT.

governor The elected chief executive of a state government. A governor's responsibilities sometimes parallel those of a U.S. President, on a smaller scale, but each governor has only the powers granted to the office by the state constitution. Some states severely limit executive powers, while others give their governors powers such as the item veto (*see* VETO, ITEM), which are greater than those possessed by the President of the United States. The term of office for a governor is four years, except in four states (Arkansas, New Hampshire, Rhode Island, and Vermont), where it is two. In one sense, it is a misnomer to call a governor the chief executive of a state. The reality is that most state constitutions provide for what amounts to a plural executive, because governors, in marked contrast to the U.S. President, typically must share powers with a variety of other independently elected executive branch officers, such as a secretary of state, an attorney general, a treasurer, and an auditor (or controller). Consequently, a governor's informal powers as a lobbyist for his or her initiatives and as head of his or her party may often be far more useful than the formal authority that comes with the office. Nevertheless, the management job of a governor compares favorably in terms of responsibility to those of the highest paid corporate executives. For example, in terms of revenues, 25 states rank among the top 100 corporations in America. Thirty-eight states are among the top 200. *Compare to* GUBERNATORIAL; *see also* VETO, ITEM.

governor, lieutenant The elected state official who would replace the governor should he or she be unable to complete a term of office. The lieutenant governor in a state government parallels the position of the Vice President in the national government but differs in that in many states the lieutenant governor is separately elected and thus may be of a different party from the governor. This can sometimes cause considerable friction when the two officeholders are political rivals—and especially when, as in California, the lieutenant governor has some of the governor's powers to act whenever the governor is out of the state. Seven states have felt no need for a lieutenant governor: Arizona, Maine, New Hampshire, New Jersey, Oregon, West Virginia, and Wyoming. In four of these states, the president of the state senate would succeed to the governorship; in the other three, the secretary of state succeeds.

The story is often told of Calvin Coolidge, then the Lieutenant Governor of Massachusetts, who met a woman at a dinner party. She asked: "What do you do?" He replied: "I'm the Lieutenant Governor." "How interesting, you must tell me all about it." Coolidge then said, "I just did."

graft *See* HONEST GRAFT/DISHONEST GRAFT.

Gramm-Rudman-Hollings Act of 1985 The Balanced Budget and Emergency Deficit Control Act of 1985, which set maximum deficit amounts for federal spending. If in any fiscal year the budget deficit exceeded the prescribed maximum by more than a specified sum, the act basically required across-the-board cuts in federal spending to reach the targeted deficit level. These reductions were to be accomplished under the "reporting provisions" spelled out in the act, which required the directors of the Office of Management and Budget and the Congressional Budget Office to submit their deficit estimates and program-by-program budget reduction calculations to the comptroller general, who, after reviewing the directors' joint report, reported the conclusions to the President. The President, in turn, then had to issue a "sequestration" order, mandating the spending reductions specified by the comptroller general. The sequestration order became effective unless, within a specified time, the Congress legislated reductions to obviate the need for the sequestration order. In 1986 the Supreme Court ruled in *Bowsher v Synar* (1986) that the comptroller general's role in exercising executive functions under the act's deficit reduction process violated the constitutionally imposed doctrine of SEPARATION OF POWERS, because the comptroller general is removable only by a congressional joint resolution or by impeachment, and the Congress may not retain the power of removal over an officer performing executive powers. However, in anticipation of this possibility, the act contained a fallback deficit reduction process, which eliminates the comptroller general's role. *See also* BALANCED BUDGET AMENDMENT.

The Act, which took the names of its three Senate sponsors (Phil Gramm of Texas and Warren B. Rudman of New Hampshire, both Republicans, and Ernest F. Hollings, a South Carolina Democrat), was denounced because its deficit targets have been missed and accounting gimmicks were used to hide the real dimensions of the deficit problem. To opponents who say it was a joke, supporters say that the deficit would have been even larger without it. According to Senators Gramm and Rudman: "Congress and the Administration have resorted to budget trickery in order to avoid some hard decisions. And, while gimmicks to hide the true cost of Federal programs have existed for many years, we concede that the willingness of the two branches to resort to such tricks has increased somewhat this year. Yet, even with the gimmicks, the deficit is projected to continue on its downward path in 1990" (*The New York Times*, October 25, 1989). But the Gramm-Rudman-Hollings Act was one "gimmick" that the Congress could no longer tolerate. Thus, it was substantially gutted by The Omnibus Budget Reconciliation Act of 1990.

grandfather clause Originally, a device used by some states of the Old South to disenfranchise black voters. Grandfather clauses, written into seven state constitutions during the Reconstruction Era, granted the right to vote only to persons whose ancestors—"grandfathers"—had voted prior to 1867. The Supreme Court ruled in *Guinn v United States* (1915), that all grandfather clauses were unconstitutional because of the Fifteenth Amendment. Today, a grandfather clause is a colloquial expression for any provision or policy that exempts a category of individuals from meeting new standards. For example, if a jurisdiction were to establish a policy that all managers had to have a master's degree in public administration as of a certain date, it would probably exempt managers without such degrees who were hired prior to that date. This statement of exemption would be a grandfather clause.

grant 1. A form of gift that entails certain obligations on the part of the grantee and expectations on the part of the grantor. **2.** An intergovernmental transfer of funds (or other assets). Since the New Deal, state and local governments have become increasingly dependent upon federal grants for an almost infinite variety of programs, growing to over 21 percent of all state and local expenditures in 1985. From the era of land grant colleges to the present, a grant by the federal government has been a continuing means of providing states, localities, public (and private) educational or research institutions, and individuals with funds to support projects the national government considered useful for a wide range of purposes. In recent years, grants have been made to support the arts as well as the sciences. All such grants are capable of generating debate over what the public as a whole, acting through the grant-making agencies of the federal government, considers useful and in the national interest.

Grant, Ulysses S. (1822–1885) President of the United States from 1869 to 1877. Grant, a West Point graduate who had dropped out of the Army, became the victorious general of the Civil War who went on to become one of the most inept of Presidents. Grant, the first in a series of Civil War generals to become Republican Presidents, presided over administrations full of scandal. While Grant himself was honest, he consistently showed blind loyalty to corrupt friends.

grassroots 1. The rank and file of a political party. **2.** The voters in general. **3.** Decentralized. **4.** A patronizing way of referring to the origin of political power.

grassroots lobbying Influencing government decision makers through pressure (usually in the form of letters, postcards, telegrams, and phone calls) from large numbers of constituents. This is also called indirect lobbying.

gravitas Intellectual weight. A politician must exhibit a certain degree of gravitas if he or she is to be taken seriously for high office.

Great Communicator A nickname for President Ronald Reagan, because he was so effective and likeable on television. But whether Reagan retires the title or not depends on whether or not a national political leader can ever again be as effective a "salesman" as he was on the campaign trail.

Great Depression The period between the stock market crash of October 29, 1929 and World War II, when the United States and the rest of the western world experienced the most severe economic decline in this century. The main focus of the NEW DEAL was to lessen privations caused by the depression and to create regulatory structures and economic policies that would modify the severity of the normal business cycle. It would cause President Franklin D. Roosevelt to say in his second inaugural address, January 20, 1937, that: "I see one third of a nation ill-housed, ill-clad, ill-nourished." Because the Great Depression started during the Republican Hoover Administration, the Democrats have ever since blamed Republicans in general for it. As Democratic President Harry S Truman said: "Republicans don't like people who talk about depressions. You can hardly blame them for that. You remember the old saying: Don't talk about rope in the house where somebody has been hanged" (*The Words of Harry S Truman*, 1984). The United States is extremely unlikely to ever again suffer a depression. Political rhetoric will not allow it. When economist Alfred Kahn used the word "depression" when speaking on behalf of the Jimmy Carter Administration in the late 1970s, he was so attacked by all sides that he pledged to use the word "banana" in his future economic analyses. Then he warned that if certain things were not done, the nation could suffer a "big banana." *Compare to* PANIC; RECESSION.

Great Mentioner The yet to be found Washington denizen who is always the first to "mention" someone as a possible presidential candidate. The Great Mentioner was first discovered by journalist Peter Lisagor (1915–1976). But Lisagor was never rude enough to suggest what seems to be self-evident; that the "Great Mentioner" very often turns out to be the person being mentioned.

Great Society The label for the 1960s domestic policies of the Lyndon B. Johnson administration, which were premised on the belief that social and economic problems could be solved by new federal programs. This was Johnson's effort to revive the federal reform presence in social change represented in the Progressive movement, the New Deal, and the Fair Deal. According to a May 23, 1964, speech of President Johnson, "we have the opportunity to move not only toward the rich society and the powerful society, but upward to the Great Society. The Great Society rests on abundance and liberty for all. It demands an end to poverty and racial injustice." While Richard Goodwin (1931–   ), then a Johnson speechwriter, is generally credited with coming up with the phrase, earlier authors had also used it. English jurist Sir William Blackstone (1723–1780) in his *Commentaries on the Laws of England* (1765–1769) wrote how it was "impossible for the whole race of mankind to be united in one great society." English political economist Graham Wallas (1858–1932) wrote of the utopian aims of an industrial society in his 1914 *The Great Society*. English political scientist Harold Laski (1893–1950) in his 1931 *Introduction to Politics* wrote of the "place of the state in the great society." In recent years Johnson's Great Society has been subject to considerable analysis. Various authorities (such as public policy analysts Charles Murray and John Schwartz), with equal statistical sophistication, have asserted that the Great Society was either a considerable success or a considerable failure.

green 1. Unripe or inexperienced; someone who has much to learn. 2. Having to do with the environment. Thus "green poitics" are environmental politics. A "green party" is mainly concerned with environmental issues, although it does not necessarily have to have the word "green" in its name. "Green taxes" tax things that are environmentally undesirable. "Big green" was a California environmental reform ballot initiative.

green card A small document identifying an alien as a permanent resident of the United States, entitled to legally find employment.

Gregg v Georgia *See* CRUEL AND UNUSUAL PUNISHMENT.

Grenada, invasion of The American military action of October 25, 1983, that took control of the Caribbean island nation of Grenada away from a Marxist military government, which had seized power six days earlier. President Ronald Reagan said in a speech to the nation on Lebanon and Grenada, October 27, 1983: "Grenada, we were told, was a friendly island paradise for tourism. Well it wasn't. It was a Soviet-Cuban colony being readied as a major military bastion to export terror and undermine democracy." The Ronald Reagan administration acted in response to requests for military intervention from Grenada's governor-general and from the Organization of Eastern Caribbean States; and to guarantee the safety of the approximately 1,000 American citizens (mostly medical students) on the island. Within 60 days, all U.S. combat units were gone and the island was left in the control of a civilian council, which would govern pending elections.

Griggs et al. v Duke Power Company (1971) The most significant single Supreme Court decision concerning the validity of employment examinations. The Court unanimously ruled that Title VII of the Civil Rights Act of 1964 "proscribes not only overt discrimination but also practices that are discriminatory in operation." Thus, if employment practices operating to exclude minorities "cannot be shown to be related to job performance, the practice is prohibited." The ruling dealt a blow to restrictive credentialism, stating that, while diplomas and tests are useful, the "Congress has mandated the commonsense proposition that they are not to become masters of reality." In essence, the court held that the law requires that tests used for employment purposes "must measure the person for the job and not the person in the abstract." The *Griggs* decision applied only to the private sector until the Equal Employment Opportunity Act of 1972 extended the provisions of Title VII to cover public employees.

Griswold v Connecticut (1965) The Supreme Court case that, in holding that the state regulation of birth control devices was an impermissible invasion of privacy, helped to establish privacy as a constitutionally protected right under the Ninth and Fourteenth Amendments. Justice William O. Douglas wrote, in the majority opinion: "The First Amendment has a penumbra where privacy is protected from governmental intrusion." He asked: "Would we allow the police to search the sacred precincts of marital bedrooms for telltale signs of the use of contraceptives? The very idea is repulsive to the notions of privacy surrounding the marriage relationship."

gross national product (GNP) The monetary value of all of the goods and services produced in a nation in a given year; one of the most important tools for measuring the health of a nation's economy. The U.S. Department of Commerce is responsible for gathering GNP data. All GNP figures must be adjusted for inflation or deflation if they are to accurately reflect the growth (or nongrowth) of the economy.

gross political product The total money spent in all elections in the United States in a given year. While critics have always complained that spending is excessive, when compared to other major democracies, U.S. spending is about average.

groupthink The psychological drive for consensus at any cost, which tends to suppress both dissent and the appraisal of alternatives in small decision-making groups. The term, because it refers to a deterioration of mental efficiency and moral judgment due to in-group pressures, has an invidious connotation. It was originated by Irving L. Janis in his book, *Victims of Groupthink: A Psychological Study of Foreign Policy Decisions and Fiascoes* (1972; 2nd ed., 1982).

Grove City College v Bell *See* CIVIL RIGHTS RESTORATION ACT OF 1988.

GS *See* GENERAL SCHEDULE.

GSA *See* GENERAL SERVICE ADMINISTRATION.

gubernatorial Pertaining to the office of governor, which comes from the Greek *kybernan,* meaning to direct a ship. The Romans borrowed the word from the Greeks as *guberno.* Then the French took it and sent it across the English channel as governor. When the word is used as an adjective, it goes back to its Latin roots; thus, gubernatorial.

Gucci Gulch The hallways outside of the rooms where congressional committees meet; so called because highly paid lobbyists, supposedly wearing expensive Gucci shoes, wait there to corner members of Congress as they enter and exit the committee rooms.

Gulf of Tonkin Resolution The August 10, 1964 joint resolution of the U.S. Congress that sanctioned the Johnson Administration's use of great numbers of American forces in an expansion of the VIETNAM WAR. Premised upon a presumed attack on U.S. ships in the Gulf of Tonkin by North Vietnamese naval units, it stated that Congress "approves and supports the determination of the President, as Commander in Chief, to take all necessary measures to repel any armed attack against the forces of the United States and to prevent further aggression." The Johnson administration would treat this as the moral and legal equivalent of a declaration of war. Later, those who opposed the war would denounce it as a fraud because there was no solid evidence that there ever was an attack on American ships in the Tonkin Gulf. Indeed, historian Barbara W. Tuchman in *The March of Folly* (1984) would write: "With evidence accumulating of confusion by radar and sonar technicians in the second clash, [President] Johnson said privately, 'Well, those dumb stupid sailors were just shooting at flying fish.' So much for casus belli." But there was little initial opposition. The House of Representatives passed it unanimously. In the Senate there were only two dissenting votes. Senator Jacob K. Javits, who voted for the resolution, would later write in *Who Makes War* (1973): "In voting unlimited presidential power most members of Congress thought they were providing for retaliation for an attack on our forces; and preventing a large-scale war in Asia, rather than authorizing its inception." *Compare to* CREDIBILITY GAP.

gun control Any government effort to regulate the use of firearms by the civilian population. While there are minor laws dealing with the registration of guns and the prohibition of their sale to criminals, there is no effective gun control in the United States. Proponents of free access to all kinds of weapons point to the Second Amendment of the U.S. Constitution: "A well-regulated militia, being necessary to the security of a free state, the right of the people to keep and bear arms, shall not be infringed." Opponents of easy access to guns point out that the "right" referred to in the amendment logically belongs only to members of the militia, not to all citizens. Right or wrong about the "right," gun control advocates have been consistently overwhelmed by the political strength of those who advocate free access. The basic federal law on gun control is the Gun Control Act of 1968. In 1986, the Congress significantly weakened this act and made it much easier to buy and sell rifles and shotguns and to transport them across state lines. The amending legislature was passed with the support of Republicans and Southern Democrats—the conservative coalition. A subsequent amendment in 1988 made it illegal to import, sell, or possess firearms without a minimum metal content. This was so potential terrorists carrying guns could not bypass metal detectors.

guns and butter A phrase which since the 1930s has succinctly summarized a government's policy option between military expenditures (the guns) or domestic spending (the butter). For example , Senator William Proxmire in a speech in the Senate, September 3, 1969, said: "Not too long ago it was commonplace to hear that this nation could afford both guns and butter—that we could provide for our defense, meet our world commitments and take care of pressing national problems. Now it has become fashionable to take the opposite view—we can have either guns or butter, but not both." President Richard M. Nixon wrote in *RN: Memoirs* (1978): "Seeking both guns and butter is a policy that works only in the very short term. I think that [President] Johnson belatedly came to understand this, because through the four years of my first term I cannot recall an instance when he urged me to go forward with any of his Great Society programs."

gypsy moths Those liberal and moderate Republicans in the U.S. House of Representatives who tended to deny support to President Ronald Reagan's domestic and foreign policies. They were called gypsy moths, in contrast to BOLL WEEVILS, after a leaf-eating moth found in the north, because most of these House members represented congressional districts from the Northeast and Midwest.

H

habeas corpus *See* WRIT OF HABEAS CORPUS.

hack **1.** A drudge; a petty officeholder; an inferior politician. Hack is short for hackney horse—a worn-out horse available for hire. While the political use of the term started in the last century, party hacks of one kind or another still abound. **2.** A derogatory description for a journalist of no particular distinction.

Hamilton, Alexander (1755–1804) George Washington's aide and secretary during the Revolutionary War who went on to become a Wall Street lawyer. Hamilton was a prime sponsor of the Annapolis Convention, which called for the Constitutional Convention. A strong supporter of a strong national government, he signed the U.S. Constitution and coauthored the *Federalist Papers* to help get it ratified in his native New York. When Washington became President, he made Hamilton first secretary of the Treasury. As such, Hamilton is credited with putting the new nation on sound financial footing by having the new government, with the approval of the Congress, assume the Revolutionary War debt. Even though paying off the war debts mostly benefited financial speculators, that one act of honoring the debt of the Continental Congress established the United States internationally as a nation capable of paying its bills and managing its finances. Hamilton was also a strong advocate of a national bank and national currency. He was killed in 1804 by a political enemy, Vice President Aaron Burr, in a duel.

Hamilton's *Report on Manufactures* Alexander Hamilton's 1791 analysis, written while he was secretary of the Treasury (1789–1795), of why government intervention in the economy is desirable. The *Report*, which calls for a tariff system to protect American industry and for federal public works for roads and canals, was to influence American economic policy for generations. Hamilton felt that the general welfare required that government encourage infant industries to avoid overdependence on other countries for essential supplies.

Hammer v Dagenhart (1918) The Supreme Court case that held unconstitutional a federal statute barring goods made by child labor from interstate commerce. The Court would not concede that the federal government could regulate child labor in interstate commerce until 1941, when it upheld the Fair Labor Standards Act of 1938, which put restrictions on the use of child labor. That landmark case was UNITED STATES V DARBY LUMBER COMPANY.

handlers Campaign managers and their staffs who seek to "handle" their candidate in such a way that he or she wins. It is a slightly pejorative term because it implies that the candidate can't do it all or isn't fully in control.

HARD CASES

The word comes from those who train and care for competitive animals such as gamecocks or fighting dogs. While use of the word "handler" is relatively recent, the concept goes way back. For example, the story is often told of the political candidate who dutifully read the speech prepared for him by his handlers and then told his audience: "Now I would like to say a few words of my own."

hard cases Cases in which fairness may require judges to be loose with legal principles. "Hard cases make bad law," as the saying goes, because the specific complexity of the issues may force judges to take positions that, while appropriate to the circumstances presented to them, may suggest future legal applications that are likely to be considered unjust.

hard funds *See* SOFT MONEY.

hard hat Someone who works in the construction industry or in a factory where a protective plastic hat is commonly worn. These blue collar workers, sometimes called Reagan Democrats, tend to support conservative administrations at the national level. Thus, the term "hard hat" often refers to a working-class conservative—even though many "hard hats" are not.

Harding, Warren Gamaliel (1865–1923) The DARK HORSE compromise candidate at the 1920 Republican National Convention who won election as the 29th President with a call to a "return to normalcy" after the tumult of World War I. Harding, a newspaperman, served in the Ohio state senate from 1899 to 1903 and as lieutenant governor in 1904 and 1905. In 1910 he ran unsuccessfully for governor. Four years later, Harding won a seat in the U.S. Senate. During his six years there, which he characterized as a "very pleasant place," Harding became known as a safe and conservative member, thus earning him a place at the top of the Republican ticket of 1920 as a compromise candidate through a deal made in a SMOKE-FILLED ROOM. He accomplished little in office and is usually rated by historians to be one of the 10 worse Presidents. He died suddenly in office in August of 1923, leaving to his successor a series of government scandals for which he himself was not personally responsible but which gave his administration a reputation for corruption that became representative of political attitudes in the 1920s. It was Alice Roosevelt Longworth, the daughter of President Theodore Roosevelt, in *Crowded Hours* (1933) who made the most famous assessment of Harding: "I think everyone must feel that the brevity of his tenure of office was a mercy to him and to the country. Harding was not a bad man. He was just a slob."

hard line **1.** A policy of taking a strong stand against communist expansionism. **2.** Any policy that is unyielding to compromise.

hardball A serious game, as opposed to softball which is less dangerous. According to Christopher Matthews' *Hardball* (1988), hardball "is clean, aggressive Machiavellian politics. It is the discipline of gaining and holding power, useful to any profession or undertaking, but practiced most openly and unashamedly in the world of public affairs."

Harrison, Benjamin (1833–1901) The Republican President of the United States from 1889 to 1893 (and grandson of President William Henry Harrison). In the 1888 presidential election he lost the popular vote but won the presidency with a majority of the electoral vote. While he made modest efforts at civil service and tariff reform, the rising labor movement and populist sentiment meant he would lose his 1892 bid for reelection to the man he had defeated in the previous election, Grover Cleveland.

Harrison, William Henry (1773–1841) The President of the United States with the shortest term of office. He died less than a month after he was inaugurated in 1841. Legend has it that office seekers had so crowded the White House, pushing in doors and hanging out windows, that he caught pneumonia. But at his age and in those days, the cause of death could have been almost anything. He was known as "Old Tippecanoe" after a battle he led against the Indians in 1811. His 1840 presidential campaign was the first modern presidential contest in that the candidate traveled all over the nation giving speeches, emphasized his humble LOG CABIN origins, and ignored issues in favor of image.

Hart, Gary (1931–   ) The U.S. Senator from Colorado (1975–1987) whose candidacy for the 1984 Democratic presidential nomination was effectively destroyed when his debate opponent, WALTER MONDALE, asked him: "Where's the beef?" Hart then beefed up his candidacy for the 1988 nomination and became the front runner until a widely publicized, apparently adulterous affair forced him out of the race.

Hatch Act The collective popular name for two federal statutes that restrict the political activities of federal employees. The 1939 act restricted almost all federal employees, whether in the competitive service or not. The impetus for this legislation came primarily from a decrease in the proportion of federal employees in the competitive service, a result of the creation of several score New Deal agencies outside the MERIT SYSTEM. Senator Carl Hatch (1889–1963), a Democrat from New Mexico, had worked for several years to have legislation enacted that would prevent federal employees from being active at political conventions. He feared that their involvement and direction by politicians could lead to the development of a giant national political machine.

A second Hatch Act, in 1940, extended these restrictions to positions in state employment having federal financing. Penalties for violation of the Hatch Act by federal employees have been softened considerably over time. Originally, removal was mandatory, but, by 1962, the minimum punishment was suspension for 30 days.

It has never been possible to define completely the political activities prohibited by the Hatch Act. However, the following are among the major limitations: (1) serving as a delegate or alternate to a political party convention; (2) soliciting or handling political contributions; (3) being an officer or organizer of a political club; (4) engaging in ELECTIONEERING; (5) being, with some exceptions, a candidate for elective political office; and (6) speaking to or leading partisan political meetings or rallies. The constitutionality of these regulations was first upheld by the Supreme Court in *United Public Workers v Mitchell* (1947), and reaffirmed in *Civil Service Commission v National Association of Letter Carriers* (1973). Repeal of the Hatch Act (or relaxation of some of its provisions) has been high on the legislative agenda of unions, especially since union legal challenges to the act have been unsuccessful. Both Presidents Ford and Bush have vetoed bills which would have relaxed restrictions on the partisan political activities of federal employees.

hatch acts, little State laws that parallel the federal government's prohibition on partisan political activities by employees paid with federal funds.

hat in the ring Active political candidacy. It's a term from boxing and was first applied to politics by President Theodore Roosevelt; when someone was willing to box all comers, he threw his hat in the boxing ring.

hawk Inclined toward military action. Its antithetical term is dove. A hawk is a bird of prey; a dove is a far more peaceful bird (in metaphor, if not in reality) and a symbol of peace since ancient times. Thomas Jefferson in a letter to James Madison on April 26, 1798, used "war hawks" to describe those Federalists who wanted to bring on war with France. Later, the term was applied to those who brought on the War of 1812 with England. Dove is of more recent vintage in American national politics; it was first used during the John F. Kennedy administration to describe those presidential advisors who advocated a policy of accommodation with the Soviet Union. The hardliners were, of course, hawks; and the metaphors carried on to the Vietnam period. The first modern usage of the hawk/dove dichotomy was probably by journalist Charles Bartlett writing on the Cuban Missile Crisis for the *Saturday Evening Post* (December 8, 1962): "The hawks favoured an air strike to eliminate the Cuban missile bases . . . . The doves opposed the air strike and favoured a blockade." Senator Henry M. Jackson stretched this bird metaphor just about as far as it has gone: "I'm not a hawk or a dove. I just don't want my country to be a pigeon" (*Time*, March 22, 1971).

hawk, chicken A public figure, whether congressman or movie star, who was eligible for military service during the Vietnam War but who legally avoided it, and who now advocates a hard line foreign policy that might lead to American troops being sent into combat. Also known as a "war wimp."

Hayes, Rutherford B. (1822–1893) The President of the United States from 1877 to 1871. Hayes, a major general during the Civil War, was the Governor of Ohio in 1876 and was nominated by the Republicans for the presidency that year in the wake of the Grant Administration scandals. In that election Hayes lost the popular vote to the Democratic candidate, Samuel J. Tilden (1814–1886), Governor of New York. The electoral vote, which Hayes won, was contested and the Republicans made a deal with the Democrats: accept the verdict and occupation troops would be withdrawn from the South. Enough Southern Democrats agreed that Hayes became President and ended Reconstruction.

Head Start The federal program designed to provide early education opportunities for poor children prior to kindergarten. Head Start centers exist nationwide and offer not only preacademic instruction but also health, social, nutritional, and psychological services.

Health and Human Services, U.S. Department of (DHHS) The cabinet-level department of the federal government most concerned with health, welfare, and income security plans, policies, and programs. Its largest single agency is the Social Security Administration. It was created on October 17, 1979, when the Department of Education Organization Act divided the Department of Health, Education, and Welfare in two.

Health, Education, and Welfare, U.S. Department of (HEW) A former cabinet-level department of the federal government. Created in 1953, HEW was reorganized into the Department of Education and the Department of Health and Human Services in 1979. *See also* EDUCATION, U.S. DEPARTMENT OF; HEALTH AND HUMAN SERVICES, U.S. DEPARTMENT OF.

hearing 1. A legal or quasi-legal proceeding in which arguments, witnesses, or evidence are heard by a judicial officer or administrative body. **2.** A legislative committee session for hearing witnesses. At hearings on legislation, witnesses usually include specialists, government officials, and representatives of those affected by the bills under study. Subpoena power may be used to summon reluctant witnesses. The public and press may attend open hearings but are barred from closed (executive) hearings.

hearing examiner *See* ADMINISTRATIVE LAW JUDGE.

hearsay A statement of a witness based not on direct knowledge but on what the witness heard someone else say. Hearsay evidence is generally not accepted in court.

Heart of Atlanta Motel v United States (1964) The Supreme Court case that upheld the constitutionality of Title II of the Civil Rights Act of 1964, which prohibited discrimination because of race, color, sex, religion, or national origin in restaurants, hotels, and other places of public accommodation engaged in interstate commerce.

heir apparent 1. The next in line for an hereditary office such as king. **2.** By analogy, an administrative or political figure who, it is assumed, will achieve the office or power of a current leader upon that leader's death or retirement. Many an heir apparent has turned out to be less apparent than was apparent.

hidden agenda The unannounced or unconscious goals, personal needs, expectations, and strategies that each individual or group possesses. Parallel to a group's open, public agenda are the private or hidden agendas of each of its members.

high crimes and misdemeanors Legal offenses that warrant the IMPEACH-MENT of high officeholders. In addition to treason and bribery, high crimes and misdemeanors are grounds for removal from office of "the president, vice president and all civil officers of the United States," as stated in Article II, Section 4, of the U.S. Constitution. No precise definition of this phrase has evolved.

high negatives Very low ratings in public opinion polls; a very negative image in the public mind. Vice President George Bush had very high negatives early in the 1988 presidential campaign, but he proved that year that an aggressive campaign could overcome such ratings.

higher law The notion that no matter what the laws of a state are, there remains a higher law to which a person has an even greater obligation. A higher law is often appealed to by those who wish to attack an existing law or practice that courts or legislators are unlikely or unwilling to change. In a famous speech in the Senate on March 11, 1850, William Henry Seward of New York argued against slavery by asserting that "there is a higher law than the Constitution which regulates our authority." Martyrs throughout the ages have asserted a higher law in defiance of the state, thus earning their martyrdom. The classic presentation of this concept is in Sophocles' (496–406 B.C.) play *Antigone,* in which the heroine defies the king, asserts a higher law as her justification, and forces the king to have her killed. Because the courts of any state will only enforce the law of the land, appealing to a higher law is always chancy business. Examples of Americans who have appealed to a higher law and wound up in jail as a result are Henry David Thoreau (see CIVIL DISOBEDIENCE), MARTIN LUTHER KING, JR., and Vietnam War resisters.

Hill, Anita *See* THOMAS, CLARENCE.

hill, the The U.S. Congress, because it is literally situated on a hill (it is 88 feet above sea level; the White House is 55 feet above sea level). Now there can be no doubt about which is the higher branch of government.

hired gun **1.** A mercenary. **2.** A POLITICAL CONSULTANT who works just for the money and not because of any commitment to a cause of candidate. **3.** A "neutral gun for hire"; a longstanding description of apolitical career bureaucrats.

hit men **1.** Killers for hire. **2.** By analogy, campaign consultants who are experts on NEGATIVE ADVERTISING designed to "kill" political opponents.

hit list **1.** Any group targeted for unfavorable action. **2.** Political appointees to government positions slated to be fired if the political opposition wins the next election. **3.** Incumbent elected officials targeted for defeat by a political party or political action committee.

Hobbes, Thomas (1588–1679) The English political philosopher and social contract theorist who wrote *Leviathan* (1651), a highly influential and comprehensive theory of government. Hobbes asserted that, in a state of nature, man is in a chaotic condition "of war of everyone against everyone." For safety's sake, men formed governments to which they surrendered their freedom but from which they got security and order. Hobbes' preferred form of government is absolute monarchy. While Hobbes favored monarchs who were not tyrants, his theorizing offered no recourse to those finding themselves under one. His greatest significance to students of American government is that he, as the first of the major social contract theorists (see JOHN LOCKE and JEAN-JACQUES ROUSSEAU), provided the foundation upon which the others would build and ultimately influence the American Revolution.

Hofstadter, Richard *See* PARANOID STYLE.

Holmes, Oliver Wendell, Jr. (1841–1935) The Associate Justice of the Supreme Court from 1902 to 1932 who, because of his scholarly writings and brilliant dissenting opinions (he was known as "the great dissenter"), had a profound influence on the development of American law. Many of his dissents would become the core arguments for majority opinions a generation later.

home equity district A specified part of a city which a government agency undertakes to insure homeowners against drastic home price declines caused by fears of rapid racial turnover. This is an effort to prevent WHITE FLIGHT by literally insuring homeowners that they won't lose the equity in their homes by remaining in an increasingly integrated neighborhood. In 1988 Illinois was the first state to create such a program.

home rule The ability or power of a MUNICIPAL CORPORATION to develop and implement its own CHARTER. It resulted from the urban reform movement of the turn of the century, which hoped to remove urban politics from the harmful influence of state politics. Home rule can be either a statutory or a constitutional system and varies in its details from state to state.

home style The manner in which members of the U.S. Congress project themselves to their home constituencies so they can retain constituent support and get reelected. The significant elements of home style include the personal style by which legislators present themselves, how they explain their legislative records, and how they allocate scarce resources, such as time for this or that issue or attention to this or that constituent.

Homeless Act *See* MCKINNEY ACT.

honest broker A disinterested third party who helps others negotiate an agreement. The term is often used in diplomacy when one country seeks to help two others reach agreement on a contentious issue.

honest graft/dishonest graft **1.** The classic distinction between the two genres of graft, made by George Washington Plunkitt, a politico associated with New York's Tammany Hall early in this century. Dishonest graft, as the name implies, involves bribery, blackmailing, extortion, and other obviously illegal activities. As for honest graft, let Plunkitt speak:

Just let me explain by examples. My party's in power in the city, and its goin' to undertake a lot of public improvements. Well, I'm tipped off, say, that they're goin' to lay out a new park at a certain place.

I see my opportunity and I take it, I go to that place and I buy up all the land I can in the neighborhood. Then the board of this or that makes its plan public, and there is a rush to get my land, which nobody cared particular for before.

Ain't it perfectly honest to charge a good price and make a profit on my investment and foresight? Of course, it is. Well, that's honest graft.

Compare to PREFERMENTS. For more of Plunkitt's wisdom, see William Riordon's *Plunkitt of Tammany Hall* (1963). **2.** The new style honest graft involves perfectly legal "campaign contributions" from individuals and groups. According to sociologist Amitai Etzioni: "The law forbids only explicit deals. A lobbyist may visit a member of Congress shortly before a vote. He'll express the position the lobby favors, will make a campaign contribution sometime before the vote, and—if the vote is satisfactory— another after it is cast. So long as no direct link is forged between the contribution and vote, giver and receiver are home free. Since there is no need for openly stating such a connection, in effect all that the law achieves is that certain forms of speech are respected" (*The New York Times*, November 23, 1982). *Compare to* HONORARIUM.

honeymoon period The relatively short time after taking office that an elected executive may have harmonious relations with the press, with the legislature, and with the public. Honeymoons, which may last from a few hours to a few months, tend to end once the executive (whether a President, governor, or mayor) starts to make the hard decisions that alienate one constituency or another. As political terms go, honeymoon is quite old. In a December 27, 1796 letter to Edward Rutledge, Thomas Jefferson uses it in an analysis of the presidency: "I know well that no man will ever bring out of that office the reputation which carries him into it. The honeymoon would be as short in that case as in any other, and its moments of ecstasy would be ransomed by years of torment and hatred." The word is still actively used. President Gerald R. Ford, told a joint session of Congress on August 12, 1974: "I do not want a honeymoon with you. I want a good marriage."

honorable A form of address used for many public officials, such as judges, mayors, and members of the U.S. Congress. Honorable does not necessarily imply personal honor or integrity; it merely signifies current (or past) incumbency.

honorarium 1. A symbolic sum paid to a speaker. Traditionally, an honorarium was a modest amount given to a visiting academic or other dignitary who gave a speech or otherwise contributed services. Propriety forbade any "haggling" over fees. As politicians and other public figures (in or out of office) began to command substantial speaking fees, the word "honorarium" continued to be used long after the sums involved ceased to be symbolic. **2.** A legal bribe paid to a government official for a specific act or, more likely, for a continuing sympathetic view toward the interests of those who give the honoraria. *Compare to* HONEST GRAFT/DISHONEST GRAFT.

Hoover Commission of 1947–1949 The first Hoover Commission, formally known as the Commission on the Organization of the Executive Branch of the Government, created by the Congress via the Lodge-Brown Act of 1947 for the ostensible purpose of integrating and reducing the number of government agencies generated by World War II. Former President Herbert Hoover was chosen by the commission to be its chairman. Instead of calling for a reduction of government agencies, the commission made a vigorous call for increased managerial capacity in the Executive Office of the President (EOP) through: (1) unlimited discretion over presidential organization and staff, (2) a strengthened Bureau of the Budget, (3) an office of personnel located in the EOP, and (4) the creation of a staff secretary to provide liaison between the President and the subordinates. In addition, the commission recommended that executive branch agencies be reorganized to permit a coherent purpose for each department and better control by the President. Many of its recommendations were adopted, including passage of the Reorganization Act of 1949 and the establishment of the Department of Health, Education and Welfare in 1953.

Hoover Commission of 1953–1955 The second Hoover Commission, formally known as the Commission on the Organization of the Executive Branch of the Government, was created by Congress via the Ferguson-Brown Act of 1953 for three ostensible purposes: (1) the promoting of economy, efficiency, and improved service in the transaction of the public business; (2) the defining and limiting of executive functions; and (3) the curtailment and abolition of government functions and activities competitive with private enterprise. A major recommendation was the elimination of nonessential government services and activities competitive with private enterprise, based on the assumptions that the federal government had grown beyond appropriate limits and that such growth should be reversed. In contrast to the earlier commission, the second commission's recommendations accomplished little.

Hoover, Herbert (1874–1964) The Republican President of the United States from 1929 to 1933. In accepting the Republican presidential nomination on August 11, 1928, Hoover told his national convention: "We in America today are nearer to the final triumph over poverty than ever before in the history of any land. The poorhouse is vanishing from among us." Nevertheless, Hoover had the great misfortune to become President just when the Great Depression almost destroyed the American economy. He believed that the depression was the result of the international consequences of the Versailles Treaty, rather than of any fundamental internal economic condition of the United States. A whole generation of Americans grew up holding him personally responsible for economic events that no President of that time could have controlled. Ironically, Hoover, who made a fortune early in life as an engineer, headed allied relief operations during and after World War I, served as secretary of Commerce under Presidents Warren G. Harding and Calvin Coolidge, had a worldwide reputation as a preeminent administrator. While he is remembered as a conservative President, Hoover first entered government service during the Democratic Administration of Woodrow Wilson. In 1920 he was even mentioned as a possible candidate for the Democratic nomination. His roots were much more in the progressive rather than the conservative tradition. In later life he was respected as an "elder statesman."

Hoover, J. Edgar *See* FEDERAL BUREAU OF INVESTIGATION.

horizontal federalism *See* FEDERALISM, HORIZONTAL.

horse race Competitive political campaign. Consequently, media coverage tends to concentrate on the horse race aspects of the campaign: who's ahead, who may stumble, who's a long shot, etc. Critics of the media complain that this horse race coverage so dominates overall campaign coverage that issues get neglected.

Horton, Willie The convicted murderer and rapist who did much to help George Bush become President in 1988 by becoming the symbol of his opponent Michael Dukakis' "softness" on crime. In a now famous 30-second television spot the announcer says over a photo of Bush that Bush believes in the death penalty. Then over a photo of Dukakis he says that not only does Dukakis oppose the death penalty but "allowed first-degree murderers to have weekend passes from prison." Then over a mugshot of Willie Horton, a black man, the announcer says "One man was Willie Horton, who murdered a boy in a robbery, stabbing him 19 times. Despite a life sentence, Horton received 10 weekend passes from prison. Horton fled, kidnapped a young couple, stabbing the man and repeatedly raping his girlfriend." Because the spot was produced and run by Americans for Bush, an independent group that was not formally part of the Bush campaign, Bush could and did technically disavow it while at the same time benefitting from its subtle racism. His campaign then ran reinforcing ads on what became known as the "furlough issue." Both Horton and the Horton spot became dominant issues throughout the 1988 presidential campaign. And what of Horton? Back in prison he told reporters that Bush "may just be a cheap political opportunist ... I can't help but question his moral judgment" (*Newsweek*, November 6, 1989). An editorial in *The New Republic* (August 20, 1990) said that Horton's "political legacy outweighs that of any convicted rapist in American history."

hot line 1. The telephone and teletype links between the White House and Moscow's Kremlin established for instant communications should a crisis occur. **2.** Any communications system that links chief executives of governments with each other. **3.** The communications that link a chief executive with his or her military commanders.

hot pursuit 1. The legal doctrine that allows a law enforcement officer to arrest a suspect who has fled into another jurisdiction. **2.** The doctrine of international maritime law that allows a state to seize a foreign vessel that has initiated an act of war on the territory of the invaded state and is pursued into international waters. **3.** Pursuit of an enemy while in sight of, or in contact with, it. **4.** The pursuit of an enemy across international borders.

house 1. One of the two divisions of a bicameral legislature. **2.** The lower branch of a bicameral legislature. **3.** The U.S. House of Representatives, as distinct from the Senate, although each body is a house of the U.S. Congress. ALEXANDER HAMILTON justified the creation of the House on June 27, 1788 at the New York Convention on the adoption of the Constitution: "Here, sir, the people govern; here they act by their immediate representatives." In 1790 the House had 105 members, each of whom represented less than 39,000 citizens. By 1920 the House had grown to 435 members, each representing about 200,000 citizens. In that year, the House froze by statute House membership at 435 where it remains today—except that each member now represents about 560,000 citizens.

house divided speech *See* SLAVERY.

House of Representatives See CONGRESS, UNITED STATES; HOUSE.

House Un-American Activities Committee (HUAC) A committee of the House of Representatives created in 1938 to investigate subversion and un-American propaganda that might be a danger to American government as guaranteed by the Constitution. HUAC became notorious during the post World War II RED SCARE when it sought to find communist subversion in all aspects of American life. It was heavily criticized for its abuses of civil liberties. President Harry S Truman told an audience at Columbia University in 1959: "I've said many a time that I think the Un-American Activities Committee in the House of Representatives was the most un-American thing in America!" (*Truman Speaks*, 1960).

Housing and Urban Development, U.S. Department of (HUD) The principal cabinet-level federal agency responsible for programs concerned with housing needs and with improving and developing the nation's communities. The Department of Housing and Urban Development Act of 1965 created HUD by transferring to it all of the functions, powers, and duties of the Housing and Home Finance Agency, the Federal Housing Administration, and the Public Housing Administration. By the end of the Reagan Administration massive mismanagement and corruption came to light at HUD. The federal department responsible for housing policy seemed to have had policies that favored only those builders with connections to influential Republican "consultants" who steered HUD funds to their clients for hefty fees. According to Representative Tom Lantos, who chaired House hearings on HUD mismanagement: "In some cases these individuals' knowledge and prior experience with low-cost housing was limited to Baltic and Mediterranean Avenue with one house on each property" (*The New York Times*, June 23, 1989). As Jack Kemp took over as HUD Secretary in the new Bush Administration he was faced with revitalizing a demoralized, scandal-ridden department. *Compare to* URBAN RENEWAL.

Humphrey, Hubert H. (1911–1978) The Democratic U.S. Senator from Minnesota (1949–1965; 1971–1978) who was Vice President under President Lyndon B. Johnson (1965–1969). Humphrey was the Democratic presidential nominee in 1968 who narrowly lost to Richard M. Nixon over the issue of Vietnam. Domestically, Humphrey was liberalism personified and an influential supporter of civil rights. He first came to national prominence at the 1948 Democratic National Convention when he told the delegates: "The time has arrived for the Democratic party to get out of the shadow of states' rights and walk forthrightly into the bright sunshine of human rights."

Humphrey's Executor v United States (1935) The Supreme Court case prohibiting the dismissal of commissioners of the Federal Trade Commission by the President for reasons of disagreement over policy. The Court reasoned that an FTC commissioner "occupies no place in the executive department and . . . exercises no part of the executive power," thereby distinguishing the case from MYERS V UNITED STATES. By implication, the decision applied to positions in any federal agency exercising predominantly quasi-judicial or quasi-legislative functions.

hundred days The first 100 days of Franklin D. Roosevelt's administration in 1933, when a great deal of landmark legislation was enacted to cope with the Great Depression. The term initially came from the period between Napoleon's triumphant 1815 return from Elba and his defeat at Waterloo. The first hundred days of all new administrations since FDR's have been unfavorably compared to his in terms of legislative productivity. Nevertheless, all newly inaugurated Presidents seek to use the leftover energy of their successful campaign, their honeymoon era with press and public, and the inexperience of a new Congress to generate and see passed a program of legislation that almost certainly will be more difficult to get through at a later time.

hustings Any place in which a political speech is made. A candidate on the campaign trail may be said to be on the hustings. The word is derived from an old Norse word meaning a house assembly or meeting. In British usage, the hustings is also the literal platform from which a speech is given.

I

ICC *See* INTERSTATE COMMERCE COMMISSION.

ICMA *See* INTERNATIONAL CITY MANAGEMENT ASSOCIATION.

ideologues Those who believe intensely in a certain system of political beliefs; those who put faith in abstract principles without regard to the realities of a situation. Such true believers tend to interpret all acts, whether political or apolitical, from the perspective of their ideology. A. Bartlett Giamatti, president of Yale University, said during the 1982 commencement (reported in *The Christian Science Monitor*, June 11, 1982): "In choosing between ideologues of the Right and of the Left, I choose to eschew both because they are finally, in their desire to control and exclude, not different. If you believe they are, if you believe that an ideologue of the Left is less authoritarian in impulses and acts than one of the Right, look again."

ideology 1. A comprehensive system of political beliefs about the nature of people and society; an organized collection of ideas about the best way to live and about the most appropriate institutional arrangements for society. The term first arose during the French Revolution to refer to a school of thought, separate from religion, about how a society should be organized. But the term has evolved to mean the philosophic bent of true believers of whatever belief. The mainstreams of American politics have never been rigidly ideological; only the extremes of both major parties—on the far Right and far Left—are much concerned with correct rules of thought for the party's most faithful. One writer, Daniel Bell, even discovered an "end of ideology" in America in his 1960 book *End of Ideology: On the Exhaustion of Political Ideas in the Fifties*. Many post-World War II historians and political scientists saw and still see pragmatism (a problem-by-problem approach to the solution of problems without regard to theoretically determined ends) as the American alternative to ideology. But ideology seems to be making a comeback, especially with the new Right (*see* RIGHT, NEW), and, of course, it has never left the old Left (*see* LEFT, OLD). **2.** Whatever one believes about the political process, whether it is articulated or not. **3.** An interrelated set of ideas or a world view that explains complex social phenomena in a relatively simple way. **4.** The selected and often distorted notions about how a society operates. A group may adhere to such notions as a means of retaining group solidarity and of interpreting a world from which they have become alienated.

illegal alien A person from another country who is living or working in the United States unlawfully. The U.S. Department of Labor prefers to refer to these people as undocumented workers, a term that preserves the presumption of innocence and sounds less criminal.

image makers Political consultants who take on the publicizing of a candidate much like an advertising agency takes on the publicizing of a product. The resulting public image of the candidate is intended as a clear, simple, portrait-like characterization, acceptable to all groups. The end result can be (1) a fairly accurate image of the candidate achieved through paid advertising and unpaid advertising, known as media events; (2) a made-over image—a candidate inaccurately presented in paid advertising and allowed only controlled access to the news media; or (3) something in between. *Compare to* POLITICAL CONSULTANTS.

immigration 1. Coming to a new country with the intention of permanently remaining. **2.** A government's policies which regulate the circumstances under which aliens may enter and remain. The history of the United States is to a large extent the history of succeeding waves of immigration. Historian Oscar Handlin wrote in *The Uprooted* (1951): "Once I thought to write a history of the immigrants in America. Then I discovered that the immigrants *were* American history." The most famous presidential statement on immigration came from President Franklin D. Roosevelt in remarks to the Daughters of the American Revolution in Washington D.C. on April 21, 1938: "Remember, remember always that all of us, and you and I especially, are descended from immigrants and revolutionists."

immigration, illegal The unlawful entry of a person into a state. This is a major problem in the United States because borders are so wide and essentially unguarded. There are two basic attitudes toward illegal immigration: (1) overall it is desirable because the immigrants perform low-paying jobs citizens don't want and effectively subsidize the economy; and (2) that they are a drain on the economy because they tend not to pay taxes while using government services.

Immigration and Naturalization Service (INS) The federal agency created in 1891 responsible for administering the immigration and naturalization laws relating to the admission, exclusion, deportation, and naturalization of aliens. The INS was originally part of the Department of Labor; but after more restrictive immigration laws made it necessary to more carefully monitor prospective new citizens, the INS was relocated into the Department of Justice.

Immigration and Naturalization Service v Chadha See VETO, LEGISLATIVE.

immunity 1. An exemption from a duty or obligation. For example, foreigners with diplomatic immunity cannot be prosecuted for breaking the laws of their host country; they can only be expelled. **2.** An exemption from prosecution granted to persons to force them to testify in a criminal matter without violating their Fifth Amendment protections against self-incrimination. Anyone who refuses to testify to a grand jury or a court after being granted immunity can be held in contempt and be sent to jail until he or she reconsiders. **3.** The freedom of governments in the American federal system from being taxed by other governments. **4.** An exemption from ordinary legal culpability while holding public office. Government officials generally need some protection against law suits, whether frivolous or not, which might be brought against them by people dissatisfied with their actions or adversely affected by them. Otherwise, government could be brought to a standstill by such suits or be crippled by the threat of them. In general, judges and legislators are well protected by judicial doctrines concerning immunities, whereas police officers, sheriffs, and most public administrators are not.

immunity, congressional The immunity of members of the U.S. House of Representatives and the Senate from lawsuits derived from what they say on the floors of the Congress. This limited immunity is established by the "speech and debate" portion of the Constitution, Article I, Section 6, which also holds that they may not be arrested except for "treason, felony and breach of the peace." So they are clearly subject to criminal prosecution, just as any other citizen. Furthermore, what they say in newsletters and press releases is also prosecutable. *Compare to* PRIVILEGE.

immunity, presidential The immunity of the President of the United States from judicial action. There are many reasons for this: case law (*Kendall v U.S.* [1838]); the futility of prosecuting a person who has the power of pardon; the separation of powers, which asserts that one branch of government is not answerable to another; and the need for the undisturbed exercise of the office of the President. Consequently, the only way to bring a President to account is by IMPEACHMENT.

immunity, sovereign A government's freedom from being sued for damages in all but those situations in which it passes statutes allowing it. Amendments to the Administrative Procedure Act in 1976 allow suits to be filed against the federal government.

immunity, transactional The immunity which grants that a witness will not be prosecuted for the crime about which he or she is specifically being questioned.

immunity, use The immunity that prevents a witness from being prosecuted for any crimes revealed through compelled testimony or leads derived from the testimony. This is the most common form of immunity.

immunization The party faithful's resistance to new ideas or new parties; the strength of long-term political affiliation against new attachments. Thus, diehard stalwarts are immune from political solicitations, unless of course they have a political desire so great that even this metaphorical immunity won't help.

impeachment A quasi-judicial process for removing public officials from office. Impeachment is the beginning of the process by which the President, Vice President, federal judges, and all civil officials of the United States may be removed from office if convicted of the charges brought against them. Officials may be impeached for treason, bribery, and other HIGH CRIMES AND MISDEMEANORS. The U.S. House of Representatives has the sole authority to bring charges of impeachment (by a simple majority vote), and the Senate has the sole authority to try impeachment charges. An official may be removed from office only upon conviction, which requires a two-thirds vote of the Senate. The Constitution provides that the chief justice shall preside when the President is being tried for impeachment. Only two Presidents have ever been charged with impeachable offenses by the House: Andrew Johnson in 1868 (he was acquitted by the Senate) and Richard Nixon in 1974 (his resignation stopped the impeachment process).

implied power That authority not explicitly granted by the U.S. Constitution but inferred, based on a broad interpretation of other EXPRESSED or ENUMERATED POWERS. The notion of implied power was first given voice in the case of MCCULLOCH V MARYLAND (1819), when Chief Justice John Marshall wrote: "Let the end be legitimate, let it be within the scope of the Constitution, and all means which are appropriate, which are plainly adapted to that end, which are not prohibited, but consist with the letter and the spirit of the Constitution are constitutional."

impoundment A tactic available to fiscal strategists—the withholding by the executive branch of funds authorized and appropriated by law. There are several types of impoundment decisions. The earliest example traces back to Thomas Jefferson, who impounded funds designed to finance gunboats for the Mississippi River. A primary and accepted mode of impoundment is for emergencies, as in the case of war. President Franklin D. Roosevelt impounded funds slated for numerous programs that were "superseded" by the events of late 1941. Another mode of impoundment is to confiscate funds when the program objective has been accomplished. Presidents Dwight D. Eisenhower and Harry S Truman both made use of impoundment to take back "extra" funds from programs whose objectives had been met or were clearly not in need of funds. Another mode of impoundment is for legal compliance. President Lyndon B. Johnson impounded funds and threatened to impound other funds for local governments and school districts in violation of the Civil Rights Act or federal court orders.

The case for fiscal impoundment was made by the Richard M. Nixon administration as being necessary for economic stabilization and to enable the President to accomplish his legal responsibilities under the Employment Act of 1946. However, fiscal impoundment really amounts to a form of line-item veto. Several state governments empower their governors with the right to specify a budgetary figure for each program in the budget; if the legislature exceeds the recommended sum, the governor may veto any legislatively added sum above the original recommendation. Of course, any cuts made by the legislature are binding. However, the line-item veto is not power granted to the President by either the U.S. Constitution or by subsequent legislation.

The arguments in favor of impoundment made by the Nixon administration focused on the difficulties that the executive had in planning a budget (based on the revenue estimates) and then having the Congress essentially tack on $20–30 billion more for "favorite programs." As a direct result of the impoundment controversy, the Congress set up its own parallel budget machinery in 1974 under the Congressional Budget and Impoundment Control Act. Significant for fiscal policy is the fact that the act established a new congressional budget process requiring the Congress to set a maximum limit (recognizing the fiscal implications) and to make the various subcommittees keep the total final budget under that ceiling. Of course, this doesn't prevent the Congress from establishing a very high ceiling, but it does force it to face the total fiscal issue directly.

The ad hoc impoundments of the Nixon administration were repeatedly rejected by the federal courts when they were challenged. Now Title X of the Congressional Budget and Impoundment Control Act provides for two kinds of legal impoundments: (1) deferrals which are presidential decisions not to spend funds until a later date, and (2) rescissions which are presidential decisions not to spend funds at all. Both deferrals and rescissions must also be approved by Congress.

impoundment resolution An expression of disapproval by either the U.S. House of Representatives or the Senate of a proposed rescission or deferral of budget authority. Whenever all or part of any budget authority provided by the Congress is deferred, the President is required to transmit a special message to the Congress describing the deferrals. Either house may, at any time, pass a resolution disapproving this deferral of budget authority, thus requiring that the funds be made available for obligation. When no congressional action is taken, deferrals may remain in effect until, but not beyond, the end of the fiscal year.

in re A Latin phrase meaning "in the matter of; regarding."

In re Neagle *See* NEAGLE, IN RE.

INS *See* IMMIGRATION AND NATURALIZATION SERVICE.

inalienable rights Rights derived from natural law, which all people have and which cannot be taken away or transferred. Thomas Jefferson, influenced by John Locke, asserted in the Declaration of Independence "that all men are created equal, that they are endowed by their Creator with certain unalienable rights, that among them are life, liberty, and the pursuit of happiness." (Note that Jefferson used "unalienable" instead of "inalienable." While either is acceptable, "inalienable" has become more common.) Daniel T. Rodgers' *Contested Truths* (1987) contends that: "Natural Rights was the central radical political slogan of the Revolution, an ancient phrase suddenly fashioned into a tool of defiance. . . . a phrase whose very abstractness left it permanently open to new meanings, new grievances, new uses."

inaugural address The speech that a political executive makes upon being sworn into office. These speeches are often used to set a tone for an administration. President Abraham Lincoln used his in 1861 to appeal to "the better angels of our nature." President Franklin D. Roosevelt used his in 1933 to remind the nation that "the only thing we have to fear is fear itself." President John F. Kennedy used his in 1961 to tell Americans to "ask what you can do for your country." All new executives, Presidents, governors, and mayors try to make their inaugural addresses memorable. Few succeed.

inauguration The heralding into office of a chief executive with a formal ceremony, which includes taking an oath of office. The word is derived from an ancient Roman practice that took place before a new governor assumed office: the augurs (the diviners and prophets) would study the movements of birds to foretell the future of the administration. Today, this function is performed by political columnists and television commentators—and the birds are left alone.

Income Tax Amendment *See* SIXTEENTH AMENDMENT.

incomes policy 1. A general phrase for the totality of a national government's influence upon wages, prices, and profits. **2.** Direct government control on prices and wages.

incorporation 1. The creation of a government CORPORATION by a legislature. **2.** The creation of a private corporate entity by following procedures called for in applicable state law. The corporation then created becomes a legal entity, an artificial person, subject to legal action. **3.** The selective application of the protections of the federal BILL OF RIGHTS to the states; this process is also known as absorption. This nationalization of many of the provisions of the Bill of Rights was accomplished mostly through the due process clause of the Fourteenth Amendment. The incorporation doctrine overcame the Supreme Court's ruling in *Barron v Baltimore* (1833), that the Bill of Rights limited only the actions of the federal government, not those of individual state governments.

incorporation, total The constitutional theory that the Bill of Rights was totally incorporated by the Fourteenth Amendment. This theory rejects the need for selective incorporation as discussed above.

incrementalism 1. An approach to decision making in government in which policymakers begin with the current situation, consider a limited number of changes in that situation based upon a restricted range of alternatives, and test those changes by instituting them one at a time. The contrast to incrementalism is a more radically oriented decision making process (e.g., BUDGETING, ZERO-BASED). Incrementalism is an especially important aspect of BUDGETING. **2.** A normative theory of government that views policymaking as a process of bargaining and competition involving the participation of people with conflicting points of view.

incumbency effect 1. The overwhelming advantage of political incumbents in a contest for reelection. Short of a major scandal, voters tend to be more comfortable supporting a familiar name. This is all the more true for legislators of long standing who have had the opportunity to do considerable casework for their constituents. While incumbents do have many advantages, they also hae one major disadvantage—they must run on their voting record. **2.** The ability of incumbents to raise large sums of money for campaign expenses. After all, an incumbent can actually do something for a special interest; a challenger offers only the small potential of being able to do something in the future.

Independence, Declaration of *See* DECLARATION OF INDEPENDENCE. For text, *see* Appendix A.

independent A registered voter who does not declare an affiliation with a political party. Since the overwhelming majority of a party's members will vote for the party's candidate in the general election, many a political contest is a fight for the support of the independent voters. About one third of all voters describe themselves as independents; some, of course, are undercover partisans.

independent agency A federal executive agency not included in an executive department or within the Executive Office of the President. Some, such as the Smithsonian Institution, are of long standing. Many others have been created in this century, as the responsibilities of government have increased. A *regulatory commission* is a special kind of independent agency, established by the U.S. Congress to regulate some aspect of U.S. economic life. Among these are the Securities and Exchange Commission and the Interstate Commerce Commission. Such agencies are, of course, not independent of the U.S. government. They are subject to the laws under which they operate as these laws are enacted and amended by the Congress. Independent agencies and regulatory commissions can be divided into those units under the direct supervision and guidance of the President, and therefore responsible to him or her, and those not under such supervision and guidance. The units in the first group can be categorized as independent executive agencies, while those in the second group can be subdivided into independent regulatory commissions and government-sponsored enterprises.

Independent executive agencies, with rare exceptions, are headed by single administrators appointed by the President and confirmed by the Senate. These administrators serve at the pleasure of the President and can be removed at any time. In addition, they must submit their budget requests to the Office of Management and Budget (OMB), which is located within the Executive Office of the President, for review and clearance. Examples of independent executive agencies include the Environmental Protection Agency, the General Services Administration, and the Small Business Administration.

Independent regulatory commissions (such as the ICC) and government-sponsored enterprises (such as the TVA) are bodies headed by several commissioners, directors, or governors, also appointed by the President and confirmed by the Senate. Unlike administrators of independent executive agencies, they serve for fixed terms and cannot be removed at the pleasure of the President. While all of the independent regulatory commissions and most of the government-sponsored enterprises submit their budget requests to the OMB for review and clearance, the degree of dependence on these budgets varies considerably. Nearly all of the government-sponsored enterprises generate a considerable part of their financial resources from outside sources, while the independent regulatory commissions rely on the government for their funding. Those units subject to periodic authorization and appropriations hearings (all of the independent executive agencies and independent regulatory commissions and most of the government-sponsored enterprises) must undergo a review of their activities at those congressional hearings. Note that many regulatory functions are also performed by regular cabinet departments. For example, the Food and Drug Administration is located within the Department of Health and Human Services, and there is a Food Safety and Inspection Service within the Department of Agriculture.

independent candidate An aspirant for political office who is not affiliated with a political party. The Supreme Court in *Storer v Brown* (1974) held that a state could deny a position on a ballot to an independent candidate if that person had a formal affiliation with a political party within the past year. This was to prevent losers in a primary election from continuing the fight as independents in the general election.

independent counsel A euphemism for a special prosecutor. *See* PROSECUTOR, SPECIAL.

independent expenditure Payment for political advertising expressly advocating the election or defeat of a clearly identified candidate for federal office and which expenditure is not made with the cooperation of, or in consultation with, the supported candidate or his or her agents. Individuals, groups, and political action committees may support candidates by making independent expenditures on their behalf without limit, according to the FEDERAL ELECTION CAMPAIGN ACT.

independent spending Political campaign expenditures made without the cooperation or consent of the candidate who benefits. This is a loophole in some campaign finance laws which allows rich friends and interested groups (or political action committees) to spend lavishly beyond normal campaign limitations—so long as there is no collusion with the candidate.

indexing A system by which salaries, pensions, welfare payments, and other kinds of income are automatically adjusted to account for inflation.

indictment **1.** A formal written accusation submitted to a court by a grand jury, alleging that a specified person has committed a specified crime, usually a felony. The classic statement on the ease with which public prosecutors can gain indictments is attributed to the French Cardinal Richelieu (1585–1642): "If you give me six lines written by the hand of the most honest of men, I will find something in them which will hang him." *See also* JURY, GRAND. **2.** Any accusation of wrongdoing.

industrial policy Government regulation of the manufacturing ability of a nation through law, tax incentives, and subsidies. The United States does not have a comprehensive industrial policy, compared to other nations, especially Japan, whose government exercises considerable control over industrial planning and decision making. This is because of traditional American abhorrence of central planning, which is associated with communism and considered the antithesis of the free enterprise system. But because of increasing economic competition from Japan and other nations, where government and business work cooperatively to advance industrial interests, there is now a considerable debate in the United States over whether the national government should develop a more cohesive and comprehensive industrial policy. *Compare to* COMPETITIVENESS.

infant industry argument The argument calling for a policy of temporary protection for an industry that potentially can be competitive in the world market. Often, a new industry realizes declining costs as output expands and experience in production is acquired. In the initial phase of production start-up, infant domestic industry may not be competitive with existing world producers. Thus, it is often argued that temporary protection in the form of high protective tariffs is required.

inferior federal courts All federal courts below the Supreme Court.

inflation/deflation Inflation is a rise in the costs of goods and services equated to a fall in the value of a nation's currency. Deflation is the reverse —a fall in costs and a rise in the value of money. Economist Milton Friedman has often observed that "inflation is one form of taxation that can be imposed without legislation."

influence peddler **1.** One who claims to have special access to people in power and for a fee will use that access on your behalf. **2.** One who offers bribes to public officials on behalf of a third party.

informal congressional groups *See* LEGISLATIVE SERVICE ORGANIZATIONS.

infrastructure **1.** A general term for a jurisdiction's fixed assets, such as bridges, highways, tunnels, and water treatment plants. **2.** A political party's or a government's administrative structure, the people and processes that make it work. **3.** The institutional framework of a society that supports the educational, religious, and social ideology, which in turn supports the political order. **4.** The permanent installations and facilities for the support, maintenance, and control of naval, land, or air forces.

initiative A procedure that allows citizens, as opposed to legislators, to propose the enactment of state and local laws. An initiative, the proposed new law, is placed on the ballot (often as a proposition) only after the proper filing of a petition containing signatures from 5 to 15 percent of the voters. Fewer than half of the states provide for the initiative. Initiatives are not possible with federal legislation because Article I of the U.S. Constitution prevents the Congress from delegating its legislative responsibilities. *Compare to* REFERENDUM.

initiative, constitutional Citizen-proposed amendment to a state constitution.

initiative, direct A citizen-initiated proposal that must be submitted directly to the voters at a special election or the next general election.

initiative, indirect A citizen-initiated proposal that must first be submitted to the legislature. It is submitted to the voters only if the legislature rejects it or proposes a substitute measure.

injunction A court order forbidding specific individuals or groups to perform acts the court considers injurious to the property or other rights of a person or community. There are two basic types of injunctions: (1) a temporary restraining order, which is issued for a limited time prior to a formal hearing; and (2) a permanent injunction, which is issued after a full formal hearing. Once an injunction is in effect, the court has contempt power to enforce its ruling through fines or imprisonment, or both.

in-kind transfers A welfare benefit other than cash, such as clothing, food, or food stamps.

inoculation A campaign tactic whereby a candidate anticipates an area of attack from the opposition and takes action so that the issue, if raised, is muted. For example, a Democrat who suspects that a Republican opponent might accuse him of being soft on crime could inoculate himself from such charges by coming out strongly for CAPITAL PUNISHMENT.

inspector general The job title (of military origin) for the administrative head of an inspection or investigative unit of a larger agency.

institutional discrimination Practices contrary to equal employment opportunity policies, without intent to discriminate. Institutional discrimination (also known as INSTITUTIONAL RACISM) exists whenever a practice or procedure has the effect of treating one group of employees differently from another.

integration 1. Any policy that encourages interaction between members of different races. 2. In education, the purposeful policy of having children of different races attend the same public schools. Integration was mandated by the Supreme Court in BROWN V BOARD OF EDUCATION and has often resulted in WHITE FLIGHT. *Compare to* SEGREGATION.

interest 1. A benefit or advantage that one seeks to gain through the political process. 2. The extra money a person or institution receives in return for lending money to another person; money paid for the use of money. 3. Engagement in an occupation or profession that influences one's attitudes toward other social, economic, or political actions. 4. A right to something, whether intangible, such as freedom, or concrete, such as half ownership in a cement factory. 5. A group of persons who share a common cause, which puts them into political competition with other groups or interests. Thus, the oil interests want better tax breaks for the oil industry; the consumer interests want new laws protecting consumer rights vis-à-vis the business interests, who want fewer laws protecting consumer rights. According to California State Senator Ed Davis: "About 90 percent of all legislation is conceived by special interests. It is merchandised by special interests. And probably less than 5 percent is inspired by Governors, by individual legislators, by government itself. You say, 'Oh, isn't that evil!' The answer is, hell no, it isn't evil. That's what a democracy is all about" (*Los Angeles Times*, January 19, 1981).

interest group liberalism A theory of policymaking (most associated with THEODORE J. LOWI) maintaining that public authority is parceled out to private interest groups and results in a weak, decentralized government incapable of long-range planning. Powerful interest groups operate to promote private goals but do not compete to promote the public interest. Government becomes, not an institution that makes hard choices among conflicting values, but a holding company for interests. These interests are promoted by alliances of interest groups, relevant government agencies, and the appropriate congressional committees in each issue area. *See also* COZY TRIANGLES; PLURALISM.

interest group theory A theory based on the premise that individuals function primarily through groups and that these groups act as appropriate and necessary to further group goals (based on common interests). The group process, including formulation of group objectives and development of specific group actions and response, is seen as a fundamental characteristic of the political process.

The significance of groups in the political process has been recognized for over 2,000 years: ARISTOTLE noted that political associations were both significant and commonplace because of the "general advantages" members obtained. One of the first specific references to groups in the American political process was James Madison's famous discussion of factions in *Federalist* No. 10. In Madison's view, the group was inherent in the nature of people, and its causes were unremovable. The only choice then was to control the effects of group pressure and power. A more elaborate discussion of group theory can be traced to JOHN C. CALHOUN's treatise on governance, *A Disquisition on Government* (1853). While essentially an argument for the protection of minority interests, the treatise suggested that ideal governance must deal with all interest groups, since they represent the legitimate interests of the citizens. If all groups participated on some level of parity within the policymaking process, then all individual interests would be recognized by the policymakers.

While the work of Calhoun represents the development of early group theory, modern political science group theory has taken greater impetus from the work of ARTHUR F. BENTLEY. But it remained for political scientists DAVID B. TRUMAN and Earl Latham (1907–1977) to conceptualize the theoretical implications of group action and to begin assembling a theory of the group process. Truman's principal work—*The Governmental Process* (1951)—viewed group interaction as the real determinant of public policy, the primary focal point of study, in his view.

Latham's *The Group Basis of Politics* (1952) was particularly significant, because of his conceptualization that government itself is a group just like the various private groups attempting to access the policy process. Latham ascribed to government the same characteristics and concern for power associated with all organized private groups. He contended that the basic structure of the political community is associational. The state or political community will establish "norms of permissible behavior in group relations and enforce these norms." In essence, the state becomes more than a referee between groups in conflict, because it is also developing goals as well as overseeing activity.

Latham viewed the legislature as the referee of the group struggle, responsible for "ratifying the victories of the successful coalitions and recording the terms of the surrenders, compromises, and conquests in the form of statutes." The function of bureaucrats is quite different, however. They are like "armies of occupation left in the field to police the rule won by the victorious coalition." Although Latham's description was aimed primarily at regulatory agencies, he saw the bureaucrat being deluged by the losing coalitions of groups for more favorable actions despite the general rules established. The result is that "regulatory agencies are constantly besought and importuned to interpret their authorities in favor of the very groups for the regulation of which they were originally granted." (E.E. SCHATTSCHNEIDER in *The Semisovereign People* [1960] challenged Latham's assumption that the results of political conflict can be analyzed so facilely: "To assume that the forces in a political situation could be diagrammed as a physicist might diagram the resultant of opposing physical forces is to wipe the slate clean of all remote, general and public considerations for the protection of which civil societies have been instituted.")

Latham distinguished three types of groups, based on phases of development: incipient, conscious, and organized. An incipient group is one "where the interest exists but is not recognized" by the potential members; a conscious group is one "in which the community sense exists but which has not become organized"; and finally an organized group is "a conscious group which has established an objective and formal apparatus to promote the common interest." Latham's incipient and conscious groups are essentially the same as Truman's potential groups, which always exist but don't come together until there is a felt need for action on an issue.

The concept of potential groups keeps the bureaucratic policymaking process honest (or perhaps balanced); given the possibility that new groups might surface on some issues may influence decision making. The potential groups concept also serves as a counterargument to the claim that group theory is undemocratic. Once the concept of potential group is married to the active role of organized groups, the claim can be made, in David Truman's words, that "all interests of society by definition are taken into account in one form or another by the institutions of government." *See also* PRESSURE GROUP; LOBBY.

interface 1. Any common boundary between things. For example, in tailoring it refers to a fabric that is placed between two other fabrics to give them body and shape. **2.** The point of contact, or the boundary between organizations, people, jobs, or systems. Nowadays, the verbose politician does not mix with or visit with constituents; he or she has the pleasure of interfacing with them. During the Jimmy Carter administration, Vice President Walter Mondale observed: "In the Senate, you have friends; in the executive, you interface."

intergovernmental expenditure An amount paid to other governments as political, fiscal, or programmatic aid in the form of shared revenues and grants-in-aid, as reimbursements for performance of general government activities, and for specific services for the paying government (e.g., care of prisoners, and contractual research), or in lieu of taxes. *See also* FEDERAL-ISM, FISCAL.

intergovernmental relations (IGR) The complex network of interrelation-ships among governments; political, fiscal, programmatic, and administra-tive processes by which higher units of government share revenues and other resources with lower units of government, generally accompanied by special conditions that the lower units must satisfy as prerequisites to receiving the assistance. *See also* ADVISORY COMMISSION ON INTERGOVERN-MENTAL RELATIONS; FEDERALISM.

intergovernmental revenue Amounts received from other governments as fiscal aid in the form of shared revenues and grants-in-aid, as reimburse-ments for performance of general government functions, and specific ser-vices for the paying government (e.g., care of prisoners, and contractual research), or in lieu of taxes.

Interior, U.S. Department of the (DOI) The cabinet-level federal agency created in 1849. It was chiefly responsible for the westward expansion of the nation and the control of the distribution of public lands and resources. For much of its history, it was a center of controversy over corruption and opportunism, as well as, with the War Department, the sometimes brutal control of the Indian inhabitants and their various removals from opening territories. As the nation's principal conservation agency, Interior has responsibility for most of our nationally owned public lands and natural resources; it also has a major responsibility for American Indian reservation communities and for people who live in island territories under U.S. administration. *Compare to* CONSERVATION.

intermediate nuclear forces (INF) *See* INF TREATY.

Internal Revenue Service (IRS) The federal agency, established in 1862 within the Treasury Department, responsible for administering and enforc-ing the internal revenue laws, except those relating to alcohol, tobacco, firearms, and explosives (which are the responsibility of the Bureau of Alco-hol, Tobacco and Firearms). The IRS mission is to encourage and to achieve the highest possible degree of voluntary COMPLIANCE with the tax laws and regulations.

Internal Security Act of 1950 *See* ALBERTSON V SUBVERSIVE ACTIVITIES CONTROL BOARD.

International City Management Association (ICMA) A Washington-based professional organization, formed as the City Managers' Association in 1914, for appointed chief executives of cities, counties, towns, and other local governments. Its primary goals include strengthening the quality of urban government through professional management, and developing and disseminating new concepts and approaches to management through information services, training programs, and publications. *See also* PUBLIC INTEREST GROUPS.

International Trade Commission, United States (ITC) The federal agency that makes recommendations involving international trade and tariffs to the President, the Congress, and other government agencies. It was created in 1916 as the United States Tariff Commission and changed to its present name in 1974 under provisions of the Trade Act of 1974.

interposition *See* JOHN C. CALHOUN.

Interstate Commerce Commission (ICC) The federal commission that regulates interstate surface transportation, including trains, trucks, buses, inland waterway and coastal shipping, freight forwarders, and express companies. The regulatory laws vary with the type of transportation; however, they generally involve (1) certification of carriers seeking to provide transportation for the public, (2) rates, (3) adequacy of service, and (4) purchases and mergers. The ICC, established in 1887, is considered the prototype for independent federal regulatory commissions.

interstate compacts Formal arrangements entered into by two or more states, generally with the approval of the U.S. Congress, to operate joint programs. While Article I, Section 10, of the Constitution requires that interstate compacts be approved by the Congress, as a practicality many agreements on minor matters ignore this requirement. The initial intent was to prevent states from forming regional alliances that might threaten national unity.

invisible hand ADAM SMITH's description from *The Wealth of Nations* (1776) of the capitalistic market mechanism that invisibly and automatically promotes the general welfare as long as individuals are allowed to pursue their self-interest.

Iowa bump The boost in preference polls and name recognition that a presidential candidate hopes to get by doing well in the Iowa caucus.

Iowa caucus The earliest CAUCUS in a presidential election year. A good showing in the Iowa caucus is often critical for a candidate if he or she is to establish the needed momentum to be taken seriously as a candidate. Caucuses are held at each of the 2,487 Iowa precincts. The members of each political party meet at the precinct level to select delegates to the county conventions which in turn sends delegates to the Congressional district conventions which sends delegates to the State convention which selects the delegates to the national convention. Candidates win at each level if people favorable to them are selected to go on to the next level.

Iran-Contra affair The controversy arising in the fall of 1986, when it was revealed that the Ronald Reagan administration had secretly sold arms to the government of Iran (so Iran would use its good offices to gain the release of American hostages in Lebanon) at higher than normal prices and used the "profits" to fund the CONTRAS in Nicaragua. The controversy grew into a scandal because it was illegal to sell arms to Iran, illegal to fund the Contras beyond limits set by the Congress under the BOLAND AMENDMENT, and against the expressed policy of the United States to negotiate for, let alone trade arms for, the release of hostages. Because the Iran-Contra operation was undertaken primarily by the National Security Council without the formal approval of the departments of Defense and State, the affair called into question the coherence of the Reagan administration's foreign policy.

Former President Richard M. Nixon, a man who knows much about lying and cover-ups, offered a succinct analysis of the affair. *Newsweek* (October 5, 1987) reported that Nixon told friends: "Reagan will survive the Iran-Contra scandal because when push comes to shove he can say, 'I was stupid.' After a pause, Nixon added with a sly grin: 'I never had that option.'" Nixon was exactly right. Reagan was relatively untouched by the scandal even though he admitted after he left the presidency that "It was a covert action that was taken at my behest" (*The New York Times*, February 23, 1990), because he could tell people "I don't remember" and have it accepted. Congress had neither the stomach nor the popular support to impeach this lovable old man for what were clearly impeachable offenses. Had Nixon been more lovable the whole WATERGATE scandal could have turned out differently as well. The Iran-Contra affair dragged on until late December of 1992 when lame duck President George Bush pardoned the last six former Ronald Reagan Administration officials who were being pursued by the independent prosecutor (Lawrence E. Walsh who was initially appointed in 1986). This was viewed as an outrageous abuse of the presidential pardon power by some and as a fitting end to prosecutions that never should have begun in the first place by others. *See also* TOWER COMMISSION.

Iranian hostage crisis The wholesale violation of diplomatic privileges and immunities that occurred when the Iranian government-backed "students" captured the American Embassy complex of buildings in Teheran on November 4, 1979, and held 53 Americans hostage for 444 days, until January 20, 1981. The crisis so dominated the last year of the Jimmy Carter administration that it badly damaged Carter's reelection prospects, especially after an unsuccessful rescue effort on April 24, 1980. The Iranians agreed to free the hostages only after the Carter administration agreed to some of the Iranian demands "in principle." As one last insult to the Carter administration, the hostages were freed on the day Ronald Reagan succeeded Carter as President. *See* OCTOBER SURPRISE.

iron curtain The political, social, and economic schism between the countries of eastern and western Europe. The phrase was popularized by British prime minister Winston Churchill in a March 5, 1946 speech at Westminster College, Fulton, Missouri, in which he said: "From Stettin in the Baltic to Trieste in the Adriatic, an iron curtain has descended across the continent." Now the phrase is also used to refer to any hostile and seemingly permanent political division. However, the specific curtain which Churchill referred to has gone the way of the COLD WAR.

iron triangles See COZY TRIANGLES

IRS See INTERNAL REVENUE SERVICE.

isolationism The policy of curtailing as much as possible a nation's international relations so one's country can exist in peace and harmony by itself in the world. Isolationism was the dominant U.S. foreign policy for many periods in its history, particularly during most of the nineteenth century and the two decades between the world wars. George Washington in his Farewell Address, September 17, 1796, advocated a policy of isolationism: "Why quit our own to stand upon foreign ground? Why, by interweaving our destiny with that of any part of Europe, entangle our peace and prosperity in the toils of European ambition, rivalship, interest, humor or caprice?" But modern trade, communications, and military weapons make isolationism virtually impossible for any nation today, even though such wishful thinking will continue to be a significant factor in domestic politics. Since 1945, the United States has abandoned isolationism, replacing it with a clear international commitment made evident by policies such as the TRUMAN DOCTRINE and formal alliances such as NATO. Contradicting George Washington, President Harry S Truman expressed the national consensus in a speech in St. Louis, Missouri, June 10, 1950: "Isolationism is the road to war. Worse than that, isolationism is the road to defeat in war."

issue A matter of political contention; a point in question, *the issues* are what politicians always say are important in a political campaign. However, it is these same issues that critics say they ignore. Nevertheless, all campaigns are expected to have issues. As JAMES BRYCE observed of American politics in his *The American Commonwealth* (1888): "if issues do not exist, they have to be created."

issue-attention cycle A model developed by Anthony Downs that attempts to explain how many policy problems evolve onto the political agenda. The cycle is premised on the proposition that the public's attention rarely remains focused on any one issue for a very long time, regardless of the objective nature of the problem. The cycle consists of five steps: (1) the preproblem stage (an undesirable social condition exists, but has not captured public attention); (2) alarmed discovery and euphoric enthusiasm (a dramatic event catalyzes the public attention, accompanied by an enthusiasm to solve the problem); (3) recognition of the cost of change (the public gradually realizes the difficulty of implementing meaningful change); (4)

decline of public interest (people become discouraged or bored or a new issue claims attention); and (5) the postproblem stage (although the issue has not been solved, it has been dropped from the nation's agenda). It was outlined in Down's "Up and Down with ecology—The 'Issue-Attention Cycle'" (*Public Interest*, Vol. 28, Summer 1972).

issue group A politically active organization created in response to a specific issue. For example, the Right to Life Association was created as a response to the Supreme Court's 1973 *Roe v Wade* decision legalizing abortion.

issue networks 1. The totality of public and private actors who interact and combine either to put forth and enact into law or to oppose public policy initiatives. This is an inherently chaotic process with little neatness or definition. The concept is mainly used after the fact by policy analysts to explain how a policy or issue came into being. **2.** The bureaucratic experts, professional associations, and private sector practitioners of a technical specialty that both formally and informally define standards of practice and develop consensus on public policy issues affecting their profession. *Compare to* COZY TRIANGLES.

issue voting *See* VOTING, ISSUE.

item veto *See* VETO, ITEM.

J

Jackson, Andrew (1767–1845) The commanding general at the 1815 Battle of New Orleans where the Americans, in the last engagement of the War of 1812, literally killed half of the attacking British force of 5,000, with less than a dozen casualties of their own. Elected president in 1828, he was the first westerner (being from Tennessee) to occupy the White House (1829–1837) and the first president elected by the Democratic party. Jackson opposed state nullification of federal laws and advocated a strong national government, an expanded SUFFRAGE (through the removal of property requirements for white males), and a strengthened party system. His contributions to the conduct of the presidency included vigorous use of patronage, transformation of the cabinet into a group of loyal advisors and allies, reliance on informal advisors (his "kitchen cabinet"), and highly publicized use of the veto to enforce his policy positions. During his two terms of office, Jackson was blamed for inventing the SPOILS SYSTEM. Prior to Jackson, the federal service was a stable, long-tenured corps of officials decidedly elitist in character and remarkably free of corruption. Jackson, for the most part, continued with this tradition in practice, turning out of office about as many appointees as had Jefferson. But in his most famous statement on the character of public office (his Message to Congress of December 8, 1829), Jackson asserted that the duties of public office are "so plain and simple that men of intelligence may readily qualify themselves for their performance: and I cannot but believe that more is lost by the long continuance of men in office than is generally to be gained by their experience." Jackson thus claimed that all men, especially the newly enfranchised who did so much to elect him, should have an equal opportunity for public office. In playing to his plebeian constituency, Jackson put the patrician civil service on notice that they had no natural monopoly on public office. His rhetoric on the nature of the public service was to be far more influential than his administrative example. While Jackson's personal indulgence in spoils was more limited than popularly thought, he did establish the intellectual and political rationale for the unmitigated spoils system that was to follow. *Compare to* CALHOUN, JOHN C.; *see also* CABINET, KITCHEN.

Jacksonian democracy *See* DEMOCRACY, JACKSONIAN.

Jackson, Jesse (1941–   ) The civil rights activist who in 1984 became the first African-American to mount a major national campaign for the Democratic nomination for President. Shirley Chisolm (1924–   ), as a African-American congresswoman from New York, sought the nomination in 1972; but her candidacy was more symbolic than real. Jackson is president of the National Rainbow Coalition, a decidedly left-of-center splinter group within the Democratic party for those, in Jackson's words, "who are being locked out of their party." In 1988 Jackson mounted an even more serious campaign for the Democratic presidential nomination but lost to Governor Michael Dukakis of Massachusetts, who lost to then-Vice President George Bush. Jackson, noted for his soaring rhetoric, is a major influence in Democratic Party politics. His biggest problem in being taken as a serious contender for the presidency is the fact that he has never held elected office and seems disinclined to seek any but the symbolic seat of "shadow senator" from the District of Columbia.

Jarvis-Gann Initiative *See* PROPOSITION 13.

Jefferson, Thomas (1743–1826) The primary author of the Declaration of Independence, the first secretary of State (under President George Washington), the second Vice President (under President John Adams), the third President of the United States (1801–1809), and the founder of the University of Virginia (1819). Jefferson is universally acknowledged as one of the major forces in the creation of the American political party system, and both of today's major parties trace their philosophic origins to him. (Jefferson was the leader of the Republican party, which originated in 1791. This evolved into the Democratic-Republican party, which changed its name to the Democratic party in 1828. Many disaffected Democratic-Republicans, who called themselves National Republicans, united with other splinter groups in 1834 to form the Whig party, which disintegrated in 1852. A coalition of disaffected Democrats and former Whigs formed the modern Republican party in 1856).

Jefferson was the first President to face the problem of a philosophically hostile bureaucracy. Although sorely pressed by his supporters to remove Federalist officeholders and replace them with Republican partisans, Jefferson was determined not to remove officials for political reasons alone. Jefferson rather courageously maintained that only "malconduct is a just ground of removal: mere difference of political opinion is not." With occasional defections from this principle, even by Jefferson himself, this policy became the norm rather than the exception down through the administration of Andrew Jackson.

Jefferson was so talented and so influential in so many areas that on April 29, 1962, when President John F. Kennedy invited all of the Nobel Prize winners to dine at the White House, he told them: "I think this is the most extraordinary collection of talent, of human knowledge, that has ever been gathered together at the White House—with the possible exception of when Thomas Jefferson dined here alone."

Jeffersonian democracy *See* DEMOCRACY, JEFFERSONIAN.

Jim Crow A name given to any law requiring the segregation of the races. All such statutes are now unconstitutional. But prior to the CIVIL RIGHTS ACT OF 1964 many southern states had laws requiring separate drinking fountains, separate rest rooms, separate sections of theaters, and so on for the blacks and whites. The name "Jim Crow" comes from a nineteenth-century vaudeville character who was called Jim (a common name) Crow (for a black-colored bird). Thus, the name "Jim Crow" was applied to things having to do with blacks.

Job Corps The federal training program created by the COMPREHENSIVE EMPLOYMENT AND TRAINING ACT OF 1973, which offers social and occupational development for disadvantaged youths through centers with the unique feature of residential facilities for all or most enrollees. Its purpose is to prepare them for the responsibilities of citizenship and to increase their employability by providing them with education, vocational training, and useful work experience in rural, urban, or inner-city centers. Enrollees may spend a maximum of two years in the Job Corps. However, a period of enrollment from six months to a year is usually sufficient to provide adequate training and education to improve employability to a substantial degree. Job Corps recruiting is accomplished primarily through state employment services.

Job Training Partnership Act of 1983 *See* COMPREHENSIVE EMPLOYMENT AND TRAINING ACT OF 1973.

John Birch Society A secretive, far-right, ultraconservative organization founded in 1959 to fight communism and communist influences in American life. It was named after John Birch, a U.S. army captain killed by the Chinese communists in 1945. His namesake society honors him as the first victim of the cold war. Under the leadership of its founder, Robert H. Welch, Jr. (1899–1985), the society sought (1) to impeach then Chief Justice EARL WARREN, (2) to withdraw the United States from the United Nations, (3) to end U.S. participation in NATO, and (4) to eliminate all federal welfare programs. At the local level it sought to place its members on school boards, city councils, and so on. Because of the society's paranoid anticommunism (e.g., it considered the fluoridation of drinking water to be a Communist plot), the name "Bircher" has become synonymous with a right-wing extremist. At its height, the society had about 800 local chapters and more than 100,000 members. These figures are much, much lower now.

Johnson, Andrew (1808–1875) The border state (Tennessee) Vice President who succeeded to the presidency in 1865 after Abraham Lincoln was assassinated. He was the only President to be impeached by the House of Representatives and to be tried for "high crimes and misdemeanors" by the Senate. The Radical Republicans, who were in power in the Congress, wanted to get rid of him because of his compassionate policies toward the defeated South and his hostility to programs which would help the newly freed slaves. He was acquitted by one vote, a narrow win for himself and the institution of the presidency. *Compare to* IMPEACHMENT.

Johnson, Lyndon B. (1908–1973) The Vice President who became President when President John F. Kennedy was assassinated on November 22, 1963. A member of the Congress from Texas since 1937 and the leader of the Democrats in the Senate since 1953 (majority leader from 1955 to 1961), Johnson proved extremely skillful in getting liberal legislation through a Congress still dominated by southern conservative Democrats. He won election to the presidency in his own right in 1964 by such an overwhelming landslide and carried such significant numbers of new Democratic congressmen in on his COATTAILS that there was much talk of the total disintegration of the Republican party. Yet in spite of an excellent record on civil rights and domestic programs, his questionable and ineffective tactics in pursuing the Vietnam War divided the country considerably, and, after Johnson declined to run for a second full term, gave the Republicans and Richard M. Nixon the presidency in 1968. It was sarcastically said at the time: "Roosevelt gave us the New Deal, Truman gave us the Fair Deal, but Johnson gave us the Ordeal."

Johnson v Santa Clara County *See* REVERSE DISCRIMINATION.

Joint Chiefs of Staff The primary military advisors to the secretary of Defense and to the President of the United States. The group consists of the chiefs of staff of the U.S. army and air force, the chief of naval operations, the commandant of the marine corps (but only when marine corps matters are at issue), and a chairman, who is generally considered the spokesman for the nation's military establishment. The Joint Chiefs has been heavily criticized because it does not operate as a unified command but works mainly to perpetuate interservice rivalries and identities. While an organization known as the Joint Chiefs of Staff operated during World War II, the present organization was created by the National Security Act of 1947.

The Pentagon Reorganization Act of 1986 sought to strengthen the role of the Chairman of the Joint Chiefs of Staff by making him personally the President's "principal military adviser," instead of, as before, the representative of the collective opinion of all of the service chiefs. General John W. Vessey, Jr., then Chairman, Joint Chiefs of Staff, said his job was "To give the president and secretary of defense military advice before they know they need it" (*New York Times*, July 15, 1984).

joint session A combined meeting of both Houses of Congress; usually held in the House Chamber because it is larger. The President always presents the STATE OF THE UNION MESSAGE to a joint session.

joint staff 1. A staff formed of two or more of the services of the same country. **2.** The staff of the Joint Chiefs of Staff as provided for under the National Security Act of 1947, as amended.

joker A vague clause specifically inserted into a bill that seems innocuous but has the effect of making the bill ineffective or subject to much later litigation.

Journal The official record of the proceedings of the House of Representatives and the Senate. The *Journal* records the actions taken in each chamber but, unlike the *Congressional Record*, it does not include the verbatim report of speeches and debate.

judge A judicial officer elected or appointed to preside over a court of law, whose position has been created by statute or by constitution, and whose decisions may be reviewed only by a judge of a higher court. Thomas Jefferson realized that "our judges are as honest as most men, and not more so." Judges gain their offices usually in one of three ways depending upon local law: through partisan election, through nonpartisan election, or by appointment. Robert Traver in his novel, *Anatomy of a Murder* (1958), holds that: "Judges, like people, may be divided roughly into four classes: judges with neither head nor heart—they are to be avoided at all costs; judges with head but no heart—they are almost as bad; then judges with heart but no head—risky but better than the first two; and finally, those rare judges who possess both head and a heart."

judge-made Descriptive of laws created by judicial PRECEDENTS as opposed to statutory laws.

judicial activism The making of new public policies through the decisions of judges. This may take the form of a reversal or modification of a prior court decision, the nullification of a law passed by the legislature, or the overturning of some action of the executive branch. The concept of judicial activism is most associated with the Supreme Court, which from time to time has found new laws when none were there before. However, judges at any level can be said to engage in judicial activism when their judicial positions are used to promote what they consider to be desirable social goals. The main argument against judicial activism is that it tends to usurp the power of the legislature. The counterargument holds that, because laws—being products of compromise—tend to be vague on "hot" issues, the courts are in effect forced by the nature of the cases they receive to sort things out in a manner that seems "activist" to critics. In a larger historical sense, Chief Justice John Marshall's introduction of JUDICIAL REVIEW began judicial activism by claiming a special constitutional authority for the Court over the actions of other branches of government. *Compare to* JUDICIAL SELF-RESTRAINT.

Judicial Conference of the United States The group of federal judges, chaired by the chief justice of the Supreme Court, which provides for administrative policymaking for the federal court system.

judicial officer Any person exercising judicial powers in a court of law; a judge.

judicial review 1. The power of the Supreme Court to declare actions of the President, the Congress, or other agencies of government at any level to be invalid or unconstitutional. While it was first asserted by the Supreme Court in MARBURY V MADISON (1803), it was a power used sparingly in the nineteenth century, and used commonly in the twentieth especially since the 1930s. **2.** Any court's power to review executive actions, legislative acts, or the decisions of lower courts (or quasi-judicial entities, such as arbitration panels) to either confirm or overturn them. As long ago as 1835 in

Democracy in America, ALEXIS DE TOCQUEVILLE observed: "The power vested in the American courts of justice of pronouncing a statute to be unconstitutional forms one of the most powerful barriers that have ever been devised against the tyranny of political assemblies." *See also* least dangerous branch.

judicial self-restraint A self-imposed limitation on judicial decision making; the tendency on the part of judges to favor a narrow interpretation of the laws and to defer to the policy judgment of the legislative and executive branches. Justice Harlan Fiske Stone wrote in *United States v Butler* (1936), that "while unconstitutional exercise by the executive and legislative branches is subject to judicial restraint, the only check on our own exercise of power is our own sense of self-restraint." *Compare to* JUDICIAL ACTIVISM; POLITICAL QUESTION.

judiciary 1. The courts in general; the judicial branch of government. It is the judiciary that protects citizens from real and potential abuses by the other branches. Chief Justice John Marshall said: "To what quarter will you look for protection from an infringement on the Constitution, if you will not give that power to the judiciary? There is no other body that can afford such a protection." **2.** The courts of a specific jurisdiction such as the federal judiciary.

jump bail To illegally flee while free on BAIL.

junket *See* OVERSIGHT, CONGRESSIONAL.

juridical democracy An alternative to interest group liberalism offered by THEODORE J. LOWI in *The End of Liberalism* (1969), which calls for the federal courts to take a stronger role in achieving democratic ideals by forcing the Congress into a greater "rule of law" posture. Such force would come about by increasingly declaring statutes unconstitutional if they continue to be so vague that significant policy powers are delegated to government agencies who use this discretion to play the interest group game. Lowi views the competition of interest groups for influence over program implementation as inherently undemocratic, because these decisions should be made in great detail in the legislation itself. And only the courts can force the Congress to do this.

jurisdiction 1. A territory, subject matter, or person over which lawful authority may be exercised. **2.** A union's exclusive right to represent particular workers within specified industrial, occupational, or geographical boundaries. **3.** The power of a court to act on a case. **4.** A legislative committee's area of responsibility.

jurisdictional dispute 1. A disagreement between two government entities over which should provide services to a disputed area, over who has the authority to tax a disputed source, who has the prior right to initiate prosecution in a criminal or noncompliance case, and so on. **2.** A disagreement between two unions over which should control a particular job or activity.

jurisdiction, original The power of a court to hear a case first. This is in contrast to appellate jurisdiction, which means that the court reviews cases only after they have been tried elsewhere. Article III, Section 2 of the U.S. Constitution gives the Supreme Court original jurisdiction in cases involving foreign ambassadors and disputes between the states.

jurisprudence **1.** The art and science of the law; not the laws of any given jurisdiction but the origin, form, and nature of the law in general; the structure of legal systems. **2.** The study of legal philosophy and its underlying concepts. **3.** A trend in case law; the collective course of judicial decision making on a given issue over time.

jurist **1.** Any judge. **2.** Someone who has made outstanding intellectual contributions to legal thought and legal literature.

jury A group of citizens randomly chosen to make judgments on charges in either criminal or civil cases.

jury, death qualified *See* LOCKHART V MCCREE.

jury, grand A group of citizens selected to review evidence against accused persons to determine whether there is sufficient evidence to bring the accused to trial—to indict or not to indict. A grand jury usually has from 12 to 23 members and operates in secrecy to protect the reputation of those not indicted. Grand juries have been both criticized for being easily manipulated tools in the hands of prosecutors and praised for protecting the rights of those falsely accused.

jury, hung A jury that is so irreconcilably divided in opinion that it is unable to reach a verdict.

jury panel The group of persons summoned to appear in court as potential jurors, from among whom the actual jurors are selected.

jury trial *See* TRIAL, JURY.

jury, trial A statutorily defined number of persons (usually at least six and no more than 12) selected to determine matters of fact based on evidence presented at a trial and to render a verdict. The right of a public trial by an impartial jury in all criminal prosecutions is guaranteed by the Sixth Amendment. However, many defendants waive this right and accept PLEA BARGAINING. In *Duncan v Louisiana* (1968), the Supreme Court held that trial by jury in criminal cases is fundamental to the American scheme of justice. We hold that the Fourteenth Amendment guarantees a right of jury trial in all criminal cases which—were they to be tried in a federal court—would come within the Sixth Amendment's guarantee. . . . The nation has a deep commitment to the right of jury trial and is reluctant to entrust plenary powers over the life and liberty of the citizen to one judge or to a group of judges.

The pros and cons of jury trial have often been debated. Arguments in favor include (1) the value of citizen participation in the criminal justice system; (2) the obvious advantage of 12 (or six) minds over one; (3) the likelihood that, if a jury is convinced, a case has been established; (4) the protection of civil liberties and commonsense application of the law by choosing a group at random from the lists of registered voters or licensed drivers; and (5) the great difficulty in intimidating or bribing a group that does not come together until the beginning of a trial. Arguments against juries are (1) the sheer expense of so cumbersome a process; (2) the uncertainty of whether the jurors will understand the issues at hand; (3) the almost inevitable delays associated with jury trials; and (4) the fact that a jury does not give reasons for its decision, making it more difficult to appeal.

jus sanguinis Latin meaning "right of blood"; the legal principle that a newborn child's nationality or citizenship is the same as that of the parents.

jus soli Latin meaning "right of land"; the legal principle that a newborn child's nationality or citizenship is determined by where the birth occurred. This is the case in the United States; anyone born here is automatically a citizen.

justice **1.** The title of a judge; for example, an associate justice of the Supreme Court. *Compare to* CHIEF JUSTICE. **2.** An elusive quality of treatment by one's nation that is perceived by the overwhelming majority of the citizens to be fair and appropriate. **3.** The philosophic search for perfection in governance. The Athenian historian Thucydides cynically observed in *The Peloponnesian Wars* (fifth century B.C.) that: "Into the discussion of human affairs the question of justice only enters where there is equal power to enforce it, and that the powerful exact what they can, and the weak grant what they must." Many would suggest that things haven't changed much since ancient times. Nevertheless, James Madison wrote in *Federalist* 51 that "justice is the end of government. It is the end of civil society." **4.** The ideal that each nation's laws seek to achieve for each of its citizens. According to ALEXIS DE TOCQUEVILLE in *Democracy in America* (1835): "There is one universal law that has been formed or at least adopted . . . by the majority of mankind. That law is justice. Justice forms the cornerstone of each nation's law." **5.** A cynical justification for tyranny. PLATO in *Republic* (370 B.C.) wrote that "justice is but the interest of the stronger." **6.** The name of a law enforcement agency, usually headed by an ATTORNEY GENERAL.

Justice, U.S. Department of A cabinet-level department of the federal government. As the largest law firm in the nation, the Department of Justice is supposed to represent the citizens of the United States in enforcing the law in the public interest. The department conducts all suits in the Supreme Court in which the United States is concerned. It represents the government in legal matters generally, rendering legal advice and opinions, upon request, to the President and to the heads of the executive departments. The U.S. ATTORNEY GENERAL supervises and directs these activities, as well as those of the U.S. attorneys and U.S. marshalls in the various judicial districts around the country. While the attorney general was placed in the President's cabinet in 1789, it wasn't until 1870 that the Congress created a Department of Justice.

K

Keating Five The five Senators who collected in total about $1.4 million in campaign donations from Charles Keating of the now bankrupt Lincoln Savings and Loan: Alan Cranston of California, Dennis Deconcini of Arizona, Donald Riegle of Michigan, John McCain of Arizona, and John Glenn of Ohio. After a 14-month investigation costing approximately $2 million, the Senate Ethics Committee reported that there was substantial evidence of wrongdoing only by Senator Cranston. The committee's highly publicized hearings generated considerable discussion over the ethical issue of just how far a lawmaker should go to help a constitutent who is also a substantial financial backer.

Kefauver, Estes (1903–1963) The Senator from Tennessee (1949–1963) who was the Democratic vice presidential nominee in 1956. He was the first to demonstrate that the presidential primary in the television age was a way to go over the heads of the "bosses" to the "people." His astute use of the 1956 New Hampshire primary showed how a regional politician could come "out of nowhere" and get on the national ticket.

Kennedy, Edward Moore "Ted" (1932–   ) The youngest brother of President John F. Kennedy and a Senator from Massachusetts since 1963. Kennedy, who was often mentioned as a possible Democratic nominee for President (he actively sought but lost the nomination to President Jimmy Carter in 1980), is a major voice for traditionally liberal legislation in the Senate. *See also* CHAPPAQUIDDICK.

Kennedy, John Fitzgerald (1917–1963) After service in the House of Representatives from 1947 to 1953 and in the Senate from 1953 to 1960, Kennedy became the first Roman Catholic to be elected President of the United States. His administration (1961–1963) is now more noted for its style (which has come to be known as CAMELOT) than substance. His charming and charismatic personality tended to overshadow his failure to get any major legislation through a conservative-dominated Congress and his foreign policy frustrations with Cuba in the BAY OF PIGS, the Soviet Union in the CUBAN MISSILE CRISIS, and Vietnam, where he had placed 16,000 American military "advisors." But in spite of all this, Kennedy will always be remembered as the President who brought a sense of youthful vigor to the White House and launched the space age with his decision to put Americans on the moon within a decade. Just as President Franklin D. Roosevelt used radio to create a personal relationship with the American public, Kennedy became the first President to effectively use live television on a regular basis through the PRESIDENTIAL PRESS CONFERENCE. Perhaps Kennedy's most significant decision for the future of the nation was his selection of LYNDON B. JOHNSON to be his Vice President—with all the good and ill that implied for the 1960s. Kennedy was assassinated in Dallas, Texas, on November 22, 1963. *See also* WARREN COMMISSION.

Kennedy, Joseph P. II (1952–   ) The oldest son of Robert F. Kennedy, who since 1987 has represented the Eighth District of Massachusetts in the Congress, the same seat once held by his uncle, President John F. Kennedy.

Kennedy, Robert Francis (1925–1968) The younger brother of President John F. Kennedy, his campaign manager in 1960, then his attorney general. On the day after his inauguration, January 21, 1961, President Kennedy announced the appointment of his youthful and legally inexperienced brother to his cabinet, playfully saying: "I see nothing wrong with giving Robert some legal experience as Attorney General before he goes out to practice law" (*The Kennedy Wit*, 1964). Humor and brotherhood aside, Robert Kennedy proved to be the most effective and influential member of the President's cabinet. In 1964 he was elected to the Senate from New York. He was assassinated on June 6, 1968 while campaigning for the Democratic party's presidential nomination. During his campaign he became famous for saying: "Some men see things as they are and say 'Why?' I dream things that never were and say, 'Why not?'" He took this quote from playwright George Bernard Shaw's *Back to Methuselah* (1921).

Kerner Commission The National Advisory Commission on Civil Disorders, chaired by Governor Otto Kerner (1908–1976) of Illinois, which reported in 1968 that the "nation is rapidly moving toward two increasingly separate Americas; one black and one white."

Kerr-Mills Act The popular name for the Social Security amendments of 1960, which expanded and modified the federal government's existing responsibility for assisting the states in paying for medical care for the poor.

Kestnbaum Commission The Commission on Intergovernmental Relations, created in 1953 by President Dwight D. Eisenhower and chaired by Meyer Kestnbaum, whose report (submitted in 1955) led to the creation of the permanent ADVISORY COMMISSION ON INTERGOVERNMENTAL RELATIONS in 1959.

Keyishian v Board of Regents (1967) The Supreme Court case that held that laws "which make Communist Party membership, as such, prima facie evidence of disqualification for employment in the public school system are overboard and therefore unconstitutional."

Keynes, John Maynard (1883–1946) The English economist who wrote the most influential book on economics of this century, *The General Theory of Employment, Interest and Money* (1936). Keynes founded a school of thought known as Keynesian economics, which called for using a government's fiscal and monetary policies to positively influence a capitalistic economy, and developed the framework of modern economic theory. All Presidents since Franklin D. Roosevelt have used Keynes' theories to, admittedly or unadmittedly, justify deficit spending to stimulate the economy. Even President Richard M. Nixon once said, "We're all Keynesians now." Keynes, however, observed in his *General Theory* that "practical men, who believe themselves to be quite exempt from any intellectual influences, are usually the slaves of some defunct economist." He provided the definitive economic forecast when he asserted that "in the long run we are all dead."

keynote address The major political speech (other than the candidate's acceptance speech) at a national nominating convention that is supposed to set the tone for the campaign to come. It is an opportunity to make the party's case on prime-time television to the people and is usually given by one of the party's most gifted orators.

Key, V.O., Jr. (1908–1963) The political scientist who did pioneering work in developing empirical methods to explore political and administrative behavior. His article "The Lack of a Budgetary Theory" (*American Political Science Review* 34, December 1940) posed what was soon acknowledged as the central question of budgeting—"on what basis shall it be decided to allocate X dollars to activity A instead of activity B?" His *Politics, Parties and Pressure Groups* (5th ed., 1964) was the pioneering text in the functional analysis of the various elements in the political process. His *Southern Politics in State and Nation* (1949) was the classic study of why the Democratic party dominated the South for so long after the Civil War.

kinder gentler nation President George Bush's phrase for the more compassionate country he wanted to lead; first used in his acceptance speech at the 1988 Republican National Convention.

King, Martin Luther, Jr. (1929–1968) The black southern Baptist minister who became the preeminent leader of the CIVIL RIGHTS MOVEMENT. His tactics of nonviolent confrontation with southern segregational policies aroused enough sympathy and support in the rest of the nation that they led to landmark civil rights legislation. King was assassinated in Memphis, Tennessee, on April 4, 1968. His influence as the "saint" of civil rights was so strong that his birthday was made a national holiday in 1983.

Kissinger, Henry A. (1923–   ) The Harvard University political scientist who became President Richard M. Nixon's National Security Advisor (1969–1973); then secretary of State under both Presidents Nixon and Ford (1973–1977). While he shared the Nobel Peace Prize in 1973 for his efforts to bring peace to Vietnam, he was also widely criticized for U.S. Vietnam War policies—especially for his involvement in the Cambodian incursion.

Know-Nothing party The Supreme Order of the Star Spangled Banner, formed by secret far-right patriotic societies in the late 1840s. The order wanted to restrict immigration, increase the residency requirement for citizenship to 21 years, and prohibit Catholics and the foreign born from holding elected office. Since it was a secret society, members were bound to reply "I know nothing" when asked about their organization's activities. In the early 1850s, they became the American party and won some state elections in New England. In 1856 Millard Fillmore (1800–1874), the former President (1850–1853), was the party's candidate for President. His loss was so great (he carried only one state, Maryland), that the party disintegrated. Know-nothing was an informal title given to them by the press; but the term is still used to describe anyone who is a bigot, a political reactionary, or simply stupid.

Korean War The war between communist North Korea and noncommunist South Korea, which began on June 25, 1950, when the North invaded the South. The decision on the part of President Harry S Truman and his advisors to promote intervention was a reversal of a policy previously announced by secretary of State Dean Acheson, that Korea lay outside the defense perimeter of the United States. The decision was based on the belief that the actions of North Korea reflected larger policy interests promoted by the Soviet Union and Communist China and therefore required a strong American response. The American intervention was a symbolic signal to the Soviets that the United States was determined to halt the spread of Communism. With the encouragement of the United States, the United Nations Security Council (with the Soviet Union temporarily absent) asked member nations to aid the South in resisting the invasion. Thus, the war, called a "police action," was fought under the flag of the United Nations by U.S. forces with small contingents from over a dozen other nations. The North Koreans, in turn, soon got help from Chinese Communist "volunteer" forces. After three years, an armistice was signed (July 27, 1953), which maintained the division of the Koreas almost exactly where it was before the war started. No peace treaty has ever been signed. The Korean War is an example of a limited war with ambiguous objectives. When the commander of all U.N. and U.S. forces during the first part of the war, General Douglas MacArthur (1880–1964), publicly disagreed with President Truman's limited war policies, he was dismissed from command in April 1951. In the end, more than 50,000 Americans died in the Korean War; another 100,000 were wounded.

Korematsu v United States *See* EMERGENCY POWERS.

Ku Klux Klan (KKK) The most infamous U.S. terrorist organization: a racist white supremacist group established in the South following the Civil War. The KKK has a long history of intimidation, beatings, and murders of blacks, as well as other racial and religious minorities. Lynchings are a hallmark of the KKK, as are the burning of crosses, designed to instill fear into the hearts of onlookers. Klansmen traditionally cloak themselves in the anonymity of white robes and hide their faces under hoods. Early in this century the KKK had considerable political power; it dominated politics in a dozen states and counted dozens of Congressmen as members. However, today the KKK has only the slightest influence in American politics. Thus, it has traveled from mainstream to the lunatic fringe; from millions of members to a few thousand. In recent years, successful lawsuits brought against the KKK by its victims have dealt the organization severe setbacks.

L

Labor, U.S. Department of (DOL) The cabinet-level federal agency created in 1913 to foster, promote, and develop the welfare of the wage earners of the United States, to improve their working conditions, and to advance their opportunities for profitable employment. In carrying out this mission, the DOL administers more than 130 federal labor laws guaranteeing workers' rights to safe and healthful working conditions, a minimum hourly wage and overtime pay, unemployment insurance, workers' compensation, and freedom from employment discrimination.

Labor-Management Relations Act of 1947 The federal statute, also known as the *Taft-Hartley Act*, that modified what the Congress thought was a prounion bias in the National Labor Relations (Wagner) Act of 1935. Essentially a series of amendments to the National Labor Relations Act, Taft-Hartley (1) allowed national emergency strikes to be put off for an 80-day cooling-off period, during which the President might make recommendations to the Congress for legislation; (2) delineated unfair labor practices by unions to balance the unfair labor practices by employers defined in the Wagner Act; (3) made the closed shop illegal, allowing states to pass right-to-work laws; (4) excluded supervisory employees from coverage under the act; (5) allowed suits against unions for contract violations (judgments enforceable only against union assets); (6) required a party seeking to cancel an existing collective bargaining agreement to give 60 days' notice; (7) gave employers the right to seek a representation election if a union claimed recognition as a bargaining agent; (8) allowed the National Labor Relations Board to be reorganized and enlarged from three members to five; and (9) provided for the creation of the Federal Mediation and Conciliation Service to mediate labor disputes. The act was passed over the veto of President Harry S Truman.

Labor-Management Reporting and Disclosure Act of 1959 The federal statute enacted in response to findings of corruption in the management of some unions, also known as the *Landrum-Griffin Act*. The act provided for the reporting and disclosure of certain financial transactions and administrative practices of labor organizations and employers and created standards for the election of officers of labor organizations. The Congress determined that certain basic rights should be assured to members of labor unions, and these are listed in Title I of the act as a "bill of rights." Existing rights and remedies of union members under other federal or state laws, before any court or tribunal, or under the constitution and bylaws of their unions are not limited by the provisions of Title I. Executive Order 11491 applied these rights to members of unions representing employees of the executive branch of the federal government.

labor movement **1.** An inclusive phrase for the progressive history of UNIONS and unionism in the United States. Sometimes it is used in a broader sense to encompass the fate of the workers. The political influence of American unions has been declining precipitously in recent decades. In 1955, for example, close to 40 percent of all nonfarm workers belonged to unions. But by 1990, that number had dropped to 16.4 percent. **2.** The political organization of working-class interests.

laboratories of democracy A phrase first coined by Supreme Court Justice Louis Brandeis to refer to state governments that develop innovative policies to deal with social and economic problems. The implication is that if the policies succeed, they will be adopted by other states or by the federal government. Brandeis wrote in a dissenting opinion to *New State Ice Co. v Liebmann* (1932): "It is one of the happy incidents of the federal system that a single courageous State may, if its citizens choose, serve as a laboratory; and try novel social and economic experiments without risk to the rest of the country."

Laffer curve The purported relation between tax rates and government revenues publicized by economist Arthur B. Laffer (1940–). According to Laffer, higher taxes reduce government revenues because high rates discourage taxable activity. Following this logic, a government can raise its total revenues by cutting taxes. This should stimulate new taxable activity, and the revenue from this should more than offset the loss from lower tax rates. While Laffer may have been the first to draw his curve, many others had earlier expressed the ideas behind it. For example, JOHN MAYNARD KEYNES wrote: "Taxation may be so high as to defeat its object. . . . Given sufficient time to gather the fruits, a reduction of taxation will run a better chance, than an increasing, of balancing the budget." Even President John F. Kennedy observed in a speech of December 14, 1962, that "it is a paradoxical truth that tax rates are too high today and tax revenues are too low—and the soundest way to raise revenues in the long run is to cut tax rates now." *Compare to* SUPPLY-SIDE ECONOMICS.

laissez-faire A hands-off style of governance that emphasizes economic freedom so capitalism's INVISIBLE HAND can work its will. The concept is most associated with ADAM SMITH and his book *The Wealth of Nations* (1776). While laissez-faire is still used to express a philosophic attitude toward government, it has long been rejected by the mainstream of American politics. Even conservative Republican President William Howard Taft said in a September 17, 1909 speech: "We have passed beyond the time of . . . the laissez-faire school which believes that the government ought to do nothing but run a police force."

Lakewood plan *See* SERVICE CONTRACT.

lame duck **1.** Any officeholder who is serving out the remainder of a fixed term after declining to run or being defeated or ineligible for reelection. The authority of such an officeholder is considered to be impaired, or lame.

The phrase originated in the early days of the London stock market (known as Exchange Alley until 1773). A broker who went bankrupt would "waddle out of the Alley" like a lame duck. By the time of the American Civil War, the phrase had crossed the Atlantic to refer to a bankrupt politician. **2.** Anyone in an organization whose leaving has been announced, whether for retirement, promotion, or transfer.

lame duck amendment The Twentieth Amendment to the U.S. Constitution, ratified in 1933, which provides that the terms of the President and Vice President shall end at noon on January 20 instead of March 4, the terms of senators and representatives shall end at noon on January 3 instead of March 4, and the terms of their successors shall then begin. Prior to this amendment, the annual session of the Congress began on the first Monday in December (Article I, Section 4). Since the terms of new members would not begin until March 4, members who had not been reelected in November continued to serve during the lame duck session, December through March 4. Thus, the lame duck amendment, which eliminates such a session, is in reality an anti-lame duck amendment.

lame duck appointment A political appointment made by a lame duck or outgoing executive. A lame duck appointment was one of the major questions at issue in MARBURY V MADISON.

lame duck president 1. Any President who has not been reelected. Thus, Jimmy Carter was a lame duck President from November 1980 to January 20, 1981 after he lost to Ronald Reagan. **2.** Any President in his second term, even though the Twenty-Second Amendment, making the President ineligible to run for a third term, was not intended to create an automatic lame duck President. But no matter how large a second term victory is, the amendment appears in effect to have done so. (One must also remember that two terms were an accepted limit until Franklin D. Roosevelt's unprecedented four elections, and the American experiences with two-term presidencies since passage of the amendment has been very limited.)

Landrum-Griffin Act *See* LABOR-MANAGEMENT REPORTING AND DISCLOSURE ACT OF 1959.

landslide A decidedly lopsided political victory, one in which the loser is metaphorically buried in a landslide. The Republican presidential electoral victories of 1980, 1984, and 1988 were landslides, because the opposition (Jimmy Carter in 1980, Walter F. Mondale in 1984, Michael Dukakis in 1988) carried so few states. A landslide victory is not synonymous with an unspecified MANDATE for action. There are a significant number of instances where Presidents won reelection by overwhelming landslides only to find their effectiveness seriously curtailed shortly thereafter (Franklin D. Roosevelt after 1936, Lyndon B. Johnson after 1964, Richard M. Nixon after 1972, and Ronald Reagan after 1984). In contrast, a very narrow victory may generate too much caution. For example, John F. Kennedy won by such a narrow margin in 1960 that he felt he had to wait until a hoped-for more decisive victory in 1964 before he could act boldly on critical issues, such as civil rights and Vietnam.

last hurrah The final campaign of a veteran politico. Edwin O'Connor used this as the title of his 1956 novel about Boston's James Curley (1874–1958).

laundry list That part of a political speech or document that lists goals to achieve or grievances to be redressed. The most famous of all political laundry lists was the long list of offenses by King George III included in the middle of the DECLARATION OF INDEPENDENCE.

law **1.** A generalization about nature that posits an order of behavior that will be the same in every instance where the same factors are involved. **2.** Enforceable rules that apply to every member of society. Thus, when a politician, such as Mayor Frank Hague of Jersey City, New Jersey says, "I am the law" (*The New York Times*, November 11, 1937) or when President Richard M. Nixon (in a television interview of May 20, 1977) said, "When the President does it, that means that it is not illegal," they are expressing total contempt for the whole concept of law. There is no true law if someone can get away with being above the law. **3.** A statute passed by a legislature and signed by an executive or passed over a veto. **4.** The totality of the rules and principles promulgated by a government. **5.** A codified reflection of the POLITICAL CULTURE of a community. According to essayist Ralph Waldo Emerson's "Politics" (*Essays: Second Series*, 1903): "The form of government which prevails is the expression of what cultivation exists in the population which permits it. The law is only a memorandum." **6.** The ultimate source of binding authority in a political community. Thus, even despotic governments have law; they are just not a government of laws. *Compare to* ACT; ORDINANCE; STATUTE.

law, administrative **1.** That branch of law concerned with the procedures by which administrative agencies make rules and adjudicate cases. **2.** The legislation that creates administrative agencies. **3.** The rules and regulations promulgated by administrative agencies. **4.** The law governing judicial review of administrative actions.

law and order **1.** The suppression of crime and maintenance of public order. **2.** A powerful CODE WORD for controlling domestic violence by curtailing the civil rights of minorities.

law, balance *See* BALANCE LAW.

law, blue *See* BLUE LAWS.

law, canon Laws made by a church for its organization and governance. *Compare to* LAW, ECCLESIASTICAL.

law, civil **1.** That part of the law dealing with private, as opposed to criminal, actions. **2.** The law that has evolved from ancient Roman law. **3.** Rule by civilians as opposed to military government. **4.** Codified law, such as the U.S. Code.

law, code Law that is to be found in law books, as opposed to *equity law*, which a judge makes up (based on related precedents) to deal with a new situation.

law, common The totality of laws that initially developed in England and continued to evolve in the United States. Whenever this kind of law—which is based on custom, culture, habit, and previous judicial decisions—proved inadequate, it was supplanted by statutory laws made by legislatures. But the common law tradition, based upon PRECEDENT, is still the foundation of the American legal system, even though much of what was originally common law has been converted into statutes over the years.

law, constitutional That area of the law concerned with the interpretation and application of the nation's highest law—the Constitution of the United States.

law, criminal That branch of the law which deals with crime and punishment. In a criminal court case the government (sometimes called the "state" or the "people") initiates the action because the defendant is thought to have committed an offense against public authority.

law, draconian *See* DRACONIAN.

law, ecclesiastical All of the laws that deal with a church, whether divine, secular, or natural. *Compare to* LAW, CANON.

law enforcement agency A federal, state, or local criminal justice agency of which the principal functions are the prevention, detection, and investigation of crime and the apprehension of alleged offenders.

law, ex post facto *See* EX POST FACTO LAW.

law, equity *See* LAW, CODE.

law, good samaritan *See* GOOD SAMARITAN LAW.

law, Jim Crow *See* JIM CROW.

law, labor All the laws that apply to concerns of employment, wages, conditions of work, unions, labor-management relations, etc.

law, natural The rules that would govern humankind in a STATE OF NATURE, before governments or positive law existed. Correspondingly, natural rights are the rights that all people have irrespective of the governing system under which they live. The tenets of natural law were a great influence on the American Revolution. For example, noted attorney James Otis (1725–1783) wrote in *The Rights of the British Colonies Asserted and Proved* (1764): "There can be no prescription old enough to supersede the Law of Nature and the grant of God Almighty, who has given to all men a natural right to be free, and they have it ordinarily in their power to make themselves so, if they please." *Compare to* INALIENABLE RIGHTS.

law of the land 1. The U.S. Constitution. Article VI states that "this Constitution . . . shall be the supreme law of the land." **2.** Laws enforced throughout a geographical area. **3.** A nation's customs, which over time are incorporated into the common law.

law, organic The fundamental or underlying law of a state. The U.S. Constitution is the organic law of the United States. *Compare to* STATUTE, ORGANIC.

law, Parkinson's *See* PARKINSON'S LAW.

law, positive Law that has been created by a recognized authority, such as a legislature, as opposed to natural or common law.

law, private A statute passed to affect only one person or group, in constrast to a public law.

law, public **1.** Legislative acts that deal with the citizenry as a whole; statutes that apply to all. **2.** Legal actions initiated by a government agency on behalf of the public, as opposed to private civil actions initiated by a private party for personal benefit. **3.** That branch of the law that deals with the relations between a government and its citizens.

law, public interest That portion of a legal practice devoted to broad societal interests, rather than to the problems of individual clients. A public interest law firm provides services to advance or to protect important public interests (e.g., the environment or freedom of information issues) in cases that are not economically feasible or desirable for private law firms.

law reviews The scholarly journals of the legal profession. All of the better law schools publish law reviews, which are edited by their best students. According to Harvard University law professor Morton J. Horwitz, law is "an odd profession that presents its greatest scholarship in student-run publications" (*Newsweek*, September 15, 1975).

law, Roman The body of law codified by the Romans under the Emperor Justinian in 530 A.D., which provides the underlying basis for civil law in much of the Western world. Why else are so many legal phrases and concepts in Latin? Roman law, a major example of a CODE LAW, which seeks to cover all instances of behavior, is contrasted with COMMON LAW, which evolves over long periods through court action and custom.

law, slip *See* SLIP LAW.

law, statutory All laws that are based upon STATUTES enacted by a legislature.

law, substantive The basic law of rights and duties (contract law, criminal law, accident law, law of wills), as opposed to *procedural law* (law of pleading, law of evidence, law of jurisdiction).

laws, antitrust *See* ANTITRUST LAWS.

laws, fair employment practice *See* FAIR EMPLOYMENT PRACTICE LAWS.

laws, fair housing *See* FAIR HOUSING LAWS

laws, right-to-work *See* RIGHT-TO-WORK LAWS.

leadership **1.** Those who hold formal positions of power in a legislature, such as a speaker, a majority leader, a whip, and so on; usually referred to as *the* leadership. **2.** The exercise of authority, whether formal or informal, in directing and coordinating the work of others. The best leaders are those who can simultaneously exercise both kinds of leadership: the formal, based on the authority of rank or office; and the informal, based on the willingness of others to give service to a person whose special qualities of authority they admire.

leadership fundraiser A single event sponsored by a legislature's leadership to raise campaign funds for their party's candidates for the legislature.

leadership PAC A POLITICAL ACTION COMMITTEE created by the party leadership of a legislature in order to continually raise campaign funds for their party's candidates for the legislature. Since a leadership PAC solicits funds from all sources, special interests are diluted—and the candidates who eventually benefit from the funds may not know of their origin.

leading indicators Statistics that generally precede a change in a situation. For example, an increase in economic activity is typically preceded by a rise in the prices of stocks. Each month, the Bureau of Economic Analysis of the Department of Commerce publishes data on hundreds of economic indicators in its *Business Conditions Digest*. Several dozen of these are classified as leading. The bureau's composite index of 12 leading indicators is a popular means of assessing the general state of the economy. Typical leading indicators include average work week of production workers in manufacturing, average weekly claims for state unemployment insurance, new factory orders for consumer goods, and new building permits issued.

League of Women Voters A national, nonpartisan, public interest organization with 1,300 state and local affiliates. Founded in 1920 by the delegates to the last convention of the National American Woman Suffrage Association to educate newly enfranchised women in public affairs, it has grown to be the most respected private source of nonbiased information on elections at all jurisdictional levels. In response to criticism that the League has become politicized, League President Dorothy S. Ridings said: "The very first president of the League of Women Voters once said that 'To be political without being partisan in a country where the two words are nearly synonymous has always been a delicate undertaking.' And you know, she was right. A lot of people confuse being political, which we surely are, with being partisan, which we surely are not" (*The New York Times*, March 12, 1985).

leak 1. The deliberate disclosure of confidential or classified information by someone in government who wants to advance the public interest, embarrass a bureaucratic rival, or help a reporter disclose incompetence or skulduggery to the public. As journalist James Reston (1909–) has written, "The government is the only known vessel that leaks from the top." All Presidents have had to deal with a seeming constant flood of leaks. President Ronald Reagan told a press conference on April 9, 1986: "The White House is the leakiest place I've ever been in." Patrick J. Buchanan, as the Director of Communications for the White House, said: "Leaks are like prostitution and gambling: You can control them and contain them a bit, but you're not going to eliminate them" (*Los Angeles Times*, June 9, 1986). One way to trace leaks is to "salt a memo": give ever so slightly altered versions of the same memo to different members of a group and see whose version is leaked. **2.** The inadvertent disclosure of secret information.

least dangerous branch The federal judiciary; the Supreme Court; the judicial branch in general. This is Alexander Hamilton's description of the judicial department of government in *Federalist* No. 78:

> Whoever attentively considers the different departments of power must perceive that, in a government in which they are separated from each other, the judiciary, from the nature of its functions, will always be the least dangerous to the political rights of the Constitution; because it will be least in a capacity to annoy or injure them. The Executive not only dispenses the honours, but holds the sword of the community. The legislature not only commands the purse, but prescribes the rules by which the duties and rights of every citizen are to be regulated. The judiciary, on the contrary, has no influence over either the sword or the purse; no direction either of the strength or of the wealth of the society; and can take no active resolution whatever. It may truly be said to have neither force nor will, but merely judgment; and must ultimately depend upon the aid of the executive arm even for the efficacy of its judgments.

L. Ed. The abbreviation for *Lawyer's Edition* of the UNITED STATES REPORTS.

left The liberal, sometimes socialistic, elements of the political spectrum. The political Left in all free countries tends to favor a highly regulated capitalism, socially responsible free enterprise, and a
strong welfare state. In contrast to the RIGHT, which tends to be conservative, the Left has historically been an enthusiastic advocate of change (though in welfare states, the Left has assumed a conservative position aimed at preserving the structure and benefits of that state). The extreme Left tends to consist of those radicals who would take their nation all the way to communism. The terms Left and Right have come down to us from the fact that nineteenth-century European parliaments had the nobility sit on the king's right, the place of honor; that left the left side for the ignoble masses. *Compare to* LIBERALISM; SOCIALISM.

leftist Someone who philosophically leans to the political Left. However, the word should be used cautiously, because it has taken on a taint that suggests the person being so called is a radical, a communist, or worse.

left, new The political reformers of the 1960s and 1970s who fought for civil rights for all, cheered on the war on poverty, opposed the war in Vietnam, and sought radical change in the American political and economic systems. Their influence dissipated as the war ended and the nation turned away from social reform and toward conservatism. While the term was first used to refer to those associated with the *New Left Review* journal in 1959, it was soon adopted by the mass media and the student movement of the 1960s.

left, noncommunist The post World War II New Deal liberals who sought to sustain a leftward movement in American politics that was not associated either with Marxism or with traditional Democratic party compromises with the conservative South.

left, old The between-the-World-Wars American leftists who were heavily influenced by communist ideology, were often members of the Communist party, and who felt themselves to be engaged in the Marxist class struggle.

left, radical The far-left elements of the new left.

legion 1. The basic military organization of Ancient Rome; comparable to a modern division in function but smaller in size. **2.** A special-purpose military organization, such as a Foreign Legion. **3.** Many; a large group such as the American Legion, an organization for veterans.

legiscide The lessening of a legislature's powers by the continuous enactment of laws that give more and more power to an executive.

legislation The end product of legislative action: laws, statutes, ordinances, and so on. There may not always be an end product. Depending on one's attitude toward a bill, the best legislation may be no legislation. Woodrow Wilson poetically wrote in his landmark study, *Congressional Government* (1885), that "once begin the dance of legislation, and you must struggle through its mazes as best you can to its breathless end,—if any end there be." The legislative process is inherently messy. It is so full of compromise, hypocrisy, and self-interest that its end product, legislation, is sometimes compared to sausage, in that a wise person will avoid watching either of them being made. What's worse, often the legislators who vote on a bill haven't even read it. Senator BARRY GOLDWATER complained: "Senators often don't know what they're voting on. That's a lousy way to run a lemonade stand, much less our national legislative process. . . . The final weeks of almost every session of the Congress now look and sound like a bargain-basement sale. Bills are passed so wildly that they often contain unprinted amendments. That means Congress is passing legislation it has never read!" (quoted in Robert Sherrill's *Why They Call It Politics*, 1990).

legislation, direct Laws enacted by a jurisdiction's population via an INITIATIVE, a REFERENDUM, or a TOWN MEETING, in contrast to laws enacted by an elected legislature.

legislative assistant An aide to a legislator who researches and writes bills, writes speeches for the legislator, attends committee sessions on pending bills, etc. *Compare to* ADMINISTRATIVE ASSISTANT.

legislative branch 1. Members of the Congress, supporting staffs, plus the General Accounting Office (GAO), the Government Printing Office, and the Library of Congress. Several organizations in addition to the GAO are considered support agencies of the Congress: the Congressional Research Service, a division of the Library of Congress; the Office of Technology Assessment; and the Congressional Budget Office. **2.** The representative lawmaking assembly of any level of government.

legislative clearance *See* CENTRAL CLEARANCE.

legislative council A group of state legislators, sometimes joined by administrative officers, who meet between legislative sessions to develop a legislative agenda, engage in research on policy issues, and so on.

legislative counsel The lawyer (or office) who aids legislators and legislative committees in the legal research necessary for such work as writing bills and holding hearings.

legislative court *See* CONSTITUTIONAL COURT.

legislative day The "day" extending from the time either house of the Congress meets after an adjournment until the time it next adjourns. Because the House of Representatives normally adjourns from day to day, legislative days and calendar days usually coincide. But in the Senate, a legislative day may, and frequently does, extend over several calendar days.

legislative history The written record of the writing of an act of the Congress. It may be used in writing rules, or by courts in interpreting the law, to ascertain the intent of the Congress if the act is ambiguous or lacking in detail. The legislative history is listed in the SLIP LAWS and consists of House, Senate, and conference committee reports (if any) and the House and Senate floor debates on the law. The history, particularly the committee reports, often contains the only complete explanation of the meaning and intent of the law. Members of the Congress, their staffs, and other interested parties often try to influence a legislative history to help shape the way the law is eventually administered by agencies and interpreted by the courts.

legislative immunity *See* IMMUNITY, CONGRESSIONAL.

legislative intent The supposed meaning of a statute as interpreted from its legislative history. Sometimes, during the legislative debate on a bill, a member of the legislature will specifically talk about what is intended or not intended by the bill so that the ensuing legislative history will be a better guide to future interpretations of what really was meant by the law. *Compare to* ORIGINAL INTENT.

legislative liaison The coordination of executive branch communications to the legislature. Liaison is a critical activity if an executive, whether President, governor, mayor, or executive agency, is to see his, her, or its legislative proposals enacted into law. In effect, the legislative liaison is a chief executive's or an agency's lobbyist.

legislative oversight The review of executive branch activities to ascertain that legislative mandates are properly carried out. *See also* OVERSIGHT, CONGRESSIONAL.

legislative party Those members of a political party who hold seats in a given legislature. If they hold a majority of the seats, they are the "party in power." Unlike legislative parties in parliamentary systems, American legislative parties are notoriously undisciplined and seldom work together as a cohesive unit.

Legislative Reorganization Act The 1946 law which dramatically reduced the number of standing committees in the Senate and House, provided for a major expansion of the Legislative Reference Service (now known as the Congressional Research Service), and promoted the creation of a professional, nonpartisan staff for committees, as well as increased staff for individual members. This was the Congress's first effort to establish an effective staff system to decrease its dependence on executive agencies for information.

legislative service organizations Informal groups of members of the Congress who meet to discuss policy issues of mutual concern. While such organizations have always existed, only in the last few decades have they become institutionalized and given formal staff assistance to do in-depth policy research analyses of major issues. The oldest such organization is the Democratic Study Group (DSG), organized in 1958. The success of the DSG in providing its members with information on pending legislation led other House and Senate members to organize informal groups around other issues. There are now about a hundred such groups in the Congress, among them the Republican Study Committee, the Congressional Black Caucus, the Northeast-Midwest Congressional Coalition, the Congressional Steel Caucus, the Congressional Rural Caucus, and the Congressional Hispanic Caucus.

Informal groups have traditionally been financed by members donating a portion of their staffing and equipment allowances to the group. In 1979, the House established new accounting procedures for informal groups (which the House officially calls legislative service organizations). A group above a certain size can be designated a legislative service organization and, in return for streamlined congressional funding and accounting procedures, is required to make regular public disclosure of its finances and to refrain from accepting noncongressional funds in support of legislative activities. *Compare to* CAUCUS.

legislative supremacy The notion that while there are three "co-equal" branches of government, the legislature is nevertheless supreme. After all, it has the greatest number of enumerated powers, and the executive and judicial branches must enforce its laws. As James Madison wrote in *Federalist* No. 51: "In republican government, the legislative authority necessarily predominates." President Franklin D. Roosevelt in a press conference on July 23, 1937 put it another way: "It is the duty of the President to propose and it is the privilege of the Congress to dispose."

legislative veto *See* VETO, LEGISLATIVE.

legislator A member of a legislature elected to represent the interests or the voters of a specific constituency. Legislators always tend to be in the shadow of a chief executive. But according to Senator J. William Fulbright: "The legislator is an indispensable guardian of our freedom. It is true that great executives have played a powerful role in the development of civilization, but such leaders appear sporadically, by chance. They do not always appear when they are most needed. The great executives have given inspiration and push to the advancement of human society, but it is the legislator who has given stability and continuity to that slow and painful progress" (Robert B. Heywood, ed., *The Works of the Mind*, 1947). *Compare to* EDMUND BURKE; POLITICO.

legislature **1.** The lawmaking branch of a representative government. It is not necessary for a legislature to have the word "legislature" in its formal title. It could be called an assembly or a city council. **2.** The lawmaking branch of the government of the United States. Article I, Section 1 of the U.S. Constitution states that all legislative power shall be vested in the Congress. This means that the President is specifically denied the power to make laws. All his authority must be based either on expressed or implicit powers granted by the Constitution or on statutes enacted by the Congress. **3.** According to Governor Hugh Carey of New York, a legislature is "a body that deals with unfinished business" (*The New York Times*, July 11, 1976). **4.** The lawmaking branch of a state or local government. *Compare to* STATE GOVERNMENT.

levy **1.** An assessment or collection of taxes. **2.** The conscription of men for military service.

libel The creation and use of written materials that are so false and malicious that injury is caused to a person's reputation and he or she is subjected to ridicule, hatred, or contempt. The defense for allegations of libel is to prove that what was written was true. Libel comes from the Latin word *libellus*, meaning "little book." When ancient Romans wanted to attack each other in writing, they would put their charges on posters for the public to read or on small scrolls to be passed from reader to reader. While libel is considered by the law to be unprotected speech (i.e., not free), the law treats public figures as an exception. They can only succeed at an action for libel if they can prove that "actual malice" was a motivating factor. *Compare to* DEFAMATION OF CHARACTER; NEW YORK TIMES MAGAZINE V SULLIVAN; SLANDER.

liberal **1.** An advocate of political and social reform, expanding government control of the economy, greater efforts on behalf of the poor, and more laws protecting consumers, the environment, and criminal defendants. (Because of this last concern, it is often said that a liberal is a CONSERVATIVE who has been arrested.) During the 1988 presidential election, the Republican candidate George Bush effectively used what he called "the L word" against Democratic candidate Michael Dukakis, who was trying to avoid political labels and run on the issue of competence. Only toward the end of the campaign, after it was too late to do any good, did Dukakis admit he was a liberal—and proud of it. But by that time the Republicans had effectively insinuated that "liberal" was a dirty word, and Dukakis simply wasn't competent enough to clean it up. **2.** When referring to trade policy, relative freedom of controls or restraints. The most liberal trade is free trade.

liberal, limousine A contemptuous term for a wealthy citizen who is a strong advocate of welfare state programs—that are paid for primarily by taxes on the middle class.

liberal, neo *See* NEOLIBERALISM.

liberalism 1. Originally, a political doctrine that espoused freedom of the individual from interference by the state, toleration by the state in matters of morality and religion, laissez-faire economic policies, and a belief in natural rights that exist independently of government. This is sometimes referred to as classical liberalism. While liberal concepts can be traced back to the Magna Charta of 1215 and through the writings of the major political theorists of the eighteenth-century European Enlightenment, by the nineteenth century liberalism had come to stand for a kind of limited governance whose policies most favored individual liberty and political equality. In this sense, the Founders were all liberals. 2. The use of resources by a government to achieve social change. In this century, liberalism has come to stand for the advocacy of government programs for the welfare of individuals, because without such welfare state advantages the masses have little chance to enjoy the traditional freedoms long espoused by the political theorists. So a term that meant small government and low taxation in the last century has in this century come to mean big government and high taxation. One is reminded of humorist Will Rogers' statement referring to the New Deal's domestic programs: "I can remember way back when a liberal was one who was generous with his own money."

liberalization Reductions in tariff and other measures that restrict world trade, unilaterally or multilaterally. Trade liberalization has been the objective, for example, of all GATT trade negotiations.

liberals, kneejerk A pejorative reference to liberals who, in the eyes of conservatives, automatically and unthinkingly respond favorably to causes espoused by the political left.

libertarianism A pure form of classical LIBERALISM, which asserts that a government should do little more than provide police and military protection; other than that, it should not interfere—either for good or ill—in the lives of its citizens. A major intellectual force advocating libertarianism was Ayn Rand (1905–1982), the objectivist philosopher who attacked welfare state notions of selflessness and sacrifice for a common good in novels, such as *The Fountainhead* (1943) and *Atlas Shrugged* (1957). In *Capitalism: The Unknown Ideal* (1966) she wrote: "The only proper function of the government of a free country is to act as an agency which protects the individual's rights, i.e., which protects the individual from physical violence." In 1980, a Libertarian party presidential candidate was on the ballot in all 50 states, and in 1984, in 38 states. Thus far, the Libertarian party has had little impact on American politics.

liberty 1. FREEDOM. Liberty, meaning freedom, is one of the most important themes of American history. Thomas Jefferson in a November 13, 1787 letter to W.S. Smith wrote: "The tree of liberty must be refreshed from time to time with the blood of patriots and tyrants. It is its natural manure." Thomas Paine wrote in his *Dissertation on First Principles of Government* (1795): "He that would make his own liberty secure, must guard even his enemy from oppression; for if he violates this duty, he establishes a precedent that will reach to himself." President Franklin D. Roosevelt echoed Benjamin Franklin when he said in a message to Congress, January 7, 1941: "Those who would give up essential liberty, to purchase a little temporary safety, deserve neither liberty nor safety." President John F. Kennedy was deemed prudent when in his inaugural address he said: "Let every nation know, whether it wishes us well or ill, that we shall pay any price, bear any burden, meet any hardship, support any friend, oppose any foe to assure the survival and the success of liberty." Yet Senator BARRY GOLDWATER in a speech accepting the Republican Presidential nomination in 1964 was considered radical when he said: "Extremism in the defense of liberty is no vice. And . . . moderation in the pursuit of justice is no virtue." **2.** Freedom from government interference with private actions. Abolitionist Wendell Phillips in a famous 1852 speech in Boston (reprinted in his *Speeches Before the Massachusetts Anti-Slavery Society*, 1853) asserted: "Eternal vigilance is the price of liberty—power is ever stealing from the many to the few. . . . The hand entrusted with power becomes . . . the necessary enemy of the people. Only by continual oversight can the democrat in office be prevented from hardening into a despot." Justice Louis D. Brandeis wrote in a dissenting opinion in *Olmstead v United States* (1928): "Experience should teach us to be most on our guard to protect liberty when the Government's purposes are beneficent. Men born to freedom are naturally alert to repel invasion of their liberty by evil-minded rules. The greatest dangers to liberty lurk in insidious encroachment by men of zeal, well-meaning but without understanding." *Compare to* CIVIL LIBERTY.

Library of Congress The library established under a law approved on April 24, 1800, appropriating $5,000 "for the purchase of such books as may be necessary for the use of Congress." The library's scope of responsibility has been widened by subsequent legislation. One entity, the Congressional Research Service, functions exclusively for the legislative branch of the government. As the library has developed, its range of service has come to include both the entire government establishment in all its branches and the public at large, so it has become a national library for the United States and one of the great research libraries of the world. Since 1870, the library has been responsible for COPYRIGHTS, which must be registered with its Copyright Office.

lie *See* BIG LIE.

light at the end of the tunnel The description of a safe exit from a desperate situation, which became the standard response of many American officials in the 1960s about when the war in Vietnam would be successfully concluded. They were so consistently and embarrassingly wrong that the phrase is now associated with stupid or false predictions of military or administrative success.

limited government A government that is not all-powerful. The United States is often said to be a limited government because it has only those powers assigned to it by the Constitution; a Constitution that also contains a variety of prohibitions that further limit it. For example, it cannot abridge freedom of the press, deny due process of law, or permit slavery. Indeed, the Tenth Amendment specifically denies any additional powers to the federal government when it asserts that "the powers not delegated to the United States by the Constitution, nor prohibited by it to the States, are reserved to the States, respectively, or to the people." However, the NECESSARY AND PROPER CLAUSE of the Constitution has allowed the federal government to expand its powers vastly over the years. *Compare to* CONSTITUTIONALISM.

Lincoln, Abraham (1809–1865) The sixteenth President of the United States who led the North to victory during a Civil War that was forced upon him; who, in doing so, saved the Union; and who, in an effort to deny resources to the enemy, abolished slavery in the South. (The Thirteenth Amendment, enacted after the Civil War, abolished slavery throughout the United States.) Lincoln's 1860 election to the presidency precipitated the secession of the southern states over the issue of slavery. Yet Lincoln's personal position on slavery was considered moderate for his times; he was willing to allow slavery in the South but opposed its extension to new territories. In his 1861 Inaugural Address, he told the seceded states that there would be no civil war unless they forced the issue:

> In your hands, my dissatisfied fellow countrymen, and not in mine is the momentous issue of civil war. The government will not assail you. You can have no conflict without being yourselves the aggressors. You have no oath registered in heaven to destroy the government, while I shall have the most solemn one to "preserve, protect, and defend" it.

South Carolina did force the issue when it attacked the Union Army's island fortress of Fort Sumter in Charleston harbor on April 12, 1861. Almost four years to the day, on April 9, 1865, the last effective army in the South, under General Robert E. Lee (1807–1870), surrendered to General Ulysses S. Grant (1822–1885) at Appomattox Court House in Virginia. (Grant would later be President from 1869–1877.) Five days later, on April 14, 1865, Lincoln was assassinated by an actor, John Wilkes Booth (1838–1865), while attending a play at Ford's Theater in Washington, D.C.

Over the years, Lincoln's qualities of honesty (he was known as Honest Abe), his rise from humble origins (he was truly born in a log cabin), his dramatic death immediately following his greatest victory (the surrender of the South and the salvation of the union), his granting of freedom through EMANCIPATION PROCLAMATION to millions of slaves (he was called the Great Emancipator), and his reverence for and eloquence on behalf of democratic government, particularly in the Gettysburg Address, have made him (along with George Washington) a secular saint in American political culture. One of Lincoln's biographers, the poet Carl Sandburg, was invited to address a joint session of Congress on the 150th anniversary of Lincoln's birth, February 12, 1959. He started his speech with these words: "Not often in the story of mankind does a man arrive on earth who is both steel and velvet, who is as hard as rock and soft as drifting fog, who holds in his heart and mind the paradox of terrible storm and peace unspeakable and perfect."

line-item budget *See* BUDGET, LINE-ITEM.

line-item veto *See* VETO.

linkage institution Any established group that provides the means for the will of the people to get onto a government's agenda. Political parties, because they are the links between ordinary citizens and elected policymakers, are considered linkage institutions.

litany A metaphor for a list of political complaints, often repeated, as in the pleas of a prayer order or religious service. A litany is often part of a campaign speech.

literacy test 1. An examination of one's ability to read and write. **2.** A now prohibited requirement for voting. The 1970 VOTING RIGHTS ACT amendments barred all literacy tests as a requirement for voting because they were inherently discriminatory. Some southern states went far beyond testing for mere reading and writing ability; they would also disqualify black citizens who couldn't adequately interpret many Constitutional provisions. Because the process was simply a ruse for intimidating black voters, the Supreme Court upheld the ban on literacy tests in *Oregon v Mitchell* (1970).

litmus test The test that determines the alkaline or acidic nature of a chemical solution. The term has been applied to politics as an indicator of a politician's true ideological nature. Thus, a stand or vote on any given issue may be considered a litmus test of whether the person in question is a real conservative, a true liberal, and so on.

litigation A legal dispute taken to court; a lawsuit. Litigation is a major means of influencing public policy. If an interest group dislikes a new law or the new actions of an agency based on an old law, they can challenge it in the courts by asserting that it is unconstitutional or in violation of other laws or rights.

little city hall 1. A branch office of municipal government. **2.** A very small municipal headquarters building.

loan guarantee An agreement by which a government pledges to pay part or all of the loan principal and interest to a lender or holder of a security in the event of default by a third-party borrower. The purpose of a guaranteed loan is to reduce the risk borne by a private lender by shifting all or part of the risk to the government. If it becomes necessary for the government to pay part or all of the loan's principal or interest, the payment is a direct outlay. Otherwise, the guarantee does not directly affect budget outlays. *See also* CHRYSLER CORPORATION LOAN GUARANTEE ACT OF 1979.

lobby 1. Any individual, group, or organization that seeks to influence legislation or administrative action. Lobbies can be trade associations, individual corporations, good-government public interest groups, or other levels of government. The term arose from the use of the lobbies, or corridors, of legislative halls as places to meet with and persuade legislators to vote a certain way. The right to attempt to influence legislation is based on the First Amendment to the Constitution which holds that the Congress shall make no law abridging the right of the people "to petition the government for a redress of grievances." Lobbying in general is not an evil; many lobbies provide legislators with reliable first-hand information of considerable value. However, some lobbies have given the practice an undesirable connotation, because they often contribute money to political campaigns and offer special favors to elected and appointed officials. All such contributions and favors are given, of course, in the expectation of favorable treatment on some issue in the future. In effect, they are often thinly but effectively disguised BRIBES. As humorist Will Rogers said: "A Lobbyist is a person that is supposed to help a Politician to make up his mind, not only help him but pay him" (*The Autobiography of Will Rogers*, D. Day, ed., 1949). Common forms of lobbying include testifying before a legislative hearing, formal and informal discussions with elected and appointed government officials, sending research results or technical information to appropriate officials, seeking publicity on an issue, drafting potential legislation, and organizing letter-writing campaigns. **2.** Journalists who wait upon legislators in the lobby of the legislature.

lobby terms *See* BACKGROUNDER.

Lobbying Act of 1946 The Federal Regulation of Lobbying Act of 1946, which requires that persons who solicit or accept contributions for lobbying purposes keep accounts, present receipts and statements to the clerk of the House of Representatives, and register with the clerk of the House and the secretary of the Senate. The information received is published quarterly in the *Congressional Record*. The purpose of this registration is to disclose the sponsorship and source of funds of lobbyists but not to curtail the right of persons to act as lobbyists. The constitutionality of the Lobbying Act was upheld in *United States v Harriss* (1954).

lobbying, indirect *See* GRASSROOTS LOBBYING.

local affairs, department of The generic name of a state agency with oversight responsibilities for local government. Sometimes local governments are required to submit audit and budget reports to such an agency, with the exact requirements varying from state to state.

LOCAL GOVERNMENT

local government Any government entity that is not clearly state or federal. This could include general local governments, such as counties, municipalities, and towns, as well as special-purpose local governments, such as school districts, port authorities, and fire districts.

local option The authority given by a state to its localities to determine by a local referendum election a specific policy for that locality—for example, liquor sales on Sunday.

Lochner v New York (1905) The Supreme Court case that declared unconstitutional a New York law that sought to regulate the hours of employment in a bakery. The Court held that such regulation was not part of the police powers of the state and infringed on the constitutionally protected liberty of contract. This was overruled in *Bunting v State of Oregon* (1917), which held that the regulation of working hours was a valid extension of police powers. The *Lochner* case is often considered the last gasp of judicial social Darwinism.

Locke, John (1632–1704) The English physician and philosopher whose writings on the nature of governance were a profound influence on the FOUNDING FATHERS. It is often argued that the first part of the Declaration of Independence, which establishes the essential philosophic rationale for the break with England, is Thomas Jefferson's restatement of John Locke's most basic themes. Locke's *A Letter Concerning Toleration* (1689) anticipated American thought on religious toleration: he held that a policy of toleration was only logical because it permitted all of the religious groups to support the state, while the alternative of religious persecution and suppression only led to sedition and internal discord.

But Locke's most influential works by far were his *Two Treatises of Government* (1690), in which he rejected the notion that kings had a divine right to rule, made the case for a constitutional democracy, and provided the philosophical justification for revolution later used by the Americans. Locke wrote that human beings who are "by nature free, equal, and independent," chose to live with others—to give up the "state of nature" to enter into a "social contract" to gain the security that is impossible in the "state of nature." They consent to live by the will of the majority, and it is for this purpose that governments are created. And a government formed by the people with their consent can be dissolved by the people if their trust is betrayed. According to Locke:

> Whenever the legislators endeavor to take away and destroy the property of the people, or to reduce them to slavery under arbitrary power, they put themselves into a state of war with the people, who are thereupon absolved from any further obedience, and are left to the common refuge which God hath provided for all men against force and violence.

Compare to REVOLUTION; SOCIAL CONTRACT.

Lockhart v McCree (1986) The Supreme Court case that held legal the exclusion from juries hearing capital cases those citizens who assert that they could never vote to impose the death penalty. This case upheld the use of so-called death qualified juries.

log cabin A reference to the oft-asserted humble origins of American politicians, especially presidential candidates. While most associated with Abraham Lincoln, the first presidential candidate to use the log cabin symbol was William Henry Harrison in 1840. He won in spite of the fact that his plebian past was considerably exaggerated (he was really born in a mansion). Until recently, the log cabin or some other symbol of early adversity has been a significant factor in American elections. John Nance Gardner (1867–1967), Vice President under Franklin D. Roosevelt from 1933–1939, was in 1959 presented with a birthday cake in the shape of the log cabin in which he was born. He then observed, "That log house did me more good in politics than anything I ever said in a speech."

logrolling Mutual aid among legislators: you help me, I'll help you; you scratch my back, I'll scratch yours; you vote for my bill, I'll vote for yours. Logrolling is birling, a game of skill popular among lumberjacks, which calls for two people to cooperatively maintain their balance on a floating log as they spin it with their feet. Logrolling in politics is usually associated with the passage of bills that benefit a legislator's constituency, PORK BARREL legislation, or bills that are of personal interest. Sam Taliaferro Rayburn (1882–1961), the three-time Speaker of the U.S. House of Representatives (1940–1946, 1949–1953, 1955–1961), summed it up when he told new congressmen, "If you want to *get* along, *go* along."

long-arm statute *See* STATUTE, LONG-ARM.

Long, Huey P. *See* DEMAGOGUE.

long run **1.** A vague term for the indefinite future. **2.** Any period of time beyond the current or next fiscal year. Harry L. Hopkins (1890–1946), the NEW DEAL era White House aide, is usually credited with observing: "People don't eat in the long run—they eat every day." *See also* KEYNES, JOHN MAYNARD.

loop **1.** An informal term for a communications network for policy or bureaucratic purposes. Thus, those "in the loop" regularly get information not usually available to others. Those "out of the loop" don't really know what is going on regarding a particular issue. **2.** An inner circle of high-level advisors to a chief executive.

loophole **1.** A small opening in a wall. **2.** A TAX LOOPHOLE. **3.** Any provision of a law that allows someone to be exempted from its overall provisions.

loose cannon Someone whose speech or actions are so uncontrollable that he or she is liable to cause great damage to someone else. The term comes from the obvious danger of having a loose cannon rolling about the deck of a ship. A political loose cannon may be a politician's relative or an overzealous staffer.

loose constructionist *See* STRICT CONSTRUCTIONIST.

lottery 1. A form of decision making in which a choice is made by random selection of one entry from all entries submitted; the selection of one lot from among the entirety placed in a container. For example, draft selections in World Wars I and II were made from jars of numbers, each number having been assigned to a potential draftee. The intention of a lottery is to assure the absence of favoritism or special influence; it is a form of gambling in which the luck of the draw, so to speak, controls selection. **2.** State-sponsored and state-administered gambling undertaken as an alternative to raising taxes. Government lotteries have a long tradition in America. Many of the colonies were subsidized by lotteries. Even the Continental Congress authorized a lottery in 1776 to raise funds for the War of Independence. However, after a spate of scandals in the nineteenth century, the lottery fell into disfavor and disuse. The first of the modern state lotteries began in 1964 in New Hampshire. Since then, over 30 states (plus the District of Columbia) have initiated lotteries, and most of the U.S. population now lives in states with lotteries. The lottery is praised by those who see it as a popular alternative to higher taxes and condemned by those who say it takes advantage of the poor who play it disproportionately, mostly lose, and thus subsidize the middle class, who would pay higher taxes if there were no lottery.

lower house *See* UPPER HOUSE.

Lowi, Theodore J. (1931–   ) The leading critic of interest group pluralism, who is also noted for his classification of all public policies as either distributive, regulatory, or redistributive. His book *The End of Liberalism: Ideology, Policy, and the Crisis of Public Authority* (1969; 2nd ed., 1979) provided a provocative critique of the modern democratic government and a condemnation of the paralyzing effects of interest group pluralism. Lowi asserted that public authority is parceled out to private interest groups, resulting in a weak, decentralized government incapable of long-range planning. These powerful interest groups operate to promote private goals; they do not compete to promote the public interest. Government then becomes not an institution capable of making hard choices among conflicting values but a holding company for interests. The various interests are promoted by alliances of interest groups, relevant government agencies, and the appropriate legislative committees. Lowi denied the very virtues that E. Pendleton Herring and other group theorists saw in their promotion of interest group pluralism. Lowi's analysis is a scathing indictment of a governing process in which agencies charged with regulation are seen as basically protectors of those being regulated. *See also* INTEREST GROUP THEORY; JURIDICAL DEMOCRACY; PUBLIC POLICYMAKING.

Lowi's other works include *At the Pleasure of the Mayor: Patronage and Power in New York City, 1898–1958* (1964); "American Business, Public Policy, Case-Studies, and Political Theory," *World Politics* (July 1964); *Pri-*

vate Life and Public Order (1968); *The Politics of Disorder* (1971); *The Personal President: Power Invested, Promise Unfulfilled* (1985).

loyal opposition In a two-party system, the party out of power but loyal to the interest of the nation as a whole. Former Senator J. William Fulbright has said: "The democratic system requires the existence of a loyal opposition. It's unrealistic to expect people to submerge their views in some ideal of bipartisanship . . . You don't really want a bunch of zombies over there who just support the President, come what may. People who disagree shouldn't be made to feel like skunks at a picnic" (*Los Angeles Times*, February 1, 1985).

loyalty 1. Allegiance. A loyalty oath is an affirmation of such allegiance. Loyalty may be felt toward a state or toward any organization or religious group that may expect special commitment by its members to the interests of the organization or the group. When the interests of such groups are in conflict with one another, individuals who hold membership in both groups may find themselves, or be considered by others to be, conflicted in their loyalties; hence, they may be thought inherently or potentially disloyal to one or the other. Many public employers may legitimately require their employees to swear or affirm their allegiance to the Constitution of the United States and to that of a particular state. **2.** Staying within an organization's chain of command; not going above the heads of one's administrative superiors; not complaining about policy set by those higher up in the hierarchy; following blindly the administrative team or policy. This is what President Lyndon B. Johnson meant when he told his staff what he meant by loyalty over Vietnam: "I don't want loyalty. I want *loyalty*. I want him to kiss my ass in Macy's window at high noon and tell me it smells like roses" (quoted in Larry Berman, *Planning a Tragedy*, 1982). **3.** A conspiracy for mutual inefficiency. This is military historian B.H. Liddell Hart's explanation from his *Why Don't We Learn From History* (1943) for what an artificial loyalty to one's military (or administrative) unit often amounts to.

lulu A corruption of "in lieu of"; legislative slang for payments made to state legislators in lieu of expenses. Such lump-sum payments made it unnecessary for state lawmakers to suffer the inconvenience of submitting receipts for their expenses.

lunatic fringe The overzealous and fanatical members of any political party or social movement. The term was first applied by President Theodore Roosevelt—to impatient reformers. A later President Roosevelt, Franklin D., told a press conference on May 30, 1944: "You sometimes find something good in the lunatic fringe. In fact, we have got as part of our social and economic government today a whole lot of things which in my boyhood were considered lunatic fringe and yet they are now part of everyday life."

M

McCardle, Ex parte (1869) The Supreme Court case that held that the Congress could regulate the appellate jurisdiction of the Court by passing legislation even if the legislation affected a case under active consideration. Article III, Section 2 of the U.S. Constitution gives appellate jurisdiction to the Supreme Court with "such expectations and under such regulations, as the Congress shall make."

McCarran Act The 1952 law, passed over President Harry S Truman's veto, which gave the executive branch wide powers to exclude from the United States foreigners who might "engage in activities prejudicial to the public interest." This was mainly used to exclude leftist politicians and novelists. Even novelist Graham Greene was once denied a visa because he admitted to having been a Communist Party member decades earlier. This portion of the Act was repealed in 1988. The government retains the right to exclude potential spies and terrorists. *See also* ALBERTSON V SUBVERSIVE ACTIVITIES CONTROL BOARD.

McCarthy, Eugene J. (1916–   ) The U.S. Senator from Minnesota from 1959 to 1970 who challenged incumbent President Lyndon B. Johnson in the 1968 New Hampshire Democratic presidential primary over the issue of the Vietnam War. After Johnson dropped out of contention, McCarthy continued to seek his party's nomination but lost out to Vice President Hubert H. Humphrey.

McCarthy, Joseph R. (1908–1957) The Republican U.S. Senator from Wisconsin (1947–1957) whose RED SCARE tactics made him the preeminent American DEMAGOGUE of the 1950s. He first came to national prominence after a February 9, 1950 speech in Wheeling, West Virginia, in which he held up a piece of paper and told the audience: "I have here in my hand a list of 205 persons that were known to the Secretary of State as being members of the Communist party and who nevertheless are still working and shaping policy of the State Department." These were typical of the kind of reckless charges for which McCarthy became famous. Typical also is the fact that McCarthy did not provide supporting evidence. McCarthy grew so reckless with his accusations that in 1954 he became one of the few senators in American history to be formally censured by the U.S. Senate for the fact that he "tended to bring the Senate into dishonor and disrepute." When President Harry S Truman was asked to comment on one of McCarthy's outbursts, he responded "No comment. The Senator is pathological and a liar, and I don't need to comment on that."

McCarthyism Extreme and irresponsible anticommunism. Senator Joseph R. McCarthy of Wisconsin rose to fame and influence during the early

1950s by recklessly charging that individuals or organizations were communist or were influenced by communists. The word *McCarthyism* is generally credited to *Washington Post* cartoonist Herbert Block who first used it in March 1950 as the label for a barrel of mud that a Republican elephant was hesitant to use as a platform. Block would later write in *The Herblock Book* (1952): "There's nothing particularly ingenious about the term, which is simply used to represent a national affliction that can hardly be described in any other way. And if anyone else has a prior claim on it, he's welcome to the word and to the junior senator from Wisconsin along with it." McCarthy himself embraced the term. He made the theme for his successful campaign for reelection to the U.S. Senate in 1952: "McCarthyism is Americanism with its sleeves rolled."

McCarthyism was not limited to McCarthy. The classic tactic of McCarthyism is the use of an unproven association with any individual, organization, or policy, which the accuser perceives as liberal or leftist and, as a result, either un-American or even treasonous. Today, any actions by public officials that flout individual rights and imply guilt by association would be considered—by anyone sensitive to the concept of due process of law—as examples of McCarthyism. *See also* DEMAGOGUE.

McClellan Committee The Senate committee on Improper Activities in Labor-Management Relations, chaired by Senator John L. McClellan (1896–1977) of Arkansas. The committee's findings of violence and corruption spurred the passage of the LABOR-MANAGEMENT REPORTING AND DISCLOSURE (Landrum-Griffin) ACT OF 1959.

McCulloch v Maryland (1819) The Supreme Court decision that upheld the implied powers granted to the Congress by the NECESSARY AND PROPER CLAUSE of the Constitution, upheld the supremacy of the national government in carrying out functions assigned to it by the Constitution, and established the doctrine of intergovernmental tax immunity. In stating that "the power to tax is the power to destroy," the Court held that the Bank of the United States was not subject to taxation by the State of Maryland. *Compare to* STRICT CONSTRUCTIONIST.

McGovern, George S. (1922–   ) The U.S. Senator from South Dakota from 1963 to 1981 who was the Democratic nominee for the Presidency in 1972. While he campaigned on a platform to end the war in Vietnam, cut defense spending, and institute broad social welfare reforms, he was soundly defeated by President Richard M. Nixon, who was running for reelection.

McKinley, William (1843–1901) The President of the United States from 1897 to 1901. After Civil War service as an aide to Colonel (later President) Rutherford B. Hayes, McKinley practiced law until elected to the House of Representatives in 1876. In the election of 1890 he lost his seat in Congress and returned to Ohio to win the governorship. Elected President in 1896, he expected to oversee a peaceful conservative Republican administration.

But the American victory in the Spanish-American War of 1898 and the subsequent acquisition of Puerto Rico, Guam, and the Philippines from Spain meant that the United States was suddenly an imperial power. Reelected in 1900 in a tide of public support for imperialism, McKinley was fatally shot by an anarchist, Leon Czolgosz (1873–1901), as he visited the Pan-American Exposition in Buffalo, New York. McKinley was succeeded by his Vice President, Theodore Roosevelt, who had become a national hero through his war exploits in Cuba.

McKinney Act The Homeless Assistance Act of 1987 which authorized federal funding for the homeless, including health care, emergency food and shelter, mental health services, transitional housing, and job training. The Act was named in honor of Representative Stewart B. McKinney of Connecticut, a liberal Republican who in 1987 became the first member of Congress to die of AIDS.

McNabb v United States (1943) The Supreme Court case that held that the federal courts could not convict someone of a crime because of a confession gained while the person was illegally detained (i.e., held for interrogation for an unreasonable length of time without being charged with a crime or offered the opportunity for legal counsel). This ruling was extended to the states in *Mallory v Hogan* (1964).

mace **1.** A medieval weapon, usually a heavily studded club designed to be particularly threatening and destructive. **2.** Political slang for forcing (with a figurative mace) public employees to make contributions to the party in power. **3.** A legislature's symbol of authority; there is a mace in the U.S. House of Representatives. **4.** A modern chemical spray weapon used to disable (but not kill) an opponent; often carried by police.

Machiavelli, Niccolo (1469–1527) An Italian Renaissance political philosopher and history's most famous and influential political analyst. His book of advice to would-be leaders, *The Prince* (1532), is the progenitor of all how-to-succeed books and is often considered to be the first real work of political science. Its exploration of how political power is grasped, used, and kept is the benchmark against which all subsequent analyses are judged. Machiavelli's amoral tone and detached analysis have caused him to be both soundly denounced as well as greatly imitated. For example, he asserted that "a prudent prince cannot and should not keep his word when to do so would go against his interest, or when the reasons that made him pledge it no longer apply." Such advice has made his name synonymous with political deception. But no other writer before or since has given the world such a brilliant lesson in how to think in terms of cold political power.

macroeconomics The study of the relationships among broad economic trends, such as national income, consumer savings and expenditures, capital investment, employment, money supply, prices, government expenditures, and balance of payments. Macroeconomics is especially concerned with government's role in affecting these trends. *See also* FISCAL POLICY; MICROE-CONOMICS; MONETARY POLICY.

Madisonian model The basic framework for governance in the U.S. Constitution. It is republican as opposed to democratic, and has a strong system of CHECKS AND BALANCES. Historians have called this the Madisonian model because James Madison was so influential in advocating the basic concepts contained in the Constitution. Political scientist James MacGregor Burns offers a critical analysis of the Madisonian model in his *The Deadlock of Democracy: Four Party Politics in America* (1963): "We have been too much entranced by the Madisonian model of government. . . . The system of checks and balances and interlocked gears of government . . . requires the consensus of many groups and leaders before the nation can act; . . . we underestimate the extent to which our system was designed for deadlock and inaction."

Madison, James (1751–1836) The fourth President of the United States (1809–1817), often called the chief architect of (or the father of) the Constitution because he was: (1) active in the call for the Constitutional Convention; (2) a major influence in creating a governing framework that stressed national supremacy; (3) a coauthor of the FEDERALIST PAPERS, which helped ensure ratification; (4) a major actor in the passage of the Bill of Rights; and (5) the author of a journal on the proceedings of the Constitutional Convention, which is history's prime source on the convention's deliberations. Madison is also one of America's preeminent political theorists. His intellectual framework for American government (incorporated into the Constitution) is known as the MADISONIAN MODEL. His theorizing on the nature of factions in FEDERALIST NO. 10 is the beginning of interest group theory. As President Thomas Jefferson's secretary of State, Madison was smoothly positioned to succeed him. Unfortunately, his actual time as President was one of his less successful efforts; his inept handling of the War of 1812, which saw the White House and the Capitol burned by British soldiers, caused him to lose much of his popularity. Nevertheless, there is no better example in world history of a political thinker so influential in his own lifetime—and since. For the standard biography, see Irving Brant's *James Madison* (6 vols., 1941–1961). For Madison's role in the development and adoption of the Constitution, see Max Farrand's *Records of the Federal Convention* (3 vols., 1937). *See also* COMMANDER IN CHIEF.

madman theory President Richard M. Nixon's theory that if the President of the United States seemed to be a little bit crazy and irrational, the other side would be more responsive and pliable in international dealings. Nixon's White House Chief of Staff, H.R. Haldeman, in his book *The Ends of Power* (1978), quotes Nixon: "I call it the Madman Theory. . . . I want the North Vietnamese to believe that I've reached the point where I might do anything to stop the war. We'll just slip the word to them that, 'for God's sake, you know Nixon is obsessed about Communists. We can't restrain him when he's angry—and he has his hand on the nuclear button'—and Ho Chi Minh himself will be in Paris in two days begging for peace."

magistrate A lower-level judicial official, sometimes elected, who handles misdemeanor cases. In rural areas the same duties are performed by a Justice of the Peace.

magistrate, chief A now dated term for the President of the United States.

Magna Charta 1. The charter of liberties that English nobles forced from King John in 1215. Because it is considered the beginning of limited government and the rule of law as opposed to absolute monarchy, it is an important forerunner to the U.S. Constitution. **2.** Any document offering fundamental guarantees of rights.

mainstream The most advantageous of political positions, not too far from the extremes of left or right. To be in the mainstream means to swim in the political center where most of the voters are to be found. A drier but parallel description is *middle of the road*.

majority 1. Greater than half. The story is often told that after ADLAI STEVENSON gave a presidential campaign speech a woman said to him: "Governor, your speech was magnificent. You'll get the vote of every thinking person." Stevenson replied, "It's not enough. I need a majority." **2.** Being of full legal age. **3.** The military rank or office of a major. **4.** The political party in a state or legislature with the most votes. **5.** The sovereign, in a free society. President Abraham Lincoln said in his first inaugural address, March 4, 1861: "A majority, held in restraint by constitutional checks and limitations, and always changing easily, with deliberate changes of popular opinions and sentiments, is the only true sovereign of a free people."

majority leader The chief strategist and floor spokesman for the party in nominal control in either house of a legislature. He or she is elected by party colleagues. Christopher Matthews' *Hardball* (1988) quotes Howard H. Baker, Jr., who was the majority leader of the U.S. Senate in the early 1980s: "The most important part of a Senate majority leader's education is over by the third grade: he has learned to count." And just how does one count votes or measure support for an issue? According to Senator Sam Nunn, there are some kinds "of things you don't measure by votes—you put your nose in the air and smell. . . . you give it the old sniff test" (*The Los Angeles Times*, June 7, 1985).

majority of one A single individual, so long as he or she is in the right. Essayist Henry David Thoreau (1817–1862) wrote in *On Civil Disobedience* (1849) that "any man more right than his neighbor constitutes a majority of one." And Calvin Coolidge (1872–1933), in accepting the Republican vice presidential nomination on July 27, 1920, said: "One with the law is a majority."

majority rule The underlying premise of democratic societies—that those with most of the people on their side should govern. The historic problem of majority rule has been protecting the minorities from oppression. This is why the founders created a REPUBLIC, a system of government one step removed from majority rule, and provided that the U.S. Constitution could only be changed by extraordinary majorities. But as Representative Morris K. Udall asserted: "If democracy means anything, it means that sooner or later the majority gets its way" (*The Washington Post*, June 11, 1975).

majority secretary A STAFFER who aids the Senate Majority Leader. There is also a corresponding minority secretary. They assist the leadership in counting votes, advise their party members on bills under consideration, help to schedule votes, and arrange for PAIRS, among other duties.

majority system An electoral system in which one candidate must win a majority of the votes to be elected; if all candidates get less than a majority, a runoff election is then held for the top two vote-getters.

majority whip In effect, the assistant majority leader in the U.S. House of Representatives or Senate. The whip helps marshal majority forces in support of party strategy. *Compare to* MINORITY WHIP; WHIP.

major player A slang phrase for someone, whether an individual, an organization, or a sovereign state, whose views must be taken into account on a policy issue.

make whole A legal remedy that provides for an injured party to be placed, as near as may be possible, in the situation he or she would have occupied if the wrong had not been committed. The concept was first put forth by the Supreme Court in the 1867 case of *Wicker v Hoppock*. In 1975, the Court held, in the case of *Albermarle Paper Company v Moody*, that Title VII of the Civil Rights Act of 1964 (as amended) intended a make-whole remedy for unlawful discrimination.

Making of the President A series of bestselling books on the presidential election process written by journalist Theodore H. White (1915–1986) on the campaigns of 1960, 1964, 1968, and 1972. White's reporting helped to change the nature of campaign press coverage. No longer could reporters just rewrite press handouts. White's *Making of the President* books set a new standard for political reporting, which had the juiciness of an inside story, the intimacy of a biography, and the perspective of history. White himself, however, became the victim of the success of his behind-the-scenes format. He said, in 1972: "I used to specialized in getting behind-the-scenes stuff, but now the rooms are so crowded with reporters getting behind-the-scenes stories that nobody can get behind-the-scenes stories."

malaise The medical term for a vague feeling of illness that is used in other contexts to express a lassitude or ineffectiveness not traceable to a specific source and not exhibiting a specific set of symptoms. Malaise was President Jimmy Carter's word for the political uneasiness he found in America. He first used it in a town meeting at Bardstown, Kentucky, July 31, 1979: "I thought a lot about our Nation and what I should do as President. And Sunday night before last, I made a speech about two problems of our country—energy and malaise."

malapportionment The skewed distribution of voters in a state's legislative or congressional districts. Prior to several landmark Supreme Court decisions in the early 1960s, malapportionment or maldistricting was the "normal" pattern of legislative apportionment throughout the nation. This tended to give sparsely populated rural districts a disproportionate say in state and national affairs. The Court held malapportionment to be unconstitutional in the 1964 cases of REYNOLDS V SIMS and WESBERRY V SANDERS.

malfeasance The performance of a consciously unlawful act on the part of a public official. *Compare to* MISFEASANCE.

Mallory v Hogan (1964) The Supreme Court case that held that the Fifth Amendment guarantee against self-incrimination applied to the states through the due process clause of the Fourteenth Amendment. Thus, a prisoner has the right not to answer questions of police or prosecutors if the answers would be self-incriminating. This decision reversed *Twining v New Jersey* (1908).

managed trade **1.** A reference to protectionist devices other than tariffs which governments, particularly those of the west, have adopted since the late 1970s to restrict the volume of imports from Japan and the new industrializing countries of the third world (or else to regulate trade between the United States and the European Community countries). Managed trade includes voluntary quotas, special levies, orderly marketing agreements, and government subsidies to domestic producers. Such measures have affected chiefly the steel, textile, auto, shipbuilding, and electronics industries, as well as agriculture. **2.** A trade policy that depends more heavily on negotiations with international trading partners, as opposed to solely market forces, to improve a balance of trade. **3.** A euphemism for traditional trade PROTECTIONISM.

mandamus, writ of A court order that compels the performance of an act.

mandate The perceived popular or electoral support for a public program, political party, or a particular politician. U.S. Presidents who win elections by overwhelming majorities may rightly feel the vote was a mandate to carry out their proposed policies, but Presidents who win by narrow margins may perceive no mandate to implement their programs. Thus, a President's mandate or electoral margin can often have a significant effect on legislative proposals. The greater the mandate, the more deferential the Congress is likely to be. President Ronald Reagan was especially effective—with a Congress half controlled by the opposition party—because he won election and reelection by such large margins.

mandating One level of government requiring another to offer—or pay for—a program as a matter of law or as a prerequisite to partial or full funding for either the program in question or other programs.

man of the people **1.** A politician of humble origins, such as Andrew Jackson, Abraham Lincoln, and Harry Truman. **2.** A politician not of humble origins, such as Franklin D. Roosevelt, whose followers assert that he represents the interests of ordinary folks.

man on horseback 1. A military figure, such as Napoleon Bonaparte, who is a potential dictator if the civilian regime falters. **2.** Any former military figure (usually a general) who aspires to civilian leadership. In American politics, the phrase was first applied to Ulysses S. Grant during his 1868 presidential campaign.

Mapp v Ohio (1961) The Supreme Court case that made the exclusionary rule (meaning that illegally gained evidence would be barred at trials) binding on all jurisdictions; thus, evidence obtained by means of unreasonable searches and seizures would not be admissible in court. This overruled *Wolf v Colorado* (1949). *Compare to* EXCLUSIONARY RULE.

Marbury v Madison (1803) The preeminent Supreme Court case because of its famous declaration of the Court's power of JUDICIAL REVIEW—the power to declare federal legislation or executive actions unconstitutional and consequently unenforceable through the courts. It was in this case that Chief Justice John Marshall held that it was the duty of the judiciary to say what the law is, including expounding and interpreting that law. The law contained in the Constitution, he said, was paramount, and laws repugnant to its provisions must fall. He concluded that it was the province of the courts to decide when other law was in violation of the basic law of the Constitution and, where this was found to occur, to declare that law null and void. This is the doctrine known as judicial review, the basis for the Court's application of constitutional guarantees.

marginal seat A legislative district in which it is difficult to predict whether the incumbent will be reelected. Any district in which the winning candidate receives less than 55 percent of the vote is considered a marginal seat. *Compare to* DISTRICT, OPEN; SAFE SEAT.

marginal tax rate The tax rate percentage applied to the last increment of income for purposes of computing federal or other income taxes.

marker 1. An I.O.U. (I owe you); a statement of debt, usually of gambling. **2.** A boundary indicator. In this sense the word is used in the phrase "lay down a marker" to send a signal not to cross a line whether figurative or literal. **3.** A political obligation to someone.

marketplace of ideas The public forum in which political beliefs and policy innovations compete for attention and support. In this market people buy, meaning support, the ideas they like best.

marking up a bill *See* BILL, MARKING UP A.

Marshall, George Catlett Jr. (1880–1959) The Chief of Staff of the U.S. Army during World War II and the single individual most responsible for the ultimate victory in Europe. It was he who selected Eisenhower and all other major commanders, he who allocated resources, and he who determined overall strategy. He was also a man of unstinting honor and integrity, who was revered by all who worked for or with him. According to Forrest C. Pogue's *George C. Marshall: Organizer of Victory* (1973), Marshall would have commanded the D-Day invasion of Europe, instead of Eisenhower, except for the fact the his civilian superior, President Franklin D. Roosevelt, came to the decision that Marshall would remain as Chief of Staff because, in Roosevelt's words: "Well I didn't feel I could sleep at ease if you were out of Washington." After his retirement from the Army, he was secretary of State (1947–1949), head of the American Red Cross (1949–1950), and secretary of Defense (1950–1951). In 1953 he was awarded the Nobel Prize for Peace, a result of his work in the MARSHALL PLAN.

Marshall, John (1755–1835) The revolutionary war soldier (he was actually in the same boat with George Washington as they crossed the Delaware River for the Battle of Trenton) who became the third chief justice of the Supreme Court and, by almost universal agreement, the one who did the most to establish the independent authority of the Court. From 1801 to 1835 he led the struggle for the Court to be the final arbiter of the Constitution and, by sheer force of will and legal cunning, made the federal government supreme over the states, and made the federal judiciary a true check on the power of the other two branches. There was initially much resistance to this idea. For example, in *Worcester v Georgia* (1832), the Court called for the President to act on an issue concerning the Cherokee Indians. President Andrew Jackson pointedly refused, saying: "John Marshall has made his decision: now let him enforce it!" (quoted in Horace Greeley, *The American Conflict*, 1864). This kind of presidential resistance is unthinkable today. After many years on the bench, Marshall was able to say: "The acme of judicial distinction means the ability to look a lawyer straight in the eyes for two hours and not hear a damned word he says" (quoted in A.J. Beveridge, *The Life of John Marshall*, 1919). For some of his landmark cases, *see* COHENS V VIRGINIA; DARTMOUTH COLLEGE V WOODWARD; FLETCHER V PECK; GIBBONS V OGDEN; MCCULLOCH V MARYLAND; MARBURY V MADISON.

Marshall Plan The economic aid program for post World War II Europe proposed by George Catlett Marshall Jr., U.S. Army chief of staff during the war. In 1947, President Harry S Truman made him Secretary of State. On June 5 of that year, Marshall proposed the European Recovery Program, a massive aid program that became known as the Marshall Plan, in a speech at Harvard University: "Our policy is directed not against any country or doctrine but against hunger, poverty, desperation and chaos. Its purpose should be the revival of a working economy in the world so as to permit the emergence of political and social conditions in which free institutions can exist." The plan worked so well and became so well known that the term entered the language and means any massive use of federal funds to solve a major social problem. President Harry S Truman wrote in his *Memoirs*, II (1956): "I had referred to the idea [European Recovery Program] as the 'Marshall Plan' when it was discussed in staff meetings, because I wanted General Marshall to get full credit for his brilliant contributions . . . . He had perceived the inspirational as well as the economic value of the proposal. History, rightly, will always associate his name with this program, which helped save Europe from economic disaster and lifted it from the shadow of enslavement by Russian Communism."

martial law **1.** The exercise of partial or complete military control over domestic territory in time of emergency because of public necessity. In the United States, it is usually authorized by the President, but may be imposed by a military commander in the interests of public safety. **2.** Arbitrary military rule imposed not by constitutional means, but by force.

Marxism **1.** The doctrine of revolution based on the writings of Karl Marx (1818–1883) and Friedrich Engels (1820–1895), which maintains that human history is a struggle between the exploiting and exploited classes. Marx and Engels wrote the *Communist Manifesto* (1848) "to do for history what Darwin's theory has done for biology." The basic theme of Marxism holds that the proletariat, or working class, will suffer so from alienation that it will rise up against the bourgeoisie, who own the means of production, and will overthrow the system of capitalism. After a brief period of rule by "the dictatorship of the proletariat," the classless society of communism would be forthcoming. While Marxism currently has a strong influence on the economies of the second, third, and fourth worlds, its intent has never been fully achieved. Indeed, because Marx's writings are so vast and often contradictory, serious Marxists spend considerable time arguing about just what Marx "really" meant. Marx's magnum opus, *Das Kapital* (1867), is frequently referred to as the bible of socialism. **2.** "The opium of the intellectuals," according to critic Edmund Wilson in *Letters on Literature and Politics 1912–1972* (1977). This was a play on Marx's assertion that religion was the opium of the suffering masses.

mashed potato circuit **1.** A gastronomical description of the political campaign trail. **2.** An "after dinner" speaking tour. *Compare to* RUBBER-CHICKEN CIRCUIT.

mass party A POLITICAL PARTY in which membership is open to anyone. The United States has a tradition of mass or semimass parties—in contrast to elite (or cadre) parties, such as the Communist party of the Soviet Union, in which only citizens meeting certain criteria are allowed to join.

matching funds **1.** Those funds provided for a specific purpose by one level of government as a condition for receiving additional funds for this same purpose from another level of government. Thus, a state government may agree to pay 50 percent of the cost of a local capital improvement program if the local government provides the other 50 percent. **2.** Funds provided by private foundations or government agencies that are contingent upon the donee organization raising equivalent funds from other sources. **3.** Funding for presidential elections available on an optional basis to candidates who agree to abide by contribution and expenditure limits. Primary election campaigns are funded through the presidential primary matching payment account, and general election campaigns are funded through the presidential election campaign fund; these accounts are funded by taxpayers who take the option of earmarking one dollar of their tax liability for this purpose.

A primary election candidate may be eligible for matching funds once $5,000 is raised in donations of $250 or less in each of 20 states. Thereafter, the fund matches each contribution of $250 or less until the total amount of public funds equals 50 percent of the candidate's primary expenditure limit. By requiring that private funds be raised in the primaries, the law seeks to insure that only serious candidates (i.e., those able to attract private contributors) may receive public funds.

In the general election, the nominees for President and Vice President of the two major parties are automatically eligible for a flat stipend of many millions from the presidential election campaign fund. This figure is raised every four years according to the cost-of-living increase. No private contributions may be accepted by major party candidates who receive public funds in the general election, except for a specified amount from the national committees of their respective political parties. Third-party candidates may receive public funds in an amount proportionate to the votes received by that party in the previous presidential election, and candidates of newly organized parties may be eligible for retroactive public funds after the election if they receive at least 5 percent of the popular votes cast.

Matthew effect The apparent increase in an electoral majority because the presidential candidate who gets the most votes in a state gets all of a state's electoral votes (or delegates, in a primary election). This is known as the Matthew effect because in the *Bible* (Matthew 13:12) it is said: "For whosoever hath, to him shall be given, and he shall have more abundance; but whosoever hath not, from him shall be taken away even that he hath." This is why a President who wins only 55 percent of the popular vote can wind up with 90 percent of the electoral votes.

max out Make the largest political campaign contribution allowed by law. According to Senator Alan Cranston: "Some people are able to give the maximum amount: they're accustomed to it. But people who can only afford $100 may have to think twice about it. It's not worth my time to raise it in $100 amounts. I have to concentrate on the people who can max out" (*Los Angeles Times*, February 10, 1985).

maximum feasible participation The requirement under the Economic Opportunity Act of 1964 that any community action program designed to help the poor have the maximum feasible participation of the people the program was designed to help. Thus, it was expected that the poor would help plan and implement anti-poverty programs. This was one of the most significant efforts ever of writing citizen participation requirements into federally funded programs.

Mayflower Compact The covenant for the governance of Plymouth Plantation, Massachusetts, signed by most of the male passengers aboard the ship *Mayflower* on November 21, 1620. While not a constitution, it was a social compact for local government that has since been idealized as the foundation of American constitutional thinking.

mayor The elected chief executive officer of a municipal corporation; the chief ceremonial officer of a city. In most modest-sized and small cities, the office of mayor is a part-time job. Depending on whether the job of mayor is administratively strong or weak, the mayor may simply be the first among equals on a CITY COUNCIL. while many big city mayors have become national figures, no mayor has ever been able to make the leap from city hall to the White House. The basic problem of all big city mayors was once summarized by Peter Flaherty, then Mayor of Pittsburgh: "You can't understand how lonely a Mayor feels with his problems. The people in the suburbs use our facilities but won't help pay for them. The Pittsburgh Zoo costs us $1 million a year. Three out of four people who go there come from outside the city. But when I ask the county commissioners for help, they look out the window" (*The New York Times*, March 24, 1971).

mayor-council system A system of urban government with a separately elected executive (the mayor) and an urban legislature (the city council) usually elected in partisan WARD elections. It is called a strong mayor system if the office of mayor is filled by separate citywide elections and has such powers as veto, appointment, and removal. Where the office of mayor lacks such powers, it is called a weak mayor system. This designation does not take into account any informal powers possessed by the incumbent mayor, only the formal powers of the office. Hence, Richard J. Daley (1902–1976) of Chicago was a strong mayor in a weak mayor system.

means test An income criterion used to determine if someone is eligible for government welfare or other benefits. For example, a family might be allowed certain welfare benefits only if its annual cash income is less than $12,092 (the federal government's 1988 definition of poverty for a family of four). Means-tested entitlement programs are often compared to non-means-tested programs, such as social security, which citizens are entitled to without regard to their private means. It has even been suggested that one way of reducing the nation's social security liability is to subject future benefits to a means test—that is, those people otherwise eligible for social security benefits would receive them only if their incomes were below a specified level.

media **1.** Journalistic sources of news, print or broadcast. What Walter Lippmann once said of newspapers now applies to television news as well: "The newspaper is in all literalness the bible of democracy, the book out of which a people determines its conduct. It is the only serious book most people read. It is the only book they read every day" (*Liberty and the News*, 1920). **2.** Advertising vehicles such as newspapers, magazines, television, and radio. In the context of political campaigns "unpaid media" is coverage and publicity from news organizations that is free—not paid for. "Paid media" is political advertising in the same places that must be paid for.

media advisor Originally, this was a technical advisor to a political campaign. However, as campaigns became more media-intensive over the last several decades, the media advisor has often evolved in a full-fledged POLITICAL CONSULTANT who deals with all aspects of campaign strategy.

media blitz A campaign offensive, commercially speaking. "The Blitz" was the German bombing of London during World War II; by analogy a modern-day blitz bombards the public with campaign commercials until they surrender. But it doesn't always work. Remember that London never succumbed.

media event An activity undertaken as a means of generating publicity from the news media. The defining criterion for a media event is that it would not be done if cameras and reporters were not present. Examples include protest demonstrations scheduled for the convenience of the early evening television news programs or a walk through a poor or ethnic neighborhood by a candidate for public office to demonstrate meaningful (and photogenic) concern. *Compare to* PSEUDOEVENT.

media, generative The prestige news sources such as *The New York Times*, *The Wall Street Journal*, and the major news magazines which heavily influence the nature and patterns of all news coverage. Because other news sources often follow their lead, they collectively have the ability to generate national news.

media kits The packages of candidate information given to news sources. They typically contain photos, a brief biography, campaign position papers, printed brochures, and names of contacts for additional information.

media state A society in which the media dominates the political process because, absent a strong party system, this is the only means by which those who govern as well as those who would govern can communicate with the citizenry. Kevin Phillips wrote in *Harper's* (January 1977): "Ancient Sparta was a military state. John Calvin's Geneva was a religious state. Mid-nineteenth century England was Europe's first industrial state, and the contemporary United States is the world's first media state."

media, vertical Any political advertising other than radio, television, or direct mail; includes bumper stickers, yard signs, hats, buttons, and so on.

media wave Large amounts of political advertising over a relatively short period of time, especially on television.

mediation Any attempt by an impartial third party to help settle disputes; also known as *conciliation*. A mediator has no power but that of persuasion; the mediator's suggestions are advisory and may be rejected by both parties. Mediation and conciliation tend to be used interchangeably to denote the entrance of an impartial third party into a labor dispute. However, there is a distinction. Conciliation is the less active term. It technically refers simply to efforts to bring the parties together so that they may resolve their problems themselves. Mediation, in contrast, implies that an active effort will be made to help the parties reach agreement by clarifying issues, asking questions, and making specific proposals. However, the usage of the two terms has become so blurred that the only place where it is absolutely necessary to distinguish between them is in a dictionary.

mediation service An abbreviated way of referring to the Federal Mediation and Conciliation Service or state agencies performing a similar function.

Medicaid The federally aided, state-operated, and state-administered program that provides medical benefits for certain low-income people in need of health and medical care. Authorized by 1965 amendments to the Social Security Act, it covers only members of one of the categories of people who can be eligible for WELFARE cash payment programs—the aged, the blind, the disabled, and members of families with dependent children where one parent is absent, incapacitated, or unemployed. (Under limited circumstances, states may also provide Medicaid coverage for children under 21 years of age who are not categorically related.) Subject to broad federal guidelines, states determine coverage, eligibility, payment to health care providers, and the methods of administering the program.

Medicare The national health insurance program for the elderly and the disabled, authorized by a 1965 amendment to the Social Security Act. The two parts of Medicare—hospital insurance and medical insurance—help protect people 65 years of age and over from the high costs of health care. Also eligible for Medicare are disabled people under 65 who have been entitled to Social Security disability benefits for 24 or more consecutive months (including adults who are receiving benefits because they have been disabled since childhood). Insured workers and their dependents who need dialysis treatment or a kidney transplant because of permanent kidney failure also have Medicare protection.

melting pot A sociological term that implies (1) that each succeeding wave of immigrants to the United States blends into the general society and (2) that this melting is ideally what should happen. The term originated in Israel Zangwill's (1864–1926) play *The Melting Pot* (1908), in which he wrote: "America is God's Crucible, the great Melting-Pot where all races of Europe are melting and reforming!" The phrase became the symbol of assimilation for several generations of American immigrants. President Woodrow Wilson, said in a April 19, 1915 speech: "There is here a great melting pot in which we must compound a precious metal. That metal is the metal of nationality." But studies have consistently shown that this "ain't necessarily so." Carl N. Degler's *Out of Our Past* (1970) holds: "The metaphor of the melting pot is unfortunate and misleading. A more accurate analogy would be a salad bowl, for, though the salad is an entity, the lettuce can still be distinguished from the chicory, the tomatoes from the cabbage." In recent years the term has become less fashionable and has been replaced in political rhetoric by the image of a mosaic. For example, in a speech in Pittsburgh, Pennsylvania, October 27, 1976, presidential candidate Jimmy Carter said: "We become not a melting pot but a beautiful mosaic. Different people, different beliefs, different yearnings, different hopes, different dreams."

member 1. *See* CONGRESS, MEMBER OF. **2.** An informal way of referring to a representative in the HOUSE. Congressional STAFFERS often refer to their boss as "my member." **3.** The male sexual organ. There has been much humorous juxtaposition of definitions 2 and 3.

memorial A written request to a legislative body or an executive. Memorials are usually petitions by groups seeking to influence a proposed government action. All communications to the U.S. Congress from state legislatures, both supporting and opposing legislation, are embodied in memorials, which are referred to the appropriate committees.

mending fences What legislators do when they return to their home districts to consult with constituents and generally look after their political interests.

mentor A trusted counselor. The term has become increasingly important in the context of organizational and political careers, as empirical evidence has shown that having an influential mentor is critically important to career advancement. The word comes from Homer's *The Odyssey*. When Odysseus set off for the war at Troy, he left his house and wife in the care of his friend, Mentor. When things got rough at home for Odysseus' family, Athena, the goddess of wisdom, assumed the shape of Mentor and provided Telemachus, the son of Odysseus, with some very helpful advice about how to deal with the problems of his most unusual adolescence.

merit system A public sector concept of staffing that implies that no test of party membership is involved in the selection, promotion, or retention of government employees and that a constant effort is made to select the best qualified individuals available for appointment and advancement.

Merit Systems Protection Board (MSPB) The independent federal government agency, created by the Civil Service Reform Act of 1978, designed to safeguard both the merit system and individual employees against abuses and unfair personnel actions. The MSPB consists of three members, appointed on a bipartisan basis to seven-year nonrenewable terms. The MSPB hears and decides employee appeals and orders corrective and disciplinary actions against an employee or agency when appropriate. It also oversees the merit system and reports annually to the Congress on how the system is functioning. Within the MSPB was an independent special counsel with the power to investigate charges of prohibited personnel practices (including reprisals against WHISTLE BLOWERS). However, the Whistleblower Protection Act of 1989 converted the special counsel's office into an independent agency within the Executive Branch. This Office of Special Counsel was also given expanded powers to protect whistleblowers.

metropolitan government A central government for an urban area. It is a consolidated government if all the existing local governments at the time of its formation are abolished. In contrast, under a pure federated government, each local unit retains its identity and some of its functions while other functions are transferred to the metropolitan government. However, there are so many variants and exceptions to this formula that it is impossible to generalize accurately about the structure of metropolitan governing arrangements.

metropolitan statistical area *See* STANDARD METROPOLITAN STATISTICAL AREA.

Mexican War *See* POLK, JAMES K.

microeconomics The study of the parts of an economy and how they function as opposed to the study of a total economy and its aggregate performance. Individual firms and consumers are analyzed concerning wages, prices, inputs and outputs, and supply and demand, among other things. *Compare to* MACROECONOMICS.

micromanagement 1. A pejorative term for overly close supervision by policymakers in the implementation of programs. The Congress has been accused of micromanagement when it writes detailed rules governing programs into legislation, thus denying line managers any real administrative discretion. But any manager is a micromanager if he or she refuses to allow subordinates to have any real authority or responsibility. **2.** A form of patronage that occurs when influential members of Congress insist that government programs, especially in the area of military procurement, contain elements that benefit their districts. For example, the Army may be forced into buying more of a weapon than it needs simply because the factory that makes it is in an influential member's congressional district.

middle of the road *See* MAINSTREAM.

military-industrial complex A nation's armed forces and their weapons and materiel suppliers. During his farewell address in 1961, President Dwight D. Eisenhower warned that "in the councils of government we must guard against the acquisition of unwarranted influence, whether sought or unsought, by the military-industrial complex. The potential for the disastrous rise of misplaced power exists and will persist." Malcolm C. Moos (1916–1982), Eisenhower's chief speechwriter during the second term, is usually credited with coining what has become Eisenhower's single most memorable warning: to "guard against . . . the military-industrial complex."

military intelligence *See* INTELLIGENCE.

militia *See* NATIONAL GUARD.

Mill, John Stuart (1806–1873) The English political reformer and philosopher best known for his classic argument in defense of civil liberties for those with diverse political opinions. In *On Liberty* (1859) he wrote: "Though the silenced opinion be in error, it may, and very commonly does, contain a portion of truth; and since the general or prevailing opinion on any subject is rarely or never the whole truth, it is only by the collision of adverse opinions that the remainder of the truth has any chance of being supplied."

Mills, C. Wright (1916–1962) The radical sociologist whose most famous book, *The Power Elite* (1956), asserted that the United States is basically ruled by a political, military, and business elite, whose decisional powers essentially preempted the democratic process. Mills wrote: "The leading men in each of the three domains of power—the warlords, the corporation chieftains, the political directorate—tend to come together to form the power elite of America." Most contemporary analyses of elitism in American governance have their intellectual foundations in Mills's work, even if Mills himself is not acknowledged.

minimax A technical term within GAME THEORY, the mathematical analysis of conflict situations. In a minimax strategy, attempts are made to minimize the worst eventuality, rather than to maximize the best possible outcome. Minimax is the strategy likely to be adopted, independently, by both sides, as long as they are unable to trust each other.

minimum wage The lowest hourly rate that may be paid to a worker. While many minimum wages are established by union contracts, state laws, and organizational pay policies, minimum wage usually refers to the federal minimum wage law—the FAIR LABOR STANDARDS ACT (FLSA)—established by the Congress via FLSA amendments. President Franklin D. Roosevelt in a June 16, 1933 statement advocating federal minimum wage standards said: "No business which depends for existence on paying less than living wages to its workers has any right to continue in this country. By business I mean the whole of commerce as well as the whole of industry; by workers I mean all workers—the white-collar class as well as the man in overalls; and by living wages I mean more than a bare subsistence level—I mean the wages of decent living." The minimum wage started out as 25 cents an hour in 1938; in 1991 it was $4.25 an hour. The Secretary of Labor regulates exceptions (lower rates) based on age or physical disabilities. The minimum wage has generally been favored by Democrats and opposed by Republicans. However, President Harry Truman was fond of saying: "The Republicans favor a minimum wage—the smaller the minimum the better" (*The Words of President Harry S Truman*, 1984).

ministerial function Required action. In determining the liability of government agents for the consequences of their actions, courts have created a distinction between ministerial and discretionary functions. Though often blurred in specific cases, the distinction attempted to limit liability to acts done by the agents' volition (discretionary), in comparison to actions compelled by the Constitution, a statute, a charter, or other law (ministerial).

minority 1. Less than half. **2.** A small group within a larger one, such as a city or a legislature. **3.** A group with identifiable racial or religious characteristics from the larger society of which it is a part. **4.** Being a member of such a group. **5.** Being under the legal age of adulthood.

minority district A congressional district whose population is primarily members of a minority group. The 1982 amendments to the VOTING RIGHTS ACT require states to create such districts when appropriate.

minority leader The leader of the minority party in a legislature. The Republican minority leader in the House of Representatives, Robert H. Michel of Illinois, once said of his job: "Each member is a separate entity. You can't treat two alike. I know what I can get and what I can't, when to back off and when to push harder. It's not a matter of twisting arms. It's bringing them along by gentle persuasion. Sometimes they don't realize they're being brought into the orbit. You get down to the end of the walkway and you say, 'Hey, we aren't 2 cents apart, are we?' and he says, 'Well, I guess we aren't'" (*The Washington Post*, August 10, 1981). *Compare to* MAJORITY LEADER.

minority party Any political party in a legislature with less than a majority of the members of the legislature as its party's members. When the majority party has overwhelming numbers, the minority party is in a particularly powerless position. Late in the last century, an irate Democrat asked Speaker of the House Thomas B. Reed (1839–1902), "What becomes of the rights of the minority?" Reed replied: "The right of the minority is to draw its salaries, and its function is to make a quorum."

minority secretary *See* MAJORITY SECRETARY.

minority set-asides *See* SET-ASIDES.

minority whip The legislator who performs the duties of whip for the minority party. *Compare to* MAJORITY WHIP; WHIP.

***Miranda* rights** The set of rights that a person accused or suspected of having committed a crime has during interrogation and of which he or she must be informed prior to questioning, according to the Supreme Court in its *Miranda v Arizona* decision. The act of informing a person of these rights is often called admonition of rights, or admonishment of rights. The information given is called the Miranda warning. Once rights have been read, the arrestee is said to have been "mirandized."

Miranda v Arizona (1966) The Supreme Court case that held that an arrested person must be warned of the right to be silent and the right to have a lawyer, who will be provided if the arrested person cannot afford one, as soon as the arrest is made. The Court stated that "the prosecution may not use statements . . . stemming from custodial interrogation of the defendant unless it demonstrates the use of procedural safeguards effective to secure the privilege against self-incrimination." When the police arrest individuals and "read them their rights," it is the rights embedded in the *Miranda* decision they refer to. The Court made a major exception to *Miranda* when in *New York v Quarles* (1984) it held that suspects could be questioned before advising them of their rights if there were "overriding considerations of public safety." As for Ernesto Miranda, whose confession to kidnapping and rape was the basis for this case: he was killed in a tavern fight in 1976. Thereupon, the person arrested for his murder was read his MIRANDA RIGHTS. *Compare to* ESCOBEDO V ILLINOIS.

miscegenation law Any law forbidding interracial marriages. The Supreme Court declared all such laws unconstitutional in *Loving v Virginia* (1967).

misdemeanor A crime punishable by a jail term of less than a year. *Compare to* FELONY.

misery index The total of the rates of inflation and unemployment; first used by economist Arthur Okun in the 1970s.

misfeasance The improper or illegal performance of an otherwise lawful act that causes harm to someone. *Nonfeasance* is a failure to perform at all. *Compare to* MALFEASANCE.

missile gap Presidential candidate John F. Kennedy's 1960 charge that the United States was behind the Soviet Union in nuclear missile production. Interestingly, after the election, the Kennedy administration discovered that there was no such gap after all. Because Kennedy's missile gap evaporated, the term is sometimes used to imply a nonexistent issue.

mobocracy Government by popular whim; mob rule as opposed to the RULE OF LAW.

Model Cities Program The most significant part of the Demonstration Cities and Metropolitan Development Act of 1966. It designated particular areas in demonstration cities for intensive coordinated federal programs. Though originally programmed for only a dozen or so cities as part of President Lyndon B. Johnson's GREAT SOCIETY, it quickly grew to include more than 150 cities. It was dismantled by the Richard M. Nixon administration. *Compare to* URBAN RENEWAL.

moderate Someone whose political orientation is in the middle—between conservative and liberal. Moderates often think of themselves as independents and don't affiliate with either major party. When the word is used as an adjective, as in "moderate conservative," it means someone who is more pragmatic than ideological.

modus vivendi A Latin phrase meaning "a temporary understanding pending a final agreement." It is the acceptance of a continuing working relationship, with fundamental disagreements ignored or held in abeyance.

Mondale, Walter (1928–) The U.S. Senator from Minnesota (1964–1977) who became Vice President under President Jimmy Carter (1977–1981) and the 1984 Democratic presidential nominee. He won the nomination after devastating his major opponent, Senator GARY HART, with a single question: "Where's the beef?" This was the punch line of a then current television commercial comparing the size of hamburgers. Mondale's reference was to the substance of all the "new ideas" Hart was espousing. But Mondale, an honest hard-working man who was committed to a life of public service, didn't have much beef of his own. After promising to raise taxes in his nomination acceptance speech, his campaign, not helped by his dour personality, continued downhill until President Ronald Reagan won reelection by a landslide. On the morning after his defeat, Mondale said, "All my life I've wanted to run for the Presidency in the worst way. And that's what I did."

monetarism The economic theory that changes in the supply of money are the main determinants of economic activity; it holds that if government just keeps the money supply growing at the same rate as the growth of overall productivity, the free market will work efficiently.

monetary policy A government's formal efforts to manage the money in its economy in order to realize specific economic goals. Three basic kinds of monetary policy decisions can be made: (1) decisions about the amount of money in circulation; (2) decisions about the level of interest rates; (3) decisions about the functioning of credit markets and the banking system.

Controlling the amount of money is, of course, the key variable. In 1913, the United States passed into law the Federal Reserve Act, which created a strong central bank, the Federal Reserve. Like most central banks, the FEDERAL RESERVE SYSTEM is empowered to control the amount of money in circulation by either creating or canceling dollars. The implementation of money control is achieved through the process of putting up for sale or buying government securities, usually termed open-market operations, which means that the Federal Reserve competes with other bidders in the purchasing or selling of securities. The difference is that, when the Federal Reserve buys securities, it pays in the form of new currency in circulation. If it sells some of its securities, it decreases money available, since in effect it absorbs currency held by others. This does not mean, however, that the money stock fluctuates greatly. It steadily increases. It is in the margin of the increase that money supply has its impact. Through the use of the two other tools, the Federal Reserve can attempt to affect investments and loans. First, it can change its discount rate—the interest rate it charges other banks for loans of money that these banks can use to make loans. Second, it can change the reserve requirement—the amount of money a bank must have on hand in comparison with the amount of money it may have out on loan.

Monroe Doctrine The assertion by President James Monroe in his 1823 State of the Union message that the Western Hemisphere was closed to colonization and aggressive actions by European powers. In return, the United States promised not "to interfere in the internal concerns" of Europe. The doctrine was actually formulated by Monroe's secretary of State, John Quincy Adams (who would succeed Monroe as President). The Monroe Doctrine had strong rhetorical and political usage up to the 1920s, on the eves of World Wars I and II, and in the debates that led up to the CUBAN MISSILE CRISIS, but its relevance is declining. After all, the United States had "interfered" extensively in Europe during the World Wars, and the Soviet Union has not been deterred from "colonizing" such Western Hemisphere countries as Cuba and Nicaragua.

Monroe Doctrine, Roosevelt Corollary to President Theodore Roosevelt's assertion in his message to Congress of December 6, 1904 that: "In the Western hemisphere the adherence of the United States to the Monroe Doctrine may force the United States, however reluctantly, in flagrant cases of wrongdoing or impotence, to the exercise of an international police power."

Monroe, James (1758–1831) The President of the United States from 1817 to 1825. As a young Revolutionary War soldier he was with George Washington at Valley Forge and was wounded at the Battle of Trenton in 1776. Upon returning to his native Virginia, he studied law with Thomas Jefferson. After representing Virginia in the U.S. Senate (1790–1794), he became Governor of Virginia. In 1803 on a diplomatic mission to France, he helped arrange for the Louisiana Purchase. As President James Madison's secretary of State (1811–1817), he was positioned to be easily elected President in 1816. His administration was so harmonious that it was characterized as an era of good feeling.

Monroe v Pape (1961) The Supreme Court case that held that a person whose constitutional rights were violated by a police officer might be able to sue that officer personally for damages in federal court. However, the police officer might have official IMMUNITY, depending on what had happened.

Montesquieu, Charles de *See* CHECKS AND BALANCES.

moot **1.** A hypothetical case used for purpose of discussion. **2.** A legal case in which there is no controversy; that is, one in which any formal judgment can have no practical effect. **3.** A legal issue that has already been decided.

Moral Majority A political organization of fundamentalist Christians founded in 1979 by television evangelist Jerry Falwell (1933–   ). This "majority" tended to support Republican and other conservative causes; it opposed abortion and gay rights, supported mandatory school prayers, and generated considerable hostility from some members of the public—perhaps best summarized by a bumper sticker that read "The Moral Majority is Neither." In 1986, Falwell changed the name of his increasingly attacked organization to the Liberty Federation.

moral victory An election defeat that is turned into a victory for principle by the very fact that the candidate ran and took a public stand. Consequently, the term is often used in an ironic or sarcastic sense.

morning hour The time set aside at the beginning of each legislative day in the U.S. Senate for the consideration of regular routine housekeeping business. (The "hour" is almost never used in the House of Representatives.) In the Senate it is the first two hours of a session following an adjournment, but it can be terminated earlier if the morning business has been completed. This business includes such matters as messages from the President, communications from the heads of departments, messages from the House, the presentation of petitions and memorials, reports of standing and select committees, and the introduction of bills and resolutions. During the first hour of the morning hour in the Senate, no motion to proceed to the consideration of any bill on the calendar is in order except by unanimous consent. During the second hour, motions can be made but must be decided without debate. Senate committees normally meet while the Senate is in its morning hour. Incidentally, morning hour or morning business can occur anytime of the day or night.

morning in America The "feel good" reelection theme used by President Ronald Reagan's 1984 campaign SPOTS. Over video of scenes of an idyllic American small town, an announcer read: "It's morning again in America. In a town not too far from where you live, a young family has just moved into a new home. Three years ago, even the smallest house seemed completely out of reach. Right down the street, one of the neighbors has just bought himself a new car, with all the options. The factory down the river is working again. Not long ago, people were saying it probably would be closed forever. . . . Life is better, America is back. And people have a sense of pride they never felt they'd feel again. And so it's not surprising that just about everyone in town is thinking the same thing. Now that our country is turning around, why would we ever turn back?"

mossback A political REACTIONARY; a derogatory term for hard-core conservatives—who figuratively change their positions so slowly that moss could grow on their back.

most-favored nation An international trade policy whereby countries agree to give each other the most favorable of their trade concessions offered to foreign countries.

motion A request by a member of a legislature for any one of a wide array of parliamentary actions. One "moves" for a certain procedure or for the consideration of a measure or a vote, for example. The precedence of motions and whether they are debatable are determined by parliamentary law.

motion to recommit A motion to send a bill back to the legislative committee that reported it. Generally speaking, a motion to recommit, if adopted, kills the bill unless the motion is accompanied by specific instructions to report it back to the floor, usually within a specified time period, and with modifications, amendments, deletions, and so on.

motion to table *See* TABLE.

movement A loose grouping of people and organizations which seek political change usually around a particular issue; thus, the women's movement, the civil rights movement, etc.

movers and shakers Those members of a community who lead public opinion and are active enough in politics or business that they can make things happen. The term is often used as an informal reference to a community's power structure.

Moynihan, Daniel Patrick (1927–   ) A U.S. senator from New York, first elected in 1976, former ambassador to the United Nations (1975–1976) and India (1973–1975), and former urban affairs advisor to President Richard M. Nixon (1969–1973). Moynihan first came to national attention in 1965 when, as an assistant secretary of Labor, he wrote a report ("The Negro Family: The Case for National Action") suggesting instability in black families. Moynihan once again ran afoul of black leaders when in 1970 he wrote a memorandum to President Nixon stating that "the time may have come when the issue of race could benefit from a period of 'benign neglect.'" When the memorandum was leaked to the press, its misinterpretation once again made Moynihan a *persona non grata* with many members of the black community. Nevertheless, there are both black and white academics who now consider him a prophet of significant proportions. More recently, he denounced the policy of using the Social Security Trust Fund as a budget gimmick to hide the real size of the federal deficit; and he has argued that in the post-cold war era, the United States should lead a revitalization of international law.

muckraker President Theodore Roosevelt's term, taken from John Bunyan's (1628–1688) *Pilgrim's Progress* (1678), for a journalist who writes exposés of business and government corruption. Some of the most famous muckrakers were Lincoln Steffens (1866–1935), Ida M. Tarbell (1857–1944), and Upton Sinclair (1878–1968). Today, anyone who writes an exposé of governmental corruption or incompetence might be called a muckraker.

mudslinging A political campaign tactic by which one side (or both) uses lies, malicious gossip, and/or innuendo to discredit an opponent. This is one of the oldest of American political traditions. Illinois Governor Adlai Stevenson is usually credited with the epigram: "He who slings mud generally loses ground." But that was more wishful thinking than direct observation, for history is loaded with mudslingers who won. However, today's sophisticated politician avoids mud in favor of ATTACK POLITICS or negative advertising.

Some mud is classic. Challenger George Smathers denounced Senator Claude Pepper in a bitter 1950 Democratic primary fight for the U.S. Senate: "Are you aware that Claude Pepper is known all over Washington as a shameless extrovert? Not only that but this man is reliably reported to practice nepotism with his sister-in-law, and he has a sister who was once a thespian in New York. Worst of all it is an established fact that Mr. Pepper, before his marriage, practiced celibacy." The mud stuck. Smathers won. [Quoted in *Gothic Politics in the Deep South* (1968) by Robert Sherrill.]

mugwumps **1.** Those who desert their political party to support another candidate; one who is for whatever reason unable to vote for his regular party's ticket. **2.** The Republicans who would not support the candidacy of James G. Blaine, the Republican nominee for President in 1884. The *New York Sun* called these party bolters "Little Mugwumps." A mugwump then meant an Indian chief. Because New York politics was partial to Indian terms, it came to mean any party bolter. **3.** Someone who straddles an issue; who is unwilling to take a firm stand. Thus, it is said that a mugwump has his "mug" on one side of a fence and his "wump" on the other side. **4.** Political enemies in general.

municipal **1.** Of local government concern, as in municipal bonds or municipal parks. **2.** Of internal concern to a nation (as opposed to international). **3.** Of concern to only one government, whether state or local. In Latin, *municipium* referred to any self-governing body within the Roman Empire.

municipal bonds *See* BONDS, MUNICIPAL.

municipal commercial paper Short-term promissory notes issued by local jurisdictions.

municipal corporation **1.** The political entity created pursuant to state law by the people of a city or town for the purposes of local government. **2.** Any formally created subnational government.

municipal court A local government court with exclusive jurisdiction over violations of local ordinances. State law may also grant limited jurisdiction in criminal and civil cases arising within the jurisdiction.

municipality **1.** The municipal corporation. **2.** The officials who manage the municipal corporation.

municipal law **1.** Local legislation. **2.** National law, as opposed to international law.

municipal ordinance A local law.

municipal revenue bonds State and local government debt securities, whose interest and principal are paid from the revenues of rents, tolls, or other user charges flowing from specific projects financed by the bonds.

Muskie, Edmund Sixtus (1914–   ) The U.S. Senator from Maine (1959–1979) who was HUBERT H. HUMPHREY's vice presidential running mate during the 1968 presidential election. He ran unsuccessfully for the 1972 Democratic presidential nomination. In 1979 he resigned from the Senate to be President Jimmy Carter's secretary of State for the last year of the Carter Administration. *See also* TOWER COMMISSION.

Myers v United States (1926) The Supreme Court case that presented the question of "whether under the Constitution the President has the exclusive power of removing executive officers of the United States whom he has appointed by and with the advice and consent of the Senate." The opinion of the Court was delivered by Chief Justice William H. Taft, a former U.S. President. Not surprisingly, he argued that the removal power is an executive power, vested by the Constitution in the President alone. In Taft's view, the power to dismiss the officials in the executive branch was necessary for presidential control of administration and the ability to make sure that the laws are faithfully executed. *See also* HUMPHREY'S EXECUTOR V UNITED STATES.

N

NAACP *See* NATIONAL ASSOCIATION FOR THE ADVANCEMENT OF COLORED PEOPLE.

NACo *See* NATIONAL ASSOCIATION OF COUNTIES.

Nader, Ralph (1934–   ) The archetypal champion of consumer rights whose various investigations have spawned dozens of new consumer laws and whose efforts form the backbone of the modern CONSUMER MOVEMENT. Nader, who also heralded a revival in PUBLIC INTEREST LAW, came to prominence in 1965 when his book *Unsafe at Any Speed* (1965) attacked the auto industry for faulty designs. The clumsy effort by General Motors to discredit him backfired and made Nader, the David who forced the embarrassed GM Goliath to publicly apologize for hiring private detectives to dig up "dirt" on Nader's private life (there was none), into an overnight consumer advocate celebrity. Since then, Nader has continued as a reformer and has used his celebrity status to publicize the dangers of certain food additives, the hazards of radiation from television sets, the risks of nuclear power stations, and so on.

Nader's Raiders People who work for any of Ralph Nader's Washington-based organizations, such as the Center for the Study of Responsive Law, Public Citizen, or the Center for Auto Safety, to investigate government regulatory efforts. The raiders are often college students on summer vacation.

name recognition A measure of how much the public is aware of a candidate—whether they even know his or her name. Because a known political figure always has a head start on an unknown, many aspiring politicians run in hopeless contests just to generate the name recognition that will help them in a later election.

Nast, Thomas (1840–1902) The preeminent American political cartoonist of the nineteenth century known for creating the symbols of the Republican party (the ELEPHANT) and the Democratic party (the DONKEY), and for the modern conception of Santa Claus.

nation 1. People united by a shared cultural and political life. **2.** A STATE if it includes citizens of many historically distinct nations. According to President Abraham Lincoln in his annual message to Congress, December 1, 1862: "A nation may be said to consist of its territory, its people, and its laws. The territory is the only part which is of certain durability." **3.** A left-of-center liberal weekly of political opinion published since 1865.

national 1. Pertaining to an independent political unit. **2.** Pertaining to a central government as opposed to its lower levels. **3.** A citizen of a particular state. **4.** Nationwide in scope.

National Aeronautics and Space Administration (NASA) The federal agency created by the National Aeronautics and Space Act of 1958 whose principal statutory functions are to conduct research for the solution of problems of flight within and outside the earth's atmosphere and to develop, construct, test, and operate aeronautical and space vehicles; to conduct activities required for the exploration of space with manned and unmanned vehicles; to arrange for the most effective utilization of the scientific and engineering resources of the United States with other nations engaged in aeronautical and space activities for peaceful purposes; and to provide for the widest practicable and appropriate dissemination of information concerning NASA's activities and their results.

During its growth years, NASA led a charmed life—its work mesmerized the public and the press. Faced with squeezed budgets and an unwieldy combination of public bureaucracy and private contractors, NASA programs had great difficulties following the spectacular moon voyages. Its space shuttle program exposed more than a decade of poor leadership when, in January 1986, the shuttle *Challenger* exploded moments after launching. As NASA struggled to salvage the shuttle program and rebuild public confidence, the U.S. civilian space program seemed to fall behind that of the U.S.S.R. and consortiums of European nations. On May 11, 1990 in a speech at Texas A&I University, President George Bush asserted that the United States should send astronauts to Mars as part of a "new age of exploration." This suggestion was immediately applauded by those who support an expanded space program; but the goal's sincerity was questioned by those who noted the President did not request additional funding for NASA.

national anthem A country's official song of praise and loyalty. The U.S. national anthem is the "Star-Spangled Banner," the 1814 poem of Francis Scott Key (1779–1843) that was combined with the music of an English drinking song and, by an act of the Congress, officially designated the national anthem in 1931. (Irving Berlin's "God Bless America" has often been suggested as a more singable substitute.)

National Archives and Records Administration (NARA) The federal agency responsible for managing the records of the U.S. government. The NARA assists federal agencies in documenting their activities, administering their records management programs, and retiring their noncurrent records to Federal records centers. The NARA also manages the Presidential Libraries system and is responsible for publishing legislative, regulatory, presidential, and other public documents. The NARA became an independent agency in the executive branch of the federal government in 1985. It is the successor agency to the National Archives Establishment, which was created in 1934 and subsequently incorporated into the General Services Administration as the National Archives and Records Service. The National Archives building in Washington houses the original Declaration of Independence and the Constitution; both are on view daily. Carved on its exterior is: "What's past is prologue."

National Association for the Advancement of Colored People (NAACP) The largest and historically most influential of the black interest groups. Founded in 1909, the NAACP, headquartered in Washington, is noted for its lobbying for civil rights laws and testing of civil rights cases in federal court. *Compare to* NATIONAL URBAN LEAGUE.

National Association of Counties (NACo) The Washington-based organization of county government and management officials. Founded in 1935, NACo provides research, reference, and lobbying services for its members. *See* PUBLIC INTEREST GROUPS.

National Association of Manufacturers (NAM) An umbrella organization for American business, representing 12,000 manufacturers. The NAM is generally considered the "voice" of business in Washington.

National Civic League A Denver-based membership organization founded in 1894, long in the forefront of municipal reform effects, that serves as a clearinghouse and lobby for urban concerns. Formerly (until 1981) called the National Municipal League.

national committee The formal governing structure of the major national political parties, consisting of 50 committeemen and 50 committeewomen (two from each state) elected by the various state committees and conventions along with state party chairs and other high-ranking party officials. The national committees seldom meet; their main task is to make arrangements for the NATIONAL CONVENTION. While the national party chairperson is elected by the national committee, in reality he or she is often selected by the incumbent President or the party's presidential nominee. When there is no President or presidential candidate, as after a national election defeat, the national committee plays the key role in managing the fortunes of the party.

National Conference of State Legislatures (NCSL) The Denver-based organization that in January 1975 replaced three previously existing organizations (the National Legislative Conference, the National Conference of State Legislative Leaders, and the National Society of State Legislators). The NCSL is the only nationwide organization representing all state legislators (7,600) and their staffs (approximately 10,000). It seeks to advance the effectiveness, independence, and integrity of the state legislature as an equal coordinate branch of government. It also fosters interstate cooperation and represents states and their legislatures before the Congress and federal agencies. *See* PUBLIC INTEREST GROUPS.

national convention The assembly of DELEGATES from the various state political parties who gather every four years to nominate candidates for President and Vice President, to draft and vote on a party PLATFORM, and to use their time on national television to make their candidates and policies as attractive as possible to the American people. In recent years, with the increasing popularity of presidential PRIMARY elections and the opening up of caucuses, the national convention has often functioned merely to ratify the winner of the greatest number of delegates in the primary and caucus states. The convention's processes and traditions remain available in case the primary season proves indecisive and the nomination must be "brokered"—bargained over by the various party leaders. Political scientist Byron E. Shafer has argued in *Bifurcated Politics* (1988) that the national convention has evolved "from an older era of brokerage and bargaining to a newer era of publicity and communication." Since the real decision on the nomination is determined by the presidential primaries, the convention, while in reserve as the "nominator of last resort," has a new role as a political theme park and freak show where all sorts of causes compete for a hearing amid the glow of national publicity.

national debt The total outstanding debt of a central government. The national debt of the United States was $75 million in 1790. It reached its low point in 1835, when it was a mere $38,000. By 1981, it reached $1 trillion, but by 1986 this doubled to $2 trillion; by 1991 it was about $3 trillion. The national debt is often confused with the nation's budget deficit in a given year. The debt is, in effect, the total of all the yearly deficits (borrowing) that have not been repaid, plus accumulated interest. It is President Herbert Hoover who is usually credited with first saying: "Blessed are the young for they shall inherit the national debt."

National Emergency Act of 1976 The law that terminated various emergency powers of the President that had been in effect since the 1930s. It established clear guidelines for the declaration of future national emergencies so such events will be decided jointly by the President and the Congress.

National Endowment for the Arts/Humanities *See* NATIONAL FOUNDATION ON THE ARTS AND THE HUMANITIES.

National Environmental Policy Act *See* ENVIRONMENTAL POLICY.

National Foundation on the Arts and the Humanities An independent federal agency created in 1965 consisting of national endowments (funds granted for specific purposes) for the arts and humanities.

The activities of the National Endowment for the Arts (NEA) are designed to foster the growth and development of the arts in the United States. The endowment awards grants to individuals, to state and regional arts agencies, and to nonprofit organizations in the fields of architecture and environmental arts, crafts, dance, education, expansion arts, folk arts, literature, museums, music, media arts (film, radio, and television), theater, and the visual arts. New restrictions that Congress placed on grant recipients in 1989 provide that federal funds may not "be used to promote, disseminate, or produce materials which. . . may be considered obscene, including but not limited to depictions of sadomasochism, homoeroticism, the sexual exploitation of children, or individuals engaged in sex acts and which, when taken as a whole, do not have serious literary, artistic, political, or scientific value." These restrictions were enacted in response to NEA-sponsored art that many members of Congress found objectionable. Critics have asserted that this is unwarranted censorship of creative expression.

The activities of the National Endowment for the Humanities (NEH) are designed to promote and support the production and dissemination of knowledge in the humanities, especially as it relates to the serious study and discussion of contemporary values and public issues. The endowment makes grants to individuals, groups, and institutions—schools, colleges, universities, museums, public television stations, libraries, public agencies, and private nonprofit groups—to increase understanding and appreciation of the humanities. It makes grants in support of humanities-related research of value to the scholarly and general public.

National Governors Association (NGA) A Washington-based membership organization founded in 1908, formerly known as the National Governors Conference, that includes governors of the states, territories, and Puerto Rico. The NGA seeks to improve state government, addresses problems requiring interstate cooperation, and endeavors to facilitate intergovernmental relations at the federal-state and state-local levels. *See also* PUBLIC INTEREST GROUPS.

National Guard The military forces of the states, which often are used for civil emergencies, such as major fires or floods. Normally, under the command of each state's governor, any or all of the state's individual guard units may be called (by the U.S. Congress) into federal service at any time. Once a guard unit is called into federal service, it is no longer subject to state control. The National Guard was organized in 1916. Until that time, each state had a volunteer militia.

National Industrial Recovery Act of 1933 (NIRA) The federal statute that created a massive program of public works and guaranteed employees "the right to organize and bargain collectively through representatives of their own choosing. . . free from the interference, restraint or coercion of employers." The act, which created the National Recovery Administration (NRA) to administer its provisions, was designed to establish self-government of industry through codes of fair competition, which tended to eliminate competitive practices. These codes (which fixed hours, wages, and prices—in effect, overriding the restrictions imposed by antitrust policies) were the essence of the NIRA. Companies adopting their industries' codes of fair practice were entitled to display the Blue Eagle, a flag or poster indicating compliance. The Supreme Court declared the act unconstitutional in 1935 in SCHECTER POULTRY CORPORATION V UNITED STATES, but the Wagner Act (also known as the NATIONAL LABOR RELATIONS ACT OF 1935) provided employees with even stronger guarantees.

National Institute for Occupational Safety and Health (NIOSH) The federal agency, established under the provisions of the Occupational Safety and Health Act of 1970, responsible for formulating new or improved occupational safety and health standards. Under the Occupational Safety and Health Act, NIOSH has the responsibility for conducting research designed to produce recommendations for new occupational safety and health standards. These recommendations are transmitted to the U.S. Department of Labor, which has the responsibility for the final setting, promulgation, and enforcement of the standards.

national interest 1. Those policy aims identified as the special concerns of a given nation. Violation of them either in the setting of domestic policy or in international negotiations would be perceived as damaging to the nation's future, both in domestic development and in international competition. The classic statement on this was made by Lord Palmerston in a House of Commons speech, March 1, 1848: "We have no eternal allies, and we have no perpetual enemies. Our interests are eternal, and those interests it is our duty to follow." President John F. Kennedy in a speech at Salt Lake City, September 26, 1963 confirmed this approach: "We must recognize that every nation determines its policies in terms of its own interests." President Charles de Gaulle of France was even more succinct when he said "No nation has friends—only interests" (*U.S. News & World Report*, September 19, 1966). **2.** In the context of foreign policy, the security of the state. Theorizing about the national interest is often traced back to NICCOLO MACHIAVELLI, who held that national advantage ought to be the goal of foreign policy. Secretary of State Charles E. Hughes is quoted in Charles A. Beard's *The Idea of National Interest* (1934) as saying: "Foreign policies are not built upon abstractions. They are the result of practical conceptions of national interest arising from some immediate exigency." More recently, the national interest has been held to have two aspects: (1) minimum requirements involving a country's physical, political, and cultural integrity; and (2) variables within the total context of foreign policy. Hans J. Morgenthau (1904–1980) is the international relations scholar most associated with the notion that a nation's foreign policy must further a realistic national interest and be divested of a crusading idealistic spirit. Consequently, he became one of the severest critics of American involvement in Vietnam.

National Labor Relations Act of 1935 (NLRA) Popularly known as the Wagner Act, this is the nation's principal labor relations law applying to all private sector interstate commerce, except railroad and airline operations (which are governed by the Railway Labor Act). The NLRA seeks to protect the rights of employees and employers, to encourage collective bargaining, and to eliminate stikes and other labor-management conflicts that are harmful to the general welfare. It states and defines the rights of employees to organize and to bargain collectively with their employers through representatives of their own choosing. To ensure this, the act establishes a procedure by which workers can exercise their choice at a secret ballot election conducted by the National Labor Relations Board. Furthermore, to protect the rights of employees and employers and to prevent labor disputes that would adversely affect the rights of the public, the Congress has defined certain practices of employers (such as bad faith bargaining) and unions (such as featherbedding, or requiring more workers than necessary to be paid for work) as unfair labor practices. The NLRA is administered and enforced principally by the National Labor Relations Board, which was created by the act.

In common usage, the National Labor Relations Act refers not to the act of 1935 but to the act as amended by the Labor-Management Relations (Taft-Hartley) Act of 1947 and the Labor-Management Reporting and Disclosure (Landrum-Griffin) Act of 1959. The Wagner Act limits its coverage to those businesses that are engaged in interstate commerce in a substantial way; it was originally intended that its passage would spur the creation of "little" Wagner acts in the states. The Wagner Act also excluded some forms of labor, most pointedly, household and farm workers—this was intended to protect the South against labor organization by blacks.

National Labor Relations Board (NLRB) The federal agency created by the National Labor Relations Act of 1935 that administers the nation's laws relating to labor relations in the private and nonprofit sectors. (Some public sector organizations are also under its jurisdiction, most notably the U.S. Postal Service.) The NLRB is vested with the power to safeguard employees' rights to organize, to determine through elections whether workers want unions as their bargaining representatives, and to prevent and remedy unfair labor practices.

National League of Cities (NLC) The Washington-based organization, formerly the American Municipal Association, founded in 1924 by and for reform-minded state municipal leagues. Membership was opened to individual cities in 1947, and the NLC now has more than 1,100 direct member cities. All U.S. cities with populations greater than 500,000 are NLC direct members, as are 87 percent of all cities with more than a 100,000 residents. The NLC advocates municipal interests before the Congress, the executive branch, and the federal agencies, and in state capitals across the nation where other matters of importance to cities are decided. *See also* PUBLIC INTEREST GROUPS.

National Mediation Board The federal agency that provides the railroad and airline industries with specific mechanisms for the adjustment of labor-management disputes; that is, the facilitation of agreements through collective bargaining, investigation of questions of representation, and the arbitration and establishment of procedures for emergency disputes. Created by a 1934 amendment to the Railway Labor Act, today the board's major responsibilities are: (1) the mediation of disputes over wages, hours, and working conditions that arise between rail and air carriers and organizations representing their employees; and (2) the investigation of representation disputes and the certification of employee organizations as representatives of crafts or of classes of carrier employees.

national objective Those fundamental aims, goals, or purposes of a nation—as opposed to the means for seeking those ends—toward which a policy is directed and resources are applied.

national of the United States 1. A citizen of the United States. **2.** A person who, though not a citizen of the United States, owes allegiance to the United States.

National Organization for Women (NOW) The leading public interest group for women's issues, headquartered in Washington, D.C.; founded in 1966. NOW is dedicated to using politics (it both endorses and opposes candidates), education, and legal action to improve the political and economic status of American women. Compared to the League of Women Voters, which is nonpartisan, NOW is aggressively partisan. Since the 1989 Supreme Court decision (*Webster v Reproductive Health Services*) NOW's membership has nearly doubled to 270,000. NOW is in the forefront of the PRO-CHOICE movement.

national planning 1. Comprehensive societal planning on a country-wide scale, as opposed to local or regional planning. **2.** Centralized, government-conducted or coordinated, economic planning and development. The concept has been highly controversial, because of its identification with socialistic and communistic approaches to governmental management of national economies. In the United States, concern for national planning really began with the development of national industries, like railroads, electric companies, and communications, whose needs for extensions beyond state and local regulatory boundaries called for some kind of national system of organization. In the 1980s, various approaches to national planning have been suggested for revitalizing the U.S. industrial economy. *Compare to* INDUSTRIAL POLICY.

national policy A course of action or a statement of guidance adopted by a national government in pursuit of its objectives in a specific area. Thus, there is often said to be a national policy for health, a national policy for education, and so on. All national policies are inherently vague and seldom fully achieved or even achievable. For example, the Employment Act of 1946 states it is national policy that the federal government promote full employment; and the Housing Act of 1949 states that all Americans should, as soon as possible, have a decent home.

National Railroad Adjustment Board The federal agency, created by a 1934 amendment to the Railway Labor Act, with the responsibility for deciding disputes growing out of grievances or out of the interpretation or application of agreements concerning rates of pay, rules, or working conditions in the railroad industry.

National Railroad Passenger Corporation The for-profit corporation, known as Amtrak, created by the Rail Passenger Service Act of 1970 to provide a balanced transportation system by improving and developing inter-city rail passenger service.

National Recovery Administration *See* NATIONAL INDUSTRIAL RECOVERY ACT OF 1933.

National Rifle Association The mass organization, created in 1871 to pro-mote marksmanship, which has become the preeminent "gun lobby." The NRA is generally against all efforts to legislate controls on all conventional weapons, believing any controls are a first step toward total confiscation of arms in the hands of citizens and a violation of the Second Amendment's "right to bear arms."

National Right to Life Committee The anti-abortion lobby founded in 1973 in direct response to the Supreme Court decision in ROE V WADE.

National Right to Work Committee An organization founded in 1955 that advocates legislation to prohibit all forms of forced union membership. Its National Right to Work Legal Defense Foundation, Inc., seeks to establish legal precedents protecting workers against compulsory unionism. Its head-quarters is located in Springfield, Virginia.

National Science Foundation (NSF) The federal agency created by the National Science Foundation Act of 1950 to (1) increase the nation's base of scientific knowledge and strengthen its ability to conduct scientific research; (2) encourage research in areas that can lead to improvements in economic growth, energy supply and use, productivity, and environmental quality; (3) promote international cooperation through science; and (4) develop and help implement science education programs. In its role as a leading supporter of all varieties of scientific research, NSF also has an important role in national science policy planning.

national security **1.** A condition of military or defense advantage. **2.** A favorable foreign relations position. **3.** A phrase used as justification to hide embarrassing or illegal activities on the part of a national government. *Compare to* CREDIBILITY GAP. **4.** A defense posture capable of successfully resisting hostile or destructive action from within or without, overt or covert. In this context Admiral Thomas Moorer's warning is apt: "The Xerox machine is one the biggest threats to national security ever devised" (*Time,* June 17, 1985).

National Security Act The 1947 law that combined the U.S. army, navy, and air force into the National Military Establishment. It also created the National Security Council and the Central Intelligence Agency. Amend-ments to the act in 1949 replaced the National Military Establishment with the present Department of Defense and placed the National Security Council in the Executive Office of the President.

national security adviser The assistant to the President for national secu-rity affairs, who directs the staff of the National Security Council within the Executive Office of the President. Since the 1960s, there has been a large degree of institutional competitiveness between the national security adviser and the secretary of State over control of foreign policymaking.

National Security Agency (NSA) The agency which handles the interception, decoding, and interpretation of virtually all signals intelligence, and indeed most of the other forms of electronic intelligence for the United States. Unlike the Central Intelligence Agency, it is not fully independent, but comes loosely under the control of the Department of Defense, although most of its employees are civilians.

National Security Council (NSC) The organization within the Executive Office of the President whose statutory function is to advise the President with respect to the integration of domestic, foreign, and military policies relating to national security. The actual members of the council are the President, the Vice President, and the secretaries of State and Defense. The council's staff is directed by the assistant to the President for national security affairs. In late 1986, revelations that the NSC was heavily involved with covert operations and functioning like a "little CIA" suggested that some NSC staff members went beyond their statutory authority in what came to be known as the IRAN-CONTRA AFFAIR. The ensuing scandal forced the Ronald Reagan administration to reorganize the NSC internally and substantially change its staff. Unlike the Department of Defense or the Department of State, which are independent government departments represented by cabinet secretaries fighting for their own departmental interests, the NSC is directly under presidential control. As a source of intelligence evaluation, as well as representing the President's own think-tank for developing policy in all military, strategic, and foreign affairs matters, the NSC is a natural rival to the Departments of State and Defense.

national service 1. The concept that a nation's youth should serve the state for a set time period in a military or civilian capacity prior to completing higher education and starting a career. **2.** A euphemism for conscription.

national supremacy The doctrine that national laws are superior to and take precedence over state laws. This is based upon (1) Article VI of the Constitution, which makes the Constitution the "supreme law of the land"; (2) landmark Supreme Court cases, such as *McCulloch v Maryland, Cohens v Virginia* and *Gitlow v New York*; and (3) the military outcome of the Civil War.

national technical means Methods of verification in arms control agreements; they are principally satellites which can relay sufficiently detailed photographs to reveal whether a country is building missile silos, concentrating forces, or engaging in any other activity in contravention of an arms control agreement.

National Transportation Safety Board (NTSB) The federal agency created by the Independent Safety Board Act of 1974 that seeks to assure that transportation in the United States is conducted safely. The board investigates accidents and makes recommendations to government agencies, the transportation industry, and others on safety measures and practices. The board also regulates the procedures for reporting accidents and promotes the safe transport of hazardous materials by government and private industry.

National Urban League The nonpartisan community service agency, also called the Urban League, founded in 1911 and devoted to the economic and social concerns of blacks and other minorities. The NAACP and the National Urban League are the two major membership organizations that lobby for the interests of blacks. While the NAACP has been much concerned with the overall promotion of equal rights by lobbying for civil rights law and testing cases in the federal courts, the National Urban League, headquartered in Washington (with 115 local units), has tended to concentrate its efforts on economic issues of importance to blacks.

nationalism The totality of the cultural, historical, linguistic, psychological, and social forces that pull a people together with a sense of belonging and shared values. This development tends to lead to the political belief that this national community of people and interests should have their own political order, independent from and equal to all of the other political communities in the world. The modern nation-state was forged from such nationalistic sentiment, and most of the wars of the last two centuries have been efforts to find relief for a frustrated nationalism. Nationalism has often been compared to patriotism. For example, novelist Richard Aldington wrote in *The Colonel's Daughter* (1931): "Patriotism is a lively sense of responsibility. Nationalism is a silly cock crowing on its own dunghill." And President Charles de Gaulle of France has said: "Patriotism is when love of your own people comes first; nationalism, when hate for people other than your own comes first" (*Life*, May 9, 1969). Albert Einstein may have best summed up the phenomenon when he wrote in *The World As I See It* (1934): "Nationalism is an infantile disease. It is the measles of mankind."

Nationalism, New *See* NEW NATIONALISM.

nationality The legal relation between a person and a state, which implies a duty of allegiance on the part of the person and an obligation for protection on the part of the state. Nationality is not necessarily related to national origin. A person gains nationality via CITIZENSHIP. The concept is not restricted to people; thus, corporations or ships have the nationality of the states that charter or register them.

Nationality Act of 1940 *See* AFROYIM V RUSK.

nationalization The taking over by government of a significant segment of a country's private-sector industry, land, transportation, and so on, usually with compensation to the former owners. Socialist governments tend to favor extensive nationalization. Indeed, the level of nationalization is an accurate measure of the degree of a nation's socialism. Ironically, even conservative and nonsocialist governments have resorted to nationalization, but in an effort to save a collapsing firm or service, rather than in ideological fervor. For example, the Conservative government of the United Kingdom nationalized part of Rolls-Royce in the early 1970s; and the U.S. government created Amtrak (officially known as the NATIONAL RAILROAD PASSEN-GER CORPORATION). *Compare to* EXPROPRIATION.

nationalization of the Bill of Rights *See* INCORPORATION.

nation-state 1. A country with defined and recognized boundaries whose citizens have common characteristics, such as race, religion, customs, and language. In this context, countries like the Soviet Union and South Africa are not nation-states. **2.** A country with defined and recognized boundaries and a diverse ethnic population (such as the United States) whose citizens share political ideals and practices to such an extent that unity and internal peace prevail.

NATO The North Atlantic Treaty Organization, also known as the Atlantic Alliance, consisting of the signatories of the 1949 North Atlantic Treaty, which unites Western Europe and North America in a commitment of mutual security. Article 5 states that "the parties agree that an armed attack against one or more of them in Europe or North America shall be considered an attack against them all." NATO was created at the height of the COLD WAR to contain Soviet expansionist tendencies. It seems to have worked, in that no member of NATO has ever become a Soviet satellite. A vital clause of the treaty, one which has come to be more politically sensitive than was originally expected, is Article 6, which limits the area in which treaty support of a member state is required. The simplest definition of this area is that it applies to attacks on the territories of the member states in Europe or North America, and their ships and aircraft when north of the Tropic of Cancer. Thus, it excludes areas such as the Indian Ocean and the Persian Gulf, where the U.S. nowadays tends to argue that vital NATO interests lie, and where it would like European NATO members to assist it in defense activities.

naturalization The granting of citizenship to someone who was previously an alien. Article I, Section 8 of the U.S. Constitution authorizes the Congress to enact uniform rules for naturalization. These rules are administered by the IMMIGRATION AND NATURALIZATION SERVICE.

natural law *See* LAW, NATURAL.

natural rights *See* INALIENABLE RIGHTS.

Neagle, In re (1890) The Supreme Court case that held that the President had the right to authorize protection for federal judicial officers without a need for specific statutory authorization. The President did not have to cite the specific law that allowed him to appoint a deputy federal marshal (in this case, David Neagle) to protect a federal judge, because such actions are covered under the President's broad constitutional mandate to "take care that the laws be faithfully executed." Such instances are covered by what is called the prerogative theory of presidential power, which holds that a President can act without legislative authorization because of his or her oath to "preserve, protect, and defend the Constitution of the United States." *See* PRESIDENCY, PREROGATIVE THEORY OF THE.

Near v Minnesota *See* FREE PRESS CLAUSE.

Nebraska Press Association v Stuart *See* GAG RULE.

necessary and proper clause That portion of Article I, Section 8 of the U.S. Constitution (sometimes called the *elastic clause*) that makes it possible for the Congress to enact all "necessary and proper" laws to carry out its responsibilities. Chief Justice John Marshall in MCCULLOCH V MARYLAND (1819) gave this clause broad effect when he wrote that "in the desire to remove all doubts respecting the right to legislate on that vast mass of incidental powers which must be involved in the Constitution if that instrument be not a splendid bauble" the framers had included the necessary and proper clause.

need to know A criterion used in security arrangements which requires that those who receive CLASSIFIED INFORMATION have to establish that they must have access to such information to perform their official duties. This system often fails because bureaucratic movement of secret items is often done by those who have no need to know at all. Thus, many espionage successes come from corrupting the messengers and clerks who have access to the kind of information in their departments which would be denied to senior officers in other departments on a "need to know" basis.

negative advertising **1.** Paid commercials or advertisements attacking a political opponent during a campaign. **2.** Any critical thing an opponent says about you in an ad. Your criticism of her, by contrast, is comparative advertising.

negatives, high *See* HIGH NEGATIVES.

neighborhood **1.** A specific geographic area. **2.** An informally designated subsection of a city having distinctive characteristics. **3.** A community. While the words neighborhood and community tend to be used interchangeably, neighborhood has more of a geographic focus—the residents share a common area. Community, in contrast, implies that the population consciously identifies with the community and works together for common ends.

neighborhood association An organization of residents in a common geographic area. In many American cities, neighbors in a particular area have formally organized into associations. These associations often play important political roles, lobbying local government to protect neighborhood interests at all levels of government. They often reflect a movement calling for a decentralization of local government. At the extreme are advocates for neighborhood self-sufficiency, who see economic and political power possible for poorer neighborhoods only to the extent they become independent of the dominant urban government.

neighborhood watch A crime prevention program where community groups aid police by making a neighborhood "crime conscious" and by reporting suspicious activities to police.

neo Something new about something old; a revival or a new variant of an older ideology.

neoconservatism A pragmatic form of traditional LIBERALISM that accepts many elements of the welfare state but rejects many of the statist tendencies of "big government"; that is basically supportive of current domestic policies but wanting a more aggressive, more idealistic foreign policy; and that espouses responsible free enterprise but differs from traditional CONSERVATISM and the new Right in its rejection of government regulation of personal behavior in areas of morality, school prayer, abortion, and so on. Neoconservatism, as an intellectual force, evolved in journals such as *Commentary* and *Public Interest* during the late 1960s and early 1970s by writers who were formerly considered liberals. *Compare to* RIGHT, NEW.

neoliberalism A movement of Democrats who increasingly reject the Democratic party's traditional liberal agenda in favor of more innovative approaches to social problems, incorporating ideas from across the political spectrum. Neoliberal ideas will often be found in *The Washington Monthly.* Indeed, its editor, Charles Peters, is usually credited with coining the word. According to Peters: "the liberal movement has to change and reject the liberal clichès and automatic responses of the past—for instance, pro-government and pro-union, anti-defense and anti-business—for what we like to call 'compassionate realism.' The conventional liberal position has been to spit on business. I've come to treasure the entrepreneur. I want to help the sick and needy, but somebody out there has to be making the money to pay the taxes to help support those programs" (*The New York Times*, April 22, 1982).

nepotism Any practice by which officeholders award positions to members of their immediate family. It is derived from the Latin *nepos*, meaning "nephew or grandson." The rulers of the medieval Church were often thought to give special preference to clerics' nephews in distributing churchly offices (at that time, "nephew" was a euphemism for an illegitimate son). In this regard, James H. Boren (1925–   ), president of the humorously oriented International Association of Professional Bureaucrats, has observed that "Einstein's theory of relativity, as practiced by congressmen, simply means getting members of your family on the payroll."

Neustadt, Richard E. *See* PRESIDENTIAL POWER.

neutral competence The concept that envisions a continuous, politically uncommitted cadre of bureaucrats at the disposal of elected or appointed political executives. *See also* HIRED GUN.

neutrality In international law, the attitude of impartiality adopted during periods of war by third nations toward belligerents (the warring countries) and recognized by the belligerents. Nations declaring themselves neutral expect to be accorded rights of access to the belligerent countries for purposes of travel and trade, although when that trade has included materials necessary to the survival or the military effectiveness of the belligerent nation, such access has led to frequent debates. Thus, declarations of neutrality have not been notably successful in preventing the ultimate involvement of neutral nations in the conflicts among belligerents.

new collar voters Those members of the baby boom generation caught between the blue-collar and white-collar world; they tend to hold technical and quasi-professional jobs that can be severely affected by shifts in the economy.

New Deal The domestic programs and policies of the administration of President Franklin D. Roosevelt (1933–1945). The phrase comes from his acceptance speech at the Democratic National Convention on July 2, 1932 when he said: "I pledge to you, I pledge myself, to a new deal for the American people." The New Deal marked the beginning of big government in America—its domestic programs would literally touch the lives of every citizen. And the political coalition it formed of the urban working classes, the farmers, the ethnic blocs, the southerners, and the liberal intellectuals still embraces important elements of the Democratic party. For New Deal legislation, *see* HUNDRED DAYS.

new federalism *See* FEDERALISM, NEW.

New Freedom The domestic programs and policies of the administration of President Woodrow Wilson (1913–1921). In contrast to Theodore Roosevelt's New Nationalism, which urged regulation as the basic government policy toward big business, Wilson's New Freedom (following ideas suggested by Supreme Court Justice Louis Brandeis) favored rigorous antitrust action to break up large industrial combinations. *See also* BRIEF, BRANDEIS.

New Frontier The policies and programs of the administration of President John F. Kennedy (1961–1963). He first used the phrase when he accepted his party's nomination at the Democratic National Convention on July 15, 1960, saying in part: "The New Frontier of which I speak is not a set of promises—it is a set of challenges. It sums up not what I intend to offer the American people, but what I intend to ask of them."

New Jersey plan The proposals put before the Constitutional Convention of 1787 by William Paterson of New Jersey, which called for equal representation of the states in a unicameral legislature. *Compare to* CONNECTICUT COMPROMISE.

new look *See* MASSIVE RETALIATION.

New Nationalism **1.** The domestic programs and policies urged by Theodore Roosevelt in his Progressive party campaign of 1912 against Woodrow Wilson and the Republican incumbent, William Howard Taft. The New Nationalism accepted the reality of large business combinations but called for their regulation in the public interest. *Compare to* NEW FREEDOM. **2.** A conservative movement toward a post-COLD WAR isolationism; it calls for the withdrawal of most American forces overseas.

new paradigm A vague term for the social agenda of the Bush administration, with the aim of fostering individual self-reliance by using market incentives to alleviate social problems. The phrase was coined by Bush White House aide James Pinkerton. When asked why the Bush domestic program was given this awkward title, he said: "My theory on the word paradigm is that it's like an old dog. It drools on you, it's ugly, but you remember it" (*Newsweek*, December 17, 1990).

new world order International alignments in the wake of the COLD WAR. This phrase, which has long been used in various contexts, gained widespread usage in 1990 as Eastern Europe broke away from the over-bearing influence of the Soviet Union. Then President George Bush, during the PERSIAN GULF WAR, made the phrase particularly his own. During an address to the nation as he announced the beginning of the war to liberate Kuwait on January 16, 1991, he said: "We have in this past year made great progress in ending the long era of conflict and cold war. We have before us the opportunity to forge for ourselves and for future generations a new world order, a world where the rule of law, not the law of the jungle, governs the conduct of nations." While the phrase was denounced by *The New York Times* in an editorial (January 26, 1991) as "an unfortunate phrase, reminiscent of Nazi sloganeering," it seems to have stuck and become the very definition of the Bush Administration foreign policy goals.

New York Times Magazine v Sullivan (1964) The Supreme Court case that unanimously held that a state cannot, under the First and Fourteenth amendments, award damages to a public official for defamatory falsehood relating to his or her official conduct unless the official proves "actual malice"—that the statement was made with the knowledge of its falsity or with reckless disregard of whether it was true or false. Justice William J. Brennan, Jr., in the Court's opinion, wrote that the case had to be considered "against the background of a profound national commitment to the principle that debate on public issues should be uninhibited, robust, and wide-open, and that it may well include vehement, caustic and sometimes unpleasantly sharp attacks on government and public officials. . . . Neither factual error nor defamatory content suffices to remove the constitutional shield from criticism of official conduct."

New York Times v United States *See* FREE PRESS CLAUSE.

Newlands Reclamation Act of 1902 The federal law that provided that funds from the sale of public lands would be used for irrigation and reclamation projects. This was one of the essential pieces of legislation in the development of the CONSERVATION MOVEMENT.

news advisory An announcement to the media that a newsworthy event is forthcoming; for example, a news conference or the release of a statement.

news conference *See* PRESS CONFERENCE.

news management **1.** The informal efforts of an administration to direct and control the reporting of its activities by the news media. **2.** The use of professional public relations staffs by political and administrative leaders who seek extensive media coverage and a specific media image. News management includes scheduling press conferences in time to make the evening news broadcasts, denying (or granting) access to unfavorable (or favorable) reporters, allowing (or not allowing) reporters to cover military stories, planting stories with favored reporters, and anything else that makes it easier or harder for honest and fair news coverage to proceed. All administrations at all jurisdictional levels attempt to manage news to one extent or another. They will usually deny that they are doing so. According to journalist Timothy Crouse in *The Boys on the Bus* (1972): "Every President from Washington on came to recognize the press as a natural enemy, and eventually tried to manipulate it and muzzle it."

Nineteenth Amendment   The 1920 amendment to the U.S. Constitution that gave women the right to vote. *Compare to* SUFFRAGE.

Ninth Amendment   The amendment to the U.S. Constitution that reads, "the enumeration in the Constitution, of certain rights, shall not be construed to deny or disparage others retained by the people." This amendment reflects the framers' view that the powers of government are limited by the INALIENABLE RIGHTS of the people and that, by expressly enumerating certain rights of the people in the Constitution, the framers did not intend to recognize that government had unlimited power to invade other rights. Indeed, in *Griswold v Connecticut*, some justices sought to change the amendment's status as a rule of construction to one of positive affirmation and protection of the right to privacy.

Nixon Doctrine   The U.S. foreign policy enunciated by President Richard M. Nixon at a press conference on Guam on July 25, 1969, that sought to minimize the role of the United States as world policeman. The central thesis of the doctrine is that "America cannot—and will not—conceive all the plans, design all the programs, execute all the decisions and undertake all the defense of the free nations of the world. We will help where it makes a real difference and is considered in our interest." Former secretary of State Dean Acheson said: "The 'Nixon Doctrine' is not a great contribution to the enlightenment of the world. It was a polite way of saying, 'Some of my predecessors made stupid mistakes, and I am trying to right them'" (*The Washington Post*, December 10, 1970).

Nixon in China Syndrome   The ability of someone who seemingly has a great stake in something to change or reform it more effectively than someone else who might have been for the reform all along. Because it was Nixon—the vehement anticommunist who fought all his political life to deny recognition of "Red" China—who initiated the rapprochement with China, there was far less criticism than if the initiative had been taken by almost anyone else.

Nixon, Richard M. (1913–   )   The only man ever to be forced to resign (in 1974) from the office of President of the United States in the face of almost certain impeachment by the House on charges of "high crimes and misdemeanors." In response to the scandals of WATERGATE, the House Committee on the Judiciary voted on July 27, 1974 to approve articles of impeachment which concluded: "Richard M. Nixon has acted in a manner contrary to his trust as President and subversive of constitutional government, to the great prejudice of the cause of law and justice, and to the manifest injury of the people of the United States. Wherefore Richard M. Nixon, by such conduct, warrants impeachment and trial, and removal from office." Nixon resigned before the full house could act on the committee's recommendation; so technically he was never impeached.

After navy service in World War II, Nixon was elected to the House of Representatives (from California) in 1946 and 1948. As a member of the House Un-American Activities Committee, he developed a reputation as a virulent anticommunist. In 1950, California sent him to the Senate. The Republicans selected him as Dwight D. Eisenhower's vice presidential running mate in 1952. After being twice elected Vice President (1952 and 1956), he ran as the Republican nominee for President in 1960 against the Democratic candidate, John F. Kennedy, and lost by a narrow margin. He returned to California and ran for governor in 1962. Soundly defeated, he announced his retirement from politics. But in the wake of public dissatisfaction with the Vietnam War, he won the Republican nomination and the presidency in 1968.

Nixon had some positive achievements in foreign policy, such as winding down U.S. involvement in Vietnam, opening diplomatic relations with Communist China, and accomplishing DÉTENTE with the Soviet Union; and in domestic policy, by signing initiatives from the Democratically controlled Congress on environmental policy, workplace safety, and public service jobs. But his political duplicity will mark his place in history. His second-term efforts to centralize management of the federal bureaucracy in the White House would, had they not been stopped by the Watergate affair, have transformed American national government. Nixon was able to avoid being tried for his Watergate crimes because his hand-picked successor, Gerald R. Ford, granted him a pardon for any crimes he may have committed while in office.

Even though he disgraced himself in office, the republic owes Nixon a debt of gratitude because on two occasions he had it in his power to cause great harm to his country; in each instance and at great personal sacrifice he did the honorable thing. In 1960 his defeat to President John F. Kennedy was so close and so tainted by election fraud that he had every right to contest it. But he chose not to do so because it would have thrown the country into political turmoil. Again, during Watergate he could have accepted a trial in the Senate and possibly dragged it out for the remaining two years of his term. But rather than put the nation's political institutions through the strain, he resigned. This does not mitigate his crimes in office, but it does show that honor puts limits on how much anyone will hurt their country for self-interest. For Nixon's memoirs, see Richard Nixon, *RN: The Memoirs of Richard Nixon* (1978). *See also* CHECKERS SPEECH; STAND PAT; UNITED STATES V NIXON.

NLRB *See* NATIONAL LABOR RELATIONS BOARD.

no first use A strategic policy, publicly proclaimed, of not being the first to use nuclear weapons in a potential war. The United States has never proclaimed this as a policy. Some argue that such a policy would be desirable, because it would help prevent an escalation to nuclear war.

nolo contendere A Latin phrase meaning "no contest"; a defendant's formal answer in court to a charge in a complaint or an indictment, stating that he or she will not contest the charge but neither admits guilt nor claims innocence. Both guilty and *nolo contendere* pleas can be followed by a judgment of conviction without a trial and by a prison sentence. The main difference lies in their potential use as evidence in a related civil suit. During any subsequent civil proceeding, a guilty plea can constitute evidence that relevant facts have been admitted; a *nolo contendere* plea cannot. *Compare to* AGNEW, SPIRO T.

nomination 1. The announcement of a name or slate of names for action by any governing body charged with selection. **2.** An appointment to federal office by the executive branch of the U.S. government, subject to Senate confirmation. **3.** A political party's designation of a particular person as their candidate for a particular public office. *Compare to* DRAFT.

normalcy President Warren G. Harding's word for the restoration of America to "normal" conditions after the trauma of World War I and the postwar RED SCARE. The word became a subject of ridicule, as was Harding, and took on a connotation of reaction or extreme conservatism.

norms 1. Average or standard behaviors for members of a group. The norm is what is normal. **2.** The socially enforced requirements and expectations about basic responsibilities, behavior, and thought patterns of members in their organizational roles. *Compare to* RECIPROCITY. **3.** In psychological testing, tables of scores from a large number of people who have taken a particular test.

North American Free Trade Agreement (NAFTA) The treaty that will, if ratified, create a common market between the United States, Canada and Mexico. After the United States and Canada first signed a free trade agreement in 1989, intensive discussions began on the desirability of including Mexico. A North American trading bloc seemed a natural counterweight to the economic might of the new European Community to the East and Japan to the West. In late 1992 the administrations of U.S. President George Bush, Canadian Prime Minister Brian Mulroney, and Mexican President Carlos Salinas de Gortari approved the treaty. NAFTA will gradually eliminate all trade barriers in North America if it is ratified by the respective legislatures.

North Atlantic Treaty Organization *See* NATO

no-show jobs Government positions for which the incumbent collects a salary but is not required to report to work. While no-show jobs are illegal, they are not uncommon.

notary public A semi-public official who can administer oaths, certify the validity of documents, and perform a variety of formal witnessing duties. A *notarius* was a person who took notes during legal actions in ancient Rome. Since then, notarization, a notary's certification of documents, has been a required part of legal proceedings in all Western European-oriented countries. Almost four million citizens are notaries in the United States. State requirements for notaries vary greatly. Some states require examinations; others demand only the endorsement of a small number of local citizens. Many judges and state legislators are EX OFFICIO notaries. Three states (Florida, Maine, and North Carolina) allow notaries to perform marriages.

NOW *See* NATIONAL ORGANIZATION FOR WOMEN.

NRC **1.** National Republican Committee **2.** NUCLEAR REGULATORY COMMISSION.

NSC *See* NATIONAL SECURITY COUNCIL.

NSF *See* NATIONAL SCIENCE FOUNDATION.

Nuclear Non-Proliferation Treaty The 1968 treaty on the nonproliferation of nuclear weapons, signed by over 115 nations. It calls for nuclear nations not to transfer nuclear weapons and for nonnuclear nations not to adopt them. The uses of nuclear energy for peaceful purposes are not covered by the treaty. The treaty has been of little use. The nonnuclear powers who had any desire to build such weapons simply refused to sign it. And some who did sign it have ignored it.

nuclear parity *See* PARITY, NUCLEAR.

Nuclear Regulatory Commission (NRC) The federal agency that licenses and regulates the uses of nuclear energy to protect the public health and safety and the environment. It does this by licensing individuals and companies to build and operate nuclear reactors and to own and use nuclear materials. The NRC makes rules and sets standards for these licenses and also inspects the activities of the licensed individuals and companies to ensure that they do not violate the safety rules of the commission. The NRC was created in 1975 under provisions of the Energy Reorganization Act of 1974 and supplanted the Atomic Energy Commission (AEC), which had performed similar functions since 1946. The AEC was created to separate civilian and military uses of nuclear energy. But this battle has effectively been lost now that the NRC has responsibilities for both military and civilian uses of nuclear power.

nuclear winter A theoretical climatic change caused by the effects of smoke from a full nuclear exchange among the superpowers. Because the smoke would blot out most of the earth's sunlight for weeks or months after a nuclear war, most plant and animal life that survived the initial blast would be subsequently destroyed.

nullification *See* JOHN C. CALHOUN.

Nuremberg defense The now traditional excuse of those caught performing illegal acts for their political or military superiors: "I was only following

O

OASDI *See* OLD AGE, SURVIVORS, AND DISABILITY INSURANCE.

obscenity *See* ROTH V UNITED STATES.

obstructing justice Committing any unlawful act with the intent to hinder (or obstruct) a criminal investigation or trial. Examples include coaching witnesses to lie or destroying evidence. The most famous denial of obstruction of justice occurred during the WATERGATE scandal when President Richard M. Nixon told a nationally televised news conference on November 17, 1973: "In all of my years in public life, I have never profited, never profited from public service—I have earned every cent. And in all of my years in public life, I have never obstructed justice. And I think, too, that I could say that in my years in public life, that I welcome this kind of examination, because people have got to know whether or not their President is a crook. Well, I am not a crook. I have earned everything I have got."

O'Connor, Sandra Day (1930–) The Arizona judge who in 1981 was appointed by President Ronald Reagan to be the first female justice on the Supreme Court.

Occupational Safety and Health Act of 1970 The federal government's basic legislation, also called the Williams-Steiger Act, for providing for the health and safety of employees on the job. The act created the Occupational Safety and Health Review Commission, the Occupational Safety and Health Administration, and the National Institute for Occupational Safety and Health.

Occupational Safety and Health Administration (OSHA) A federal agency established by the Occupational Safety and Health Act of 1970. The OSHA develops and promulgates occupational safety and health standards, develops and issues regulations, conducts investigations and inspections to determine the status of compliance with safety and health standards and regulations, and issues citations and proposes penalties for noncompliance.

Occupational Safety and Health Review Commission (OSHRC) An independent adjudicatory agency established by the Occupational Safety and Health Act of 1970 to adjudicate enforcement actions initiated under the act when they are contested by employers, employees, or representatives of employees.

October surprise 1. A development so late in a campaign that the opposition does not have time to adequately respond to it before the election. **2.** A reference to the allegation that the Reagan-Bush campaign of 1980 somehow made a secret deal with Iran to defer the release of American hostages until after the presidential election of that year. The IRANIAN HOSTAGE CRISIS was one of the major factors in Jimmy Carter's defeat for reelection. In

1991 the Congress started a formal investigation into the allegation. In January 1993 a report of the House Foreign Affairs Committee concluded that there was no credible evidence to support the allegation.

off-budget federal agencies Agencies, federally owned in whole or in part, whose transactions have been excluded from the budget totals under provisions of law (e.g., the Federal Financing Bank). The fiscal activities of these agencies are not included in either budget authority or outlay totals but are presented in an appendix to the federal budget.

off the record A politician's statement that is not to be quoted or attributed in the media. Behind every "off the record" statement is the implied threat that the speaker has the right to deny ever having said it. This is in contrast to "on the record" statements, which are intended to be made public.

off year 1. Any year in which there is not a presidential election. **2.** A year in which a politician loses an election. **3.** Any year in which a government's tax revenues decline.

office 1. A place of work. **2.** A government agency. **3.** A government job. **4.** A patronage appointment. President Woodrow Wilson said on May 15, 1916: "Every man who takes office in Washington either grows or swells, and when I give a man an office, I watch him carefully to see whether he is swelling or growing."

Office of Economic Opportunity The anti-poverty agency within the Executive Office of the President created by the Economic Opportunity Act of 1964; it was the main combat arm of the WAR ON POVERTY. It was abolished in 1975 when what was left of its functions were melded into other agencies.

Office of Federal Contract Compliance Programs (OFCCP) The agency within the Department of Labor delegated to ensure (1) that there is no employment discrimination by government contractors because of race, religion, color, sex, or national origin; and (2) that there is affirmative action to employ Vietnam era veterans and handicapped workers.

Office of Management and Budget (OMB) The office that supplanted the Bureau of the Budget in the Executive Office of the President on July 1, 1970. The OMB (1) assists the President in the preparation of the budget and the formulation of fiscal policy; (2) assists in developing coordinating mechanisms to expand interagency cooperation; (3) assists the President by reviewing the organizational structure and management procedures of the executive branch to ensure that they are capable of producing the intended results; (4) supervises and controls the administration of the budget; (5) clears and coordinates departmental advice on proposed legislation and makes recommendations about presidential action on legislative enactments; (6) assists in the development of regulatory reform proposals; and (7) assists in the consideration, clearance, and, where necessary, the preparation of proposed executive orders and proclamations. The Director of OMB is second only to the President in sheer political clout, for the agency is the tool by which the President exercises power over every facet of the Executive Branch.

Office of Personnel Management (OPM) The central personnel agency of the federal government, created by the Civil Service Reform Act of 1978. The OPM took over many of the responsibilities of the U.S. Civil Service Commission, including central examining and employment operations, personnel investigations, personnel program evaluation, executive development, and training. The OPM administers the retirement and insurance programs for federal employees and exercises management leadership in labor relations and affirmative action. As the central personnel agency, the OPM develops policies governing civilian employment in executive branch agencies and in certain agencies of the legislative and judicial branches. It also delegates certain personnel powers to agency heads, subject to OPM standards and review.

Office of Science and Technology Policy The unit within the Executive Office of the President, created by the National Science and Technology Policy, Organization, and Priorities Act of 1976, that serves as a source of scientific, engineering, and technological analysis and judgment for the President with respect to major policies, plans, and programs of the federal government.

Office of Technology Assessment (OTA) The legislative branch's support office created by the Technology Assessment Act of 1972 to help the Congress anticipate and plan for the consequences of uses of technology. The OTA provides an independent and objective source of information about the impacts, both beneficial and adverse, of technological applications, and identifies policy alternatives for technology-related issues.

Office of Thrift Supervision The office within the Department of the Treasury that charters and monitors the "thrift" industry—that is, savings and loan associations.

officialese *See* GOBBLEDYGOOK.

Old Age, Survivors, and Disability Insurance (OASDI) A federal program created by the Social Security Act that taxes both workers and employers to pay benefits to retired and disabled people, their dependents, widows, widowers, and children of deceased workers. *Compare to* SOCIAL SECURITY.

Older Americans Act of 1965 (OAA) The federal law that aids and encourages state and local programs to meet the needs of senior citizens by providing community service jobs for the elderly, supporting volunteer programs by and on behalf of the elderly, forbidding age discrimination in programs supported by federal funds, and so on. The OAA is administered mainly by the Administration on Aging of the U.S. Department of Health and Human Services.

old guard **1.** Very conservative or REACTIONARY Republicans. **2.** The most determined STALWARTS of a political party; the diehards of any organization.

OLIGARCHY

The phrase refers to Napoleon's Imperial Guard at the Battle of Waterloo. When asked to surrender, legend has it that they responded: "The guard dies but does not surrender." While their exact words have often been disputed by historians, there is no dispute that they futilely died. An old guard is often known by its efforts to slow down, or transform, inevitable changes.

oligarchy 1. Rule by a political elite who govern mainly for the benefit of themselves and their class. **2.** Rule by a self-appointed elite, who wield informal but effective power because of wealth or position. **3.** Minority rule.

OMB *See* OFFICE OF MANAGEMENT AND BUDGET.

ombudsman/ombudswomen An official whose job is to investigate the complaints of the citizenry concerning public services and to assure that these complaints will reach the attention of those officials at levels above the original providers of service. The word is Swedish for "a representative of the king." Ombudsmen and ombudswomen are now found in many countries at a variety of jurisdictional levels. Many of their functions in American state, and local, and national governments are performed by members of their respective legislatures as CASEWORK.

Omnibus Claims Bill *See* CALENDAR, PRIVATE.

on the record *See* OFF THE RECORD.

one man, one vote *See* REYNOLDS V SIMS.

one-minute speeches Addresses by House of Representative members at the beginning of a legislative day. The speeches may cover any subject but are limited strictly to one minute. By unanimous consent, members may also be recognized to address the House for longer periods after completion of all legislative business for the day. Senators, by unanimous consent, are permitted to make speeches of a predetermined length during MORNING HOUR.

open convention A national nominating convention that starts without any candidate having a lock on the nomination because of the possession of a sufficient number of committed delegates.

open-end program An ENTITLEMENT PROGRAM for which eligibility requirements are determined by law (e.g., Medicaid). Actual fiscal obligations and the resultant outlays are limited only by the number of eligible persons who apply for benefits and the benefits paid to them.

open-market operations The purchase and sale in the open market by the Federal Reserve System of various securities, chiefly marketable federal government securities, for the purpose of implementing Federal Reserve monetary policy. Open-market operations, one of the most flexible instruments of monetary policy, affect the reserves of member banks and thus the supply of money and the availability and cost of credit.

open seat An open district (*see* DISTRICT, OPEN).

opinion 1. Someone's beliefs on an issue. *See also* PUBLIC OPINION. **2.** The formal announcement of a decision by a court, often giving the reasons for the decision. While a judge can deliver an opinion about any aspect of a case at almost any time, an opinion usually appears only in connection with final decisions in appeal proceedings. In the United States, the most significant legal opinions have been those of the Supreme Court. While the decisions are made by the justices, the supporting opinions are often a collective effort with their law clerks. Retired Justice Lewis Powell explains how he and his clerks would write an opinion: "I would write a memorandum myself in which I summarized how I thought the case should be decided and how the opinion should be written. I would give that to a law clerk who would then give me what we call a bench memo. If the case was assigned to me to write, that law clerk in all probability would submit in triple-space form a draft of an opinion that reflected the views I had already set forth. Before a draft opinion was circulated to the other Justices, all four of my law clerks would review it, and we would all work it over very carefully" (*Time*, July 9, 1990).

opinion, advisory A statement by a judge or regulatory agency about a question that has been informally submitted. The U.S. federal courts never issue advisory opinions. The International Court of Justice (The World Court) does. Article 96 of the United Nations Charter states that any organ of the UN may ask the World Court for an advisory opinion on a dispute. The Court has no obligation to issue advisory opinions. And should the same case come before the Court for actual settlement, a previous advisory opinion is not binding on the Court. *Compare to* DECLARATORY JUDGMENT.

opinion, concurring The opinion of a judge who agrees with a decision, but who explains his or her agreement on grounds different from those used by the other judges.

opinion day The day, usually a Monday, on which the Supreme Court gives its opinions in open court on cases it has considered.

opinion, dissenting *See* OPINION, MINORITY.

opinion, extended A separate opinion that partly concurs and partly dissents from an opinion of the court.

opinion, full A lengthy written opinion presenting in detail the reasons and reasoning leading to a decision.

opinion leaders 1. The minority of the population who take an active interest in political affairs, who regularly talk about political issues with their friends, coworkers, and family, and who therefore tend to influence public opinion. In what is called the *two-step flow theory*, opinion leaders function as mediators between the news media and the public. But as access to news via television becomes more and more pervasive, people tend to rely less and less on these traditional leaders and more and more on the media itself. **2.** Those political figures who are able to significantly influence the attitudes of the general public on political issues. **3.** Journalists and the experts journalists tend to consult on specialized matters, who often have the public's attention via the media to state their opinions on the facts at hand.

opinion, majority The opinion of most of the judges hearing a case. The majority opinion is the opinion of the court. In a Supreme Court case, the chief justice, if he or she has voted with the majority, designates the justice who will write the majority opinion; if the chief justice has voted with the minority, then the senior associate justice designates who will write the opinion.

opinion, memorandum A brief written statement of the reasons for a decision, without detailed explanation.

opinion, minority The *dissenting opinion* of one or more judges who disagree with the decision of a court. On the Supreme Court, minority opinions have sometimes been extremely significant because they have so often established the intellectual framework for subsequent reversals of decisions. Chief Justice Charles Evans Hughes (1862–1948) observed that dissents are "appeals to the brooding spirit of the law, to the intelligence of another day." Associate Justice Felix Frankfurter (1882–1965) concluded that "in this Court, dissents have gradually become majority opinions." Associate Justice William O. Douglas said: "Dissent is a tradition of this Court... A person writing a dissent is free-wheeling. When someone is writing for the Court, he is hoping to get eight others to agree with him, so many of the majority opinions are rather stultified" (*The New York Times*, October 29, 1973).

opinion, per curiam An opinion issued by a court as a whole, without indication of individual authorship.

opinion poll *See* PUBLIC OPINION SURVEY.

opinion vote The coalition vote of the majority of judges on an appeals court, whose opinion becomes law.

OPM *See* OFFICE OF PERSONNEL MANAGEMENT.

ordinance A regulation enacted by a local government. It has the force of law but must be in compliance with state and national laws. It is issued under the authority derived from a grant of power (such as a city charter) from a sovereign entity (such as a state).

original intent What the 1789 framers of the U.S. Constitution really meant; what they intended the government to be, as discerned, by their words, phrases, and sentences used in the document. "The original intent of the framers" is a debatable issue, often espoused by STRICT CONSTRUCTIONISTS, and used as a CODE WORD (or phrase) for conservative attempts to reverse Supreme Court decisions on social policy and individual rights. *Compare to* LEGISLATIVE INTENT.

original jurisdiction *See* JURISDICTION, ORIGINAL.

origination clause That portion of Article I, Section 7 of the U.S. Constitution that requires that "all bills for raising revenue [meaning taxes] shall originate in the House of Representatives."

other body 1. A reference to the Senate by a member of the House of Representatives. 2. A reference to the House by a member of the Senate.

outing The intentional public exposure of someone, often a man in political life, who is secretly homosexual. It has its origins in the phrase "come out of the closet," which is what homosexuals do when they voluntarily tell the public of their sexual orientation.

outlays What a government spends over a given time period; this includes checks issued, interest accrued on debts and on other payments, less refunds and reimbursements.

Oval Office 1. The oval-shaped White House office of the President of the United States. Although the Oval Office was built in the 1930s as part of an expansion of the west wing of the White House, the term did not come into general usage until the Richard M. Nixon administration. Until then the President's office was just called the President's office. **2.** The presidency itself, as in "The order comes from the Oval Office."

overbreadth doctrine The judicial policy that holds that laws may be declared unconstitutional because of their overbreadth (meaning that they reach too far) if they attempt to punish activities protected by the Constitution (such as free speech) even as they seek to engage in otherwise legitimate regulation. For example, in *Village of Schaumburg v Citizens for a Better Environment* (1980) the Supreme Court struck down a local ordinance prohibiting door-to-door solicitations from organizations not using at least 75 percent of their collections for charitable purposes. While a laudable effort to curtail charitable fraud, this ordinance went overboard in also prohibiting legitimate political organizations who didn't meet the 75 percent test from making door-to-door calls.

overclass The new rich created by the Reagan Administration's policies that benefited them at the expense of the middle class and poor. *Compare to* UNDERCLASS.

oversight, congressional The total means by which the U.S. Congress monitors the activities of executive branch agencies to determine if the laws are being faithfully executed. Oversight takes many forms. The most obvious are the annual congressional hearings on agency budget requests, in which agency activities have to be justified to thesatisfaction of the Congress. But any member of the Congress or a congressional committee can instigate an investigation. Most of these investigations are small matters properly falling under the rubric of CASEWORK. But if something more significant turns up worthy of a larger inquiry, an appropriate committee or subcommittee always has the right to initiate a further examination.

The entire Congress is in effect a permanently sitting grand jury always waiting to learn of improper acts by executive branch agencies so that hearings can be launched and witnesses called. Some members of the Congress are so zealous in their oversight concerns that they will go to the trouble of traveling all over the world (at government expense) to see how federal programs and policies are operating. These visits are derisively called junkets, but they are an important part of the oversight process. Some members of the Congress simply cannot understand why it is necessary to vote for money for American forces in NATO unless they first visit Europe and make a thorough investigation of the situation.

oversight, political The use of the legislative oversight function for partisan advantage. Political oversight often happens when the executive and legislative branches of a government are controlled by opposing parties, when its purpose may be to embarrass the administration. Of course, whether an oversight action is simply in the interest of good government or a play in a game of partisan one-upmanship is in the eye of the beholder.

P

PAC *See* POLITICAL ACTION COMMITTEE.

pack journalism News coverage, particularly political, that is essentially the same in all media outlets; the tendency of reporters to all have the same insights and pursue the same stories, often following the lead of a breaking story developed by one reporter who broke out of the "pack."

PADs Program Associate Directors; the chief staff aides to the Director of the OFFICE OF MANAGEMENT AND BUDGET.

page **1.** A young attendant to nobility. In medieval times pages were youths in training for knighthood. **2.** Any uniformed attendant who carries messages, runs errands, etc. **3.** A congressional patronage position for about 100 high school students each year. They attend classes early in the day; then mainly run errands for members of Congress for the rest of the day. They are supervised by the House Door Keeper in the House of Representatives and the Sergeant-at-arms in the Senate.

Paine, Thomas (1737–1809) The Revolutionary War pamphleteer whose *Common Sense* (1776) became a sensational "bestseller" and helped crystallize sentiment for a total break with England. As a member of George Washington's army during the darkest days of retreat at Valley Forge, Paine in the first of a series of pamphlets entitled *The American Crisis* (1776) wrote his immortal justification of why the Americans should persevere with the war effort:

These are the times that try men's souls. The summer soldier and the sunshine patriot will, in this crisis, shrink from the service of his country; but he that stands it *now*, deserves the love and thanks of man and woman. Tyranny, like hell, is not easily conquered; yet we have this consolation with us, that the harder the conflict, the more glorious the triumph. What we obtain too cheap, we esteem too lightly; 'tis dearness only that gives everything its value. Heaven knows how to put a proper price upon its goods; and it would be strange indeed, if so celestial an article as *freedom* should not be highly rated.

pair Historically, an informal agreement between two lawmakers on opposite sides to withhold their votes on roll-call votes so that the absence of either will not affect the outcome of the recorded vote. In this way, opposing viewpoints cancel each other out. Legislators are often paired on controversial issues when they, for political reasons, may not want to have their votes put on record. Pairing allows them to both avoid the issue and not tip the balance of the vote in either direction. There are several types of pairs: a "live pair" publicly indicates how a legislator would have voted; a "general pair" gives no such indication; a "special pair" applies to all votes on a given subject. *Compare to* VOTE TRADING.

palace guard Once upon a time, the armed guards who protected the body of the king; now the staff aides who protect a President's (or any high executive's) time and sometimes worsen the inherent isolation of the office.

Palmer raids *See* RED SCARE.

Panama Canal treaties The 1977 documents signed by the Republic of Panama and the United States that transferred ownership of the Panama Canal from the United States to Panama by the year 2000 and that guaranteed the permanent neutrality and operation of the canal. The treaties were ratified by a plebiscite in Panama in 1977 and by the U.S. Senate in 1978.

Panama intervention The U.S. invasion of Panama, beginning on the night of December 19–20, 1989, to rid that nation of its dictator's rule. General Manuel Antonio Noriega became the sole dictator of Panama in 1983. In February 1988 he was indicted in Miami by a federal grand jury on drug charges. After diplomatic efforts failed to remove him from power, Noriega escalated tensions throughout the latter part of 1989. On December 15, 1989 he declared that Panama was in a state of war with the United States. The following day his troops killed an American Marine, and four days after that President George Bush ordered American troops to forcibly remove the Noriega regime from power. Noriega escaped immediate capture and hid in the Vatican Embassy in Panama City. After 10 days in the embassy he surrendered to American Drug Enforcement Agency personnel and was immediately taken to the United States to face criminal charges in connection with his drug activities. The invasion was widely popular with both the American and Panamanian public, and came about after gross abuses of human rights and the electoral process in Panama and repeated efforts by the United States to resolve the problem by diplomatic means. Columnist George Will assured the nation that "this intervention is a good-neighbor policy. America's role in Panama. . . is an act of hemispheric hygiene" (*The Washington Post National Weekly*, December 25–31, 1989). William Safire's psychological analysis concluded: "This was not the result of an accused wimp's need to prove himself macho; we've had too much of that personal-motive pap since Lyndon Johnson" (*The New York Times*, December 21, 1989).

Panama Refining Co. v Ryan (1935) The Supreme Court case invalidating Section 9(c) of the NATIONAL INDUSTRIAL RECOVERY ACT OF 1933, which allowed the President to exclude from interstate commerce oil produced in excess of state regulations. The Court held that the section was an unconstitutional delegation of legislative power to the executive in contravention of the separation of powers. This was the first NEW DEAL statute rejected by the Court as an unconstitutional delegation of power. Known as the hot oil case, because it involved oil illegally produced or withdrawn from storage, it is considered a harbinger of the Court's negative attitude toward the New

Deal that would be more fully expressed in SCHECHTER POULTRY CORPORATION V THE UNITED STATES.

panic What economic RECESSIONS and DEPRESSIONS were called in the nineteenth century—because the word was so descriptive of the behavior of many people.

paper tiger A Chinese expression for someone or some institution that is not as strong or powerful as appearances or reputation would suggest.

paramilitary forces 1. Large local police departments. 2. Forces or groups which are distinct from the regular armed forces of any country, but resembling them in organization, equipment, training, or mission.

paranoid style The recurrent belief by various differing American political groups that there is a nationwide conspiracy against them. Examples include homosexuals who believe that AIDS was "invented" by the government to destroy them; blacks who believe that the drug epidemic is encouraged by the government to hurt them; and politicians who believe that a communist conspiracy is on the verge of taking over the country. The concept was first identified by historian Richard Hofstadter (1916–1970). He wrote in his book *The Paranoid Style in American Politics* (1965): "There is a vital difference between the paranoid spokesman in politics and the clinical paranoiac: although they both tend to be overheated, oversuspicious, overaggressive, grandiose, and apocalyptic in expression, the clinical paranoid sees the hostile and conspiratorial world in which he feels himself to be living as directed specifically against him; whereas the spokesman of the paranoid style finds it directed against a nation, a culture, a way of life whose fate affects not himself alone but millions of others."

parasite Members of society who live off the efforts of others without making any meaningful contribution to society themselves. Political cynics often call politicians parasites.

pardon An executive's granting of a release from the legal consequences of a criminal act. This may occur before or after indictment or conviction. The U.S. President's power to pardon people for federal offenses is absolute except for convictions in impeachment cases. A pardon prior to indictment stops all criminal proceedings. This is what happened when President Gerald Ford pardoned Richard M. Nixon in 1974 for all offenses that he "has committed or may have committed or taken part in while President." Ford's forgiving of Nixon's complicity in the WATERGATE scandals, for which several dozen of Nixon's associates went to jail, probably cost Ford the presidential election in 1976. State governors have comparable powers to pardon individuals for state crimes; but some governors must share their pardoning authority with the state senate or a parole board.

pardon, absolute A pardon that restores a person to his or her legal position prior to the crime in question.

pardon, conditional A pardon that becomes effective only when the person involved meets stipulated conditions.

pardon, general *See* AMNESTY.

parish **1.** The term for a county in Louisiana. **2.** An ecclesiastical district; a local church and its members. **3.** An administrative district in some countries.

parity Equality; essential equivalence.

parity, effective A measure of the overall balance of destructive nuclear capability. One country might, for example, have superiority in launchers and megatons, another in warheads and accuracy. If both were thus able to carry out their respective war plans, this situation could represent effective parity.

parity, employment The long-term goal of all AFFIRMATIVE ACTION efforts, which will be achieved after all categories of an organization's employees are proportionately representative of the population in the organization's geographic region. Employment parity exists when the proportion of protected groups in the external labor market is equivalent to their proportion in an organization's total workforce without regard to job classifications. Occupational parity exists when the proportion of an organization's protected group employees in all job classifications is equivalent to their respective availability in the external labor market.

parity, farm A price, guaranteed by the government, designed to allow a farmer to maintain a purchasing power equal to a previous base period. In theory, the parity price that the government is willing to pay gives a farmer a fair return on investment when contrasted with cost. Since the 1930s, the federal government has been using *price supports* (accompanied by production controls) to stabilize the prices of agricultural commodities. In this context, a price support is a guarantee to buy farm products at set prices. The U.S. Congress determines general parity support prices, while parity prices for specific commodities are the responsibility of the U.S. Department of Agriculture.

parity, nuclear A vague term for maintaining a rough equivalency in nuclear forces. If a superpower goes below parity, it is yielding "superiority" to the other side. President Richard Nixon wrote in *RN: Memoirs* (1978) that: "it was clear to me by 1969 that there could never be absolute parity between the U.S. and the U.S.S.R. . . . Consequently, at the beginning of my administration I began to talk in terms of *sufficiency* rather than *superiority* to describe my goals for our nuclear arsenal." Mikhail Gorbachev agreed: "Everybody must realize and agree: Parity in the potential to destroy one another several times over is madness and absurdity" (*The Christian Science Monitor*, March 18, 1987).

parity, racial A situation in which the economic status of all racial groups in a community is essentially equivalent.

parity, wage The requirement that the salary level of one occupational classification be the same as for another. The most common example of wage parity is the linkage between the salaries of police and firefighters. Over two thirds of all cities in the United States have parity policies for their police and firefighters.

Parkinson's law British author C. Northcote Parkinson's (1909–　) famous law that "work expands so as to fill the time available for its completion." It first appeared in his *Parkinson's Law and Other Studies in Administration* (1957). With mathematical precision, he "discovered" that any public administrative department will invariably increase its staff an average of 5.75 percent per year. In anticipation of suggestions that he advise what might be done about this problem, he asserted that "it is not the business of the botanist to eradicate the weeds. Enough for him if he can tell us just how fast they grow."

Parks, Rosa (1913–　) The black woman who, by refusing to take a seat in the back of a Montgomery Alabama bus, sparked the modern CIVIL RIGHTS MOVEMENT in 1955. Her subsequent arrest (she was charged with a misdemeanor) led to a year-long bus boycott by black citizens. This gave the boycott leader, DR. MARTIN LUTHER KING, JR., national exposure which he used to good effect. According to Ramsey Clark: "If Rosa Parks had not refused to move to the back of the bus, you and I might never have heard of Dr. Martin Luther King" (*The New York Times*, April 14, 1987).

parliamentarian The official charged with advising the presiding officer of a legislature regarding questions of procedure.

parliamentary inquiry A question about a legislative body's rules or procedures. Parliamentary inquiries almost always take precedence over any other business of the legislature.

parliamentary procedure The rules by which a deliberative meeting or legislature conducts itself in an orderly fashion according to established precedents. In the United States, the most commonly followed parliamentary procedures are *Robert's Rules of Order*, written (in response to an unruly church meeting) by Henry Martyn Robert (1837–1923), a U.S. army officer. First published as the *Pocket Manual of Rules of Order for Deliberative Assemblies* in 1876, it has since been revised many times. More comprehensive rules can be found in Lewis Deschler's book, *Deschler's Rules of Order* (1976).

parliamentary system A means of governance whose power is concentrated in a legislature, which selects from among its members a prime minister and his or her cabinet officers. The government—that is, the prime minister and the cabinet—stays in power so long as it commands a majority of the parliament. The government may lose its majority through a VOTE OF CONFIDENCE, or in the elections that must be held within a prescribed time period (or at least every five years in British practice). The main differences between a parliamentary system (which most of the democratic countries of the world use) and the American system are (1) the ease with which parliamentary systems of government can be changed if they fall out of favor with a majority in the legislature, and (2) the lack of checks or balances in a parliamentary system. In a parliamentary system, the legislative and the executive branch are one. The prime minister represents the legislature and, through them, the voters. The major check on his or her power is the constant possibility that his or her party will lose its working majority. *Compare to* CABINET GOVERNMENT.

parole 1. The freedom granted to a convicted offender after he or she has served a period of confinement and so long as certain conditions of behavior are met. *Compare to* PROBATION. **2.** The practice of releasing prisoners of war upon their swearing not to take up arms again during the war. This was a common practice during the early part of the American Civil War.

partisanship Extreme partiality toward the candidates, elected officials, and policies of a particular political party. While partisanship is the glue that holds political parties together, this glue has been gradually losing much of its strength in recent decades as the ranks of independent voters have grown and PARTY IDENTIFICATION has decreased. One who is nonpartisan is not influenced by, affiliated with, or supportive of, a political party. *Compare to* ELECTION, NONPARTISAN.

party *See* POLITICAL PARTY.

party, doctrinal A minor party whose principles appeal to a loyal, if small, cadre of voters and that is stable enough to place presidential candidates on the ballot over several elections. Examples include the Libertarian party and the Socialist party.

party government A political process in which opposing parties put forth comprehensive programs of action that, if elected, they implement.

party identification Loyalty to a political party; in terms of survey research, the response to the question: "Generally speaking, do you consider yourself to be a Republican, a Democrat, an independent, or something else?" While party identification has long been the single most significant factor in determining electoral behavior, the impact of party identification on voting has been declining in the last two decades because of the weakness of the parties, the increase of voters who consider themselves independents, and the growth of issue voting.

party in government Those members of a political party who have obtained elected or appointive office. Theoretically, their goal is to further the party's platform and principles.

party leader 1. Any prominent politician in his or her party; often the highest member of the party holding elected office. **2.** The candidate running for office at the head of his or her party's ticket. **3.** A member of a legislature chosen by a party to advocate its policies and viewpoints on various issues. Party leaders play a prominent role in floor debates and help determine the legislative program. The leader of the party with the greater number of members is known as the MAJORITY LEADER. The leader of the party in the minority is known as the MINORITY LEADER. The majority and minority leaders in the U.S. House of Representatives and in the Senate are elected party officials, not constitutional officers or officials of the Congress.

party, legislative *See* LEGISLATIVE PARTY.

party line **1.** A disparaging term applied to statements of belief that parrot those of a particular group, rather than resulting from individual judgment. **2.** A political party's formal position on questions of policy or ideology. When used in connection with American political parties, it is considered a point of departure from which party members are free to deviate. When used in connection with a communist party, it is the official pronouncements that a party member must accept without deviation. **3.** The figurative lines separating parties. **4.** The line (or column) on a ballot listing a party's nominees. **5.** The official point of view of an intelligence agency.

party, minor A POLITICAL PARTY so small and uninfluential that it is not a major force in American politics. Support for minor parties is often localized, such as for the Liberal party in New York, or widely dispersed, such as for the Socialist party. Minor party movements are usually based on a single theme, such as prohibition or libertarianism, which is unable to gain widespread support. In comparison, a third party is a new party strong enough to possibly influence the outcome of an election. While there are significant differences between minor and third parties, in common usage they tend to be lumped together. *Compare to* PARTY, THIRD.

party platform *See* PLATFORM.

party realignment *See* REALIGNMENT.

party, splinter A third party created when a group breaks off from a major party. Examples include the Progressive (or Bull Moose) party that broke off from the Republicans in 1912 and the DIXIECRATS who broke off from the Democrats in 1948.

party, third **1.** A temporary political party that often arises during a presidential election year to affect the fortunes of the two major parties. A third party, in contrast to a minor party, whose members tend to be ideologues, is often composed of independents and those disaffected from a major party who feel the country is ready for a new alternative. It often is hastily formed by a candidate who failed to win—and perhaps never had any prospect of winning—a major party presidential nomination. The best example of third party influence in a presidential election occurred in 1912, when former President, Theodore Roosevelt, lost the Republican nomination to the sitting President, William Howard Taft, in spite of Roosevelt having won the primary elections. Roosevelt then ran as the candidate of the Progressive "Bull Moose" Party. This split the majority Republican vote and allowed the Democrat, Woodrow Wilson, to win with a plurality. **2.** Technically, according to the Presidential Election Campaign Fund Act of 1971, a third party is a minor political party "whose candidate for the office of President in the preceding presidential election received, as the candidate of such party, 5 percent or more but less than 25 percent of the total number of popular votes received by all candidates for such office." Such a designation makes the party eligible for federal campaign funds.

party, transient A minor party that emerges from a protest or secessionist movement, runs a candidate for President, and may never be heard from again; for example, the States' Rights (DIXIECRAT) party of 1948.

party unity 1. The return of all of the party's faithful to rally around the party's candidates to prevail in the general election. After a harshly fought primary, there is invariably a call for party unity—to put private grumblings aside and forget the ill feelings generated by the usual rhetoric—for the greater good of defeating the other party. **2.** The common support that all party members in a legislature are supposed to give to their party's legislative proposals. Technically, a party unity vote is one in which a majority of one party opposes a majority in the other party. Party unity scores, such as those often reported by the *Congressional Quarterly Weekly Report*, represent the percentage of times that a member of Congress votes with his or her party on such votes.

party vote A vote in a legislative body that is basically along party lines: at least 90 percent of the members of one party vote one way, while at least 90 percent of the members of the other party vote the opposite way. Because party discipline is much less rigorous than it used to be, party votes are relatively rare today.

paternalism 1. In the United States, a derogatory reference to an organization's "fatherly" efforts to better the lot of its employees. Historically, the U.S. labor movement has considered paternalistic efforts to be a false and demeaning charity, inhibiting the growth of union membership. In societies where there are well-established paternalistic traditions, the derogatory connotations of the word may be absent. Japan is undoubtedly the most paternalistic of all the major industrial societies. **2.** A sexist attitude by males toward females; treating women as one would treat children. Men who conscientiously provide for the needs of women but who at the same time refuse to give women real responsibility or to respect them as free-thinking individuals may be said to be paternalistic. **3.** An overconcern by government for the welfare of its citizens. Those who strongly believe in self-reliance denounce a government's paternalistic interference with their lives.

patronage The power of elected and appointed officials to make partisan appointments to office or to confer contracts, honors, or other benefits on their political supporters. While subject to frequent attack from reformers, patronage has traditionally been the method by which political leaders assure themselves a loyal support system of people who will carry out their policies and organize voters for their continued political control. Patronage has always been one of the major tools by which executives at all levels in all sectors consolidate their power and attempt to control a bureaucracy. In the 1990 case of *Rutan v Republican Party*, the Supreme Court ruled that traditional patronage in public employment is unconstitutional. Writing the majority opinion, Justice William J. Brennan, Jr. said: "To the victor belong only those spoils that may be constitutionally obtained." In earlier cases, *Elrod v Burns* (1976) and *Branti v Finkel* (1980), the Court held that the First Amendment forbids government officials to discharge or threaten to discharge public employees solely for not being supporters of the political party in power, unless party affiliation is an appropriate requirement for the position involved. In the *Rutan* case, the Court was asked to decide the constitutionality of several related political patronage practices—"whether promotion, transfer, recall and hiring decisions involving low-level public employees may be constitutionally based on party affiliation and support. We hold that they may not." In a stinging dissent Justice Antonin Scalia said: "The new principle that the Court today announces will be enforced by a corps of judges (the members of this Court included) who overwhelmingly owe their office to its violation. Something must be wrong here, and I suggest it is the Court." The Supreme Court notwithstanding, patronage will in all probability turn out to be like prostitution: it can be outlawed but it cannot be stopped. Laws barring either will merely drive the practice underground.

patronage, direct Benefits that a legislator can provide constituents, such as PORK BARREL projects, intervening with the bureaucracy, or traditional jobs.

patronage, pinstripe The awarding of government contracts to large campaign contributors—so called because of the "pinstripe" suits sometimes worn by such business owners.

patronage, social The ability of a chief executive to use the prestige aspects of his or her office to wine and dine and otherwise personally impress critical political actors whose support is desired. Because this depends as much upon force of personality as anything else, some executives, such as Ronald Reagan, have been far more successful at getting political mileage out of social patronage than others. Senator Robert C. Byrd once complained about how effective Reagan was with social patronage: "I do not know what there is about the Presidency, when it comes to a [phone] call from that august and lofty position. I just cannot understand what it is that is so awesome about it. There is something that likens it to lockjaw. Some individuals [in Congress], when they receive a call from the President, apparently do not know how to say 'no'" (*The New York Times*, July 26, 1985).

Then there was the time President George Bush spent two hours schmoozing with guests at a summer lawn party. Thomas M. DeFranks of *Newsweek* (April 16, 1990) reports that he "was asked by a guest, 'Hasn't anyone told you you're the President of the United States? You don't have to do this anymore.' Bush just smiled and replied, 'How do you think I got here?'"

pay as you go **1.** The automatic withholding of income tax liabilities by means of a payroll deduction. **2.** A FISCAL POLICY calling for a BALANCED BUDGET. **3.** A pension plan in which employers pay benefits to retired employees out of current income.

paying your dues The experiences that one must have before being ready for advancement. In effect, you have to pay your dues before you can be perceived as a legitimate occupant of a higher position. Many political activists must pay their dues by performing good works for their party before they can be considered "serious" candidates for higher positions.

payroll-padding Adding unneeded jobs to a government agency to create patronage positions for political supporters. This may or may not be illegal. Padded payrolls may be to one person what essential positions for effective government are to another.

Peace Corps A program established by the Peace Corps Act of 1961 to help peoples of other countries in meeting their needs for skilled workers. The Peace Corps was the most successful and lasting of the foreign policy initiatives of the John F. Kennedy administration.

peace dividend **1.** The money that is supposed to become available with the winding down of the COLD WAR. **2.** A similar fiscal windfall that was supposed to have become available at the end of the Vietnam War. Neither has materialized.

peaking The high point of a political campaign's effectiveness, the moment when a candidate has greatest public support—enough to win the election. It's best if the campaign "peaks" right before election day. Otherwise, it may gradually lose support and the election. This is the danger of "peaking too soon." Most modern campaigns are planned to peak at election day by a gradual build-up of enthusiasm and momentum.

Pendleton Act of 1883 The Act to Regulate and Improve the Civil Service of the United States that introduced the merit concept into federal employment and created the U.S. Civil Service Commission. While this body was termed a commission, it was by no means independent. It was an executive agency that for all practical purposes was subject to the administrative discretion of the President. The act gave legislative legitimacy to many of the procedures developed by the earlier, unsuccessful, Civil Service Commission during the Ulysses S. Grant administration. *See also* CIVIL SERVICE REFORM ACT OF 1978.

Pension Benefit Guaranty Corporation (PBGC) The federal agency that guarantees basic pension benefits in covered private plans if they terminate with insufficient assets. Title IV of the Employee Retirement Income Security Act of 1974 (ERISA) established the corporation as a self-financing, wholly owned government corporation governed by a board of directors consisting of the secretaries of Labor, Commerce, and the Treasury.

Pentagon **1.** The building that has become the symbol of the U.S. Department of Defense. In 1941 it was proposed by the army as an alternative to the erection of a variety of temporary buildings. In less than four days, plans were made for a mammoth three-story facility to house office space for 40,000 people. (The pentagonal design derived from the fact that the original construction site was bounded by five existing roads.) Immediately after the Pearl Harbor attack, a fourth floor was added to the plan, and later a fifth. While parts of the building were occupied as early as eight months after groundbreaking, it wasn't finished until January 15, 1943. About 28,000 people, both civilians and military, work at the Pentagon. **2.** Either the High Command of America's military forces, especially the Joint Chiefs of Staff, the civilian authorities in the DOD, or both. In this sense the use is figurative, because important parts of both of these institutions are not located in the Pentagon building at all.

Pentagon Papers An unedited and unexpurgated record of the step-by-step judgments that brought American involvement in Vietnam to its peak point by the end of the Lyndon B. Johnson administration. A historian's dream because of the raw data involved, this essentially shapeless body of material was destined to become a cause cèlébre when 47 volumes of these secret documents were leaked in 1971 to the *New York Times* and the *Washington Post* by Daniel Ellsberg (1931–), a former Defense Department employee. The Richard M. Nixon administration got an injunction to prevent their publication, but in the case of *New York Times v United States* (1971), the Supreme Court dissolved the injunction and the papers were published beginning June 13, 1971. Ellsberg was then charged with espionage, but the case was dismissed when it was shown that the administration authorized a burglary to steal Ellsberg's medical records from his psychiatrist's office. The then Chairman of the Senate Foreign Relations Committee, J. William Fulbright, said of the papers: "Most of the material should not have been secret in the first place. . . . I still don't see the harm that came from it, other than the fact that there is involved a violation of the law. . . . I can disapprove of the leaking of documents, but at the same time I disapprove just as heartily of the abuse of the classification power" (*The Christian Science Monitor*, July 18, 1973).

Bernard Brodie would write in *War and Politics* (1973): "Hardly mentioned in the voluminous discussion of those papers is the fact that shortly before his death President Kennedy approved a plan for the phased withdrawal of U.S. military personnel from Vietnam. They were supposed to be reduced to about 12,000 by the middle of 1964, bottoming out by the middle of 1968 at the level of 1,500, which would simply provide for a headquarters for the Military Assistance Advisory Group (MAAG)."

Pentagon Reorganization Act of 1986 *See* JOINT CHIEFS OF STAFF.

people, the 1. The sovereigns who are also the subjects in the American political system. The original draft of the Constitution began: "We the people of the states of. . ." and the original 13 states were listed. But because the drafters did not know which states would in fact ratify the Constitution, they changed the wording to "We the people of the United States." This more aptly reflected the idea that the people were the source of authority and sovereignty. Thomas Jefferson wrote in a letter to Henry Lee, August 10, 1824: "Men. . . are naturally divided into two parties: 1. Those who fear and distrust the people, and wish to draw all powers from them into the hands of the higher classes. 2. Those who identify themselves with the people, have confidence in them, cherish and consider them as the most honest and safe, although not the most wise depository of the public interests." **2.** The linguistic symbol of majoritarian democracy. **3.** A euphemism for "the state." **4.** The general public. Of them Abraham Lincoln said in a speech at Clinton, Illinois on September, 8, 1858: "You can fool all the people some of the time and some of the people all of the time, but you can't fool all of the people all of the time." **5.** A mob subject to manipulation by DEMA-GOGUES. Alexander Hamilton is supposed to have once said to Thomas Jefferson during one of their many political arguments: "Your people, sir, is nothing but a great beast!"

per capita A Latin phrase meaning "by heads." In a *per capita* election, each member has one vote.

per capita tax 1. A tax on each head. **2.** The regular payment made on the basis of membership by a local union to its national organization.

per curiam 1. Latin meaning "by the court"; an opinion by *all* the judges of an appeals court. **2.** An unsigned decision by an appeals court refusing to review a lower court's decision.

peremptory challenge The right of either side in a jury trial to reject a prospective juror without giving any reason. The number of peremptory challenges available varies with state law.

Perez v Brownell *See* AFROYIM V RUSK.

perjury The intentional making of a false statement as part of testimony by a sworn witness in a judicial proceeding on a matter material to the inquiry.

Perot, H. Ross (1930–   ) The Texas billionaire who in 1992 became the most successful third party presidential candidate since former President Theodore Roosevelt ran as a BULL MOOSE progressive in 1912. Perot has long been a public figure because of his outspoken views on the Vietnam War, education, the national debt and other public policy issues. In early 1992 he announced on a Cable News Network television talk show that he would be a candidate for President if volunteers placed him on the ballot in all fifty states. After a vast outpouring of volunteers placed him on the ballot in most states and polls showed him with close to a third of the national vote, he announced his withdrawal from the race on the same day in July that Arkansas Governor WILLIAM J. CLINTON accepted the Democratic Party's presidential nomination. Then in October Perot reentered the race (asserting that he only got out in the first place because of his belief that his daughter's wedding would be disrupted by people associated President George Bush's campaign) and participated on equal terms with President

Bush and Governor Clinton in all three presidential debates. He appeared often on television with half-hour programs in which he lectured the nation on the dangers of the federal DEFICIT, on the need to raise taxes, and the necessity of cutting ENTITLEMENTS. After spending an estimated $60 million of his own funds on the campaign (mostly for television advertising), he won almost twenty percent of the popular vote. In January 1993 Perot announced the formation of "United We Stand," a membership organization that will monitor the Clinton Administration's fiscal reforms—and possibly be available to work for a future Perot candidacy.

perjury, subornation of The intentional causing of another person to commit the crime of perjury by persuasion, bribery, or threats.

Persian Gulf War The war that began on August 2, 1990, when Iraq conquered its much smaller neighbor, Kuwait, in a matter of hours—and ended on February 27, 1991, when President Bush declared victory for the allied forces. While the war was an astounding military success (only 148 American soldiers were killed in action compared to more than an estimated 100,000 Iraqi dead), it was an equally astounding diplomatic victory. Immediately after the Iraqi invasion on August 2, President Bush, using his long-standing personal contacts with world leaders and working through the United Nations, began assembling the diplomatic coalition that evolved into the military coalition against Iraq. Critical to this was the earlier ending of the COLD WAR with the Soviet Union. This made it possible to bring the Soviets into the diplomatic coalition against Iraq even though the Soviets had supplied and trained the Iraqi military.

Militarily, the war was immensely popular. It made national heroes out of General Colin Powell, the Chairman of the Joint Chiefs of Staff, and General H. Norman "Stormin' Norman" Schwarzkopf. It was the first war since World War II in which the country was, for the most part, enthusiastically united. And it became all the more popular as it was seen that casualties would be low. The military campaign called for the greatest bombing of any nation since World War II Germany. It proved that American high-tech weapons did work and could save American lives. And it showed that Iraqi leader Saddam Hussein's million-man third world army (once the world's fourth largest) was a PAPER TIGER when confronted with the American, British, and French high-tech forces. As President Bush, gloating over victory, said: "By God, we've kicked the VIETNAM SYNDROME once and for all" (*Newsweek*, March 11, 1991).

Domestically, the war sent President Bush's popularity to new highs. Of course, had the war dragged on and American casualties been considerable, his popularity might have gone to new lows. But he took the risks and earned the glory. Critics contend that this is just the problem. Despite the WAR POWERS resolution, Bush single-handedly sent more than half a million U.S. troops in harm's way without any formal approval of Congress. While the Congress, at the last minute (on January 12), gave him legal authority to commit troops to combat, he contended that he didn't really need it—that his authority under the Constitution as COMMANDER IN CHIEF was sufficient to send the cream of America's combat forces to the other side of the world to liberate a country that the United States was under no treaty obligations to help. While this issue is troubling, there is certainly no doubt after the fact that President Bush's diplomatic and military initiatives had the support of the American people. The question remains if the war will ultimately contribute to President Bush's concept of a NEW WORLD ORDER or if it will be just another episode in Middle Eastern squabbles.

persona non grata **1.** Someone who is out of favor. **2.** In diplomacy this has a very specific meaning: a diplomat formally declared to be "persona non grata" must leave the host country. The expulsion can be caused by the diplomat's own behavior, or the diplomat can be entirely innocent and expelled for larger foreign policy considerations.

Peter principle The principle promulgated by author Laurence J. Peter in his worldwide bestseller, *The Peter Principle: Why Things Always Go Wrong,* with Raymond Hull (1969). The principle holds that "in a hierarchy every employee tends to rise to his level of incompetence." Corollaries of the Peter principle hold that "in time, every post tends to be occupied by an employee who is incompetent to carry out its duties." In answer to the logical question of who then does the work that has to be done, Peter asserts that "work is accomplished by those employees who have not yet reached their level of incompetence."

petition **1.** Any formal request to a public agency or official. The First Amendment guarantees the right of citizens to communicate with the government without hindrance. **2.** A request of a court to take some specific judicial action. **3.** A usual requirement for placing a candidate on a ballot, for initiating a referendum on laws, and for seeking a recall of an elected official. The petition process usually requires that a certain percentage of a jurisdiction's voters sign the petition document.

petition, congressional A request or plea sent to one or both chambers of the U.S. Congress from an organization or private citizen's group asking for support of particular legislation or for favorable consideration of a matter not yet receiving congressional attention. Petitions are referred to appropriate committees for action. *Compare to* MEMORIAL.

photo opportunity **1.** Often shortened to *photo op,* a specific time when high-ranking officials or political candidates allow the press to take pictures. The usual rules allow for no questions, but reporters' questions are often responded to in a self-serving manner. **2.** A specifically staged incident designed to get TV news coverage, usually as part of a political campaign. For example, during the 1988 presidential campaign, Governor Michael Dukakis drove a tank to show he was strong on defense, and Vice President George Bush visited a flag factory to show he was patriotic. *Compare to* MEDIA EVENT.

picketing 1. A political demonstration in which demonstrators walk about a symbolic area (e.g., in front of the White House) carrying signs with political messages. Picketing of this kind is often done to gain media attention for some issue. **2.** An act that occurs when one or more persons are present at an employer's place of business in order (1) to publicize a labor dispute, (2) to influence others (both employees and customers) to withhold their services or business, or (3) to demonstrate a union's desire to represent the employees of the business being picketed. The Supreme Court held, in the case of *Thornhill v Alabama* (1940), that the dissemination of information concerning the facts of a labor dispute was within the rights guaranteed by the First Amendment. However, picketing may be lawfully enjoined if it is not peaceful, is for an unlawful purpose, or is in violation of a state or federal law.

Pierce, Franklin (1809–1869) The President of the United States from 1853 to 1857. He was a Northern Democrat from New Hampshire who sought to deal with the increasingly divisive issue of slavery by appeasing the South. For example, he made Jefferson Davis (soon to be President of the Confederacy) his Secretary of War. This policy proved so unpopular that his party wouldn't even consider him as a serious candidate for renomination in 1856. JAMES BRYCE in *The American Commonwealth* (1914) wrote: "Who now knows or cares to know anything about the personality of James K. Polk or Franklin Pierce? The only thing remarkable about them is that being so commonplace they should have climbed so high."

pigeonholing The virtual killing of a bill by a congressional committee by refusing to vote on whether or not to allow it to go to the entire House of Representatives or Senate for consideration. The committee figuratively puts the bill in a tight hole, and there it stays. Typically, over 90 percent of all bills referred to congressional committees are pigeonholed.

pinko *See* RED.

PIRG *See* PUBLIC INTEREST RESEARCH GROUP.

plaintiff The person who initiates a civil lawsuit.

planning The formal process of making decisions for the future of individuals and organizations. Planning never occurs in a vacuum; it is an inherently political process. Consequently, the success of a plan of any kind is often a function of the political astuteness of the planner. This as true today as it was when ALEXANDER HAMILTON advised in *The Federalist* No. 70 (1788): "Men often oppose a thing merely because they have had no agency in planning it, or because it may have been planned by those whom they dislike."

There are two basic kinds of planning: strategic and operational. Strategic planning, also known as long-range, comprehensive, integrated, overall, and managerial planning, has three dimensions: the identification and examination of future opportunities, threats, and consequences; the process of analyzing an organization's environment and developing compatible objectives along with the appropriate strategies and policies capable of achieving those objectives; and the integration of the various elements of planning into an overall structure so that each unit of the organization knows in advance what must be done, when, and by whom. Operational planning, also known as divisional planning, is concerned with the implementation of the larger goals and strategies that have been determined by strategic planning; with improving current operations; and with the allocation of resources through the operating budget.

planning programming budgeting system (PPBS) A budgeting system that requires agency directors to identify program objectives, to develop methods of measuring program output, to calculate total program costs over the long run, to prepare detailed multiyear program and financial plans, and to analyze the costs and benefits of alternative program designs. The system was developed in the U.S. Department of Defense during the late 1950s. In the 1960s, the PPBS took the budgeting world by storm. It began by insisting that it could interrelate and coordinate the three management processes constituting its title. Planning would be related to programs that would be keyed to budgeting. To further emphasize the planning dimension, the system required five-year forecasts for program plans and cost estimates. It placed a whole new emphasis on program objectives, outputs, and alternatives and stressed the new watchword of evaluation—the effectiveness criterion. President Lyndon B. Johnson made the PPBS mandatory for all federal agencies in 1965. Johnson—at the height of his political powers after his landslide election win—envisioned PPBS as the steering mechanism for his Great Society programs.

By 1970, the PPBS, as a formal system, was expanding in some jurisdictions, contracting in others. Opposition to the system came from various quarters, especially from bedeviled agency administrators and staff who experienced one difficulty after another in complying with the PPBS's submission requirements. The system was formally abandoned in the federal government when the Richard M. Nixon administration discontinued it in 1971. State and local governments, in the meantime, were rapidly modifying their PPBS programs and installing hybrid versions.

platform A statement of basic principles put forth by a political party, usually at its national convention, to be adopted by its candidates in the election campaign. The platform, which does not formally bind either the party or its candidates, also contains specific short-term goals or proposals for legislation, known as *planks*. The planks of a party's political platform are often hotly contested at a national convention, as party ideologists seek to nail down their favorite planks and supporters of the likely nominees strive to keep the platform so general that it will have wide appeal. Those who believe that "there is not a dime's worth of difference" between the two major parties should read their 1988 platforms. For example, the Republicans are PRO-LIFE, against MINIMUM WAGE increases, and opposed to new taxes. The Democrats are PRO-CHOICE, favor INDEXING the minimum wage, and pledge to raise taxes on the wealthy.

platform committee At a national convention this is the committee that does the initial drafting of a party's platform. Their draft, before it becomes the party's platform, must be ratified on the convention's floor.

Plato (427–347 B.C.) The Greek philosopher who, because of his *The Republic* (370 B.C.), is often considered to be the first political scientist. *The Republic* is the western world's first systematic analysis of the political process and the reason for a state. Plato provided an intellectual rationale for the "divine right of kings" even before Christianity sanctioned the notion. To Plato, only an elite of philosopher kings or "guardians" had the political wisdom necessary to govern, a wisdom that could be transmitted to others by selective breeding. Thus, a just society would be one where each knew his place—with the guardians on top (*compare to* BIG LIE). Because Plato wrote his philosophy in the form of dialogues in which Socrates directs discussion among varying groups of people, questioning them rather than asserting his own positions, there are a multitude of interpretations of the meanings Plato himself would have intended had he stated them in more systematic form. Programs suggested in *The Republic,* for example, may appear to be contradicted by programs discussed in another of his works, *The Laws*.

Plato became a small part of the 1988 presidential campaign when Marilyn Quayle, wife of the Republican Vice Presidential nominee, responded to suggestions that her husband was an intellectual lightweight by asserting: "He tries to read Plato's *Republic* every year" (*Newsweek*, September 26, 1988). Many pundits responded sympathetically when they opined that they hope he succeeds in reading it one year—real soon.

play in Peoria To be acceptable in a Peoria-like American city: traditional, middle-sized, and more-or-less homogeneous, the mainstream of traditional social attitudes. Politicians often ask themselves of proposed national policies, "Will it play in Peoria?"

play politics To put personal political or partisan advantage over the public interest. No competent politician would ever admit to playing politics; such reprehensible activities are only engaged in by the political opposition. Besides, one person's play may be another's astute furtherance of the public interest.

plea A defendant's formal answer in court to a charge contained in a complaint or indictment. The three possible pleas are guilty, not guilty, or *nolo contendere* (no contest). If a defendant stands mute and says nothing, it is considered a plea of not guilty.

plea bargaining The negotiations between a prosecutor and a criminal defendant's legal counsel over the severity and number of charges to which the defendant will plead guilty in exchange for the dropping of more serious charges or a promise to ask the court for a less severe sentence. Plea bargaining has grown to be an essential element in the American criminal justice system. Without it, the courts would be overwhelmed with demands for trials, which are both expensive and time-consuming. However, the plea-bargaining process may not be in the best interests of the defendant or of justice, particularly when the threat of an even harsher sentence is used to produce a guilty plea that may not itself be justifiable. Nevertheless, plea bargaining is the most usual process of criminal case disposition, because the overwhelming majority of criminal defendants accept a plea bargain in lieu of going to trial. The Supreme Court, in *Bordenkircher v Hayes* (1978), agreed that prosecutors should have broad discretion in negotiating pleas.

plebiscite 1. A direct vote on an important issue by the entire electorate of a nation. **2.** Any means of expression for popular opinion. In this sense, a REFERENDUM is a plebiscite. **3.** Informally, a vote for a party or an individual associated with a particular policy. For example, some historians have contended that the 1920 national election, when the Democrats supported U.S. membership in the League of Nations (and lost), while the Republicans opposed it (and won), was a plebiscite on whether the United States should join the league.

pledge of allegiance *See* ALLEGIANCE, PLEDGE OF.

plenary session Any meeting of a legislature, convention, and so on, with all members present.

Plessy v Ferguson *See* SEPARATE BUT EQUAL.

plum 1. Something thought to be especially desirable. **2.** A political appointment. **3.** Any advantage obtained as a political reward. The term is an abbreviated version of the phrase "shake the plum tree," which in the nineteenth century was slang for the dispensing of political largess.

plum book The book *Policy and Supporting Positions*, first published in 1960, which lists high-level jobs in the U.S. government. The plum book is often viewed as a list of political jobs available to a new administration to which it can make appointments. The available jobs include a large variety of positions exempt from competitive civil service rules as well as vacancies in the judiciary and jobs in the legislative branch filled by presidential appointment. The plum book is prepared by the Committee on Post Office and Civil Service of the House of Representatives after every presidential election and is printed quadrennially by the Government Printing Office. *See also* PATRONAGE.

plural executive *See* EXECUTIVE, PLURAL.

pluralism 1. Cultural diversity in a society stratified along racial lines. This concept was developed by historian John S. Furnival to describe the unstable colonial domination of an alien minority over an indigenous majority. *Compare to* PLURALISM, CULTURAL. **2.** Any political system in which there are multiple centers of legitimate power and authority—for example, medieval Europe, where the various monarchies and the Catholic church had power in different spheres of society. *Compare to* PLURALISM, POLITI-

CAL. **3.** In the U.S. context, a theory of government that attempts to reaffirm the democratic character of society by asserting that open, multiple, competing, and responsive groups preserve traditional democratic values in a mass industrial state. In democratic theory, pluralism is distinguishable from GENERAL WILL theory, which posits the capacity to incorporate mass aims in a single conception of the public purpose. Thus, traditional democratic theory, with its emphasis on individual responsibility and control, is transformed into a model that emphasizes the role of competitive groups in society. Pluralism assumes that power will shift from group to group as elements in the mass public transfer their allegiance in response to their perceptions of their individual interests. However, power-elite theory argues that, if democracy is defined as popular participation in public affairs, then pluralist theory is inadequate as an explanation of modern U.S. government. Pluralism, according to this view, offers little direct participation, since the elite structure of government is closed, pyramidal, consensual, and unresponsive. Under this theory, society is divided into two classes: the few who govern and the many who are governed; that is, pluralism is covert elitism, instead of a practical solution to preserve democracy in a mass society. *See also* INTEREST GROUP LIBERALISM.

pluralism, cultural 1. The belief that a nation's overall welfare is best served by preserving ethnic cultures, rather than by encouraging the integration and blending of cultures. This is in contrast to the assimilationist belief that all immigrants should take their turn in a national MELTING POT and come out homogenized. **2.** A social and political condition in which diverse ethnic groups live in relative peace and harmony.

pluralism, hyper- A governing situation wherein so many groups so successfully compete for political power that power becomes decentralized and nothing much can get done. *Compare to* INTEREST GROUP LIBERALISM.

pluralism, political A governing arrangement with a SEPARATION OF POWERS, such as in the United States. Because power is distributed among several entities, which can check each other if need be, no single institution is all powerful or sovereign.

plurality The number of votes cast for a candidate who obtains the greatest number of votes, though not a majority, in a contest of more than two candidates. Primary elections, which often have many candidates, are often won by pluralities. In some elections, such as that for President, a plurality is enough to win. In others, a run-off election must be held between the highest vote-getters so that one wins with a majority.

pocket veto *See* VETO, POCKET.

pocketbook issues Political issues that directly affect the disposable income of voters; for example, the rate of inflation and mortgage interest rate.

point man 1. The front line soldier most exposed to enemy fire; when the shooting starts, he is most likely to be hit. **2.** By analogy, a politician who is purposely exposed to criticism to protect others who stay "above the battle." Richard M. Nixon wrote in his *Memoirs* (1978) of his time as President Eisenhower's running mate: "Eisenhower also knew that to maintain his above-the-battle position he needed a running mate who was willing to engage in all-out combat, and who was good at it. In a sense, the hero needed a point man." **3.** The leading candidate in a primary election; the one most exposed to criticism and attack.

point of order An objection raised by a participant that a formal meeting is departing from rules governing its conduct of business. The objector cites the rule violated; the chair sustains the objection if correctly made. Order is restored by the chair's suspending proceedings until it conforms to the pre-scribed order of business.

pol **1.** A POLITICO. **2.** Slang for someone professionally engaged in politics. **3.** A low level political worker. A "party pol" is a functionary of a political orga-nization.

polarization The political views on an issue taken to extremities; a situation where the degree of opposition appears to make compromise or rational adjudication of differences impossible. There are perennial discussions about how the United States is becoming increasingly polarized between those who would abolish abortion and those for freedom of choice, between those who favor school busing for integration and those who don't, and between those who favor protectionist policies and those for free trade.

police Paramilitary state and local government organizations whose most basic responsibilities include maintaining public order and safety (through the use of force if necessary), investigating and arresting persons accused of crimes, and securing the cooperation of the citizenry. The term police, while referring to all law enforcement officers in general, is usually a reference to municipal law enforcement officers. County officers are sheriffs; state offi-cers are usually called the state police, state troopers, or highway patrol. There is no national police force in the United States, nor has there ever been much support for one. The Federal Bureau of Investigation functions as a national police force only in direct response to crimes in violation of fed-eral law. Supreme Court Justice Robert H. Jackson in his *The Supreme Court in the American System of Government* (1955) explains why: "I cannot say that our country could have no central police without becoming totalitar-ian, but I can say with great conviction that it cannot become totalitarian without a centralized national police... A national police... will have enough on enough people, even if it does not elect to prosecute them, so that it will find no opposition to its policies." *Compare to* CONSTABLE.

police action **1.** Military intervention by a state whose proclaimed purpose is to uphold international law. **2.** The KOREAN WAR because the war was fought with the approval and under the flag of the United Nations.

police power The inherent power of a state to use physical force if needed to regulate affairs within its jurisdiction in the interests of the safety and welfare of its citizens. Police power goes far beyond the criminal justice system; it is the legal basis by which governments regulate such areas as public health, safety, and morals.

police review board A panel of ordinary citizens given the formal authority by their municipality to review specific acts of police officers about which citizens have complained and to make recommendations for disciplinary or other administrative actions. The most common issue before police review boards is whether, in a given instance, police have used excessive or unwarranted force.

police state 1. A totalitarian society in which citizens are heavily supervised by police forces, both open and secret. A police state is an inherent tyranny, which rules by explicit or implied terror and which denies its citizens many of the most obvious civil liberties. In a police state, sheer force replaces the legal system and due process of law. **2.** A reference to the United States when it is felt that the government is violating basic freedoms and abusing the Bill of Rights.

policeman of the world A role the United States has sometimes played through its foreign policy. Both the Korean and Vietnam interventions have often been described as police efforts. As UN Ambassador Jeane J. Kirkpatrick wrote in *Commentary* (November 1979): "Vietnam presumably taught us that the United States could not serve as the world's policeman; it should also have taught us the dangers of trying to be the world's midwife to democracy when the birth is scheduled to take place under conditions of guerrilla war."

policing, soft A style of law enforcement that deliberately seeks to minimize community conflict in inner city areas by not rigorously enforcing laws; the more important mission is to maintain public order.

policy A statement of goals that can be translated into a plan or program by specifying the objectives to be obtained. Goals are a far more general statement of aims than are objectives. Goal-objective ambiguity may exist for a variety of reasons. The original sponsors of the policy or program may not have had a precise idea of the end results desired. Formal statements of objectives may be intentionally ambiguous, if such vagueness makes it easier to obtain a consensus on action: value judgments underlying the objectives may not be shared by important groups. Consequently, the end result intended may be perceived by some as implying ill effects for them. So explicit statements of objectives, which tend to imply a specific assignment of priorities and commitment of resources, may be purposely avoided. *Compare to* PUBLIC POLICY.

policy agenda The issues that OPINION LEADERS and the general public consider important enough for political debate and possible government action. *Compare to* AGENDA SETTING.

policy analysis A set of techniques that seeks to answer the question of what the probable effects of a policy will be before they actually occur. A policy analysis undertaken on a program that is already in effect is more properly called a program evaluation. Nevertheless, the term is used by many to refer to both before- and after-the-fact analyses of public policies. All policy analysis involves the application of systematic research techniques (drawn largely from the social sciences and based on measurements of program effectiveness, quality, cost, and impact) to the formulation, execution, and evaluation of public policy to create a more rational or optimal administrative system.

policy committee A political candidate's primary advisory committee, consisting of the campaign manager, the treasurer, and the finance chair, among others.

policy entrepreneur A political actor who makes major investments of POLITICAL CAPITAL in a specific issue in the expectation that the issue can be used to political advantage. Policy entrepreneurs can be either in or out of office. For example, Senator Edward Kennedy has long been an entrepreneur for national health insurance; and Ralph Nader, who has never sought public office, has been the preeminent entrepreneur for consumer protection. *Compare to* PUBLIC ENTREPRENEUR; PUBLIC POLICY ENTREPRENEUR.

policymaking *See* PUBLIC POLICYMAKING.

policy studies A phrase used to describe interdisciplinary academic programs that focus on aspects of public policy.

policy wonk Someone who is a compulsive student of public policy analysis. Wonk is slang for a student who is a grind or a nerd. Policy wonk came to the fore of American politics during the 1992 presidential election when it was used to describe Governor William J. Clinton of Arkansas.

polis 1. The Greek word for city. **2.** The Greek concept of a political community. *Compare to* POLITY.

political 1. Having to do with the state and its governing institutions. **2.** Having to do with the processes by which people gain and use power in social settings, whether the setting is the city, a factory or office, or the family.

political access *See* ACCESS.

political action Any organized attempt to influence the political process, from lobbying legislators to seeking the election (or defeat) of particular candidates.

political action committee (PAC) An organization whose purpose is to raise and then distribute campaign funds to candidates for political office. Because federal law restricts the amount of money a corporation, union, trade association, or individual can give to a candidate, PACs have evolved as the major means by which large contributions can influence an election. The PACs were developed by labor unions during and after World War II to acknowledge and encourage the new and potentially significant political power of the American labor movement and to separate specific labor interests from larger public interests in the effort to blunt public criticism of "big labor's" political influence.

There are two kinds of PACs: (1) the segregated fund type, which is wholly accountable to its parent organization and may not solicit funds from the public; and (2) the nonconnected political committee, which raises money from the general public (mostly by direct mail) to independently support candidates—that is, to spend money on a candidate's behalf because federal law limits the amounts that candidates and parties can spend on their own. John Terry Dolan, as chairman of the national Conservative Political Action Committee, explained how this second category of PACs can be potentially dangerous to the political process. "We could be a menace, yes. Ten independent expenditure groups, for example, could amass this great amount of money and defeat the point of accountability in politics. We could say whatever we want about an opponent of a Senator Smith and the senator wouldn't have to say anything. A group like ours could lie through its teeth and the candidate it helps stays clean" (*The Washington Post*, August 10, 1980).

The PACs were encouraged by the FEDERAL ELECTION CAMPAIGN ACT of 1972 and its amendments, which sought to curtail the political campaign abuses disclosed by the WATERGATE scandals. But PACs have proved too popular, in a sense. There were 608 PACs in 1975; by 1982, that number jumped to 3,371. By 1990, the number exceeded 4,500. In the 1988 election alone, PACs gave more than $172 million to candidates.Their sheer numbers and the vast amounts of money they spend have greatly escalated the costs of running for office. Now, members of the U.S. Congress are more dependent upon large amounts of campaign money from PACs than they once were on the relatively small amounts of money from the traditional fat cats and special interests—who are as influential as ever, because they now have their own PACs. *Compare to* TARGETING.

political activism Organized efforts outside of the regular channels of political influence undertaken specifically to change or direct policy. *Compare to* ACTIVIST.

political activists The small minority of citizens who are actively and consistently involved in politics, either in running for office or in support of others who run.

political advertising The totality of the means by which campaigns sell their candidate to the voters. These include (1) radio and TV SPOTS, (2) newspaper and magazine ads, (3) DIRECT MAIL, and (4) campaign paraphernalia such as bumper stickers, yard signs, buttons, and other novelties.

political alienation *See* ALIENATION.

political amateurs Political activists who get involved with a candidate or issue out of an ideological or personal commitment. Political amateurs are often known by their reluctance to compromise and by being more interested in fighting the good fight than in winning. While they are not permanently committed, not visibly accountable, and not predictable actors in the political process, they may still be important in a given campaign. According to James Q. Wilson's *The Amateur Democrat* (1962): "An amateur is one who finds politics intrinsically interesting because it expresses a conception of the public interest. The amateur politician sees the political world more in terms of ideas and principles than in terms of persons. . . . The principal reward of politics to the amateur is the sense of having satisfied a felt obligation to 'participate.'"

political ambiguity The purposeful use of words, phrases, or acts that are susceptible to multiple interpretation to seek the support of differing constituencies. This is why many members of legislatures avoid roll-call votes, offer hazy statements on policy issues, and make vague campaign promises. From the politician's point of view, ambiguity is a time-tested strategy that works; unless, of course, the voters are sophisticated enough to see through it.

political animal 1. In ARISTOTLE's *Politics*, that aspect of human behavior that requires community organization. It is a term of praise when it is seen as a capacity for compromise and effective action, and of criticism when it is perceived as destructive to fundamental values. **2.** Someone who assesses the political implications of every action, no matter how minor.

political apathy Indifference to politics, as demonstrated by a failure to vote or to take an interest in public affairs. On the one hand, apathy indicates contentment or at least the lack of discontent with the political process. But it can also be argued that apathy is an indication of despair and the lack of a sense of political efficacy.

political appointee A person given a job in government mainly because of political connections (or occasionally because of preeminence in a specific field) as opposed to a person who gains his or her job through the MERIT SYSTEM. While a political appointee is any patronage appointment, the phrase tends to be reserved for high-level managerial positions, which elected officials use to take over the bureaucracy. *See also* ELROD V BURNS; SPOILS SYSTEM.

political base A candidate's hard core of support; it can be anything a candidate can count on from a safe district from which to launch a state-wide race, strong support among an ethnic or religious group, or a solid core of FAT CAT contributors.

political campaign 1. A formal effort established by law to obtain elective office; the contest for popular support between rival candidates that occurs prior to an election. Aspirants to public office once took their campaigns to the people; now they take them to the television station. Much of any major political campaign is fought via competing 30-second SPOTS for consumers who have learned to tke their politics in the same way they learn to "vote" for their favorite deodorant, toilet tissue, and denture glue. It was Senator Paul D. Laxalt of Nevada who said: "Campaigning is like trying a law suit:

The jury's a little bigger, but there's a verdict in each case" (*The Christian Science Monitor*, January 22, 1975). **2.** Any effort to obtain a political objective by convincing relevant individuals or groups of its importance, as in lobbying.

political capital Influence of the kind that will further a politico's ambitions. Just as the private sector uses capital in the form of money or property to create more wealth, the political world has its own "coins" with which to buy political wealth. A politician makes political capital by doing favors for others, by exposing a scandal that embarrasses the opposition, and so on. Political capital, like any currency, can be saved; and when the time is right, the debts can be called in. According to columnist Patrick J. Buchanan: "Political capital is not something that is dissipated. It is a renewable resource. The more that you invest in it, the greater the return. [For example,] the idea that the President [Reagan] gave up political capital on the [Nicaraguan] contras is ridiculous. He put all his chips on the table up there [on Capitol Hill], and he won, and it's redoubled. The investment of political capital is something that, when invested wisely, doubles and redoubles itself" (*USA Today*, July 18, 1986).

political clearance The process by which qualified applicants for both PATRONAGE and MERIT SYSTEM appointments are hired only after there is an appropriate indication of partisan political sponsorship. While it is illegal to require political clearance for merit system appointments, it remains a common practice.

political club A local civic organization that focuses on maintaining the fortunes of particular political party but that also engages in social, educational, and charitable works that will indirectly advance the interests of the party.

political commissar 1. In the Soviet Union, a civilian assigned to a military unit to insure that its commanders follow the policies of the government. **2.** By analogy, any representation of a central executive assigned to line agencies to insure that new employees and their policies are politically acceptable. The Richard M. Nixon administration placed political commissars in many federal agencies to assure that new appointees, both patronage and merit system, had POLITICAL CLEARANCE.

political committee As defined by the Federal Election Commission, any committee, club, association, or group of persons that for the purposes of influencing federal elections receives contributions or makes expenditures in excess of $1,000 during a calendar year.

political consultants 1. Professionals in campaign management who provide a wide range of services, from advertising to polling, to a candidate; in effect, a "store" from which a candidate can "buy" all the things needed to get elected. **2.** Advertising specialists who are for hire to sell political candidates. The underlying premise is that a political personality can be sold in the same way as songs or soft drinks. Adlai Stevenson (1900–1965), who was the Democratic party candidate for President in 1952 and 1956, at the dawn of the television age, said in accepting his party's nomination on August 18, 1956, that "the idea that you can merchandise candidates for high office like breakfast cereal. . . is. . . the ultimate indignity to the democratic process." Indignity it may be, but it hasn't stopped most major candidates of both parties from suffering such in the hope of being elected—for their image if not for their substance. Mark Hanna's (1837–1904) management of William McKinley's Presidential campaign in 1896 is generally considered the beginning of the modern form of national political advertising. The introduction of the idea of "Madison Avenue" in the Stevenson-Eisenhower campaigns of the 1950s is generally thought to be the beginning of the professionalization of the process. The ultimate reasons why candidates in all major contests need a political consultant was succinctly explained by journalist Theodore H. White: "There are plants that are called heliotropic because they turn to the sun regardless of where you plant them. All politicians today are videotropic: They turn to a television" (*U.S. News & World Report*, July 5, 1982). *Compare to* IMAGE MAKERS.

political corruption *See* CORRUPTION, POLITICAL.

political culture A community's attitudes toward the quality, style, and vigor of its political processes and government operations. The only way to explain the extreme variations in public bureaucracies is by the cultural context of the host jurisdictions. The quality of bureaucratic operations varies for a variety of reasons—not the least of which is the substantial disagreement on just what constitutes a quality operation. But the quality or style of operations is determined only in the lesser part by critics and public officials; the crucial determinant is the political will of the community. It determines the values to be applied to any given public problem; helps establish the obligations of the public role; and establishes the parameters of activities an official may participate in. Even when corruption is rife, it is the political culture that sets the limits and direction of such corruption. *Compare to* POLITICAL SOCIALIZATION.

political culture, Elazar's The division of American political culture into three major subcultures: the individualistic, the moralistic, and the traditional. This viable classification of the various American political cultures was not achieved until the mid-1960s with the work of Daniel J. Elazar of Temple University. Elazar classified the political subcultures of the United States (and of the individual states) by examining three sets of factors for each locality studied: (1) the sources of political culture, such as race, ethnicity, and religion; (2) the manifestations of political culture, such as political attitudes, behavior, and symbols; and (3) the effects of political culture, such as political actions and public policies. In this manner, he was able to identify the political subcultures for each of several hundred American communities in his book *American Federalism: A View from the States* (2nd ed., 1972).

The individualistic political culture "holds politics to be just another means by which individuals may improve themselves socially and economically." In the moralistic political culture, politics is conceived "as a public activity centered on some notion of the public good and properly devoted to the advancement of the public interest." The traditionalistic political culture is reflective of "an older precommercial attitude that accepts a substantially hierarchical society as part of the ordered nature of things, authorizing and expecting those at the top of the social structure to take a special and dominant role in government."

political economy The conjunction of politics and economics; the study of relations between the economy and the state that was practiced before either political science or economics became distinct disciplines. Political economy is a public policy concern because of the primacy of economic prosperity to U.S. governments. Not only does the government account for one third of the GROSS NATIONAL PRODUCT, it also regulates the basic economic conditions of society: for example, it can specify production of a product, regulate the wages of the production workers, prescribe working conditions, and establish standards for and inspect the quality of the finished product. *See also* ECONOMIC POLICY; FISCAL POLICY.

political efficacy A citizen's belief (1) that he or she can understand and participate in political affairs and (2) that the political system will be responsive. Political scientists Angus Campbell, Philip E. Converse, Warren E. Miller, and Donald E. Stokes, in their classic analysis of voting behavior, *The American Voter* (1960), found that there existed a very high positive correlation between an individual's "sense of political efficacy" and his inclination to vote. Those with a high sense of political efficacy (a belief that they could influence the political process) almost always voted; those with a low sense of political efficacy tended to vote only in about half the instances when there was an opportunity to vote.

political executive **1.** An individual, such as a President, governor, or mayor, whose institutional position makes him or her formally responsible for the governance of a political community. He or she gains this responsibility through election by the people and can have it taken away by not being reelected, by being impeached, or by being recalled. **2.** A high-level PATRONAGE appointee. **3.** The institutions of a government responsible for governing; the totality of the departments, agencies, and bureaus of a government.

political junkie One who is addicted to politics either as a player who gets actively involved or as a viewer who constantly reads about and follows political affairs.

political language An inversion of the usual meanings of words. According to English essayist George Orwell: "Political language—and with variations this is true of all political parties, from Conservatives to Anarchists—is designed to make lies sound truthful and murder respectable, and to give an appearance of solidity to pure wind" ("Politics and the English Language," *Shooting an Elephant*, 1950).

politically correct (PC) 1. Attitudes toward public issues that are socially acceptable according to prevailing norms in a regime. **2.** A catch-all description for new social attitudes that emerged on American university campuses in the early 1990s. PC activists seek to repress ideas, statements, or behavior that they consider to be racist or sexist. Another major theme is the rejection of literary and political works by DWEMs (Dead White European Males) and the replacement of such traditional classics with works by women and by nonwhite or third world writers. Because the PC movement is sometimes led by faculty who teach students to be intolerant of views that are not PC, the whole movement has been referred to as a new MCCARTHYISM.

political machine 1. Historically, an informal organization that controlled the formal processes of a government through corruption, patronage, intimidation, and service to its constituents. A political machine usually centered on a single politician—a boss—who commanded loyalty through largess, fear, or affection. The phrase is usually pejorative, because the machine works to achieve political control through those who run the machine, rather than through the popular will. The classic story of a political machine concerns Tammany Hall in New York City. John P. O'Brien (1873–1951), the newly installed mayor in 1932, was asked who his new police commissioner would be. He responded: "I haven't had any word on that yet." Tammany Hall soon gave him the "word." **2.** A grudging compliment to a modern political campaign or organization that is effectively managed—with or without some of the elements of the traditional political machine. **3.** A government agency used to disperse patronage. For example, when DuBois L. Gilliam, a former high official at HUD, told a Congressional committee of the pervasive political favoritism and fraud at HUD during the 1980s, he said: "The Department of Housing and Urban Development was the best domestic political machine I've ever seen. We dealt strictly in politics" (*The New York Times*, May 1, 1990). *See also* BOSSISM.

political neutrality The concept that public employees should not actively participate in partisan politics. The Hatch Acts of 1939 and 1940 restrict the political activities of almost all federal employees and those in state employment having federal financing. Many states have "little" Hatch Acts which further limit the possible political activities of public employees.

political obligation 1. The mutual responsibilities that citizens and states have to each other. **2.** The informal sense of debt that one political actor may have toward another because of past favors. Someone under political obligation is expected to return the favor at an appropriate time.

political officer A career foreign service officer who specializes in political as opposed to economic or consular matters.

political orientation 1. One's political beliefs. **2.** One's political party.

political party An organization that seeks to achieve political power by electing members to public office so that their political philosophies can be reflected in public policies. There are always three elements to a viable political party: (1) the party in the electorate consisting of all those citizens who identify with it; (2) the party organization which is its formal structure and includes all party officers and workers; and (3) the party in government consisting of all those members the party got elected to public office. American political parties are inherently decentralized entities. While they annually engage in statewide and local campaigns of greatly varying intensity, they organize to mount national campaigns only in Presidential election years.

It has often been said that the party system is the oil that makes the constitutional machinery work. Throughout their history, Americans have taken to political parties with great enthusiasm in spite of the fact that George Washington in his Farewell Address of September 17, 1796 warned his fellow citizens "in the most solemn manner against the baneful effects of the spirit of party." Washington felt that this "spirit of party". . . "serves always to distract the public councils and enfeeble the public administration. It agitates the community with ill-founded jealousies and false alarms; kindles the animosity of one part against another; foments occasionally riot and insurrection." Washington and the other founders hoped to create a partyless government. Their failure to do so led to the Twelfth Amendment, which changed the means by which the ELECTORAL COLLEGE elects the President.

EDMUND BURKE two centuries ago provided the first modern definition of a political party: "A body of men united for promulgating by their joint endeavors the national interest, upon some particular principle in which they are all agreed." Joseph A. Schumpeter disagreed. To him a party was not a group, in the Burkean sense, "who intend to promote public welfare." His party was "a group whose members propose to act in concert in the competitive struggle for political power." Most modern analysts would agree that they are both right; both principle and power are major motivations for people to join parties. As for the famous sentence, "Now is the time for all good men to come to the aid of the party"; it was simply devised to test the speed of the first typewriter in the fall of 1867, during "an exciting political campaign," according to Charles E. Weller's *The Early History of the Typewriter* (1918).

political period *See* POLITICAL RATE.

political question **1.** An issue that a court chooses not to decide because of the court's judgment that the issue is inappropriate for a judicial determination; the question is better left to another branch of government. For example, in *Colegrove v Green* (1946), the Supreme Court denied federal jurisdiction over cases of legislative malapportionment because it felt the issue was a political question. However, the Court later reversed itself in BAKER V

CARR. **2.** The doctrine of self-imposed restraint on the part of the Supreme Court, through which it defers to the judgment of the legislature and executive branches when a political question is at issue. Such questions include decisions to recognize foreign governments, and determinations of when amendments to the Constitution have been ratified. For example, in *Coleman v Miller* (1939), the Supreme Court held that the efficacy of a constitutional amendment's ratification by a state following a previous rejection by that same state is a political question, for determination by the Congress. *Compare to* JUSTICIABILITY. **3.** A question that is understood as having no clear-cut, technical answer, and hence, as subject to debate among holders of competing opinions.

political rate The rate radio and TV stations, according to FCC rules, must charge for political advertising; it must not be more than what they charge their best regular customers. But this political rate exists only for a "political period"; 45 days before a primary and 60 days before a general election. Otherwise candidates can be treated as regular low-volume customers and charged much more.

political rights **1.** All of the implicit (constitutionally guaranteed) and implied (by natural law) rights of a citizen in a free society. **2.** Whatever rights a dictatorial government allows its citizens to have.

political risk The chance a company takes by engaging in business in a politically unstable state; the business could be expropriated or social upheavals might make it impossible to operate—employees could even be killed. In response to this problem, political risk insurance does a thriving trade.

political science The academic discipline that studies political phenomena; originally, the contention by eighteenth-century theorists that the political behavior of individuals as well as states could be subjected to the same criteria of analysis as natural phenomena. While this idea can be traced back certainly to Greek theorists like Plato and Aristotle, its development in Enlightenment thought rested on the transfer of conceptions of a mechanical celestial universe to the universe of human action. The constitution— the makeup—of governments could thus be defined in the form of mechanisms that limit and control the judgment and authority of individual leaders. The modern enlargement of that conception of science has led to recurring debates over the study of the mechanisms of government, the behavior of the governed, and the actions of those who govern—debates that assert either the applicability of scientific study or the relevance of the political arts of leadership that cannot be subjected to scientific analysis. While the growth of psychology, sociology, and the other social science disciplines have expanded our understanding of what a science of politics might be, the essential role of individual choice pointed out by Aristotle has kept the debate—science or art—alive. Indeed, John Adams in a July 9, 1814 letter to Thomas Jefferson bemoaned: "While all other Sciences have advanced, that of Government is at a stand; little better understood; little better practiced now than 3 or 4 thousand years ago."

And playwright George Bernard Shaw (1856–1950) gave early voice to what has become the standard complaint: that "political science, the science by which civilization must live or die, is busy explaining the past whilst we have to grapple with the present. It leaves the ground before our feet in black darkness whilst it lifts up every corner of the landscape behind us."

political socialization The transition from generation to generation of the ethos of a political system by the conscious and unconscious instilling of the values of a POLITICAL CULTURE. This is one of the most critical political processes; it starts in the home and continues in public school civics classes. ARISTOTLE thought that the real constitution of a society was to be found in the political attitudes of the people. Without these supportive predispositions in the psyche of the society, their paper manifestations—such as a written constitution—would be worthless and ineffective no matter how well written.

political stability The ability of a political system to maintain an equilibrium; to retain the support of its people for government policies within a stable range; to avoid radical and sudden changes in the premises of its political and economic systems. The United States has long been considered a country of great political stability.

political subculture 1. *See* POLITICAL CULTURE, ELAZAR'S. 2. The specific political timber of an ethnic group, which differs in significant ways from the dominant political culture of the community.

political system The institutions and processes that allow the citizens of a polity to make, implement, and revise public policies. According to David Easton, the political system essentially consists of those interactions through which values (such as equality and security) are authoritatively allocated for a society. Easton's model of the political system can be thought of as an input-output box, which takes in political demands and supports and puts out public policies, such as laws, court decisions, and regulations. These outputs then return to influence the system as feedback.

political warfare 1. An election campaign. 2. Aggressive use of political means to achieve national objectives; A constant policy of taking political action against the interests of another power in the expectation that the opposing nation will be worn down by the constant demands of internal and international political problems. Political warfare was a major weapon in the cold war arsenal.

politician 1. One who makes a career of seeking or serving in elective or appointive public office; one devoted to the service of a *polis*, a political community; one engaged in the professional practice of politics. President Ronald Reagan often liked to say: "Politics is said to be the second-oldest profession. Sometimes I think it's close to the first" (*Los Angeles Times*, October 25, 1974.) 2. A political party boss; someone engaged in politics for personal gain. Any public service done is purely incidental. **3.** According to Ambrose Bierce's *The Devil's Dictionary* (1911), "An eel in the fundamental mud upon which the superstructure of organized society is reared. When he wriggles he mistakes the agitation of his tail for the trembling of the edifice. As compared with the statesman, he suffers the disadvantage of being alive." This national antipathy was recognized by Abraham Lincoln who, speaking on January 11, 1837 to the Illinois legislature, asserted that politicians are "a set of men who have interests aside from the interests of the people, and who, to say the most of them, are, taken as a mass, at least one long step removed from honest men. I say this with the greater freedom, because, being a politician myself, none can regard it as personal." It was also noted by John F. Kennedy when he said: "Mothers all want their sons to grow up to be president, but they don't want them to become politicians in the process." *Compare to* STATESMAN.

politician, crossover A member of a minority group who as a political actor is capable of getting substantial numbers of votes from members of the larger public as well as from minority voters.

politician, honest "One who, when he is bought, will stay bought." This definition is usually credited to Simon Cameron (1799–1889), who as Abraham Lincoln's first secretary of War administered his office so corruptly that Lincoln appointed him minister to Russia just to get him out of town.

politician, pot-house A tavern or bar room politician; one who may be perpetually drunk or otherwise not worthy of respect. The "pot" here refers to a "pot of ale." It has nothing to do with the modern use of pot to mean marijuana.

politico 1. An elected official. **2.** A politician who is mainly concerned with reelection, patronage, and personal advancement and enrichment. **3.** An unofficial hanger-on and MOVER AND SHAKER of the political process, such as a campaign worker, a wealthy contributor, or a POLITICAL CONSULTANT. **4.** A role adopted by legislators that is a pragmatic mix between EDMUND BURKE's notions of trustee and delegate.

politics 1. The art and science of governance; the means by which the will of the community is arrived at and implemented; the activities of a government, politician, or political party. **2.** The pursuit and exercise of the political power necessary to make binding policy decisions for the community and to distribute patronage and other government benefits. **3.** The socialization of conflict. This definition comes from E.E. SCHATTSCHNEIDER in his *The Semi-Sovereign People* (1960). He sees the political process as a sequence: "conflicts are initiated by highly motivated, high-tension groups so directly and immediately involved that it is difficult for them to see the justice of competing claims. As long as the conflicts remain *private*. . . no political process is initiated. Conflicts become political only when an attempt is made to involve the wider public." *Compare to* PRIVATIZATION OF CONFLICT. **4.** The policymaking aspect of government, in contrast to its administration. **5.** The interpersonal negotiation that leads to consensus within, and action by, groups. **6.** A profession engaged in by those who move from one political office to another in an upward spiral toward greater public responsibility and power. As President John F. Kennedy told students in a speech at the University of North Carolina on October 12, 1961: "Those of you who regard my profession of political life with some disdain should remember that it made it possible for me to move from being an obscure lieutenant in the United States Navy to Commander-in-Chief in fourteen years with very little technical competence." **7.** According to Ambrose Bierce's *The Devil's Dictionary* (1906): "A strife of interests masquerading as a contest of principles. The conduct of public affairs for private advantage." **8.** Defined by what it isn't by Finley Peter Dunne's Mr. Dooley as "ain't beanbag"; meaning not a children's game but a tough quest for power. **9.** According to attorney Edward Bennett Williams, "Politics is the gentle art of getting votes from the poor and campaign contributions from the rich by promising to protect each from the other," quoted in Gerald Gardner's *The Mocking of the President* (1988). This definition probably originated with editor Oscar Ameringer (1870–1943). **10.** According to historian Henry Adams in his *The Education of Henry Adams* (1907): "Politics, as a practice, whatever its professions, had always been the systematic organization of hatreds." **11.** Popular entertainment. Americans have always looked to politics for amusement and fun. Those who decry the lack of seriousness in current political campaigns miss a major point: American politics has always been serious—serious entertainment. **12.** That which makes strange bedfellows because necessity so often forces unlikely pairs to work together for a common goal. The statement that "politics makes strange bedfellows" is usually traced to author Charles Dudley Warner's (1829–1900) *My Summer in a Garden* (1871). *Compare to* ART OF THE POSSIBLE.

politics, attack A new name for an old tactic; throwing political mud at an opponent, usually via TV SPOTS. Such tactics are on the increase at every level of government because of the effectiveness of negative campaigning, because the public shows little toleration for informal debate, and because of the general decline of the political parties. Candidates thus strive to create appeal by attacking opponents with rumor, innuendo, and half-truths.

politics, checkbook A description of the present-day reality in congressional elections, the fact that special interest groups (through their PACs) and FAT CAT donors dominate the elections process and have concomitant influence with the Congress.

politics, germ theory of *See* HERBERT BAXTER ADAMS.

politics is local The essence of former Speaker of the House Tip O'Neill's political philosophy: that if you want to understand the political behavior of members of Congress, you must know what issues affect their home districts, what their constituents really care about.

politics, peanut **1.** Petty, insignificant, sometimes lowdown political acts. By analogy, a peanut politician is one so unimportant that he or she never deals with "big" issues. **2.** The politics of President Jimmy Carter. The use of the peanut in reference to politics goes back well into the last century. As recently as 1973 Robert F. Wagner, the former Mayor of New York, said: "In political life, you get used to being attacked by peanut politicians" (*The New York Times*, March 26, 1973). President Carter, who was formerly in the peanut business, gave peanut politics a new life in Washington.

politics, power A translation of the German word *Machtpolitik,* referring to an aggressive foreign policy that substitutes threats and the actual use of military power for international law; in short, the notion that might makes right. According to Ely Culbertson's *Must We Fight Russia?* (1946): "Power politics is the diplomatic name for the law of the jungle." *Compare to* REALPOLITIK.

politics, practical **1.** Expedient political actions; those that are on the edge of legality and morality. The first use of the phrase is usually credited to British prime minister Benjamin Disraeli's novel *Vivian Grey* (1826). **2.** Those political acts that go over the edge of legality and morality and are indeed illegal and immoral. **3.** A cynical approach to political affairs. It was journalist H.L. Mencken who wrote in *The Smart Set* (December 1921) that: "The whole aim of practical politics is to keep the populace alarmed (and hence clamorous to be led to safety) by menacing it with an endless series of hobgoblins, all of them imaginary."

politics, retail Person-to-person political dealings, selling yourself or your program one-on-one. Susan Brophy, an aide to Governor Michael Dukakis, explained how his campaign for the Democratic presidential nomination courted super-delegates before the party's 1988 national convention: "It's totally retail politics. We know who they are, what they do for a living, what their dogs and cats are named. We send them speeches, hold receptions. And the governor usually talks to at least 10 of them on the phone every day" (*Newsweek*, March 28, 1988).

politics, wholesale Mass, large-scale political communication via conventions or television; selling yourself or your programs to a large audience. Senator Abraham A. Ribicoff of Connecticut divided politicians into "wholesalers" and "retailers": "Wholesalers undertake the big issues, the big picture and the big problems, while retailers devote their lives to all the petty things—door-to-door salesmen who cultivate the political vineyards, backslapping, greeting, doing minor retailing" (*The New York Times*, July 30, 1974).

polity **1.** An organized society, such as a state. **2.** The governing structures of a political community. **3.** ARISTOTLE's notion of the constitution, written or unwritten, that governs a body of people. *Compare to* POLIS.

Polk, James K. (1795–1849) The President of the United States from 1845 to 1849. Polk, a Congressman from and then Governor of Tennessee, was the first major DARK HORSE candidate in American presidential politics. Promising manifest destiny and "Fifty-four forty or fight" (this referred to the latitudinal boundary with Canada), he won the Democratic nomination and the presidency in 1844. When Mexico refused an offer of $30 million for New Mexico and California, Polk sent the Army to provoke a war. The Mexicans obliged, were conquered, and forfeited (with payment by the United States of $18 million) land comprising the present states of California, Nevada, Utah, and most of New Mexico and Arizona. Polk was able to peacefully settle the dispute with Great Britain over Canada at the 49th parallel of latitude. He had promised to serve only one term, and he returned to Tennessee after the inauguration of his successor, Zachary Taylor. He died three months later.

poll **1.** The counting of votes in an election. Poll is derived from *polle,* an old Teutonic word meaning "the top or crown of the head." In a head-counting situation in the olden days, someone would stand on high and count the tops of heads. **2.** The place (usually plural: polls) where people vote. **3.** The result of an election in terms of vote count. **4.** Private and informal (meaning not legal or binding) surveys of public opinion or of the opinions of any group. *Compare to* PUBLIC OPINION SURVEY; SAMPLE.

poll, benchmark A beginning poll used as a campaign strategy planning tool; it identifies opinion before the campaign starts.

poll, panel back A survey which continuously interviews the same individuals (the panel) during a campaign to measure their evolving perceptions.

poll, straw A test of the opinions of a voting group deliberately intended to have no effect other than suggesting to members of the group the direction in which opinion might be headed.

poll tax *See* TAX, POLL.

poll, tracking A means of measuring the public's reaction to developing events; continuous short surveys over several days or weeks that indicate trends in public sentiment. Tracking polls help major campaigns to fine-tune their political advertising.

pollbook A register of eligible voters. Today, a pollbook is more likely to be a printout from a computer.

polling, tactical Designing the questions in a poll so that respondents are effectively led to the "right" answers. Tactical polling is used when the sponsors of the poll are not interested so much in truth as in poll results that support their position or candidate.

Pollock v Farmer's Loan & Trust Co. *See* SIXTEENTH AMENDMENT.

polls, exit Interviews with voters (asking how they voted) just after they have finished voting and are exiting the polling places. This information is then aggregated, and projections of who has won or lost are made. As with all polls, an exit poll might select a scientific sample of the voting population or it might sample the man in the street (those interviews so loved by local TV news programs). Consequently, the reliability of exit polls can vary enormously. The reporting of exit poll results in presidential elections has become controversial because the United States is geographically divided into four time zones. Sometimes the winner is projected on the basis of exit polling by the news media on the East Coast many hours before the polls close on the West Coast. This seems to have discouraged many voters on the West Coast from voting at all, to the adverse interest of many state and local candidates.

pollster A person or organization that conducts public opinion polls. Thus, a pollster could be the individual interviewer or the organization he or she works for. Pollsters are used both by the media, which make the results public, and by campaign organizations, which often base their strategy and tactics on them—and which may make their results public if it is to their advantage to do so. Pollsters have tremendous influence on modern campaign strategies mainly because they are the only advisors to a candidate who can offer hard data to justify recommendations for action. Many political leaders are their own pollsters in that they have informal ways of knowing their standing in public opinion. Jimmy Carter once boasted: " My esteem in the country has gone up substantially. It is very nice, now, that when people wave at me, they use all their fingers" (*Time*, October 30, 1978). *See also* GEORGE HORACE GALLUP.

pollwatcher An individual who, on behalf of a candidate or a party, observes the voting process on election day to encourage proper procedures and to report irregularities. This function varies in importance depending on the historical integrity of the voting process in any given jurisdiction.

pool reporter The reporter(s) who represent all the press when it is impractical for a large number of media people to go with a political figure on an airplane, to a meeting, etc. Pool reporters are then obligated to share their information with their media colleagues.

popular sovereignty **1.** The concept that ultimate political authority resides with the people. This idea is at the heart of American government; the notion that the people are sovereign is inherent in the Declaration of Independence and in the Constitution. **2.** In the pre-Civil War debates on slavery, popular sovereignty was advocated by the South; in this context it referred to the right of new states coming into the union to decide the issue of slavery on an individual basis. Because the western lands preparing for statehood were said to be "squatted upon" by its new residents, this option for slavery was also called "squatter sovereignty."

popular vote *See* VOTE, POPULAR.

populism 1. A general term for any of a variety of mass political movements that began in both Europe and the United States toward the end of the nineteenth century. Populism is noted for mobilizing the poorer sectors of a society, often rural people who have suffered the dislocations of industrialization and urbanization, against existing institutions. In this sense, both fascism and national socialism (the nazism of Hitler's Germany) have their origins in populist movements—which, however, came under control of charismatic leaders. But any political movement that has mass popular backing and is generally perceived to be acting in the interests of the people can be called populist. **2.** A recurring political theme in the United States that stresses the role of government in defending small voices against the powerful and the wealthy. As a political force, populism, which grew out of a farmers' protest movement in the 1890s, is ideologically ambiguous. Economically, it has been decidedly to the Left, with its concerns for government aid for the little people. But at the same time, it has been decidedly to the Right on social issues, because its core support has often come from religious fundamentalists. Jim Hightower, Commissioner of Agriculture of Texas, says: "Populism addresses the problem that too few people have too much money and power. . . . It doesn't seek a liberal solution, to give welfare to the farmer who's been forced off his land, or a conservative solution, which is to say 'I got mine, so long sucker.' The idea is to put the tools of self-help in people's hands, to free up their enterprise so that prosperity doesn't trickle down, it percolates up" (*The Washington Post,* May 10, 1986).

pork Government largess obtained not on merit or because of legal entitlement but because of political patronage. A new "cut" of pork is increasingly favored in Washington in recent years: regulatory loopholes and tax breaks for those who have given large campaign contributions to members of Congress.

pork barrel 1. Favoritism by a government in the allocation of benefits or resources; legislation that favors the district of a particular legislator by providing for the funding of public works or other projects (such as post offices or defense contracts) that will bring economic advantage to the district and political favor for the legislator. **2.** The treasury of a state or national government when it is perceived as a means of providing funds for local interests regardless of their utility to the state as a whole.

position classification The use of formal job descriptions to organize all jobs in a civil service MERIT SYSTEM into classes on the basis of duties and responsibilities, for the purposes of delineating authority, establishing chains of command, and providing equitable salary scales.

position paper A formal statement of opinion or of proposed policies on political or social issues; often issued by candidates for public offices, public interest groups, unions, and so on.

positioning Marketing research applied to politics. First, opinion polling establishes what the public thinks on an issue; then the candidate takes a position on the issue in the way that appeals to the majority of voters.

positive law *See* LAW, POSITIVE.

Potomac fever An overwhelming desire to obtain or retain a high-status job, elective or appointive, in Washington, D.C., which sits on the banks of the Potomac River. Senator George D. Aiken of Vermont once said: "When the Presidential bug gets into your veins, the only thing that will get it out is embalming fluid" (*The New York Times*, May 1, 1975).

poverty   Defined by the U.S. Bureau of the Census in 1991 as an annual cash income of less than $13,924 for a family of four. This is the subsistence approach. Another way to approach poverty is in terms of relative deprivation, in which the poor are those with less than most others, even if everyone's economic level is well above subsistence level. Poverty has long been perceived as a natural, normal condition for some members of a society. The *New Testament* teaches that "ye have the poor always with you" (Matthew 26:11). But in more recent times, poverty has come to be thought of as an essentially unnatural or undemocratic condition, a measure of the weakness of a society that claims equality for all of its citizens. As President John F. Kennedy said in his inaugural address of January 20, 1961: "If a free society cannot help the many who are poor, it cannot save the few who are rich." *Compare to* WAR ON POVERTY; LEADERSHIP.

poverty, feminization of   The increasing tendency for impoverished households to be headed by an unmarried mother. The number of single-mother families living in poverty has more than doubled in the 1980s.

poverty line   The statistical measures, expressed in terms of yearly income, that households of varying sizes need to stay above poverty, used by the federal government to define poverty. This has become a contentious practice even though the line is raised each year to account for inflation. The poverty line is determined by taking the amount of money that the Department of Agriculture determines a household needs for a minimally adequate diet and multiplying it by three. Some say the formula for calculating poverty created in the 1960s doesn't reflect current spending patterns because it doesn't take into account items such as higher housing expenses and day care for children. Others contend that the formula only exaggerates the level of poverty because it doesn't include benefits such as food stamps and subsidized public housing.

poverty trap   The dilemma that families on means-tested WELFARE benefits often face. The welfare system is such that they chance losing benefits if their income rises; consequently, they are discouraged from seeking employment that pays only marginally better than welfare alone—employment that might eventually take them off the welfare rolls.

Powell v Alabama   *See* GIDEON V WAINWRIGHT.

power   **1.** The ability or the right to do something; the ability to exercise authority over others. **2.** A national strength, such as a strong economy. **3.** That which, according to Mao Zedong, "grows out of the barrel of a gun" (*Quotations from Chairman Mao*, 1966). Traditionally, the power of regimes was a function of their military prowess; their ability to coerce their populations internally and defend themselves from external threats. **4.** Legal or official authority; formal responsibility for affairs of government. In this context power is value neutral. As playwright George

Bernard Shaw wrote in *Major Barbara* (1905): "You cannot have power for good without having power for evil too. Even mother's milk nourishes murderers as well as heroes." **5.** An individual state; a great power has a strong military, a small power does not. **6.** Military forces in general. **7.** That which makes you attractive to others who hope some perceived power or influence will rub off. This is what secretary of State Henry A. Kissinger meant when he said: "Power is the ultimate aphrodisiac" (*New York Times*, October 28, 1973). **8.** That which corrupts when it is unlimited. The most famous statement on this come from English historian Lord Action (John Dahlberg): "Power tends to corrupt, and absolute power corrupts absolutely. Great men are almost always bad men. . . . There is no worse heresy than that the office sanctifies the holder of it," letter to Bishop Mandell Creighton, April 5, 1887, reprinted in *Life and Letters of Mandell Creighton* (1904). **9.** According to comedian Dick Gregory, in *Dick Gregory's Political Primer* (1972): "[Power is] exerted energy and capacity for action. When followed by the word structure, it refers to a group which includes America's most wealthy and influential citizens. When prefixed by the word black, it creates terror in the minds of the power structure."

Power implies a hierarchy of control of stronger over weaker. Social scientists John R.P. French and Bertram Raven, in "The Bases of Social Power" (Dorwin Cartwright, *Studies in Social Power*, 1959), suggest that there are five major bases of power: (1) expert power, which is based on the perception that the leader possesses some special knowledge or expertise; (2) referent power, which is based on the follower's liking, admiring, or identifying with the leader; (3) reward power, which is based on the leader's ability to mediate rewards for the follower; (4) legitimate power, which is based on the follower's perception that the leader has the legitimate right or authority to exercise influence over him or her; and (5) coercive power, which is based on the follower's fear that noncompliance with the leader's wishes will lead to punishment. Subsequent research on these power bases has indicated that the first two (expert and referent power) are more positively related to subordinate performance and satisfaction than the last three (reward, legitimate, and coercive power).

power base A politician's most dependable support. It is a vague phrase, which could mean a home state or district, a wing of the party, or a cadre of FAT CAT campaign contributors.

power broker 1. A person who controls a bloc of votes that can be delivered in exchange for a price. The price could be a promise of appointive office, the acceptance of a specific policy, the placement of a favored candidate on the ticket, or plain old-fashioned money. **2.** Someone who is so trusted by the contesting sides of an issue that he or she can arrange an agreement. **3.** An *èminence grise*—who runs government from behind the scenes.

power, corridors of The official world, the bureaucracy, the places where leaders make decisions for the rest of us. The phrase comes from the title of a 1964 novel by C.P. Snow.

power curve The cutting edge of high level decision making. Someone who is "behind the power curve" is unaware of the latest decision.

power-elite theory *See* MILLS, C. WRIGHT; PLURALISM.

power, inherent 1. An authority that is an integral part of sovereignty and that, while not expressly stated, is implied by the nature of government and necessary for a government to function. **2.** A power not expressly granted by the U.S. Constitution but that came about through the NECESSARY AND PROPER CLAUSE.

power of attorney A legal document authorizing one person to act as attorney for, or in the place of, the person signing the document.

power of the purse 1. Control of a treasury or other source of funding. The power to control the distribution of funding for public expenditure has been the basis of disputes between executives and legislatures for centuries. **2.** The ability of political figures to direct government appropriations to the programs they favor. Under Article I, Section 7, of the U.S. Constitution, the power of the purse belongs to the House of Representatives because "all bills for raising revenue shall originate" there.

power politics *See* POLITICS, POWER.

PPBS *See* PLANNING PROGRAMMING BUDGETING SYSTEM.

preamble 1. The first paragraph of the U.S. Constitution, which begins "We the people. . . " and goes on to explain the reasons for the Constitution ("to form a more perfect union, establish justice, insure domestic tranquility. . . "). **2.** An introduction to a legal document, such as an administrative agency rule or a statute, that explains why it was written. A preamble is not legally enforceable but may be referred to by the courts to ascertain the ORIGINAL INTENT.

precedent The legal principle that previous decisions influence future decisions unless explicitly overruled. It is the basis for stability in law, built on the expectation that judgments will be consistent with one another unless there is reason for change. According to satirist Jonathan Swift (1667–1745) in *Gulliver's Travels* (1726), "It is a maxim among lawyers that whatever hath been done before may be done again: and therefore they take special care to record all the decisions formerly made against common justice and the general reason of mankind. These, under the name of *precedents*, they produce as authorities to justify the most iniquitous opinions."

precinct 1. A local government subdivision for organizing the voting process, typically containing less than a thousand voters; the next larger unit is a WARD. As such, the precinct is the basic unit of political party organizations. The precinct workers are the frontline troops in election campaigns. Modern political consultants often say: "There's a precinct worker in every home now. It's called a television." The traditional precinct worker is the committeeman or committeewoman (sometimes called a PRECINCT CAPTAIN), usu-

ally elected every two years. **2.** A municipal subdivision for police administration, which may or may not be coterminous with election precincts.

precinct captain The person responsible for the interests of a political party
in a voting precinct. Typical duties include supervising party volunteer
workers, registering voters, cultivating voters by doing favors for them, and
getting out the vote on election day.

precinct, key A representative locality used to estimate election night
trends and make predictions of winners and losers. A key precinct should
ideally be a microcosm of the overall electorate.

preemption doctrine The legal principle that federal laws take precedence
over state laws. This principle is grounded in the portion of Article VI of
the U.S. Constitution that asserts that the Constitution "and all the laws of
the United States which shall be made in pursuance thereof. . . shall be the
supreme law of the land."

preferments The modern version of HONEST GRAFT/DISHONEST GRAFT; the
advantages politicians gain because of their position or connections. Examples include contracts to provide insurance on government property, contracts to supply government institutions, and retainers paid to a politician's
law firm by an interested lobbyist. Journalist Mike Royko in *Boss: Richard
J. Daley of Chicago* (1971) reported that Mayor Daley was once asked by a
real estate agent newly elected to the state legislature how he should conduct himself. Daley advised him, "Don't take a nickel; just hand them your
business card." Preferments are often quietly solicited through seemingly
innocent business cards.

preferred position doctrine The notion, not fully accepted by the Supreme
Court, that First Amendment rights are more important than other parts of
the Bill of Rights and thus may take precedence.

prerogative theory of presidential powers *See* NEAGLE, IN RE.

prerogative theory of the presidency *See* PRESIDENCY, PREROGATIVE THE-
ORY OF THE.

presidencies, two Aaron Wildavsky's division of the presidency into two
differing spheres of influence: foreign policy and domestic policy. Wildavsky contended that presidential leadership in foreign policy will, generally speaking, find greater support among the public than leadership in
domestic policy. To test his hypothesis, Wildavsky examined congressional
action on presidential proposals from 1948 to 1964. For this period, the
Congress approved 58.5 percent of the foreign policy bills; 73.3 percent of
the defense policy bills; and 70.8 percent of general foreign relations, State
Department, foreign aid bills, and treaties. During this same period, the
Congress approved only 40.2 percent of the President's domestic policy
proposals. Thus, the two-presidencies thesis was confirmed. Wildavsky's
work has spawned a bevy of research articles, none of which has materially
diminished the original thesis put forth in "The Two Presidencies" (*Trans-
Action*, December 1966).

presidency, American The U.S. institution and office of the presidency. The American President has been compared to an elective monarch, but there are few kings or queens today who exercise the same degree of authority as does the President of the United States. The office simultaneously encompasses several titles that are often split among two or more incumbents in monarchies and parliamentary democracies.

Presidents are traditionally accorded the unofficial designation "chief of state," a position that most closely parallels that of a king or queen in a monarchy. As such, they are recognized as the symbolic embodiment of the United States and its citizens, and thus are accorded the same honors due a reigning sovereign. But President Harry S Truman warned in *Plain Speaking* (1973): "When you get to be President, there are all those things, the honors, the twenty-one gun salutes, all those things. You have to remember it isn't for you. It's for the Presidency." Presidents also perform many of the functions of prime ministers or premiers in parliamentary democracies. As chief executive, an office held under the Constitution, they preside over the cabinet and manage the executive branch. As political leader, they direct the operations of their party's national organization and serve as leader of its members in the Congress. The Constitution also vests Presidents with powers to make treaties and to appoint ambassadors, cabinet officers, and judges of federal courts, with the advice and consent of the Senate. They also hold the position of commander in chief of the armed forces. Unlike prime ministers, Presidents are not members of the legislature, nor is their tenure in office dependent on the approval of a majority of the legislators. Elected by the citizens, they serve a definite term, from which they can be removed only by the process of impeachment. At the same time, presidential tenure is usually limited to two four-year terms, as opposed to hereditary monarchs, who reign for life.

presidency, bifurcated A presidency that willingly shares power with the other branches of government on domestic policy issues but at the same time totally rejects the notion that power should also be shared in foreign policy. However, there are many who say that the Constitution does not give a President the option of which powers to share—they are all shared.

presidency, imperial A phrase that implies that the President of the United States has grown to be the head of an international empire as well as the head of a domestic political state. It suggests that the presidency has grown too powerful, that it has assumed more authority than is justified by its constitutionally granted powers. This suggestion is reinforced when the office takes on more and more of the trappings of traditional European monarchy. The high-water mark of these trappings occurred during the Richard M. Nixon administration, when the civilian White House guards were dressed in uniforms reminiscent of a Gilbert and Sullivan comic opera. The "imperial" uniforms were so ridiculed by the press that they were soon retired. The phrase "imperial presidency" is usually credited to the 1973 book of the same title by historian Arthur Schlesinger, Jr. The book came out just as the Watergate scandal broke and all of the excesses of the Nixon administration were bared to the world. While Schlesinger's phrase was a convenient way to summarize Nixon's corrupting of the presidential office, the book, written before the scandal broke, was not an attack on Nixon but rather an analysis of the gradual enhancement of presidential powers in modern times. Schlesinger wrote: "The American democracy must discover a middle ground between making the President a czar and making him a puppet. The problem is to devise means of reconciling a strong and purposeful Presidency with equally strong and purposeful forms of democratic control. Or, to put it succinctly, we need a strong Presidency—but a strong Presidency *within the Constitution*."

presidency, prerogative theory of the Abraham Lincoln's belief, supported by JOHN LOCKE's *Second Treatise of Government* (1688), that under certain conditions the chief executive possesses extraordinary power to preserve the nation. This power, as Lincoln saw it, might not only exceed constitutional bounds but act against the Constitution. A President, according to this view, could at least for a short while assume dictatorial powers. Lincoln explained in an April 4, 1864, letter to A.G. Hodges:

. . . that my oath to preserve the Constitution to the best of my ability imposed upon me the duty of preserving, by every indispensable means, that government—that nation, of which that Constitution was the organic law. Was it possible to lose the nation and yet preserve the Constitution? By general law, life and limb must be protected, yet often a limb must be amputated to save a life; but a life is never wisely given to save a limb. I felt that measures otherwise unconstitutional might become lawful by becoming indispensable to the preservation of the Constitution through the preservation of the nation. Right or wrong, I assumed this ground, and now avow it.

presidency, restricted view of A limited (or literalist) view of presidential power that holds, according to President William Howard Taft in *Our Chief Magistrate and His Powers* (1916), that "the president can exercise no power which cannot be fairly and reasonably traced to some specific grant of power or justly implied and included within such express grant as proper and necessary to its exercise." Furthermore (and directly contrary to President Theodore Roosevelt's stewardship view), "there is no undefined residuum of power which he can exercise because it seems to be in the public interest."

presidency, rhetorical A description of the American presidency that refers to its ever-increasing reliance on rhetoric for political success, as opposed to its historic reliance on political parties and party organization. Political scientists James Caeser, Glen Thorow, Jeffrey Tulis, and Joseph

Bessette in "The Rise of the Rhetorical Presidency" (*Presidential Studies Quarterly*, Spring 1981) argue that, historically, leadership through rhetoric was suspect, that Presidents rarely spoke directly to the people, and that, in any event, Presidents relied much more heavily on party and political leadership in the Congress for their electoral and programmatic support. But today's Presidents attempt to move mass opinion by speeches that exhort the public to support their policies and programs. Presidents are obliged to do this for three reasons: the modern doctrine of the presidency, which avers that the presidency is a place of moral leadership and should employ rhetoric to lead public opinion; the advent of the modern mass media, especially television, which facilitates the use of rhetoric; and the modern presidential campaign, which blurs campaigning and governing.

presidency, stewardship theory of the　President Theodore Roosevelt's view that the President, because he represents and holds in trust the interests of all the people, should be free to take any actions in the public interest that are not specifically forbidden by the Constitution or statutory law. But he articulated this doctrine in his autobiography published in 1913 after he left office. *Compare to* BULLY PULPIT.

President　**1.** The head of state in a republic. The powers of such Presidents vary enormously. The President of the United States, who is also the head of the government, has great powers. In contrast, most other Presidents (such as those in Israel and Germany) have mainly ceremonial and informal authority. **2.** One appointed or elected to preside over a formal assembly. **3.** A chief executive officer of a corporation, board of trustees, university, or other institution.

President, acting　The title of the Vice President of the United States when temporarily assuming the powers of the presidency under the provisions of the Twenty-Fifth Amendment.

President elect　The elected President of the United States, other than an incumbent President, from the time the election results are known in November until inauguration in January. This informal title is superfluous for a sitting President who wins reelection.

President, Making of the　*See* MAKING OF THE PRESIDENT.

president of the Senate　The presiding officer of the U.S. Senate, normally the Vice President of the United States. In his or her absence, a president pro tempore (president for the time being) presides. Normally, the Vice President presides over the Senate only if an upcoming vote is expected to be close, because the U.S. Constitution (Article I, Section 3) provides that the Vice President can vote only in the event of a tie.

president pro tempore　The chief presiding officer of the United States Senate in the absence of the Vice President. The recent practice has been to elect to this office the Senator of the majority party with longest continuous service. This is a largely symbolic position that has never become politically powerful in itself.

presidential character Political scientist James David Barber's (1930–   ) theory of how a President's personality or character influences the success of his administration. In *The Presidential Character: Predicting Performance in the White House* (3rd ed., 1985), Barber classified all Presidents according to whether they take an active or passive role in the presidency and whether their personal enjoyment of or emotional attitude toward the job of President is positive or negative. This puts all Presidents into one of four quadrants: active-positive, active-negative, passive-positive, or passive-negative. Barber finds that the best Presidents tend to be active-positive; they have great self-confidence, enjoy the give and take of politics, and are results-oriented. Examples include Franklin D. Roosevelt, Harry S Truman, and John F. Kennedy. In contrast, the worst Presidents tend to be active-negative; they are often driven personalities with compulsive-aggressive behavior patterns and who are more interested in power than politics. Examples include Woodrow Wilson, Lyndon B. Johnson, and Richard M. Nixon. Barber's framework for evaluating Presidents, while widely read and highly influential, has been severely criticized for being superficial, long-distance psychoanalysis.

presidential commission *See* COMMISSION, PRESIDENTIAL.

presidential debates Joint televised press conferences by the major party candidates for U.S. President. These head-to-head confrontations (which are not true debates) have become an expected part of each presidential election season. They have two main aspects: the predebate negotiations over whether there will be a debate, and the post-debate analysis of who did how well. The debates themselves, while compelling to watch, seldom offer anything new. The basic strategy is to hope the opponent will make a mistake. But few candidates have been as lucky as Jimmy Carter was in 1976, when his opponent, President Gerald Ford, boldly asserted that "there is no Soviet domination of Eastern Europe." History has shown Ford's statement to be simply premature; but at the time it confirmed public perceptions that he was an intellectual lightweight. In the first of the modern presidential debates in 1960, Richard M. Nixon made the mistake of actually trying to debate, while his opponent, John F. Kennedy, concentrated on style and on presenting the correct presidential image. People listening to the debate on radio thought that Nixon had won, but Kennedy's style won him the television audience and the election. Ever since, presidential debates have been a game of style over substance.

presidential directive A formal instruction from the President of the United States. Unlike EXECUTIVE ORDERS, which apply broadly to the entire executive branch, presidential directives tend to be narrowly focused, deal with a single subject, and apply to only a handful of federal government agencies.

presidential election campaign fund The fund taxpayers may contribute to by checking a box on their federal income tax return. The tax form gives each taxpayer an opportunity to assign one dollar from their taxes (two dollars on a joint return) to pay for the public financing of presidential elections. Even though this does not increase their tax liability, only about 25 to 30 percent of all taxpayers contribute. *See* MATCHING FUNDS.

presidential electors The people who compose the ELECTORAL COLLEGE, which elects the President and Vice President of the United States—the only elective federal officials not elected by a direct majority vote of the people. In the presidential election held on the first Tuesday after the first Monday in November of every fourth year, each state chooses as many presidential electors as it has senators and representatives in the Congress. The District of Columbia also chooses three presidential electors.

presidential form of government A governing system in which the executive branch is separate from and independent of the legislature, as in the United States, in contrast to a PARLIAMENTARY SYSTEM, in which the executive is integrated with the legislature. Walter Bagehot wrote in his *The English Constitution* (1867): "The independence of the legislative and executive powers is the specific quality of Presidential government, just as their fusion and combination is the precise principle of Cabinet government." *Compare to* CABINET GOVERNMENT.

presidential power 1. The right and the means to enforce and execute the nation's laws. Article II of the U.S. Constitution vests the executive power in the President. There is dispute among scholars about whether the executive power consists solely of those powers enumerated for the President or whether it includes also those powers that are implied in Article II. Most authorities lean toward the latter interpretation. The distinction between the President and the presidency—that is, between the individual elected to the office and the power of the office itself—is essentially a modern distinction, which has its origins in the writings of political scientists of Woodrow Wilson's generation. The ability of individuals to effect the power of the office at given periods is distinguishable from the inherent powers of the office. The powers expressly granted to Presidents are few in number. They act as commander in chief of the army and navy and of the state militias when they are called into the service of the United States. They may require the written opinion of executive officers and are empowered to grant reprieves and pardons except in the case of impeachment. Presidents are granted the power, by and with the advice and consent of the Senate, to make treaties, provided that two thirds of the Senators present concur. They also nominate and, by and with the advice and consent of the Senate, appoint ambassadors, other public ministers and consuls, justices of the Supreme Court, and other federal officers whose appointments are established by law. Presidents have the power to fill all vacancies that occur during recesses of the Senate. (Those commissions expire unless the Senate consents to them when it reconvenes.) The Constitution also directs Presidents to inform the Congress periodically on the state of the union and to recommend legislation considered necessary and expedient. They may, on extraordinary occasions, convene both houses of the Congress, or either of them, and, in case the two houses disagree about the time of adjournment, may adjourn them to such time as he or she considers proper. Presidents also receive ambassadors and other public ministers, and commission all officers of the United States. The President may veto acts of the Congress. A two-thirds vote of those present and voting is required in both the House and the Senate to override a presidential veto. Finally, Presidents are instructed to "take care that the laws be faithfully executed."

In addition to these express powers, Presidents derive certain implied authority from the Constitution. This implied authority, like the expressed powers, has been in the past and remains today a subject of dispute and debate. Major implied constitutional powers flow from the presidential authority as commander in chief. Though the Congress has the explicit power to declare war, Presidents have the authority not only to protect the nation from sudden attack but also to initiate military activities without a formal declaration of war. American Presidents have used military force hundreds of times, but only on five occasions has the Congress declared war: the War of 1812, the Mexican War, the Spanish-American War, and the two World Wars. On all other occasions, it merely recognized, after executive initiatives, that hostilities did in fact exist. In recent years, the Congress has sought to define more clearly (most notably through the War Powers Resolution of 1973) the conditions under which Presidents could take unilateral military action. **2.** Persuasion. Historian Richard E. Neustadt's *Presidential Power* (1960) asserts that a President's real powers are informal, that presidential power is essentially the power to persuade. Neustadt quotes President Harry S Truman contemplating General Dwight D. Eisenhower becoming President: "He'll sit here, and he'll say, 'Do this! Do that!' And nothing will happen. Poor Ike—it won't be a bit like the Army. He'll find it very frustrating." *See also* UNITED STATES V CURTISS-WRIGHT EXPORT CORPORATION; UNITED STATES V NIXON; YOUNGSTOWN SHEET AND TUBE CO. V SAWYER.

presidential press conference A formal meeting between a President and groups of representatives of the press. Prior to William McKinley, Presidents met with individual reporters as they chose, or responded to pursuit. McKinley held the first group press meeting, and his successor, Theodore Roosevelt, used both individual and group meetings. By the 1920s, it was the custom for Presidents to hold sporadic meetings with groups of reporters, using various methods of controlling the exchanges. Some Presidents required that questions be submitted in advance; Herbert Hoover established the practice of distinguishing between what could or could not be quoted.

But the modern press conference began with Franklin D. Roosevelt, who, in his first one, established three classes of information: statements that could be directly quoted, statements that could be used for background but not directly attributed to him, and statements that were strictly off the record. Since none of the transcripts of the conferences were ever published, and since the President retained the power to exclude reporters from meetings, his control over the process was absolute. Roosevelt established regular meetings, and Harry S Truman continued the process; but only in the last year of the Truman administration were edited transcripts available for publication. Dwight D. Eisenhower, although under pressure to open press conferences to live television, insisted on allowing only edited films and radio transcripts, a fact that gave print news media and radio a distinct advantage over television news coverage, then in its infancy. His reason for exercising such control was the possibility that accidental statements could endanger national policy. John F. Kennedy's 1961 decision to hold live press conferences was a revolution in modern communications history and in the character not only of news conferences but television news in general. Television made all public figures immediately quotable and without the protective controls their predecessors had enjoyed.

Since President Kennedy owed his election in large measure to his performance on televised debates with his opponent Richard M. Nixon, he had no fear of using this medium to consolidate and extend his political support from the public. All Presidents since Kennedy have used televised press conferences as part of an overall program of NEWS MANAGEMENT with varying degrees of success. But it is always a loaded deck and the press has little chance of either embarrassing a President with a question (all Presidents are skillful enough to deal with awkward questions) or to gain an unintended revelation. The last time these press conferences were genuinely hostile was during the WATERGATE era when President Richard Nixon was moved to say at a press conference on October 26, 1973: "Don't get the impression that you [the press] arouse my anger. You see, one can only be angry with those he respects. . ." By tradition, the first two reporters recognized at a presidential news conference are the representatives of the two major wire services, the Associated Press and United Press International.

presidential succession Under Article II, Section 1, of the U.S. Constitution, the Vice President exercises the power and duties of the President in the event of the President's death, resignation, disability, or removal from office. The Twenty-Fifth Amendment, ratified by the required three fourths of the states on February 10, 1967, provides: (1) that a Vice President who succeeds a President acquires all powers of the office; (2) that when the vice presidency is vacant, the President shall nominate a Vice President who shall take office when confirmed by a majority vote of both houses of the Congress; (3) that when the President informs the Congress in writing that he is unable to discharge his duties and until he informs the Congress in writing otherwise, the Vice President shall be the acting President; and (4) a procedure by which the Congress would settle disputes between a Vice President and a President as to the latter's ability to discharge the powers and duties of his office.

Two Vice Presidents have been appointed under the provisions of the Twenty-Fifth Amendment: Gerald R. Ford, installed on December 8, 1973 (to succeed Spiro T. Agnew), and Nelson A. Rockefeller, installed on December 16, 1974 (to succeed Gerald Ford, who had succeeded to the presidency with the resignation of President Richard M. Nixon on August 9, 1974). Nixon was the first President in history to resign from the presidency and Ford was the first to succeed to that office without having been elected by the people. Prior to the Truman administration, the secretary of State was designated to become President if both a President and Vice President had vacated their offices. But the Presidential Succession Act of 1947 arranged for elected officials—first the Speaker of the House of Representatives, and then the Senate President pro tempore—to take over the office before unelected cabinet members.

President's Committee on Administrative Management *See* BROWNLOW COMMITTEE.

presiding officer **1.** Any member of the U.S. Senate designated by the president pro tempore to preside during Senate sessions. Usually, only senators from the majority party preside, normally for one hour at a time. **2.** A member of the majority party of the House of Representatives who is appointed by the SPEAKER to preside over the House in the speaker's absence. **3.** Any formal chair of a meeting.

press conference **1.** A formal opportunity for mass media representatives as a group to ask questions of a public figure. **2.** Political theater by which a President or other major political personality matches wits with obstreperous and obsequious reporters. But the game, played mainly for the benefit of the TV cameras, is fixed. Politicos can so easily prepare for and parry questions that they almost always look good. If they can throw in a few jokes, they look even better. *See also* PRESIDENTIAL PRESS CONFERENCE.

press secretary **1.** The official who speaks for a government agency. **2.** A politician's chief public relations assistant. According to George E. Reedy, former Press Secretary to President Lyndon B. Johnson: "A Press Secretary hasn't been elected to anything and no one gives a damn what he thinks. They only care what the President thinks. . . [the President is] a monarch, a sort of king, and if he wants to say something stupid, a Press Secretary should say something stupid. If [the President] wants to lie, it's the responsibility of a Press Secretary to lie" (*Los Angeles Times*, October 24, 1974). This nonresponsive attitude continues. According to Marlin Fitzwater, President George Bush's press secretary: "The people's right to know is guaranteed by the Constitution. But it doesn't say when they get to know" (*The New York Times*, January 18, 1990).

pressing the flesh **1.** The now-expected act of a politician as he or she wades into a crowd to shake as many hands as possible before moving on to the next campaign stop. **2.** Any campaign tactic that has the candidate touching people. Presidents have often been criticized for this because of safety concerns. According to Harvard law professor Paul Freund: "The President should be less disposed to engage in a rather meaningless mingling with crowds. The pressing of flesh as a way of gauging public sentiment means nothing. . . . It's better for a President to judge public response by mail, telegrams. Certainly, it has more significance than having someone reach out and touch the hem of his garment" (*The New York Times*, September 24, 1975).

pressure group 1. Any organized group that seeks to influence the policies and practices of government. The difference between a pressure group and a LOBBY is that a pressure group is a large, often amorphous group that seeks to influence citizens as well as the political system; lobbyists are relatively small groups that seek to influence specific policies of government. Pressure groups are usually composed of committed amateurs. Lobbyists (usually full-time professional entreators) may be hired by pressure groups to help make their pressure more effective. **2.** A less-than-kind way of referring to legitimate lobbying organizations. *Compare to* LOBBY.

pretrial detention The holding in custody, pending a trial, of someone suspected of committing a crime because there is evidence that the person meets specific conditions for the denial of bail.

preventive detention Legally holding a person against his or her will because it is suspected that the person might commit a crime if allowed to go free. The Bail Reform Act of 1984, which permits preventive detention for those suspected of having committed a federal crime who might endanger the "safety of any other person and the community," was upheld by the Supreme Court in *United States v Salerno* (1987).

previous question An issue before the U.S. House of Representatives for a vote but superseded by another issue for the attention of the chamber. A motion for the previous question, when carried, has the effect of cutting off all debate and forcing a vote on the subject originally at hand. If, however, the previous question is moved and carried before there has been any debate on the subject at hand and the subject is debatable, then 40 minutes of debate is allowed before the vote. The previous question is sometimes moved to prevent amendments from being introduced and voted on. The motion for the previous question is a debate-limiting device and is not allowed in the Senate.

price support *See* PARITY, FARM.

primary An election held before a general election to nominate a political party's candidates for office. In some states, other officials, such as delegates to party conventions, are also elected at this time. Primaries developed during the early twentieth century as part of the reform agenda of the progressive movement. It was argued that leaving the nomination process to the political party bosses was inherently undemocratic, and that real democracy was possible only with rank and file participation, especially since nominations in jurisdictions where one party was dominant were often tantamount to election. Dates for primaries are set by the states and vary considerably. In some states, a separate primary is held by each of the principal parties. A major criticism of primaries is that those who vote in them tend to be unrepresentative not only of the general public but even of their party. The Supreme Court has made several rulings on primaries. In *Democratic Party v LaFollette* (1982) it held that a state could not force a delegate to a national convention to support the winner of his state's presidential primary. In *Tashijan v Republican Party of Connecticut* (1986), it held that states could not require political parties to make their primary elections open only to previously registered party members. *Compare to* CAUCUS.

primary, advisory A primary election that is not binding but merely indicative of the voter's preferences.

primary, beauty contest A presidential primary election in which voters elect a favored candidate in party caucuses and county and state conventions but do not elect national delegates. Michigan has a beauty contest primary. In 1988 Michigan Democrats selected delegates by designating places where on primary election day anyone could show up and vote. The Republicans selected representatives in precinct caucuses. These representatives then gathered at a state-wide convention to select national delegates.

primary, blanket An open primary election that allows voters to participate in the nominations of candidates from multiple parties on the same day by voting for a gubernatorial candidate of one party, a senatorial candidate from another party, a mayoral candidate from a third, and so on. Alaska and Washington state have blanket primaries.

primary, closed A primary election in which a voter must declare (or have previously declared) a political party affiliation and vote only that party's ballot in the primary election. *Compare to* PRIMARY, OPEN.

primary, contested A primary election in which a candidate has some competition. An *uncontested primary*, in contrast, presents no competition to the candidate. Many political figures of both major parties, especially in legislative offices, are so entrenched with their party and constituents that it would be futile for another member of the same party to challenge them; so they run unopposed.

primary, crossover An open primary; one in which members of one party can "cross over" to vote for another party's candidates. *Compare to* CROSS-FILING.

primary, direct A primary election in which political party nominees are selected directly by the voters.

primary, divisive A primary so hard-fought by the various party factions that it is difficult, if not impossible, to later create the PARTY UNITY needed for victory in the general election.

primary, New Hampshire Historically, the first primary election in the presidential election year and, consequently, a critically important one for generating the political and financial support that will allow candidates to continue. *Compare to* IOWA CAUCUS.

primary, nonpartisan A primary election in which voters and candidates from all parties use a single ballot. This is common in judicial elections and in certain local elections. Runoff elections (*see* ELECTIONS, RUNOFF) are often required if no candidate wins a majority of the vote. Louisiana is the only state with nonpartisan primaries for statewide and congressional offices.

primary, open A primary election in which a voter may vote for the nomination of any of the candidates regardless of his or her political party affiliation. Open primaries, used in 29 states, often lead to "strategic" voting, wherein voters cross over to vote for the weaker opposition candidate. *Compare to* PRIMARY, CLOSED.

primary, preference A primary election in which the voters indicate their preference for particular candidates. Such indications may or may not be binding upon the states' delegates to the party's national convention. Some states automatically enter in their presidential preference primaries all candidates being seriously mentioned in the press. It then becomes the obligation of noncandidates to withdraw their names. No candidate's name stays on the ballot if he or she formally asks that it be withdrawn.

primary, presidential The statewide elections that allow rank-and-file political party members to select (or to indicate preference for) delegates to their party's national nominating convention. Delegates may or may not be legally bound to support the candidate who wins the primary. Some delegates run already pledged to certain candidates, some run uncommitted. In 1984, about as many states used CAUCUSES as used primaries. The primary game from the point of view of the candidate is to win so many delegates along the primary campaign trail that uncommitted delegates increasingly climb on the bandwagon as convention time approaches.

The modern criteria for winning a primary is not that a candidate gain the most votes but that he or she does better than expected. Thus, a dark horse can "win" even if he or she loses. And a front runner who literally wins the primary may lose if the win is not as big as expected.

primary, regional A presidential primary in which all of the states in a region have primary elections on the same day. Although there are no formal regional primaries, whenever many states in a region have primaries on the same day it is, in effect, a regional primary. Many political analysts are against this practice because it may give the winner too great of an advantage too early in the game; others are in favor of it for the same reason. *Compare to* SUPER TUESDAY.

primary, white A primary election in which black participation was forbidden or discouraged. White primaries were common in the early part of the twentieth century in the South. The Supreme Court ruled that white primaries were illegal in *Smith v Allwright* (1944).

prior restraint The power (which has usually been denied by the Supreme Court to the federal government) to prevent the publication of something or to require approval prior to publication. Generally speaking, any government effort to constrain any kind of freedom of expression is prior restraint and is prohibited under the First Amendment. The major exception has been obscenity cases, but even there, according to the Supreme Court in *Organization for a Better Austin v Keefe* (1971), the "government carries a heavy burden of showing justification for the imposition of such a restraint." During wartime, censorship—the ultimate in press restraints—has been imposed through the Trading-with-the-Enemy Act of 1917. However, most censorship of military affairs has been voluntary on the part of the press. This cooperative approach worked quite well during World War II and the KOREAN WAR. However, during the VIETNAM WAR this system broke down and there was considerable conflict between the U.S. military and the press over reporting. The military sought to prevent any possible press conflicts during the PERSIAN GULF WAR by simply refusing to allow reporters free access to the troops. Because reporters could only see and hear what the military wanted them to see and hear, this amounted to *de facto* censorship. *Compare to* FREE PRESS CLAUSE; PENTAGON PAPERS.

prisoner's dilemma *See* GAME THEORY.

Privacy Act of 1974 The federal statute that reasserts the fundamental right to privacy as derived from the Constitution of the United States and that provides a series of basic safeguards for the individual to prevent the misuse of personal information by the federal government. The act provides for making known to the public the existence and characteristics of all personal information systems kept by every federal agency. It permits a person access to records containing one's own personal information and allows the person control of the transfer of that information to other federal agencies for nonroutine uses. The act also requires all federal agencies to keep accurate accountings of transfers of personal records to other agencies and outsiders, and to make the accountings available to the individual. It further provides for civil remedies for the person whose records are kept or used in contravention of the requirements of the act.

Virtually all agencies of the federal government have issued regulations implementing the Privacy Act. These regulations generally inform the public how to determine if a system of records contains information on themselves, how to gain access to such records, how to request amendment of such records, and how to appeal an adverse agency determination on such a request. *See also* FREEDOM OF INFORMATION ACT OF 1966.

private regardingness An attitude on the part of some citizens that places their personal short-term benefit over the welfare of the community as a whole. *Compare to* PUBLIC REGARDINGNESS.

privatization The process of returning to the private sector property (such as public lands) or functions (such as trash collection or fire protection) previously owned or performed by government. Republican administrations and conservative Republicans in general tend to be in favor of privatizing those government functions that can be performed (in their opinion) less expensively or more efficiently by the private sector. In this context, the terms privatization and reprivatization tend to be used interchangeably. Some extreme advocates of a wholesale privatization of government functions would even return social security, education, and public health to the private sector. The ultimate statement on privatization comes from novelist Joseph Heller in *Catch-22* (1961): "I'd like to see the government get out of war altogether and leave the whole feud to private industry."

privatization of conflict E.E. SCHATTSCHNEIDER's concept from *The Semi-Sovereign People* (1960) that there exists "a whole battery of ideas calculated to restrict the scope of conflict or even to keep it entirely out of the public domain." Consequently, "a tremendous amount of conflict is controlled by keeping it so private that it is almost completely invisible." This is in contrast to the socialization of conflict, Schattschneider's definition of POLITICS.

privilege 1. An advantage that a person or group has that others do not. **2.** An exemption from a duty or obligation that others have. For example, attorneys often have the privilege of being exempt from jury duty. **3.** The opportunity to make otherwise defamatory statements. For example, a senator cannot be held accountable in court for anything said on the floor of the Senate. Such remarks, no matter how scurrilous, are privileged. But the same thing said in another forum can bring a lawsuit for SLANDER. For example, when a senator read the still secret Pentagon Papers into the *Congressional Record,* the Supreme Court held that this was privileged speech in *Gravel v United States* (1972). However, the Court held in *Hutchinson v Proxmire* (1979) that a senator could be sued for statements made in a press release, because it does not represent speech on the floor of the Senate. **4.** A basic right or implied set of rights. For example, the privilege of U.S. citizenship. **5.** The obligation to withhold information. For example lawyers, priests, and physicians cannot be forced to divulge confidential discussions with clients, parishioners, and patients. *Compare to* EXECUTIVE PRIVILEGE. **6.** Rights of members of the Congress as to the relative priority of the motions and actions they may make in their respective chambers. Privileged questions concern legislative business. Questions of privilege concern legislators themselves (*see* PRIVILEGE, QUESTIONS OF).

privileged communication Information that a court cannot require disclosures of in evidence. Examples generally include (but may vary with local laws): communications between husbands and wives; physicians', psychologists', and lawyers' communications with their clients; and journalists' communications with their sources *Compare to* EXECUTIVE PRIVILEGE; *see also* SHIELD LAWS.

privileged questions Concerning the order in which bills, motions, and other legislative measures may be considered by the Congress. This order is governed by strict priorities. For instance, a motion to recommit can be superseded by a motion to table, and a vote would be forced on the latter motion only. A motion to adjourn, however, takes precedence over this one, and is thus considered of the highest privilege.

privilege, questions of Matters affecting members of the Congress individually or collectively. Questions affecting the rights, safety, dignity, and integrity of proceedings of the House of Representatives or of the Senate as a whole are questions of privilege of the House or Senate. Questions of personal privilege relate to individual members of the Congress. A member's rising to a question of personal privilege is given precedence over almost all other proceedings. An annotation in the House rules points out that the privilege of the member rests primarily on the Constitution, which gives him or her a conditional immunity from arrest and an unconditional freedom to speak in the House.

privileges and immunities clause **1.** Article IV, Section 2, of the U.S. Constitution, which holds that "the citizens of each state shall be entitled to all privileges and immunities of citizens in the several states." This ensures that U.S. citizens from out of state have the same legal rights as local citizens in any state. **2.** That portion of the Fourteenth Amendment that provides that "no state shall make or enforce any law which shall abridge the privileges and immunities of citizens of the United States." This was enacted in response to the BLACK CODES of some post-Civil War southern states, which denied blacks the same citizenship rights as whites. *See also* SLAUGHTER-HOUSE CASES.

pro choice A policy position of those who are not necessarily in favor of ABORTION but who are in favor of allowing each woman to decide the question for herself. Pro choice political candidates seek to deemphasize advocacy of abortion and stress the libertarian position that government has no business, indeed no right, to make this decision for a woman. *Compare to* PRO LIFE.

pro bono publico A Latin phrase meaning "for the public good." Often abbreviated to *pro bono*, it usually stands for work done by lawyers without pay for some charitable or public purpose.

pro death An unkind way of referring to someone who favors society allowing both abortion and capital punishment.

pro forma A Latin phrase meaning as "a matter of form" or "a mere formality." The phrase applies to requirements or agreements that are presumed to have no real effect on behavior.

pro life A policy position of those opposed to ABORTION, opposed to the Supreme Court's decision in ROE V WADE, and opposed to giving women the option of abortion. Some pro life proponents believe that abortion should be allowed in the case of rape or incest. Others, such as Illinois Congressman Henry Hyde, would not allow this option saying: "Rape and incest are tragedies, but why visit on the second victim, the unborn child. . . capital punishment?" (*Time*, July 9, 1990). *Compare to* PRO CHOICE.

pro memoria The formal record of a conversation between a foreign minister (or agent) and the head of a diplomatic mission (or agent). This is usually written in the third person but not signed, only initialed.

pro se A Latin term meaning "in one's own behalf." Its expanded meanings are acting as one's own defense attorney in criminal proceedings; representing oneself.

probable cause A set of facts and circumstances that would induce a reasonably intelligent and prudent person to believe a particular person had committed a specific crime; reasonable grounds to make or believe an accusation. Probable cause is required to justify arrest and the beginning of prosecution. The Supreme Court established the criteria for probable cause in *Draper v United States* (1959).

probate **1.** The process of proving that a will is genuine and then distributing the property of an estate. **2.** In some states, the name for a court that handles the distribution of decedents' estates (dead persons' property) and other matters.

probation **1.** The freedom granted to a convicted offender as long as he or she meets certain conditions of behavior. Conditions typically include maintaining regular employment, abstaining from drugs and alcohol, and not associating with known offenders. Not committing another offense is always a condition of probation. *Compare to* PAROLE. **2.** A period of service in a job during which the probationer is expected to prove his or her abilities to justify continued employment. Most civilian positions in government have mandatory probation periods. During this time, the employee usually has no seniority rights and may be discharged without CAUSE, as long as such a discharge does not violate laws concerning union membership and equal employment opportunity.

procedural law *See* LAW, SUBSTANTIVE.

procedural rights The various DUE PROCESS protections that all citizens have against arbitrary actions by public officials.

progressive movement A designation applied to the American experience with the consequences of urbanization and industrialization that affected western society in the decades between 1890 and 1920 (a period often known as the progressive era). While the term has its origins in religious concepts that argued for the infinite improvability of the human condition (rather than ordained class distinctions), by the end of the nineteenth century it had come to mean a responsibility of classes for one another and a willingness to use all government and social institutions to give that responsibility legal effect. In the United States, the movement was associated with two extremes: the search for greater democratic participation by the individual in government, and the application of science and specialized knowledge and skills to the improvement of life.

Politically, the movement reached its national climax in 1911, with the creation of the Progressive party as a break between the Republican party professionals, who backed the incumbent, William Howard Taft, and the Republican opponents of machine politics and party regularity, who nominated former Republican President Theodore Roosevelt. The split in the Republican party caused the Democratic candidate, Woodrow Wilson, to be elected. Wilson in fact represented many of the programs the Progressives had supported (banking reforms, antitrust laws, and business regulation), but he did not support many of the Progressive interests in national social policy. The NEW DEAL inherited many of these latter concerns.

The progressives got their name from the fact that they believed in the doctrine of progress—that governing institutions could be improved by bringing science to bear on public problems. It was a disparate movement, with each reform group targeting a level of government, a particular policy, and so on. Common beliefs included that good government was possible and that "the cure for democracy is *more* democracy." And to achieve this, they only had to "throw the rascals out." At the national level, they achieved civil service reform; at the state level, they introduced the direct primary, the initiative, the referendum, and the recall; at the local level, they spawned the commission and council-manager forms of government. And it was the progressive influence that initially forged the fledgling discipline of public administration. *See also* CIVIL SERVICE REFORM.

promise *See* CAMPAIGN PROMISE

propaganda **1.** A government's mass dissemination of true information about its policies and the policies of its adversaries. **2.** Similar dissemination that is untruthful (sometimes called *black propaganda*). The concept was introduced into American political science after World War I when British news reports of German atrocities (both real and imagined) were indicted as having influenced American attitudes toward entry into the war. Ever since World War II, when the German Ministry of Propaganda under Joseph Goebbels broadcast one lie after another, the term has taken on a sinister connotation. Goebbels musically advised to: "Think of the press as a great keyboard on which the government can play" (*Time*, March 27, 1933). Propaganda was so associated with the Nazis that historian Harrison E. Salisbury, writing of the period immediately following the 1941 Pearl Harbor attack, noted in *A Journey for Our Times* (1983): "It is almost impossible to locate an offensive-minded, realistic, hard-boiled thinker in the [American] army high command. To a suggestion that propaganda might be utilized as a military weapon, they throw up their arms in horror, exclaiming: 'Of course, we wouldn't think of using a Nazi method!'" **3.** The manipulation of people's beliefs, values, and behavior by using symbols (such as flags, music, or oratory) and other psychological tools. British author J.B. Priestley wrote in *Outcries and Asides* (1974) that: "Almost all propaganda is designed to create fear. Heads of governments and other officials know that a frightened people is easier to govern, will forfeit rights it would otherwise defend, is less likely to demand a better life, and will agree to millions and millions being spend on 'Defense.'" As novelist Aldous Huxley wrote in *The Olive Tree* (1937), propaganda is an effort "to make one set of people forget that certain other sets of people are human." **4.** According to British general Sir Ian Hamilton, *The Soul and Body of an Army* (1921), making the "enemy appear so great a monster that he forfeits the rights of a human being." This makes it emotionally easier to kill him. Hamilton further observes that since the enemy cannot bring a libel action, "there is no need to stick at trifles." **5.** According to Cambridge University philosopher Francis M. Cornford (1874–1943): "That branch of the art of lying which consists in nearly deceiving your friends without quite deceiving your enemies" (*New Statesman*, September 15, 1978). *Compare to* DISINFORMATION.

property tax *See* TAX, REAL-PROPERTY.

proportional representation An electoral system policy of allocating seats in a legislature or national nominating convention to the various interests, minorities, and parties in proportion to their strength in the electorate. Thus, a group that is 10 percent of the electorate would be entitled to 10 percent of the legislative seats. Proportional representation systems require complicated voting practices (such as the Hare system) and are not widely used in the United States.

Proposition 2-1/2 A 1980 tax limitation measure approved by the voters of Massachusetts that requires local governments to lower property taxes by 15 percent a year until they reach 2-1/2 percent of fair market value.

Proposition 13 A state constitutional amendment approved by California voters (it was put on the ballot as the Jarvis-Gann initiative) in 1978 which rolled back and set ceilings on property taxes. Proposition 13 is an important landmark in a national tax-relief movement. *See also* TAX REVOLT.

Proposition III *See* TAX REVOLT.

prorogation **1.** A mutually agreed extension on the expiration date of an international agreement. **2.** Any extension of a deadline for a debate, an adjournment, etc.

prosecutor An attorney employed by a government agency whose official duty is to initiate and maintain criminal (and sometimes civil) proceedings on behalf of the government against people accused of committing criminal offenses. The prosecutor is the attorney acting on behalf of the government (the people) in a criminal case. A public prosecutor has one of the most powerful offices in government. According to Governor James R. Thompson of Illinois (a former prosecutor): "You take the power of a prosecutor; this probably is the most restrained and unrestrainable power possessed by any public official in the United States. I recognized that, so I've already in my career possessed more power to affect people's lives without check than I ever will again, either as a Governor or as a President" (*The Christian Science Monitor*, April 20, 1977).

prosecutor, special A prosecutor appointed to consider the evidence in a case and, if necessary, to undertake the prosecution of a case that presents a possible conflict of interest for the jurisdiction's regular prosecutor. This usually happens in the federal government when someone who is or has been personally and professionally close to the U.S. attorney general must be investigated.

protectionism The use of government policy to determine the prices of foreign manufactured goods on domestic markets; a policy of high tariffs or low import quotas to protect domestic industries. Protectionism is the opposite of a FREE TRADE policy. Protectionist legislation is invariably proposed by members of the Congress from districts whose industries are adversely affected by foreign imports. Laid-off factory workers don't want to hear about the theoretical benefits of free trade; they want protectionist legislation that would put import duties on the foreign-made products that have cost them their jobs.

protocol 1. The generally accepted practices of international courtesy that have evolved over the centuries; codes prescribing strict adherence to set etiquette, precedence, and procedure between diplomats and among military services. **2.** A supplementary international agreement or an annex to a treaty. **3.** A preliminary draft of a treaty. **4.** The conventions about computer software that allow different parts of a computer system and different computer systems to communicate. **5.** The records or minutes of a diplomatic conference. **6.** The plan of a scientific experiment or medical procedure.

proxy 1. A person authorized to request or fill out registration forms or to obtain an absentee ballot on behalf of another person. A proxy may not cast a ballot for another person. **2.** A person who acts for another in a formal proceeding. **3.** A political candidate who represents not him or herself but another person; for example, a senator might run as a proxy for a sitting President who is reluctant to enter a presidential primary, or a governor's wife might run for his office if he is constitutionally ineligible to succeed himself.

psephology The study of electoral behavior. This Greek word was given currency by Richard Scammon and Ben Wattenberg's *The Real Majority* (1970).

pseudoevent Historian Daniel J. Boorstin's (1914–   ) term for nonspontaneous, planted, or manufactured "news," whose main purpose is to gain publicity for the person or cause which arranged the "event." As described in Boorstin's *The Image: A Guide to Pseudo-Events in America* (1961), an orchestrated news LEAK and the releasing of TRIAL BALLOONS are typical pseudoevents. *Compare to* MEDIA EVENT.

public 1. The people in general. **2.** The citizens of a jurisdiction. **3.** A subset of a larger public, such as a novelist's public (those who read his books) or the reading public (those who regularly read books).

public administration 1. The executive function in government; the execution of public policy; the means by which political values are implemented. **2.** Organizing and managing people and other resources to achieve the goals of government. **3.** The art and science of management applied to the public sector. Public administration is a broader term than public management, because it does not limit itself to management but incorporates all of the political, social, cultural, and legal environments that affect the managing of public institutions.

public affairs 1. Those aspects of corporate PUBLIC RELATIONS that deal with political and social issues. **2.** A more genteel-sounding name for a public relations department. **3.** The totality of a government agency's public information and community relations activities. **4.** An expansive view of the academic field of public administration. Accordingly, a graduate school of public affairs might include, in addition to degree programs in public administration, programs in police administration, urban studies, and so on.

public assistance Local government welfare programs. Such programs are a right, an entitlement, to those who meet specific criteria for the determination of need. They are often, as in the case of Aid to Families with Dependent Children and food stamps, heavily subsidized by the federal government. *Compare to* ENTITLEMENT PROGRAM.

public, attentive The minority of citizens who are consistently interested in and regularly read about and follow political affairs.

public choice economics An approach to public administration and politics based on microeconomic theory that views the citizen as a consumer of government goods and services. It would attempt to maximize administrative responsiveness to citizen demand by creating a market system for government activities in which public agencies would compete to provide citizens with goods and services. This might replace a portion of the current system, under which most administrative agencies in effect act as monopolies under the influence of organized pressure groups, which, the public choice economists argue, are institutionally incapable of representing the demands of individual citizens.

public defender An attorney employed by a government agency or subdivision whose official duty is to represent criminal defendants who are unable to hire private counsel.

public domain 1. Land owned by the government. **2.** Any property right held in common by all citizens; for example, the content of U.S. government publications, expired copyrights, and expired patents. **3.** The right of government to take property, with compensation, for a public purpose. *See also* FIFTH AMENDMENT.

public employee Any person who works for a government agency. Public employees constitute the core of government in developed nations. They carry on the day-to-day business of government with expertise that is generally unavailable elsewhere in the society. Although many public service tasks are technical and highly structured, a substantial proportion of civil servants are inevitably engaged in making decisions that have an impact on public policy. For example, the use of AFFIRMATIVE ACTION in the sense of quotas or goals has been an important political issue in the United States for over two decades, yet it is a policy created by administrative fiat and has yet to be fully mandated either by legislation or executive order. The U.S. political system enhances the policymaking role of the public service in several ways. Elected officials often prefer to avoid making decisions on hotly contested political issues. In consequence, these matters are often thrust upon the judicial and administrative arms of government. And the Congress, recognizing both its own limitations and the expertise of career administrators, has in recent decades delegated authority in a vast array of policy areas to the bureaucracy.

public entrepreneur A nonelective government executive who creates, or radically alters, and expands a public organization; then leads it on to significant accomplishment. Admiral Hyman Rickover (1900–1986), the "father" of the atomic submarine, and J. Edgar Hoover (1895–1972) of the FBI are classic examples. *Compare to* POLICY ENTREPRENEUR; PUBLIC POLICY ENTREPRENEUR.

public finance An imprecise term that refers to the totality (1) of the raising and spending of funds by governments and (2) of the management of government debt. *Compare to* FISCAL POLICY; MONETARY POLICY.

public financing 1. Paying for something out of government funds. **2.** In the context of elections, efforts to exclude the influence of special interests by having government pay for the costs of political campaigns. Since 1976 presidential campaigns have been financed by the public. Both major parties also have their national conventions subsidized by the public. Presidential primary candidates are eligible for matching funds after they raise at least $5,000 in each of 20 states. There has been much discussion about the public financing of congressional elections, but no action. It is commonly said that there are three groups generally opposed to public financing: the public, challengers, and incumbents. The public is hostile to plans that can only mean higher taxes; challengers don't want limitations on what they feel they must spend to defeat an incumbent; and incumbents oppose it because they do not want to encourage challengers who want their jobs.

public goods Commodities typically provided by government that cannot, or would not, be separately parceled out to individuals, since no one can be excluded from their benefits. Public goods, such as national defense, clean air, and public safety, are neither divisible nor exclusive. This definition applies only to pure public goods. Many goods supplied by governments (public housing, hospitals, and police protection) could be and often are supplied privately.

public hearing A meeting to receive public input—both informational and opinionated—on a designated need, issue, problem, or pending policy or program. Public hearings are held by local, state, and national elected bod ies (such as a U.S. Senate subcommittee or a board of county commissioners) and public agencies (e.g., the U.S. Environmental Protection Agency or a state highway department).

public housing Dwelling units paid for or subsidized by government. Public housing is usually available only after a MEANS TEST. Public housing has been severely criticized because it tends to concentrate the poor and members of minority groups in high-density units that breed crime and other social problems.

public interest A phrase used by those who seek to identify concerns generally considered to be private with concerns that are perceived to affect the public as a whole. This is the universal label in which political actors wrap the policies and programs that they advocate—but would any lobbyist, public manager, legislator, or chief executive ever propose a program that was not "in the public interest?" Because the public interest is generally taken to mean a commonly accepted good, the phrase is used both to further policies that are indeed for the common good and to obscure policies that may not be so commonly accepted as good.

A considerable body of literature has developed about this phrase, because it represents an important philosophic point that, if found, could provide considerable guidance for politicians and public administrators alike. In *The Public Philosophy* (1955), Walter Lippmann wrote: "The public interest may be presumed to be what men would choose if they saw clearly, thought rationally, acted disinterestedly and benevolently."

public interest groups **1.** A national network of quasi-public voluntary associations. The so-called "big seven" include the Council of State Governments (CSG), the National Governors Association (NGA), the National Conference of State Legislatures (NCSL), the National Association of Counties (NACo), the National League of Cities (NLC), United States Conference of Mayors (USCM), and the International City Management Association (ICMA). The CSG has several relevant affiliated organizations: the NGA, and associations of attorneys general, lieutenant governors, state budget officers, state purchasing officials, and state planning agencies. The various state leagues of municipalities are constituent bodies of the NLC. Furthermore, the American Society for Public Administration (ASPA), the National Academy of Public Administration (NAPA), and the National Association of Schools of Public Affairs and Administration (NASPAA) are the principal important voices in the intergovernmental network. More specialized are the associations of planning, personnel, and finance officials. **2.** Organized PRESSURE GROUPS seeking to develop positions and to support national causes relating to a broader definition of the public good, as opposed to a specific social or economic interest. Such groups are often characterized by efforts to obtain a national membership and high participation. Examples of public interest groups are Common Cause, the Nader organizations, the League of Women Voters, the Sierra Club, and Consumer's Union. *See also* INTEREST GROUP THEORY.

public interest law *See* LAW, PUBLIC INTEREST.

public interest movement A loose phrase for the continuous efforts of public interest groups to gain the passage of legislation that will advance broad societal interests. The movement, whose origins can be traced back to the progressive era, consistently advances a heterogeneous public policy agenda through a threefold approach: (1) lobbying for legislation; (2) bringing civil suits in the federal courts, and (3) supporting political candidates who support their views.

public interest research group (PIRG) One of the consumer advocacy organizations inspired by RALPH NADER that operate out of colleges and universities. While presumably nonpartisan, they tend to lobby in behalf of traditional liberal positions, and at least one chapter has even endorsed a presidential candidate.

public office 1. An elected or appointed government job. **2.** A public trust; a responsibility to act in the public interest. The notion that a "public office is a public trust" goes back to antiquity. President Grover Cleveland used it as his slogan during the 1884 presidential campaign.

public opinion 1. The GENERAL WILL; the aggregate of the individual feelings of a political community on a given issue; a force of such intangible power that it sets limits on what a government can do. American public opinion, while often tested in opinion polls, is really made known only through elections. **2.** The mass media manipulated attitudes of an ill-informed public. According to Walter Lippmann's classic analysis, *Public Opinion* (1922), the media has increased the gap between citizens' stereotyped impressions of politics and the complex realities of politics by putting out selected simplified explanations of political phenomena. Lippmann, in the best Burkean tradition (*see* EDMUND BURKE), was concerned that political leaders would defer too much to a basically ill-informed public and follow opinion instead of leading it. He would later write that "the notion that public opinion can and will decide all issues is in appearance very democratic. In practice it undermines and destroys democratic government. For when everyone is supposed to have a judgment about everything, nobody in fact is going to know much about anything." **3.** Elite opinion. As George F. Kennan in *American Diplomacy, 1900–1950* (1951) wrote: "what purports to be public opinion in most countries that consider themselves to have popular government is often not really the consensus of the feelings of the mass of the people at all but rather the expression of the interests of special highly vocal minorities—politicians, commentators, and publicity-seekers of all sorts: people who live by their ability to draw attention to themselves and die, like fish out of water, if they are compelled to remain silent."

public opinion leader *See* OPINION LEADER.

public opinion survey A scientifically designed process to measure public opinion using a statistically sampled cross-section of the population in question. Also referred to as public opinion polls, they are used descriptively (e.g., to describe public attitudes about crime in America) and predictively (e.g., to project voting patterns in a forthcoming election or to gauge public support for a pending bond issue). President Harry S Truman warned in a campaign speech on October 26, 1948: "Polls are like sleeping pills designed to lull the voters into sleeping on election day. You might call them 'sleeping polls.'" *Compare to* POLL, SAMPLE.

public policy Whatever a government decides to do or not to do; what a government does in response to a political issue. Public policies are made by authoritative actors in a political system, who are recognized because of their formal position as having the responsibility for making binding choices for society. British statesman Lord Salisbury (1830–1903) is usually credited with first remarking: "There is no such thing as a fixed policy, because policy like all organic entities is always in the making." There are essentially two kinds of literature on public policy. One is process-oriented and attempts to understand and explore the dynamic social and political mechanics and relations of how policies are made. The other is prescriptive and attempts to examine how rational analysis can produce better policy decisions.

public policy cycle A conceptual model that views the public policy process as moving through the following stages in succession: agenda setting (or the identification of a policy issue), policy or decision making, implementation, program evaluation or impact analysis, and finally feedback which leads to revision or termination; thus, the process comes full circle—which is why it is called a "cycle."

public policy entrepreneur A political actor who takes a political issue and runs with it. Thus, a senator might make a particular issue her own by sheer force of expertise which, if respected, "forces" colleagues to take cues on the matter from her. Or a staffer might become such an expert on an issue that he can heavily influence legislation dealing with it. Thus, a public policy entrepreneur can be anyone in the political environment whose expertise and actions can affect an issue. *Compare to* POLICY ENTREPRENEUR; PUBLIC ENTREPRENEUR.

public policymaking The totality of the decisional processes by which a government decides to act or not act on a particular problem or concern. In seeking an explanation for the mechanisms that produce policy decisions or nondecisions, one is immediately confronted with two early, distinct, and opposite theories.

What might be called the rational decision-making approach generally has been attributed to Harold Lasswell's *The Future of Political Science* (1963), which posited seven significant phases for every decision: (1) the intelligence phase, involving an influx of information; (2) the promoting or recommending phase, involving activities designed to influence the outcome; (3) the prescribing phase, involving the articulation of norms; (4) the invoking phase, involving the establishment of correspondence between prescriptions and concrete circumstances; (5) the application phase, in which the prescription is executed; (6) the appraisal phase, assessing intent in relation to effect; and (7) the terminating phase, treating expectations (rights) established while the prescription was in force.

The rejection of this approach was urged by charles e. lindblom, who proposed the incremental decision-making theory, popularly known as the science of muddling through. Lindblom sees a rational model as unrealistic. The policymaking process was above all, he asserted, complex and disorderly. Disjointed incrementalism as a policy course was in reality the only truly feasible route, since incrementalism "concentrated the policymaker's analysis on familiar, better-known experiences, sharply reduced the number of different alternative policies to be explored, and sharply reduced the number and complexity of factors to be analyzed."

The opposition of the rational and incremental models seemingly has produced no real obstacles for subsequent study of policymaking. One later policy analysis scholar simply has contended that the reality of the policy process should not negate attempts to establish ideal models. Political scientist Charles O. Jones, in *An Introduction to the Study of Public Policy* (3d ed., 1984), finds that, while Lindblom's thesis accurately describes most policy processes, there is "no particular reason why those who want change should limit their actions because the system is 'incremental.'" A question then remains, How can one accept that the incremental model is the reality but use the rational model as a conceptual framework for policy analysis? There is no ready answer to such a question other than to go back to Jones. Scholars use the rational model because it affords a dissective capability that can be used to focus on policy specifics and stages, regardless of how well constructed or formulated any given decisions may be.

Another significant theorist, THEODORE J. LOWI, holds that different models should be constructed for different types of public policies. His now classic article, "American Business, Public Policy, Case Studies and Political Theory" (*World Politics*, July 1964), argued that policy contents should be an independent variable and that there are three major categories of public policies: distribution, regulation, and redistribution. "Each arena tends to develop its own characteristic political structure, political process, elites, and group relations." As one might expect, distribution policies involve actions that provide services and products to individuals and groups; regulatory policies involve transfers or transactions that take from one party and provide to another.

It seems fair to conclude that there is no single policymaking process that produces all policies. Rather, there are numerous policy processes, each capable of producing different policy contents and applicable only in a particular environment.

public power   Energy produced by government-owned and -operated power plants, such as those of the TENNESSEE VALLEY AUTHORITY in the eastern United States, and the Western Area Power Administration in the west. Only about 20 percent of the electricity annually produced in the United States is generated in publicly owned power stations, and most of this is sold to privately owned public utilities, which distribute it to households and businesses. Ever since the 1930s, when the federal government first got into the power-generating business, there has been considerable debate over whether the government should stay in it. The political Right tends to say no: Sell all the power plants to private investors. The political Left tends to say yes: Stay in it and build more.

The single most controversial area of public power is nuclear. While the federal government owns outright some nuclear plants (e.g., TVA), it regulates them all through the NUCLEAR REGULATORY COMMISSION. With the development of nuclear weapons in the 1950s, the federal government actively encouraged utility companies to use nuclear power (*see* ATOMS FOR PEACE)—the safe and cheap power of the future. But as the 1979 accident at Three Mile Island in Pennsylvania and the 1986 accident at Chernobyl in the Soviet Union showed, nuclear power is not necessarily safe; nor has it proved inexpensive.

public-private partnerships   Joint efforts on the part of local governments and the business community to plan for, generate public support for, and pay for major social programs or construction projects that will be mutually beneficial.

public regardingness   An attitude on the part of citizens in some income and ethnic groups that is broader than narrow self-interest; that, in marked contrast to the attitudes of others, takes the welfare of the community as a whole into account in decisions about voting and political support. Those who have a high degree of public regardingness would vote for higher school property taxes—even though they might not have children in public schools—because adequately financed schools are important for the general welfare of the community. *Compare to* PRIVATE REGARDINGNESS.

public relations   1. Building and maintaining good relationships with other organizations, groups, or "publics" such as employees, clients, legislators, and so on. **2.** The totality of informing and influencing the public about an agency's activities. President Harry S Truman once complained in a November 14, 1947 letter to his sister: "All the President is, is a glorified public relations man who spends his time flattering, kissing, and kicking people to get them to do what they are supposed to do anyway" (quoted in Robert H. Ferrell, *Off the Record*, 1980).

public service **1.** Participation in public life; voluntary acts for one's community. JEAN JACQUES ROUSSEAU wrote in *Social Contract* (1762): "As soon as public service ceases to be the chief business of the citizens, and they would rather serve with their money than with their persons, the state is not far from its fall." **2.** Government employment; the totality of a jurisdiction's employees; the totality of a nation's public sector employees. **3.** What a government does for its community: police protection, trash collection, and so on. **4.** A local public utility. **5.** One's DUTY to the STATE. Perhaps the classic statement on this is Nathan Hale's comment to his friend, William Hull, who in 1776 was trying to dissuade him from volunteering to be a spy (Hale was later caught by the British and hung): "I am not influenced by the expectation of promotion or pecuniary reward. I wish to be useful, and every kind of service necessary for the public good, becomes honorable by being necessary" (quoted in Isaac William Stuart's *Life of Captain Nathan Hale*, 1856).

public service corporation A private, regulated corporation that provides an essential service or commodity to the public, such as an electric or a gas utility company; not to be confused with a public sector organization or a publicly supported organization.

public trust **1.** A PUBLIC OFFICE. Grover Cleveland's 1884 presidential campaign slogan was: "A public office is a public trust." **2.** A formally established charity that benefits the general public.

public utilities A legal designation encompassing those organizations producing essential services, usually in a monopolistic fashion; originally, a designation of services—like water, gas, and electricity—to large numbers of the public provided by private corporations and paid for by community users. The public nature yet monopolistic character of such corporations eventually subjected them to public scrutiny and regulation, if not public ownership. They are all characterized as public now, despite differences in ownership, management, and regulation.

public utilities commissions State agencies that regulate power companies, railroads, and so on. They typically set rates, hold hearings on the quality and level of services, and do economic analyses on regulated industries.

public welfare **1.** Government support of and assistance to needy persons contingent upon their need. *Compare to* WELFARE. **2.** A legal basis for government action. For example, a governor may be bound by a state constitution to protect the public welfare and thus to send National Guard troops to a major disaster site. **3.** The general welfare of the United States. *Compare to* GENERAL WELFARE CLAUSE.

public works A generic term for government-sponsored construction projects. Initially, it was applied to any construction useful to the public, regardless of its potential for private profit. But the use of such projects as a means of providing employment during times of recession or as a potential for distribution of federal resources to states or cities has given the term a new meaning in economic planning. Since the 1930s, public works projects have sometimes been used in times of economic recession or depression to stimulate the economy (*see* PUMP PRIMING). Public works are also major elements in PORK BARREL legislation, designed to benefit an individual congressional district. *See also* BENEFIT DISTRICT.

PUC *See* PUBLIC UTILITIES COMMISSION.

pump priming 1. Pouring water into a dry pump to lubricate seals and valves and rapidly increase the efficiency of the pump, even though this may waste the initial water. **2.** The concept, originating in the NEW DEAL, of stimulating the economy during a time of economic decline by borrowing money to spend on public works, defense, welfare, and so on. In theory, the prosperity generated by such expenditures would increase tax revenues, which in turn would pay for the borrowing. *Compare to* JOHN MAYNARD KEYNES.

pundit 1. An expert who writes on public affairs; a person who appears on political TV news programs to comment on current affairs because of some presumed expertise. **2.** A political columnist. The word, which is derived from the Hindi word "pandit" meaning "wise man," when originally used in English had a mocking connotation which it seems to have lost.

Q

quasi-judicial agency An agency, such as a regulatory commission, that may perform many functions ordinarily performed by the courts. Its interpretation and enforcement of rules gives these rules the authority of law. It adjudicates (*see* ADJUDICATION) and may bring charges, hold hearings, and render judgments. (*Quasi* is Latin for "as if" or "almost.")

quasi-legislative Descriptive of the rule-making authority of administrative agencies. The authority of an administrative agency to make rules gives those rules the authority of law; that is, makes them enforceable as though they had been passed by a legislature.

Quayle, J. Danforth (1947–   ) The U.S. Senator from Indiana who was George Bush's surprise choice as a vice presidential running mate in 1988. As Vice President from 1989 to 1993 he has had more than the traditional problems of not being taken seriously by the public because of his extremely youthful looks and his reputation as an intellectual lightweight. *See also* PLATO.

questions of privilege *See* PRIVILEGE, QUESTIONS OF.

quid pro quo A Latin phrase meaning "something for something"; initially meaning the substitution of one thing for another. In politics it suggests actions taken, because of some promised action in return.

quorum The number of members who must be in attendance to make valid the votes and other actions of a formal group. In the Supreme Court, a quorum is six. In the U.S. Senate and the House of Representatives, it is a majority of the membership. In the Committee of the Whole House, it is 100. If a point of order is made that a quorum is not present, the only business that is in order is either a motion to adjourn or a motion to direct the sergeant at arms to request the attendance of absentees.

quorum call A method of determining whether a legislative quorum is present by calling the roll of the legislature's members. In the U.S. Senate, a quorum call is used mainly as a kind of parliamentary "time out," while senators meet on and off the Senate floor to decide how to proceed on a particular piece of legislation. It is a routine way of suspending debate without recessing or adjourning the Senate. Usually, there are several quorum calls on any given day the Senate is in session. A call is triggered when a senator says, "I suggest the absence of a quorum," and the clerk of the Senate begins slowly to call the role of senators. Regular business resumes when a senator says, "I ask unanimous consent that further proceedings under the quorum call be dispensed with."

quorum call, notice In the Committee of the Whole House, a notice quorum call may be made by the chair when the point of order is made that a quorum is not present. If 100 members, which constitute a quorum in the Committee of the Whole House, appear within the specified time period, the notice quorum call is not recorded. If 100 members fail to appear, a regular quorum call, which is recorded, is made.

quotas 1. Any quantitative restriction. Quotas are often used in the context of protectionist trade policies and AFFIRMATIVE ACTION. **2.** GOALS.

R

race **1.** A grouping of human beings with common characteristics presumed to be transmitted genetically. Which characteristics are properly included has been a subject of debate. They range from physical characteristics that are immediately observable, such as color of hair, skin, and eyes, to the subtler aspects of intelligence and aptitudes. Some races have genetic susceptibility to certain diseases or physical disorders. **2.** The human race as distinguished from other animals. **3.** Ancestry, tribal, or national origin. The latter definition was common up to the middle of the twentieth century as a way of distinguishing among national groups and is traceable to eighteenth-century distinctions among people according to language. It became a method of attempting to define a hierarchy of races, with the so-called Anglo-Saxons at the top and others arranged along supposedly developmental lines. German philosopher Friedrich Nietzsche's (1844–1900) conception of a superman or super-race became a tragic caricature as used by dictator Adolf Hitler (1889–1945) in his attempt to establish a German *volk* (people) destined to dominate the world. **4.** In recent times, in American political language, race has come to designate issues or attitudes concerning blacks. Other minority groups are called ethnics or subcategories of ethnic, to satisfy government requirements for administration of certain programs. Race has thus moved from a term signifying high distinction or complex scientific differentiation to one that implies an unacceptable prejudice. **5.** An election contest. **6.** An armaments buildup, as in an arms race. *See also* MINORITY.

race categories The racial-ethnic categories that the Equal Employment Opportunity Commission requires for reporting purposes. These are: *white, not of Hispanic origin*, people having origins in any of the peoples indigenous to Europe, North Africa, or the Middle East; *black, not of Hispanic origin*, people having origins in any of the black racial groups of Africa; *Hispanic*, people of Mexican, Puerto Rican, Cuban, Central, or South American, or other Spanish-speaking American origin, regardless of race; *American Indian or Alaskan native*, people having origins in any of the peoples indigenous to North America and who maintain cultural identification through tribal affiliation or community recognition; *Asian or Pacific islander*, people having ancestry in any of the original peoples of the Far East, Southeast Asia, the Indian subcontinent, or the Pacific islands (these areas include China, Japan, Korea, the Philippine Islands, and Samoa).

The Supreme Court has also recognized additional race categories that are protected by the federal civil rights laws. In *Shaare Tefila Congregation v Cobb* (1987), it held that Jews could bring charges of racial discrimination against defendants who were also considered Caucasian. And in *Saint Francis College v Al-Khazraji* (1987), it held that someone of Arabian ancestry was protected from racial discrimination under the various civil rights statutes.

racism, institutional *See* INSTITUTIONAL DISCRIMINATION.

race norming A controversial practice used by some government agencies whereby they make an upward adjustment on the aptitude test scores of minorities. This "within-group score conversions" makes minority applicants more competitive in the job market.

racist 1. Any person or organization that either consciously or unconsciously discriminates against a person on the basis of race or supports the supremacy of one race over others. **2.** Someone who is insensitive to the feelings of racial minorities and uses racially demeaning language or diction in all innocence out of genuine ignorance. Such people might deny they are racist as in definition 1; however, offended minority groups might still perceive them to be so.

radical 1. Any political activist who advocates drastic changes in the operating premises of the nation—often, but not necessarily, by violent means. Radicals exist on both the extreme Left and extreme Right. Mark Twain said, "The radical of one century is the conservative of the next. The radical invents the views. When he has worn them out the conservatives adopt them" (*Notebooks*, 1935). President Franklin D. Roosevelt told the nation in a radio address on October 26, 1939: "A radical is a man with both feet firmly planted—in the air." **2.** After the Civil War, a Republican opponent of Presidents Lincoln and Johnson's policy of compassion for the defeated South.

raison d'etat A reason of state; for the good of the country; a critically important motive for otherwise unjustified government action. If the life of the state is in question, *raison d'etat* is then the rationale to do anything, no matter how otherwise illegal, to save it.

rally 1. A gathering of people for common action. Thus, soldiers would traditionally "rally" 'round the flag in prepartion for an attack. **2.** A political meeting, usually with a major candidate. In the old days, before television, the candidate was expected to be the major entertainment—speeches of several hours were not uncommon. But today rallies are primarily MEDIA EVENTS with enough entertainment value to be worthy of TV news. **3.** The attitude that the public tends to take when the President first becomes involved in an international crisis; presidential popularity and approval ratings go up as public opinion rallies to support him. Of course, if the President doesn't quickly resolve the crisis, this mood will dissipate.

ranking member The member of a legislative committee who has the greatest seniority. The ranking member of the majority party often becomes the committee's chair. A ranking minority member is the senior committee member from the minority party.

ratification 1. The power of a legislature to approve or reject TREATIES, constitutional amendments, or even a new constitution itself. The U.S. Constitution was ratified by the states over a three-year period from December 7, 1787 (when Delaware became the first state to ratify) to May 29, 1790 (when Rhode Island became the last of the original 13 states to do so). Article VII of the Constitution provided that any nine states were enough for it to go into effect (it would not have been binding on states that did not ratify it). George Washington is supposed to have said upon his signing of the Constitution on September 17, 1787: "Should the states reject this excellent Constitution, the probability is that an opportunity will never again offer to make another in peace—the next will be drawn in blood." **2.** The U.S. Senate's ADVISE AND CONSENT function. **3.** The formal confirmation by the union membership of a contract that has been negotiated and signed on their behalf by union representatives.

reactionary One who would return to outmoded ideas of the past. It is a derogatory reference to those political activists who are so discontent with maintaining the status quo that they yearn for a previous status quo. According to John Lukacs' *Confessions of an Original Sinner* (1990), a reactionary "will recognize how. . . an idea whose time has come may not be any good." *Compare to* CONSERVATISM.

Reagan Democrat The traditional blue-collar backbone of the Democratic Party who votes for the Republican candidate for President out of a feeling that Democrats put up such unattractive candidates for national office. The Presidential election of 1988 proved that the Reagan Democrats were still very supportive of a Republican for President—even if he wasn't Reagan.

Reagan Doctrine The media term, usually credited to journalist Charles Krauthammer (1950–), for the Ronald Reagan Administration's policy (in conjunction with the Congress) of militarily supporting guerrilla insurgencies against communist governments in third world countries, such as Afghanistan, Angola, Cambodia, and Nicaragua. According to White House Communications Director Patrick Buchanan: "The doctrine says we don't have to resign ourselves to the fact that once a country has become a member of the socialist or Communist camp it must remain there forever. Where genuine national-liberation movements seek to recapture their country from a Communist tyranny imposed from without, America reserves the right—and may indeed have the duty—to support those people" (*U.S. News & World Report*, January 27, 1986). Columnist Michael Kinsley found the Reagan Doctrine to be "a specific rejection of international law as the illogical elevation of sovereignty over more important values such as democracy and freedom" (*The New Republic*, October 1, 1990).

Reagan revolution 1. The resurgence of the Republican party in the 1980s under the leadership of President Ronald Reagan. **2.** The radical changes in the nation's fiscal and tax policies under the Reagan administration, which redefined domestic priorities and curtailed federal programs designed to solve social problems. As Reagan often said: "Government is not the solution to our problems. Government is the problem." In other words, the national welfare would be better served with general economic prosperity, brought about by tax cuts than with expanded welfare programs. *See also* SUPPLY-SIDE ECONOMICS.

Reagan, Ronald W. (1911–   ) The President of the United States from 1981 to 1989. Reagan, a movie actor since the late 1930s, took part in the early introduction of Hollywood to labor organization and Democratic party politics. He became a successful television promoter of General Electric products in the 1950s and joined the Republican party. His active involvement in the ill-fated 1964 presidential campaign of BARRY GOLDWATER made him a major voice in national Republican politics. This led to Reagan's election as governor of California (1967–1975) and eventually to his successful 1980 presidential campaign against Jimmy Carter; and his even more successful 1984 campaign for reelection against Walter Mondale.

Reagan's engaging personality made him personally popular even with those who disagreed with his policies. After a severe recession early in his first term, he initiated a program of unparalleled deficit spending for a military buildup that supporters contended both brought domestic prosperity and broke the back of communism in the Soviet Union and Eastern Europe. Critics argued that it provided artificial prosperity at the cost of enormous debt. Reagan was masterful at using the media. His stage-managed public appearances rightfully earned him the title of the "Great Communicator." After the middle of his last term, his reputation began to suffer as the IRAN-CONTRA AFFAIR unravelled, as it was revealed by his former Chief of Staff, Donald T. Regan, that some presidential decisions were being made by an astrologer employed by First Lady Nancy Reagan, and as the HUD and SAVINGS AND LOAN SCANDALS became known. Nevertheless, he retired with his popularity largely intact, the first President to successfully complete two terms in office since Dwight D. Eisenhower.

Reaganomics *See* SUPPLY-SIDE ECONOMICS.

realignment **1.** A new order of demonstrated political loyalties, whether of the electorate or of the parties and voting blocs in a legislature. A realignment could be a temporary response to a charismatic political figure, a one-time alliance on behalf of an issue, or (as the term is most often used) a permanent change in the electorate, such as when the South, which was once solidly Democratic, developed a two-party system—at least in national elections. The last major realignment in American national politics occurred in the 1930s, when Franklin D. Roosevelt forged the New Deal coalition, and the Democrats became the majority party. Political scientist Everett Carll Ladd wrote in "On Mandates, Realignments, and the 1984 Presidential Election" (*Political Science Quarterly*, Spring 1985): "For two decades now, political scientists and other commentators have stumbled and sloshed around a conceptual swamp called realignment that we have created for ourselves. The main reason we have had such difficulty dealing with contemporary partisan realignment is that we have expected it to be like the one acted out in the 1930s—the great New Deal realignment." The question is still unanswered about whether Ronald Reagan has laid the political foundation for a realignment that will make the Republicans supplant the Democrats as the majority party. *See also* DEALIGNMENT; ELECTION, CRITICAL; SOUTHERN STRATEGY. **2.** in international politics, the latest adjustments to diplomatic, military, or trade policies to reflect the current realities of international relationships. *Compare to* BALANCE OF POWER.

realism The belief that power and self-interest are the main realities of international politics; and that considerations of ideology, morality, political rights, etc., are inherently secondary. The intellectual prophet of realism is international relations scholar Hans J. Morgenthau. *Also see* NATIONAL INTEREST.

realpolitik A German word, now absorbed into English, meaning "realist politics." The term is applied to politics—whether of the organizational or societal variety—premised on material or practical factors rather than on theoretical or ethical considerations. It is the politics of realism; an injunction not to allow wishful thinking or sentimentality to cloud one's judgment. It has taken on more sinister overtones, however, particularly in modern usage. At its most moderate, 'realpolitik' is used to describe an overcynical approach, one that allows little room for human altruism, that always seeks an ulterior motive behind another actor's statements or justifications. At its strongest, it suggests that no moral values should be allowed to affect the single-minded pursuit of one's own or one's country's self-interest, and an absolute assumption that any opponent will certainly behave in this way.

reapportionment **1.** A new assignment to a state of a new number of congressional seats in response to changes in population as determined by the decimal census. The U.S. Congress takes the fixed size of the House of Representatives (435 members) and, after assigning one seat to each state as required by the Constitution, allots the remaining 385 on the basis of population. **2.** A parallel apportionment of state legislature seats. *Compare to* GERRYMANDER; REDISTRICTING; SUNBELT-SNOWBELT TENSION.

reappropriation Legislative action to restore or extend the obligational availability, whether for the same or different purposes, of all or part of the unobligated portion of budget authority, which otherwise would lapse.

reasonable doubt *See* BEYOND A REASONABLE DOUBT.

rebellion *See* REVOLUTION.

recall **1.** A procedure that allows citizens to vote officeholders out of office between regularly scheduled elections. For a new election to be called, a recall petition must be presented with a prescribed percentage of the jurisdiction's voters' signatures. **2.** The rehiring of employees from a layoff. **3.** The returning of defective products to their manufacturers (often via a retailer) either at the manufacturer's initiative or because of an order from a government regulatory agency enforcing a consumer protection law. *Compare to* REFERENDUM.

recess **1.** A break in a formal proceeding, such as a trial or hearing, that may last from a few minutes to a few hours. **2.** A break in a legislative session. It is distinguished from adjournment in that it does not end a legislative day and so does not interfere with unfinished business. **3.** The time between court sessions. For example, the Supreme Court is usually in recess during the summer months.

recess appointment **1.** A presidential appointment to federal office of a person to fill a vacant position, one that requires the advice and consent of the Senate to be filled, while the Senate is not in session. People appointed to office while the Senate is in recess may begin their duties before their names have been submitted to the Senate. However, the President must submit each such nomination when the Senate reconvenes, and the recess appointment expires at the end of the next session unless the Senate has confirmed each one by a majority vote. Moreover, the recess appointment expires and the office is declared vacant even earlier than the end of the next session if the Senate acts before that time to reject the nominee. **2.** A similar appointment by a state governor.

recession A decline in overall business activity that is pervasive, substantial, and of at least several months' duration. Historically, a decline in real GROSS NATIONAL PRODUCT for at least two consecutive quarters of a year has been considered a recession. While the distinction between a recession and a depression is a matter of usage, recession is generally perceived as a temporary low point in a normal BUSINESS CYCLE, while a depression suggests more fundamental, underlying shifts in the economy—shifts that are likely to be permanent and that require basic changes. President Ronald Reagan once observed: "A recession is when your neighbor loses his job. A depression is when you lose yours" [quoted in Lou Cannon's *Reagan* (1982)]. The last depression in the United States was the GREAT DEPRESSION of the 1930s.

recession, growth A time when the economy is growing but at a below-normal rate. This should not be confused with euphemisms for recession, such as "rolling readjustment" or "extended seasonal slump."

reciprocal trade agreement A formal understanding concluded with one or more foreign countries under which U.S. tariffs or other trade barriers are reduced in return for reductions of foreign barriers against American goods.

reciprocity **1.** The giving of privileges to the citizens of one jurisdiction by the government of another, and vice versa. **2.** A mutuality in the terms of trade between two nations. This usually refers to the negotiated reduction of a country's import duties or other trade restraints in return for similar concessions from another country. Because of the frequently wide disparity in their economic capacities and potential, the relationship of concessions negotiated between developed and developing countries is generally not one of equivalence. Thus, the phrase "relative reciprocity" is used to characterize the practice of developed countries seeking less than full reciprocity from developing countries in trade negotiations. **3.** One of the key NORMS in a legislature, whereby members exchange favors in order to further their own, their constituents', and the public's interests.

recognition 1. DIPLOMATIC RECOGNITION. **2.** An employer's acceptance of a union as the bargaining agent for all of the employees in a particular bargaining unit.

recommit to committee *See* COMMITTEE, RECOMMIT TO.

reconciliation The process used by the U.S. Congress to adjust amounts for a fiscal year (determined by tax, spending, and debt legislation) to match the ceilings enacted in the second required concurrent resolution on the budget for that year. Changes to laws, bills, and resolutions—as required to conform with the binding totals for budget authority, revenues, and the public debt—are incorporated into either a *reconciliation resolution* or *reconciliation bill*.

record 1. The written account of a legal or administrative case, containing the complete history of all actions taken concerning it. **2.** The past performance of a political party or an individual politician. New York Governor Alfred E. Smith (1873–1944) was famous for saying "Let's look at the record," when he was the unsuccessful Democratic nominee for President in 1928.

recorder of deeds The local official responsible for filing public land records.

record, public A document filed with, or put out by, a government agency and open for public review.

red A communist, because the red flag is the international symbol of communism. This is why someone thought to be leaning toward communism might be called *pink* or a *pinko*.

red-baiting Accusing someone, usually falsely and often a political opponent, of being a communist or being supportive of communist policies. Since World War II this has been an often-used tactic in political campaigns. One of the most famous instances of red-baiting occurred during the 1950 race for the U.S. Senate from California. Richard M. Nixon won by accusing his opponent, Helen Gahagan Douglas, of being "pink down to her underwear" and she never recovered. Christopher Matthews in *Hardball* (1988) tells how Representative Jack Brooks did recover from red-baiting charges in his first House race in 1952. Brooks spoke to a large group of voters and explained what the fake charges were against him. Then he said: "I fought the fascists for five years in World War II; I own a shotgun back at home and I'll shoot any man who calls me a Communist." That ended one candidate's problem with red-baiting.

red herring 1. Originally, smoked herrings that people opposed to fox hunting might drag along a fox's trail to divert the hunting dogs to a false scent; by analogy, something used to divert attention from the real issue. **2.** An advance copy of a prospectus that must be filed with the Securities and Exchange Commission before a corporation can sell its stocks or bonds. It is "for information only" and marked in red for identification.

red scare **1.** A time of unreasoning and unreasonable fear of communist subversion. **2.** The period immediately following World War I and the Russian Revolution of 1917, when American hysteria over radicals, anarchists, and communists resulted in the wholesale arrest and often deportation of people thought to be subversive. The best known aspect of the red scare of this period was the "Palmer raids," conducted by agents of Attorney General A. Mitchell Palmer (1872–1936), in which thousands of citizens and aliens alike were arrested without specific charges. The raids were noted for their lack of due process and violations of civil liberties. They came to an end along with Palmer's presidential ambitions in 1920, when Palmer's predicted uprising of reds in an effort to overthrow the government never materialized. **3.** The period of MCCARTHYISM after World War II. *See also* DUCK TEST.

red tape A symbol of excessive formality and attention to routine. It has its origins in the red ribbon with which clerks bound official documents in the nineteenth century. The ribbon has disappeared, but the practices it represents linger on.

redistribution Taking from the rich and giving to the poor; domestic policies and programs whose goal is to shift wealth or benefits from one segment of the population to another. The WELFARE STATE is founded on the notion of redistribution. The basic mechanism for redistribution is taxation. However, the laws themselves can sometimes redistribute benefits. For example, tax loopholes benefit one group of taxpayers at the expense of others; and the Civil Rights Act, through equal employment opportunity mandates, gave economic benefits to one segment of the population at the theoretical expense of another.

Redistribution is one leg of a three-part classification of all domestic public policies into distribution, regulation, or redistribution, as outlined by THEODORE J. LOWI. It is more popular with some classes of society than with others. ALEXIS DE TOCQUEVILLE observed in *Democracy in America* (1835): "Countries. . . when lawmaking falls exclusively to the lot of the poor cannot hope for much economy in public expenditure; expenses will always be considerable, either because taxes cannot touch those who vote for them or because they are assessed in a way to prevent that." As the playwright George Bernard Shaw (1856–1950) said in *Everybody's Political What's What?* (1944): "A government which robs Peter to pay Paul can always depend on the support of Paul."

redistricting **1.** The action of a state legislature (or a court if the legislature fails to act) in redrawing congressional district boundaries in response to a

REAPPORTIONMENT of congressional seats among the states. The Constitution requires (in Article I, Section 2) that an "enumeration," a census, be undertaken every 10 years specifically for the purpose of adjusting the number of congressional seats to which each state is entitled. This is a major means by which national political power peacefully follows the population as it shifts from one state or region to another. The reassignment of the numbers of congressional seats that each state will have is reapportionment; a state's redrawing of its congressional districts is redistricting. *Compare to* BAKER V CARR; GERRYMANDERING; REYNOLDS V SIMS. **2.** A parallel process for state legislative districts.

redlining A practice allegedly followed by some urban financial institutions in which they refuse loans for home mortgages and improvements in areas thought to be poor risks. People living or wishing to live in these areas are denied such loans regardless of their particular financial situation. In consequence, the areas denied financing are unable to upgrade their housing and thus go into an economic decline. (The term derives from the drawing of red lines around such areas on a map.) Some states have laws prohibiting redlining.

referendum A procedure for submitting proposed laws or state constitutional amendments to the voters for their direct approval or rejection. A petition signed by an appropriate percentage of the voters can force a newly passed law onto the ballot, or it could be put on the ballot by the recommendation of the legislature. While only a minority of the states provide for statutory referenda, practically all states require them for constitutional amendments. Local governments also use the referendum, especially when the law requires that certain issues, such as capital project borrowing, must be submitted directly to the voters. *Compare to* RECALL.

reflagging *See* FLAG OF CONVENIENCE.

reform movement 1. What an out-of-power political party often considers itself. **2.** Good-government advocates of changes in governing structures. **3.** A loose term for efforts to weed out corruption in public office. New York Mayor Jimmy Walker (1881–1946) is usually credited with saying: "A reformer is a guy who rides through the sewer in a glass-bottom boat." In 1932, these reformers forced Walker to resign as mayor amid charges of vast corruption. New York political boss Roscoe Conkling (1829–1888) is quoted in David M. Jordan's *Roscoe Conkling of New York* (1971) as saying: "When Dr. Johnson defined patriotism as the last refuge of a scoundrel, he ignored the enormous possibilities of the word reform." **4.** The PROGRESSIVE MOVEMENT, which advocated municipal reforms, such as the council-manager form of government, civil service reform, the short ballot, and nonpartisan elections.

registration, periodic A voter registration policy that requires voters to register before each election or at designated intervals between elections.

registration, permanent A voter registration policy which allows voters to remain continuously registered unless they fail to vote for several elections in a row.

registration, voter The process whereby a prospective voter is required to establish his or her identity and place of residence prior to an election to be declared eligible to vote in a particular jurisdiction. The reasons for registration are to prevent electionday fraud by making it difficult for one person to vote at more than one location and to ensure that those who do vote have previously established that they are eligible residents. Prior to any major election, all political parties make significant efforts to get their potential supporters registered. In recent years, many jurisdictions have made major efforts to make it easier for citizens to register by combining registration with driver's license application, by allowing registration in supermarkets and shopping centers, and so on. Public service announcements on television encourage all segments of the population to register so that they can later vote. Cable TV outlet MTV took a humorous approach when singer Cyndi Lauper asked the audience: "Are your shoes too tight? Are your feet too small? Well, the answer to this and many other problems is to register and vote." *Compare to* VOTER REQUIREMENTS.

regulation The rule-making process of those administrative agencies charged with the official interpretation of a statute. These agencies (often independent regulatory commissions), in addition to issuing rules, also tend to administer their implementation and to adjudicate interpretative disputes. The Interstate Commerce Commission in 1887 became the prototype of the modern regulatory agency. *See also* DELEGATION OF POWER; DEREGULATION; HUMPHREY'S EXECUTOR V UNITED STATES; INDEPENDENT AGENCY.

Rehnquist Court The Supreme Court under the leadership of Chief Justice William H. Rehnquist, who has been on the Court since 1972 (appointed by President Richard M. Nixon) and was appointed Chief Justice of the U.S. by President Ronald Reagan in 1986.

relief A term that usually refers to the public assistance programs available during the GREAT DEPRESSION of the 1930s. *Direct relief* referred to straight WELFARE payments. *Work relief* referred to any of the numerous public works projects initiated specifically to provide jobs for the unemployed.

religious test A legal requirement that someone must profess faith in a particular religion to qualify for public office. This is expressly forbidden by that portion of Article VI of the U.S. Constitution that reads: "No religious test shall ever be required as a qualification to any office or public trust under the United States." Together with the First Amendment, this guarantee expresses the principle that church and government are to remain separate, and that citizens' religious beliefs are no indication of their patriotism or their ability and right to serve their country. Thus, citizens need not fear that their religious affiliations or convictions will legally bar them from holding office.

rendezvous with destiny A special mission. President Franklin D. Roosevelt gave currency to the phrase in his speech accepting renomination for the presidency, June 27, 1936. He said in part: "There is a mysterious cycle in human events. To some generations much is given. Of other generations much is expected. This generation of Americans has a rendezvous with destiny." The phrase became all the more poignant once the United States entered World War II.

rent control Local laws that regulate the amount by which landlords can raise rents on residential properties. The Supreme Court in *Fisher v City of Berkeley* (1986) held that municipal rent control laws did not violate federal antitrust statutes. Frustrated by their inability to remove rent controls at the local level, opponents have sought state laws that preempt local ordinances. They have been successful in varying degrees in at least a dozen states. For example, Colorado and Georgia now have total bans on any form of rent control, while Minnesota requires a local referendum for enactment of controls.

repeal The nullification of a law by the body that previously enacted it. Thomas Paine wrote in *The Rights of Man* (1791): "A law not repealed continues in force, not because it cannot be repealed, but because it is not repealed, and the nonrepealing passes for consent." Later, President Ulysses S. Grant, would state in his inaugural address of March 4, 1869: "I know no method to secure the repeal of bad or obnoxious laws so effective as their stringent execution."

report The document setting forth a congressional committee's explanation of its action on a bill. Reports by the House of Representatives and the Senate are numbered separately and are designated "H. Rept." and "S. Rept." Conference reports are numbered and designated in the same way as regular committee reports. Most reports favor a bill's passage. Adverse reports are occasionally submitted, but more often, when a committee disapproves a bill, it simply fails to report it at all. When a committee report is not unanimous, the dissenting committee members may file a statement of their views, referred to as a *minority report*. Sometimes a bill is reported without recommendation; this means that the committee was divided on its merits.

representation, actual A mode of legislative representation in which legislators vote the will of their constituents regardless of their own judgments. *Compare to* TRUSTEE.

representation, agency A situation that exists when the people represented have the power to hire and fire their representatives.

representation, proportional *See* PROPORTIONAL REPRESENTATION.

representation, sociological Having elected or appointed representatives with the same racial, ethnic, or religious characteristics as the people they serve.

representation, virtual **1.** Having elected or appointed representatives with differing sociological characteristics from the people they serve. **2.** A style of legislative representation in which representatives vote in the best interests of their constituents as opposed to simply reflecting their will. Also known as the TRUSTEE model.

representative A member of the U.S. House of Representatives or of a lower house in a state legislature. *See* CONGRESSMAN/CONGRESSWOMAN; CONGRESS, MEMBER OF.

representative bureaucracy A concept that asserts that all social groups have a right to participate in their governing institutions. In recent years, the concept has become even more value-laden; now it implies that all social groups should occupy bureaucratic positions in direct proportion to their numbers in the general population.

representative government A governing system in which a legislature freely chosen by the people exercises substantial power on their behalf. EDMUND BURKE distinguished representation from delegation.

republic A Latin word meaning "the public thing": the state and its institutions; that form of government in which sovereignty resides in the people who elect agents to represent them in political decision making. The United States is a republic. The founders specifically wanted a governing structure that was one step removed from a pure DEMOCRACY. And they also wanted a governing structure that could function over a large area. As James Madison wrote in *The Federalist* No. 14: "In a democracy the people meet and exercise the government in person; in a republic, they assemble and administer it by their representatives and agents. A democracy, consequently, will be confined to a small spot. A republic may be extended over a large region." Yet the Founders all knew that many republics in history, such as the Roman republic, had been replaced by despots. Consequently, when Benjamin Franklin was asked what sort of government had been hatched at the Constitutional Convention, he replied, "a republic, if you can keep it." He knew that "keeping it" was far from certain.

republican One who believes in a government where the people exercise their sovereignty through elected representatives. *Compare to* DEMOCRAT.

Republican A member of the Republican party.

Republican party 1. The first American political party to develop in opposition to the Federalist Party in 1791. Led by Thomas Jefferson, this party later evolved into the Democratic-Republican party, which became the Democratic party in 1828. **2.** The 1854 coalition of antislavery Whigs and Jacksonians that went on to win the presidency with Abraham Lincoln in 1860. It dominated national politics from the Civil War to the New Deal. During that time, only two Democrats were elected President (Grover Cleveland and Woodrow Wilson). Since the New Deal, the Democrats have been the majority party, but the Republicans have still been able to consistently win the White House with a hero of World War II (Dwight D. Eisenhower); in the wake of domestic disunity over Vietnam (Richard M. Nixon); in a contest against a Democratic President seemingly unable to control inflation or maintain a competent foreign policy (Ronald Reagan); and against Democratic candidates unable to present themselves or their ideas in a palatable way to the American people (Reagan and George Bush). To the extent that presidential politics has degenerated to a duel of 30-second television spots, the Republicans have been the better duelists by far. The party has been less successful at the congressional and state levels, however. So the question remains as to whether it will forge a new political REALIGNMENT with a Republican majority.

The Republican party has long been considered the conservative party in American politics; they have favored increased spending on defense, decreased spending on domestic, educational, and welfare programs, and a general reduction in the size of government by curtailing government regulation and increasing the privatization of selected government programs. As President Ronald Reagan told a Republican congressional dinner on May 4, 1982, the Republican Party is "the party that wants to see an America in which people can still get rich."

res judicata A Latin term for "a settled matter, a closed case." It means that a court has passed judgment on a case and consequently will not reexamine it.

rescission A bill or a joint resolution that cancels in whole or in part budget authority previously granted by the U.S. Congress. Rescissions proposed by the President must be transmitted in a special message to the Congress, which must approve such proposed rescissions under procedures in the Budget and Impoundment Control Act of 1974 for them to take effect.

reservation   1. In the context of international relations, a nation's formal declaration that, while it accepts a treaty in general, it must modify or expand its terms before it is fully acceptable. Once the reservation is agreed to by the other party, it is then considered part of the original agreement. **2.** Land set aside by a government for a specific purpose. **3.** Any of the approximately 400 land units reserved for American Indians and supervised by the Bureau of Indian Affairs of the U.S. Department of the Interior.

reserve   1. Portion of a body of troops which is deep to the rear, or withheld from action at the beginning of an engagement, available for a decisive movement. **2.** Members of military services who are not in active service but who are subject to call to active duty once war begins. **3.** That portion of a budget appropriation or contract authorization held or set aside for future operations or contingencies and in respect to which administrative authorization to incur commitments or obligations has been withheld.

reserved powers The principle of American federalism embodied in the Tenth Amendment of the U.S. Constitution that gives the states (or the people) the residue of powers not granted to the federal government or withheld from the states. Chief Justice Harlan F. Stone wrote in UNITED STATES V DARBY LUMBER that the Tenth Amendment is "but a truism that all is retained which has not been surrendered." *Compare to* DELEGATED POWER.

reserve requirements The percentage of deposit liabilities that U.S. commercial banks are required to set aside at their Federal Reserve bank, as cash in their vaults, or as directed by state banking authorities. The reserve requirement is one of the tools of monetary policy. Federal Reserve officials can control the lending capacity of the banks (thus, influencing the money supply) by varying the ratio of reserves to deposits that commercial banks are required to maintain.

residency requirement 1. The requirement that a citizen live in a jurisdiction for a specific length of time before being eligible to vote or hold public office. The Supreme Court held in *Dunn v Blumstein* (1972), that a "durational" residency requirement to vote is unconstitutional. However, as a practical matter the Court recognized the necessity of closing voter registration rolls 30 to 50 days before an election. **2.** The requirement that a person be (or become) a resident of a jurisdiction to be eligible for employment within its government. **3.** The requirement that a person be a resident of a jurisdiction for a specific time period before becoming eligible for WELFARE benefits. The Supreme Court has ruled in *Shapiro v Thompson* (1969) that jurisdictions cannot discriminate against newer residents in the provision of social benefits.

resident commissioner *See* DELEGATE.

resolution A congressional action (designated H. Res. or S. Res.) that deals with matters entirely within the prerogatives of one house or the other. It requires neither passage by the other chamber nor approval by the President, and it does not have the force of law. Most resolutions deal with the rules of one house. They also are used to express the sentiments of a single house, as condolences to the family of a deceased member, or to give "advice" on foreign policy or other executive branch business.

resolution, concurrent A congressional action (designated H. Con. Res. or S. Con. Res.) that must be passed by both houses but does not require the signature of the President and does not have the force of law. Concurrent resolutions generally are used to make or amend rules applicable to both houses or to express the sentiment of the two houses. For example, a concurrent resolution is used to fix the time for adjournment of the Congress.

resolution, joint A congressional action (designated H. J. Res. or S. J. Res.) that requires the approval of both houses and the signature of the President, just as a bill does, and has the force of law if approved. There is no real difference between a bill and a joint resolution. The latter is generally used in dealing with limited matters, such as a single appropriation for a specific purpose. Joint resolutions also are used to propose amendments to the Constitution. They do not require presidential signature but become a part of the Constitution when three fourths of the states have ratified them.

resolution on the budget, concurrent A resolution passed by both houses of the Congress, but not requiring the signature of the President, setting forth, reaffirming, or revising the congressional budget for the U.S. government for a fiscal year. Two such resolutions are required preceding each fiscal year. The first, due by May 15, establishes the congressional budget. The second, due by September 15, reaffirms or revises it. Other concurrent resolutions may be adopted at any time following the first required concurrent resolution.

Resolution Trust Corporation The organization created by the federal government in the wake of the SAVINGS AND LOAN SCANDAL of 1989 to manage the sale of the hundreds of thousands of properties the federal government may end up owning by taking over the assets of failed banks.

restrictive covenant *See* COVENANT.

retainer 1. A servant or attendant. **2.** The act of a client employing a lawyer. **3.** An initial or continuing fee paid to a lawyer either for specific services or simply to be available if needed. Legislators have traditionally solicited bribes by informally suggesting that special interests keep their law firms "on retainer." In a now famous December 21, 1833 letter to Philadelphia banker Nicholas Biddle, Senator Daniel Webster told him, "I believe that my retainer has not been renewed, or refreshed as usual," and that if he wanted his interests to be represented in Congress, "it may be well to send me the usual retainers." Today such solicitations are more subtle, at least at the national level.

retaliation 1. A military attack in response to an earlier action of those being attacked. **2.** Action taken by a country against another because of the imposition of tariffs or other trade barriers. Retaliation can take a number of forms, including imposition of higher tariffs, import restrictions, or withdrawal of trade concessions previously agreed to. According to GATT, restrictive action by one country legally entitles the aggrieved party to compensatory action.

revenue anticipation notes Forms of short-term borrowing used by a jurisdiction to resolve a cash flow problem occasioned by a shortage of necessary revenues or taxes to cover planned or unplanned expenditures.

revenue gainer 1. Euphemism for a tax increase (also *revenue enhancement*). **2.** The manipulation of existing tax laws (or methods) to increase revenues as opposed to the more straightforward approach of raising or creating new taxes.

revenue neutral A characteristic of a tax reform law whose net effect would be to neither increase nor decrease the total taxes raised. Instead, it would readjust tax burdens, presumably to make the overall tax system fairer or simpler.

revenue reform 1. A TAX EXTENSION. **2.** Taxing things or people that were not previously taxes; for example, taxing social security benefits as regular income.

revenue sharing The distribution of federal tax revenues among subnational levels of government. First proposed in its present form in the early 1960s by Walter Heller, then chairman of President John F. Kennedy's

Council of Economic Advisers, revenue sharing was designed to arrest the rising fiscal burdens of many state and local governments. Part of its original rationale was the concern of some economists about the accumulation of federal budget surpluses. Given today's record federal deficits, this sounds a bit unreal; nevertheless, it was a true concern of the early 1960s. The theory was that a budget surplus would produce a fiscal drag on the economy and that the money ought to be put back into the economy in some efficient way. Revenue sharing was a natural. Another justification for revenue sharing was its ability to mitigate fiscal imbalances among the states, where variances in per capita personal income are significant. Finally, the argument was made that revenue sharing is economically justified by the federal government's monopolization of the most efficient and progressive tax source—the federal income tax.

In 1972, revenue sharing was introduced to the nation with the passage of the State and Local Fiscal Assistance Act. With the advent of the Ronald Reagan administration, general revenue sharing was subject to increased scrutiny. The General Revenue Sharing Program was allowed to expire in 1986. The burgeoning of federal budget deficits remains the major obstacle to renewal.

reverse discrimination A practice generally understood to mean discrimination against white males in conjunction with preferential treatment for women and minorities. The practice had no legal standing in civil rights laws. Indeed, Section 703(j) of TITLE VII of the Civil Rights Act of 1964 holds that nothing in the title shall be interpreted to permit any employer to "grant preferential treatment to any individual or group on the basis of race, color, religion, sex or national origin." Yet affirmative action programs necessarily put some white males at a disadvantage that they would not have otherwise had. Reverse discrimination is usually most keenly per- ceived when affirmative action policies conflict with older policies of granting preferments on the basis of seniority, test scores, and so on. The practice of reverse discrimination was finally given legal standing when the Supreme Court in *Johnson v Santa Clara County* (1987) upheld an affirmative action plan which promoted a woman ahead of an objectively more qualified man. Critics contended that this turned Title VII's requirement that there be no "preferential treatment" upside down because for the first time the Court sanctioned and gave legal standing to reverse discrimination.

revising and extending The process by which members of Congress make additions and revisions to their remarks which would otherwise appear in the CONGRESSIONAL RECORDS without the cleaning up of grammar and expansion of remarks that "revising and extending" allows.

Revlon President A critical reference to George Bush, suggesting that he "proposes only cosmetic solutions for big problems." According to the *Pittsburgh Post-Gazette* (October 14, 1989), the phrase was coined by free-lance writer Peter Edelman. *Compare to* TEFLON PRESIDENT.

revolution **1.** Any social, economic, agricultural, political, or intellectual change involving major transformations of fundamental institutions. Those institutions may be class structures (as in MARXISM), economic structures (as in industrial revolution), methods of producing food supplies (as in green revolution), ideas and approaches to knowledge (as in a scientific revolution), or systems of governance. Political revolutions in which one leader uses violent means to take power from another without transforming the system are also often called revolutions, although the use of the term since the eighteenth century has tended to be confined to fundamental changes, rather than to mere changes in power. Political commentators who see major changes, say, from one presidential administration to another are often inclined to refer to the changes as a revolution (thus, the REAGAN REVOLUTION, the Roosevelt revolution) to indicate a large degree of supposed transformation. **2.** A right of the citizens of a society to overthrow bad, incompetent, or unjust rulers—by violence if necessary—to establish a better government. The founders, heavily influenced by JOHN LOCKE, believed this strongly. Thomas Jefferson wrote in a letter to William Stevens Smith on November 13, 1787, that "the tree of liberty must be refreshed from time to time with the blood of patriots and tyrants. It is its natural manure." In this context, revolution is a right that helps insure proper government, and one that threatens only the government of tyrants. This right of revolution has often been turned into a religious obligation. Both the American Thomas Jefferson and the Iranian Ayatollah Khomeini (1901–1989) have preached that resistance to tyrants is obedience to God. The right of revolution serves as a continuous check on potential tyrants. According to Abraham Lincoln in his first inaugural address, March 4, 1861: "This country, with its institutions, belongs to the people who inhabit it. Whenever they shall grow weary of the existing government, they can exercise their constitutional right of amending it, or their revolutionary right to dismember or overthrow it." Unfortunately, as novelist Franz Kafka (1883–1924) is alleged to have warned: "Every revolution evaporates, leaving behind only the slime of a new bureaucracy" (*Newsweek*, October 14, 1968). **3.** Evolution. Americans have come to suspect foreign revolutions and revolutionaries, even as they continue to revere their own. The association of the term with Marxism has led Americans to a more evolutionary concept of government change, one that denies anyone the right to overthrow the Constitution by force. While the concept of revolution by peaceful means is difficult for oppressed people to accept, here or anywhere else in the world, it has come to be the basis for the affirmation of American government as a successful system for carrying out the will of the people through established procedures. As President John F. Kennedy said in his speech to the diplomatic corps of the Latin American republics on March 13, 1962: "Those who make peaceful revolution impossible will make violent revolution inevitable."

Revolution must be contrasted with *rebellion*. Theoretically, those in rebellion seek power for its own sake. In seeking domination, they violate the structures of a civil society. In this context, the worst rebels are tyrannical rulers who have violated both their personal honor and their political mandates and thus deserve to be overthrown. The ability of those fighting to overthrow a government to sustain their cause ultimately affects whether history calls them revolutionaries or rebels—as the Confederate states discovered when they lost the American Civil War. As Thomas B. Reed said in a speech in the House of Representatives, April 12, 1878: "The only justification of rebellion is success."

Reynolds v Sims (1964) The Supreme Court case that established the criterion of ONE MAN, ONE VOTE for legislative apportionment. The Court held that legislative districts must be apportioned on the basis of population to comply with the equal protection of the laws guaranteed by the Fourteenth Amendment. In so ruling, it rejected the federal analogy, which suggested that one house of a state legislature (paralleling the U.S. Senate) could be apportioned on a basis other than population. It held that the analogy was invalid, because the political subdivisions of a state are not sovereign entities, as the states are. In holding that legislatures should "represent people, not trees, or acres," the Court did much to curb the rural bias of the state legislatures. *Compare to* BAKER V CARR.

rider A provision that may have no relation to the basic subject matter of the bill it is riding on. Riders become law if the bills in which they are included become law. They are often added to appropriation bills, though technically this is banned. The U.S. House of Representatives, unlike the Senate, has a strict germaneness rule; thus, riders are usually Senate devices.

right **1.** Correct; truthful; moral. This is what Henry Clay (1777–1852) meant when he said "I had rather be right than President." (Clay was neither; what he thought he was "right" about was a defense of slavery.) Another famous use of this sentence occurred in 1890. Samuel McCall's *The Life of Thomas Brackett Reed* (1914) records how Representative William Springer, speaking in the House, quoted Henry Clay: "As for me, I would rather be right than be President." Speaker of the House Reed corrected Springer: "The gentleman will never be either." **2.** The conservative, sometimes reactionary, elements of the political spectrum. The political Right in all countries tends to favor traditional free enterprise, capitalism, a strong military, a vigorous executive, and cultural conservatism. *Compare to* LEFT. **3.** A legally enforceable power or privilege; or a power or privilege believed to have been conferred by God or nature, hence incapable of being subverted by man. As Ramsey Clark once explained: "A right is not what someone gives you; it's what no one can take from you" (*The New York Times*, October 2, 1977). *Compare to* CIVIL RIGHTS.

right, natural *See* LAW, NATURAL.

right, new Traditional conservatism with an evangelical and intolerant edge to it; that is why it is also known as the "religious Right." The new Right expresses the politics of resentment: it rejects much of government's involvement in the economy and with traditional WELFARE programs. It advocates a strong anticommunist foreign policy and traditional moral virtues regarding religion, school prayer, abortion, and pornography. The new right believes so strongly in its views that it seeks constitutional amendments and other changes in the law to enforce them. According to Senator Thomas J. McIntyre of New Hampshire: "The new Right cannot comprehend how people of opposing viewpoints can find common ground and work together. For them, there is no common ground. And this, in my judgment, is the best indication of what they truly are—radicals, whose aim is not to compete with honor and decency, not to compromise when necessary to advance the common good, but to annihilate those they see as 'enemies'" (*The Washington Post*, March 3, 1978). *Compare to* MORAL MAJORITY.

right-of-way Also known as *easement*, the legal right to use the land of another, typically for right of passage of a person, vehicle, underground cables, and so on. In the case of "scenic easement," it is the right to a view.

right, old The traditional conservative Right. It is called old or "paleo" Right just to differentiate it from the new Right.

right, radical Far Right conservatives, many of whom believe that those who advocate policies that differ from their own are motivated by treason. The radical Right is as intolerant of differing political opinions as is the radical Left.

right to life The movement to reverse the present legal status of ABORTION in the United States. *See also* ROE V WADE.

right-to-work laws State laws that make it illegal for collective bargaining agreements to contain maintenance of membership, preferential hiring, union shop, or any other clauses calling for compulsory union membership. A typical right-to-work law might read: "No person may be denied employment and employers may not be denied the right to employ any person because of that person's membership or nonmembership in any labor organization." The Labor-Management Relations (Taft-Hartley) Act of 1947 authorized right-to-work laws in Section 14(b): "Nothing in this Act shall be construed as authorizing the execution or application of agreements requiring membership in a labor organization as a condition of employment in any State or Territory in which such execution or application is prohibited by State or Territorial law." The law does not prohibit the union or closed shop; it simply gives each state the option of doing so. Twenty states have done so to some degree: Alabama, Arizona, Arkansas, Florida, Georgia, Iowa, Kansas, Louisiana, Mississippi, Nebraska, Nevada, North Carolina, North Dakota, South Carolina, South Dakota, Tennessee, Texas, Utah, Virginia, and Wyoming.

riot commission *See* KERNER COMMISSION.

ripper act Any legislative measure abolishing offices held by opposition partisans, thereby lessening the powers of administrative agencies controlled by opposition appointees, transferring the authority to grant contracts, and so on. All ripper acts are done in a spirit of partisanship and revenge.

rise above principle What a politician does when he or she compromises and agrees to measures that may be contrary to his or her professed principles but may better meet the perceived public need.

Robert's Rules of Order *See* PARLIAMENTARY PROCEDURE.

Roe v Wade (1973) The Supreme Court case that (by a vote of seven to two) made ABORTION legal in the United States by ruling that governments lacked the power to prohibit them. Associate Justice Harry Blackmun wrote regarding this case that "freedom of personal choice in matters of marriage and family life is one of the liberties protected by the due process clause of the Fourteenth Amendment. . . . That right necessarily includes the right of a woman to decide whether or not to terminate her pregnancy." This has been one of the most controversial Supreme Court decisions, heralded by some groups as a landmark for women's rights and denounced by others, especially the new Right, as the legalization of murder. The *Gallup Report* (January/February 1986) showed that Americans were evenly divided between those who oppose and those who support the *Roe v Wade* decision. *Compare to* GRISWOLD V CONNECTICUT.

roll-call 1. The calling of the names of the members of a legislature to determine whether a quorum is present so that formal business may be conducted. **2.** An individually recorded vote of the members of a legislature. A roll-call vote is in contrast to a voice vote, in which there is no way to hold a legislator accountable for how he or she voted. Roll calls have often been replaced by electronic devices, but the effect is the same—the way each legislator voted becomes a matter of public record. **3.** The name of a twice-weekly newspaper on congressional affairs published in Washington, D.C.; it calls itself the "newspaper of Capitol Hill."

roorback A false media account of something designed to embarrass a political candidate. The word dates from 1844, when a Baron Roorback reported in the *Ithaca (N.Y.) Chronicle* that Democratic presidential candidate James K. Polk had bought slaves—and then had his initials branded on them. Ever since then, a roorback has been synonymous with political slander.

Roosevelt, Eleanor (1884–1962) The wife of President Franklin D. Roosevelt. She was the first First Lady to publicly play a major political role in her husband's administration. Her example has made her a major influence in the modern women's movement. She continued in public life after her husband's death, serving as a delegate to the United Nations and continuing as a significant voice in liberal causes and humanitarian issues.

Roosevelt, Franklin Delano (1882–1945) The President of the United States (1933–1945) whose NEW DEAL policies are often said to have saved the capitalistic system, who led the nation through the Great Depression of the 1930s and to victory in World War II, and who is on every leading historian's list, along with Abraham Lincoln and George Washington, as one of the most important U.S. Presidents. Roosevelt entered public life as a member of the New York Senate (1910–1913). He became assistant secretary of the Navy (1913–1920) in the Woodrow Wilson administration, the unsuccessful Democratic nominee for Vice President in 1920, and governor of New York (1929–1933).

Roosevelt reached the height of political power despite the fact that, after 1921, when he contracted polio, he was basically confined to a wheelchair. Yet because he was able to stand (with braces) to give speeches, and because reporters were not allowed to take pictures that made him appear to be disabled, much of the American public was unaware of his handicapped condition—even though it was not a secret. But this did not stop his critics, who attacked him, his New Deal policies, and his wife, Eleanor, as being either socialist or fascist. The hatred of Roosevelt was so intense that his opponents were often too furious to pronounce his name; thus, he was often called "that man in the White House." This reference is now used for any occupant of that house with whom one is exasperated.

Roosevelt, Theodore "Teddy" (1858–1919)   The colonel who led the Rough Riders in Cuba during the 1898 Spanish-American War; who was elected governor of New York on the basis of his war record; who was made Vice President under William McKinley by the party bosses who wanted him out of New York; and who became President after an assassin shot McKinley in 1901. Roosevelt, who won election in his own right in 1904, took an expansive view of the presidency (regarding it as, in his own words, a BULLY PULPIT) and thus set the tone for most of the Presidents who followed. He was the first to advocate consumer protection and the CONSERVATION of natural resources. His memoirs were published as *An Autobiography* (1913). *See also* BIG STICK; NEW NATIONALISM; PRESIDENCY, STEWARDSHIP THEORY OF.

rose garden strategy   "The" rose garden is a part of the White House grounds often used for brief ceremonies or outdoor press conferences. A rose garden strategy has an incumbent President running for reelection largely by staying home and acting presidential; to use the symbolic trappings of the office for all they are worth. Often a rose garden strategy will call for "rose garden rubbish"—the virtually meaningless comments a President makes to visiting groups.

Roth v United States (1957)   The Supreme Court case that asserted that obscenity was not protected free speech under the First Amendment because it was "utterly without redeeming social importance or value." But how is it to be determined whether some expression is obscene enough to forgo First Amendment protection? According to the Court, the test of obscenity is "whether to the average person, applying contemporary community standards, the dominant theme of the material taken as a whole appeals to prurient interest." This test of obscenity has been modified by the Court in *Miller v California* (1973), wherein "contemporary community standards" were replaced by "national standards."

rotten borough A legislative district with a disproportionately small population compared to its representation. In the 1960s, the Supreme Court via BAKER V CARR and REYNOLDS V SIMS mandated the elimination of the traditional rotten boroughs.

Rousseau, Jean-Jacques (1712–1778) The Swiss-born French Enlightenment philosopher whose theories of democracy and the social contract were major influences on the American and French revolutions. His most important book, *The Social Contract* (1762), opens with the poignant: "Man is born free, and everywhere he is in chains." Rousseau found free, natural human beings, the "noble savages," to be good; but the institutions of society had corrupted them. The only form of social organization that could get them back to the state of natural liberty was direct democracy. Only this kind of popular sovereignty offered legitimacy; only the general will as expressed by the people could make valid law. Rousseau's notions fell on fertile intellectual ground. His basic ideas, that ordinary people had the right to govern themselves and had the right to overthrow kings who claimed a competing divine right, can be found in both the Declaration of Independence and the U.S. Constitution.

rubber-chicken circuit A gastronomic description of the political campaign trail. Often the trail includes fund-raising dinners for which participants are charged excessive amounts to dine with the candidate. The charges are referred to as "per plate," meaning "per diner." Thus, a $100 per plate dinner might net the candidate or party approximately $70 per diner after deducting actual expenses. When Senator John F. Kennedy was campaigning for the presidency, he attended such a dinner in Salt Lake City on September 23, 1960, and was moved to say after a round of applause: "I am deeply touched—not as deeply touched as you have been coming to this dinner, but nevertheless it is a sentimental occasion." Journalist Charles Krauthammer described campaigning for the presidency as "a three-year diet of rubber chicken and occasional crow" (*Time*, May 14, 1982).

rule 1. A regulation made by an administrative agency. **2.** A decision of a judge or presiding officer. **3.** A standing order governing the conduct of business in the House of Representatives or Senate and listed in the chamber's book of rules. The rules deal with duties of officers, order of business, admission to the floor, voting procedures, and so on. **4.** In the House, a decision made by its Rules Committee about the handling of a particular bill on the floor. The committee may determine under which standing rule a bill shall be considered, or it may provide a special rule in the form of a resolution. If the resolution is adopted by the House, the temporary rule becomes as valid as any standing rule. A special rule sets the time limit on general debate. It may also waive points of order against provisions of the bill or against specified amendments to the bill. It may even forbid all amendments or all amendments except those proposed by the legislative committee that handled the bill. In this instance, it is known as a closed rule, or GAG RULE, as opposed to an open rule, which puts no limitation on floor amendments. *Compare to* RULES, SUSPENSION OF.

rule making authority The powers, which have the force of law, exercised by administrative agencies. Agencies begin with some form of legislative mandate and translate their interpretation of that mandate into policy decisions, specifications of regulations, and statements of penalties and enforcement provisions. The exact process to be followed in formulating regulations is only briefly described in the federal Administration Procedure Act (APA). The APA does distinguish between rule making that requires a hearing and rule making that requires only notice and the opportunity for public notice and comment. Whether the formal or informal procedure is to be used is determined by the enabling statute: the Supreme Court's decision in *United States v Florida East Coast Railway* (1973) held that formal rule making need only be followed when the enabling statute expressly requires an agency hearing prior to rule formulation. The APA also requires that rules be published 30 days before their effective date and that agencies afford any interested party the right to petition for issuance, amendment, or repeal of a rule. In effect, while the APA establishes a process of notice and time for comment, it accords administrative rule makers the same prerogatives as legislatures have in enacting statutes. There is, of course, the additional requirement that the rule enacted be consistent with the enabling statute directing the rule making.

rule of four The Supreme Court's policy of granting a petition for a writ of CERTIORARI if four or more justices consider a case to be worthy of review.

rule of law A governing system in which the highest authority is a body of law that applies equally to all (as opposed to the "rule of men," in which the personal whim of those in power can decide any issue). The idea of the desirability of a "government of laws, and not of men" can be traced back to Aristotle. The earliest American reference is in the 1779 Massachusetts Constitution. John Marshall also used this succinct legal description in *Marbury v Madison* (1803): "The government of the United States has been emphatically termed a government of laws, and not of men. It will certainly cease to deserve this high appellation, if the laws furnish no remedy for the violation of a vested legal right." The rule of law and the concomitant notion that no one is above the law have been continuously critical concepts. When President Gerald R. Ford succeeded President Richard M. Nixon (who was forced to resign because of his illegal activities during the WATERGATE scandal), he told the nation right after taking the oath of office (August 9, 1974): "My fellow Americans, our long national nightmare is over. Our Constitution works; our great Republic is a government of laws and not of men." *Compare to* GOV-ERNMENT.

rule of three The practice of certifying to an appointing authority the top three names on an eligible list. The rule of three is intended to give the appointing official an opportunity to weigh intangible factors, such as personality, before making a formal offer of appointment. The rule of one certifies only the highest-ranking person on the eligible list. The rule of the list gives the appointing authority the opportunity to choose from the entire list of eligibles.

rule, restrictive A legislative rule that limits the number and kind of amendments that can be offered to a bill being debated.

rules, suspension of A time-saving procedure for passing bills in the U.S. House of Representatives. The wording of the motion, which may be made by any member recognized by the Speaker, is: "I move to suspend the rules and pass the bill." A favorable vote by two thirds of those present is required for passage. Debate is limited to 40 minutes, and no amendments from the floor are permitted. If a two-thirds favorable vote is not attained, the bill may be considered later under regular procedures. The suspension procedure is in order on the first and third Mondays and Tuesdays of each month.

run ahead of the ticket To get more votes in an election than the party's standard bearer. A candidate for the U.S. Congress runs ahead of the ticket when he or she gets more votes than the party's nominee for President.

run scared A campaign strategy of not taking any chances of complacency; of campaigning heavy and hard even if you are way ahead in the opinion polls.

runaway shop A business that moves out of a jurisdiction specifically to avoid its high taxes, strong unions, strenuous safety regulations, etc.

running dog A political lackey; the Chinese communist term for someone subservient to capitalist masters.

rustbelt Those parts of the northeastern and midwestern United States where traditional manufacturing industries are in decline, literally rusting away. Rustbelt is often used synonymously with *snowbelt*. *See also* SUN-BELT-SNOWBELT TENSION.

Rutan v Republican Party *See* PATRONAGE.

S

safe seat A legislative district in which the incumbent is virtually guaranteed reelection; normally a seat that is captured with 60 percent or more of the vote. This could be because of the candidate's strong political appeal, an overwhelming registration of voters from the candidate's party, or the candidate's many years of CASEWORK service to the district's citizens. In recent U.S. House of Representative elections, a majority of districts have been won by 65 percent or more of the vote. *Compare to* MARGINAL SEAT.

safety net President Ronald Reagan's term for the social WELFARE programs that, in his opinion, assure at least a subsistence standard of living for all Americans. The Reagan Administration's use of the term is often credited to Congressman Jack Kemp's 1980 book, *An American Renaissance*, in which he states: "Americans have two complementary desires. . . . They want an open, promising ladder of opportunity. And they want a safety net of social services to catch and comfort those less fortunate than themselves."

sample Any deliberately chosen portion of a larger population that is representative of that population as a whole. Scientifically selected samples—random samples in which each person in a population has an equal chance of being selected—are the foundation of PUBLIC OPINION polling. The size of a sample can be very small in relation to the overall population. It is possible to accurately measure public opinion in a nation of over two hundred million with a sample of a few thousand—if the sample is properly selected. The pollsters often report that sample results are accurate to within plus or minus 3 or 4 percentage points. This may not be terribly helpful in a close race, but the cost of making the survey marginally more accurate by interviewing 10 or 20 times as many subjects quickly becomes prohibitive. When opinion sampling was first introduced in the period between the World Wars, it was difficult for political leaders to believe that such a small portion of a large population could provide an accurate measure of the whole population. Now most politicians are true believers about sampling, and no major campaign is without its pollsters. This situation has created a larger danger: that those in or seeking public office will merely parrot their pollsters' perceptions of public opinion rather than forging new opinions. Modern sampling makes it all too easy to tell the public what they want to hear as opposed to what they need to hear. *Compare to* OPINION LEADER.

sample, probability A sample in which each member of the population has an equal chance of being selected as a respondent; thus, equal weight is theoretically given to all segments of the population.

sampling, area Selecting a sample that is confined to a specific geograhic area, such as a county, a city, or a ward. Within each area the sample is randomly selected.

sampling error The error caused by generalizing the behavior of a population from a sample of that population that is not totally representative of the population as a whole. For example, it is often reported that a specific survey of public opinion is accurate to plus or minus 4 percentage points. This 8 point spread represents the sampling error. There would be no sampling error if an entire population (e.g., 240 million Americans) were surveyed instead of a few thousand.

sampling, haphazard Not a true sample at all; a nonscientific man in the street type poll.

sampling, quota Selecting respondents from groups that have specific geographic, religious, racial, or other characteristics.

sampling, systematic Selecting as respondents every tenth, twelfth, twentieth, etc., name from a large list.

sanction 1. The penalties attached to a law to encourage people to obey it. **2.** Ratification by a higher (or another) authority. **3.** Foreign policies that range in a continuum from the suspension of diplomatic or economic relations to outright military intervention, designed to force another nation to change its behavior. *See also* CONSTRUCTIVE ENGAGEMENT.

sandbagging Setting a political opponent up for a fall by creating unreasonable expectations, by building him or her up far beyond anyone's capabilities. Then when they "fail" to adequately perform, they can be criticized for their ineptness.

sanitize 1. To make clean, to sterilize, or to disinfect. **2.** To revise a document to prevent the identification (1) of sources, (2) of the actual person and places concerned, or (3) of the means by which it was acquired.

savings and loan scandal The largest financial scandal in American history brought about by the 1980s' loosening of bank regulations and the reduction of oversight by the federal government. Now that hundreds of banks (typically savings and loan institutions) have failed, the U.S. government is stuck with an estimated $500 billion bill to pay off federally insured depositors. The scandal started with the Garn-St. Germain Depository Institution Decontrol Act of 1982, which allowed for a wider range of investments by savings and loan institutions—including unsecured business loans. At the same time that the law said banks could go beyond traditional conservative home mortgage investments, the Reagan Administration dramatically cut the number of federal bank auditors. Thus, thousands of bankers, especially those in the south and southwest, were able to literally loot their own banks because hardly anybody was looking. (Depositors weren't concerned because they were largely insured against loss. The Congress had raised deposit insurance to $100,000 from $40,000 in 1980.) This "looting" took the form of sweetheart deals, land flips (banks selling land back and forth to raise its price), organized crime involvement, and outright incompetence. When the enormous dimension of the scandal became apparent in the late 1980s the Democratically controlled Congress sought to blame the Republican administrations of Presidents Reagan and Bush for their lax supervision of the banking industry. The Republicans sought to lay the blame on the Congress for allowing decontrol in the first place. Only one thing was certain; there was plenty of blame to go around. *See also* FEDERAL DEPOSIT INSURANCE CORPORATION; FINANCIAL INSTITUTIONS, REFORM, RECOVERY, AND ENFORCEMENT ACT OF 1989; OFFICE OF THRIFT SUPERVISION; RESOLUTION TRUST CORPORATION.

scandal 1. In religion, an offense committed by a holder of high office. The term has been popularized to cover the commission of any action considered a demeaning of the responsibilities of office by the holder of that office. **2.** The exposure of corruption in public office. The corrupting nature of political power makes scandals inevitable. Remember English historian Lord Acton's (1834–1902) maxim: "Power tends to corrupt; absolute power corrupts absolutely." The question to be asked of scandal is not why, but when. *See also* IRAN-CONTRA AFFAIR; WATERGATE. **3.** Perfectly legal political acts that are ethically dubious. As *New Republic* editor Michael Kinsley has often said: "The scandal in Washington is not what's illegal, it's what's legal." This is also known as Kinsley's Law.

scapegoating 1. The Old Testament ritual of selecting a goat to be sent into the wilderness symbolically bearing the sins of a whole community. **2.** Shifting the blame for a problem or failure to another person, group, or organization—a common bureaucratic and political tactic. Sometimes it is the responsibility of an elected official to be a scapegoat. As President John F. Kennedy said during a press conference on June 15, 1962: "I know when things don't go well, they like to blame the President, and that is one of the things Presidents are paid for."

scenario An imaginary account of how a crisis which could occur in the future might play itself out. A scenario, for example, might depict a conventional attack by the Soviet Union on western Europe, or a superpower confrontation over the Middle East crisis.

scenario, rosy An all too optimistic estimate of economic growth and interest rate levels made by federal budgeteers so that the estimated federal deficit will seem less than realistic estimates would suggest.

Schattschneider, E. E. (1892–1971) A significant analyst of the role of POLITICAL PARTIES and PRESSURE GROUPS in American life. His *Politics, Pressures and the Tariff* (1935) established the intellectual framework for the next generation of political analysis on the role of pressure groups. Schattschneider argued for strong parties and was against direct primaries, which he felt to be destructive of party organization and inconsequential to the larger questions of democratic representation. In *Party Government* (1942) he wrote that "democracy is not to be found *in* the parties but *between* the parties." Schattschneider clashed with many of his pluralistically oriented contemporaries because, as he wrote in his *The Semi-sovereign People* (1960), the "flaw in the pluralist heaven is that the heavenly chorus sings with a strong upper-class accent." *See also* INTEREST GROUP THEORY; POLITICS; PRIVATIZATION OF CONFLICT.

Schechter Poultry Corporation v United States (1935) The Supreme Court case concerning the constitutionality of congressional delegations of authority that invalidated much of the NATIONAL INDUSTRIAL RECOVERY ACT OF 1933—then the heart of the New Deal's effort to fight the Great Depression. The Court held that the separation of powers provided for in the Constitution means that "Congress is not permitted to abdicate or to transfer to others the essential legislative functions with which it is vested." Consequently, legislative delegations would be constitutional only if the Congress "has itself established the standards of legal obligation." Based upon these premises, the Court held that the promulgation of a "live poultry code" under the National Industrial Recovery Act was constitutionally defective. Although *Schechter* has never been directly overruled, the courts have subsequently taken a more flexible view of legislative delegations. Had the *Schechter* rule been forcefully applied since 1935, the discretion exercised by the federal bureaucracy would have been severely constricted.

Schenck v United States *See* CLEAR AND PRESENT DANGER.

school district A SPECIAL DISTRICT for the provision of local public education for all children in its service area. An elected board, the typical governing body, usually hires a professional superintendent to administer the system. School districts, having their own taxing authority, are administratively, financially, and politically independent of other local government units. The total number of school districts has been constantly shrinking because mergers of two or more districts has become such a common phenomenon. There were over 108,000 school districts in 1942; today there are less than 15,000.

School District of Abington Township v Schempp (1963) The Supreme Court case that held that school prayers or other religious exercises violated the establishment of religion clause of the First Amendment as applied to the states by the Fourteenth Amendment. *Murray v Curlett* (1963) was decided at the same time on the same grounds. In *Engle v Vitale* (1962), the Court also held unconstitutional a nondenominational prayer because it was inappropriate for school authorities to advocate any official prayer. In *Stone v Graham* (1980), the Court forbade posting the Ten Commandments in classrooms; but in *Widmar v Vincent* (1981), the Court allowed on First Amendment grounds that state university classrooms can be used for student religious group meetings.

school prayer *See* SCHOOL DISTRICT OF ABINGTON TOWNSHIP V SCHEMPP.

Scott v Sandford *See* DRED SCOTT V SANDFORD.

search and seizure The ability of governments to look for, examine, and take as evidence the property and persons of citizens. The Fourth Amendment specifically forbids "unreasonable" searches and seizures. There is considerable debate and a multitude of court cases over what "unreasonable" means in this context. Criminal cases are often dismissed because "tainted evidence" (evidence obtained by an unreasonable search or seizure) is inadmissible. *See also* EXCLUSIONARY RULE; MAPP V OHIO; WARRANT.

SEC *See* SECURITIES AND EXCHANGE COMMISSION.

secession **1.** Withdrawing one's membership in an organization. **2.** The withdrawal of a polity from a large political union. **3.** The now discredited notion that the American states retained so much of their sovereignty that they could withdraw from the union if they wished. This extreme states' rights position was rejected by the Lincoln Administration; when the South tried to secede in 1861, the issue was settled by the Civil War.

Second Amendment The amendment to the U.S. Constitution that provides for the freedom of the collective citizenry to protect itself—to have a "right to bear arms" against both disorder in the community and attack from foreign enemies. Many GUN CONTROL opponents think of this amendment as an absolute prohibition against government regulation of firearm ownership. In America's frontier days, each person's own arms were indeed vital to the national "militia" and were "necessary to the security of a free state." But in today's modern, urbanized society, military and police forces are supposed to supplant the need for individual reliance upon firearms. The Supreme Court, as a result, has upheld state and federal laws prohibiting the carrying of concealed weapons, requiring the registration of firearms, and limiting the sale of specified firearms for other than military uses. Former Supreme Court Justice Lewis Powell told a meeting of the American Bar Association convention: "It is not easy to understand why the Second Amendment, or the notion of liberty, should be viewed as creating a right to own and carry a weapon [handguns] that contributes so directly to the shocking number of murders" (*Newsweek*, August 22, 1988).

second-class citizen One who does not have all of the civil rights of other citizens. Historically, blacks were called, and because of segregation and discrimination often considered themselves to be, second-class citizens. But since the CIVIL RIGHTS MOVEMENT and the new laws that flowed from it, there can legally be no second-class citizens in the United States. Nevertheless, the phrase is still used in various contexts: by minorities who wish to emphasize economic disparities, by women who feel that they have not achieved social equity with men, by prisoners who complain they can't vote.

secretariat **1.** An office, headed by a secretary-general, that is responsible for the administrative affairs of a legislature or an international organization. **2.** The United Nations secretariat, whose secretary-general is appointed to a five-year term of office by the General Assembly upon the recommendation of the Security Council.

secretary **1.** The head of a cabinet agency of the U.S. government; for example, the secretary of State, the secretary of Defense. **2.** A diplomatic rank for those in positions that support the activities of the chief of a mission. For example, a first secretary is a career foreign service officer who is second in command to the ambassador, the second secretary is third in command, and so on. **3.** A service person whose function is defined by an executive whom he or she supports. While such functions are often considered stenographic or clerical, the association of a secretary with an executive is a major relationship in carrying out the responsibilities of the executive, as well as in controlling access to executive judgment and responsibilities. The word comes from the Latin *secretarius,* meaning "a confidential officer, one who can be trusted with secrets."

secretary-general The administrative head of a SECRETARIAT. The best-known secretary-general is that of the United Nations. Since the beginning of the United Nations, this office has been filled by a career diplomat from a country perceived as relatively neutral by both the western alliance and the Soviet bloc.

secretary of State **1.** The senior cabinet officer and chief foreign policy officer of the United States. The secretary of State (who is fourth in line of succession to the presidency after the Vice President, the Speaker of the House of Representatives, and the president pro tempore of the Senate) directs the Department of State and all diplomatic missions abroad. While formally in charge of foreign policy, all post World War II secretaries of State have had to, in effect, share power with other institutional and personal influences on the foreign policymaking process. Recent secretaries have often found themselves competing for foreign policy dominance with the secretary of Defense, the head of the Central Intelligence Agency, and the President's national security advisor. Overall, the secretary of State is only as strong or as influential as a President allows him or her to be. The only postwar secretaries to dominate the foreign policymaking process vis-à-vis the other actors were John Foster Dulles (1888–1959) under Dwight D. Eisenhower and Henry Kissinger (1923–) under Richard M. Nixon and Gerald Ford. The basic problem of the office was summed up by Dean Rusk when he was secretary of State (1961–1969): "Physicists and astronomers see their own implications in the world being round, but to me it means that only one-third of the world is asleep at any given time, and the other two-thirds is up to something" (*The Atlanta Constitution*, October 23, 1964). **2.** A state government official (elected in 36 states and appointed by the governor in 14 states) who is responsible for official papers, the administration of elections, motor vehicle registration, business licensing and incorporation, and other jobs.

secretary of the Senate The chief administrative officer of the Senate, overseeing the duties of Senate employees, the education of the pages, the administration of oaths, the registration of lobbyists, and other activities necessary for the operation of the Senate.

Secret Service, United States The federal agency created in 1860 that is authorized to detect and arrest any person committing any offense against U.S. laws relating to coins, currency, and other obligations, and securities of the United States and of foreign governments. In addition, subject to the direction of the secretary of the Treasury, the Secret Service is authorized to protect the person of the President of the United States, the members of his or her immediate family, the President elect, the Vice President or other officer next in the order of succession to the presidency, the immediate family of the Vice President, the Vice President elect, major presidential and vice presidential candidates, former Presidents and their wives during their lifetimes, widows of former Presidents until their deaths or remarriages, minor children of a former President until they reach age 16, and visiting heads of a foreign state or foreign government. *Compare to* G-MEN.

sectionalism Seeking to further the interests of a specific portion of a country; defining a particular group of geographical political bodies in terms of a pressure group interest they have in common. The distinction between regions and sections in American history has sometimes rested on geographical common interests, such as rivers, woodlands, and other resources shared across state boundaries; and social, racial, and other cultural and historical concerns that tied them together as common political forces. The changing of such interests and their use of political rallying points has transformed, periodically, the meaning of both sectionalism and regionalism in American politics. Sectionalism is practiced by the congressional delegations of one part of the country presumably at the expense of the rest of the country. Nevertheless, astute practitioners of sectional politics will always be able to rationalize sectional programs as being in the overall national interest.

Securities and Exchange Commission (SEC) The federal regulatory commission created by the Securities Exchange Act of 1934 that oversees the nation's stock and financial markets. It seeks the fullest possible disclosure to the investing public and strives to protect the interests of the public and investors against malpractices in the securities and financial markets.

security clearance An administrative determination that an individual is eligible for access to classified information.

Security Council The most powerful of the elements created by the United Nations Charter for dealing with questions of international peace and security. The Security Council has five permanent members (China, France, the Soviet Union, the United Kingdom, and the United States) and representatives of 10 other nations, five of which are chosen each year for two-year terms. Each of the permanent members has a VETO over decisions of substance, which provides the major powers with protection against majority decisions in the larger U.N. GENERAL ASSEMBLY, where each member nation has only one vote. The Security Council was originally conceived to function as a kind of board of directors for the world.

security risk 1. A public employee thought to be so susceptible to the influence of foreign agents that he or she cannot be trusted with continued employment or continued access to sensitive information. **2.** Any disloyal or generally untrustworthy citizen.

sedition Advocating resistance to or rebellion against a legally established government. *Compare to* ALIEN AND SEDITION ACTS.

segregation The separation of people by any particular identifying characteristic. Historically, segregation has been practiced in schools, businesses, and public places against racial minorities (primarily blacks), women, and persons with obvious handicaps. All local laws calling for racial segregation have been invalidated by federal legislation, such as the CIVIL RIGHTS ACT OF 1964 and by Supreme Court cases such as BROWN V BOARD OF EDUCATION.

selective incorporation *See* INCORPORATION.

selectman or selectwoman An elected local government governing board member usually in a New England town or township.

self-government 1. Democratic government in which citizens participate in governance either directly or through their representatives. **2.** HOME RULE; the autonomy possessed by substate jurisdictions.

self-incrimination clause That portion of the Fifth Amendment that holds that no person "shall be compelled in any criminal case to be a witness against himself." However, a witness may waive this privilege or have it waived by the court with a grant of IMMUNITY. This constitutional protection applies only to criminal prosecutions; the courts may still compel testimony that may adversely affect someone's economic interests or reputation. Although those accused may waive their rights under the Fifth Amendment, they generally must know what they are doing and must not be forced to confess, for any confession obtained by use of force or threat will be excluded from the evidence presented at trial. However, the Supreme Court has ruled that, even where an in-custody defendant initially exercises his or her right to remain silent, an incriminating statement procured after a significant time lapse and a fresh set of warnings operates as a waiver and is not violative of MIRANDA RIGHTS. Furthermore, if defendants or witnesses fail to invoke the Fifth Amendment in response to questions addressed to them while on the witness stand, such a failure may operate as a waiver of the right and they will not be permitted to object later to a court's admitting their statements into evidence on the basis that it was self-incriminating. The guarantee against self-incrimination applies only to testimonial actions. Thus, it has been held that government actions, such as obtaining handwriting samples and blood tests, are not violative of the Fifth Amendment.

self-restraint *See* JUDICIAL SELF-RESTRAINT.

senate 1. The Latin word for "a group of old men." A senate was the governing body of the ancient Roman Republic. **2.** The upper chamber of the

U.S. Congress. (The House of Representatives does not, however, accept that the Senate is upper; it acknowledges the Senate only as a coequal chamber.) The Roman origins of the word can be found in the constitutional provision that senators be at least 30 years old, while House members need only be 25—remember that 200 years ago, when life expectancy was far less than today, 30 was considered old. The Senate has always been a conservative force in American society. Initially created as part of the compromise that protected the interests of the small states at the Constitutional Convention of 1787, it still functions to give disproportionate power to small (in population), essentially rural states. While an institution that allocates power according to land (only two senators per state) as opposed to population is hard to defend in the abstract, the Senate as an institution has seldom been attacked for its essentially unrepresentative nature. This was not always so. Until the Seventeenth Amendment, ratified in 1913, which called for the direct election of senators, the Senate was routinely vilified for being largely representative of corrupt state legislatures. *Compare to* CONGRESS, UNITED STATES. **3.** The upper chamber of a state legislature.

senator One who serves as a legislator in the upper house of a legislature. For the qualifications of U.S. senator, *see* CONGRESS, MEMBER OF.

senatorial courtesy The customs of the Senate as they are applied to presidential nominations for executive branch appointments. It means that nominations from a state will generally not be confirmed unless they have been approved by the senators of the President's party from that state, with other senators following their lead (this is the courtesy) in the attitude they take toward such nominations.

senators, senior and junior The two senators from a state. Regardless of age, the senior senator is the one who was elected first; the junior senator is the one elected last.

senior executive service (SES) The federal government's top management corps, established by the Civil Service Reform Act of 1978. The large majority of the approximately 11,000 SES executives are career managers; there is a 10 percent government-wide ceiling on the number who may be noncareer. In addition, about one third of SES positions are career reserved; that is, they can be filled only by career executives. *See also* CIVIL SERVICE REFORM ACT OF 1978.

seniority, congressional The custom whereby a member of the Congress who has served longest on the majority side of a committee becomes its chair or, if on the minority, its ranking member. Members are ranked from the chairman down, according to length of service on the committee. Modifications made during the 1970s' congresses caused the seniority rule to be less rigidly followed than previously. In both chambers, nominees for committee chairs are subject to public votes in caucus meetings of their party colleagues. Members who lose their seats in the Congress and then return (or who change committees) start at the bottom of the list again, except that they outrank those members beginning their first terms. The seniority system has always had its critics. What Shirley Chisholm wrote in *Unbought and Unbossed* (1970) is typical: "The seniority system keeps a handful of old men. . . in control of the Congress. These old men stand implacably across the paths that could lead us toward a better future. But worse than they, I think, are the majority of members of both Houses who continue to submit to the senility system." She has a real point about senility. Representative Morris K. Udall in discussing Representative Henry Reuss' elevation to Chairmanship of the House Banking and Currency Committee, said: "He's 62. He defeated a man who was 81. They say he led a youth rebellion. The House is the only place you can lead a youth rebellion and take your grandchildren with you" (*The Wall Street Journal*, February 24, 1975). Nevertheless, as former speaker of the House Carl Albert said: "I look upon [the seniority system] as Churchill looked on democracy: It's the worst system ever devised, except for every other one suggested to take its place" (*The Washington Post*, January 10, 1971).

separate but equal   The doctrine espoused by the Supreme Court in *Plessy v Ferguson* (1896), which held that segregated railroad facilities for blacks, facilities that were considered equal in quality to those provided for whites, did not violate the equal protection clause of the Fourteenth Amendment. In a dissenting opinion Justice John Marshall Harlan wrote: "We boast of the freedom enjoyed by our people .. . . But it is difficult to reconcile that boast with a state of the law which, practically, puts the brand of servitude and degradation upon a large class of our fellow citizens, our equals before the law. The thin disguise of 'equal' accommodations for passengers in the railroad coaches will not mislead anyone, or atone for the wrong this day done." In BROWN V BOARD OF EDUCATION, the Court nullified this doctrine when it asserted that separate was "inherently unequal."

separation of church and state   The absolute independence from each other of government and religious institutions that is mandated by the First Amendment of the U.S. Constitution. When the Constitution was first written, for example, only two states—New York and Virginia—did not have religious qualifications for public office. In New Jersey, New Hampshire, South Carolina, and Georgia, a person had to be a Protestant to hold office. In Maryland and Massachusetts a public official had to be of the "Christian religion." Pennsylvania demanded a "belief in God and the inspiration of the Scriptures." Delaware required that only "Protestants who accepted the Holy Trinity could serve in the legislature." However, Article VI of the Constitution holds that "no religious test shall ever be required as a qualification to any office or public trust under the United States." This was created by the ESTABLISHMENT CLAUSE of the First Amendment which states that "Congress shall make no law respecting an establishment of religion." *See also* RELIGIOUS TEST.

separation of powers The allocation of powers among the three branches of government so that they are a check upon each other. This separation, in theory, makes a tyrannical concentration of power impossible. The U.S. Constitution contains provisions in separate articles for three branches of government—legislative, executive, and judicial. There is a significant difference in the grants of power to these branches: the first article, dealing with legislative power, vests in the Congress "all legislative powers herein granted"; the second article vests "the executive power" in the President; and the third article states that "the judicial power of the United States shall be vested in one Supreme Court, and in such inferior courts as the Congress may from time to time ordain and establish." The drafters of the Constitution were very familiar with Sir William Blackstone's *Commentaries on the Laws of England* (1783) which asserted that: "In all tyrannical governments the supreme magistracy, or the right both of making and of enforcing the laws, is vested in one and the same man, or one and the same body of men; and wherever these two powers are united together, there can be no public liberty." Thus, Justice Louis D. Brandeis writes in *Myers v. United States* (1926): "The doctrine of the separation of powers was adopted by the Convention of 1787, not to promote efficiency but to preclude the exercise of arbitrary power. The purpose was, not to avoid friction, but, by means of the inevitable friction incident to the distribution of the governmental powers among three departments, to save the people from autocracy." *Compare to* CHECKS AND BALANCES; FEDERALIST 51.

sequestration   **1.** Automatic cuts in federal spending imposed by the GRAMM-RUDMAN-HOLLINGS ACT if budget targets are not met. **2.** A judge's order to keep a jury isolated from the public during a trial; this is usually so that they will not have their opinions contaminated by sensationalism in the media.

sergeant at arms The officer charged with maintaining order in a formal meeting, under the direction of the presiding officer. In the early British parliaments, a sergeant at arms enforced laws and arrested people. While a modern sergeant at arms may no longer be armed, the limited police powers remain. In the U.S. Senate, the sergeant at arms is the Senate's principal law enforcement and executive officer, responsible for the enforcement of all rules made by the Committee on Rules and Administration, for the regulation of the Senate wing of the Capitol, and for the Senate office buildings. The sergeant at arms in the House of Representatives tends to the security of the Capitol and House office buildings and is in charge of the MACE, the symbol of legislative power and authority.

service contract An agreement between local units of government for one unit (usually larger) to provide a service, such as garbage collection, for another (usually smaller). It is often called the LAKEWOOD PLAN, because it was first extensively used between the County of Los Angeles and the City of Lakewood, California.

service fee **1.** User charges for government services not fully paid for by general taxation. Examples include water fees from municipal governments and admission fees for national parks. **2.** The equivalent of union dues that nonunion members of an agency shop pay the union for negotiating and administering the collective bargaining agreement.

SES *See* SENIOR EXECUTIVE SERVICE.

session **1.** The time between the convening and the adjournment of a legislature or court. This can be a few weeks, a few months, or almost all year. **2.** The daily meetings of a legislature or court. Thus, a session can last many months and at the same time begin anew at 9:00 am each morning.

session, executive *See* EXECUTIVE SESSION.

session, special The formal convening of a legislature, outside of its constitutionally scheduled meetings, at the initiative of a chief executive. Article II, Section 3, of the U.S. Constitution gives the President the authority to call the entire Congress or either house into special session "on extraordinary occasions." All state governors have similar authority. Prior to the ratification of the LAME DUCK AMENDMENT in 1933, a new President came into office in March without a Congress in session until the next December. Early twentieth-century Presidents often found it necessary to call special sessions to ask for new legislation at the opening of their administrations if they wanted to take advantage of the momentum of their election the previous November.

set aside A higher court's reversing of a lower court's decision; the decision is literally set aside—made void.

set asides Government purchasing and contracting provisions that allocate a certain percentage of business for minority-owned companies. The use of set asides was upheld by the Supreme Court in Fullilove v Klutznick and Metro Broadcasting v FCC but restricted in city of richmond v j.a. croson.

Seventeenth Amendment The 1913 amendment to the U.S. Constitution that changed the electoral process for U.S. senators from selection by state legislatures to a popular vote. By the early 1900s, it had become a concern that, under the system of indirect election by state legislatures, many senators were indifferent to popular demands and obligated to corporations that could often influence their elections. Another objection to the selection of senators by legislatures was that often a state went unrepresented or only half-represented in the Senate because of the inability of many legislatures to agree on any one candidate.

Seventh Amendment The amendment to the U.S. Constitution that guarantees a jury trial in most federal civil suits.

sewer money *See* SOFT MONEY.

sex discrimination Any disparate or unfavorable treatment of a person in an employment situation because of his or her gender. The Civil Rights Act of 1964 (as amended by the Equal Employment Opportunity Act of 1972) makes sex discrimination illegal in most employment, except where a bona fide occupational qualification is involved. In 1980, after the federal courts had decided that sexual harassment was sex discrimination in a variety of cases, the Equal Employment Opportunity Commission issued legally binding rules clearly stating that an employer has a responsibility to provide a place of work that is free from sexual harassment or intimidation. In 1986, the Supreme Court reaffirmed this, when in the case of *Meritor Saving Bank v Vinson*, it held that sexual harassment creating a hostile or abusive work environment, even without economic loss for the person being harassed, was in violation of Title VIII of the Civil Rights Act of 1964.

sexual harassment *See* SEX DISCRIMINATION; THOMAS, CLARENCE.

shadow senator A position created by the city council of Washington D.C.; the occupant is expected to lobby the Congress for statehood for the District of Columbia.

sheriff The elected (in all states but Rhode Island) chief officer of a county law enforcement agency, usually responsible for law enforcement in unincorporated areas of the county and for the operation of the county jail. The sheriff—whose title comes from the Middle English *schirreff*, Old English *shire-reeve*, the king's representative in a shire (an English county)—is also the officer of the local court who serves papers, enforces court orders, and so on.

Sherman Antitrust Act of 1890 The federal statute that held "every contract, combination in the form of trust or otherwise, or conspiracy, in restraint of trade or commerce . . . is hereby declared to be illegal." While the statute was directed at industrial monopolies, the courts used the act punitively against the budding union movement. Subsequent legislation (the Clayton Act of 1914) exempted unions from the Sherman Act prohibitions on the restraint of trade.

Sherman statement *See* DRAFT.

shield laws **1.** Statutes that permit reporters to protect the confidentiality of their sources. While many states have shield laws to encourage people to talk freely to the press without fear that their identity will be publicly exposed, the federal government does not. Indeed, the Supreme Court in *Branzburg v Hayes* (1972) rejected the notion that reporters have special protections under the First Amendment. Thus, reporters may be required to reveal sources if called as a witness in a trial; and held in contempt of court (and possibly jailed) if they do not. **2.** Any statute that shields victims or witnesses from questioning in open court—for example, statutes that protect the anonymity of children or statutes that prevent defense lawyers from asking rape victims about their previous and unrelated sexual activities.

silent majority The mass of ordinary Americans, especially those who don't demonstrate or get involved in political causes. President Richard M. Nixon gave the phrase currency when in an address to the nation on November 3, 1969 he said: "And so tonight—to you, the great silent majority of my fellow Americans—I ask for your support [for the Vietnam War]."

sine die *See* ADJOURNMENT SINE DIE.

single-issue politics Situations in which decisions of political support or nonsupport are made on one factor to the exclusion of all others. The factor is usually quite specific, such as opposition to abortion, support for protectionist legislation to help a particular industry, and so on. Senator Thomas F. Eagleton reminds us in *The Washington Post* (October 31, 1986): "This country's had single-issue politics before. Slavery was single-issue politics; prohibition was single-issue. . . . But today we have the most unlimited proliferation of single-issue politics, and the filibuster gives the single-issue politician his powerful voice. . . So the single-issue politician can hold up [an] appropriation bill by amendments on abortion, amendments on [school] busing, amendments on [school] prayer." Senator Patrick J. Leahy feels that "single-issue politics of either the left or the right destroys the concept of a pluralistic nation, destroys the idea of representative democracy" (*Los Angeles Times*, September 16, 1981). *Compare to* ISSUE VOTING.

Sixteenth Amendment The 1913 amendment to the U.S. Constitution that allows the federal government to tax income "from whatever source derived." This overturned the Supreme Court's decision in *Pollock v Farmer's Loan and Trust Co.* (1895), which held that a direct income tax from the federal government was unconstitutional. The Supreme Court had earlier upheld the Civil War income tax in *Springer v United States* (1881). The *Pollock* decision reversed *Springer,* which was, in turn, reversed by the Sixteenth Amendment.

Sixth Amendment The amendment to the U.S. Constitution that sets forth specific rights guaranteed to persons facing criminal prosecution in federal courts—and in state courts by virtue of the Fourteenth Amendment. The right to a speedy and public trial requires that the accused be brought to trial without unnecessary delay and that the trial be open to the public. Intentional or negligent delay by the prosecution that prejudices the defendant's right to prepare a defense has been held as grounds for dismissal of the charges. Trial by an impartial jury supplements the earlier guarantee contained in Article III of the U.S. Constitution. The right to jury trial does not apply to trials for petty offenses, which the Supreme Court has suggested to be those punishable by six months confinement or less. In trials where a jury is used, the jury must be impartially selected, and no persons can be excluded from jury service merely because of their race, class, or sex.

The Sixth Amendment also requires that defendants be notified of the particular factual nature of the crimes they have been accused of committing, so that they can prepare their defense. This also means that the crime must be established by statute beforehand, so that all persons are on public notice about the existence of the prohibition. The statute must not be so vague or unclear that it does not inform people of the exact nature of the crime. Generally, those accused are entitled to have all witnesses against them present their evidence orally in court and to cross-examine them.

Moreover, the accused is entitled to the aid of the court in having compulsory process issued, usually a subpoena, which orders into court as witnesses those persons whose testimony the accused desires at the trial.

Finally, the Sixth Amendment provides a right to be represented by counsel. For many years, this was interpreted to mean only that the defendant had a right to be represented by a lawyer if the defendant could obtain one. The Supreme Court held in GIDEON V WAINWRIGHT, however, that the amendment imposes an affirmative obligation on the part of federal and state governments to provide at public expense legal counsel for those who cannot afford it.

slander Oral statements that are so false and malicious that injury is caused to a person's reputation. Slander is often confused with LIBEL (false and malicious written statements).

slate **1.** The party ticket; the lists of candidates of a party in a particular election. **2.** Those candidates in a primary election that have been endorsed by their party.

slate card A hand-sized card with the names and ballot locations of a political party's candidates; often given out on election day so that voters can easily take it into voting booths.

Slaughterhouse Cases (1873) The Supreme Court cases that drew a sharp distinction between the rights of U.S. citizens and the rights of citizens of the various states. The Court held that civil rights were derived from state citizenship and thus were not protected by the U.S. Constitution (especially the Fourteenth Amendment) against state action. This ruling was the Supreme Court's first interpretation of the Fourteenth Amendment. The ruling has since been overruled, as the Court has gradually made most of the protections of the Bill of Rights applicable to the states through INCORPORATION.

slavery Involuntary servitude. Slavery existed in parts of the United States until it was prohibited by the Thirteenth Amendment in 1865. Slavery was addressed, albeit obliquely, in various parts of the Constitution. In Article I, Section 2 slaves are to be counted for purposes of congressional appointments as "three fifths" of a person. Article I, Section 9 says that Congress cannot pass any law banning the importation of slaves until 1808 (which it did). Article IV, section 2 said that persons "held in service" who escaped had to be returned. This was upheld by DRED SCOTT V SANDFORD. Abraham Lincoln was, even before he became President, a most eloquent spokesman against slavery. He told the Illinois Republican State Convention on June 16, 1858: "'A house divided against itself cannot stand' [*The Bible*, Mark 3:25]. I believe this government cannot endure, permanently half slave and half free. I do not expect the Union to be dissolved—I do not expect the house to fall—but I do expect it will cease to be divided. It will become all one thing, or all the other." He was right. *See also* EMANCIPATION PROCLAMATION.

sleaze factor The phrase that critics used to sum up the fact that so many top officials of the Reagan Administration were found in violation of ethical or legal norms. Sleaze is a vague word for shoddy or tricky behavior. After President Ronald Reagan left office and the full dimensions of the SAVINGS AND LOAN and HUD scandals became apparent, it was realized that the sleaze factor was far greater than even his worst critics had imagined.

slip law The first official publication of a bill enacted into law by the U.S. Congress. Each is published separately in unbound, single-sheet, or pamphlet form. Slip laws usually become available two to three days after presidential approval.

slush fund **1.** Money collected by the military services in the nineteenth century by selling grease and other refuse (the slush). The resulting funds were used to buy small luxuries for the soldiers and sailors. **2.** Discretionary funds appropriated by a legislature for the use of an agency head. **3.** Private monies used for campaign expenses. **4.** Funds used for bribery. **5.** Secret funds. All slush funds because of their lack of formal accountability have an unsavory connotation—even when they are perfectly legal. *Compare to* CHECKERS SPEECH.

Smith Act *See* ALIEN REGISTRATION ACT OF 1940.

Smith, Adam (1723–1790) The Scottish economist who provided the first systematic analysis of economic phenomena and the intellectual foundation for laissez-faire capitalism. In *The Wealth of Nations* (1776), Smith discusses an INVISIBLE HAND that automatically promotes the general welfare as long as individuals are allowed to pursue their self-interest. It has become customary for organization theorists to trace the lineage of present-day theories to Smith's concept of the division of labor. Greater specialization of labor was one of the pillars of the invisible hand market mechanism, in which the greatest rewards would go to those who were the most efficient in the competitive marketplace. As Smith's work marks the beginning of economics as an identifiable discipline, he is often referred to as the father of economics. *See also* ABILITY TO PAY.

Smithsonian Institution The organization created by an act of the U.S. Congress in 1846 to carry out the terms of the will of James Smithson of England, who, in 1829, bequeathed his entire estate to the United States "to found at Washington, under the name of the Smithsonian Institution, an establishment for the increase and diffusion of knowledge among men." To carry out Smithson's mandate, the institution, as an independent trust establishment, performs fundamental research; publishes the results of studies, explorations, and investigations; and preserves for study and reference over 70 million items of scientific, cultural, and historical interest; maintains exhibits representative of the arts, U.S. history, technology, aeronautics and space explorations, and natural history.

smoke-filled room The stereotypical description of any place of political deal-making, where political bosses dictate the "will" of the people. In the old days when behind-the-scenes politicos got together to cut a deal or seal a nomination at a national convention, the room quickly filled up with the exhalations of their cigars and cigarettes. The slightly sinister connotations of "smoke-filled room" first developed when the phrase was applied to the hotel room where the Republican party leaders decided on the nomination of Warren G. Harding in 1920.

smoking gun Irrefutable evidence of a crime, just as if someone were caught standing over a murder victim with a smoking gun in his hand. The term, while widely used in detective fiction, came into politics with the WATERGATE scandal. Smoking gun became the term for the evidence that would justify President Richard M. Nixon's impeachment. The "gun" in this case was found in the Watergate tapes. During the IRAN-CONTRA AFFAIR, President Ronald Reagan proclaimed his innocence by saying: "There ain't no smoking gun" (*Newsweek*, June 29, 1987).

SMSA *See* STANDARD METROPOLITAN STATISTICAL AREA.

snakecheck The final review of a political speech to make sure that nothing potentially embarrassing stays in it; the analogy is to checking a tent or sleeping bag for snakes before going to sleep.

snowbelt *See* RUSTBELT; SUNBELT-SNOWBELT TENSION.

sobriety checks An anti-drunk driving program whereby police stop motorists at random points to look for signs of intoxication. The Supreme Court in *Michigan v Sitz* (1990) held that such programs were constitutional.

social contract 1. The philosophic notion that the obligations that individuals and states have toward each other originate in a theoretical social contract they have made with each other. If the state breaks the social contract, then grounds for REVOLUTION exist. This was an important consideration in the Declaration of Independence. *Compare to* STATE OF NATURE. **2.** The social welfare policies of a government. They are considered a contract because citizens have grown to expect and depend upon them. **3.** EDMUND BURKE's concept from *Reflections on the Revolution in France* (1790) that "Society is indeed a contract. . . .[But] as the ends of such a partnership cannot be obtained in many generations, it becomes a partnership not only between those who are living but between those who are living, those who are dead, and those who are yet to be born. . . . Changing the state as often as there are floating fancies. . . no one generation could link with the other. Men would be little better than the flies of a summer." This concept has been one of the historical foundations of conservatism in the modern world.

social contract theorists *See* THOMAS HOBBES (1588–1679), JOHN LOCKE (1632–1704), and JEAN-JACQUES ROUSSEAU (1712–1778).

social Darwinism English natural historian Charles Darwin's (1809–1882) concept of biological evolution applied to the development of human social organization and economic policy. The major influence on American social Darwinism was the Englishman, Herbert Spencer (1820–1903), who spent much of his career working out the application of concepts such as "natural selection" and "survival of the fittest" to his ideas of social science. American social Darwinists, generally speaking, occupied a wide range of theories, from an absolute rejection of the idea of government intervention in social development to elaborate methods of developmental influence that could affect the various races (into which they believed civilization was divided).

social democracy The democratization of all social institutions, as opposed to the democratization of only governing institutions. *Compare to* DEMOCRACY.

social equity A normative standard holding that equity, rather than efficiency, is the major criterion for evaluating the desirability of a policy or program.

social indicators Statistical measures that aid in the description of conditions in the social environment (e.g., measures of income distribution, poverty, health, physical environment).

social insurance Any benefit program that a state makes available to the members of its society in time of need and as a matter of right.

social responsibility of business The belief that business organizations have a moral and ethical duty to contribute to social well-being; that they have an obligation to society other than seeking a profit in a legal manner. But others, such as economist Milton Friedman, feel that the resolution of social problems is the task of governments, not businesses, and managers who so spend money on them act irresponsibly.

social security The popular name for the Old Age, Survivors, and Disability Insurance (OASDI) system established by the Social Security Act of 1935. At first, social security covered only retired private sector employees. In 1939, the law was changed to cover survivors when the worker dies and to cover certain dependents when the worker retires. In the 1950s, coverage was extended to include most self-employed persons, most state and local employees, household and farm employees, members of the armed forces, and members of the clergy. Today, almost all jobs are covered by social security. Disability insurance was added in 1954 to give workers protection against loss of earnings due to total disability. The social security program was expanded again in 1965 with the enactment of Medicare, which assured hospital and medical insurance protection to people 65 years of age and over. Since 1973, Medicare coverage has been available to people under 65 who have been entitled to disability checks for two or more consecutive years and to people with permanent kidney failure who need dialysis treatment or kidney transplants. Amendments enacted in 1972 provide that social security benefits increase automatically with the cost of living. The biggest problem with Social Security is demographics. In 1950 the ratio of taxpaying workers to pensioners was 120 to 1. In the year 2030 it will be 2 to 1. This is why social security payroll taxes have risen from 1 percent (with a $30 yearly maximum) in 1940 to 7.65 percent (with a yearly maximum of $3,924) in 1990.

Social Security Administration The agency of the Department of Health and Human Services that administers the national program of contributory social insurance whereby employees, employers, and the self-employed pay contributions that are pooled in special trust funds.

Social Security Trust Fund The fictional account into which social security tax payments are deposited until needed to pay benefits. The reality is that these payments are used to reduce the federal deficit and that actual payments to pensioners come out of general revenues. The so called "trust fund" is just an accounting and public relations gimmick.

socialism A system of government in which many of the means of production and trade are owned or run by the government and in which many human welfare needs are provided directly by the government. The system may or may not be democratic. Socialism is one of the most "loaded" words in American politics. To the Right it represents the beginnings of communist encroachment on traditional American values and institutions. To the Left it represents the practical manifestation of America's pragmatic and generous spirit. To others it is simply an unpopular government program or one that benefits someone else. However, while American political culture will countenance limited socialistic measures, it will not tolerate socialistic rhetoric. Thus, the social security program was labeled an insurance system when its proponents knew that it was always designed to be an income transfer program. On the whole, Americans abhor the symbol represented by the word *socialism,* but are very much in favor of limited socialistic measures, so long as they are espoused as pragmatic responses to difficult problems. *Compare to* MARXISM.

socialism, creeping The gradual advance of socialist principles and practices into governing policies and institutions. The United States is often said to be a "victim" of creeping socialism because of the enactment of so many social welfare programs in this century. During a June 11, 1953 speech in South Dakota President Dwight D. Eisenhower told Republican Party leaders: "I believe that for the past twenty years there has been a creeping socialism spreading in the United States." When asked what he meant by that at a June 17, 1953 press conference, Robert J. Donovan's *Eisenhower* (1956) reports that he replied: "Continued Federal expansion of the T.V.A. He reiterated for what he said was the thousandth time that he would not destroy the T.V.A., but he said that he thought it was socialistic to continue putting money paid by all the taxpayers into a single region which could then attract industry away from other areas." When ADLAI STEVENSON was accused of favoring creeping socialism during this same time period, Gerald Gardner's *The Mocking of the President* (1988) reports that he responded: "I am no more in favor of socialism than anybody else, and I particularly dislike things that creep. But if I don't like what they call creeping socialism, there is something else I dislike just as much, and that is galloping reaction."

socialized medicine 1. A medical care system in which the organization and provision of medical care services are under direct government control, and providers are employed by or under contract with the government. **2.** A medical care system believed to be subject to excessive government control.

soft money 1. Funds given by national political parties to their state and local parties for nonfederal uses, such as voter registration drives. The money is soft because its use is not watched carefully by the states and its collection by the national party is often unreported because of its nonfederal character. This is a backdoor and dishonorable way of effectively channeling fat cat contributions, in excess of legal limits, to federal candidates. It is also known as *sewer money* because of its suspicious odor. **2.** Funds for a program that are not received on a recurring basis from a steady source. For example, grant or gift funds on a one-time or even a several-year basis are soft in comparison to the hard funds that come each year from a legislative appropriation.

Solicitor General of the United States The official of the Department of Justice who is the actual attorney who represents the federal government before the Supreme Court and any other courts. It is the solicitor general who must approve any appeal that the U.S. government might take to an appellate court. When appearing before the Supreme Court the Solicitor General traditionally wears a formal attire of striped pants and a dark gray morning coat.

solid South A reference to the once solidly Democratic South. The solid South was also solidly white, because most blacks were discouraged from voting by poll taxes, intimidation, and other means. Those few blacks who did vote tended to be Republican. This began to change with the NEW DEAL of the 1930s and the FAIR DEAL of the 1940s and rapidly changed with the CIVIL RIGHTS MOVEMENT of the 1960s. The event that more than anything else broke the solid South was the advocacy of equal rights for blacks by the national Democratic party. Blacks have consequently become pivotal elements in the Democratic electorate of all southern states. Today the South is certainly not solid for the Democrats and, based on presidential elections since 1980, may well be solid for the Republicans. *See also* V.O. KEY, JR.

sound bite 1. A very brief statement made by a political candidate that can be effectively used on broadcast spots or regular news coverage. **2.** Any snippet of audio or video tape of a politician's speech that can be used for political news or advertising purposes. Sound bites are getting smaller. According to Massachusetts Governor Michael Dukakis, the Democratic presidential nominee in 1988, in 1968 the average TV news sound bite was 42 seconds. Twenty years later in 1988, it was 9.8 seconds. Dukakis complained: "If you couldn't say it in less than 10 seconds, it wasn't heard because it wasn't aired" (*The New York Times*, April 22, 1990). **3.** A political campaign slogan or short statement that summarizes a candidate's beliefs. Such simplistic policies can backfire if they promised more than anyone can deliver. George Bush became President by shouting: "Read my lips: no new taxes." But less than two years into his presidency he was forced to eat his sound bite and agree to raise taxes.

source **1.** A person, thing, or activity from which intelligence information is obtained. **2.** In clandestine activities, a person (agent), normally a foreign national, in the employ of an intelligence activity for intelligence purposes. **3.** In interrogation activities, any person who furnishes intelligence information, either with or without the knowledge that the information is being used for intelligence purposes. In this context, a *controlled source* is in the employment or under the control of the intelligence activity and knows that the information is to be used for intelligence purposes. An *uncontrolled source* is a voluntary contributor of information and may or may not know that the information is to be used for intelligence purposes. **4.** A person who provides information to a journalist. Often these sources demand that their identities be kept secret. In some states, SHIELD LAWS allow this. *See also* AGENT.

southern primary *See* SUPER TUESDAY.

southern strategy The Republican party's efforts beginning in the late 1960s (1) to encourage significant numbers of traditional southern white Democratic voters to defect to the Republican party and (2) to appeal to Hispanic voters, especially in Texas, California, and Florida.

sovereign immunity *See* IMMUNITY, SOVEREIGN.

sovereignty The quality of being supreme in power, rank, or authority. In the United States, the people are sovereign and government is considered their agent. In a January 29, 1916 speech President Woodrow Wilson rhetorically asked: "Just what is it that America stands for? If she stands for one thing more than another, it is for the sovereignty of self-governing people." The sovereignty of the sovereign states of the United States is largely a myth, however, because so much power on most crucial issues now lies with the federal government. It was always so. As President Abraham Lincoln said in a message to Congress, July 4, 1861: "Much has been said about the 'sovereignty' of the States, but the word even is not in the National Constitution, nor, as is believed, in any of the state Constitutions." The literature on sovereignty is immense and freighted with philosophy. *Compare to* TENTH AMENDMENT.

sovereignty, consumer The power of individual customers in a free market economy to, as an unorganized group, determine what products get produced. They literally use their money to "vote" on goods and services.

Speaker The presiding officer of the U.S. House of Representatives, elected by its members. The U.S. Constitution (Article I, Section 2) says that the House "shall choose their speaker and other officers." Although the membership may vote on officers as they do on any other question, in most cases it is strictly a party vote. Republicans and Democrats meet separately before the House organizes for a new Congress and each chooses a slate of officers. These two slates are presented at the first session of the House, and the majority party slate is, of course, selected. The vote is *viva voce* ("by voice"), except for election of the Speaker. The Speaker (who, according to the Constitution, does not have to be an elected member, but always has been) presides over the House, appoints the chairs to preside over the committees of the Whole, appoints all special or select committees, appoints conference committees, has the power of recognition of members, and makes many important rulings and decisions in the House. He or she may vote, but usually does not, except in case of a tie. The Speaker and the majority leader determine administrative policies in the House, often confer with the President, and are regarded as spokespersons for the administration if they and the President belong to the same political party. Otherwise, they are major advocates for their own party.

Speaker of the House John W. McCormack once said: "I think it is correct to say that the Speaker of the House does occupy the second most powerful position in our government. In theory, the Vice President is second to the President; but in actual terms of power and influence in our government, the Speaker ranks second. I don't say that to downgrade in any way the office of the Vice President. That is just the way it is" (*U.S. News & World Report*, July 27, 1970). Carl Albert, who succeeded McCormack as Speaker, elaborated on this power: "Most people think of me as the presiding officer of the House and nothing else. Yet I'm also the political leader in the House. I'm the House chief executive officer. I appoint lots of committees and commissions. I am the House's chief administrative officer. Everyone I see working in this building is working for me" (*The Christian Science Monitor*, April 15, 1971).

special assessment   A real estate tax on certain landowners to pay for improvements that will, at least in theory, benefit them; for example, a paved street. *See also* BENEFIT DISTRICT.

special committee   *See* COMMITTEE, SELECT.

special district   A unit of local government typically performing a single function and overlapping traditional political boundaries. Examples include transportation districts, fire protection districts, library districts, water districts, sewer districts, and so on. Because special districts are such useful devices, they have been multiplying rapidly. In 1942 there were only 8, 299 of them in the entire United States. Today there are almost 30,000. They constitute one third of all American government entities.

special order   **1.** A RULE from the House Rules Committee which establishes procedures for the consideration of a bill on the floor of the House. **2.** A House or Senate member's advance reservation of a block of time to speak on the floor at the very beginning or end of a daily session.

speech and debate clause   *See* IMMUNITY, CONGRESSIONAL.

spellbinder 1. A political speaker (or the speech itself) that can really hold an audience's attention, as if putting them under a bewitching spell. **2.** A DEMAGOGUE with charismatic speaking abilities.

spillover effects Benefits or costs that accrue to parties other than the buyer of a good or service, also known as *externalities*. For the most part, the benefits of private goods and services inure exclusively to the buyer (e.g., new clothes, a television set). In the case of public goods, however, the benefit or cost usually spills over onto third parties. An airport, for example, benefits not only its users but spills over onto the population at large in both positive and negative ways. Benefits might include improved air service for a community, increased tourism, and attraction of new businesses, while costs might include noise pollution and traffic congestion.

spin control Efforts by an administration or an individual political actor to manipulate the media to contain, deflect, and minimize an unraveling scandal or other embarrassing or politically damaging revelation. The purpose is to keep the situation from spinning out of control. Spin control efforts are easily seen after a political debate between candidates when their managers seek to persuade the media that their candidate really won.

spin doctor A practitioner of SPIN CONTROL. The term is often used in the plural. For example, after each of the presidential debates in 1988, both parties unleashed an array of spin doctors upon the media in an attempt to affect public opinion regarding the debate.

spoiler A candidate for public office who obviously cannot win but stays in the race to ensure that a rival or political enemy cannot win either. Few spoilers will ever admit to the role; they usually see themselves as candidates of principle.

spoils system 1. The widespread practice of awarding government jobs to political supporters as opposed to awarding them on the basis of merit. **2.** A critical reference to the PATRONAGE practices of one's political opposition.

spot A broadcast (radio or TV) political commercial ranging from 10 seconds to five minutes. Spots are growing increasingly shorter. There is a truism among political consultants that whenever a campaign simultaneously airs a five-minute spot on all local stations, the locality experiences a severe drop in water pressure—because so many viewers use it as an opportunity to use the toilet.

There have been many complaints that spots are having a CHILLING effect on legislative behavior. According to Representative David R. Obey: "When the main question in a member's mind every time he votes is, 'What kind of a 30-second spot are they going to make out of this vote,' then truly the ability of the political system to make complicated and tough decisions in the long-range interest of the United States is atomized" (*The New York Times*, March 8, 1990).

spot, contrast Negative broadcast advertising that highlights the differences between rival political candidates.

spot, daisy The most famous and arguably the most effective political commercial ever made. Media consultant Tony Schwartz created it for President Lyndon Johnson during his 1964 presidential race against Barry Goldwater. Schwartz describes the spot in his book, *The Responsive Chord* (1973): "The spot shows a little girl in a field counting petals on a daisy. As her count reaches ten the visual motion is frozen and the viewer hears a countdown. When the countdown reaches zero we see a nuclear explosion and hear President Johnson say, 'These are the stakes, to make a world in which all God's children can grow, or go into the darkness. Either we must love each other or we must die.' As the screen goes to black at the end, white lettering appears stating 'on November 3rd, vote for President Johnson.'" The spot was shown only once. It was so controversial that its subsequent showings were cancelled. But since the Republicans were so angry at the Democrats' implication that Goldwater would blow up the world, the ad became news and was shown on all the networks.

spot, generic A political commercial that is akin to institutional advertising; it boosts the company and not one specific product. Thus, a generic spot will sell a political party and its policies instead of specific candidates.

spot, Willie Horton *See* HORTON, WILLIE.

spot zoning *See* ZONING, SPOT.

square deal President Theodore Roosevelt's term for his domestic policies. As he said in a speech in Dallas, Texas on April 5, 1906: "When I say I believe in a square deal I do not mean. . . it['s] possible to give every man the best hand. If the cards do not come to any man, or if they do come, and he has not the power to play them, that is his affair. All I mean is that there shall not be any crookedness in the dealing."

squatter's rights The right to ownership of land merely by occupying it for a certain period. During the settling of the American West, this was a legal means of acquiring title to land. Today, squatting is generally not recognized as legal. But this has not stopped some urban social activists from squatting in abandoned housing, fixing it up somewhat, and then demanding ownership.

SSI *See* SUPPLEMENTAL SECURITY INCOME.

staff 1. The subordinate employees of an organization. **2.** Specialists who assist line managers in carrying out their duties. (Line managers are those responsible for the primary purpose of the organization. In a civilian context, they provide goods or services. In the military, they do the actual fighting.) Generally, staff units do not have the power of decision, command, or control of operations. Rather, they make recommendations to executives and line managers.

staff, chief of 1. The military title for the officer who supervises the work of the other officers on a commander's staff. **2.** A civilian supervisor of an overall management team who reports directly to the chief executive officer. **3.** The top aide to the President of the United States. White House chiefs of staff have often been criticized for isolating the President and for exercising enormous authority as a *de facto* deputy President when nobody elected them to that office. Presidents from Dwight D. Eisenhower to George Bush have had chiefs of staff; some have had greater power than others, and some functioned as a chief of staff without the title.

staff, general A group of officers in the headquarters of divisions or similar larger units that assist their commanders in planning, coordinating, and supervising operations.

staff out The process that involves soliciting a variety of views or recommendations on an issue so that a decision maker will be aware of all reasonable options.

staff, paid Those who work for a political campaign that receive a salary as opposed to the usually far greater numbers of volunteers.

staff, personal **1.** Those members of an organization who report directly to an executive, rather than through an intermediary, such as a chief of staff. Personal staff members could be relatively low-level, such as secretaries or chauffeurs, or high-level technical experts. **2.** The staffs who serve individual legislators either in their capital offices or their home state/district offices, as opposed to the staff of the legislative body or its committees. Personal staffs handle correspondence, publicity, CASEWORK, and local political affairs for the legislators.

staff principle The principle of administration that states the executive should be assisted by officers who are not in the line of operations but are essentially extensions of the personality of the executive and whose duties consist primarily of assisting the executive in controlling and coordinating the organization and, secondly, of offering advice.

staffer Originally, any full-time employee of a politician's campaign organization or elected public office. The term has grown to include all legislative committee staffs as well. Before World War I, the members of Congress outnumbered their full-time staff. Today, each senator has a paid staff of from 13 to 71 members; they average 36. House staffs average 17. In addition to helping with legislative matters and casework, each staffer is a personal political machine looking after the political fortunes of his or her boss. Congressional staff members have few employment rights (due to congressional exemption) and may be hired and fired at will.

Because "staffer" is an all-inclusive term equally applied to clerical and professional workers, it may be considered poor usage by those who rightly consider themselves more than just a staffer by virtue of their professional attainments. Nevertheless, diminutive and condescending as the term may be, it covers those who are clerical and those who are professional, those who are accomplished experts and those who are not, and those who are offended by the term as well as those who are not.

staffing process The procedure by which presidential statements and speeches are systematically reviewed and corrected by the federal agencies affected. According to Ronald Reagan's White House speechwriter Peggy Noonan in her memoir *What I Saw at the Revolution* (1990): "In staffing, a speech was sent out to all of the pertinent federal agencies and all the important members of the White House staff and the pertinent White House offices. If the speech was relatively unimportant perhaps twenty people in all would see it and comment on it. An important speech would be gone over by fifty or so. The way the system was supposed to work was that the reviewers were to suggest changes, additions, and deletions. The key word here is suggest."

stagflation High unemployment and inflation at the same time. This was something new in the 1970s because historically high unemployment tended toward deflation.

stalking horse A politician who is a front for another. The phrase comes from hunting, when a hunter might literally hide behind his horse to better stalk his unsuspecting prey.

stalwarts **1.** Faithful party followers. **2.** Republican party loyalists during the last quarter of the nineteenth century. When Charles Guiteau shot President James A. Garfield in 1881 because the President had not given him a patronage appointment, he is supposed to have shouted, "I am a stalwart and Arthur is president now." Obviously, Guiteau, who was hanged the next year, felt that Chester Arthur, the vice President, would be more receptive to his petitions for office than Garfield had been. He wasn't.

stand A lawmaker's position, for or against, on a given issue or vote. A member of Congress can make his or her stand known in one of three ways: (1) by answering yea or nay on a roll-call vote, (2) by pairing with another legislator for or against, or (3) by announcing his or her position to the House or Senate.

standard metropolitan statistical area (SMSA) A creation of the U.S. Census Bureau to more accurately portray urban population; it includes the population in all counties contiguous to an urban county (i.e., one with a city over 50,000 in a common total), if the population of those counties is involved in the urban county workforce. Being designated an SMSA is important to cities and counties because only SMSAs are eligible for certain federal government grants.

standing **1.** Permanent, as in a standing committee of the Congress; a standing rule; or a standing order. **2.** A person's right to initiate legal action because he or she is directly affected by the issues raised.

stand pat To accept a present situation; to maintain an existing policy. The phrase comes from poker, where it means you will play the cards initially dealt you and not draw additional cards in hopes of a better hand. Early in the twentieth century, to stand pat came to mean being REACTIONARY, especially in contrast to the members of the PROGRESSIVE MOVEMENT. Nobody in American politics today is in favor of standing pat. There is a classic piece of film from the 1960 presidential campaign in which Richard Nixon, with his wife, Pat, seated behind him, energetically tells an audience that "we can't stand pat." Subsequently, to Mrs. Nixon's presumed relief, he changed that line to "America cannot stand still."

stare decisis A Latin term meaning "let the decision stand"; the legal principle that once a precedent is established all similar cases should be decided the same way. *Compare to* PRECEDENT.

stars and stripes **1.** The flag of the United States. On June 14, 1777, the Continental Congress resolved "that the flag of the thirteen United States be thirteen stripes, alternate red and white; that the UNION be thirteen stars, white in a blue field, representing a new constellation." As new states came into the union, a star was added for each. **2.** The newspaper published by and for the U.S. army. It was started during World War I, revived for World War II, and has continued ever since.

Star-Spangled Banner **1.** The flag of the United States. **2.** The NATIONAL ANTHEM of the United States.

state **1.** A political unit having territory, population, and sovereignty over its internal and external affairs. While it is true, as Woodrow Wilson wrote in *The State* (1889), that: "The state exists for the sake of society, not society for the sake of the state"; sociologist William Graham Sumner, *Commercial Crises* (1879) would have us always remember that "When all the fine phrases are stripped away, it appears that the state is only a group of men with human interests, passions, and desires, or, worse yet, the state is only an obscure clerk hidden in some corner of a governmental bureau. In either case the assumption of superhuman wisdom and virtue is proved false." **2.** A component government in a federal system, such as an American state government. **3.** One of the 50 states of the United States. In many federal laws, the term also includes the District of Columbia, the Commonwealth of Puerto Rico, and any territory or possession of the United States. **4.** A short form of reference to the U.S. Department of State. **5.** An abstract concept referring to the ultimate source of legal authority.

state central committee The formal leadership body of a political party within a state. It is composed, variously, of representation of congressional districts, counties, or state legislative districts.

state committee The governing body of a political party within a state; sometimes called the state central committee.

state department, little The President's foreign policy advisors who work directly as part of the White House staff.

state, department of A state government agency that typically maintains official documents, issues licenses for businesses as well as certificates of incorporation and administers elections among other varied duties. All states have such a department headed by a secretary who is usually elected.

state government A subnational government in the United States that consists of legislative, executive, and judicial branches and all departments, boards, commissions, and other organizational units thereof. It also includes any semiautonomous authorities, institutions of higher education, districts, and other agencies that are subject to administrative and fiscal control by the state through its appointment of officers, determination of budgets, approval of plans, and other devices. The state governments of the original independent colonies formed the union under the U.S. Constitution in 1787. The priority of these governments over the union was a claim that was finally ended by the Civil War, even though STATES' RIGHTS and the distinction between state and federal power remained highly controversial issues in American government well into the twentieth century.

state of nature What SOCIAL CONTRACT theory assumes to be the condition of mankind before the establishment of a social contract and organized government. THOMAS HOBBES found life in it to be "nasty, brutish, and short." JEAN-JACQUES ROUSSEAU thought it idyllic. And JOHN LOCKE wrote that "the state of nature has a law of nature to govern it, which obliges every one; and reason, which is that law, teaches all mankind who will but consult it, that, being all equal and independent, no one ought to harm another in his life, health, liberty or possessions."

state of the union message The annual message of the President of the United States to the Congress wherein legislative initiatives are usually proposed. Article II, Section 3, of the U.S. Constitution requires that the President "shall from time to time give to the Congress information of the state of the Union, and recommend to their consideration such measures as he shall judge necessary and expedient." George Washington and John Adams appeared before the two houses in joint session to read their messages. Thomas Jefferson discontinued the practice in 1801, transmitting his message to the Capitol to be read by clerks in both houses. Jefferson's procedure was followed for a full century. On April 8, 1913, Woodrow Wilson revived the practice of delivering the state of the union message in person. With the exception of Herbert Hoover, Wilson's example has been followed by subsequent Presidents. In 1965 President Lyndon B. Johnson shifted the time of the state of the union message from midday to evening—in recognition that the "message" was designed for a prime-time national audience. Since 1976 the opposing party has offered a televised rebuttal immediately after the President's speech.

State, secretary of *See* SECRETARY OF STATE.

State, U.S. Department of The cabinet-level department of the federal government whose primary objective is the execution of foreign policy to promote the long-range security and well-being of the United States. The Department of State is the oldest of all cabinet departments. It was the first of three departments created in 1789; this makes the secretary of State the RANKING MEMBER of the cabinet.

state visit An official visit, attended by appropriate ceremonies, by one head of state (or government) to another.

statecraft **1.** The art and science of governance, of leadership, and of politics. **2.** Machiavellian cunning or duplicity in government. **3.** DIPLOMACY.

statehouse **1.** The building in the state where the legislature meets; a state CAPITOL. **2.**. A governorship. The question is often asked: "Can [any governor] go from the statehouse to the White House?"

state's attorney **1.** The ATTORNEY GENERAL of a state. **2.** A local prosecutor (e.g., a district attorney) who represents the state (the people) in a criminal trial.

state's evidence In a criminal trial, evidence or testimony on behalf of the state (the prosecution). State's evidence is what an accomplice to a crime gives to the state in a negotiated effort (in PLEA BARGAINING) to get a lesser personal penalty for the crime at issue.

statesman A respectful reference to a political leader of considerable national or international prominence. According to President Harry S Truman, "A statesman is a politician who's been dead ten or fifteen years" (*The New York Telegram and Sun*, April 12, 1958). According to British Prime Minister Harold MacMillan (1894–1987), "When you're abroad you're a statesman; when you're home, you're just a politician."

states' rights **1.** Those rights that, according to the U.S. Constitution, have been neither given to the federal government nor forbidden to the states. What remains is the essence of state sovereignty. **2.** A CODE WORD for opposition to federal civil rights legislation, federal land-use policies, or other federal policies perceived to be violations of state sovereignty.

statism **1.** A belief in the sovereignty of individual states. **2.** Oppressive policies on the part of a state whereby individual liberty suffers as the social and economic powers of the state are increased.

statistics **1.** That branch of mathematics concerned with the correlation of data. **2.** Facts in the form of descriptive data to be used in the formation of government policy. **3.** Lies, because so many statistical presentations are based upon inaccurate data or used in self-serving ways. British Prime Minister Benjamin Disraeli (1804–1881) is usually credited with being the first to observe: "There are three kinds of lies: lies, damned lies and statistics."

Statistical Abstract of the United States The statistical portrait of American life published annually by the U.S. Bureau of the Census. It summarizes in tabular form an almost infinite variety of numerical data about the political, economic, and social life of the United States. Included are major sections on government finances and employment, elections, and law enforcement.

statute A law passed by a legislature; legislative-made as opposed to JUDGE-MADE law.

statute, long-arm A law that allows the courts in one state to claim jurisdiction over a matter in another state; often used in cases involving nonresident defendants.

statute, organic The legislative act which creates an agency.

statutes at large A collection of all statutes passed by a particular legislature (such as the U.S. Congress), printed in full and in the order of their passage.

statutes of limitations Laws that place limits on the time authorities have to charge someone with a crime after its commission, limits on the time someone has to contest a contract in a civil lawsuit, and so on.

statutory offense An act which is made a crime by statute as opposed to common law. For example, statutory rape is considered to be rape because a statute holds that males who have sexual relations with females below a certain age are "automatically" rapists.

steel seizure case *See* YOUNGSTOWN SHEET AND TUBE CO. V SAWYER.

Stevenson, Adlai E. (1835–1914) Vice President of the United States (1893–1897) during President Grover Cleveland's second term.

Stevenson, Adlai E., II (1900–1965) The Governor of Illinois (1948–1952) who was the Democratic Party's nominee for President in 1952 and 1956. In both years he lost to President Dwight D. Eisenhower. Throughout the 1950s Stevenson was the leading voice for liberalism and internationalism. He ended his career as the U.S. Ambassador to the United Nations (1961–1965), an organization he helped create in 1946. Stevenson II was the grandson of the original Adlai Stevenson.

Stevenson, Adlai E., III (1930–   ) The son of Stevenson II who was the U.S. Senator from Illinois (1970–1981).

Stone v Graham *See* SCHOOL DISTRICT OF ABINGTON TOWNSHIP V SCHEMPP.

strategic planning *See* PLANNING.

street money Cash given to campaign workers on election day to reimburse volunteers for expenses, buy gas for driving voters to polls, print sample ballots, and so on. Such cash, also known as *walking around money*, has also been used to simply buy votes.

strict constructionist One who believes the U.S. Constitution should be interpreted narrowly and literally. Strict constructionists tend to be against JUDICIAL ACTIVISM and in favor of JUDICIAL SELF-RESTRAINT. This is what President Ronald Reagan meant on June 23, 1986 when he said: "The one thing that I do seek are judges that will interpret the law and not write the law." A LOOSE CONSTRUCTIONIST, in contrast, believes that the Constitution should be interpreted liberally in order to reflect changing times. Chief Justice John Marshall first made the case for loose construction in MCCULLOCH V MARYLAND, when he asserted: "Let the end be legitimate, let it be within the scope of the Constitution, and all means which are appropriate, which are plainly adapted to that end, which are not prohibited, but consist with the letter and spirit of the Constitution, are constitutional." *Compare to* ORIGINAL INTENT.

Structural Impediments Initiative The totality of the overall U.S. effort to get the Japanese to change their methods of doing business to make them more compatible with western business practices. For example, some

Japanese retail outlets will only buy products of Japanese origins, even when imported goods are less expensive. This is especially true with agricultural products.

stump 1. To give campaign speeches in a great variety of locations in an electoral jurisdiction. Before empty soap boxes were commonly available, candidates would use a convenient tree stump, quite literally, as their political platform. The standard campaign speech, the one given on most occasions during a campaign, is the *stump* speech. **2.** Any bombastic, exuberant, sometimes inflammatory, but always entertaining political oratory.

subcommittee A subset of a larger COMMITTEE. Much of the business of the U.S. Congress is conducted in its approximately 230 subcommittees. These subcommittees give many junior members of the Congress their only opportunity to chair a committee—to "take an issue and run with it."

subgovernments The COZY TRIANGLES of congressional committees or subcommittees, agency executives, and interest group lobbyists that often dominate public policymaking in a given area. Subgovernments, with a relatively small number of participants which, as a group, can function pretty much autonomously, are often contrasted with ISSUE NETWORKS—large numbers of people with vastly varying degrees of interest, mutual commitment, and power to influence an issue. While a subgovernment or iron triangle is a relatively stable unit both for purposes of exercising power and political analysis, an issue network is so loose that it almost defies definition.

subnational government State and local government.

subpoena 1. A written order issued by a judicial officer requiring a specified person to appear in a designated court at a specified time, either to serve as a witness in a case under the jurisdiction of that court or to bring material to that court. **2.** A formal order to appear before a legislature; usually a legislative committee. This has the same force of law as a subpoena issued by a judicial officer.

subpresidencies The notion that the duties of the President of the United States can be grouped into logical and relatively independent categories of policies, actions, and political patterns, each representing a subpresidency. Examples include the foreign policy presidency, the economic policy presidency, the domestic policy presidency.

substantive bill clearance *See* CENTRAL CLEARANCE.

substitute A motion, an amendment, or an entire bill introduced in place of pending business. Passage of a substitute measure kills the original measure by supplanting it. A substitute may be amended.

Subversive Activities Control Board *See* ALBERTSON V SUBVERSIVE ACTIVITIES CONTROL BOARD.

suffrage The right to vote. Property ownership was commonly required for voters in the early years of the United States, but, by the time Andrew Jackson became President in 1829, universal white male suffrage had been effectively achieved. Since then, various constitutional amendments have been devoted to expanding the suffrage. In 1870, the Fifteenth Amendment held that suffrage shall not be denied "on account of race, color, or previous condition of servitude." In 1920, the Nineteenth Amendment held that citizens of either sex had the right to vote. This was quite controversial at the time. The prevailing feeling against women's suffrage was summed up by President Grover Cleveland (*Ladies' Home Journal*, April 1905): "Sensible and responsible women do not want to vote. The relative positions to be assumed by man and woman in the working out of our civilization were assigned long ago by a higher intelligence than ours." In 1964, the Twenty-Fourth Amendment prohibited the poll tax in federal elections. And in 1971, the Twenty-Sixth Amendment lowered the voting age to 18 years.

summit 1. A meeting between the highest level executives of independent organizations, usually governments. The word in its diplomatic sense may first have been used by British historian Walter Bagehot in *The English Constitution* (1867): "The old-world diplomacy of Europe was largely carried on in drawing-rooms, and, to a great extent, of necessity still is so. Nations touch at their summits." But British prime minister Winston Churchill, who certainly read Bagehot, is generally credited with the first modern use of the term in the early 1950s. When governments have summits, there is a great tendency to personalize the outcomes—to believe that new-found interpersonal relations suddenly become more important than continuing national interests. But former Secretary of State Henry A. Kissinger warns: "This reflects a profound American temptation to believe that foreign policy is a subdivision of psychiatry and that relations among nations are like relations among people" (*Time*, June 17, 1985). This is why some analysts, such as Senator Barry M. Goldwater in *Why Not Victory?* (1962), have concluded: "The only summit meeting that can succeed is the one that does not take place." The COLD WAR summits between the U.S. and the U.S.S.R. were so portentous and dramatic because they were meetings of adversaries, meetings of two sides that had good reason to feel hostile toward each other. Now that the Cold War is over, summits as we have known them may no longer be possible; they may simply become routine state visits. **2.** A meeting between the President and the leaders of Congress to reach agreement on the annual federal budget. They are usually eleventh-hour affairs that seek myriad budget gimmicks to disguise the true size of the budget deficit.

summit diplomacy. *See* DIPLOMATIC SUMMIT.

summit, economic The annual, since 1975, meeting of the leaders of the seven major industrialized countries (known as the Group of 7 or G-7): the United States, France, Britain, Germany, Canada, Italy, and Japan—plus the President of the European Community.

summons 1. A written order issued by a judicial officer requiring a person who is a party to a lawsuit to appear in a designated court at a specified time. **2.** A court order to appear as a witness in a case or for jury duty. **3.** A traffic citation issued by a police officer.

sumptuary laws Laws that attempt to control the sale or use of socially undesirable, wasteful, or harmful products.

sunbelt-snowbelt tension The problems caused by the post World War II era movement of jobs and population from states in the Northeast and the Midwest to the states of the South, Southwest, and West. Political power (in terms of congressional seats) and economic power (in terms of jobs) continues to shift. *Compare to* RUSTBELT.

sunset laws Laws that fix termination dates on programs or agencies. The laws were pioneered by Colorado, after a major lobbying effort by Common Cause. Many other jurisdictions have now enacted sunset laws. They require formal evaluations and subsequent affirmative legislation if the agency or program is to continue. Although the purpose of a finite life span of, say, five years is to force evaluation and to toughen legislative oversight, the effect is to subject programs to automatic termination unless the clock is reset. Despite its widespread popularity, such time-bomb evaluation is not without risks. There are limits to the abilities of any legislature's staff to do the kind of thorough evaluation required to make sunset meaningful. And, of course, the political reality is that the evaluation might become a tool of bipartisan infighting. Requiring organizations to submit evaluation data for review and to justify their programs may amount to little more than burying the legislature in an avalanche of insignificant paper—something at which agencies have a demonstrated prowess. Furthermore, some agencies, such as police, prisons, and mental health institutions, will be rightly skeptical of the chances of their programs being shut down.

sunshine laws Requirements that government agencies hold their formal business meetings open to the public. Many state and local governments have sunshine laws. The federal government's Sunshine Act of 1977 requires all independent regulatory commissions to give advance notice of the date, time, place, and agenda of their meetings. Closed meetings are allowed if circumstances warrant, but citizens have the right to take agencies to federal court if they feel that closed meetings were not justified.

sunshine rules The rules adopted by the U.S. House of Representatives in 1973 and the Senate in 1975 that require committee meetings to be open to the public (including the press and lobbyists) unless a majority of the committee publicly votes to hold a closed, or executive, session.

superfund *See* COMPENSATION AND LIABILITY ACT OF 1980.

superpowers The United States and the former Soviet Union, because of their large military forces and nuclear arsenals. However, it is often argued that the United States is the only true superpower because it is economically strong while the economy of the Soviet Union was more comparable to that of a third-world or developing country.

supervisors, board of The governing body for a county government. Membership on the board is determined either by election or by *ex officio* appointment of other local officials.

super delegate *See* DELEGATE, SUPER.

super Tuesday A presidential primary election day in March in which many states participate. It was first created in 1988 to downplay the importance of the earlier Iowa caucuses and New Hampshire primary; and to force candidates to early on face a broader electorate. Since so many of the states are in the South, it is sometimes called the *Southern Primary*.

supplemental bill *See* BILL, DEFICIENCY.

Supplemental Security Income (SSI) The federal program that assures a minimum monthly income to needy people with limited income and resources who are 65 years of age or older, blind, or disabled. Eligibility is based on income and assets. Although the program is administered by the Social Security Administration, it is financed from general revenues, not from social security contributions.

supply-side economics The belief that lower tax rates, especially on marginal income, encourage fresh capital to flow into the economy, which in turn generates jobs, growth, and new tax revenue. Because this concept was adopted by President Ronald Reagan and his advisors, it has been popularly called *Reaganomics*, even though Reagan's actual economic policies have been a melange of supply-side thinking, monetarism, old-fashioned conservatism, and even Keynesianism. While economist Arthur Laffer is generally credited with having "discovered" supply-side economics, the underlying premises of it were established almost 200 years ago by Alexander Hamilton in *Federalist* No. 21. Hamilton argued that:

It is a signal advantage of taxes. . . that they contain in their own nature a security against excess. They prescribe their own limit; which cannot be exceeded without defeating the end proposed—that is, an extension of the revenue. When applied to this object, the saying is as just as it is witty, that, "in political arithmetic, two and two do not always make four." If duties are too high, they lessen the consumption; the collection is eluded; and the product to the treasury is not so great as when they are confined within proper and moderate bounds.

George Gilder's *Wealth and Poverty* (1981), sometimes called the "supply-side Bible," is the most comprehensive explanation and justification for Reaganomics. *See* VOODOO ECONOMICS.

supremacy clause That portion of Article VI of the U.S. Constitution that asserts that the Constitution, treaties, and laws made on its behalf "shall be the supreme Law of the Land," implying that federal law will take precedence over state law.

Supreme Court, United States The highest United States court. Since 1869, the Court has been composed of the CHIEF JUSTICE of the United States and eight associate justices. The Congress, which governs its organization by legislation, has varied the number of associate justices from six to 10. The Congress now requires six justices for a quorum. The power to nominate the justices is vested in the President, and appointments are made by and with the advice and consent of the Senate. Article III, Section 1 of the Constitution further provides that "the judges, both of the supreme and inferior courts, shall hold their offices during good behavior, and shall, at stated times, receive for their services, a compensation, which shall not be diminished during their continuance in office."

The Constitution provides that "in all cases affecting ambassadors (to the United States), other public ministers and consuls, and those in which a State shall be party," the Supreme Court has ORIGINAL JURISDICTION. This was modified by the Eleventh Amendment to preclude citizens from suing a state. Additionally, the Constitution provides that the Congress may regulate the appellate jurisdiction of the Court. The Congress has authorized the Supreme Court to, among other things, review decisions of the lower federal courts and the highest courts of the states. Because instances of original jurisdiction are rare, the overwhelming majority of cases heard by the Court are appeals from the federal and state court systems.

The internal review process of the Court has largely evolved by custom, while the procedures to be followed by petitioners to the Court are established in rules set forth by the Court. After individually examining each case submitted, the justices hold a private conference to decide which cases to schedule for oral argument, which to decide without argument, and which to dismiss. If at least four justices agree, a case will be taken by the Court for a decision, with or without argument. If oral argument is heard, a total of one hour is generally allowed the parties to argue the issues and respond to questions of the justices. Later, in conference, the justices make their decision by simple majority vote. A tie vote means that the decision of the lower court is allowed to stand. Such a vote could occur when one or three justices do not take part in a decision. When the justices have decided a case, the chief justice, if he or she voted with the majority, assigns an associate justice to write the opinion of the Court. If the chief justice is in the majority, the senior associate justice in the minority makes the assignment. The individual justices may, of course, write their own opinions in any decision.

Article VI of the Constitution provides that the Constitution and the laws of the United States made "in pursuance thereof" shall be the supreme law of the land. Thus, when the Supreme Court decides a case, particularly on constitutional grounds, it becomes guidance for all the lower courts and legislatures when a similar question arises. As Justice Robert Jackson observed: "The Court is not final because it is infallible; the Court is infallible because it is final," *Brown v Allen* (1952). While the Court's greatest power is that of JUDICIAL REVIEW, this ability to negate acts of other branches of government is used sparingly. Whenever possible, the Court seeks other grounds if it is necessary to reverse a lower court decision. Each year, the Court receives for review nearly 4,000 decisions from lower state and federal courts. The justices examine each case submitted and agree to hear arguments on less than 200 each term; another 100 or so are disposed of by decision of the Court without oral argument; and the rest are either denied or dismissed. *Compare to* BRETHREN; UNITED STATES REPORTS.

supreme law of the land The U.S. Constitution, laws of the United States made "in pursuance of" the Constitution, and treaties made under authority of the United States. Judges throughout the country are bound by them, regardless of anything in separate state constitutions or laws.

surrogate An official substitute for a political candidate at an event, usually a "name" who is associated with the candidate's policies, but often a literal member of the family. Political wives have always made great surrogates; sometimes, as with Betty Ford, they become more popular than their husbands.

surtax An additional tax, or surcharge, on what has already been taxed; that is, a tax on a tax. For example, if you must pay a $1,000 tax on a $10,000 income (10 percent), a 10 percent surtax would be an additional $100.

suspend the rules *See* RULES, SUSPENSION OF.

Swann v Charlotte-Mecklenburg Board of Education (1971) The Supreme Court case that decreed that extensive school busing could be used as part of a racial desegregation plan. This decision established the legal framework for all future school BUSING decisions.

symbolic speech Nonverbal behavior, such as hand movements, facial expressions, wearing certain items of clothing. Symbolic speech, as opposed to symbolic actions (which may be disruptive or destructive), is generally protected by the First Amendment. For example, the Supreme Court held in *Tinker v Des Moines School District* (1969) that students who wore black armbands to protest the Vietnam War could not be punished because this was a "silent, passive expression of opinion" that was not disruptive.

system 1. Any organized collection of parts united by prescribed interactions and designed for the accomplishment of a specific goal or general purpose. **2.** The political process in general. **3.** The ESTABLISHMENT; the powers that be who govern; the domain of a ruling elite. **4.** The BUREAUCRACY.

System, The American government in general; the American political process.

T

table **1.** A legislative or procedural motion to suspend the consideration of a proposal. The motion to "lay on the table" is not debatable in either house of the U.S. Congress, and it is usually a method of making a final—and adverse—disposition of a matter. In the Senate, however, different language is sometimes used. The motion is worded to let a bill "lie on the table," perhaps for subsequent "picking up." This motion is more flexible, merely keeping the bill pending for later action, if desired. **2.** In British usage exactly the opposite; there "to table" means to bring something up for discussion.

Taft, William Howard (1857–1930) The only person to be both President of the United States (1909–1913) and Chief Justice of the Supreme Court (1921–1930). Taft, at 321 pounds, also holds the record as the largest of all Presidents. While he was the handpicked successor of President Theodore Roosevelt, Taft quickly lost Roosevelt's support once in office. Roosevelt found him so unacceptably conservative that both men competed for the Republican nomination in 1912. When Roosevelt won the primaries but lost the nomination to Taft, he ran for President as a "Bull Moose" Progressive. This split the Republican vote and allowed Woodrow Wilson, the Democrat, to win. *See* PRESIDENCY, RESTRICTED VIEW OF.

Taft Commission The 1912 Commission on Economy and Efficiency, chaired by the President, which called for a national budgetary system. Its recommendations were incorporated into the BUDGET AND ACCOUNTING ACT OF 1921.

Taft-Hartley Act *See* LABOR-MANAGEMENT RELATIONS ACT OF 1947.

Tammany Hall A building in New York City used by the Tammany Society (founded in 1789 and named after a Delaware Indian chief), which became a symbol of all that is associated with political machines, because the New York County Democrats also met in the building.

targeting **1.** A tactic used by POLITICAL ACTION COMMITTEES (PACs) through which specific members of the U.S. Congress are identified (targeted) for defeat. They then channel campaign funds to the candidate's opposition, or spend funds on behalf of the opposition. The PACs that engage in this kind of negative campaigning have been called "attack PACs." **2.** The process of selecting military targets and matching the appropriate response to them, while taking account of operational requirements and capabilities. This has vast implications for nuclear policy. For example, warheads targeted on nonmilitary targets would not be considered first-strike weapons. **3.** The process of making a campaign resource-allocation decisions aimed at those voters (target groups) most likely to be susceptible to your candidate's message.

tariff A list of taxes imposed on imported products. *Compare to* DUTY.

Tashjian v Republic Party of Connecticut *See* PRIMARY.

tax A compulsory contribution exacted by a government for public purposes. This does not include employee and employer assessments for retirement and social insurance purposes, which are classified as "insurance trust revenue." Taxes are generally perceived by a public to be legitimate if they are levied by that public's elected representatives. Indeed, one of the causes of, and principal rallying cries for, the American Revolution was that there should be "no taxation without representation" because "taxation without representation was tyranny." Consequently, practically all taxes at all levels of government are now enacted by popularly elected legislatures. While Benjamin Franklin wrote in a letter to Jean-Baptiste Leroy on November 13, 1789 that "in this world nothing can be said to be certain but death and taxes," and Justice Oliver Wendell Holmes wrote in a 1904 Supreme Court opinion that "taxes are what we pay for civilized society," it remained for novelist Margaret Mitchell to observe in *Gone With the Wind* (1936): "Death and taxes and childbirth! There's never any convenient time for any of them!"

Taxes are one of the most volatile of political issues. Walter Mondale in accepting the Democratic Party's presidential nomination in 1984 said: "Taxes will go up. And anyone who says they won't is not telling the truth." He lost by a landslide. George Bush in accepting the Republican Party's presidential nomination in 1988 said: "Read my lips, no new taxes." He won by a landslide. There is a lesson in this. *See also* REVENUE GAINERS; TAXATION.

tax abatement The relinquishment of a tax that would ordinarily be due; also known as *tax remission*. For example, a local government might temporarily abate certain property taxes to encourage the renovation of slum housing.

taxable income Under federal tax law, either the gross income of businesses or the adjusted gross income of individuals minus deductions and exemptions—against which income tax rates are applied.

tax amnesty A government's forgiving of the failure to pay taxes previously due if they are paid within an announced period. This saves the taxpayer the interest and penalties that would have been due and gains the government far more in revenues than it would obtain through normal enforcement. During the 1980s at least 30 states have used tax amnesty programs to increase their income tax collections. The federal government has yet to have a tax amnesty program. Many complain that all such programs are inherently unfair to people who pay their taxes on time.

tax anticipation notes *See* REVENUE ANTICIPATION NOTES.

tax assessment *See* ASSESSMENT.

tax avoidance Planning one's personal finances to take advantage of all legal tax breaks, such as deductions and tax shelters. The very wealthy J.

Pierpont Morgan (1836–1913) provided the intellectual foundation of tax avoidance when he said, "No citizen has a moral obligation to assist in maintaining the government. If Congress insists on making stupid mistakes and passing foolish tax laws, millionaires should not be condemned if they take advantage of them." The Tax Reform Act of 1986 was designed to make tax avoidance more difficult by closing many TAX LOOPHOLES. *Compare to* TAX EVASION.

tax base The thing or value on which taxes are levied. Some of the more common tax bases include individual income, corporate income, real property, wealth, motor vehicles, sales of commodities and services, utilities, events, imports, estates, and gifts. The rate of a tax to be imposed against a given tax base may be either specific or *ad valorem*. Specific taxes raise a specific, nonvariable amount of revenue from each unit of the tax base (e.g., 10 cents per gallon of gasoline). *Ad valorem* taxes are expressed as a percentage, and the revenue yield varies according to the value of the tax base (e.g., a mill levy against real property).

tax, broad based Any tax levied on all eligible taxpayers whether or not they receive any benefits from the levy.

tax, capital gains A tax on the profit made on the increase in value of capital assets (such as a house or stocks) when they are sold. Tax rates on capital gains may be lower than for personal income if the assets are held longer than a prescribed period. The TAX REFORM ACT OF 1986 eliminates the special treatment of capital gains for federal income tax purposes. The Bush Administration has sought to have it reinstated; that is, to make taxes on capital gains lower than taxes on income.

tax collections *See* TAX YIELD.

tax, corporate income A tax on the privilege of operating a business. Various deductions can be made for depreciation, capital gains, research and development costs, and so on, to determine taxable income.

tax credits The provisions of law that allow a dollar-for-dollar reduction in tax liabilities.

tax, direct A tax paid to a government directly by a taxpayer (e.g., an income tax). Article I, Section 9 of the U.S. Constitution holds that "no capitation, or other direct, tax shall be laid, unless in proportion to the census or enumeration herein before directed to be taken." This inhibited the enactment of the federal income tax until the Sixteenth Amendment of 1913 changed the Constitution to allow for direct taxation. *Compare to* TAX, INDIRECT.

tax, earmarked A tax whose revenues must, by law, be spent for specific purposes. For example, a state gasoline tax may be earmarked for highway construction.

tax elasticity The relation between the percentage of tax revenue raised compared to the percentage of change in personal income. A perfectly elastic tax would always be able to collect the same percentage of the income of its jurisdiction's population.

tax, estate The federal and state taxes on a deceased person's property made prior to the estate's distribution to heirs.

tax, estimated That portion of income tax that individuals with other significant income than salaries must declare to the Internal Revenue Service and pay every three months.

tax evasion Taking illegal and criminal actions to avoid paying one's tax obligations. *Compare to* TAX AVOIDANCE.

tax extension **1.** The expansion of the coverage of a tax; for example, a state sales tax which covered only certain items might be "extended" by new legislation to cover additional items. **2.** Adjusting progressive tax rates so that more people qualify for the highest marginal tax brackets.

tax, excess profits A supplement to corporate income taxes, usually imposed during a national emergency.

tax, excise A tax on the manufacture, sale, or consumption of a product such as gasoline or tobacco.

tax exemption **1.** The immunity from taxation of certain activities and institutions. Such exemption may be temporary, such as a 10-year exemption to encourage new housing in a particular area, or permanent, as in the exemptions enjoyed by most schools and churches. **2.** The immunity from taxation of certain kinds of income, such as child-support payments and income from municipal bonds.

tax-exempt municipal bonds *See* BONDS, MUNICIPAL.

tax exempts **1.** Land, buildings, or businesses that do not pay taxes because of legal exemptions. **2.** Investments, such as municipal bonds, that are tax-free. **3.** Nonprofit organizations that meet legal requirements for tax exemption.

tax expenditure The losses of tax revenue attributable to provisions of the federal tax laws that allow a special exclusion, exemption, or deduction from gross income or that provide a special credit, preferential rate of tax, or deferral of tax liability. When an individual or a corporation gets a TAX SUBSIDY, the federal government counts it as a tax expenditure. *Compare to* TAX LOOPHOLE.

tax, exported A tax paid by nonresidents of a community (e.g., a city wage tax paid by commuters).

tax, flat A tax that charges the same rate to each taxpayer. The concept has been put forward in a variety of proposals for reform of the federal income tax. *Compare to* TAX REFORM ACT OF 1986.

tax, gift *See* TAX, TRANSFER.

tax incentive A provision in a tax law that encourages particular economic activity. For example, provisions for accelerated depreciation encourage businesses to buy new equipment; provisions that allow the deducibility of the interest on a home mortgage encourage people to buy houses.

tax incidence The effects of a particular tax burden on various socioeconomic levels.

tax, income *See* TAX, PERSONAL INCOME.

tax, indirect A tax paid to a third party, who in turn pays it to the government (e.g., a sales tax). *Compare to* TAX, DIRECT.

tax-increment financing The ability of local government to finance large-scale development through the expected rise in the property tax to be collected after the development is completed. This permits the issuance of bonds based on the expected tax increase.

tax, inheritance A tax (usually progressive) on an individual's share of a deceased person's estate.

tax, kiddie The federal income tax provision that significant amounts earned on accounts in the name of children under age 14 are taxed at the parents' marginal rate, the rate paid on the last dollar of income. This is not what self-styled hotel queen Leona Helmsley meant when she said: "Only the little people pay taxes" (*Newsweek*, July 24, 1989).

tax, license A tax exacted (either for revenue raising or for regulation) as a condition to the exercise of a business or nonbusiness privilege.

tax lien Legally executed charges on a property because of unpaid taxes. The lien can result in a foreclosure and tax sale; that is, the property can be forcibly sold to pay the taxes due.

tax loophole An inconsistency in the tax laws, intentional or unintentional, that allows the avoidance of some taxes. An intentional tax loophole is a TAX EXPENDITURE. A tax expenditure for one person is often viewed as a loophole by another. Tax loopholes are perfectly legal; but they have an unsavory reputation as the handiwork of special interest lobbyists. *Compare to* TRANSITION RULE.

tax, marriage Not an actual tax, but the simple fact that under some income tax laws two wage earners who happen to be married to each other and file a joint tax return will often pay more in taxes than if they were single and filed separately.

tax, negative income A welfare program in which citizens with incomes below a specified level receive cash payments.

tax, personal income A tax based on the ABILITY TO PAY principle, in that the tax rate is applied against income. But income is more than just money—it is any asset that increases one's net worth; and yet income taxes are not necessarily a straight tax on all of one's income in a given year. Remember all those millionaires that the press annually discovers who do not pay any tax on their income? They are able to do this because it is not their large incomes that are subject to taxation, but their adjusted gross incomes. All taxpayers have the right to exclude certain kinds of incomes from their gross incomes for tax purposes. For example, interest from state and local bonds is exempt from federal taxation. Thus, a millionaire whose sole income came from investments in such bonds would pay no federal income tax. The taxpayer may also subtract deductions and exemptions from taxable income. Then the taxpayer can deduct a host of expenses, as long as they are allowed by the tax laws: medical care, state and local taxes (if a federal return), home mortgage interest, and charitable contributions. A taxpayer can itemize deductions or take a minimum standard deduction, which is a precalculated weighted average. Progressive tax rates are then applied to the taxable income to determine how much tax is due.

All states but Florida, Nevada, South Dakota, Texas, Washington, and Vermont have personal income taxes, as do many cities. Residents of Baltimore, Cleveland, Detroit, New York, and Philadelphia, for example, must pay personal income taxes to three different governments: federal, state, and local.

tax, personal property Tax on the assessed value of (1) tangible property, such as furniture, animals, or jewelry; or (2) intangible property, such as stocks and bonds.

tax, property *See* TAX, REAL-PROPERTY.

tax, poll **1.** A tax required of voters; once widely used by southern states to discourage blacks from voting. The Twenty-Fourth Amendment to the U.S. Constitution prohibits denial of the right to vote for federal officials because a person has not paid a tax. This amendment was designed to abolish the requirement of a poll tax which, at the time of its ratification, was imposed by five states as a condition to voting. The Supreme Court in *Harper v Virginia State Board of Elections* (1966) subsequently held that poll taxes were unconstitutional under the equal protection clause of the Fourteenth Amendment, on the basis that the right to vote should not be conditioned on one's ability to pay a tax. Accordingly, poll taxes are now prohibited in all state and federal elections. **2.** A capitation tax; a per capita assessment. In the United Kingdom the poll tax, formally known as a "community charge," has been used to replace local real estate taxes.

tax, progressive Any tax that requires people of greater wealth to pay a larger percentage in tax than people of lesser means. Income taxes are often progressive. *Compare to* TAX, FLAT; TAX, REGRESSIVE.

tax rate The percentage of taxable income (or of inherited money, purchases subject to sales tax, and so on) paid in taxes. The federal income tax has a graduated tax rate. This means that the first $10,000 of a person's taxable income might be taxed at a 20 percent rate (or $2,000) and the next $1,000 to $2,000 at a 25 percent rate. This percentage rate is what most people think of as their *tax bracket*.

tax, real-property Any tax on land and its improvements; usually referred to simply as *property tax*. This tax is the mainstay of most local governments; it provides nearly half of the revenues that local governments get from their own sources. To administer a property tax, the tax base must first be defined—that is, housing and land, automobiles, other assets, whatever. Then an evaluation of the worth of the tax base must be made—this is the ASSESSMENT. Finally, a tax rate, usually an amount to be paid per $100 value of the tax base, is levied. Since the value of the tax base will appreciate or depreciate substantially over time, continuing assessments must be made.

Arguments for the property tax resemble a good news/bad news joke. The good news is that the property tax provides a stable revenue source and has a good track record as a strong revenue raiser. The bad news is that its stability can also be considered inflexibility, as it does not keep pace with income growth. The good news is that, since property is generally unmovable, it is hard to miss and, therefore, provides a visible tax base for relatively unskilled local tax officers to administer. The bad news is that the administration and assessment of property tax is at best erratic and at worst a horrendous mess. The result is that the property tax base tends to erode over time; that the property of the wealthy and the politically influential may be undervalued; that there is a strong incidence effect on newcomers; and that the elderly are being increasingly pressed to meet property tax burdens.

tax reform The recurrent effort to produce a more equitable tax system at all levels of government. As a process, it is never-ending and full of semantic traps—for one person's tax reform often winds up as another's tax increase. Sometimes tax reform is not as much reform as the addition of new kinds of taxes. New things to tax come about by the inventiveness of fiscal experts or by new technology. For example, James Kendall's biography *Michael Faraday* (1955) tells that when Faraday, one of the pioneers in the development of electricity, was first explaining his invention to the British Chancellor of the Exchequer, he was interrupted with "the impatient inquiry: 'But, after all, what use is it?' Like a flash of lightning came the response: 'Why, sir, there is every probability that you will soon be able to tax it!'"

Tax Reform Act of 1986 A comprehensive revision of the federal income tax law that collapsed 14 tax brackets into two (15 and 28 percent), eliminated most tax shelters and deductions (with the major exceptions of those for home mortgage interest, donations to charity, state and local income and property taxes), raised the personal exemption to over $2,000, and eliminated the special treatment of income from capital gains. The law has been both praised and criticized for marking the federal government's retreat from using the tax code for economic and social engineering. Under the new law, investment decisions will, for the most part, have to be made on the merits of investments and not on their tax implications. While not a pure flat tax, the law is considered a victory for those who advocated simplifying the income tax rate structure. Because the act's large standard deduction ($5,000 for joint filees) and increased personal exemption, the law was designed to have the effect of taking millions of low-income taxpayers off the rolls. Thus, the act has been praised as an important piece of antipoverty legislation. While there have been minor amendments to the law (rates were raised in 1990), its basic provisions remain intact—for now.

tax, regressive Any tax that has people with lower incomes paying a higher overall percentage of their income in tax than people of greater income. Sales taxes are examples of regressive taxes. *Compare to* TAX, FLAT; TAX, PROGRESSIVE; TAX, SALES.

tax, regulatory A tax levied for purposes other than raising revenue; examples include taxes on tobacco or gasoline to reduce consumption.

tax revolt A nationwide grassroots movement, heralded by California's PROPOSITION 13 in 1978 to decrease or limit the rate of increase possible on property taxes. In a sense, this was a revolt by the middle class against the rising cost of government services, which created a period of fiscal stress for state and local government. The tax revolt, it is important to note, was not over the unfairness or uneven distribution of the tax burden but over the levels of taxation, especially on real estate, which were increasing dramatically in a period of double-digit inflation. By 1980, the tax revolt movement forced 38 states to reduce or at least stabilize tax rates. When California passed Proposition III in 1990, which among other things would double the state gasoline tax over five years to pay for new highways, many analysts hailed this as the end of the "tax revolt." According to Speaker of the House Thomas Foley: "The tax revolt which allegedly started in California has been tempered by a realization that we have to make investments in the country" (*USA Today*, June 8, 1990).

tax, sales A tax on consumption, rather than income. This favorite of many state and local governments calls for a fixed tax rate, ranging from 2 to 9 percent, to be charged on most purchases. A variety of items tend to be excluded from sales taxation—for example, medicine and foods. The major criticism of the sales tax is equity. Sales taxes tend toward regressivity, in that higher-income groups pay a lesser percentage of their income in tax than do lower-income groups. To illustrate, a family of four with an annual income of $8,000 would spend half of that in direct consumption and might pay a 5 percent sales tax of $200, or 2.5 percent of their income. But another family of four with an $80,000 income will have a much lower percentage of direct consumption (say 25 percent) and, although they pay 5 percent on this amount ($1,000), the proportion of their income taken by the sales tax is 1.2 percent—or half that of the lower-income family.

tax, school A local real-property tax imposed by a school district. Because school taxes are largely dependent upon the value of housing, rich districts have always tended to have more revenue, and therefore better overall educational programs, than poor ones. However, two things happened in 1990 that could substantially change local education financing: (1) New Jersey decided not to provide state aid to their wealthiest school districts so that more revenue could be given to the poorest; and (2) the Supreme Court in *Missouri v Jenkins* (1990) held that a federal judge had the authority to order a school district to raise taxes—in this instance to pay for a magnet school plan designed to remedy past practices of school segregation. Justice

Byron R. White in the opinion of the Court said: "A court order directing a local government body to levy its own taxes is plainly a judicial act within the power of a Federal Court." Nevertheless, Justice Anthony M. Kennedy in a dissent said: "Today's casual embrace of taxation imposed by the unelected, life-tenured Federal judiciary disregards fundamental precepts for the democratic control of public institutions."

tax, self-employment The means by which persons who work for themselves are provided social security coverage. Each self-employed person must pay self-employment tax on part or all of his or her income to help finance social security benefits, which are payable to self-employed persons as well as to wage earners.

tax, severance A tax imposed by more than half of the states for the privilege of "severing" natural resources, such as coal, from the land.

tax, shared A tax imposed and administered by a higher level of government whose revenues it shares, according to a predetermined percentage formula, with lower units of government. For example, states commonly collect sales taxes and return a portion to counties and municipalities.

tax shelter An investment in which any profits are fully or partially tax-free or that creates deductions and credits that reduce one's overall taxes.

tax, stamp 1. A tax on certain legal documents, such as deeds, when it is required that revenue stamps be bought and put on the documents to make them valid. The British Parliament's Stamp Act of 1765 sought to increase revenues from the American colonies and helped trigger the movement toward revolution. This tax, which required stamps on legal papers, newspapers, pamphlets, almanacs, cards, and so on, was so resented and caused such turmoil that it was repealed in 1766. **2.** A tax on illegal drug sales. This is not a real tax; it is a legal gimmick that makes it easier to arrest and convict drug dealers. Fifteen states do this both to increase revenue and because it is often easier to obtain a conviction on tax evasion than drug trafficking.

tax subsidy A tax advantage designed to encourage specific behavior that furthers public policy; for example, mortgage interest deductions to encourage citizens to buy houses and investment tax credits to encourage businesses to expand and create new jobs. *Compare to* TAX EXPENDITURE.

tax, transfer A tax on large transfers of property or money, which are made without something of value given in return. Often called a *gift tax*.

tax, unitary A business tax of a percentage of worldwide profits, not just profits earned in the taxing jurisdiction. For example, if a corporation has 20 percent of its payroll, property, and sales in a given state, that state might tax 20 percent of the corporation's worldwide income.

tax, value-added (VAT) A type of national sales tax imposed by almost all Western European countries as a major source of revenue, levied on the value added to a product at each stage of its production and distribution; sometimes called a *business transfer tax*. Proponents of VAT in the United

States argue that the system rewards efficiency and, thus, is superior to the corporate income tax in allocating economic resources; it can encourage savings and capital formation because it is a tax solely on consumption; it can help balance-of-payments problems because it can be imposed on imports and rebated on exports; and it can be a major new source of revenue for meeting domestic spending needs, especially social security costs. Opponents of VAT in the United States charge that it is a regressive tax (i.e., it falls most heavily on the poor); that it is inflationary, in that it causes prices to consumers to go up; and that it would be an additional tax, rather than a substitute for present taxes.

tax, wage Tax on salaries levied by a government. Many cities have wage taxes that have the indirect benefit of forcing suburban commuters to help pay for the services provided to the region by the central city.

tax, withholding Sums of money that an employer takes out of an employee's pay and turns over to a government as prepayment of the employee's federal, state, or local tax obligations.

tax yield The amount of tax that could potentially be collected. Tax collections are the portion of the tax yield that is actually collected. It was Ralph Waldo Emerson who observed: "Of all debts men are least willing to pay the taxes. What a satire is this on government! Everywhere they think they get their money's worth, except for these" ("Politics," *Essays*, 1844).

taxation Government revenue collection. There are major differences between the federal and state-local revenue systems. The federal system has experienced a trend toward less diversity; over two thirds of its general revenue are provided by the federal income tax and the several insurance trust funds (such as social security). State and local revenue systems, in contrast, depend on a greater variety of revenue sources (such as property taxes, income taxes, sales taxes, user charges, lotteries, and federal grants). While local governments still rely primarily on the property tax, their states—with a few exceptions—rely largely on the state personal income tax. In addition, state sales and business taxes provide a significant source of income. This melange of taxing authorities creates great disparities in the state-local tax burden. A resident of New York may pay hundreds or thousands of dollars in state income taxes while a resident of Texas—which has no state income tax—pays none. Virginians have to pay more than double the sales taxes paid by Vermonters. There are even greater variations in property taxes. Given two identical houses, one may be assessed at x dollars in one jurisdiction while the other may be taxed at three times that amount in another jurisdiction. *See also* ABILITY TO PAY; DUTY; TAX, DIRECT; TAX, INDIRECT.

taxation, art of "So plucking the goose as to obtain the largest amount of feathers with the least possible amount of hissing." This definition is usually attributed to Jean-Baptiste Colbert (1619–1683), France's controller general of finance under Louis XIV.

taxation, double 1. The illegal imposition of two taxes on the same property by the same government during the same time period for the same purpose. **2.** Taxing the same money twice. One legal form of double taxation is taxing a corporation on its profits, then taxing its stockholders on dividends from the corporation. Another is the taxation of the income of foreign nationals who will be taxed on the same income when they return home.

taxation, progressive A tax policy in which people in each successively higher income bracket pay a progressively higher tax rate. The federal higher income bracket pay a progressively higher tax rate. The federal graduated personal income tax is the best example of progressive taxation.

taxation, proportional A tax policy in which people pay an identical percentage increase in their tax rates as their incomes rise. Some taxes that are actually proportional in structure, such as sales taxes or property taxes, function as regressive taxes when the tax paid is compared against income; the point being that people in a low-income bracket will pay a higher percentage of their incomes for sales tax than will people with higher incomes.

taxation, regressive A tax policy in which the effective tax rate falls as the tax base increases. *Compare to* TAX, SALES.

taxes, green Measures that raise revenue at the same time that they reduce pollution; for example, additional taxes on gas or diesel fuel.

taxes, payments in lieu of Annual sums paid to local governments by tax-exempt organizations. For example, some universities make payments in lieu of taxes to their cities to help pay for such services as trash removal and police and fire protection.

Taylor, Zachary (1784–1850) The President of the United States from 1849 to 1850. He was the victorious general of the Mexican War. "Old Rough and Ready," as he was admirably called, won the 1848 Whig nomination for President over such political heavyweights as Henry Clay and Daniel Webster. He won the election but died suddenly after about 15 months in office. He was succeeded by his Vice President, Millard Fillmore.

Technology Assessment Act of 1972 *See* OFFICE OF TECHNOLOGY ASSESSMENT.

teflon president A reference to Ronald Reagan because of his ability to avoid being blamed for the mistakes of his subordinates. He was so well liked that it was claimed "nothing sticks," much like Teflon brand non-stick cookware. The phrase was first used by Congresswoman Patricia Schroeder, a Democrat from Colorado, in 1983. Walter Cronkite, the former CBS News anchorman, later said: "I'm amazed at this Teflon Presidency. This Administration had had scandals, rumors of major influence-peddling and the like, yet it has no effect on the popularity of the President. Reagan is even more popular than [Franklin] Roosevelt, and I never thought I'd ever see anyone that well-liked. Roosevelt, you'll remember, had his major critics, major figures who actually disliked him. Nobody hates Reagan. It's amazing" (*USA Today*, May 12, 1986). While nothing else may have stuck, this phrase did—at least until the TOWER COMMISSION report of 1987. *Compare to* REVLON PRESIDENT.

telephone bank A campaign tactic which organizes volunteers to call potential voters to read them a scripted pitch on why they should vote for their candidate. This is sometimes still called a "boiler room" operation because such banks of telephones were once commonly located in the basements or boiler rooms of buildings.

Tennessee Valley Authority (TVA) The government-owned corporation created in 1933 that conducts a unified program of resource development for the advancement of economic growth in the Tennessee River Valley region. The authority's program includes flood control, navigation development, electric power production, fertilizer development, recreation improvement, and forestry and wildlife development. While its power program is financially self-supporting, other programs are financed primarily by appropriations from the Congress.

Tenth Amendment The last part of the Bill of Rights that holds that the "powers not delegated to the United States by the Constitution, nor prohibited by it to the states, are reserved to the states respectively, or to the people." The Tenth Amendment embodies the principle of federalism, which reserves for the states the residue of powers not granted to the federal government or withheld from the states. In recent years, it has not served as much of a constraint on the expansion of the powers of the national government. *Compare to* RESERVE POWERS; TREATY.

term bonds *See* BONDS, TERM.

term limitation **1.** A provision in constitutions limiting elected executives or legislators to no more than a specific number of terms. For example, the U.S. Constitution limits a President to two terms. Many state constitutions and city charters also limit the terms of their chief executives. **2.** A movement to limit the number of terms a Senator or Representative may serve in the U.S. Congress. Because the INCUMBENCY EFFECT is so strong many believe this may be the only way to insure healthy legislative turnover. **3.** Parallel state and local movements.

Terminiello v Chicago (1949) The Supreme Court case that held that a local ordinance calling for restrictions on free speech (if such speech was likely to cause a breach of the peace) was an unconstitutional infringement on the First Amendment guarantee of free speech. Justice William O. Douglas wrote in this case: "Freedom of speech, though not absolute. . . is nevertheless protected against censorship or punishment, unless shown likely to produce a clear and present danger of a serious substantive evil that rises far above public inconvenience, annoyance, or unrest. . . . There is no room under our Constitution for a more restrictive view. For the alternative would lead to standardization of ideas either by legislatures, courts, or dominant political or community groups."

Third Amendment The amendment to the U.S. Constitution that holds that "no soldier shall, in time of peace be quartered in any house, without the consent of the owner, nor in time of war, but in a manner to be prescribed by law." Prior to the Revolution, American colonists had frequently been required against their will to provide lodging and food for British soldiers. The Third Amendment prohibited the continuation of this practice. Ironically, during World War II many American soldiers were quartered in British homes—at the insistence of the British government.

Third House of Congress 1. Congressional conference committees, which so often allow for the passage of legislation by effecting critical compromises. *See also* COMMITTEE, CONFERENCE. **2.** The great number of lobbyists who constantly attend the congressional process; usually pejorative.

Thirteenth Amendment The 1865 amendment to the U.S. Constitution that prohibits slavery. This amendment is the only part of the Constitution that regulates purely private relationships and the first amendment to increase the jurisdiction of the federal government in discriminatory issues by overruling state law.

With the secession of the southern states from the Union and the subsequent outbreak of the Civil War in April 1861, the controversy over slavery intensified. A necessary consequence of the southern states' secession was their forfeiture of representation in the Congress. As a result, congressmen advocating the abolition of slavery faced little opposition, and they were quick to act. On April 16, 1862, the Congress abolished slavery in the District of Columbia. In June, the law was extended to include all territories. In September 1862, President Abraham Lincoln, acting as commander in chief during a time of war, issued the Emancipation Proclamation, which became effective on January 1, 1863. The proclamation declared that all people held in slavery "are, and henceforth shall be, free; and the executive government of the United States, including the military and naval authorities thereof, will recognize and maintain the freedom." The Emancipation Proclamation was contested on several grounds. Opponents strongly questioned the President's constitutional authority to issue such a decree. Others argued that, while the proclamation had freed the slaves in the seceded states, it had not, in effect, made slavery illegal. This left the status of border states and the already defeated Confederate states in question with regard to slavery. The Thirteenth Amendment was proposed and passed to quell the controversy over the constitutionality of the Emancipation Proclamation and to settle the issue of slavery in the United States forever.

Thomas, Clarence (1948–   ) An Associate Justice of the U.S. Supreme Court since 1991. After serving as Chairman of the Equal Employment Opportunity (EEOC) from 1982 to 1990 and as a judge on the U.S. Court of Appeals (1990–1991), he (as an African-American) was appointed by President George Bush to succeed Thurgood Marshall, the only previous African-American on the Supreme Court. His October 1991 confirmation hearings became exceedingly controversial when Anita Hill (1956–   ), a professor at the University of Oklahoma School of Law, accused Thomas of sexual harassment when she worked for him at the EEOC. This was all the more shocking, if true, because Thomas, as chair of the EEOC, bore the primary responsibility for enforcing the nation's laws against sexual harassment. While the truth of this accusation was never determined, Thomas was confirmed by a narrow margin and Hill became a national heroine to many. The hearings, which showed the all male Senate Judiciary Committee hostilely interrogating Hill, helped revitalize the efforts of women to gain elective office.

thousand points of light President George Bush's metaphor, first used in his acceptance speech at the Republican Convention on August 18, 1988, for volunteerism and charity in American life. In his inaugural address of January 20, 1989, he further defined the "points" as "all the community organizations that are spread like stars throughout the nation doing good." Peggy Noonan, who wrote Bush's acceptance speech, said in her memoirs *What I Saw at the Revolution* (1990) that the "thousand points of light. . . became Bush's shorthand way of referring to the network of helping organizations throughout the country, and it became in some circles the object of derision, or at least of good-natured spoofing."

throw the rascals out An oft-heard campaign slogan of the party not in power. Sometimes all it really means is that it's time for a change of rascals. According to James R. Thompson, Governor of Illinois: "The policies of today are negative. It is not so much who you elect, it's who you throw out" (*Chicago Tribune Magazine*, July 26, 1981).

ticket The list of a particular party's candidates for a given election.

ticket balancing *See* BALANCED TICKET.

ticket, kangaroo One in which the second spot, for Vice President or lieutenant governor, is stronger than the first. The kangaroo is known for its strong hind legs and weak front legs.

ticket-punching A career strategy which calls for a military officer or civilian official to get all the appropriate assignments and training to qualify for the next promotion. Ticket-punchers are more interested in being able to say that they were in charge of something than what really happened to what they were charged with

ticket splitting Voting for candidates of differing political parties for various offices, as opposed to voting for all of the candidates of a given party (a straight ticket). Independents are most likely to split their tickets because they have no party loyalty. But even the party faithful split their tickets if provoked by unattractive candidates. To discourage voters from splitting their tickets, parties nominate someone to head the ticket (a candidate for President, governor, and so on) who might have sturdy COATTAILS and thus drag other members of the ticket along to victory. The last presidential coattail vote of any consequence was in 1964, when Lyndon

B. Johnson's landslide victory carried a large number of new Democratic members of the Congress into office. In recent presidential elections, about 60 percent of all voters have voted split tickets. While Republican Presidents Reagan and Bush won the White House in 1980, 1984, and 1988, their coattails were simply not sufficient to bring along a Republican Congress.

ticket, straight Voting for all of one party's candidates on a ballot.

title 1. The legal right to own something, such as a car or a house. **2.** A formal document proving such ownership. **3.** A section of a larger piece of legislation; for example, Title VII. **4.** The formal name of a bill. George F. Will wrote: "It is said that the titles of most bills in Congress are like the titles of Marx Brothers movies ('Duck Soup,' 'Animal Crackers'): they do not tell much about the contents" (*Newsweek*, October 3, 1977).

Title VII The backbone of the equal employment opportunity effort, part of the Civil Rights Act of 1964 as amended. Title VII prohibits employment discrimination because of race, color, religion, sex, or national origin and created the Equal Employment Opportunity Commission as its enforcement vehicle. The federal courts have relied heavily upon Title VII in mandating remedial action on the part of employers.

titular leader The nominal leader of a political party. In American politics, this phrase is generally reserved for defeated presidential candidates who remain the leader of their party, a leader in name only, until the party selects a new presidential nominee at its next national convention.

Tocqueville, Alexis de (1805–1859) The French historian who visited the United States in the early 1830s and went home to write *Democracy in America* (1835), a landmark description of American governance and a classic analysis of American political culture. According to Tocqueville, "The great advantage of the Americans is that they have arrived at a state of democracy without having to endure a democratic revolution; and that they are born equal instead of becoming so." While Tocqueville was the first to identify this notion of equality as the fundamental aspect in the development of American political culture, he also warned about the "tyranny of the majority," whereby minorities are forced into conformity by the "tyrannical" rule of the majority.

Tocqueville was quite taken with the American constitutional system, 40 years old when he saw it, and was particularly impressed with the political independence of the judiciary and their power of judicial review, which he considered a stabilizing influence comparable to the position of privilege enjoyed by European aristocracy. "Within these limits the power vested in the American courts of justice of pronouncing a statute to be unconstitutional forms one of the most powerful barriers that have ever been devised against the tyranny of political assemblies." And it was Tocqueville who was the first to note that "there is hardly a political question in the United States which sooner or later does not turn into a judicial one."

tokenism In the context of EQUAL EMPLOYMENT OPPORTUNITY, an insincere EEO effort by which a few minority group members are hired to satisfy government affirmative action mandates or the demands of pressure groups.

Tonkin Gulf Resolutions *See* GULF OF TONKIN RESOLUTION.

tort Legal harm done to another person that can be the cause of a civil court suit. For example, libel can be a tort.

totalitarianism A governing system in which a ruling elite holds all power and controls all aspects of society. No opposition is allowed, and power is maintained by internal terror and secret police. Nazi Germany and the Soviet Union under Stalin are two examples of totalitarian states. *Compare to* AUTHORITARIANISM; FASCISM; MARXISM.

Tower Commission The President's Special Review Board established by President Ronald Reagan in the fall of 1986 to investigate the IRAN-CONTRA AFFAIR and the operations of the National Security Council. The commission, named for its chairman, John G. Tower, former U.S. Senator from Texas, had two other members: Edmund S. Muskie, former U.S. senator from Maine and former secretary of State; and Brent Scowcroft, national security adviser to President Gerald Ford. The commission's 1987 report found that President Reagan had been "disengaged" and "did not seem to be aware" of the White House foreign policy process; that the National Security Council had indeed arranged to trade arms for hostages with Iran and sought to use funds from the arms sale to illegally aid the CONTRAS in Nicaragua; and that certain members of the White House staff sought to cover up these facts as the Iran-contra affair evolved. The most immediate effects of the report was the resignation of Donald Regan, the President's chief of staff, and his replacement by Howard Baker, former U.S. senator from Tennessee.

town **1.** An urban entity, with powers less than those possessed by cities. The powers of towns are strictly controlled by state statutes. **2.** The New England town combines the role of both city and county. It usually contains one or more urban areas plus surrounding rural areas.

town meeting **1.** A method of self-government, suitable for only the smallest jurisdictions, where the entire citizenry meets to decide local public policy. The town meeting is still the governing body for 88 percent of all New England municipalities. According to Robert Preer—in "Town Meetings Don't Work" (*The Washington Post*, June 13, 1986)—town meetings today are most likely to be controlled by special interests and the town's bureaucracy. Attendance is slight. Even though quorums are set at only 1 or 2 percent of registered voters, meetings are often canceled because of the lack of a quorum. "Raises and promotions pass with ease because meetings are so often packed with employees and their families and friends." Preer concludes that the modern town meeting "is a microcosm of national politics. In both cases, power has shifted from an apathetic and unorganized public to special interests, the mass media, and a bureaucratic-technocratic elite."

2. A common technique for legislators to keep in touch with their constituents; various "town meetings" are scheduled at town halls, high schools, or other public halls so that the legislator can report to constituents and answer their questions.

township A subdivision of a county traditionally having six miles on each side and varying in importance as a unit of government in the 16 states that have them. Townships in the Midwest are sometimes referred to as congressional townships because public land surveys in the last century initially labeled them thus on maps authorized by the Congress.

transfer payments Payments by a government made to individuals who provide no goods or services in return. All of the social welfare programs at all levels of government that provide subsistence income support are transfer payment programs. They are often referred to as ENTITLEMENT PROGRAMS because one becomes entitled to transfer payments if one meets criteria established by the authorizing legislation.

transition rule The euphemism for a TAX LOOPHOLE for special interests retained in the Tax Reform Act of 1986.

Transportation, U.S. Department of (DOT) The cabinet-level Washington-based department established in 1966 that manages the nation's overall transportation policy. Under its umbrella are eight administrations, whose jurisdictions include highway planning, development, and construction; urban mass transit; railroads; aviation; and the safety of waterways, ports, highways, and oil and gas pipelines. In peacetime, the U.S. Coast Guard is part of the DOT.

treason Disloyalty as defined by Article III, Section 3 of the U.S. Constitution. Treason is the only crime defined by the Constitution. (It "shall consist only in levying War against them [the United States], or in adhering to their enemies, giving them aid and comfort. No person shall be convicted of treason unless on the testimony of two witnesses to the same overt act, or on confession in open court.") The precise description of this offense reflects an awareness that persons holding unpopular views might be branded as traitors. Recent experience in other countries with prosecutions for conduct loosely labeled as treason confirms the wisdom of the authors of the Constitution in expressly stating what constitutes this crime and how it shall be proved.

treason, high What the modern world considers TREASON. It was once distinguished from petit, or small, treason, which was the killing of someone to whom one owed obedience, such as a husband or overlord. Today, acts of petit treason are treated as any other murder.

treasurer 1. An officer in charge of an organization's money; but not necessarily the same person making its financial decisions. **2.** The state official responsible for the safeguarding of public funds and payment of public debts. Most state treasurers are elected and are responsible for tax collection.

Treasurer of the United States The federal official who is responsible for formally taking in and paying out public moneys. This is not a policymaking position and, as federal appointments go, is relatively unimportant.

Treasury, U.S. Department of the One of the first cabinet-level departments of the United States. Created in 1789, the Department of the Treasury formulates and recommends financial, tax, and fiscal policies; serves as financial agent for the U.S. government; manufactures coins and currency; and enforces related laws. Its agencies include the Customs Service, the Bureau of Engraving and Printing, the Internal Revenue Service, the U.S. Mint, and the Secret Service.

treaty A formal international agreement between two or more sovereign states that establishes rights as well as obligations for the parties. In the United States, treaties, once they have been negotiated with foreign states, in essence become executive branch proposals that, to take effect, must be submitted to the Senate for approval by two thirds of the senators present. Before acting on such foreign policy matters, senators usually send them to committee for scrutiny. Treaties are read and debated in the Senate, much like legislative proposals, but are rarely amended. After approval by the Senate, they must be ratified by the President. A ratified treaty binds the states as well as the federal government. Indeed, the Supreme Court held in *Missouri v Holland* (1920) that a treaty may interfere with some of the rights reserved to the states by the Tenth Amendment.

But while a President cannot make a treaty without the Senate, can one be abrogated without their approval? This issue arose when President Jimmy Carter recognized the People's Republic of China effective January 1, 1979, and withdrew recognition from Taiwan effective the same date. Commensurate with this action, Carter announced that the 1955 National Defense Treaty with the Nationalist Chinese government of Taiwan would terminate on January 1, 1980, in accordance with the treaty's proviso permitting termination by either party with one year's notice. Carter obviously assumed that there existed presidential authority to abrogate treaties. Senator Barry Goldwater did not, and he filed an appeal with the federal district court that granted Goldwater and his colleagues from the Congress standing to sue. The Court then ruled President Carter's abrogation of the treaty unconstitutional. Eventually, in *Goldwater v Carter* (1979), the Supreme Court ordered, without hearing argument, that the case be dismissed; thus, upholding the President's power to terminate treaties.

trial The examination in a court of the issues of fact and law in a case for the purpose of reaching a judgment. There are basically two kinds of trials: criminal, in which the state seeks to punish a wrongdoer; and civil, in which private citizens take legal action against other citizens (or sometimes governments). While all citizens have the right to take someone to court, according to Judge Shirley M. Hufstedler of the U.S. Court of Appeals: "A regular civil trial today, with or without a jury, is beyond the economic reach of all except the rich, the nearly rich, or the person seriously injured by a well-insured defendant" (*The New York Times*, February 10, 1974).

trial balloon A deliberate LEAK of a potential policy to see what public response will be. The term comes from the meteorological practice of sending up a balloon to test weather conditions. If public response is hostile, the new policy proposal can be quietly dropped (or deflated).

trial, bench *See* TRIAL, NONJURY.

trial de novo The Latin term meaning a "new trial."

trial, jury A trial in which a JURY, a panel of community members, determines the issue of facts in a case.

trial, nonjury A trial in which a judge determines the issues of fact and law in a case. Because no jury is used, those involved must waive any constitutionally or statutory rights to a jury trial. This is the same as a *judge trial*, a *bench trial*, and a *court trial*.

trial, political 1. A highly publicized trial in which standards of fair play and due process are not followed and the verdict is predetermined by the state. **2.** A highly publicized trial in which the defendants and their supporters assert that they are being brought to trial because of their political views, even though all procedural safeguards and due processes have been allowed. **3.** A trial in which defendants specifically seek to generate community support for an issue they espouse.

trial, public The Sixth Amendment right of a defendant "in all criminal prosecutions" to "enjoy. . . a speedy and public trial." The Supreme Court has ruled in *Richmond Newspapers v Virginia* (1980) that "absent an overriding interest criminal trials had to be open to the public and the press."

trial, speedy A prompt trial, as guaranteed by the Sixth Amendment provision that "in all criminal prosecutions, the accused shall enjoy the right to a speedy and public trial." Although the federal constitution and the constitutions of almost all the states provide that the accused shall enjoy the right to a speedy trial, the precise requirements are not clear. Most states and the federal government (Speedy Trial Act of 1974) have enacted statutes setting forth the time within which a defendant must be tried following the date of arrest, detention, and first appearance or the filing of charges in court. If the accused is not brought to trial within the specified period, the case is dismissed. Most statutes also provide a method for computing excludable delay—delay not counted for the purposes of determining if a trial is speedy. Examples of excludable delay include other proceedings concerning the defendant, such as a hearing on mental competency to stand trial, pending trials on other charges, probation or parole revocation hearings, continuances granted at the request of the defendant, and the absconding of the defendant. The speedy trial provision of the Sixth Amendment was made applicable to the states in *Klopfer v North Carolina* (1967).

trickle-down theory 1. A basis for government policies that seeks to benefit the wealthy in hopes that prosperity, in turn, will trickle down to the middle and lower economic classes. The term was first coined by humorist Will Rogers (1879–1935), when he analyzed some of the depression remedies of the Herbert Hoover Administration and noted that "the money was all appropriated for the top in the hopes it would trickle down to the needy." However, this sentiment was expressed by Congressman and orator William Jennings Bryan, in his famous "Cross of Gold" speech at the Democratic National Convention in Chicago, July 8, 1896: "There are those who believe that if you will only legislate to make the well-to-do prosperous, their prosperity will leak through on those below. The Democratic idea, however, has been that if you make the masses prosperous, their prosperity will find its way up through every class which rests upon them." **2.** The belief that housing is upgraded for all groups as they move into housing left vacant by other groups progressing up the economic ladder. **3.** The notion that the party that wins the presidency will eventually have that success "trickle down" to lower offices; that, as columnist George Will put it: "Repeated Republican successes in presidential contests cannot be hermetically sealed at that level" (*The New Season*, 1988).

true believer A strongly committed IDEOLOGUE; someone whose political beliefs are not likely to be influenced by normal political campaign efforts.

Truman, David B. (1913–   ) A political scientist and one of the most influential interest group theorists. Truman's principal work, *The Governmental Process* (1951), views group interaction as the real determinant of public policy and as the proper focal point of study. Truman defines the interest group as "a shared attitude group that makes certain claims upon other groups in the society. If and when it makes its claims through or upon any of the institutions of government, it becomes a public interest group." Group pressure is assured through the establishment of lines of access and influence. Truman notes that the administrative process provides a multitude of points of access, comparable to those of the legislature. What Truman provides for group theory is a complete description and analysis of how groups interact, function, and influence the overall political system. Two types of groups are identified by Truman: existing groups and potential groups. The potential group is constituted by people who have common values and attitudes but do not yet see their interests being threatened. Once they do, Truman argues, they form a group to protect their interests. *See also* INTEREST GROUP THEORY.

Truman Doctrine The policy of the Harry S Truman administration of giving military and economic aid to those countries (Greece and Turkey, specifically) seeking to resist "totalitarian aggression." This doctrine, which was presented by President Truman in 1947 in his address to a joint session of the Congress in support of the Greek-Turkish aid bill, became a cornerstone of the U.S. policy of CONTAINMENT. According to defense analysts James Chace and Caleb Carr, *America Invulnerable* (1988): "It was [Dean] Acheson who was primarily the author of the doctrine that would bear Truman's name, filling much the same role that John Quincy Adams had played for James Monroe in 1823—and producing the most important American foreign policy declaration since that same Monroe Doctrine." *Compare to* NIXON DOCTRINE.

Truman, Harry S (1884–1972) The President of the United States (1945–1953) who (as Vice President) became President upon the death of Franklin D. Roosevelt. It was Truman who made the decision to drop the first atomic bomb on Japan to quickly end World War II, whose foreign policy of communist CONTAINMENT is still the cornerstone of American foreign policy, and whose MARSHALL PLAN led to the economic recovery of Western Europe after World War II.

Truman started political life as part of the (Thomas J.) Pendergast political machine of Kansas City, Missouri. The machine arranged his appointment and then election to various county posts. While the machine sent him to the U.S. Senate in 1934, Truman's personal integrity remained unquestioned. Truman first gained national prominence during the early part of World War II, when he saved the federal government millions of dollars as chairman of a Senate watchdog committee on defense spending—the "Truman committee." This went far in making him acceptable to President Franklin D. Roosevelt as a vice presidential running mate in 1944. A true apostle of the NEW DEAL, he tried with varying success to expand and sustain it with his own FAIR DEAL. His greatest domestic triumph was his 1948 election as President in his own right. In spite of the fact that all the pollsters and political pundits predicted he would certainly lose to Thomas E. Dewey, the Governor of New York, Truman won decisively.

trust A group of companies that work together to maintain an effective monopoly; this inhibits competition—thus, raising prices for consumers and profits for the trusts. *See also* ANTITRUST LAWS.

trust funds Funds collected and used by the federal government for carrying out specific purposes and programs according to terms of a trust agreement or statute, such as the social security and the unemployment trust funds. Trust funds are administered by the government in a fiduciary capacity and are not available for the general purposes of the government. Trust fund receipts that are not anticipated to be used in the immediate future are generally invested in interest-bearing government securities and earn interest for the trust fund. A special category of trust funds called trust revolving funds is used to carry out a cycle of business-type operations, such as with the Federal Deposit Insurance Corporation.

trustee 1. A person who holds property for another. **2.** The role that elected representatives adopt when they vote according to their conscience and best judgment, rather than according to the narrow interests of their immediate constituents. Senator Bill Bradley sees this as his role: "For a member of Congress, the question is this: Do you believe your role is to represent the general interest, or is it your job to represent narrower interests—this one, that one—and put together a quilt of service? I believe a legislator's job is to represent the general interest" (*The New York Times*, May 9, 1986). *Compare to* BURKE, EDMUND; POLITICO.

truth squad **1.** A group of opposition party members who follow a candidate to tell their version of the truth about the candidate's campaign statements. The main purpose of a truth squad is to make an opposing candidate seem to be a liar. **2.** An interest group that makes a point of correcting the inaccurate political campaign rhetoric of wayward, loose-with-the-truth candidates. For example, *Newsweek* (April 16, 1990) has reported that the Sierra Club has developed a policy of telling voters when candidates exaggerate their pro-environment voting records.

turnout The number of voters who actually vote, compared to the number of voters eligible to vote. Turnout is a significant indicator of voter apathy, though whether it also indicates voter ALIENATION is hotly debated. Certainly turnout varies directly with socioeconomic status. A low turnout tends to favor Republicans, because Republicans are more likely to vote in any case. As a group, they have many of the attributes of conscientious voters—being older, more formally educated, and wealthier than Democrats. A large turnout tends to favor Democrats simply because they are the majority party. Theoretically, then, they should almost always win. But they don't because of alienation from the political system, apathy (which is an indication of acquiescence with the status quo), or institutional blocks, such as voter registration (*see* REGISTRATION, VOTER), and the difficulties of absentee ballots. The highest turnouts are almost always for presidential elections. But even then, the United States has among the lowest turnouts in the western world. According to political analyst Richard M. Scammon: "The idea that high voter turnout necessarily means good government and low turnout means bad government is nonsense. It's something that we've been fed in high-school civics class. We've salivated over this thing like a Pavlovian dog, and it just isn't true. The Soviet Union, Hitler's Germany, Italy under Mussolini—all had very high participation, but not many people would hold them up as examples to be emulated. What it boils down to is that freedom means the freedom not to vote, as well as the right to vote" (*U.S. News & World Report*, October 25, 1976).

TVA *See* TENNESSEE VALLEY AUTHORITY.

Twelfth Amendment The 1804 amendment to the U.S. Constitution that required electors to vote separately for President and Vice President. This was necessitated by the development of a national party system; something not anticipated by the framers. *See* ELECTORAL COLLEGE.

Twentieth Amendment Commonly known as the LAME DUCK AMENDMENT, and ratified in 1933, the Constitutional amendment that provided new starting dates for the terms of the U.S. President, senators, and representatives.

Twenty-Fifth Amendment The 1967 amendment to the U.S. Constitution that provides for the Vice President to become the acting President in the event that the President "is unable to discharge the powers and duties of his office." In outlining the duties and functions of the President, the framers of the Constitution included provisions regarding the continuity of the executive. Article II, Section I reads in part: "In case of the removal of the President from office, or of his death, resignation, or inability to discharge the powers and duties of the said office, the same shall devolve on the Vice President." In several respects, this provision of the Constitution is unclear, and eventually it presented a number of questions insufficiently answered by the document. For example, when President William Henry Harrison died in 1841, Vice President John Tyler was left unsure whether he should serve as an "acting" or "official" President of the United States. Although Tyler did ultimately take the oath of office as President, the decision to do so by no means met with unanimous approval. The controversy that ensued was, however, finally quieted when both houses of the Congress voted to recognize Tyler as the official President of the United States. The action taken by Tyler established the precedent followed by eight future Vice Presidents faced with similar circumstances: Millard Fillmore, Andrew Johnson, Chester Arthur, Theodore Roosevelt, Calvin Coolidge, Harry S Truman, Lyndon Johnson, and Gerald Ford—each of whom became President of the United States through succession.

Another uncertainty arose about presidential succession in cases when a President was unable to "discharge the powers and duties" of his office. Again, the Constitution provided no clear answer to the problem. In three instances in American history the President was considered unable to perform his duties. In all three cases, largely because of uncertainty over correct procedure, the Vice President did not assume the incapacitated President's responsibilities.

The first occasion arose in 1881, when President James Garfield fell victim to an assassin's bullet. Garfield lingered for nearly 80 days, during which he was able to perform only one official act—the signing of an extradition paper. In 1919, President Woodrow Wilson suffered a severe stroke, leaving him largely disabled for the rest of his term. Finally, at least three times during his administration, President Dwight D. Eisenhower was considered unable to perform as President because of poor health. He chose to solve the problem by means of an informal working agreement with Vice President Richard M. Nixon, rather than an amendment to the Constitution. The Twenty-Fifth Amendment provides a formal process for such situations.

The assassination of President John F. Kennedy and the succession of Vice President Lyndon B. Johnson in 1963 reminded the nation of yet another gap in the succession clause—the lack of a mechanism for choosing a Vice President when the previous Vice President succeeds to the presidency. The framers foresaw the need to have a qualified Vice President in office should the President die, but they neglected to establish a procedure whereby a vice presidential vacancy could be filled. The Twenty-Fifth Amendment provides such a process. This procedure was first used in 1973, when President Richard M. Nixon nominated Gerald Ford to be Vice President after Spiro Agnew resigned in disgrace. It was next (and last) used in 1974, when Ford nominated Nelson Rockefeller to be his Vice President. This was the only time when both the offices of President and Vice President were held by people who had not been elected to either one. *See also* PRESIDENTIAL SUCCESSION.

Twenty-First Amendment The 1933 amendment to the U.S. Constitution that repealed the Eighteenth Amendment and prohibition.

Twenty-Fourth Amendment The 1964 amendment to the U.S. Constitution that prohibits the use of POLL TAXES by states.

Twenty-Second Amendment The 1951 amendment to the U.S. Constitution that provides that no one person can be elected to the office of President more than twice. This was enacted to prevent any subsequent President from repeating Franklin D. Roosevelt's unparalleled record of being elected President four times (in 1932, 1936, 1940, and 1944).

Beginning with George Washington, the tradition of a two-term presidency was established. Thomas Jefferson followed Washington's precedent, as did succeeding Presidents—until Franklin D. Roosevelt. Although the two-term tradition was regarded as an unwritten law prior to Roosevelt's extended administration, numerous attempts had been made throughout America's history to secure it through an amendment to the Constitution. It was not until the Eightieth Congress that an amendment to limit the President to two terms was finally successful. The Congress, convening in 1946, was the first to have a Republican majority since 1928. During the previous years, dominated by the Roosevelt administration, the Republicans had been unable to halt the President and his New Deal legislation. During the debates over the Twenty-Second Amendment, the Republicans argued that Roosevelt had accumulated inappropriate power due to his long tenure as President. Ironically, when the Republicans finally had a President popular enough to be able to possibly get elected for a third term, Ronald Reagan, many, including Reagan, expressed regret over the Twenty-Second Amendment. Historian Daniel J. Boorstin has said that this amendment "was a very short-sighted and, I think, malicious Constitutional amendment. . . . the notion that it is desirable to have a President who can give his full attention to the 'Presidency' and not worry about re-election is quite a mistake. What we want is a President who will be thinking about the prospects of re-election and will wonder what reaction the public will have to what he's doing as President. That's what we mean by representative government" (*The Washington Post*, July 21, 1973).

Twenty-Seventh Amendment The 1992 amendment to the U.S. Constitu-

tion which bars members of Congress from voting themselves any pay raises that would take effect before the next congressional election. Originally proposed by JAMES MADISON more than 200 years ago, it only became law in 1992 when Michigan became the 38th state to ratify it.

Twenty-Sixth Amendment The 1971 amendment to the U.S. Constitution that lowered the voting age to 18 years. At the time, there was great concern about the impact of the youth vote; but young voters are far less likely to vote than those who are older. Communications theorist Marshall McLuhan was correct when he said in *Understanding Media* (1964): "American youth attributes much more importance to arriving at driver's license age than at voting age."

Twenty-Third Amendment The 1961 amendment to the U.S. Constitution that allots presidential electors to the District of Columbia. This allowed the people who lived in the same city as the President to vote for (or against) presidential candidates in national elections. When the Twenty-Third Amendment was proposed in the Congress, the District of Columbia had over 800,000 residents—a population greater than 13 of the states. Those who lived in the nation's capital had all the obligations of citizenship, including payment of federal and local taxes and service in the armed forces, yet they were prevented from voting in national elections, since the Constitution reserved that privilege to residents of the states. Article II, Section 1 of the Constitution states that only "states" are eligible to appoint electors. The Twenty-Third Amendment changed that.

two congresses *See* CONGRESS, MEMBER OF.

two-party system The political system in the United States, which, because of electoral provisions and cultural traditions, makes it almost impossible for a significant THIRD PARTY to emerge. Because most candidates for public office are chosen on the basis of single-member districts with plurality elections, where only one party's candidate can win, the party that comes in second can assert that it is the reasonable alternative. Third-party voters are made to feel that their vote is wasted. Each major party also has distinctive sectional strength; the second party, accordingly, is never wiped out. In addition, in spite of an abundance of rhetoric to the contrary, the United States is a society without great ideological disagreements. Political feeling tends toward the center. Consequently, third parties, which tend to be started by fringe groups, have little chance to attract significant numbers of voters. *Compare to* DUVERGER'S LAW.

Two Party System, Toward a More Responsible A 1950 report by the Committee on Political Parties of the American Political Science Association (published in *American Political Science Review*, Vol. 44, supplement, September 1950) that called on the major American political parties to be "more responsible" in the sense of offering the public clear alternatives by adopting the kind of party discipline found in parliamentary systems. In this case, the party voted in would have a clear mandate to install its policies and, if the voters did not like these, they would know exactly who to vote out in the next election. This strong call to be more ideological fell on infertile intellectual ground. While this responsible party model has been much talked about by political scientists, politicians have all but ignored it. Nonetheless, the national government sometimes functions in the responsible party mode; particularly good examples would be the Eighty-Ninth Congress (with Lyndon B. Johnson as President) and the Ninety-Seventh Congress (with Ronald Reagan as President).

two presidencies *See* PRESIDENCIES, TWO.

Tyler, John (1790–1862) President of the United States from 1841 to 1845. Elected Vice President on a Whig ticket with William Henry Harrison ("Old Tippecanoe"), he was the Tyler in the 1840 slogan "Tippecanoe and Tyler Too." When Harrison died less than a month after his inauguration, Tyler became the first Vice President to succeed to the presidency. His administration accomplished little save for the annexation of Texas. Tyler retired from public life in 1845 until 1861 when, as a Virginian, he endorsed secession and was elected to the Confederate Congress. Historians have not thought highly of him. For example, Theodore Roosevelt wrote in *Thomas Hart Benton* (1897) that Tyler "has been called a mediocre man; but this is unwarranted flattery. He was a politician of monumental littleness."

tyranny 1. Oppressive or nonrepresentative government. James Madison defined tyranny in *The Federalist* No. 47 (1788): "The accumulation of all power, legislative, executive, and judiciary, in the same hands, whether of one, a few, or many, and whether hereditary, self-appointed, or elective, may justly be pronounced the very definition of tyranny." During the American Revolution THOMAS PAINE wrote in *The American Crisis* (1776) that: "Tyranny, like hell, is not easily conquered; yet we have this consolation with us, that the harder the conflict, the more glorious the triumph. What we obtain too cheap, we esteem too lightly: it is dearness only that gives every thing its value." **2.** Anarchy. William Pitt, Earl of Chatham, in a famous speech in the House of Lords, January 9, 1770, said: "Where law ends, tyranny begins." JOHN LOCKE said the same in his *Second Treatise of Government* (1690). **3.** Taxation without representation. One of the slogans of the American Revolution, usually attributed to Boston attorney James Otis (1725–1783), was that "Taxation without representation is tyranny."

tyranny of the majority *See* TOCQUEVILLE, ALEXIS DE.

U

umbrella groups Lobbying organizations that speak for a large number of disparate interests. Examples include the U.S. Chamber of Commerce, the National Association of Manufacturers, and the AFL-CIO.

umbrella party An oft-used description of the major American political parties, because they unite a large variety of ideologies and interests under one overarching umbrella, the party itself. Because of this, they are sometimes also described as *catchall parties*.

unalienable rights *See* INALIENABLE RIGHTS.

unanimous consent A request of a legislative body made by a member that the entire body agree to a usually noncontroversial motion "without objection." This is a frequently used time-saving measure that avoids voting on minor procedural issues. For example, it is common for a U.S. senator to ask unanimous consent to insert a statement in the *Congressional Record*.

Uncle Sam The mythical old man who personifies the U.S. government. The name is traced back to the Troy, New York *Post* of September 7, 1813. Legend has it that Samuel Wilson (1766–1854), a government inspector of Army supplies during the War of 1812, was given "Uncle Sam" as a nickname. Nevertheless, it was political cartoonist Thomas Nast who popularized the modern version of an Uncle Sam with a top hat, frock coat, and striped trousers. The most famous Uncle Sam is James Montgomery Flagg's World War I "I Want You" recruiting poster.

underclass 1. That portion of the American population mired, from generation to generation, in a cycle of poverty. **2.** A CODE WORD for inner-city blacks.

underdog A candidate for elective office who is not leading in the polls; a candidate who starts a political campaign with a decided disadvantage; an apparent loser. Because underdogs often come from behind and win, candidates are seldom ashamed to admit that they are underdogs when it is obvious; besides, it might get them some sympathy votes. *Compare to* FRONT RUNNER.

underground 1. A covert unconventional warfare organization established to operate in areas generally controlled by the enemy. **2.** Descriptive of political events and publications that are neither secret nor unknown to a public, but which are of such limited interest or low circulation that they are almost invisible to the general public. Typically, an "underground" press thrives in a large university community.

underground economy Economic activity that evades tax obligations; work done "off the books," for cash only. Examples of underground economic activity include a medical doctor accepting cash from a patient and not recording the payment for income tax purposes; a carpenter doing work for a small business and accepting an in-kind payment, whose value is not recorded for income tax purposes; and, of course, traditional criminal activity. Underground in this context does not necessarily mean secret—except to the Internal Revenue Service.

unicameral *See* BICAMERAL LEGISLATURE.

unincorporated area An urban area that has not become a municipality and has no local government structure of its own other than its county.

union 1. A worker's organization formed to advocate the needs of its members—wages, working conditions, and benefits—through collective bargaining. **2.** The United States—which is a union of its component states. **3.** A single-purpose international organization; for example, a customs union. **4.** The merging of two or more countries to form a single new one. **5.** That part of a national flag that signifies the union of two or more states; thus, the blue part of the American flag on which are located the 50 white stars representing the 50 states in the union.

United Nations 1. The World War II allies, led by the United States and the United Kingdom, who defeated the Axis powers of Germany, Japan, and Italy. The phrase "united nations" was devised by President Franklin D. Roosevelt and was first used in the Declaration of United Nations on January 1, 1942. **2.** The international peacekeeping agency that replaced the League of Nations. The U.N. charter, drawn up at a conference in San Francisco, was signed on June 25, 1945, by 50 nations; the United Nations formally came into existence on October 24, 1945, when a majority of the signatory nations had ratified the charter. By the 1980s, it had three times the members it had when it started. The United Nations' business is conducted primarily through its GENERAL ASSEMBLY and SECURITY COUNCIL. The United Nations is funded by assessments on its member states by means of an elaborate formula; the United States annually contributes about one third of the U.N.'s budget. Many U.N. activities are carried out by its specialized agencies, such as the International Atomic Energy Agency (founded in 1957), the International Civil Aviation Organization (founded in 1947), the International Labor Organization (founded in 1946), and the World Health Organization (founded in 1948).

United States-Canada Free Trade Agreement of 1988 The bilateral treaty designed to eliminate all tariffs between the two countries by 1998. While many trade issues remain unresolved, the agreement creates mechanisms for resolving them. *Compare to* NORTH AMERICAN FREE TRADE AGREEMENT.

United States Civil Service Commission The central personnel agency of the United States from 1883 through 1978. It was abolished by the CIVIL SERVICE REFORM ACT OF 1978. *See also* MERIT SYSTEM PROTECTION BOARD; OFFICE OF PERSONNEL MANAGEMENT.

United States Code A consolidation and codification of the general and

permanent laws of the United States arranged by subject under 50 titles, the first six dealing with general or political subjects, and the other 44 alphabetically arranged from agriculture to war and national defense. The code is now revised every six years and a supplement is published after each session of the Congress.

United States Conference of Mayors (USCM) A Washington-based organization of city governments founded in 1933. It is a national forum through which this country's larger cities express their concerns and actively work to meet U.S. urban needs. By limiting membership and participation to the 750 cities with populations over 30,000 and by concentrating on questions of federal-city relations, the conference seeks to become a focus for urban political leadership. *See also* PUBLIC INTEREST GROUPS.

United States Court of Appeals *See* COURT OF APPEALS.

United States District Court *See* DISTRICT COURT.

United States Government Manual An annual publication of the federal government that provides detailed information on all agencies of the executive, legislative, and judicial branches of government. The *Manual*, available from the Government Printing Office, also includes the names of major federal officeholders.

United States International Trade Commission *See* INTERNATIONAL TRADE COMMISSION, UNITED STATES.

United States Reports The official record of cases decided by the Supreme Court. In citations, *United States Reports* is abbreviated to U.S. For example, the legal citation for the case of *Pickering v Board of Education* is 391 U.S. 563 (1968). This means that the case will be found on page 563 of volume 391 of the *United States Reports* and that it was decided in 1968. Prior to 1882, the *Reports* used the names of the court reporters. For example, the citation for *Marbury v Madison* is 1 Cranch 137 (1803). Cranch was the reporter from 1801 to 1815. *Compare to* L. ED.

United States Statutes at Large Bound volumes issued annually containing all public and private laws and concurrent resolutions enacted during a session of the Congress, reorganization plans, proposed and ratified amendments to the Constitution, and presidential proclamations.

United States Tariff Commission *See* INTERNATIONAL TRADE COMMISSION, UNITED STATES.

United States Trade Representative (USTR) A cabinet-level official with the rank of ambassador who is the President's principal advisor on international trade and commodity policies. The USTR also has lead responsibility for the conduct of all international trade negotiations.

United States v Curtiss-Wright Export Corporation (1936) The Supreme Court case defining the President's constitutional position in foreign affairs. In 1934 the Congress adopted a joint resolution authorizing the President by proclamation to prohibit the sale (within the United States) of arms to some South American nations. The President issued such a proclamation.

Curtiss-Wright attacked such constraint on its business on the grounds that the joint resolution constituted an unconstitutional delegation of legislative authority to the President. The Supreme Court upheld the resolution and proclamation on the grounds that the Constitution created the "very delicate, plenary and exclusive power of the President as the sole organ of the federal government in the field of international relations" and that, in the international sphere, the President must be accorded "a degree of discretion and freedom from statutory restriction which would not be admissible were domestic affairs alone involved."

United States v Darby Lumber (1941) The Supreme Court case that upheld the Fair Labor Standards Act of 1938, which established minimum wages and maximum hours for workers in businesses engaged in, or producing goods for, interstate commerce.

United States v Eichman See FLAG.

United States v Nixon (1974) The Supreme Court case dealing with President Richard M. Nixon's claim that the Constitution provided the President with an absolute and unreviewable EXECUTIVE PRIVILEGE; that is, the right not to respond to a subpoena in connection with a judicial trial. The court held that "neither the doctrine of separation of powers, nor the need for confidentiality of high-level communications, without more, can sustain an absolute, unqualified, presidential immunity from judicial process under all circumstances." The Court allowed there was a limited executive privilege that might pertain in the areas of military, diplomatic, or security affairs, and where confidentiality was related to the President's ability to carry out his constitutional mandates. This was the decision which, in effect, forced Nixon to resign as President.

unit rule The requirement that state delegations to a national nominating convention must cast all of their votes for the issue or candidate that has the majority of the votes of the state delegates. Since 1972, both major political parties have put severe restrictions on the use of the unit rule.

upper house That branch of a BICAMERAL LEGISLATURE that tends, in contrast with the *lower* house, to be both less representative of and less responsive to the public. (This is because upper houses have fewer members and longer terms of office than lower-house members.) The term comes from the fact that at one time many European parliaments had a house that represented the upper class, the aristocracy, and a "lower" house that represented the people.

urban enterprise zone See ENTERPRISE ZONE.

urban homesteading A local program that gives a family a substandard home in a distressed urban area on condition that the structure be renovated and lived in by that family. Sometimes these programs provide for low-interest home improvement loans or charge token amounts for the homes.

Urban League See NATIONAL URBAN LEAGUE.

urban planning   The formal process of guiding the physical and social development of cities and their regions. While urban planning is first of all a highly technical process, it is also highly politicized because the various community interests are always ready to fight for their version of beneficial change. *See also* PLANNING.

urban renewal   The national program for city redevelopment, started in 1949 to rejuvenate urban areas through large-scale physical projects. Originally a loan program primarily for housing, it was quickly transformed by political pressures into a grant program for redoing large sections of central business districts or other commercial areas. It has been severely criticized for its uprooting of communities, especially black neighborhoods, and replacing them with commercial developments. The Housing and Community Development Act of 1974 put urban renewal, the MODEL CITIES program, and a variety of other categorical urban development programs under the Community Development Block Grant program administered by the Department of Housing and Urban Development.

U.S.   *See* UNITED STATES REPORTS.

U.S.C.   *See* UNITED STATES CODE.

USDA   See agriculture, u.s. department of.

user changes   Specific sums, also known as *user fees,* that consumers of a government service pay to receive that service. For example, a homeowner's water bill, if based upon usage, would be a user charge. Other examples include road and bridge tolls, and charges to use public swimming pools.

utilitarianism   The political philosophy which holds that it is the ethical duty of a government to do the greatest good for the greatest numbers. jeremy bentham is considered the preeminent utilitarian philosopher. However, Thomas Jefferson nicely summed up the principles of utilitarianism in a March 22, 1812 letter to F.A. van der Kemp: "The only orthodox object of the institution of government is to secure the greatest degree of happiness possible to the general mass of those associated under it."

utopia   1. The Greek word meaning "nowhere." **2.** A model of a society that meets the needs of all its citizens as they perceive those needs; in their terms, the perfect society. **3.** A literary form that posits a carefully designed polity that will, by its character, raise contrasts with reality. While conceptions of ideal societies go back to ancient times, it was English cleric Sir Thomas More's 1516 book, *Utopia,* that gave the concept its modern name.

V

VA *See* VETERANS AFFAIRS.

Van Buren, Martin (1782–1862) The President of the United States from 1837 to 1841. As governor of New York he perfected the modern POLITICAL MACHINE known as the Albany Regency. He threw his machine behind the candidacy of Andrew Jackson in 1828 and was rewarded with the post of secretary of State (1829–1831). When JOHN C. CALHOUN resigned as Jackson's Vice President, Van Buren replaced him for Jackson's second term (1833–1837). As heir apparent to Jackson, he won the presidency in his own right in 1836. A severe economic decline and an unpopular war against the Seminole Indians in Florida caused him to lose his bid for re-election in 1840.

veep A slang term for Vice President.

velcroid A person at a political reception who attaches him or herself (like velcro) to a candidate—and can only be pulled away with difficulty.

venire facias A Latin term for "you should cause to come"; the WRIT that orders a sheriff to assemble a jury.

venireman A member of a jury.

venue 1. The locality in which a criminal trial takes place. **2.** The locality where a crime occurred. *Compare to* CHANGE OF VENUE.

Veterans Affairs, Department of (VA) The federal agency, created in 1930, that administers benefits for former members of the military and their dependents. In 1988 the Veterans Administration was elevated to cabinet status with a name change to Department of Veterans Affairs.

veterans' benefits Any government advantages available to those who served in the armed forces of the United States that are not available to citizens who did not serve. Veterans' benefits may include government-supplied health care, advantageous home mortgage terms, and pensions.

veterans' preference The concept that dates from 1865, when the Congress, toward the end of the Civil War, affirmed that "persons honorably discharged from the military or naval service by reason of disability resulting from wounds or sickness incurred in the line of duty, shall be preferred for appointments to civil offices, provided they are found to possess the business capacity necessary for the proper discharge of the duties of such offices." The 1865 law was superseded in 1919, when preference was extended to all "honorably discharged" veterans, their widows, and wives of disabled veterans. The Veterans' Preference Act of 1944 expanded the scope of veterans' preference by providing for a five-point bonus on federal examination scores for all honorably separated veterans (except for those with a service-connected disability, who are entitled to a 10-point bonus).

Veterans also received other advantages in federal employment, such as protections against arbitrary dismissal and preference in the event of a reduction in force.

All states and many other jurisdictions have veterans' preference laws of varying intensity. New Jersey, an extreme example, offers veterans absolute preference; if a veteran passes an entrance examination, he or she must be hired (no matter what the score) before nonveterans can be hired. Veterans competing with each other are rank-ordered, and all disabled veterans receive preference over other veterans. Veterans' preference laws have been criticized because they have allegedly made it difficult for government agencies to hire and promote more women and minorities. Although the original version of the Civil Service Reform Act of 1978 sought to limit veterans' preference in the federal service, the final version contained a variety of new provisions strengthening veterans' preference.

veto 1. The Latin word for "I forbid." **2.** Disapproval by the President of a bill or joint resolution, other than one proposing an amendment to the Constitution. When the Congress is in session, the President must veto a bill within 10 days, excluding Sundays, after he has received it, or it becomes law without signature. When the President vetoes a bill, it is returned to the house of its origin with a message stating the reasons for its rejection. *Compare to* VETO OVERRIDE. **3.** The right of any of the five permanent members of the United Nations Security Council (China, France, the United Kingdom, the United States, and the U.S.S.R.) under Article 27 of the U.N. charter to prevent any decision by withholding agreement. **4.** The disapproval of proposed legislation by any chief executive who has formal authority to do so.

veto, absolute Any veto that is final because there is no legal way to override it. For example, a veto by a permanent member of the United Nations SECURITY COUNCIL is absolute.

veto, congressional *See* VETO, LEGISLATIVE.

veto, item The executive power to block separate points of a bill. Many state governors have this authority; the President of the United States does not, although President Ronald Reagan repeatedly requested that the Congress grant him this power. An item veto would allow a President to remove a RIDER from a bill and thus make it more difficult for members of the Congress to hold important legislation hostage to PORK BARREL or other special interest provisions. According to then Speaker of the House Thomas P. O'Neill, Jr.: "There's never been any enthusiasm for the line-item veto in the House. [President] Reagan's argument to me is that with nearly every [state] governor doing it, why can't the President? My answer to him is that the Founding Fathers intended equality in our government" (*U.S. News & World Report*, September 16, 1985).

veto, legislative A statutory measure that subjects a President's proposal to the approval or disapproval of the Congress. Either action must be taken usually within 60 or 90 days. The legislative veto may take the form of a committee veto, a simple resolution passed by either house, or a concurrent resolution.

The legislative veto was first provided for in the Economy Act of June 30, 1932, when the Congress authorized President Herbert Hoover to reorganize executive departments and agencies, subject to disapproval by a simple majority of either house within 60 days. Since 1932, several hundred pieces of legislation have included some version of the legislative veto. Until 1973, the legislative veto was used mainly for executive reorganization proposals. Then the War Powers Resolution unleashed a new conception of the legislative veto. For the first time, it became the only check on major presidential policy initiatives, such as war, as opposed to being an after-the-fact sanctioning of management reforms.

In 1983, the Supreme Court ruled in *Immigration and Naturalization Service v Chadha* (1983) that the one-house (meaning either house) congressional veto violated the separation of powers principle and was therefore unconstitutional. The Court reasoned that the congressional veto bypassed the President, who was given no opportunity to sign or veto the measure at hand. The Congress could accomplish the same ends and not violate the separation of powers by using the regular legislative processes to achieve its will; then the President would not be bypassed. Nevertheless, the legislative veto continues to be widely used. According to Louis Fisher of the Congressional Research Service, more than 140 legislative vetoes have been enacted since the *Chadha* decision "by open defiance and subtle evasions" (*The New York Times*, March 31, 1989).

veto override A legislature's approval, usually by an extraordinary majority, of a bill over the veto of the executive. If the President disapproves a bill and sends it back to the Congress with a list of objections, the Congress may override the veto by a two-thirds vote in each chamber. The Constitution requires a yea-and-nay roll call for this action. The question put to each house is: "Shall the bill pass, the objections of the President to the contrary notwithstanding?"

veto, pocket The act of the President in withholding approval of a bill after the Congress has adjourned—either for the year or for a specified period—thus, effectively vetoing it without express disapprovals. When the Congress is in session, a bill becomes law without the President's signature if he or she does not act upon it within 10 days, excluding Sundays, from the time of receipt. But if the Congress adjourns within that 10-day period, the bill is killed without the President's formal veto. In many cases in the past, where bills have been sent to the President toward the close of a session, he has taken advantage of this provision and has held until after adjournment those measures of which he disapproved but which he did not wish to return with his objections to the Congress for its further action.

vice president The second highest elected official in the United States who succeeds to the presidency in the event of the death, removal, or resignation of the President of the United States. The Vice President's only other constitutional responsibility is to preside over the U.S. Senate (except when it is trying a President for impeachment) and vote in the case of a tie.

John Adams (1735–1826), the first Vice President, wrote in a December 19, 1793 letter to his wife, Abigail: "My country has contrived for me the most insignificant office that ever the invention of man contrived or his imagination conceived." And Thomas R. Marshall (1854–1925), Woodrow Wilson's Vice President, is supposed to have said that "the vice president of the United States is like a man in a cataleptic state: he cannot speak; he cannot move; he suffers no pain; and yet he is perfectly conscious of everything that is going on around him." John Nance Garner (1868–1967), the Texan who was Franklin D. Roosevelt's first Vice President (1933–1941), is usually credited with saying that "the vice presidency of the United States isn't worth a pitcher of warm spit." ("Spit" is not the actual word he used for the bodily excretion he had in mind, but that is how the reporters cleaned it up.) Recent Presidents, however, have tended to give their Vice Presidents significant domestic and foreign policy assignments.

The presidency was seldom within the reach of early twentieth-century Vice Presidents because they tended to be obscure figures selected to balance tickets by representing states or regions whose votes were important to the presidential candidate. But television has changed the situation significantly. As their party's most visible candidates after four or eight years of highly visible public service, Vice Presidents now find themselves to be logical front runners. However, if the policies of the President they have served are unpopular, Vice Presidents seeking their party's nomination for President may have a particular difficulty disassociating themselves from those policies, especially under the watchful eyes of a President sensitive to criticism.

Nine Vice Presidents have succeeded to the presidency upon the death (or resignation) of a President: John Tyler (1841), Millard Fillmore (1850), Andrew Johnson (1865), Chester A. Arthur (1881), Theodore Roosevelt (1901), Calvin Coolidge (1923), Harry S Truman (1945), Lyndon Johnson (1963), and Gerald Ford (1974). Others, such as John Adams, Martin Van Buren, Richard Nixon, and George Bush won election as President after completing terms as Vice President. But the ultimate significance of the vice presidency was long ago summed up by then-professor Woodrow Wilson in his *Congressional Government* (1885): "There is very little to be said about the Vice President. . . . His importance consists in the fact that he may cease to be Vice President."

victim impact statements *See* booth v maryland.

Vietnam syndrome The perceived reluctance of the American people to see their military forces involved in a long drawn out war for no purpose that they could overwhelmingly understand or support.

Vietnam War The 1956 to 1975 war between the noncommunist Republic of Vietnam (South Vietnam) and the communist Democratic Republic of Vietnam (North Vietnam), which resulted in the victory of the North over the South and the unification of the two countries into the communist Socialist Republic of Vietnam on July 2, 1976. The United States first offered financial support to South Vietnam during the Dwight D. Eisenhower administration. Military assistance began with the John F. Kennedy administration in 1961. By 1963, the United States had 16,000 military "advisors" in South Vietnam. In 1964, the GULF OF TONKIN RESOLUTION allowed the administration of Lyndon B. Johnson to expand U.S. involvement in spite of the fact that Johnson had promised, notably in a campaign speech in Akron, Ohio, on October 21, 1964: "We are not about to send American boys nine or ten thousand miles away from home to do what Asian boys ought to be doing for themselves." By 1968, the United States had over 500,000 men engaged in the most unpopular foreign war in American history. As a direct result, the Democrats lost control of the White House to Republican Richard M. Nixon. The Nixon administration's policy of "Vietnamization" called for the South Vietnamese to gradually take over all the fighting from the Americans. The Americans continued to pull out, and the South held off the North for awhile. As the American forces dwindled, the North got more aggressive and successful. Finally, the North's January 1975 offensive led to the South's unconditional surrender by April.

More than 58,000 Americans died in the Vietnam War; another 150,000 were wounded. President Ronald Reagan said on February 24, 1981 that American soldiers "came home without a victory not because they had been defeated but because they had been denied permission to win." Graham A. Martin, the last American Ambassador to South Vietnam, was quoted in *The New York Times* (April 30, 1985) as saying: "In the end, we simply cut and ran. The American national will had collapsed." President George Bush in his Inaugural Address of January 20, 1989, observed: "That war cleaves us still. But, friends, that war began in earnest a quarter of a century ago; and surely the statute of limitations has been reached. This is a fact: The final lesson of Vietnam is that no great nation can long afford to be sundered by a memory."

village 1. An unincorporated settlement within a county. **2.** A small municipal corporation.

Virginia plan The proposals for abolishing the Articles of Confederation and creating a strong central government, submitted to the Constitutional Convention in 1787 by Edmund Randolph (it is also called the Randolph plan, even though it was mostly written by James Madison) on behalf of the entire Virginia delegation. Many of the plan's elements eventually found their way into the Constitution: for example, a bicameral legislature, a national executive, a national judiciary, and legislative representation based on population as determined by a census.

vision thing President George Bush's one-time description of his political philosophy. According to *Newsweek* (May 23, 1988) he used this phase to refer to his "alleged lack of a grand world view." The press teased him about this strange usage but he had his quiet revenge. After treatment for early glaucoma in one eye, he told reporters: "I'm taking drops now, one in the morning and one at night, but the vision thing is very good" (*Newsweek*, April 23, 1990).

VISTA *See* ACTION.

vital statistics The data on a country's births, deaths, marriages, and so on, maintained by national governments.

viva voce voting Oral voting; a VOICE VOTE.

voir dire **1.** A French term meaning "to speak the truth." **2.** The formal examination of potential jurors by the judge and lawyers for the defense and prosecutions to learn if they are acceptable for jury service in the case at hand. **3.** The preliminary examination of witnesses in a case to learn if they should testify. **4.** An examination, out of the presence of the jury, of some issue or fact in a case.

Volcker Commission The National Commission on the Public Service created in 1987 to examine the "quiet crisis" in government personnel management. It was popularly called the Volcker Commission after its chairman, Paul Volcker (1927–   ), former Chairman of the Board of Governors of the Federal Reserve System. The Commission issued a major report in 1989 bemoaning the low quality, low pay, and low morale of the federal service.

voluntary restraint agreements (VRAs) Informal bilateral or multilateral agreements in which exporters voluntarily limit exports of certain products to a particular country, in order to avoid economic dislocation in the importing country and the imposition of mandatory import restrictions.

voodoo economics Presidential candidate George Bush's 1980 description of Republican primary opponent Ronald Reagan's economic policy proposals. After joining Reagan as the vice presidential nominee on the 1980 and 1984 tickets, Bush thought he had better not say it anymore. And he didn't. But the press never let him forget it. When in 1982 he denied ever having said it ("I didn't say it. I challenge anyone to find it"), NBC News then showed a videotape of him using the phrase. Since then he hasn't denied saying it.

vote, bullet A vote for a single issue or candidate without regard or interest for other parts of the ballot; so called because the voting is done as fast as a bullet.

vote, clothespin A vote for the lesser of two evils, for the least objectionable of two objectionable candidates; so called because of the image of putting a clothespin over one's nose to keep out the bad smell of the candidate as one casts a ballot.

vote, cemetery Fraudulent votes; traditional political machines would often "allow" residents of a cemetery to vote for their party's candidates.

vote, crossover A vote in an open primary election for a candidate of the opposition party. The usual motivation is to help gain a nomination for the opposition party's weakest candidate, but some crossover voting is also a sincere effort to support a favored candidate who just happens to belong to another party. *See also* PRIMARY, OPEN.

vote, floating Voters who constantly drift from one political party to another instead of sticking to a single party and developing a strong sense of party identification.

vote, free A vote in a legislature on which the leaderships of the various parties have not taken a position; thus, legislators are free to vote any way they please without incurring party disfavor.

vote of confidence In a PARLIAMENTARY SYSTEM of government, the formal approval that an administration needs from a majority of the legislature if it is to continue in power. A majority that has become disenchanted with the current government may call for a "vote of no confidence" to force the government to resign or to call an election. If the government wins this vote, it stays in power.

vote, party *See* PARTY VOTE.

vote, party unity *See* PARTY UNITY.

vote, popular The actual numbers of votes cast for the various presidential candidates in a national election, as opposed to the number of votes each wins in the ELECTORAL COLLEGE. There is always the concern in presidential elections that a candidate will win the popular vote but lose the election, because the electoral college vote is based on winning individual states.

vote, protest A vote for a candidate who has no real chance of winning (e.g., a third-party candidate) to show unhappiness with the other options. More people talk of protest voting than actually do it, because once alone in the voting booth most people are reluctant to "throw their vote away." Consequently, most third-party candidates in national elections, such as George Wallace (1968) and John Anderson (1980), have higher preelection polls than postelection vote counts.

vote, reconsider a A legislative motion to reopen debate on an issue that has just been decided by vote. It has, until it is disposed of, the effect of suspending the action. In the Senate, the motion can be made only by a member who voted on the prevailing side of the original question or by a member who did not vote at all. In the House, it can be made only by a member on the prevailing side. A common practice after close votes in the Senate is a motion to reconsider, followed by a motion to table the motion to reconsider. On this motion to table, senators vote as they voted on the original question, to enable the motion to table to prevail. The matter is then finally closed, and further motions to reconsider are not entertained. In the Congress, as a routine precaution, a motion to reconsider usually is made every time a measure is passed. Such a motion almost always is tabled immediately.

vote, recorded A legislative vote upon which each member's stand is individually made known. In the Senate, this is accomplished through a *roll call* of the entire membership, to which each senator on the floor must answer "yea," "nay," or (if he or she does not wish to vote) "present." Since January 1973, the House has used an electronic voting system both for yeas and nays and for other recorded votes. The Constitution requires a recorded vote on the question of overriding a veto. In other cases, a recorded vote (or a recorded teller vote) can be obtained by the demand of one fifth of the members present. *Compare to* VOTE, TELLER.

vote, roll call *See* VOTE, RECORDED.

vote, soft Voters who will vote if they just happen to be walking by the polls on election day; voters nobody can count on. Jody Powell, an aide to President Jimmy Carter, defined the soft vote as "The voters who don't care enough to come vote for you in the rain" (quoted in M. Schram's *Running for the President*, 1976).

vote, standing A nonrecorded vote used in both the House and the Senate. A standing vote, also called a division vote, is taken as follows: those in favor of a proposal stand and are counted by the presiding officer; then members opposed stand and are counted. There is no record of how individual members voted. In the House, the presiding officer announces the numbers for and against. In the Senate, usually only the result is announced.

vote, straw An unofficial, nonbinding vote. It is derived from the adage that "straws show which way the wind blows."

vote, swing A voter who has no loyalty to a political party and leans toward one candidate or another depending on their policies or personalities.

vote, teller A means of voting in the House in which members file past tellers and are counted as for or against a measure but are not recorded individually. The teller vote is not used in the Senate. In the House, tellers are ordered upon demand of one fifth of a quorum. (This is 44 in the House, 20 in the COMMITTEE OF THE WHOLE.) The House also has a recorded teller vote procedure, introduced in 1971 (now largely supplanted by electronic voting), under which the individual votes of members are made public just as they would be on a yea-and-nay vote. *Compare to* VOTE, RECORDED.

vote trading A legislative tactic in which one legislator votes for a bill favored by a second legislator, with the understanding that the second legislator will vote in favor of a bill advocated by the first legislator. Vote trading may be explicit, where the two make an informal agreement, or implicit, where the trade is the result of an unspoken understanding. *Compare to* PAIR; RECIPROCITY.

vote, voice **1.** A voting procedure in which those eligible to vote answer "aye" or "nay" in chorus. The presiding officer then decides the result. **2.** UNANIMOUS CONSENT, or without objection.

vote, write-in A vote for someone other than one of the candidates on the official ballot. While often legal, this is usually a futile protest against the available candidates.

voter A citizen who indicates ballot choices in an election. The terms *voter* and *elector* tend to be used interchangeably; but there is a distinction. An elector has the right to vote. A voter is an elector exercising this right.

voter, core One who votes in practically every election in which he or she is eligible. Core voters tend to be major party loyalists.

voter, peripheral One who usually votes only in presidential elections, and not in state and local off-year elections.

voter registration *See* REGISTRATION, VOTER.

voter requirements Conditions that citizens must meet to be eligible to vote. Minimum requirements for voting in every state are citizenship of the United States and being 18 years of age or older. Some states permit 17-year-olds to vote in primary elections if they will be 18 by the date of the general election.

voter, undecided A citizen eligible to vote who has not yet made a decision on how to vote. The undecided vote is often large enough to confound the pollsters and to be the critical factor in close elections.

voting The exercise of the right of SUFFRAGE; participating in an election by indicating a preference among candidates. This is the only means by which most citizens can participate in political decision making.

voting, absentee Voting by citizens who, for whatever reasons, cannot go to their normal polling places on election day and therefore take advantage of state and federal laws that allow them to vote in advance or by mail. *Compare to* BALLOT, ABSENTEE.

voting, approval An electoral process whereby voters can vote for (approve of) as many of the candidates on a ballot as they desire but cannot cast more than one vote for each candidate. The candidate with the greatest vote total wins. This voting system is rarely used but much discussed.

voting behavior 1. The total means by which citizens express their opinions on political candidates and issues at the polls. **2.** The subfield of political science that seeks to discover (or explain) voting patterns and trends.

voting, bloc Voting done in collusion with others according to commonly agreed policies. This can occur either in legislatures, when all of the members of a party cast the same vote or when a bipartisan coalition (such as the conservative coalition in the Congress) forms; or in a general election, when all of the members of an ethnic or interest group vote the same way. In 1970, George C. Wallace won reelection as governor of Alabama by actively campaigning against the bloc vote. Because his pronunciation of the words "bloc" and "black" was indistinguishable, he played to the white backlash vote while being able to deny any racial attack.

voting, bullet A tactic used by supporters of a candidate running for one of several identical local offices on a school board, county commission, or city council. Voters who are allowed to vote for more than one person for the same office, vote for only one—thereby increasing that candidate's chances by denying "extra" votes to others.

voting, compulsory A legal requirement that eligible voters vote. The Supreme Court has held in *Lane v Wilson* (1939) that penalties for not voting are unconstitutional and a violation of the Fifteenth Amendment.

voting, cumulative An electoral process whereby each voter has more than one vote which can then be distributed among various candidates or given solely to one. Cumulative voting makes it easier for third parties to gain seats in a legislature.

voting, early Voting prior to the formal election day. This can be done through absentee ballots or in states, such as Texas, that allow for early voting—casting a ballot in person up to several weeks before the formal election. Early voting has been praised as one answer to low turnout because citizens have a greater period of time in which to vote. It also allows candidates an opportunity to "lock in" votes and protect themselves from last-minute negative advertising. (This has nothing to do with the phrase "vote early and vote often," which developed in the last century as encouragement for vote fraud.)

voting, electronic A method of voting by legislatures which calls for members to insert a plastic card in a voting station and then vote by pressing buttons. Votes are then immediately presented on a highly visible electronic display. The House of Representatives has used electronic voting since 1973.

voting, issue 1. The casting of a vote for a candidate on the basis of one issue alone, such as the candidate's support for or against legal abortion. **2.** Voting for a candidate because of his or her stand on issues, rather than because of the candidate's party affiliation.

voting, negative 1. Voting against, as opposed to voting for, something. **2.** Voting against the party in power as a protest of its policies.

voting, plural A voting system whereby some elite voters are legally entitled to more than one ballot, more than one vote. This is not legal in the United States.

voting, pocketbook Voting decided on the basis of personal economic issues; on whether a candidate's or an initiative's policies would cost the voter money in terms of additional taxes, fewer jobs, and so on.

voting, preferential A voting system in which electors indicate first, second, third, and so on, choices of candidates.

voting, proportional 1. *See* PROPORTIONAL REPRESENTATION. **2.** The option of assigning a portion of one's total vote to more than one candidate. The Hare system is a variant of proportional voting.

voting, prospective Voting for a candidate on the assumption that he or she will advocate or implement specific policies in the future. Prospective voting is a major element in presidential elections. *Compare to* VOTING, RETROSPECTIVE.

voting residence Generally, a voter's DOMICILE. However, the voting residence of an American voter pursuant to the Overseas Citizens Voting Rights Act and no longer domiciled in the United States is the place where he or she was domiciled immediately prior to departure from the United States. The Constitution originally left to the states the right to determine eligibility for voting. Consequently, residency in a state and registration as a voter became essential requirements for voting. In a series of steps, especially over the last 20 years, the Supreme Court has moved in the direction of creating a national presumption of the right to vote, although a national registration still does not exist. *Compare to* RESIDENCY REQUIREMENTS.

voting, retrospective Voting for candidates on the basis of their past performance in political office. Retrospective voting is often a factor in returning incumbent legislators to office, because they have had time to be of service to their constituents, get public works for their district, and so on. *Compare to* VOTING, PROSPECTIVE.

Voting Rights Act of 1965 The law that extended the elective franchise to millions of once-excluded members of minority groups, and arguably the most important civil rights legislation ever passed (with the possible exception of the Civil Rights Act of 1964). At the heart of the act are the Section 4 triggering formula (providing for automatic coverage of jurisdictions with low minority electoral participation) and the Section 5 requirement of preclearance of all voting law changes by such jurisdictions with the attorney general or the Federal District Court for the District of Columbia. Other sections authorize the appointment of federal examiners to enforce the right to vote and permit federal observers to monitor elections. The act, which was amended in 1970, 1975, and 1982, also bans literacy tests, requires bilingual elections in some jurisdictions, and encourages the creation of predominantly minority districts. The constitutionality of the act was upheld by the Supreme Court in *South Carolina v Katzenbach* (1966).

voting, split ticket Voting for candidates of more than one party. *See* TICKET SPLITTING.

voting, straight ticket Voting only for candidates of the same party. Voting machines often allow voters to pull one lever to select the straight party ticket. Only 43 percent of all voters cast a straight ticket in 1984.

voting, strategic Voting that is not sincere but is intended to bring about some other result, such as when voters cross over in a primary to vote in favor of the weaker candidate of the opposition party or when legislators vote in favor of an amendment to a bill that they believe will cause its ultimate defeat.

voting, tactical Voting not for one's preferred choice in an election but for a candidate that is more likely to win. Thus, a member of a minor party may vote for a major party candidate in hopes of actually influencing the election.

voting, weighted A voting system in which each voter's vote is proportionate to something, such as shares of stocks owned or numbers of constituents represented.

voucher system A government program that issues redeemable coupons to eligible citizens to purchase services on the open market. For example, housing vouchers have been suggested as an alternative to public housing, and education vouchers have been suggested as an alternative to public education. The idea was popularized by economist MILTON FRIEDMAN in *Capitalism and Freedom* (1962).

vox populi A Latin phrase meaning "the voice of the people." The original saying, from an eighth-century letter to the Emperor Charlemagne from Alcuin, an English theologian, is *vox populi, vox dei*—"the voice of the people is the voice of God." Even then it was disputed.

W

Wagner Act *See* NATIONAL LABOR RELATIONS ACT OF 1935.

walking-around money *See* STREET MONEY.

wall of separation The phrase used to describe the First Amendment prohibition against the establishment of a national church. The idea is that there should be a "wall of separation" between church and state. *See also* ESTABLISHMENT CLAUSE.

Wallace, George C. (1919–   ) The Democratic governor of Alabama who was a presidential candidate in 1968 and 1972. Shot in an assassination attempt while campaigning in 1972, he was thereafter partially paralyzed and wheelchair-bound. He was a rabid segregationist early in his career. His most famous public statement of that time was: "I say segregation now, segregation tomorrow, segregation forever" (*Life*, December 26, 1969). He later moderated his racial views and apologized for his past bigotry; the last time he was reelected governor in 1982, he had substantial black support.

Wallace, Henry A. (1888–1965) The Secretary of Agriculture (1933–1940) who became President Franklin D. Roosevelt's Vice President from 1941 to 1945. Because of his pro-left views, Wallace was unacceptable to the conservative wing of the Democratic Party; thus, he was dumped as Vice President during FDR's campaign for a fourth term in 1944. His "dumping" paved the way for Senator Harry S Truman to become FDR's Vice President and successor. In 1948 Wallace unsuccessfully ran for President on the Progressive Party ticket.

war on poverty The phrase used by the Lyndon B. Johnson administration for its 1960s GREAT SOCIETY programs designed to eliminate the causes and effects of poverty in the United States. In his January 8, 1964 State of the Union Message, President Johnson said: "This administration today, here and now, declares unconditional war on poverty in America. I urge this Congress and all Americans to join with me in that effort. It will not be a short or easy struggle—no single weapon or strategy will suffice—but we shall not rest until that war is won." After two decades, it is clear who won the war—poverty. But the fact that poverty has yet to be defeated takes nothing away from the great intentions and limited accomplishments of the "military" effort. The policy question to be asked is not whether the war was worth fighting (it was); but what would be the best strategies and tactics to employ the next time the nation makes a major effort to fight this perennial enemy. *See also* OFFICE OF ECONOMIC OPPORTUNITY.

war powers The legal authority to initiate war. The U.S. Constitution gives to the Congress the authority to declare war, but the President, as commander in chief, has implied powers to commit the military forces to action. In

World War II, the last war the Congress actually declared, the Congress was called into emergency joint session by President Franklin D. Roosevelt the day after the attack on Pearl Harbor (December 8, 1941) and voted to declare war on Japan. More recently, the Congress, concerned with presidential military initiatives during the Vietnam War, has sought to place substantial controls on the President's power to commit American troops to combat. The War Powers Resolution of 1973 clarifies the respective roles of the President and the Congress in cases involving the use of military forces without a declaration of war. The President "in every possible instance" shall consult with the Congress before introducing troops and shall report to the Congress within 48 hours. The use of the armed forces is to be terminated within 60 days (with a possible 30-day extension by the President) unless the Congress acts during that time to declare war, enacts a specific authorization for use of armed forces, extends the 60- to 90-day period, or is physically unable to meet as a result of an attack on the United States. At any time before the 60 days expires, the Congress may direct by concurrent resolution that American military forces be removed by the President. But according to Senator Alan Cranston: "The Act has been a failure. It has not prevented Presidents from pursuing risky military adventures before enlisting Congressional support" (*The Los Angeles Times*, October 26, 1987). It continues to be a failure. The best example of this is the fact that during the PANAMA INTERVENTION and the PERSIAN GULF WAR, President George Bush never invoked the War Powers Resolution Act—and Congress never formally challenged him on it.

war, total **1.** A conflict which threatens the survival of a nation, in which all available weapons are used. **2.** A war effort which mobilizes all sectors of a nation's economy. It was Karl von Clausewitz who first developed the modern concept of total war in the early 1800s.

ward A subdivision of a city, often used as a legislative district for city council elections, as an administrative division for public services, or as a unit for the organization of political parties. A ward is often further divided into PRECINCTS.

ward heeler A local political functionary; someone who is involved with, but insignificant in, party affairs. A heeler is not worthy of much respect. The term comes from the way a dog is brought to heel by its master; ward heelers are likewise known by their obedience to their masters. According to Representative Les Aspin in *U.S. News & World Report* (March 2, 1981): "In the old days, you had the ward heeler who cemented himself in the community by taking care of everyone. But city machines died once Franklin D. Roosevelt brought in the Federal government to take care of everybody. Now the Congressman plays the role of ward heeler—wending his way through the bureaucracy, helping to cut through red tape and confusion."

Wards Cove Packing Co. v Atonio (1989) The Supreme Court case that held the burden of proof is upon the plaintiff in equal employment opportunity cases to prove that employer practices which resulted in a racial imbalance are not justified by legitimate business reasons. This ruling makes it more difficult for workers to make a prima facie case of discrimination by simply citing statistics which demonstrate underrepresentation of various racial categories in the workforce.

warrant 1. In criminal proceedings, a WRIT issued by a judge directing a law enforcement officer to do something; for example, to search some premises (a search warrant) or to arrest some person (an arrest warrant). Warrants are required because of the Fourth Amendment's assertion that the people be free from unreasonable searches and seizures. *Compare to* PROBABLE CAUSE. **2.** A short-term obligation issued by a government in anticipation of revenue. The instrument (a draft much like a check), when presented to a disbursing officer, such as a bank, is payable only upon acceptance by the issuing jurisdiction. Warrants may be made payable on demand or at some time in the future. Local governments, in particular, have used delayed payment of warrants as a way to protect cash flow.

Warren Commission The group established by President Lyndon B. Johnson to investigate the assassination of President John F. Kennedy in 1963. Chaired by Chief Justice Earl Warren (1891–1974), it concluded that assassin Lee Harvey Oswald had acted alone in shooting the President. The ensuing Warren Report has since been largely discredited by subsequent congressional and other investigations. By the time there was consensus that Kennedy was more likely killed by a conspiracy, too many years had passed, too many of the principals involved were dead by natural or other causes, and it was simply too late. Because of the ineptness of the Warren Commission, the question "Who killed President Kennedy?" will never be satisfactorily answered.

Warren, Earl (1891–1974) The chief justice of the United States from 1953 to 1969 who became the symbol of judicial activism and led the Supreme Court to many landmark decisions on desegregation, civil rights, First Amendment freedoms, and the rights of criminal defendants. President Dwight D. Eisenhower, who appointed Warren to the Supreme Court, disagreed with the activist approach of the Warren Court and was quoted as saying that Warren's appointment was the "biggest damfool mistake I ever made" (*The New York Times Magazine*, July 28, 1968).

Washington 1. The capital city of the United States. While Washington refers to the physical location of the federal government's central offices, it is frequently used as a collective noun to refer to the policymaking processes and actors of the national government (as in "Washington said". . . "Washington decided". . . or "it is Washington's policy". . .). It was President John F. Kennedy who said during a November 14, 1961 speech that Washington was the "city of Northern charm and Southern efficiency." Elliot Richardson, one of the few of President Richard M. Nixon's cabinet secretaries to come out of WATERGATE with his reputation enhanced, called

Washington a "city of cocker spaniels. It's a city of people who are more interested in being petted and admired, loved, than rendering the exercise of power" (*The New York Times*, July 13, 1982). But the most poignant analysis belongs to Fanny Dixwell Holmes (wife of Justice Oliver Wendell Holmes), who told President Theodore Roosevelt at a White House reception on January 8, 1903 that "Washington is full of famous men and the women they married when they were young" (quoted in C.D. Bowen's *Yankee From Olympus*, 1944). **2.** Washington State, located in the northwestern United States. **3.** The District of Columbia, the "D.C." in Washington, D.C., which occupies the same territory as the capital city of Washington. **4.** A code word implying vast bureaucracy, endless red tape, and the arrogant use of power. In this sense some political candidates, most notably Presidents Jimmy Carter and Ronald Reagan, have "run against" Washington.

Washington, George (1732–1799) The plantation owner and land surveyor from Virginia who was the victorious commander of the American revolutionary army, the chairman of the Constitutional Convention of 1787, and first President of the United States (1789–1797). In each instance, Washington's service brought enormous benefits to his country and honor to himself. Washington is that rare case in which a man's mythic qualities of integrity, patriotism, and honor actually live up to what he was in real life. Historian James Flexner was correct in calling Washington the "indispensable man." It was his leadership that brought victory in the Revolutionary War. It was his great prestige that made the Constitutional Convention of 1787 a success and ratification possible. It seems fair to say that, were it not for Washington's character, personal presence, and dedication to republican principles, the history of the fledgling United States would have taken a radically different turn—for the worse. He is the closest thing the United States has to a secular saint, and deservedly so. Thomas Jefferson in a January 2, 1814 letter to Dr. Walter Jones offered this assessment: "His mind was great and powerful, without being of the very first order. . . and as far as he saw, no judgment was ever sounder. It was slow in operation, being little aided by invention or imagination, but sure in conclusion. . . . He was incapable of fear, meeting personal dangers with the calmest unconcern. . . . His integrity was most pure, his justice the most inflexible I have ever known, no motives of interest or consanguinity, of friendship or hatred, being able to bias his decision. He was, indeed, in every sense of the word, a wise, a good, and a great man." Upon learning of Washington's death, the House of Representatives adopted a resolution, introduced by John Marshall but written by Henry "Light Horse Harry" Lee, that Washington was: "First in war, first in peace and first in the hearts of his countrymen." As for being the "Father of His Country," that phrase was probably first used in German (*Des Landes Vater*) in a 1779 calendar published by Francis Baily, a printer, in Lancaster, Pennsylvania. Within a few years it was a generally used epithet for Washington. *Compare to* CINCINNATUS, LUCIUS QUINCTIUS.

Watergate The scandal that led to the resignation of President Richard M. Nixon. Watergate itself is a hotel-office-apartment complex in Washington, D.C. When individuals associated with the Committee to Reelect the President were caught breaking into the Democratic National Committee Headquarters (then located in the Watergate complex) in 1972, the resulting cover-up and national trauma was condensed into one word—Watergate. The term has come to refer to any political crime or instance of bureaucratic corruption that undermines confidence in governing institutions.

Watergate analogy Ever since the Watergate scandal, political activities that seem to smell of corruption have had a "-gate" suffix added in analogy. Thus, when Ronald Reagan's 1980 campaign organization was accused of "somehow" getting hold of President Jimmy Carter's debate briefing book, the affair was dubbed "debategate." President Carter's problems with his brother's connection to Libya was called "Billygate." Of course, "-gate" charges are often denounced as pseudogates.

ways and means **1.** A government's financial resources. **2.** The methods by which a state gains its funds, supplies, and other necessities. The English House of Commons has had a Committee on Ways and Means since at least 1644. The U.S. House of Representatives has had a Ways and Means Committee since 1795. All national tax legislation must originate in the House Ways and Means Committee.

Weber, Max (1864–1920) The German sociologist who produced an analysis of an ideal-type bureaucracy that is still the most influential statement—the point of departure for all further analyses—on the subject. Weber also pioneered the concepts of the Protestant ethic, charismatic authority, and a value-free approach to social research. His major works can be found in *Protestant Ethic and the Spirit of Capitalism*, trans. Talcott Parsons (1904–1905, 1958) and *From Max Weber: Essays in Sociology* (H.H. Gerth and C. Wright Mills, eds., 1946). *See also* BUREAUCRACY; CHARISMA.

wedge issue Something that can be used to divide or polarize people. For example, in the 1980s the Republicans used affirmative action quotas as a wedge to split the working class vote. Whites who feared that blacks would gain an unfair advantage in job seeking were then more easily persuaded to vote Republican.

welfare Public financial or in-kind assistance available to citizens as a matter of right if they meet eligibility requirements, such as a MEANS TEST of income or assets below a preset minimum. Welfare is not only for the poor; it can cover a wide range of people of various means. Senator Hubert H. Humphrey provided one of the most eloquent defenses of government welfare programs at the dedication of the Hubert H. Humphrey Building of the Department of Health and Human Services on November 1, 1977: "It was once said that the moral test of government is how that government treats those who are in the dawn of life, the children; those who are in the twilight of life, the elderly; and those who are in the shadows of life—the sick, the needy and the handicapped." The Family Support Act of 1988 is the latest revision in federal welfare laws which, among other things, makes fathers more financially responsible for their children and puts single mothers under an obligation to work. *See also* ENTITLEMENT PROGRAM; RELIEF.

welfare clause *See* GENERAL WELFARE CLAUSE.

welfare queens A derogatory reference for people who use food stamps or other means-tested government benefits to buy luxuries. This was one of President Ronald Reagan's favorite terms for those who abuse welfare programs, which is why Senator Charles Grassley once told him, "You've got to realize that there are welfare queens in the Pentagon, too. They're the big contractors" (quoted in A. Ernest Fitzgerald's *The Pentagonists*, 1989).

welfare state A governing system in which it is a public policy that government will strive for the maximum economic and social benefits for each of its citizens. The differences between a welfare state and socialism are semantic only. Political scientist Andrew Hacker in *The New York Times Magazine* (March 22, 1964) offered this formal definition: "A welfare state is one that guarantees a broad series of economic protections that any citizen can claim when he is no longer able to provide for himself. In a welfare state, the benefits an individual receives are political rights, not charity, and there should be no occasion for apology or embarrassment in applying for them. Moreover, the services made available by a welfare state will parallel in quality and coverage those open to individuals who are able to draw on private resources."

Wesberry v Sanders (1964) The Supreme Court case that, in holding that congressional districts had to be substantially equal in population, created the legal basis for ending the rural bias in congressional representation. Justice Hugo L. Black in the majority opinion wrote: "While it may not be possible to draw Congressional districts with mathematical precision, that is no excuse for ignoring our Constitution's plain objective of making equal representation for equal numbers of people the fundamental goal for the House of Representatives." *Compare to* REYNOLDS V SIMS.

West Coast Hotel v Parrish (1937) The Supreme Court case that upheld the minimum wage law of the State of Washington by declaring that a minimum wage law did not violate the freedom of contract provided by the due process clause of the Fourteenth Amendment. This case overruled the Court's earlier decision, *Adkins v Children's Hospital* (1923), which held unconstitutional a federal law establishing minimum wages for women and children in the District of Columbia.

Whig party 1. An American political party established in 1836 by opponents of Andrew Jackson's policies. It elected Presidents in 1840 (William Henry Harrison) and 1848 (Zachary Taylor) but then divided over the slavery issue. By 1852 it had completely disintegrated, with one faction going on to found the modern Republican party. **2.** The seventeenth-century English political party whose goal was the transfer of power from the king to parliament. In the nineteenth century, it was succeeded by the Liberal party.

whip A fox-hunting term applied to a key aspect of the legislative process. During a hunt, a whipper-in keeps fox-sniffing dogs from straying by whipping them back into the pack. The British Parliament first used the term, then shortened it to whip, to describe those members of the legislature responsible for party discipline—for literally rounding up the party members when it was time for a vote.

While the U.S. Congress borrowed the term from the British, it has been far less successful in maintaining party discipline. The whips (of both the majority and minority parties) keep track of all important political legislation and endeavor to have all members of their parties present when important measures are to be voted upon. When a vote appears to be close, the whips contact absent members, advise them of the vote, and determine if they wish to PAIR vote. The whips assist the leadership in managing the party's legislative program on the floor of the chambers and provide information to party members about important legislative-related matters. The office of whip is unofficial and carries no special salary. *Compare to* MAJORITY WHIP.

whip, regional Any of a dozen "sub" whips that assist his or her party's whip in the House of Representatives. The Democratic leadership in the House prefers the word "zone," while the Republicans prefer "regional" whips.

whistle blower An individual who believes the public interest overrides the interests of his or her organization and publicly exposes corrupt, illegal, fraudulent, or harmful activity. Whistle blowers in our society are not well-received. Children have long been taught not to be a "squealer." In blowing the whistle, one runs the risk of being ostracized by one's coworkers, losing one's job, and being blacklisted in one's field. The Civil Service Reform Act of 1978 provided specific protection for federal whistle-blowers. *See also* MERIT SYSTEMS PROTECTION BOARD.

whistle stop 1. The now dated campaign technique of having the candidate use a special train that would stop at every station along a major route so the candidate could give a rousing speech to his awaiting supporters. **2.** Any campaign PHOTO OPPORTUNITY involving a train.

white citizens' councils *See* CITIZENS' COUNCILS.

white flight 1. The movement of white residents from central cities, sometimes as a response to public school busing to achieve school racial integration. If they could afford it, many whites moved out of the central cities and into the suburbs so that their children could attend neighborhood schools. White flight most often occurred when the school population became overwhelmingly black and when bus rides were deemed excessively long. **2.** More recently, as in the case of Miami, it is the movement of English-speaking citizens from an area that has become increasingly Hispanic in language and culture. *See also* HOME EQUITY DISTRICT. **3.** A gradual exodus of middle-class families of all races from a central city to the suburbs because they seek to escape both high crime and high tax rates. Their leaving further dilutes the tax base, thus forcing higher taxes (or lower services) on those who remain, which in turn encourages others to leave as well.

White House 1. The official residence of the President of the United States. While President George Washington chose the site, John Adams, the second President of the United States, was the first to actually live there. On the day after he moved into the White House, November 2, 1800, President Adams wrote to his wife, Abigail: "I Pray Heaven to Bestow The Best of Blessing on this house, and on All That shall hereafter Inhabit it. May none but Honest and Wise Men ever rule under This Roof!" President Franklin D. Roosevelt had this prayer inscribed over the fireplace in the State Dining Room of the White House. It just goes to show how some prayers are only partially answered. **2.** The formal main office of the executive branch of the government of the United States. **3.** The modern symbol of the presidency. **4.** A building that can speak. Reporters and political commentators frequently state that the "White House said. . . " this or that. The building speaks because it is the architectural embodiment of the bureaucratic institution that is the modern presidency. Thus, the building speaks through press releases, news conferences, deep as well as shallow background briefings, and LEAKS. While the President is the main and most desired speaker, there are a few thousand other people who also work there and who give it voice. **5.** A complex of buildings that includes the original White House, its two wings (east and west), the old Executive Office Building, the new Executive Office Building, and Blair House (an official guest house).

White House Office The personal office of the President of the United States, containing the staff and facilities that allow the President to communicate with the Congress, his appointed agency heads, the press, and the public. *Compare to* EXECUTIVE OFFICE OF THE PRESIDENT.

White House tapes The recorded Oval Office conversations that were the main issue in UNITED STATES V NIXON: Did the President have to turn over incriminating tape recordings to the special prosecutor? The Supreme Court said yes, and within days Richard M. Nixon had resigned as President. In 1986, Nixon was asked at a press luncheon what he thought was the greatest lesson of Watergate; he unrepentantly replied, "Just destroy all the tapes."

white paper Any formal statement of an official government policy, with its associated background documentation.

White, Theodore H. *See* MAKING OF THE PRESIDENT.

WIC A federal supplemental food program for Women, Infants and Children. It provides vouchers to "pregnant, postpartum and breast-feeding women, infants and children from low-income families who are determined by a competent professional authority to be at nutritional risk." The program services about 4.5 million people and costs the federal government over $2 billion a year.

Williams-Steiger Act *See* OCCUPATIONAL SAFETY AND HEALTH ACT OF 1970.

Willie Horton spot *See* HORTON, WILLIE.

Wilson, (Thomas) Woodrow (1856–1924) The President of the United States from 1913 to 1921. Wilson, who served as president of Princeton University (1902–1910) and governor of New Jersey (1911–1913), was also a president of the American Political Science Association; he is considered one of the most influential early voices of both political science and the study of public administration. Domestically his administration created the FEDERAL RESERVE SYSTEM, the FEDERAL TRADE COMMISSION, and the modern income tax. Internationally he brought the United States into World War I on the side of Great Britain and France against Germany. After the war he became the foremost advocate of the League of Nations but was frustrated by his inability to get the U.S. Senate to agree to American participation.

It has become customary to trace the origins of the academic discipline of public administration to Wilson's 1887 article, "The Study of Administration." Wilson attempted nothing less than to refocus political science. Rather than be concerned with the great maxims of lasting political truth, he argued that political science should concentrate on how governments are administered. In his words: "It is getting to be harder to run a constitution than to frame one." It was in this essay that Wilson put forth the then radical notion that politics should be separate from administration.

wimp A public figure who seems to lack a strongly perceived political character, whose stand on the issues may be fuzzy, and who is generally seen as a weak indecisive person.

wimp factor The media's term for the effect of then-Vice President George Bush's ill-defined image on the early part of the 1988 presidential campaign. Bush helped dissipate his wimp image when he vigorously attacked journalist Dan Rather on a live interview on the January 25, 1988 edition of the "CBS Evening News."

witness A person who has knowledge of the circumstances of a case and who may present such knowledge as evidence in a court. Under the Sixth Amendment, someone accused of a crime has the right to confront in court the witnesses to the alleged facts and to compel the attendance of favorable witnesses. Forcing the attendance of witnesses who may not wish to testify is known as *compulsory process*. This practice was upheld by the Supreme Court in *Washington v Texas* (1967).

womb to tomb *See* CRADLE TO GRAVE.

workfare Any public WELFARE program that requires welfare payment recipients to work (work + welfare = workfare) or to enroll in a formal job-training program.

working the fence 1. A political candidate's interaction with supporters (by shaking hands, kissing babies, etc.) who are kept behind a fence or barrier as at an airport rally. **2.** Any hands-on contact by a candidate with a large number of supporters.

work relief *See* RELIEF.

writ A document issued by a judicial officer ordering or forbidding the performance of a specified act. Writs include arrest warrants, search warrants, subpoenas, and summonses.

writ of certiorari *See.* CERTIORARI.

writ of habeas corpus A writ directing a person detaining a prisoner to bring him or her before a judicial officer to determine the lawfulness of the imprisonment. (*Habeas corpus* is a Latin phrase meaning "you have the body.") This writ is one of the oldest protections of personal liberty and is considered fundamental to due process of law. Originally, the writ of habeas corpus was a pretrial device that enabled persons imprisoned pursuant to executive order to attack the legality of their detention. Subsequently, the concept of the writ has been expanded so that anyone whose freedom has been officially restrained may petition a federal court to test whether that restraint was legally imposed. In this manner of use, it has become an important means of postconviction attacks upon criminal convictions in state and federal courts. The Supreme Court has curtailed the availability of this device in state convictions by requiring full compliance with and exhaustion of state remedies before permitting the issuance of a writ of habeas corpus from a federal court.

Article I, Section 9 of the Constitution provides that "the privilege of the writ of habeas corpus shall not be suspended, unless when in cases of rebellion or invasion the public safety may require it." The privilege of the writ is significant because it guarantees that someone arrested will be brought before a judge and not simply be left to rot in prison. During the Civil War, President Abraham Lincoln temporarily suspended the writ of habeas corpus. But after the war, in *Ex parte Milligan* (1866), the Supreme Court held that he had had no authority to do so. This was the last attempt to suspend habeas corpus in the United States.

Because habeas corpus is a vital safeguard against unlawful imprisonment, it is strange that it is explicitly mentioned only in the context of its suspension; nowhere in the Constitution is this right affirmatively conferred. Nevertheless, there is a long-standing statutory authorization to federal courts to exercise the habeas corpus power. *See also* ABLEMAN V BOOTH.

writ of mandamus *See* MANDAMUS.

Y

yield **1.** Profits as measured by a percentage of money invested. **2.** The interest rate on funds deposited in a bank. **3.** The net return of a tax after the expenses of collecting and administering it are deducted. **4.** A parliamentary procedure whereby a legislator holding the floor allows another member to speak. This kind of yielding can be temporary (as in yielding for a question) or permanent (if the yielder must be officially recognized to speak again). **5.** The energy produced by a nuclear explosion usually measured in terms of tons of TNT. For example, the yield of a nuclear explosion of one megaton is the equivalent to one million tons of TNT.

Youngstown Sheet and Tube Co. v Sawyer (1952) The Supreme Court case involving the constitutionality of President Harry S Truman's executive order directing the secretary of Commerce to take possession of and operate the nation's steel mills in connection with a labor dispute that threatened to disrupt war production. By a vote of six to three, the Supreme Court held that the President had exceeded his constitutional powers.

Z

zoning The process by which local government can designate the types of structures and activities for a particular area. Zoning began in the 1920s to protect residential neighborhoods from the encroachments of business and industry and to preserve their economic and social integrity. It involves a highly complex legal process, which is often impacted by local politics.

zoning, aesthetic A zoning policy operating in the interests of beauty. According to Justice William O. Douglas' majority opinion in the Supreme Court case of *Berma v Parker* (1954): "It is within the power of the legislature to determine that the community should be beautiful as well as healthy."

zoning, affirmative Land-use regulations that seek neighborhood development that will benefit the disadvantaged.

zoning, cluster A zoning policy that allows builders to reduce lot sizes below normal standards so that the "extra" land is retained as open space for the community.

zoning, Euclidian A zoning policy that keeps apartments and businesses out of single-home residential areas. This kind of zoning was adopted by Euclid, Ohio, and was the subject of the Supreme Court case of *Village of Euclid v Ambler Realty Company* (1926), which asserted that zoning was a valid exercise of local government powers.

zoning, exclusionary A zoning policy that specifically excludes certain types of usages, such as home sites on lots smaller than an acre. This is sometimes known as *snob zoning*, because it is often used to preserve the exclusivity of the area.

zoning, inclusionary A zoning policy that requires builders to provide (at reduced rates) a portion of new housing units for moderate and low-income families.

zoning, open-space A zoning policy requiring developers to provide a certain amount of open space, depending upon the size of their project.

zoning, spot Changing the zoning of a parcel of land without regard for the zoning plan of the entire area.

zoning variance A lawful deviation from normal zoning policy.

The Declaration of Independence

When in the course of human events, it becomes necessary for one people to dissolve the political bands which have connected them with another, and to assume among the Powers of the earth, the separate and equal station to which the Laws of Nature and of Nature's God entitle them, a decent respect to the opinions of mankind requires that they should declare the causes which impel them to the separation.

We hold these truths to be self-evident, that all men are created equal, that they are endowed by their Creator with certain unalienable Rights, that among these are Life, Liberty and the pursuit of Happiness. That to secure these rights, Governments are instituted among Men, deriving their just powers from the consent of the governed. That whenever any Form of Government becomes destructive of these ends, it is the Right of the People to alter or abolish it, and to institute new government, laying its foundation on such principles and organizing its powers in such form, as to them shall seem most likely to effect their Safety and Happiness. Prudence, indeed, will dictate that Governments long established should not be changed for light and transient causes; and accordingly all experience hath shown, that mankind are more disposed to suffer, while evils are sufferable, than to right themselves by abolishing the forms to which they are accustomed. But when a long train of abuses and usurpations, pursuing invariably the same Object evinces a design to reduce them under absolute Despotism, it is their right, it is their duty, to throw off such Government, and to provide new Guards for their future security. Such has been the patient sufferance of these Colonies; and such is now the necessity which constrains them to alter their former Systems of Government. The history of the present King of Great Britain is a history of repeated injuries and usurpations, all having in direct object the establishment of an absolute tyranny over these States. To prove this, let Facts be submitted to a candid world.

He has refused his Assent to Laws, the most wholesome and necessary for the public good.

He has forbidden his Governors to pass Laws of immediate and pressing importance, unless suspended in their operation till his Assent should be obtained; and when so suspended, he has utterly neglected to attend to them.

He has refused to pass other Laws for the accommodation of large districts of people, unless those people would relinquish the right of Representation in the Legislature, a right inestimable to them and formidable to tyrants only.

He has called together legislative bodies at places unusual, uncomfortable, and distant from the depository of their Public Records, for the sole purpose of fatiguing them into compliance with his measures.

He has dissolved Representative Houses repeatedly, for opposing with manly firmness his invasions on the rights of the people.

He has refused for a long time, after such dissolutions, to cause others to be elected; whereby the Legislative Powers, incapable of Annihilation, have returned to the People at large for their exercise; the State remaining in the meantime exposed to all the dangers of invasion from without, and convulsions within.

He has endeavoured to prevent the population of these States; for that purpose obstructing the Laws of Naturalization of Foreigners; refusing to pass others to encourage their migrations hither, and raising the conditions of new Appropriations of Lands.

He has obstructed the Administration of Justice, by refusing his Assent to Laws for establishing Judiciary Powers.

He has made Judges dependent on his Will alone, for the tenure of their offices, and the amount and payment of their salaries.

He has erected a multitude of New Offices, and sent hither swarms of Officers to harass our people, and eat out their substance.

He has kept among us, in times of peace, Standing Armies without the Consent of our legislatures.

He has affected to render the Military independent of and superior to the Civil Power.

He has combined with others to subject us to a jurisdiction foreign to our constitution, and unacknowledged by our laws; giving his Assent to their acts of pretended Legislation:

For quartering large bodies of armed troops among us:

For protecting them, by a mock Trial, from Punishment for any Murders which they should commit on the inhabitants of these States:

For cutting off our Trade with all parts of the world:

For imposing taxes on us without our Consent:

For depriving us in many cases, of the benefits of Trial by Jury:

For transporting us beyond Seas to be tried for pretended offences:

For abolishing the free System of English Laws in a neighbouring

Province, establishing therein an Arbitrary government, and enlarging its Boundaries so as to render it at once an example and fit instrument for introducing the same absolute rule into these Colonies:

For taking away our Charters, abolishing our most valuable Laws, and altering fundamentally the Forms of our Governments:

For suspending our own Legislatures, and declaring themselves invested with Power to legislate for us in all cases whatsoever.

He has abdicated Government here, by declaring us out of his Protection and waging War against us.

He has plundered our seas, ravaged our Coasts, burnt our towns, and destroyed the lives of our people.

He is at this time transporting large armies of foreign mercenaries to compleat the works of death, desolation and tyranny, already begun with circumstances of Cruelty & perfidy scarcely paralleled in the most barbarous ages, and totally unworthy the Head of a civilized nation.

He has constrained our fellow Citizens taken Captive on the high Seas to bear Arms against their Country, to become the executioners of their friends and Brethren, or to fall themselves by their Hands.

He has excited domestic insurrections amongst us, and has endeavoured to bring on the inhabitants of our frontiers, the merciless Indian Savages, whose known rule of warfare, is an undistinguished destruction of all ages, sexes and conditions.

In every stage of these Oppressions We have Petitioned for Redress in the most humble terms: Our repeated Petitions have been answered only by repeated injury. A Prince, whose character is thus marked by every act which may define a Tyrant, is unfit to be the ruler of a free people.

Nor have We been wanting in attentions to our British brethren. We have warned them from time to time of attempts by their legislature to extend an unwarrantable jurisdiction over us. We have reminded them of the circumstances of our emigration and a settlement here. We have appealed to their native justice and magnanimity, and we have conjured them by the ties of our common kindred to disavow these usurpations which, would in-evitably interrupt our connections and correspondence. They too have been deaf to the voice of justice and of consanguinity. We must, there-fore, acquiesce in the necessity, which denounces our Separation, and hold them, as we hold the rest of mankind, Enemies in War, in Peace Friends.

We, therefore, the Representatives of the united States of America, in General Congress, Assembled, appealing to the Supreme Judge of the world for the rectitude of our intentions, do, in the Name, and by authority of the good People of these Colonies, solemnly publish and declare, That these United Colonies are, and of Right ought to be Free and Independent States;

that they are Absolved from all Allegiance to the British Crown, and that all political connection between them and the State of Great Britain, is and ought to be totally dissolved; and that as Free and Independent States, they have full power to levy War, conclude Peace, contract Alliances, establish Commerce, and to do all other Acts and Things which Independent States may of right do. And for the support of this Declaration, with a firm reliance on the Protection of Divine Providence, we mutually pledge to each other our Lives, our Fortunes and our sacred Honor.

John Hancock
(Massachusetts)

New Hampshire
Josiah Bartlett
William Whipple
Matthew Thornton
Massachusetts
Samuel Adams
John Adams
Robert Treat Paine
Elbridge Gerry
Delaware
Caesar Rodney
George Read
Thomas McKean
New York
William Floyd
Philip Livingston
Francis Lewis
Lewis Morris
New Jersey
Richard Stockton
John Witherspoon
Francis Hopkinson
John Hart
Abraham Clark

North Carolina
William Hooper
Joseph Hewes
John Penn
Maryland
Samuel Chase
William Paca
Thomas Stone
Charles Carroll of
Carrollton
South Carolina
Edward Rutledge
Thomas Heywood,
Jr.
Thomas Lynch, Jr.
Arthur Middleton
Rhode Island
Stephen Hopkins
William Ellery
Connecticut
Roger Sherman
Samuel Huntington
William Williams
Oliver Wolcott

Pennsylvania
Robert Morris
Benjamin Rush
Benjamin Franklin
John Morton
George Clymer
James Smith
George Taylor
James Wilson
George Ross
Virginia
George Wythe
Richard Henry Lee
Thomas Jefferson
Benjamin Harrison
Thomas Nelson, Jr.
Francis Lightfoot
Lee
Carter Braxton
Georgia
Button Gwinnett
Lyman Hall
George Walton

The Constitution of the United States

We the People of the United States, In Order to form a more perfect Union, establish Justice, insure domestic Tranquility, provide for the common defense, promote the general Welfare, and secure the Blessings of Liberty to ourselves and our Posterity, do ordain and establish this Constitution for the United States of America.

Article I

Section 1. All legislative Powers herein granted shall be vested in a Congress of the United States, which shall consist of a Senate and House of Representatives.

Section 2. The House of Representatives shall be composed of members chosen every second Year by the People of the several States, and the Electors in each State shall have the Qualifications requisite for Electors of the most numerous Branch of the State Legislature.

No person shall be a representative who shall not have attained to the Age of twenty five Years, and been seven Years a Citizen of the United States, and who shall not, when elected, be an Inhabitant of that State in which he shall be chosen.

Representatives and direct Taxes shall be apportioned among the several States which may be included within this union, according to their respective Numbers, which shall be determined by adding to the whole Number of free Persons, including those bound to Service for a Term of Years, and excluding Indians not taxed, three fifths of all other Persons. The actual Enumeration shall be made within three Years after the first Meeting of the Congress of the United States, and within every subsequent Term of Ten Years, in such Manner as they shall by Law direct. The Number of Representatives shall not exceed one for every thirty Thousand, but each State shall have at Least one Representative; and until such enumeration shall be made, the State of New Hampshire shall be entitled to chuse three, Massachusetts eight, Rhode-Island and Providence Plantations one, Connecticut five, New York six, New Jersey four, Pennsylvania eight, Delaware one, Maryland six, Virginia ten, North Carolina five, South Carolina five, and Georgia three.

When vacancies happen in the Representation from any State, the Executive Authority thereof shall issue Writs of Election to fill such Vacancies.

The House of Representatives shall chuse their speaker and other Officers; and shall have the sole Power of Impeachment.

Section 3. The Senate of the United States shall be composed of two Senators from each State, chosen by the Legislature thereof, for six Years; and each Senator shall have one Vote.

Immediately after they shall be assembled in Consequence of the first Election, they shall be divided as equally as may be into three Classes. The Seats of the Senators of the first Class shall be vacated at the Expiration of the second Year, of the second Class at the Expiration of the fourth Year, and of the third Class at the Expiration of the sixth Year, so that one third may be chosen every second Year; and if Vacancies happen by Resignation, or otherwise, during the Recess of the Legislature of any State, the Executive thereof may make temporary Appointments until the next Meeting of the Legislature, which shall then fill such Vacancies.

No Person shall be a Senator who shall not have attained to the Age of thirty Years, and been nine Years a Citizen of the United States, and who shall not, when elected, be an Inhabitant of that State for which he shall be chosen.

The Vice President of the United States shall be President of the Senate, but shall have no Vote, unless they be equally divided.

The Senate shall chuse their other Officers, and also a President pro tempore, in the Absence of the Vice President, or when he shall exercise the Office of the President of the United States.

The Senate shall have the sole Power to try all Impeachments. When sitting for that Purpose, they shall be on Oath of Affirmation. When the President of the United States is tried, the Chief Justice shall preside; And no Person shall be convicted without the Concurrence of two thirds of the Members present.

Judgment in Cases of Impeachment shall not extend further than to removal from Office, and disqualification to hold and enjoy any Office of honor, Trust or Profit under the United States: but the Party convicted shall nevertheless be liable and subject to Indictment, Trial, Judgment and Punishment, according to law.

Section 4. The Times, Places and Manner of holding Elections for Senators and Representatives, shall be prescribed in each State by the Legislature thereof; but the Congress may at any time by Law make or alter such regulations, except as to the Places of chusing Senators.

The Congress shall assemble at least once in every Year, and such Meeting shall be on the first Monday in December, unless they shall by Law appoint a different Day.

Section 5. Each House shall be the Judge of the Elections, Returns and Qualifications of its own Members, and a Majority of each shall constitute a Quorum to do Business; but a smaller Number may adjourn from day to day, and may be authorized to compel the Attendance of absent Members, in such Manner, and under such Penalties as each House may provide.

Each House may determine the Rules for its Proceedings, punish its Members for disorderly Behaviour, and, with the Concurrence of two thirds, expel a Member.

Each House shall keep a Journal of its Proceedings, and from time to time publish the same, excepting such Parts as may in their Judgment require Secrecy; and the Yeas and Nays of the Members of either House on any question shall, at the Desire of one fifth of those Present, be entered on the Journal.

Neither house, during the Sessions of Congress, shall, without the Consent of the other, adjourn for more than three days, nor to any other Place than that in which the two Houses shall be sitting.

Section 6. The Senators and Representatives shall receive a Compensation for their Services, to be ascertained by Law, and paid out of the Treasury of the United States. They shall in all Cases, except Treason, Felony and Breach of the Peace, be privileged from Arrest during their Attendance at the Session of their respective Houses, and in going to and returning from the same; and for any Speech or Debate in either House, they shall not be questioned in any other Place.

No Senator or Representative shall, during the Time for which he was elected, be appointed to any civil Office under the Authority of the United States, which shall have been created, or the Emoluments whereof shall have been encreased during such time; and no Person holding any Office under the United States, shall be a Member of either House during his Continuance in Office.

Section 7. All bills for raising Revenue shall originate in the House of Representatives; but the Senate may propose or concur with Amendments as on other Bills.

Every Bill which shall have passed the House of Representatives and the Senate, shall, before it become a Law, be presented to the President of the United States; If he approve he shall sign it, but if not he shall return it, with his Objections to that House in which it shall have originated, who shall enter the Objections at large on their Journal, and proceed to reconsider it. If after such Reconsideration two thirds of that House shall agree to pass the Bill, it shall be sent, together with the Objections, to the other House, by which it shall likewise be reconsidered, and if approved by two thirds of that House, it shall become a Law. But in all such Cases the Votes of both

Houses shall be determined by Yeas and Nays, and the Names of the Persons voting for and against the Bill shall be entered on the Journal of each House respectively. If any Bill shall not be returned by the President within ten Days (Sundays excepted) after it shall have been presented to him, the Same shall be a Law, in like Manner as if he had signed it, unless the Congress by their Adjournment prevent its Return, in which Case it shall not be a Law.

Every Order, Resolution, or Vote to which the Concurrence of the Senate and House of Representatives may be necessary (except on a question of Adjournment) shall be presented to the President of the United States; and before the Same shall take Effect, shall be approved by him, or being disapproved by him, shall be repassed by two thirds of the Senate and House of Representatives, according to the Rules and Limitations prescribed in the Case of a Bill.

Section 8.   The Congress shall have Power To lay and collect Taxes, Duties, Imposts and Excises, to pay the Debts and provide for the common Defence and General Welfare of the United States; but all Duties, Imposts and Excises shall be uniform throughout the United States;

To borrow Money on the credit of the United States;

To regulate Commerce with foreign Nations, and among the several States, and with the Indian Tribes;

To establish an uniform Rule of Naturalization, and uniform Laws on the subject of Bankruptcies throughout the United States;

To coin Money, regulate the Value thereof, and of foreign Coin, and fix the Standard of Weights and Measures:

To provide for the Punishment of counterfeiting the Securities and current Coin of the United States;

To establish Post Offices and post Roads;

To promote the Progress of Science and useful Arts, by securing for limited Times to Authors and Inventors the exclusive Right to their respective Writings and Discoveries;

To constitute Tribunals inferior to the supreme Court;

To define and punish Piracies and Felonies committed on the high Seas, and Offences against the Law of Nations;

To declare War, grant Letters of Marque and Reprisal, and makes Rules concerning Captures on Land and Water;

To raise and support Armies, but no Appropriation of Money to that Use shall be for a longer Term than two Years;

To provide and maintain a Navy;

To make Rules for the Government and Regulation of the land and naval Forces;

To provide for calling forth the Militia to execute the Laws of the Union, suppress Insurrections and repel Invasions;

To provide for organizing, arming, and disciplining, the Militia, and for governing such Part of them as may be employed in the Service of the United States, reserving to the States respectively, the Appointment of the Officers, and the Authority of training the Militia according to the discipline prescribed by Congress;

To exercise exclusive Legislation in all Cases whatsoever, over such District (not exceeding ten Miles square) as may, by Cession of particular States, and the Acceptance of Congress, become the Seat of the Government of the United States, and to exercise like Authority over all Places purchased by the Consent of the Legislature of the State in which the Same shall be for the Erection of Forts, Magazines, Arsenals, dock-Yards, and other needful Buildings;—And

To make all Laws which shall be necessary and proper for carrying into Execution the foregoing Powers, and all other Powers vested by this Constitution in the Government of the United States, or in any Department or Officer thereof.

Section 9. The Migration or Importation of such Persons as any of the States now existing shall think proper to admit, shall not be prohibited by the Congress prior to the Year one thousand eight hundred and eight, but a Tax or duty may be imposed on such Importation, not exceeding ten dollars for each Person.

The Privilege of the Writ of Habeas Corpus shall not be suspended, unless when in Cases of Rebellion or Invasion the public Safety may require it.

No Bill of Attainder or ex post facto Law shall be passed.

No Capitation, or other direct, Tax shall be laid, unless in Proportion to the Census or Enumeration herein before directed to be taken.

No Tax or Duty shall be laid on Articles exported from any State.

No Preference shall be given by any Regulation of Commerce or Revenue to the Ports of one State over those of another: nor shall Vessels bound to, or from, one State be obliged to enter, clear, or pay Duties in another.

No Money shall be drawn from the Treasury, but in Consequence of Appropriations made by Law; and a regular Statement and Account of the Receipts and Expenditures of all public Money shall be published from time to time.

No Title of Nobility shall be granted by the United States: And no Person holding any office of Profit or Trust under them, shall, without the Consent of the Congress, accept of any present, Emolument, Office, or Title, of any kind whatever, from any King, Prince, or foreign States.

Section 10. No State shall enter into any Treaty, Alliance, or Confederation; grant Letters of Marque and Reprisal; coin Money; emit Bills of Credit; make any Thing but gold and silver coin a Tender in Payment of Debts; pass any Bill of Attainder, ex post facto Law, or Law impairing the Obligation of Contracts, or grant any Title of Nobility.

No State shall, without the Consent of the Congress, lay any Imposts or Duties on Imports or Exports, except what may be absolutely necessary for executing its inspection Laws: and the net Produce of all Duties and Imposts, laid by any State on Imports and Exports, shall be for the Use of the Treasury of the United States; and all such Laws shall be subject to Revision and Control of the Congress.

No State shall, without the Consent of Congress, lay any Duty of Tonnage, keep Troops, or Ships of War in time of Peace, enter into any Agreement or Compact with another State, or with a foreign Power, or engage in War, unless actually invaded, or in such imminent Danger as will not admit of delay.

Article II

Section 1. The executive Power shall be vested in a President of the United States of America. He shall hold his Office during the Term of four Years, and, together with the Vice President, chosen for the same term, be elected, as follows:

Each State shall appoint, in such Manner as the Legislature thereof may direct, a Number of Electors, equal to the whole Number of Senators and Representatives to which the State may be entitled in the Congress: but no Senator or Representative, or Person holding an office of Trust or Profit under the United States, shall be appointed an Elector.

The Electors shall meet in their respective States, and vote by Ballot for two Persons, of whom one at least shall not be an Inhabitant of the same State with themselves. And they shall make a List of all the persons voted for, and of the Number of Votes for each; which List they shall sign and certify, and transmit sealed to the Seat of the Government of the United States, directed to the President of the Senate. The President of the Senate shall, in the Presence of the Senate and House of Representatives, open all the Certificates, and the Votes shall then be counted. The Person having the greatest Number of Votes shall be the President, if such Number be a Majority of the whole Number of Electors appointed; and if there be more than one who have such Majority, and have an equal Number of Votes, then the House of Representatives shall immediately chuse by Ballot one of them for President: and if no Person have a Majority, then from the five highest on the List the said House shall in like Manner chuse the President. But in chusing the President, the Votes shall be taken by States, the Representation from each State having one Vote; A quorum for this Purpose shall consist of a Member or Members from two thirds of the States, and a Majority of all the States shall be necessary to a Choice. In every Case, after the Choice of the President, the Person having the greatest Number of Votes of the Electors shall be the Vice President. But if there should remain two or more who have equal Votes, the Senate shall chuse from them by Ballot the Vice President.

The Congress may determine the Time of chusing the Electors and the Day on which they shall give their Votes; which Day shall be the same throughout the United States.

No Person except a natural born Citizen, or a citizen of the United States, at the time of the Adoption of this Constitution, shall be eligible to the Office of President; neither shall any person be eligible to that Office who shall not have attained to the Age of thirty five Years, and been fourteen Years a Resident within the United States.

In Case of the Removal of the President from Office, or of his Death, Resignation, or Inability to discharge the Powers and Duties of the said Office, the Same shall devolve on the Vice President, and the Congress may by Law provide for the Case of Removal, Death, Resignation or Inability, both of the President and Vice President, declaring what Officer shall then act as President, and such Officer shall act accordingly, until the Disability be removed, or a President shall be elected.

The President shall, at stated Times, receive for his Services a Compensation, which shall neither be encreased nor diminished during the Period for which he shall have been elected, and he shall not receive within that Period any other Emolument from the United States, or any of them.

Before he enter on the Execution of his Office, he shall take the following Oath of Affirmation:—"I do solemnly swear (or affirm) that I will faithfully execute the Office of President of the United States, and will to the best of my Ability, preserve, protect and defend the Constitution of the United States."

Section 2. The President shall be Commander in Chief of the Army and Navy of the United States, and of the Militia of the several States, when called into the actual Service of the United States; he may require the Opinion, in writing, of the principal Officer in each of the executive Departments, upon any Subject relating to the Duties of their respective Offices, and he shall have power to grant Reprieves and Pardons for Offences against the United States, except in Cases of Impeachment.

He shall have Power, by and with the Advice and Consent of the Senate, to make Treaties, provided two thirds of the Senators present concur; and he shall nominate, and by and with the Advice and Consent of the Senate, shall appoint Ambassadors, other public Ministers and Consuls, Judges of the supreme Court, and all other Officers of the United States, whose Appointments are not herein otherwise provided for, and which shall be established by Law; but the Congress may by Law vest the Appointment of such inferior officers, as they think proper, in the President alone, in the Courts of Law, or in the Heads of Departments.

The President shall have Power to fill up all Vacancies that may happen during the Recess of the Senate, by granting Commissions which shall expire at the End of their next Session.

Section 3. He shall from time to time give to the Congress Information of the State of the Union, and recommend to their Consideration such Measures as he shall judge necessary and expedient; he may, on extraordinary Occasions, convene both Houses, or either of them, and in Case of Disagreement between them, with Respect to the Time of Adjournment, he may adjourn them to such Time as he shall think proper; he shall receive Ambassadors and other public Ministers; he shall take Care that the Laws be faithfully executed, and shall Commission all of the officers of the United States.

Section 4. The President, Vice President and all civil Officers of the United States, shall be removed from Office on Impeachment for, and Conviction of, Treason, Bribery, or other High Crimes and Misdemeanors.

Article III

Section 1. The judicial Power of the United States, shall be vested in one supreme Court, and in such inferior Courts as the Congress may from time to time ordain and establish. The Judges, both of the supreme and inferior Courts, shall hold their Offices during good Behaviour, and shall, at stated Times, receive for their Services, a Compensation, which shall not be diminished during their Continuance in Office.

Section 2. The judicial Power shall extend to all Cases, in Law and Equity, arising under this Constitution, the Laws of the United States, and Treaties made, or which shall be made, under their Authority;-to all Cases affecting Ambassadors, other public Ministers and Consuls;-to all Cases of admiralty and maritime Jurisdiction;-to Controversies to which the United States shall be a party;-to Controversies between two or more States; between a State and Citizens of another State;-between Citizens of different States;-between Citizens of the same State claiming Lands under Grants of different States, and between a State, or the Citizens thereof, and foreign States, Citizens or Subjects.

In all Cases affecting Ambassadors, other public Ministers and Consuls, and those in which a State shall be Party, the supreme Court shall have original Jurisdiction. In all the other Cases before mentioned, the supreme Court shall have appellate Jurisdiction, both as to Law and Fact, with such Exceptions, and under such Regulations as the Congress shall make.

The Trial of all Crimes, except in Cases of Impeachment, shall be by Jury; and such Trial shall be held in the State where the said Crimes shall have been committed; but when not committed within any State, the Trial shall be at such Place or Places as the Congress may by Law have directed.

Section 3. Treason against the United States, shall consist only in levying War against them, or in adhering to their Enemies, giving them Aid and Comfort. No Person shall be convicted of Treason unless on the Testimony of two Witnesses to the same overt Act, or on Confession in open Court.

The Congress shall have Power to declare the Punishment of Treason, but no Attainder of Treason shall work Corruption of Blood, or Forfeiture except during the Life of the Person attainted.

Article IV

Section 1. Full Faith and Credit shall be given in each State to the public Acts, Records, and judicial Proceedings of every other State. And the Congress may by general Laws prescribe the Manner in which such Acts, records, and Proceedings shall be proved, and the Effect thereof.

Section 2. The Citizens of each State shall be entitled to all Privileges and Immunities of Citizens in the several States.

A Person charged in any State with Treason, Felony, or other Crime, who shall flee from Justice, and be found in another State, shall on Demand of the executive Authority of the State from which he fled, be delivered up, to be removed to the State having Jurisdiction of the Crime.

No Person held to Service or Labour in one State, under the Laws thereof, escaping into another, shall, in Consequence of any Law or Regulation therein, be discharged from such Service or Labour, but shall be delivered up on Claim of the Party to whom such Service or Labour may be due.

Section 3. New States may be admitted by the Congress into this Union; but no new State shall be formed or erected within the Jurisdiction of any other State; nor any State be formed by the Junction of two or more States, or Parts of States, without the Consent of the Legislatures of the States concerned as well as of the Congress.

The Congress shall have power to dispose of and make all needful Rules and Regulations respecting the Territory or other Property belonging to the United States; and nothing in this Constitution shall be so construed as to Prejudice any Claims of the United States, or of any particular State.

Section 4. The United States shall guarantee to every State in this Union a Republican Form of Government, and shall protect each of them against Invasion; and on Application of the Legislature, or of the Executive (when the Legislature cannot be convened) against domestic Violence.

Article V

The Congress, whenever two thirds of both Houses shall deem it necessary, shall propose Amendments to this Constitution, or, on the Application of the Legislatures of two thirds of the several States, shall call a Convention for proposing Amendments, which, in either Case, shall be valid to all Intents and Purposes, as Part of this Constitution, when ratified by the Legislatures of three fourths of the several States, or by Conventions in three fourths thereof, as the one or the other Mode of Ratification may be proposed by the Congress; Provided that no Amendment which may be made prior to the Year One thousand eight hundred and eight shall in any Manner affect the first and fourth Clauses in the Ninth Section of the first Article; and that no State, without its Consent, shall be deprived of its equal Suffrage in the Senate.

Article VI

All Debts contracted and Engagements entered into, before the Adoption of this Constitution, shall be as valid against the United States under this Constitution, as under the Confederation.

This Constitution, and the Laws of the United States which shall be made in Pursuance thereof; and all Treaties made, or which shall be made, under the Authority of the United States, shall be the supreme Law of the Land; and the Judges in every State shall be bound thereby, any Thing in the Constitution or Laws of any State to the Contrary notwithstanding.

The Senators and Representatives before mentioned, and the Members of the several State Legislatures, and all executive and judicial Officers, both of the United States and of the several States, shall be bound by Oath or Affirmation, to support this Constitution; but no religious Test shall ever be required as a Qualification to any Office or public Trust under the United States.

Article VII

The Ratification of the Conventions of nine States shall be sufficient for the Establishment of this Constitution between the States so ratifying the Same.

Done in Convention by the Unanimous Consent of the States present the Seventeenth Day of September in the Year of our Lord one thousand seven hundred and Eighty seven and of the Independence of the United States of America the Twelfth. In witness whereof We have hereunto subscribed our Names.

Amendment 1

Congress shall make no law respecting an establishment of religion, or prohibiting the free exercise thereof; or abridging the freedom of speech, or of the press; or the right of the people peaceably to assemble, and to petition the Government for a redress of grievances.

Amendment 2

A well regulated Militia, being necessary to the security of a free State, the right of the people to keep and bear Arms, shall not be infringed.

Amendment 3

No Soldier shall, in time of peace be quartered in any house, without the consent of the Owner, nor in time of war, but in a manner to be prescribed by law.

Amendment 4

The right of the people to be secure in their persons, houses, papers, and effects, against unreasonable searches and seizures, shall not be violated, and no Warrants shall issue, but upon probable cause, supported by Oath or affirmation, and particularly describing the place to be searched and the persons or things to be seized.

Amendment 5

No person shall be held to answer for a capital, or otherwise infamous crime, unless on a presentment or indictment of a Grand Jury, except in cases arising in the land or naval forces, or in the Militia, when in actual service in time of War or public danger; nor shall any person be subject for the same offence to be twice put in jeopardy of life or limb; nor shall be compelled in any criminal case to be a witness against himself, nor be deprived of life, liberty, or property, without due process of law; nor shall private property be taken for public use, without just compensation.

Amendment 6

In all criminal prosecutions, the accused shall enjoy the right to a speedy and public trial, by an impartial jury of the State and district wherein the crime shall have been committed, which district shall have been previously ascertained by law, and to be informed of the nature and cause of the accusation; to be confronted with the witnesses against him; to have compulsory process for obtaining witnesses in his favor, and to have the Assistance of Counsel for his defense.

Amendment 7

In Suits at common law, where the value in controversy shall exceed twenty dollars, the right of trial by jury shall be preserved, and no fact tried by a jury, shall be otherwise reexamined in any Court of the United States, than according to the rules of the common law.

Amendment 8

Excessive bail shall not be required, nor excessive fines imposed, nor cruel and unusual punishments inflicted.

Amendment 9

The enumeration in the Constitution, of certain rights, shall not be construed to deny or disparage others retained by the people.

Amendment 10

The powers not delegated to the United States by the Constitution, nor prohibited by it to the States, are reserved to the States respectively, or to the people.

Amendment 11
[Ratified February 7, 1795]

The Judicial power of the United States shall not be construed to extend to any suit in law or equity, commenced or prosecuted against one of the United States by Citizens of another State, or by Citizens or Subjects of any Foreign State.

Amendment 12
[Ratified July 27, 1804]

The Electors shall meet in their respective states and vote by ballot for President and Vice-President, one of whom, at least, shall not be an inhabitant of the same state with themselves; they shall name in their ballots the person voted for as President, and in distinct ballots the person voted for as Vice-President, and they shall make distinct lists of all persons voted for as President, and of all persons voted for as Vice-President, and of the number of votes for each, which lists they shall sign and certify, and transmit sealed to the seat of the government of the United States, directed to the President of the Senate;-The President of the Senate shall, in the presence of the Senate and House of Representatives, open all the certificates and the votes shall then be counted;-The person having the greatest number of votes for President, shall be the President, if such number be a majority of the whole number of Electors appointed; and if no person have such majority, then from the persons having the highest numbers not exceeding three on the list of those voted for as President, the House of Representatives shall choose immediately by ballot, the President. But in choosing the President, the votes shall be taken by states, the representation from each state having one vote; a quorum for this purpose shall consist of a member or members from two-thirds of the states, and a majority of all the states shall be necessary to a choice. And if the House of Representatives shall not choose a President whenever the right of choice shall devolve upon them, before the fourth day of March next following, the Vice-President shall act as President, as in the case of the death or other constitutional disability of the President.-The person having the greatest number of votes as Vice-President, shall be the Vice-President, if such number be a majority of the whole number of Electors appointed, and if no person have a majority, then from the two highest numbers on the list, the Senate shall choose the Vice-President; a quorum for the purpose shall consist of two-thirds of the whole number of Senators, and a majority of the whole number shall be necessary to a choice. But no person constitutionally ineligible to the office of President shall be eligible to that of Vice-President of the United States.

Amendment 13
[Ratified December 6, 1865]

Section 1. Neither slavery nor involuntary servitude, except as a punishment for crime whereof the party shall have been duly convicted, shall exist within the United States, or any place subject to their jurisdiction.

Section 2. Congress shall have the power to enforce this article by appropriate legislation.

Amendment 14
[Ratified July 9, 1868]

Section 1. All persons born or naturalized in the United States, and subject to the jurisdiction thereof, are citizens of the United States and of the State wherein they reside. No State shall make or enforce any law which shall abridge the privileges or immunities of citizens of the United States; nor shall any State deprive any person of life, liberty, or property, without due process of law; nor deny to any person within its jurisdiction the equal protection of the laws.

Section 2. Representatives shall be appointed among the several States according to their respective numbers, counting the whole number of persons in each State, excluding Indians not taxed. But when the right to vote at any election for the choice of electors for President and Vice President of the United States, Representatives in Congress, the Executive and Judicial Officers of a State, or the members of the Legislature thereof, is denied to any of the male inhabitants of such State, being twenty-one years of age, and citizens of the United States, or in any way abridged, except for participation in rebellion, or other crime, the basis of representation therein shall be reduced in the proportion which the number of such male citizens shall bear to the whole number of male citizens twenty-one years of age in such State.

Section 3. No person shall be a Senator or Representative in Congress, or elector of President and Vice President, or hold any office, civil or military, under the United States, or under any State, who, having previously taken an oath, as a member of Congress, or as an officer of the United States, or as a member of any State legislature, or as an executive or judicial officer of any State, to support the Constitution of the United States, shall have engaged in insurrection or rebellion against the same, or given aid or comfort to the enemies thereof. But Congress may by a vote of two-thirds of each House, remove such disability.

Section 4. The validity of the public debt of the United States, authorized by law, including debts incurred for payment of pensions and bounties for services in suppressing insurrection or rebellion, shall not be questioned. But neither the United States nor any State shall assume or pay any debt or obligation incurred in aid of insurrection or rebellion against the United States, or any claim for the loss or emancipation of any slave; but all such debts, obligations and claims shall be held illegal and void.

Section 5. The Congress shall have power to enforce, by appropriate legislation, the provisions of this article.

Amendment 15
[Ratified February 3, 1870]

Section 1. The right of citizens of the United States to vote shall not be denied or abridged by the United States or by any State on account of race, color, or previous condition of servitude.

Section 2. The Congress shall have power to enforce this article by appropriate legislation.

Amendment 16
[Ratified February 3, 1913]

The Congress shall have power to lay and collect taxes on incomes, from whatever source derived, without apportionment among the several States, and without regard to any census or enumeration.

Amendment 17
[Ratified April 8, 1913]

The Senate of the United States shall be composed of two Senators from each State, elected by the people thereof for six years; and each Senator shall have one vote. The electors in each state shall have the qualification requisite for electors of the most numerous branch of the State legislatures.

When vacancies happen in the representation of any State in the Senate, the executive authority of such State shall issue writs of election to fill such vacancies: *Provided,* That the legislature of any State may empower the executive thereof to make temporary appointments until the people fill the vacancies by election as the legislature may direct.

This amendment shall not be so construed as to affect the election or term of any Senator chosen before it becomes valid as part of the Constitution.

Amendment 18
[Ratified January 16, 1919]

Section 1. After one year from the ratification of this article the manufacture, sale, or transportation of intoxicating liquors within, the importation thereof into, or the exportation thereof from the United States and all territory subject to the jurisdiction thereof for beverage purposes is hereby prohibited.

Section 2. The Congress and the several States shall have concurrent power to enforce this article by appropriate legislation.

Section 3. This article shall be inoperative unless it shall have been ratified as an amendment to the Constitution by the legislatures of the several States, as provided in the Constitution, within seven years from the date of the submission hereof to the State by the Congress.

Amendment 19
[Ratified August 18, 1920]

The right of citizens of the United States to vote shall not be denied or abridged by the United States or by any State on account of sex. Congress shall have the power to enforce this article by appropriate legislation.

Amendment 20
[Ratified January 23, 1933]

Section 1. The terms of the President and Vice-President shall end at noon on the 20th day of January, and the terms of Senators and Representatives at noon on the 3d day of January, of the years in which such terms would have ended if this article had not been ratified; and the terms of their successors shall then begin.

Section 2. The Congress shall assemble at least once in every year, and such meeting shall begin at noon on the 3d day of January, unless they shall by law appoint a different day.

Section 3. If, at the time fixed for the beginning of the term of the President, the President elect shall have died, the Vice-President elect shall become President. If a President shall not have been chosen before the time fixed for the beginning of his term, or if the President elect shall have failed to qualify, then the Vice-President elect shall act as President until a President shall have qualified; and the Congress may by law provide for the case wherein neither a President elect nor a Vice-President elect shall have qualified, declaring who shall then act as President, or the manner in which one who is to act shall be selected, and such person shall act accordingly until a President or Vice-President shall have qualified.

Section 4. The Congress may by law provide for the case of the death of any of the persons from whom the House of Representatives may choose a President whenever the right of choice shall have devolved upon them, and for the case of the death of any of the persons from whom the Senate may choose a Vice-President whenever the right of choice shall have devolved upon them.

Section 5. Sections 1 and 2 shall take effect on the 15th day of October following the ratification of this article.

Section 6. This article shall be inoperative unless it shall have been ratified as an amendment to the Constitution by the legislatures of three-fourths of the several states within seven years from the date of its submission.

Amendment 21
[Ratified December 5, 1933]

Section 1. The eighteenth article of amendment to the Constitution of the United States is hereby repealed.

Section 2. The transportation or importation into any State, Territory, or Possession of the United States for delivery or use herein of intoxicating liquors, in violation of the laws thereof, is hereby prohibited.

Section 3. This article shall be inoperative unless it shall have been ratified as an amendment to the Constitution by conventions in several States, as provided in the Constitution, within seven years from the date of the submission hereof to the States by the Congress.

Amendment 22
[Ratified February 27, 1951]

Section 1. No person shall be elected to the office of the President more than twice, and no person who has held the office of President, or acted as President, for more than two years of a term to which some other person was elected President shall be elected to the office of the President more than once. But this Article shall not apply to any person holding the office of President when this article was proposed by the Congress, and shall not prevent any person who may be holding the office of President, or acting as President, during the term within which this Article becomes operative from holding the office of President or acting as President during the remainder of such term.

Section 2. This article shall be inoperative unless it shall have been ratified as an amendment to the Constitution by the legislatures of three-fourths of the several States within seven years from the date of its submission to the States by the Congress.

Amendment 23
[Ratified March 29, 1961]

Section 1. The District constituting the seat of Government of the United States shall appoint in such manner as the Congress may direct:

A number of electors of President and Vice President equal to the whole number of Senators and Representatives in Congress to which the District would be entitled if it were a state, but in no event more than the least populous State; they shall be in addition to those appointed by the States, but they shall be considered, for the purposes of the election of President and Vice President, to be electors appointed by a State; and they shall meet in the District and perform such duties as provided by the twelfth article of amendment.

Section 2. The Congress shall have power to enforce this article by appropriate legislation.

Amendment 24
[Ratified January 23, 1964]

Section 1. The right of citizens of the United States to vote in any primary or other election for President or Vice President, for electors for President or Vice President, or for Senator or Representative in Congress, shall not be denied or abridged by the United States or by any State by reason or failure to pay any poll tax or other tax.

Section 2. The Congress shall have power to enforce this article by appropriate legislation.

Amendment 25
[Ratified February 10, 1967]

Section 1. In case of the removal of the President from office or of his death or resignation, the Vice President shall become President.

Section 2. Whenever there is a vacancy in the office of the Vice President, the President shall nominate a Vice President who shall take office upon confirmation by a majority vote of both Houses of Congress.

Section 3. Whenever the President transmits to the President pro tempore of the Senate and the speaker of the House of Representatives his written declaration that he is unable to discharge the powers and duties of his office, and until he transmits to them a written declaration to the contrary, such powers and duties shall be discharged by the Vice President as Acting President.

Section 4. Whenever the Vice President and a majority of either the principal officers of the executive department or of such other body as Congress may by law provide, transmit to the President pro tempore of the Senate and the Speaker of the House of Representatives their written declaration that the President is unable to discharge the powers and duties of his office, the Vice President shall immediately assume the powers and duties of the office as Acting President.

Thereafter, when the President transmits to the President pro tempore of the Senate and the Speaker of the House of Representatives his written declaration that no inability exists, he shall resume the powers and duties of his office unless the Vice President and a majority of either the principal officers of the executive department or of such other body as Congress may by law provide, transmit within four days to the President pro tempore of the Senate and the Speaker of the House of Representatives their written declaration that the President is unable to discharge the powers and duties of his office. Thereupon Congress shall decide the issue, assembling within forty-eight hours for that purpose if not in session. If the Congress, within twenty-one days after receipt of the latter written declaration, or, if Congress is not in session, within twenty-one days after Congress is required to assemble, determined by two-thirds vote of both Houses that the President is unable to discharge the powers and duties of his office, the Vice President shall continue to discharge the same as Acting President; otherwise, the President shall resume the powers and duties of his office.

Amendment 26
[Ratified June 30, 1971]

Section 1. The right of citizens of the United States, who are eighteen years of age or older, to vote shall not be denied or abridged by the United States or by any State on account of age.

Section 2. The Congress shall have the power to enforce this article by appropriate legislation.

Amendment 27
[Ratified May 7, 1992]

No law, varying the compensation for the service of the Senate and Representatives, shall take effect, until an election of Representatives shall have intervened.